OLD CHURCHES

MINISTERS

AND

FAMILIES OF VIRGINIA

By Bishop William Meade

Reprinted with
DIGESTED INDEX and GENEALOGICAL GUIDE
Compiled by
Jennings Cropper Wise

IN TWO VOLUMES
Volume II

Baltimore
GENEALOGICAL PUBLISHING COMPANY
1 9 6 6

Originally Published
Philadelphia, 1857

Library of Congress Catalogue Card No. 65-28854

283.755L

M461
1966
v.2

162468

CONTENTS OF VOL. II.

ARTICLE LIX.

ARTICLE LX.

ARTICLE LXI.

ARTICLE LXII.

ARTICLE LXIII.

ARTICLE LXIV.

ARTICLE LXXI.

ARTICLE LXXII.

ARTICLE LXXIII.

ARTICLE LXXIV.

ARTICLE LXXV.

ARTICLE LXXVI.

ARTICLE LXXVII.

ARTICLE LXXVIII.

Old Churches, Ministers, and Families

OF

VIRGINIA.

ARTICLE XLVI.

Antrim Parish, Halifax County.

WHEN Halifax county was divided from Lunenburg, in 1752, it comprehended all that is now Pittsylvania, Henry, Franklin, and Patrick. Antrim parish was coextensive with the county. At the time of its establishment it is probable, from certain entries in the vestry-book, that there were no churches or chapels in its wide extent, for the readers who had been appointed before the separation—four in number—were reappointed, and several gentlemen were allowed to have services in their own houses, doubtless for the benefit of their neighbours as well as their own families. Besides this, when the first minister was settled among them he was required to officiate at six different places, at no one of which was there a church or chapel, though at some of them buildings were about to be erected. Four were ordered at some of the earliest meetings of the vestry, and others afterward. One of the places of reading is recognised as being on Pigg River, in Franklin county that now is. The buildings were small, either log or frame, and not very durable, generally. The first movement toward getting a minister was in the year 1752, when a title to the parish was given to a Mr. William Chisholm, a candidate for Orders, who wished to be prepared with that indispensable qualification when he should present himself to the Bishop 'of London; but, as usual, there was this condition:—"Provided, on his return, the vestry approved of him for their minister, or should not have accepted any other in his

9

absence." Nothing more is heard of Mr. Chisholm; nor can I find his name on any of the lists of clergy ordained by the Bishop of London for any part of America.

What follows in regard to the parish of Antrim I take from a letter of the Rev. Mr. Dresser, in the year 1830, addressed to the Rev. Drs. Hawks and Rutledge, who were then engaged in writing a history of the different dioceses of the Church in this country.

THE REV. MR. DRESSER'S LETTER.

" The earliest mention of a clergyman in the minutes of the vestry is in 1753, when it was 'ordered that two thousand pounds of tobacco be paid to the Rev. Mr. Proctor, for services by him done and performed for this parish.' And at the same meeting, 'on motion of James Foulis, clerk, and for reasons appearing to this vestry, he is received and taken as minister of this parish.' The name of Mr. Foulis continues to appear on the minutes of the vestry until 1759, when tradition relates that he went away, nobody knew whither, and that he was not for a long time, if ever afterward, heard from. In 1762 the Rev. Thomas Thompson officiated a few months, and then resigned his charge, in consequence of his age and the extent of the parish. The next spring the Rev. Alexander Gordon, from Scotland, became rector of the parish, and continued to officiate until the commencement of our Revolution, when, being disaffected toward the new order of things, he retired, and spent his remaining days near Petersburg. Some of his descendants are still remaining in the parish, among whom are some of the brightest ornaments and chief supporters of the Church. Of his own morals, however, and those of his predecessor, (Foulis,) tradition does not speak in unmeasured terms.

" From the time of his departure until 1787, I find no parish records, and know but little of the Church during that interval. The Rev. James Craig, of Cumberland parish, Lunenburg, however, officiated a part of the time in this county during three or four of the last years,—a gentleman highly esteemed both as a man and a preacher.

" In May, 1787, a Convention of the deputies from the several parishes of the State was held at Richmond, and an ordinance passed, regulating the appointment of vestries, &c. The same year a new vestry was elected in this county, and, in 1790, Rev. Alexander Hay, likewise from Scotland, was inducted into the parish. He is represented as having been a man of superior talents and attainments, and, from some specimens of his sermons which I have met with, he seems to have been strictly orthodox and evangelical; but, if report speak truly, he was not endowed by nature with a very mild temper, and he soon found himself in a situation not the most favourable for the cultivation of the passive virtues of our religion. He was hardly inducted into the parish before petitions began to be presented to the Legislature for the sale of the glebe, but without success. As serving to throw some light on the condition of the parish and Church at that time, I shall send you herewith two manuscripts from the pen of Mr. Hay,—one an address to the vestry or parish generally, and the other a remonstrance to the Legislature. The ill temper manifested by him in these and other transactions, or some other cause, made several of the most influential gentlemen in the county his personal enemies, and they neglected no means to harass and thwart him. Some of them he prosecuted for slander, but obtained no damages. Under the operation of such causes, as you may well suppose, the Church continued to decline. To give you some idea of the rapidity of this decline, I will make a few extracts from the parish register during the first twenty years of Mr. Hay's ministry :—

"'1792. Baptisms, 89 whites, 35 blacks. Marriages, 11. Funerals, 1.'

"'1802. Baptisms, 31 whites, 6 blacks. Marriages, 3. Funerals, 6.'

"'1810. Baptisms, 6 whites, 7 blacks. Marriages, none. Funerals, none.'

"During the same time the whole amount of subscriptions in the parish for his support, the glebe then being occupied by him, was three hundred and forty-five pounds six shillings and elevenpence,—a little more than seventeen pounds per annum. 'For the last seven years of this time,' he says, 'during which my attendance was not constant, and my services partly discontinued, from an almost total want of encouragement of any kind, there was nothing subscribed.'

"I neglected to say, in the proper place, that measures were early taken for the erection of churches in different parts of the parish. Of these, one was rebuilt by subscription in 1793–94, but, no title to the land having been secured, it was afterward converted into a dwelling-house. Another, having fallen into disuse and being out of repair, was taken down and the materials used in the erection of a Baptist meeting-house. A third, having been sometimes used for the double purpose of a tobacco-barn and stable, was demolished and some of the timbers used in building a store on the same site. The last, having been repaired in 1795–96, was burned to the ground a few years since, having been set on fire by some one, it is said, who wished to obtain the nails. It is proper to remark that it had been some time unused, and was probably in a dilapidated state.

"In 1816 or 1817, after the Church had begun to revive in other parts of the State, and the late Bishop Ravenscroft was beginning to make her claims known in the adjoining county of Mecklenburg, a small edifice was erected about three miles from this place, in which Mr. Hay preached a few times before his death, which occurred in 1819. Here also Mr. Ravenscroft occasionally preached before his elevation to the Episcopacy, and admitted three or four persons to the communion. The situation of this church not proving favourable for an Episcopal congregation, it has recently been sold to the Methodists and the proceeds appropriated toward the erection of another in this village.

"In 1814, Evan Ragland, Esq., dying, left a large estate, consisting of land, negroes, &c., to the Church, with various provisions, but designed primarily and chiefly for the support of a minister or ministers in this parish. This will was contested by the heirs-at-law of said Ragland, and its execution opposed on several grounds. Accordingly a suit was commenced by Mr. Hay on the part of the Church, he being particularly interested, and the case was decided in his favour in the Court of Chancery. From thence it was carried up to the Court of Appeals, where the decision was likely to be reversed. After the death of Mr. Hay, however, agents or commissioners were appointed by the Convention on the part of the Church, who were authorized to make a compromise with the heirs of Mr Ragland. This they effected, and the case was of course dismissed from court. By the terms of the compromise, the land, which in the mean time had considerably depreciated in value, was sold, and bonds to one-fourth of the amount were executed to the agents for the purposes specified in the will. The last of the bonds is now due, and the Convention is expected to determine at its next meeting what shall be done with the money, amounting to one thousand seven hundred or one thousand eight hundred dollars.

"In 1820 or 1821, the Rev. Mr. Wingfield—now of Portsmouth parish, near Norfolk, but then residing with Mr. Ravenscroft—officiated several months, perhaps a year, in the county, with the view of permanently establishing himself; but he did not meet with sufficient encouragement to persevere. Four or five years since, Mr. Steel, the successor of Bishop Ravenscroft in Mecklenburg, was called to the county to perform some official duty. This led to an arrangement for him to preach once a month at Mount Laurel Church, which had been built a few years previous, chiefly by Episcopalians, but with the condition that it should be free to others when not used by them. Subsequently he made an arrangement to preach one Sunday in a month also in the court-house, which he continued to do until the close of 1828. In the spring of the same year I received ordination, and was directed by the Bishop to make this the field of my labours. These I commenced the first Sunday in June, and was well received by a few, though I found great ignorance of the Church prevailing, and, among many, the most bitter prejudices against her. These prejudices, I am happy to say, appear to be dying away, and the Prayer-Book is becoming more and more popular. During the last year I have admitted to the Communion eight persons, and baptized three adults and six children. A commodious brick church is now nearly ready for consecration in this village, and a smaller place of worship has been erected for me during the past year in another part of the county. My Sunday labours are divided between these congregations, but I am often invited to preach in Baptist and Methodist meeting-houses; and, did my stated duties permit, I might preach much oftener than I do, where twenty years ago a minister of our Church would have had little but the bare walls for an auditory. This I mention merely to show the decline of prejudice.

"Thus I have given the annals of my parish as far as I have been able to collect them; and, lest I should prove tediously prolix, I will touch upon but one point more. It is stated, in an article which I saw some time ago, from the 'Protestant Episcopalian,' and, I presume, from one of you, that Patrick Henry was once an infidel, &c. His widow and some of his descendants are residing in this county, and I am authorized by one of them to say that the anecdote related is not true. He ever had, I am informed, a very great abhorrence of infidelity, and actually wrote an answer to 'Paine's Age of Reason,' but destroyed it before his death. His widow has informed me that he received the Communion as often as an opportunity was offered, and on such occasions always fasted until after he had communicated, and spent the day in the greatest retirement. This he did both while Governor and afterward. Had he lived a few years longer, he would have probably done much to check the immoral influence of one of his compatriots, whose works are now diffusing the poison of infidelity throughout our land."

Mr. Dresser became the minister of this parish in 1828, and continued in it until 1838, when he was succeeded by its present rector, the Rev. John Grammar. Under his ministry the congregation has become one of the largest in the diocese. A church at

Meadville was built many years since, but has failed to effect what was hoped from it. A large and costly church has been built at the court-house, in place of the one mentioned by Mr. Dresser, in which one of our largest country-congregations assemble every Sabbath.

List of the old Vestrymen of Antrim Parish, from 1752 *to* ——

James Terry, Richard Echols, Thos. Dillard, Thos. Calloway, Richard Brown, William Irby, Merry Webb, Peter Wilson, William Wynne, John Guillingtine, John Owen, Nathaniel Terry, Geo. Currie, Samuel Harris, Andrew Wade, Jas. Dillard, Robert Wooding, Archibald Gordon, John Bates, Edward Booker, Hugh Junis, Geo. Watkins, Alexander Gordon, Thomas Tunstall, John Donaldson, Evan Ragland, Benjamin Dickson, William Thompson, George Boyd, Moses Terry, William Sims, Walter Coles, Edward Wade, Isaac Coles, John Coleman, William Terry, Michael Roberts, John Ragland, Armistead Washington, Joseph Hobson, George Carrington, Thomas Davenport, John Faulkner, Edmund King, Joseph Sandford, Thomas Thweat, John Ervine, Daniel Wilson, Thomas Clark, Evan Ragland, Jr., Joseph Haynes, Thomas Lipscomb, John B. Scott, Francis Petty, Daniel Parker, George Camp, William Thomas, Jno. Wattington, Achilles Colquett, Hansom Clark, John A. Fowlkes, Chas. Meriwether, Adam Toot, Edward Boyd, Thomas Clark, Beverly Syndor, Jos. Hewell, Samuel Williams, Littlebury Royster, Benjamin Rogers, Chilton Palmer, John Haynes, Sceevor Torian, Robt. Crute, Granville Craddock, Edward Carlton, William Fitzgerald, Isham Chasteen, Icare Torian, Isaac Medley, John R. Cocke, William Scott.

To them we may add other names, though not vestrymen, yet from the time of efforts for reviving the Church, taking an interest in it and contributing to it,—such as the Bruces, Ligons, Greens, Wimbishses, Leighs, Banks, Logans, Borums, Edmundsons, Fontaines, Carringtons, Baileys, &c.

In another part of the county of Halifax the Rev. Mr. Clark has been for many years doing a good work, chiefly among the poor and servants, to whom he has devoted time and labour without compensation, being enabled by Providence so to do. Under his auspices, and not without considerable pecuniary aid on his part, three new churches have been erected in that part of the county.

ARTICLE XLVII.

Parishes in Pittsylvania, Henry, Campbell, and Bedford.—
Camden Parish, Pittsylvania.

THE names of this county and parish tell their own origin. Pitt
and Camden are names familiar to the English and American ear.
They were divided from Halifax and Antrim in the year 1767. At
different times, subsequent to this, Henry, Patrick, and Franklin
were taken from Pittsylvania, but no new parishes established,
except in Henry, the Church and State having been separated,
so that the two last of them were, according to Colonial law, in
the parish of Camden, until the Episcopal Convention made other
arrangements. There are no records of the vestry-meetings in this
parish; yet the records of the court show that vestrymen were
regularly elected, and had the same duties assigned them as in
other places. To them were assigned the processioning of lands,
the binding out poor and unfortunate children, and the punishment
of offences against the moral law. Rude as was the state of society, it is a fact that these officers did sometimes punish certain
violations of the law of God, as Sabbath-breaking, profane swearing,
and incontinence, which now are never noticed. It is also a fact
that the sins of the fathers being visited upon children to the third
and fourth generation, and children's teeth being set on edge by
the eating of sour grapes on the part of their parents, is remarkably exemplified in the case of the descendants of those who nearly
a century ago were bound out on account of the immorality of
the parents. These descendants, bearing the same name, are
objects of the same action by the overseers of the poor as their
ancestors were by the churchwardens.

As to the ministers of Camden parish before the revival of the
Church in Virginia, we find but one on all our lists. In the year
1774,—seven years after the establishment of the parish,—we find
the name of the Rev. Lewis Guilliam. Would that we could find
it nowhere else! but, alas, on examining the records of the court,
we there find his name, not connected with the registry of baptisms
and marriages, as perhaps none would call on him for these offices,
but with continual petty law-suits, in which he was almost always
the loser. Shame and contempt covered his whole life. He was

a Scotchman, and never married. As to churches, I have heard of one about twenty miles from the court-house. In the year 1773, Mr. Richard Chamberlaine, of St. Peter's Church, New Kent, conveyed to the vestry, for one hundred and sixty pounds, five hundred and eighty-eight acres of land. On this land the Rev. Mr. Guilliam lived. One of the vestrymen, to whom the land was conveyed,—John Donelson,—emigrated to Tennessee, and was the father of Mrs. General Jackson. The glebe lay on the road to Henry Court-House, a few miles from "Callands." It doubtless shared the fate of other glebes. The other vestrymen were John Pigg, Crispin Shelton, John Wilson, Peter Perkins, Thomas Dillard, Hugh Innes, Theodoric Lacy, Abram Shelton, George Rowland, Robert Chandler, and William Witcher.

The descendants of the above, by the same and other names, are scattered over this and the surrounding counties. There is one family in the county which has contributed so much to keep alive the hope of the Church in this parish, in her darkest days, that I must give it a passing notice. Colonel Isaac Coles, ancestor of a number of that name in this region, and uncle of those in Albemarle, married first a Miss Lightfoot, of York, (a maid-servant of whom, one hundred and ten years old, is still alive and in the family,) and had one son by her,—Mr. Isaac Coles, of Halifax. His second wife was a Miss Thompson, from New York, with whom he became acquainted while member of Congress, and whose sister married Elbridge Gerry.* By this marriage he had a numerous offspring, who are dispersed through this county and other places. At a time when the venerable widow, and her daughter Mary, who married James M. Whittle, were almost the whole Church in that region, I always made the old mansion in which they lived a stopping-place and a house of prayer, for the mother had long been confined to it. The Lord's Supper was always administered to her. Many baptisms and confirmations of children, and children's children, have I performed, and happy religious seasons enjoyed in that "Church in the House."

The mother and the daughter above mentioned were, in person and character, striking and impressive. Great was the parental anxiety of the widow and the mother for all her children's welfare, and tender and faithful was the filial piety of the daughter, who devoted herself to the comfort of the aged mother. May the descendants of both of them follow their holy example, and not

---

* They were married in the year 1790, by Bishop Provost.

only, like them, love and nourish the Church of their ancestors, but the holy standard of religion which it lifts up on high.

By the exertions of this family, and a few others,—the Smiths and Slaughters, Millers and Sheltons,—and under the auspices of the Rev. Mr. Dresser, then minister in Halifax, now at Jubilee College, in Illinois, a church (St. Andrew's) was built in this part of the county, and, for a time, hopes were entertained that a permanent congregation might be established there; but deaths and removals have disappointed these hopes. In relation to Danville and the court-house, after a visit from the Rev. Mr. Towles, and numerous visits from the Rev. Mr. Clark, the services of the Rev. Mr. Dame were secured in 1840, for the joint purpose of teaching young females and building up the Church. At his first coming there were only eight communicants, and they all females, in the three counties of Pittsylvania, Franklin, and Henry. Since his ministry, one hundred and twenty have been added, exclusive of those coming from other parishes. A new church has been built in Danville, and another at the court-house, since Dr. Dame's coming, in 1840. He is still the minister of the parish, and will, I hope, long continue to be so.

HENRY COUNTY, PATRICK PARISH.

The county of Henry was separated from Pittsylvania in the year 1776, and the parish of Patrick from Camden in 1778; but no steps, we believe, were ever taken to build churches and procure ministers. Our fathers were then in the midst of the war, and every thing was unfavourable for such an enterprise. Patrick Henry, after whom both the county and parish were probably called, was then, I believe, a delegate from this part of the State, having his abode and much land here. Some of his descendants are here to this day. Some readers were probably exercising their functions in private houses in this county, but we hear of no settled pastor. The first efforts at the establishment of the Church, in later days, were made by the Rev. Mr. Webb, while a teacher of youth, candidate for the ministry, and lay reader at Henry Court-House.

He was succeeded by the Rev. Mr. Wade, a native of the county, and descendant of some whose names have hitherto appeared among the vestrymen of adjoining parishes. During his ministry a church has been erected at the court-house, and the foundation of a promising congregation laid. He occasionally officiated in Franklin county. No parish was ever established by law, or otherwise, in either Franklin or Patrick, until of late years, when one was erected in the former, where there is a prospect of our having a respectable settlement, as we trust, before many years.

CAMPBELL COUNTY.

Campbell was separated in 1781, just at the close of the war, when the civil Legislature was ceasing to act for the affairs of the Church. Nothing is said of a parish. That was reserved for our Convention at a later period. The first minister in Lynchburg—the Rev. Amos Tredway—is said to represent Lynchburg parish, and by that name does it still go. Subsequently, Moore parish is established in the county. In Lynchburg, the Rev. Franklin G. Smith succeeded Mr. Tredway, in 1825, and continued for about fourteen years. The Rev. Thomas Atkinson (now Bishop) succeeded Mr. Smith, and the Rev. William H. Kinckle, the present rector, succeeded him in 1844. An excellent brick church was erected in the time of Mr. Smith, and a larger and much costlier one in the time of Mr. Kinckle.

In Moore parish, the Rev. Mr. Osgood was the first who taught school and ministered. Under his care, St. John's Church was erected. In its loft was his vestry-room and chamber, and, near at hand, his school-house. The present location of St. John's is not the same with its original one, it having been found that a more convenient one might be had a mile off, to which it was moved on rollers. After the removal of Mr. Osgood to the West,—where he died,—the Rev. Mr. Tompkins took his place in both departments for many years, preaching at St. John's, and at another position some twelve miles off. Since his removal to Western Virginia, the Rev. Mr. Kinckle, of Lynchburg, has, by occasional services, kept alive the hopes of our few but zealous members in that part of the county, sometimes aided by the visits of the Rev. Mr. Clark, of Halifax, until, during the last year, the Rev. Mr. Locke, having settled himself at Campbell Court-House, took charge of both of the congregations, and added to it a new one at the place of his residence. A church has recently been purchased and consecrated at that place, and the friends of the Church in that part of the county are encouraged to hope for better times.

RUSSELL PARISH, BEDFORD COUNTY.

The county of Bedford was separated from Lunenburg in 1753. The parish of Russell was established in it at the same time. Both were enlarged in the year 1754 by the addition of a part of Albemarle, then of large extent. The present county of Campbell was included in the original bounds of the parish of Russell and county of Bedford.

On our list of clergy for 1754 and 1758, we find no minister from Bedford. In the years 1773–74–76, we find the Rev. John Brandon. Doubtless there were ministers there during the twenty years of which there are no records. Our Conventions under the independent system, after the Revolution, commenced in 1785 and continued until 1805; but there is no representation, either clerical or lay, during that period. The first representation from that region was in the year 1823, when the Rev. Amos Tredway appears as a delegate from Lynchburg, then in Campbell county. But Mr. Tredway officiated also at New London, in Bedford, as had also the Rev. Mr. Dashiel, who had the academy at New London, though he was never in regular connection with the diocese.

In the year 1825 the Rev. Nicholas H. Cobbs appears as the first regular representative from Russell parish. Its revival is to be ascribed under God to his zealous, and for a long time almost gratuitous, services, since his support was mainly derived from a school. Under his ministry St. Stephen's and Trinity Churches were built, and other positions, as Liberty, and Mr. Wharton's, occupied, where churches are now to be seen. Mr. Cobbs continued his indefatigable labours until the year 1835, when he removed to the University of Virginia, and, after two years' service as chaplain, returned to Bedford, and continued until 1839, when he removed to Petersburg. Mr. Cobbs was succeeded, for a short time, by the Rev. Mr. Doughen, after which the Rev. Mr. Marbury took charge of the parish, and was succeeded by the Rev. Mr. Cofer. The Rev. Mr. Kinsolving followed, and, after some years, was succeeded by the Rev. R. H. Wilmer, the present minister.

The Rev. Mr. Sale has been for many years occupying other parts of the county of Bedford, as at St. Thomas's Church, built under his auspices, at Liberty, at Trinity Church, when separated from St. Stephen's, and at Pedlar's Church, in Amherst county. While labouring on a farm and raising a large family, he has performed the duties of minister for a very small pecuniary compensation.

A new church was built at Liberty, in this county, during the ministry of the Rev. Mr. Caldwell, who spent some time at that place after the removal of Mr. Cobbs. After the removal of Mr. Caldwell the Rev. Mr. Sale took charge of it, and still is its canonical rector, although the duty of preaching is performed by the Rev. John Wharton, who has for some years been acting as sub-deacon. There are now no less than four parishes in that part of old Russell parish which lay in Bedford county, as now reduced in its dimensions. No parish register is found to supply a list of the old vestrymen of this parish.*

---

* I have been told of two other old churches in Bedford county, and as many other ministers, and had a promise of their names, but something has prevented its fulfilment.

ARTICLE XLVIII.

Parishes in Amelia, Nottoway, and Prince Edward.

AMELIA county was cut off from Prince George in the year 1734. Raleigh parish was established in the following year. In the year 1754 the Rev. Musgrave Dawson was minister of Raleigh parish,—how long, if before, not known. He was not the minister in 1758. The Rev. John Brunskill was minister in 1773–74–76.*

---

* The following is from an aged lady:—

The Egglestons are of Irish extract, but came over to this country from England, and settled first on the Eastern Shore of Virginia. After some time two brothers—William and Joseph—came to Amelia county, and located near the central position, where they lived to the time of their death. They, with Mr. Thos. Tabb, Colonel Archer, and Mr. Edward Booker, of Winterham, built Grubhill Church, which was supplied by a minister sent from England,—Parson Brunskill,—who, although not an acceptable preacher, always had large congregations, composed of the families immediately around, and many from a distance. Those who had galleries in the church were the Tabbs, Egglestons, and Bookers,—one public gallery.

On one occasion, when the house was full, just before the Revolutionary War, when the whole Colony was incensed against England, Parson Brunskill arose, and, seeing Colonel Archer and one or two other gentlemen dressed in regimentals, called them rebels, and expressed himself indignant to see such indications of a general rebellion, and said he should write immediately to the King and inform against them. Whereupon nearly every one in the church got up and left the house, not before warning him, however, never to repeat such language, or he would receive harsh treatment added to disrespect. He never attempted to preach afterward, but lived a quiet secluded life at the glebe, about five miles from Grubhill. Mr. McCreary was his successor,—a most pious and worthy man, whose sons fought in the Revolution.

The following is from high authority:—

Joseph Eggleston, Sen. moved to Amelia county in 1758 or '59, as shown by the baptism of his third child by the Rev. John Fox, in Ware parish, Gloucester county, in 1758, and of his fourth child by the Rev. John Brunskill, in Raleigh parish, Amelia county, in 1759, as recorded in his Bible, now in the possession of his family. This proves that the Rev. John Brunskill was in this parish in 1759, where he continued till his death in 1803 or 1804. The Rev. John Brunskill was thought to be an amiable man and an indulgent master, but stood very low for piety, and the ruin of the Church here was attributed to him. He died at his glebe, near Amelia Court-House, in 1803 or 1804, in good circumstances, leaving his servants free, and every thing else to a Mr. Richard Booker.

It does not appear to have been represented in any of the Conventions subsequent to the Revolution, until some years after the revival of the Church, except in the years 1790 and 1791, by a lay delegate,—Mr. John Royall. It is believed that Mr. Brunskill lived for many years to be a dead weight upon the Church. He never married, and lived a solitary, uncomfortable life. It is stated of him, and on authority entirely to be relied on, that, upon the declaration of war, he proclaimed from the pulpit that to take part in it was rebellion; upon which the gentlemen arose and carried their families out of the church, and, on consultation, determined to inflict punishment upon him, which was only prevented by the interference of two of the elder and most influential gentlemen present. But he was never permitted to officiate again, a lay reader being appointed to take his place. He continued until his death to hold the glebe and to live upon it.

Of the churches in Amelia I have received accounts from two of the oldest persons now living in it. There was one called Huntington, (long since in ruins,) about five miles northwest of the court-house. There was another called Chinquapin Church, in the upper part of the county, built about the year 1749 or 1750, at a place since called Paineville. There were three other churches, called Rocky Run, Avery's, and Pride's, in different parts of the county, two of which have been claimed as private property, taken down, and used for farming-purposes. Of old Grubhill Church we have more particular accounts. A venerable lady, now living, and in her ninetieth year, remembers, when a child, to have accompanied her parents to this church, and knows that the timber for it was furnished from her father's and uncle's lands, (Messrs. William and Joseph Eggleston.) Another old lady, now deceased, is known to have said that in the year 1768 she saw the workmen laying the floor of the wing of the church, the main body having probably been built some years before. I have been visiting that old building since the year 1827 or 1828. It was even then in a somewhat tottering condition as to the galleries, which had been put up, with the permission of the

---

The families who attended Grubhill Church were the Bookers, Tabbs, Egglestons, Archers, Royalls, and Meades.

The plate was kept by Joseph Eggleston, Sen. and Jr., till the death of the latter, and was sold by order of the court a few years after,—in 1815.

The Archer family is one of early settlement in Virginia, and of high respectability. Some of them formed a part of that happy and interesting circle of which Judge Tucker speaks as dwelling in York before the Revolutionary War.

vestries, by some of the old families of Egglestons, Banisters, Tabbs, Archers, &c., for their own use. Although cold in winter, hot in summer, at all times dark and uncomfortable, (being high up, and near the roof,) yet such was the old family feeling of attachment to them on the part of the descendants of those who built and first occupied them, that even after it became somewhat unsafe to sit in them, being propped up with large poles and in other ways, they could not be induced to abandon them. This presented an obstacle for some time to remodelling and improving other parts of the church; and the attachment to the whole building, such as it was, though decaying and very uncomely and uncomfortable, for a long time stood in the way of a new and better one.

At length old feelings were so much subdued as to permit a new one to be erected and the old one to be removed. The attachment to the old name, Grubhill, though neither classical nor scriptural, was so great, that not even a compromise, by which it should be called St. Paul's, Grubhill, would be accepted by those whose antiquarian feelings were distressed by the change of the name given it by their ancestors and so long in use. The history of the transaction is on the pages of the vestry-book.

As *names* are not always *things*, we trust that the divine blessing will be as abundantly poured out on the religious services performed in it under the old and homely name of Grubhill, as of any other. Of the two extremes, an undue attachment to old things, or an undue fondness for new, we prefer the former, as most conservative; but " *medio tutissimus ibis.*"

Having had access to the vestry-book of Raleigh parish, commencing in 1790, we are enabled to furnish a list of the vestrymen from that date. At an election at that time we find the name of William Giles, John Pride, Richard Eggleston, John Wiley, John Archer, Joseph Eggleston, Rowland Ward, John Towns, Jr., Daniel Hardaway,—John Archer and Richard Eggleston being made churchwardens. From that time until the year 1827 there does not appear to have been any election of vestrymen, or any thing done in the parish. In that year the Rev. William F. Lee was elected minister, and the following gentlemen vestrymen:— Hodijah Meade, John R. Robertson, Charles Eggleston, T. R. Banister, W. A. Mileston, Benjamin L. Meade, W. J. Barksdale, William Murray; to whom were added, at different times, John Booker, James Allen, Jaqueline Berkeley, Dr. Thomas Meaux, Dr. Skelton, Daniel Worsham, William Barksdale, Jr., Dr. Skelton,

Jr., B. M. Jones, Thomas G. Tabb, Egbert Leigh, J. W. Lane, Thomson Walthall. Here my list ends.

I have already said that the Rev. Mr. Lee, of whom I have spoken more fully in another place, became the minister in 1827. In the year 1835 the Rev. Farley Berkeley, the present minister, took charge of it, connecting with it the pastorship of either the church in Chesterfield, or that at Genito Bridge, in Powhatan, or sometimes of both. I see from the vestry-book, that he has ever insisted on an annual election, though the vestry protest against it as unnecessary, and record the same. How different from former days, when, though Governors, Commissaries, and clergy ever protested against annual elections, the vestries insisted on them. The difference arises from the great difference in the character of the clergy generally. I know of but one parish in the diocese which follows this ancient custom, and peculiar circumstances in its past history led to this. The clergy of our day are ready to relinquish their charges the moment they believe their services are unacceptable and unprofitable, while the people are anxious to retain as long as possible the labours of a worthy, pious, and zealous minister.

I have only to add, in relation to Raleigh parish, that the Rev. Mr. Chevers, a few years since, devoted himself very diligently to the effort at establishing the congregation at Chinquapin Church, but, after two years' faithful services, relinquished it as a hopeless task at the present time. *"Non si male nunc et olim sic erit."*

NOTTOWAY PARISH, NOTTOWAY COUNTY.

Nottoway county was separated from Amelia in the year 1788. Nottoway parish was established in the county of Amelia, being separated from Raleigh parish before the year 1752 and after the year 1748. There being no account of the Acts of Assembly for 1749–51, in Henning, I am unable to decide the precise year. In the year 1754, and again in 1758, the Rev. Wm. Proctor was the minister,—the same, no doubt, of whom mention is made in the vestry-book of Halifax. In the years 1773–74–76, the Rev. Thomas Wilkinson is the minister. Of him I have found a good account. The Rev. Mr. Jarratt informs us that Dr. Cameron was its minister for about two years after leaving Petersburg in 1793, but was obliged to resign for want of support. This was, no doubt, the last of Episcopal services in this parish, except some occasional ones of late years. As to the churches in this parish, all that I have been able to learn is from the Act of Assembly in 1755, by which the parish of St. Patrick is established in the county of Prince Edward. It seems that the county of Prince Edward had been separated from Amelia the previous year, and from that part of it in which the parish of Nottoway lay, but no new parish was then cut off from it and established in Prince Edward. But now, in 1775, the parish of St. Patrick is taken from Nottoway and made to correspond with the bounds of Prince Edward. At a later period (1788) Nottoway county is established, corresponding, I presume, with the bounds of old Nottoway parish in Amelia. The Act speaks of two new churches being recently built in the lower part of Nottoway parish, and requires the parish to refund a portion of the money which had been raised from the whole parish for their erection, to be refunded to the new parish in Prince Edward. Where these churches are situated, and what were their names, and what others had been there before, I am unable to say.*

ST. PATRICK'S PARISH, PRINCE EDWARD COUNTY.

We have seen that the county was established in 1754 and the parish in 1755. In the year 1758 the Rev. James Garden is its minister. We find him there also in 1773,—fifteen years after. In the years 1774 and 1776 the parish has no minister. In the years 1777 and 1778 the Rev. Archibald McRoberts was the minister. We have already spoken of his relinquishment of our ministry in the year 1779. With his ministry Episcopal services no doubt

---

* I have an old leaf from a vestry-book, without the name of the parish on it, in which I find the Rev. John Brunskill minister in 1753, Major Thomas Tabb and Major Peter Jones churchwardens, William Craioby, Wood Jones, William Archer, Richard Jones, and Samuel Cobb, vestrymen. This must certainly be a part of the old vestry-book of Raleigh parish, and Mr. Brunskill must have been its minister in 1753. In the following year (1754) he was certainly in another parish, and Mr. Dauson in this. He must have returned to this before the year 1773, or else one of the same name, for there were three John Brunskills in Virginia at this time.

"In the year 1829 or 1830," writes a friend, "while riding with a friend from Prince Edward Court-House to Nottoway Court-House, I noticed, near to a farm-house on the road, a barn of singular appearance. 'Yonder barn,' I remarked, 'looks much like some of the old Colonial churches I have seen.' 'It was a church of the Old Establishment,' was his reply. 'The present owner of the farm, (which I think had been the glebe,) finding it vacant and on land which was once a part of the tract he purchased, and as it was near his house, had it put on rollers and removed to its present position for the use you see. There was no one to forbid the sacrilege, or, if so, it was without avail; but the act, I believe, is condemned by the general sentiment of this community as that of a coarse-minded, unscrupulous votary of mammon.'"

ceased in Prince Edward, as we see no representative, either clerical or lay, in any Convention.

There were in Mr. McRoberts's time three churches in Prince Edward, one of which, or the congregation thereof, separated with him. Their names were—1st. The Chapel or Watkins's Church, about eighteen miles from Prince Edward Court-House, on the Lynchburg Road, which was the one whose congregation followed Mr. McRoberts in his movement toward an Independent Church. It is now occupied by different denominations. 2d. French's Church, which was about a mile from the court-house and is now gone down. 3d. Sandy River Church, on Sandy River, about eight miles from the court-house on the Petersburg Road. This last church is now, I am told, occupied by the Baptist denomination. I have in my possession a pamphlet of some twenty-two pages, containing an account of a controversy concerning it between the Methodists and Baptists in the years 1832–34. When deserted by the Episcopalians it had been repaired by general subscription, and at several different times occupied as a free church. In the year 1832 the Baptists obtained a title to it and claimed sole right to it, though not refusing to allow the Methodists the use of it at such times as the owners might choose. The Methodists were unwilling to accept these terms, and much unhappy disputation ensued. At one time two ministers of each denomination met on the same day and were in the pulpit together, and the vote of the congregation as to who should preach was taken. The matter was referred to two men eminent in the law,—Judge Thomas Bouldin and Mr. Charles Smith. They determined that the deed recently given to the Baptists was not good, that the one given to the churchwardens at the first creation of the church was the legal title, and that it belonged now to the Commonwealth of Virginia, unless there was an older and better title than that of those who made one to the church-wardens, and to this they were inclined, and therefore advised that the line be run in order to decide the point. A line was run, and it passed through the church; and so a part of it only was legally the property of the churchwardens and afterward of the Common-wealth. The result was that the Baptists retained possession, though the Methodists maintained that a wall might be raised through the church according to the line run; but it was not done. If either Mr. Chapman Johnson's opinion—that the churches were the property of Episcopalians—was true, or that of Judge Bouldin and Mr. Smith, then, in the first case, the Episcopalians in the county ought to have been applied to to decide the question, or else the public authorities, either of which would, I think, have settled it more amicably and more to the honour of religion. Other unhappy disputes have occurred concerning our old churches in other places. I knew of one where, after much strife between two denominations, the church was set up by them to the highest bidder. Who gave the title, or what was it worth? About another, two parties preached in different pulpits,—one in the old Episcopal pulpit and the other in a new one in a different part of the church. So far from their being always respected as equally common property, I have myself been refused admission into one, while on an Episcopal visitation, by those who claimed it by the right of use. In relation to the suggestion that the Episcopalians in Prince Edward were the most proper persons to decide the question as to the occupancy of Old Sandy River Church, if it be said that there were scarcely any left unto whom application might have been made, I reply that, from all the information I have been able to get, there have always been some few of high respectability there. One at least there was, whose firm attachment to the Church, yet catholic spirit to all others, and great weight of character, were felt and acknowledged by all. I allude to Mr. William Berkeley, son of the old lady of Hanover who bade the overseers of the poor who sent a deputation to her for the Communion-plate to come themselves and take it. He inherited all his mother's devotion to the Church, and when at our Conventions, and on other occasions, opportunity was presented for displaying it, never failed to do so. He was not, however, a bigot to a particular Church, but loved the whole Catholic Church. In evidence of which, being in the providence of God placed beyond the reach of an Episcopal place of worship, and near the Presbyterian College in Prince Edward, he not only attended the religious services held there, but was an active member of the board of trustees thereof. For a long period of time he presided over that board, fulfilling the duties of his station faithfully, and yet always having it distinctly understood that he was a true son of the Episcopal Church. So amiable, pious, and dignified a Christian gentleman as he was is not easily found.

In the list of vestrymen in Brunswick, Lunenburg, Halifax, and elsewhere, we meet with certain persons some of whose descendants are enrolled on other registers than those of the Episcopal Church, such as Read, Venable, Watkins, Carrington, Cabell, Morton, &c., and we know not where in the progress of our work we can more properly introduce some notice of them than in connection with

Prince Edward county and the College of Hampden-Sydney. We have seen how the Presbyterians from Ireland and Scotland, settling first in Pennsylvania, began to emigrate to the Valley of Virginia about the year 1738,—how, under Mr. Samuel Davies, they were established in Hanover and some parts around between 1740 and 1750. From thence, in a short time, they found their way into what is now Charlotte and Prince Edward, and made strong and permanent settlements there. This was in a great measure effected by the establishment of Hampden-Sydney College, a brief history of which, taken from the Sketches of the Presbyterian Church of Virginia, by the Rev. Mr. Foote, will best enable us to understand the subject. In the year 1774 the ministers and members of the Presbytery of Hanover determine to establish a public school in that part of the State,—Prince Edward,—understanding that they can procure the services of Mr. Samuel Stanhope Smith, then a candidate for the ministry in the New Castle Presbytery, and teacher of languages in Princeton College, afterward the distinguished President of the same. Sufficient funds being raised and a place selected, in November, 1774, Mr. Smith, with his brother, J. B. Smith, a candidate for the ministry, and a third person, are regularly chosen to commence the work. The first, being now ordained, was called also to the congregation in that place. Under this most eminent scholar and eloquent preacher and his yet more zealous and laborious brother, Mr. J. B. Smith, the institution flourished, notwithstanding all the obstacles of the war. In the year 1779 the elder brother resigned and accepted a call to a professorship in Princeton College. The Presidency of Hampden-Sydney devolved upon his most excellent and devoted brother, J. B. Smith, who continued to promote its welfare and the religious interests of the country around until the year 1788, when he accepted a call to a church in Philadelphia. During the Presidency of the younger Mr. Smith a charter was obtained for the College.

On the list of trustees we find names to which our eyes have become familiar on the pages of the old vestry-books, as those of Carrington, Nash, Watkins, Morton, Read, Booker, Scott, Meade, Allen, Parker, Foster, Johnson. Now, though some of them were doubtless still attached to the Episcopal Church, since it was declared at the outset that the institution should be conducted "on the most catholic plan," and it was the best policy to enlist general favour by appointing some of the Episcopal Church, yet a considerable number of them had doubtless given in their adhesion to the Presbyterian Church. Whereupon, ever since that time, we have found most of the above-mentioned names in each denomination.

Let these remarks introduce the following genealogy of the Reads and Carringtons, who may be regarded as common to the Episcopal and Presbyterian Churches of Virginia, though more of the former belonged to the Presbyterian and more of the latter to the Episcopal. I take them chiefly from the Rev. Mr. Foote's Sketches of the Presbyterian Church.

Colonel Clement Read (so often mentioned as the active vestry-man in Brunswick and Lunenburg) was born in the year 1707. He was a trustee of William and Mary College in 1729. Being President of the Council at the departure of Governor Gooch for England, in 1749, he became Governor of the Colony, but died a few days after. He had been educated at William and Mary under Commissary Blair. He married the daughter of William Hill, an officer in the British navy and second son of the Marquis of Lansdowne. Mr. Read, having, with Colonel Richard Randolph, of Curls, purchased large tracts of land in what was then Lunenburg, moved to that county and was clerk of the same for many years. He frequently served in the House of Burgesses with the great leaders of the Revolution. He died in the year 1763 and was buried at Bushy Forest. His wife was laid by his side in 1780. She was (says Mr. Foote) a pious woman and an exemplary member of the Episcopal Church. Their eldest son, Colonel Isaac Read, married a daughter of Henry Embra, (another vestryman of the Lunenburg Church,) who represented the county with his father, Clement Read. He himself represented the county with Paul Carrington, who married one of his sisters. They were both associated with Washington, Jefferson, and Henry in their patriotic movements. Paul Carrington was a zealous friend of the Episcopal Church. What were the partialities of Mr. Isaac Read, whether he followed in the footsteps of his father or not, we are unable to say. He was made colonel in a Virginia regiment, and soon after died, being laid with military honours in a vault in Philadelphia. He left a son by the name of Clement, who became a distinguished minister of the Presbyterian Church, after having for a time officiated among the Methodists. He married a descendant of Pocahontas,—a Miss Edmonds, of Brunswick,—by whom he had thirteen children.

I take from the same source (Foote's Sketches) the following notice of the Carrington family, whose members abound in this part of Virginia. Mr. Paul Carrington and his wife (who was of the

Henningham family) emigrated from Ireland to Barbadoes, where he died early in the eighteenth century, leaving a widow and a numerous family of children. The youngest child, George, came to Virginia about the year 1727 with the family of Joseph Mayo, a Barbadoes merchant. Mr. Mayo purchased and occupied the ancient seat of Powhatan, near the Falls of Jamestown. Young Carrington lived for some years with Mr. Mayo as his storekeeper. About 1732, when in his twenty-first year, he married Anne, the eldest daughter of William Mayo, brother of Joseph, who had settled in Goochland. They went to reside on Willis's Creek, now in Cumberland county. They had eleven children,—viz.: Paul, William, (who died in infancy,) George, William again, Joseph, Nathaniel, Henningham, Edward, Hannah, (who married a Cabell and was mother of Judge Cabell,) Mayo, Mary, (who married a Watkins.) The parents, George Carrington and his wife, both died in 1785. From them sprung the numerous families of Carringtons in Virginia; and in the female line the descendants have been numerous. · Their eldest child, Paul Carrington, married, as we have already said, the daughter of Colonel Clement Read, of Lunenburg,—now Charlotte,—who left a memory of great virtues. Their children were Paul, Clement, George, Mary, and Anne. Her youngest child, Paul, became Judge of the General Court of Virginia, and died in 1816. The elder Paul Carrington was married a second time, to Miss Priscilla Sims. Two of their children died in infancy. The rest were Henry, Robert, Letitia, and Martha. A very interesting account is given of this, the elder Carrington, in Mr. Grigsby's book,—the Convention of 1776. He was a member of that body, and filled various departments of duty during the Revolutionary struggle, while furnishing three sons to the army, two of whom were eminently distinguished. He was an able lawyer in his day, and after the close of the war was promoted to the General Court, and then to the Court of Appeals, where he was associated with his old friend, Edmund Pendleton, from whom he seldom if ever differed on all the great questions which came before them during the scenes of the Revolution. Agreeing with Pendleton on the subject of religion and in attachment to the Episcopal Church, when the question of the constitutionality of the law for selling the glebes came before the Court of Appeals, we find them united in giving their voice against the law. Mr. Grigsby informs us that "in middle life, and until the war of the Revolution was past, he was of a grave turn. Before the troubles began he had lost the bride of his youth. During the war, and when the Southern

States were almost the reconquered Colonies of Britain, he was never seen to smile. Day succeeded day in his domestic life, and not only was no smile seen to play upon his face, but hardly a word fell from his lips. He was almost overwhelmed with the calamities which assailed his country. But his latter years were cheered by its prosperity and glory. He died in the eighty-sixth year of his age."

That some of the descendants of such men as Paul Carrington and Clement Read, born and living in Prince Edward and the counties around, should have forsaken a Church many of whose ministers had forsaken them in times of trial, or else proved most unworthy, is not to be wondered at, when we remember the ministers of the Presbyterian Church who were sent into Virginia, and were reared in it just before, during, and after the Revolution. Samuel Davies led the way. The two Smiths were men of superior abilities. Old David Rice was himself a host. Dr. Graham, Dr. Alexander, and Dr. Hodge, following soon after, and having the powerful influence of a college in their hands, could not but make a deep impression on the public mind in all that region. It is not to be wondered at that Episcopalians should wish well to the institution, and that we should find among the trustees the names of Paul Carrington, William Cabell, Sr., James Madison, General Everard Meade, and others, who with their families were attached to the Episcopal Church, and so many of whose descendants have continued so to be. It was, in opposition to some fears expressed at the time, most solemnly pledged that it should not be a sectarian proselyting institution, though the forms of the Presbyterian Church would be observed in it; and the fact that Episcopalians have often been in some measure concerned, as trustees or professors, in its management, proves that the pledge has been redeemed as far as perhaps is practicable in such institutions. The long and prosperous Presidency over it by the late Mr. Cushing, whose memory is held in respect by all who knew him, and who, although a member of the Episcopal Church, enjoyed the confidence of the trustees of the College, and the fact that the Rev. Mr. Dame, of Danville, and Colonel Smith, of Lexington, with their well-known Episcopal attachments, were professors in the institution, are proofs that it was conducted in as catholic a spirit as circumstances would admit of. Whether in the lapse of time any change has taken place in its constitution or administration, I am unable to say.

The articles in which the Presbyterian Church has been spoken

ement of his ministry.   He has recently relinquished the
ne of them, which has connected itself with a congregation
on parish, Cumberland, St. Luke's being in Powhatan.

THE CHURCHES IN SOUTHAM PARISH.

rst church determined on was on Tear or Tar Wallett Hill.
rch has long been called Tar Wallett.   It was built on the
Daniel Coleman, in what is now Littleton parish, Cumber-
The next was ordered to be on James River, on Thomas
land.   The next to be at or near the reading-place called
's.   At the same time Peterville Church is spoken of as
a reader, and another chapel, called Ham, is ordered to be
ed.   These last were doubtless built before the division of
rish.   Additions are made at different times to some of these
es, as to those of Tear Wallett and South Chapel.   Mr.
der Trent is allowed to build a gallery for his family.   Ni-
Davies and Carter Henry Harrison are allowed to put addi-
o Ham Chapel for their families.   John Mayo and Benjamin
y are allowed to build galleries in Peterville Church for their
es.

e vestry appears to have performed their duty in regard to a
and glebe-houses for the ministers, and to have complied with
forbidding a vestryman to be a lay reader, by displacing two
were lay readers, or rather by accepting their resignation.
reader of disorderly behaviour is also summoned to answer
e vestry.

he following is a list of the vestrymen:—William Randolph,
ably the second of that name; George Carrington, probably
first of that name who settled on Willis Creek; (these were
first churchwardens;) Alexander Trent, James Barnes, James
y, Benjamin Harrison, Charles Anderson, Samuel Scott, Ste-
Bedford, Thomas Turpin, John Baskerville, (in 1748, in room
William Randolph, removed,) Benjamin Harris, (in place of
jamin Harrison, resigned,) Archibald Cary, Thomas Davenport,
place of Archibald Cary, removed in 1750,) Abraham Sally,
lliam Barnit, Creed Haskins, Wade Netherland, Alexander
nt, Jr., John Fleming, Thompson Swann, Littlebury Moseby,
nry Macon, Roderick Easly, John Netherland, Maurice Lang-
rne, John Railey, George Carrington, Jr., Edward Haskins,
n Mosely, John Hughes, Edmund Logwood, William Mayo,
chard Crump, George Williamson, William Ronald, Edmund

of having been read by a gentleman well versed in its history, he
has kindly sent me the following letter :—

"RIGHT REV. AND DEAR SIR:—I have lately read your articles on
Lunenburg, Charlotte, Halifax, Prince Edward, &c. with special interest,
as my early years were spent in the latter county, where my maternal relatives reside, and who were connected with many families in the other
counties mentioned, by blood, or affinity, or religious sympathy.   Your
papers embody much that I have often heard, with considerable additions.
Knowing that, while traversing this region, "Incedis per ignes, suppo-
sitos cineri doloso," I must needs be curious to see how you would bear
yourself, and I cannot refrain from intimating my admiration of the spirit
in which you have handled a somewhat difficult theme.   I will even add
something more in this connection,—reflections occasioned by your notices,
and which I must beg you to excuse, if at all trenching on propriety.

"My mother, as you may have heard, though firmly attached to her
own faith and Church, has a sincere, and, of late years, growing, respect
for that over which you preside.   I read your articles above mentioned to
her, and while she was pleased with their spirit, she is ready to confirm most
of the facts, saying of that concerning Prince Edward in particular, 'It
is all true; and he might have added more in the same strain.'

"The decline of Episcopacy in that region was no doubt hastened by
the causes to which you have adverted,—such as the defection of one
minister, the character of others, the rise of Hampden-Sydney College,
&c.; but the falling off of certain families, whose influence ultimately
gave a caste to religious opinion, was prepared long before.   Thus, Anne
Michaux, daughter of one of the original refugees, and who, having fled
from France on the revocation of the Edict of Nantes, settled at Manakin,
married Richard Woodson, Esq., of Poplar Hill, Prince Edward, sometimes called Baron Woodson on account of his large possessions.   This
lady, to whom I referred in my former letter, lived herself to a great age,
but of a numerous offspring only two daughters survived, one of whom
was married to Nathaniel Venable, son of that Alvan Venable whom you
have mentioned as one of the vestrymen of a parish in Louisa,—the other
to Francis Hopkins, Esq., clerk of Prince Edward.   The tradition of Mrs.
Woodson's many virtues is preserved among her numerous descendants to
this day.   Her strong character and devoted piety appear to have made
an indelible impression on such of them as had the happiness to know her.
And this it was, I believe, that gave them a respect not only for religion
in general, but a bias toward that particular type of Protestantism of which
she was so brilliant an ornament.

"Joseph Morton, the ancestor of the most numerous branch of the
Mortons, of Charlotte, married a sister of Richard Woodson.   The pro-
genitor of the Mortons of Prince Edward and Cumberland married a Michaux.   Other families of Scots or Scotch-Irish and Huguenot race were
settled in both counties.   But the families of Venable and Watkins, and
afterward the Reads, of Charlotte, did not become thoroughly Scotched
until the tide of Presbytery, which had now set in from Hanover through
Cumberland, was met in that county by a corresponding wave from the
Valley through Bedford.   The rise of the College, which was in part the
effect of this movement, became the cause of its increase, and this institution, together with the Theological Seminary, may be said to have com-

pleted it. That the spiritual children of Calvin and Knox should have formed an alliance under such circumstances was perhaps natural. But that a portion of the Carringtons should more recently have taken the same direction may be ascribed in some measure to the influence of family connections.

"I must say, however, that I have never regarded either the Venables or Watkinses as 'bigots to Presbytery' as such. And in this connection it would be false delicacy in me to refrain from stating a fact which was notorious in that county. The leading mind in that whole region, whether among the clergy or laity, was that of Colonel Samuel W. Venable, (eldest son of Colonel Nathaniel Venable above mentioned,) and of whom you will find some notice in the memoir of Dr. Alexander, of Princeton. Two of his brothers, Abraham and Richard, were known as public characters, while he remained in private life; but they always veiled their pretensions in his presence, partly from affection, but more from deference to the ascendent intellect and acknowledged wisdom of their elder brother, which impressed all who approached him. His early life, it is believed, was unstained as to morality; but, although an alumnus of Princeton, it was not until after the Revolution that he gave in his adhesion to the religion of his mother and grandmother, which had now also become that of his wife. He had fought bravely in the war, and was a decided republican in his political sentiments. Would it be too much to suppose that his settled hostility to the spirit of the English Government had somewhat jaundiced his view of the Constitution of her Church? Colonel V. was eminently a practical man,—a stern patriot and friend of good order in society, public spirited, and a patron of all improvement. Now, the bitter waters of infidelity, which had begun to appear in other parts of the State, were not unknown there, and on the outbreak of the French Revolution society in Virginia was menaced as it were with a deluge of false philosophy and its train of evils. It was to stem this tide that he and those who co-operated with him set themselves. It was not for a party that he contended, but for the substance of Christianity itself, which he believed to be in peril. As this was essential to the very existence of free society, all other questions were regarded as secondary. His numerous engagements did not permit him to enter deeply into any scriptural investigation of the relative claims of the different forms of Church Government; and, had it been otherwise, there were few to aid or sympathize with him."

ARTICLE

Parishes in Cumberland, Bucking...
James Southam, C...

IN 1745, Southam parish was cut o... in Goochland county, which county... River and to the Appomattox. That... River was called Southam parish. Sou... hatan county, which was separated at a...

A vestry-book of this parish, whose... continued until 1791, furnishes the follow... 30, 1746, the Rev. John Robertson enter... parish, being recommended by Governor... Dawson, having been ordained the previou... London. He ceased to be minister in 17... then received on probation for twelve mon... his death in 1772. Mr. Jarratt, in his a... him as a pious man.* The Rev. Jesse Cart... Hyde Saunders, at the death of Mr. McClau... for the parish, each preaching some time... in November, 1773, and continues so to be... when the record ends. In the year 1793 ... journal of the Convention for the first and... more is heard of the parish until the Rev. M... his care in connection with Goochland and... 1827. The Rev. Farley Berkeley, who succ... also connected a new church at Genito, in... church in Amelia. For the last eleven years... has been the minister of Southam parish, pre... and St. Luke's Churches, each of which have ...

---

* Of Mr. McClaurine, other favourable accounts of his pi... lence have come to me. He preached at Tar Wallett, M... Churches: beneath the chancel-floor of the latter he was bur... of his name in Virginia. He left three sons and three da... lived and died in Cumberland, and the third at Norfolk, duri... the daughters, one married a Hobson, another a Swann, and... Their mother was a Miss Blakely, from the Eastern Shore of V...

Vaughan, Peter F. Archer, William Bentley, Edward Carrington, Brett Randolph. The clerks or lay readers were Messrs. Hubbard, Anderson, Terry, Turpin, &c.

LITTLETON PARISH, CUMBERLAND COUNTY.

This was separated from Southam parish in the year 1771. Its early history is very brief,—at least such of it as has come down to us. The Rev. Christopher Macrae appears on our lists of clergy as minister of Littleton parish, Cumberland, in the years 1773–74–76, and 1785; after which he appears no more. In the next year Mr. Mayo Carrington appears as the lay delegate, without any clerical representation. In the year 1790 he appears again with the Rev. Elkanah Talley as the minister. He continues the minister for three years, and then removes to Ware parish, Gloucester. In 1797 the parish is represented by two laymen,—Alexander Brand and James Deane. In the year 1799 the Rev. James Dickenson and Mr. Alexander Trent are in the Convention. There being no journal, and perhaps no Convention, between 1799 and 1805, and none between 1805 and 1812, and having no other means of information, we are unable to say how long Mr. Dickenson continued in the parish, or whether he had any successor until some time after the revival of the Church commenced. Still, there were laymen there who, at the first signs of reviving life, came forward to declare their readiness to help on the good cause. In the first of our renewed Conventions—that of 1812—Mr. Codrington Carrington is the delegate, and, in 1813, Mr. Samuel Wilson.

A long interval again appears where all seemed hopeless. At length, in 1843, the Rev. Mr. Kinckle takes charge of it in connection with some other of the waste places around. He is succeeded in 1844 by the Rev. Mr. Bulkley, who, after some years, was succeeded in part by the present minister, the Rev. Mr. Meredith, who, in connection with the church in Buckingham, serves the congregation at Ca-Ira. Of the ministers yet alive it is not my purpose in these sketches to speak. Of those whom we have named as the ministers of this parish before 1800 we know nothing, either by report or otherwise, with the exception of Mr. Elkanah Talley and Mr. Macrae. Of the former we have spoken elsewhere in terms which it was our regret to use. Of the latter the testimony of those who ought to have known him best is most satisfactory. He was by birth and education a Scotchman,—probably ordained about 1765 by the Bishop of London. He was a man of prayer, retiring from his family three times a day for purposes of private devotion and study. He was a Scotchman, and not a modern Virginian, in his notions and habits of governing his children and the boys committed to his care, and was therefore complained of as too strict. He did not enter with spirit into the American Revolution, and was suspected of favouring the other side, though he said and did nothing, so far as we can learn, to give just offence. He had a right to a conscientious opinion on the subject; but the temper of the times did not allow this, and some violent young men either waylaid him at night or took him out of his bed, and severely chastised him, leaving him naked in the woods. Tradition says that he was prudent in the affair, and never opened his lips in the way of complaint or sought to find out his nocturnal and cowardly assailants, well knowing that it was too good a story to be kept secret, and that if he did not they would reveal it. Accordingly, in due time, they boasted of the deed and were witnesses against themselves. They were summoned before a tribunal of justice, which did not allow any patriotic feeling to prevent the punishment of such an outrage. A heavy fine was accordingly inflicted upon them. Patrick Henry, who was then in the Legislature, being well acquainted with Mr. Macrae, took some public occasion to animadvert upon the conduct of these young men, and spoke in the highest terms of Mr. Macrae. The sons of Mr. Macrae, I believe, are all dead, but three daughters and grandchildren are yet alive, and love the Church and the religion of their fathers.*

---

* The following is an extract from a letter received from one of the daughters of Mr. Macrae:—

"We were young at the time of our father's death, and regret not being able to give a more satisfactory history of his life. He was educated in Edinburgh, I believe, at the same college with Beattie, author of the celebrated *Hermit*. They were classmates, and corresponded in after-life. A professorship was offered him as soon as he graduated, and he was told all that would be required was that he should sign his belief in the Confession of Faith. He said he had never read it, but would do so immediately. On perusing the volume, there were portions he could not conscientiously subscribe. He therefore came to America, and settled in Surrey county, Virginia, where his health failed, and during that attack he became interested on the subject of religion, returned to England, and was ordained by the Bishop of London; came back to Surrey county, (where he married Miss Harris, in 1778, the daughter of Mr. John Harris, one of his vestry,) where he laboured for several years. His own and family's ill health determined him to remove to Cumberland county, where he preached for many years at Tar Wallett and Turkey Cock. During the Revolutionary War he was called out to visit (*the messenger said*) a dying neighbour who was anxious to see him. He had not proceeded a mile from home, when three men, armed with clubs, assailed and knocked him off his horse. The servant that accompanied him rode with speed to friends, who came immediately to his rescue. They left, supposing he would not survive. One of the men was

I have no record from which to derive the names of vestrymen or their doings in this parish. I know nothing of its former

---

killed, on that very spot, by a tobacco-hogshead, and another revealed the whole matter just before he was hung for some capital offence. A petition was sent to the Legislature, then in session at Williamsburg, praying that he, Mr. Macrae, might be *banished*. Patrick Henry instantly rose, and said that there were many fictitious names on that paper; that he knew Mr. Macrae intimately, and that if he was banished they would lose one of their best citizens; he hoped nothing would be done till he could send an express to Cumberland, who returned with a counter-petition, signed by the most respectable portion of the community, praying that he might remain with them; which was granted. Letters were put in the pulpit threatening his life if he ever dared to preach there again, but he knew no fear when in the path of duty, and never in a single instance omitted going to church. The Rev. Christopher Macrae died at his residence in Powhatan county, on the 22d of December, 1808, in the seventy-fifth year of his age. Dr. Cameron preached his funeral sermon."

Parson Buchanon has often lamented to us that his brother Macrae would not consent to be nominated as Bishop. He gave his advanced age as the reason for declining.

We have received an old manuscript sermon of Mr. Macrae, on the death of Colonel George Carrington and his lady, who died in the year 1785, within a few days of each other. We have already spoken of this, the first of Carringtons in Virginia, and of his wife Anna, daughter of Mr. William Mayo, one of the two brothers who first came to this country; but it is due to departed worth and piety to add the following testimony from the pulpit. The text is from the 35th Psalm, 37th verse:—"Mark the perfect man and behold the upright, for the end of that man is peace." The sermon itself, I am very sorry to say, is too much like those so common at that day, which, while containing no heretical doctrines, and some-times having passages recognising the true ones, yet are of the moralizing rather than of the evangelical cast. For instance, although in one place, and in one only, he speaks of "a firm affiance and unshaken confidence in the mercy of God through Christ," yet he often speaks in a manner well calculated to encourage the belief that virtue and integrity must be our reliance. He quotes from Pope, "The soul's calm sunshine and the heartfelt joy are virtue's prize;" says that "Heaven is our reward for a well-spent life;" that "peace is the result of integrity of life;" that "peace and serenity of mind can only be secured by a virtuous life;" of the "reward due to our actions." Now, I doubt not but that some had juster views of the plan of salvation than the language used by them would seem to indicate, and that they intended more by virtue, and goodness, and integrity, than is due to such words; but, after all the allowance that charity can make, we must acknowledge that there was a dreadful deficiency of the Gospel in such preaching, and that sermons of that cast would never awaken sinners to a sense of their lost condition and conduct them to a Saviour. With these remarks, which truth and fidelity require of me, I proceed to the close and application of the sermon :—

"Having now done with the text, give me leave to observe, that though I very rarely say any thing concerning the character of a departed friend [an honest ex-ample, worthy of imitation] on any occasion, I thought it not consistent with duty to pass over the character of persons so eminently distinguishable for the practice of piety and virtue, as our worthy departed friends, Colonel Carrington and his lady, without recommending their exemplary life as a pattern of imitation to those churches, except that old Tar Wallett has long been in the service of other denominations. Two new ones, one at Ca-Ira and another near Cartersville, have been erected of late years, and are in constant use.

TILLOTSON PARISH, BUCKINGHAM COUNTY.

These come next in geographical order, although not taken from Cumberland county and Littleton parish.

At the time that Albemarle county and St. Anne's parish, in the same, were separated from Goochland, they comprehended all that is now Buckingham, Fluvanna, Nelson, and Amherst, as well as Albemarle. In the year 1757, Tillotson parish was separated from St. Anne's parish, and, in the year 1761, the county of Buckingham was taken from Albemarle.

We have a list of ministers for 1758,—the year after the parish was formed,—but there is none belonging to it. Our next list is for 1773, when the Rev. Mr. Peasly is minister, and continues to be in the years 1774 and 1776. How much longer, if at all, or who, if any, succeeded, is not known, as there are no records until

---

who survive them. I have had the pleasure of being personally acquainted with them both for more than twelve years past, and can confidently affirm that they have always appeared to me to be as punctual and exact in the performance of the duties of their several stations, as it is possible for persons clothed with flesh and blood to be. And I have reason to believe, from general report and the relation of their acquaintances, that the same uniformity of conduct and regularity of life had always secured to them an unexceptionable good character in the opinion of all good men of their acquaintance; of which they have left sufficient proof in the world in a numerous offspring, (eleven children,) who all behave themselves as children of such worthy parents. They were generous and charitable without ostentation, and religious without noise. The gentleman filled the chair of a legislator with the integrity of a Cato, and that of a magistrate with the justice of an Aristides. All the public offices which he undertook (and they were many) he filled with credit and discharged with honour. His benevolent disposition enabled him to serve the public with so much punctuality and exactness, when there was no prospect of any other reward but the pleasure of doing good, that it is rare to meet with an instance of the same kind in an age. I have reason to conclude that both our departed friends had many friends, and no foes—if any—but such as a good man would be ashamed to number among his friends. They had as many virtues and as few failings as we can expect to meet with in any of Adam's fallen race; and, in short, I know not whether I ever knew two characters more perfect that were heads of the same family. It is certain they were both an ornament to human nature, an honour to their country, and a blessing to their neighbourhood. Time would fail me to enumerate their good qualities: suffice it, therefore, to observe that their lives were truly exemplary, and that it is our duty to imitate their virtues, that we may after death partake of their felicity, which, I firmly hope, they do now, and ever will enjoy through the endless ages of eternity.'"

1785,—nine years after. No delegation then appears, and the name of Tillotson disappears from the journal until the year 1830, when the Rev. Mr. Osgood, minister of Moore parish, Campbell county, reports some services in it. In the year 1833, the Rev. Mr. Swift was there. In the year 1838, the Rev. Mr. Cofer,—how long before or after we have not the present means of ascertaining. In the year 1845, the Rev. Mr. Meredith appears as its minister, and has continued so to the present time. A new church has been erected in this parish, which now stands at Curdsville, having been originally placed a few miles from its present site, but recently removed to its present more convenient position.

No vestry-book remains to furnish the names of the old vestrymen and families of this parish.

There were two old churches in Buckingham. At one of them, called Goodwin, near the court-house, we have officiated. The locality of the other we cannot specify, but think that it was somewhere near the Methodist Female College.

PARISH OF FLUVANNA, IN FLUVANNA COUNTY.

These were separated at the same time by an Act of Assembly, in 1777, from Albemarle county and St. Anne's parish. Just entering on the war, during which little or nothing was done, even in the old parishes, it is doubtful whether a vestry was elected or any steps taken toward building a church. At any rate, there is no record of it. The following extract, from the letter of a friend to whom I applied for information, tells nearly all that is known of this parish:—

"Our annals do not go far back. From 1835 to 1849 we were connected with St. James parish, Goochland. At the Convention of 1849 we were admitted into union with it, as Rivanna parish.* Our first minister was the Rev. Mr. Pleasants in 1835, and, I think, the first who ever preached stately in the county. He only remained about three months. The next was the Rev. Mr. Doughen, who remained less than two years. He was followed by the Rev. J. P. B. Wilmer in 1838 and 1839. He was succeeded by the Rev. R. H. Wilmer in April, 1839, who continued until the fall of 1843. The Rev. J. P. B. Wilmer returned to the parish and continued until Easter, 1849. After our separation from Goochland, the Rev. Lewis P. Clover was with us from October, 1850, to April, 1852. The Rev. Mr. Bulkley succeeded him, and was with us from July, 1852, to December, 1855. The only Episcopal Church which has ever been in

---

* The name given it by Act of Assembly, in 1777, was Fluvanna parish. Perhaps this fact was not known or thought of at the time of its new name.

the county is St. John's, Columbia, which was consecrated on the 30th of July, 1850. The only Episcopal families prior to 1835 were the Carys and General Cocke's.

Since that time the two Mr. Galts, Mr. Archy Harrison's, Mr. Bryant's, Mr. Brent's, and a goodly number of other families, have been added.

ARTICLE L.

Fredericksville and Trinity Parishes, in Louisa and Albemarle Counties.

AFTER the separation of Louisa county from Hanover, in the year 1742, and of Fredericksville parish, Louisa, from St. Martin's, Hanover, the parish of Fredericksville was enlarged by taking in a part of Albemarle lying north and west of the Rivanna. After some years Fredericksville parish was divided into Fredericksville and Trinity, the former being in Albemarle and the latter in Louisa. We first treat of it in its enlarged and undivided state. It was then without a place of worship, except an old mountain-chapel (age not known) where Walker's Church afterward stood. The first meeting of the vestry was in 1742. The vestry-book has some documents worthy of introduction as historical antiquities. They were the tests required of vestrymen at that period of England's history:—

"I. *Oath of Allegiance.*

"I, A. B., do sincerely promise and swear that I will be faithful and bear true allegiance to his Majesty King George the Second, so help me God.

"*Oath of Abjuration.*

"I, A. B., do swear that I do from my heart abhor, detest, and abjure, as impious and heretical, that damnable doctrine and position that Princes excommunicate or deprived by the Pope, or any authority of the See of Rome, may be deposed or murdered by their subjects or any other whatsoever. And I do declare that no foreign Prince, Prelate, Person, State, or Potentate, hath, or ought to have, any jurisdiction, power, superiority, pre-eminence, or authority, ecclesiastical or spiritual, within this realm. So help me God.

"II. *Oath of Allegiance.*

"I, A. B., do truly and sincerely acknowledge and promise, testify and declare, in my conscience, before God and the world, that our sovereign Lord, King George the Second, is lawful and rightful King of this realm and all other his Majesty's dominions and countries hereunto belonging; and I do solemnly and sincerely declare that I do believe in my conscience that the person pretended to be Prince of Wales during the life of the late King James, and since his decease pretending to be, and taking upon himself the style and title of, the King of England, or by the name of James the Third, or of Scotland by the name of James the Eighth, or the style and title of King of Great Britain, hath not any right whatsoever to the crown of this realm, or any other dominions hereto belonging. And I do renounce, refuse, and abjure any allegiance or obedience to him, and I do swear that I will bear faithful and true allegiance to his Majesty King George the Second, and him will defend to the utmost of my power against all traitorous conspiracies and attempts whatsoever which shall be made against his person, crown, or dignity; and I will do my utmost to endeavour to disclose and make known to his Majesty and his successors all treasonable and traitorous conspiracies which I shall know to be against him, or any of them; and I do faithfully promise to the utmost of my power to support, maintain, and defend the successor of the crown against him, the said James, and all other persons whatsoever, which succession, by an Act entitled 'An Act for the further limitation of the crown and better securing the rights and liberties of the subjects,' is, and stands limited to, the Princess Sophia, late Electress and Duchess-Dowager of Hanover, and the heirs of her body, being Protestants; and all other these things I do plainly and sincerely acknowledge and swear, according to these express words by me spoken, and according to the plain and common-sense understanding of the same words, without any equivocation, mental evasion, or secret reservation whatsoever; and I do make this recognition, acknowledgment, abjuration, renunciation, and promise, heartily, willingly, and truly, upon the true faith of a Christian, so help me God.

" THOMAS PAULETT,	ROBERT LEWIS,
" A. I. SMITH,	CHARLES BARRETT,
" DAVID COSBY,	JOHN POINDEXTER,
" THOMAS B. SMITH,	ABRM. VENABLE,
" ROGER THOMPSON,	EPHM. CLARK,
" T. MERIWETHER,	JOHN STARK.

" Test-Oath.

" I do declare that I do believe that there is not any transubstantiation in the Sacrament of the Lord's Supper, or in the Elements of bread and wine at or after the consecration thereof by any person whatsoever."

From the foregoing it is evident that the apprehension of Popery and the success of the Pretender was quite strong, and that the English Church and Government endeavoured, not only at home, but in the Colonies, through her officers, to guard most effectually against both.

Those who signed the above tests were the first vestrymen after the organization of the parish in 1742. The following were added at different times until the division of the parish in 1762:—Thomas Walker, John Meriwether, Nicholas Meriwether, David Mills, Robert Harris, Robert Anderson, Tyree or Tyrce Harris, William Johnson, John Harvie, Thomas Johnson.

After the division, a new vestry was elected from Fredericksville parish. Some of the old ones continued, and others were added, as Morias Jones, Isaac Davis, Thomas Caw, William Barksdale, John Foster, Hezekiah Rice, Robert Clark, Nicholas Lewis, and at different times afterward John Walker, Henry Fry, Thomas Jefferson,* William Tims, John Rodes, John Harvie, Mordecai Ford, Isaac Davis, James Quarles, William Dalton, Dr. George Gilmer, David Hooks, James Marks, Thomas Walker, Jr., Robert Michie, James Minor, Peter Clarkson, William Michie, Reuben Tinsley, Francis Walker, George Nicholas, Joseph Tunstall, William D. Meriwether. The last election of vestrymen was in 1787; and the last act recorded in the vestry-books was the election of Mr. John Walker as lay delegate to the Convention of that year.

Having thus drawn from our record all that relates to the vestrymen, we will return and gather up whatever else is worthy of notice.

There being no churches in the parish, the services were held at Louisa Court-House and at various private houses at different points in the county. These were performed by lay readers on Sundays, and for some years by the Rev. Mr. Barrett, from Hanover, twenty-four times in the year during the days of labour, three hundred and twenty pounds of tobacco being paid for each sermon. In the year 1745 it was determined to build three frame churches, one in some central place in Louisa county, called the Lower Church, and sometimes Trinity Church; another in Albemarle, called Middle Church, and which was doubtless the same with Walker's Church; and the third between the mountains on the Buckmountain Road, which is doubtless the same with that now called Buckmountain Church. Each of these was built at different times during the few following years. In the year 1763 another church was resolved on nearer to Orange,—whether built or not I cannot say. In the year 1747 the Rev. Mr. Arnold was chosen for one year, and continued until his death, in 1754, when his funeral was preached by Mr. Barrett.

---

* Mr. Jefferson, then living at Shadwell Mills, on the west side of the Rivanna, was in Fredericksville parish, and appears to have been an active vestryman for some years. Himself and Nicholas Meriwether were ordered to lay off two acres of land including a space around Walker's Church,—land given by Mr. Walker.

Of the Walkers, four of whom appear repeatedly on the vestry-book, I have only been able to obtain the following notices. Dr. Thomas Walker is believed to have been the first discoverer of Kentucky in 1750. In 1755 he was with Washington at Braddock's defeat. In 1775 he was one of the committee of safety appointed by the Convention of 1775 on the breaking out of the troubles with England. He was also repeatedly a member of the General Assembly.

Colonel John Walker, his eldest son, was for a short time aid to General Washington during the war. He was also for a short time a member of the Senate of the United States. Colonel Francis Walker, the youngest son, was repeatedly member of the State Legislature, and represented the counties of Albemarle and Orange in Congress from 1791 to 1795.

A Rev. Mr. Beckett then performed some services in the parish, as also the Rev. James Maury, who became the minister in the same year, and who married a Miss Walker. Soon after he settled in the parish a good glebe of four hundred acres was purchased for him, near Captain Linsey's, and a parsonage built, which, with the outhouses and other improvements, seem during his life to have been well attended to by the vestry. In the year 1763 the parish was divided into Trinity, in Louisa, and Fredericksville, in Albemarle. Of Trinity we now lose sight altogether, I fear, as I know of no source from which to obtain information. By an Act of the Legislature the vestry of Fredericksville was ordered to pay two hundred pounds—half the price of their glebe—to the new vestry of Trinity for the purchase of a glebe.

The Rev. James Maury continued until his death, in 1770, to officiate in this parish. Of him and his Huguenot ancestors I have written in my article on Manakintown,—of him particularly in my notices of the Option Law, or Two-Penny Act, and in my remarks on toleration. He was a very deserving man. He was succeeded by his son, Matthew Maury, who was ordained the preceding year. Mr. Matthew Maury continued to be the minister of the parish until his death, in 1808, though his name does not appear on the vestry-book as receiving a salary after the year 1777. From that time forward he received little or nothing for his services as a minister. He retained the glebe for the benefit of his mother and family, who lived on it, while he taught school on an adjoining farm, and educated a large number of the citizens of Virginia. He lived very near to, and on the most intimate terms with, the old blind preacher, Mr. Waddell, who officiated at the death of his wife, there being no Episcopal minister at that time in any of the surrounding counties, and but few in the State.*

---

* The Rev. James Maury, father of Matthew Maury, had twelve children,—Matthew, James, Walker, Abraham, Benjamin, Richard, Fontaine, Ann, Mrs. Strahan, Mrs. Barrett, Mrs. Lewis, Mrs. Eggleston. His son James was the old consul at Liverpool, filling that station for forty-five years, and leaving five children. His son Matthew raised ten children,—Matthew, Thomas Walker, Francis, Fontaine, Reuben, John, Mrs. Michie, Mrs. Fry, Mrs. Lightfoot, Elizabeth Walker. His son Walker was a teacher of youth in Williamsburg, Norfolk, and Albemarle, also a minister in Norfolk for a short time. His children were James, William, Leonard, Mrs. Hite, Mrs. Hay, and Mrs. Polk. Space, if not time, would fail us, even if we had the information, to mention the names of all the descendants of the old patriarch, the Rev. James Maury. They are scattered all over our land, and are to be found in various professions. One of them is a worthy minister of our Church in Kentucky, while two are married to worthy clergymen,—the Rev. Mr. Berkeley, of Lexington, Kentucky, and Rev. Mr. Nash, of Ohio. Another descendant presides

Before we make our brief mention of the ministers of this parish, since the revival of the Church during the present century, a few words are due to the two old churches at Walker's and Buckmountain, which we have said were determined upon in the year 1745, and built within a year or two afterward. Old Walker's Church, built upon the site of a still older and ruder house, stood on the side of the road from Orange Court-House to Charlottesville, at the end of a noble avenue of oaks—now no more—leading down to Mr. Walker's old seat, Belvoir,—itself no more, having been consumed by fire, but for a long time the seat of hospitality, especially to ministers and persons coming to church from a distance. The church being of wood—a framed one—of course must decay much sooner than one of more solid material.

In the year 1827, when Judge Hugh Nelson, Mr. William C. Rives, and Dr. Page, occupied their old seats, (having married into the families of the Walkers,) and the descendants of other old families were still around, the duty of repairing it was felt. But the vestry not being able, as of old, to order a levy of tobacco for building and repairing churches, it was not so easy to accomplish the work. One of the females of the parish on that occasion made the following very interesting appeal. It is believed to be from the pen of one who has since taken so active a part in procuring the new one which has recently been erected.*

THE CHURCH'S PETITION.

"Ye friends and kind neighbours, in pity draw near,
    And attend to my sorrrowful tale ;
Should you grant me but misery's portion,—a tear,—
To my grief-burden'd heart will that tribute be dear,
    While I my misfortunes bewail.

"Stern winter is o'er, nor his sway will resume,
    Though sullen and scowling he flies ;
Soft May greets us now, with her beauty and bloom,
And her whispering airs, breathing varied perfume,
    Bear her incense of flowers to the skies.

"All nature is lovely and verdant around ;
    New charms to creation are given,—
From the modest wild violet that droops on the ground,
To the oak in the forest with majesty crown'd
    And proudly arising to heaven.

---

over a National Institute at Washington, and by his learning, zeal, and great discoveries, is conferring benefits on the whole human race, rendering the ocean almost as safe as the dry land.
    * Mrs. W. C. Rives.

"But, alas! not to me does the season return,
    With reviving and soul-breathing powers:
While all nature around me is smiling, I mourn
My glory departed, my aspect forlorn,
    Contrasted with freshness and flowers.

"Through my windows dismantled and dreary as night
    The wild birds in my court seek their rest!
The owl and the bat wheel their ominous flight
O'er my altar once hallow'd by heaven's own light,
    And there is the swallow's rude nest.

"Then pity, kind friends, and your timely aid lend,
    Or soon I shall sink to decay;
'Build up the waste places,' your Zion befriend,
And gently on you shall my blessing descend.
    Oh, let me not moulder away!

"Should this world e'er forsake you, your friends become foes,
    While a wreck, tempest-tost, you are driven,
Then fly to my arms, on my bosom repose;
I can dry every tear, I can soften your woes,
    And lead you triumphant to heaven."

The result of this poetic appeal, in co-operation with other means, was the raising a sufficient sum for the repairs of the church. But, time still going on with its ravages, it was felt that a new and more durable one should be had.   A gentleman, some years since, then in prosperous circumstances, promised several thousand dollars toward the erection of a new one, though by adversity he was disabled from the full performance of his promise.   This stimulated the desire for a more expensive building than would otherwise have been attempted.   It was commenced under the auspices of one family,* although the people around, during its progress, contributed about five thousand dollars to it.   False calculations were made as to the expense of the style and manner of its execution, which caused great delay in the work, and led to various efforts and solicitations in Virginia and elsewhere in order to raise the needful amount.   Could all the disappointments and miscalculations and costs have been foreseen, it would have been improper to have attempted such a building, as a much cheaper one would have answered all the needs of the neighbourhood. But it was at length completed, and is in its exterior appearance a most beautiful building, without any thing gaudy about it, while the materials and manner of its execution give the promise of its long continuance.

As to Old Buckmountain Church, at the time that measures were

---

* The family of the Hon. W. C. Rives, of Castle Hill.

commenced for the resuscitation of our Zion in Virginia, it had been so long in the use of some other denomination that it was claimed, not merely by right of possession, but on the ground of having been repaired. It will amuse the reader to learn the kind and the amount of repairs on which this claim was grounded. When I first saw it, more than thirty years ago, it was—though said to be repaired—a mere shell, with many an opening in the clapboard walls, through which the wind might freely pass. The inward repairs consisted in removing the old pews into the gallery, where they were piled up, and in their room putting benches made of the outside slabs from the sawmill, with legs as rude thrust through them, and of course no backs. The old pulpit was left standing, but by its side was a platform made by laying a few planks across the backs of two pews, which the preacher preferred to the old-fashioned pulpit. A few years after the revival of our Church began, the Episcopalians around, not thinking that either these repairs or the occasional occupancy of the building had deprived them of their right, put in their claim, which, though stoutly resisted by some, being as stoutly insisted on by others, was finally admitted, and the old church, being much better repaired than before, has ever since been in our possession and use.

As to the ministers who have officiated in Fredericksville parish since the revival of the Church, we have but little to say. The Rev. Mr. Bausman took charge of it in 1818, and remained less than one year. The Rev. Mr. Hatch succeeded him in 1820 and continued until 1830. He was succeeded by the Rev. Zachariah Mead, who continued three or four years, and, as did Mr. Hatch, served the whole county. From 1833 to the fall of 1838, the Rev. W. G. Jones, from Orange, officiated at Walker's Church. In the year 1839 the present minister, the Rev. Mr. Boyden, took charge of the parish, and for some years ministered also to the congregation on the Green Mountain. The church on Buckmountain has for many years been served in conjunction with other congregations, which will be mentioned when we speak in our next article of St. Anne's parish.

ARTICLE LI.

St. Anne's Parish, Albemarle County.

In the year 1761, Albemarle, besides its present territory, embraced all of Fluvanna, Buckingham, Nelson, and Amherst. By various Acts between that time and 1777, it was reduced to its present dimensions. St. Anne's parish covered the whole of this region at its first organization in 1742, and by successive Acts was reduced to the same dimensions with the present county of Albemarle, with the exception of that part which forms Fredericksville parish. The dividing-line, after running some distance along the Rivanna, crosses the same and passes through Charlottesville. Of late years some other parishes have been formed within St. Anne's parish, as that on Green Mountain, &c. Our first knowledge of any churches in that part of St. Anne's parish now in Albemarle, as at present bounded, is of two which began about the year 1746 or 1747, under the direction of the Rev. Robert Rose, who moved from Essex to what is now Amherst, and extended his labours, during a short period, to that part of Albemarle called the Green Mountain, where were built Ballenger's Church, not very far from Warren, and the Forge Church, not far from Mr. John Cole's, the ancestor of those now bearing that name, and who appears from the vestry-book in my possession to have been the most active member of the vestry, until the year 1785, when the record closes. After Mr. Rose's death, in 1751, the Rev. Mr. Camp probably succeeded to all his churches. He lived in the neighbourhood of New Glasgow. The old glebe-house is still to be seen on the land of Dr. Hite, near the road-side. He moved with his family to the West just before the Revolution, and it is said was murdered by the Indians near the fort of Vincennes on the Wabash. Previously to this the Rev. Mr. Ramsay had settled in Albemarle and become the minister of St. Anne's parish with its reduced dimensions. He is represented as a very unacceptable minister. The Rev. Charles Clay followed him. He was near relative of our statesman, Mr. Henry Clay,—probably first-cousin,—and inherited no little of his talents and decision of character. He was ordained by the Bishop of London in 1769, and on 22d October of the same year was received as minister of St. Anne's parish. The vestry-book opens in 1772 and closes in 1785, during all of which time, as well as the three preceding years, Mr. Clay was the minister, living at the glebe, somewhere in the Green Mountain neighbourhood, and preaching at the two churches,—Ballenger and The Forge,—and sometimes at the courthouse, and at various private houses in Albemarle ; also, at the Barracks during the war, which was probably the place where the British prisoners under General Philips were kept, first by Colonel Bland, and afterward by General Wood. He also preached in Amherst and Chesterfield occasionally. The places of his preaching I ascertain from the notes on a number of his sermons, which have been submitted to my perusal. The sermons are sound, energetic, and evangelical beyond the character of the times. One of them, on the new birth, is most impressive and experimental. Another on the atonement, for Christmas-day, is very excellent as to doctrine, and concludes with a faithful warning against the profanation of that day by "fiddling, dancing, drinking, and such like things," which he said were so common among them.

In the year 1777, on the public fast-day, he preached a sermon to the minute-company at Charlottesville, in which his patriotic spirit was displayed. " Cursed be he (in the course of his sermon he said) who keepeth back his sword from blood in this war." He declared that the " cause of liberty was the cause of God,"—calls upon them to "plead the cause of their country before the Lord with their blood." And yet he said, " There might be some present who would rather bow their necks to the most abject slavery, than face a man in arms." It was at this time and under these circumstances that he became acquainted with Mr. Jefferson, who, having removed into this parish from Fredericksville, was now elected to the vestry of St. Anne's, though it does not appear that he ever acted. This intimacy was kept up until his death in Bedford county, in the year 1824, where he and Mr. Jefferson each had farms, and where, during the visits of the latter, there was much friendly intercourse. During the latter years of his ministry in St. Anne's parish, the connection of Mr. Clay with his vestry was very unhappy. The salary of one year was the occasion of it. There appears to have been some division in the vestry about it. The majority, however, was against Mr. Clay, and a law-suit was the result. The decision was not satisfactory to Mr. Clay, and he refused taking the amount offered, and told the vestry if they would not pay him what he considered right, he would receive none. The vestry ordered Mr. Fry, the collector, to lay it out in a land-warrant, thinking that he might change his mind. Nothing more appeared on the vestry-book about it, and how it was ended I know not. Mr. Clay must have left St. Anne's in 1784, for we find him representing the Church in Chesterfield in the Episcopal·Convention at Richmond, in the year 1785, but never afterward. The Church was daily sinking, and, his mind being soured perhaps by his controversy with the vestry, and discouraged by the prospects before him as a minister, he moved to Bedford, and betook himself to a farmer's life, only officiating occasionally at marriages, funerals, &c. to the few Episcopalians of that region. He married a most estimable and pious lady of that neighbourhood, who survived him many years and contributed greatly to the revival of the Church under the Rev. Mr. Cobbs of that county. He left a numerous and most respectable family of sons and daughters, who have adhered to the Church of their parents. At his death the Rev. Mr. Ravenscroft performed the funeral services. There was something peculiar in the structure of Mr. Clay's mind, in proof of which it is mentioned that by his will he enjoined, what has been strictly observed, that on the spot where he was buried, and which he had marked out, there should be raised a huge pile of stones for his sepulchre. It is about twenty feet in diameter and twelve feet high, and being first covered with earth, and then with turf, presents the appearance of one of those Indian mounds to be seen in our Western States.

In looking over the vestry-book, which extends from 1772 to 1785, we find nothing requiring notice except the list of vestrymen and what is said of churches.

The list of vestrymen is as follows :—John Coles, Jacob Moore, John Ware, Patrick Napier, James Hopkins, James Garland, Michael Thomas, William Coxe, John Fry, Roger and George Thompson, William Burton, John Harris, John Scott, Thomas Jefferson, Orlando Jones, William Oglesby, Richard Farrar, Philip Mazzei, William Hughes, Samuel Shelton, Wm. Ball, Charles Lewis, Nathaniel Garland, Nicholas Hamner, Richard Davenport, John Old, Joshua Fry, Charles Irving, John Jordan. The vestry appears throughout to have been attentive to the glebe-house and its appurtenances. As to churches, in 1774 it was ordered that a church be built at a place to be chosen by Henry Martin and Patrick Napier, and that Messrs. Roger and George Thompson might each build a pew, adjoining, at their own expense. In 1777 a church was contracted for with Mr. Edward Cobbs, at whose house services had been held. It was not finished for some years. It is also stated that in 1777 Mr. James Minor, Dabney Minor, and John Napier were appointed to examine a church built by a Mr. Anderson. During the ministry of Mr. Clay there was also a Mr. Holmes acting as a teacher and preacher in Albemarle. He was also American in his feelings, and rejoiced in the capture of Cornwallis.

After the resignation of Mr. Clay the Rev. Mr. Darneile performed some services here and in Nelson. We learn that he became involved in debt, and studied law; but, not extricating himself, he left his family, and, going to the South, spent some years there. From the year 1795 to 1812 the Rev. William Crawford occasionally officiated at the churches in St. Anne's parish.

After that period there were no services until the year 1818, when the Rev. Mr. Bausman divided his labours between the few remaining Episcopalians about Charlottesville in St. Anne's parish, and Walker's Church, in Fredericksville. The Episcopal Church, under new auspices, now began to revive a little. The Gospel was preached in a clearer and more forcible manner than had been common in Virginia, and the ministers exhibited more zeal. In the year 1820, the Rev. Frederick Hatch succeeded to Mr. Bausman, and extended his efforts to the Green Mountain, finding a considerable number of the old families still attached to the Church. Old Ballenger Church was in ruins, and that called The Forge was in little better condition. Still, service was held in it for some years. The first time I ever saw it was in company with Bishop Moore, not long after his coming to Virginia. It was a cold, cloudy, stormy day, and the wind whistled not only around but within its tattered walls. The Holy Communion was administered to a few of the old adherents of the church. General Cocke, from Fluvanna, had come that morning from his home, between twenty and thirty miles, to partake of his first Communion, as he has continued to do ever since on Episcopal visitations. The resolve was taken that day, that a new and better house must be provided for the worship of God, which has been faithfully fulfilled. Some miles off, in a more central position and on a beautiful site, a neat and excellent brick church has been erected, and near it, more recently, a parsonage and small glebe have been added. A parish has been established in that part of the county. A succession of ministers either in whole or in part have ministered unto it. The Rev. Mr. Hatch stands first. Then follow the Rev. Zachariah Mead, the Rev. Joseph Wilmer, the Rev. Mr. Boyden, the Rev. Charles Ambler, and their present rector, the Rev. W. M. Nelson. But few of the old families are represented now.   The Fryes, Cobbs, Nicholases, Harrises, Lewises, Garlands, Thomases, Thompsons, Joneses, Napiers, are gone, but the descendants of John Cole, in considerable number, the Tompkinses, Riveses, Carters, Gants, Randolphs, and others, have taken their places, and will, I trust, fulfil them well.   In that part of the parish called North Garden, and near which an old church stood, a new brick church was also erected by the zeal and liberality of a few devoted friends, and the same was done also on the road leading from Charlottesville to Staunton, and the two, being brought into one parish, have generally been supplied with a minister. The Rev. Mr. Christian acted for some time as missionary in that part of the county.   Then the Rev. William Jackson, who recently fell victim to the fever in Norfolk, was the settled pastor for some years.   After him came the Rev. Mr. Slack, and at present the Rev. Mr. Davis, who, as well as most of his predecessors, connect with them the church on Buckmountain, in Fredericksville parish, and sometimes the church at Rockfish, in Nelson county.

To the zeal and enterprise of the Rev. Mr. Hatch, is, under God, to be ascribed the building of the church in Charlottesville, which stands just within the bounds of Fredericksville parish.   For a long time the court-house was the only place in Charlottesville or round about for public worship.   The four leading denominations in the State equally divided the Sabbaths, and some thought that this was sufficient, and calculated to promote peace and love among them all.   Mr. Jefferson used to bring his seat with him on horseback from Monticello, it being some light machinery which, folded up, was carried under his arm, and unfolded served for a chair on the floor of the court-house.   But the great body of the people felt the need of a more convenient place of worship, where more persons could be accommodated and in a better manner.   It was proposed that all denominations should unite in one; but that was found full of difficulties, and was soon abandoned.   It was then proposed that two should unite,—the Episcopalians and Presbyterians; which also came to nothing.   Mr. Hatch, who was opposed to either scheme, then circulated a subscription for an Episcopal church, which immediately succeeded, and was soon followed with the same success by all the others; and the village is now filled with well-built churches.   The plan of the Episcopal church was furnished by Mr. Jefferson, and, though far from being the best, is much better for the purposes of worship and preaching than most of those which now come from the hands of ecclesiological architects, who, if hired to injure the voices and energies of ministers, and to frustrate the main purposes for which temples of religion are built, could not have succeeded much better than they have done by their lofty ceilings, their pillars, recesses, and angles, besides the heavy debts into which they have led their employers. The church in Charlottesville has been recently enlarged and much improved.

The Rev. Mr. Hatch was succeeded in this parish by the Rev. Zachariah Mead, an alumnus of our Seminary. For the encouragement of young men of weak constitutions to choose a country parish, let me give the experience of Mr. Mead. When he left the Seminary he was thought to be far gone in that disease of which he eventually died,—consumption,—so that he required assistance to get into the stage which was to convey him to the place where it was soon to be determined whether a speedy death or a prolonged life was to be his portion. The latter was his portion. By little and little he enlarged his sphere of labour, until on horseback he rode over the whole hilly and mountainous country of Albemarle, taking charge of all the congregations in both parishes, which now employ, and fully employ, the labours of four ministers, and in less than a year swam the Rivanna River, on horseback, on a bleak day, without taking cold. He became a hearty man, and continued so until he returned to the North, took charge of a congregation in Boston, lost his health, and was obliged to seek its restoration in the milder climate of Richmond and in the editorial chair. Had he returned again to the labours of a country ministry, his days and services might have been prolonged. Mr. Z. Mead was succeeded for two years in the church at Charlottesville by the Rev. Mr. Cobbs, (now Bishop,) while performing the duties of Chaplain to the University. He was followed by the present minister, the Rev. R. K. Meade, who has been in this position ever since his ordination,—more than twenty years. Every fourth year at first, and, of late, every two years in eight, the Chaplaincy of the University is filled by an Episcopal minister, which deserves to be mentioned in the history of the Church in this parish. It was just before the Chaplaincy of Mr. Cobbs, that a circumstance occurred deserving some notice, as it occasioned much excitement at the time, and not a little misapprehension. A pestilential disease had visited the students of the Institution for two successive years, or twice in the same year, sweeping a number of them into untimely graves. There was something most unaccountable, mysterious, and awful in all the circumstances of it. Though there was confessedly much of irreligion and even infidelity in the faculty of that day, yet such an awe rested upon them, that at the instance of a pious member of it, Judge Lomax, the Law Professor, it was determined to celebrate the event in the most solemn manner.   The Episcopal Convention was to meet in Charlottesville the ensuing spring, and that was selected as the proper time for it. The author of these pages was requested to prepare and deliver a discourse at that time and on the occasion referred to.   It was a most trying and responsible undertaking, but he dared not refuse. At the time appointed there was present, on Sabbath morning, in the great rotunda of the University, a large number of the clergy and laity then in attendance on the Convention, with the Professors, students, and people around.

The sermon was preached from those words of the Prophet Amos, (3d chap. 6th verse,) "Shall a trumpet be blown in the city and the people not be afraid?   Shall there be evil in the city and the Lord hath not done it?"   I need not say that the doctrine of an overruling special providence was drawn from these words, in opposition to atheism, chance, or some general divine providence which attends only to great things, which governs and directs the spheres, but lets the atoms fly at random,—that a warning was given to take heed to this judgment, and carefully inquire what was the righteousness that God called on us to learn.   The importance of literary institutions was dwelt upon, and especially the great duty of calling in the aid of Heaven in the conduct of them.

I hope the reader will excuse the insertion of the following passages:—

"The design of God, therefore, in these dispensations, and the use to be made of them by us, are as plain as they are important.   When God visits us with the rod of affliction, it is that we may search our hearts and try our ways and turn to him.   When his judgments are abroad in the earth, it is that the inhabitants may learn righteousness.   Does it not, then, become all concerned in this Institution to ask, May not these judgments have been intended to stir us up to more zeal in rendering it holy and acceptable to God?   Should they not ask, With what views and hopes have we entered upon this work?   Did we acknowledge the Almighty, and feel that without his blessing we could not prosper? or was our hope from the talents and favour of man?   Have we not only invoked the aid and placed it under the guardian care of God, but sincerely dedicated it to him, wishing to make it an instrument of glory in our land, by training up youths, not merely in human literature, but in the sublimest of all sciences and the noblest of all virtues,—the knowledge and love of God?   If such have not been the principles upon which this Institution was raised, or on which it is now conducted, is it superstition or weakness to ask whether these visitations have not been sent to show the rulers thereof their entire dependence upon God?   See how easily the Almighty can blast all their high hopes and dash all their noble schemes to the earth. See how quickly he can send a plague or pestilence through these buildings, and scatter far and wide the young tenants thereof, and strike such a panic through the hearts of parents and friends that you can scarce recall them. Oh, it is a hazardous experiment to undertake to conduct such an institution, in which the minds of young immortal and rational beings are to be instructed, and their passions restrained and their actions regulated, without constantly and earnestly imploring and seeking the aid of God in the way of his appointment. It cannot be done. I know the difficulties of this work; I am well aware of the peculiar difficulties of it in this place; and am not upbraiding those who are sincerely desiring to do all that is right. But still, as the minister of God requested to speak on this occasion, I can take no other view of the subject than that which has been presented, and am firmly convinced, from the word of God and the past history of man, that any attempt to succeed in such a work without invoking and securing the blessing of God must fail of permanent success.

"In every age of the world the instructors of youth have been deeply impressed with the importance of inculcating reverence to the gods, and making religion take its due part in their public exercises. The philosophers of Greece and Rome—Socrates and Plato, Seneca and Epictetus—failed not in this duty. The Rabbis in Judea made this a principal science in their schools. And has it pleased the Almighty to clear away all the shadows and clouds and reveal the true light to us? Has he visited the earth and brought life and immortality to light by the Gospel? Has he set this in opposition to all the wisdom of man,—philosophy, falsely so called,—saying, 'Where is the wise, where is the scribe, where is the disputer of this world? Hath not God made foolish the wisdom of this world?' And shall this be neglected and left out of the wide range of scientific research? Shall we be content to be wise for a few years only, and not for everlasting ages? From the circle of sciences shall the most important and sublime and interesting be excluded? In an institution bearing in its very name a determination to take the widest range of intellectual improvement, shall that be omitted in which all are equally because all are infinitely concerned? Shall the roving and adventurous mind of youth be permitted to wander through all the labyrinths and mysteries of science without the sure light of heavenly truth to guide it? Oh, might I be permitted to speak to all the friends and patrons and directors of this College in the language of plain but affectionate entreaty, I would beseech them, as they would have it to find favour with God and man and be a mighty blessing to our State and country, that they solemnly dedicate it to Almighty God, and place it under his guardian care. In his name and by his laws let them rule over it. Let them see that the high motives and awful sanctions of religion be continually and eloquently presented to the minds of the youth committed to their care. Let the divine philosophy of the Bible be here studied. Let the morality here taught be the morality of the Bible. Let the Bible, which is the religion of Protestants, be the text-book of first esteem and most constant reference. Let the history of our religion be learnt; let the proofs of Christianity be investigated; let the prophecies of the most ancient and venerable books be read and compared with all other histories that attest their fulfilment. Let it not be said that nothing is taught contrary to Christianity; that the mind is left free to its own choice: rather let it be announced to the world that every thing which can be said is said in its behalf, and every thing which can be done is done in order to lead those immortal souls, who come hither for the high improvement of their faculties, to the saving knowledge of Him who is 'the true God and eternal life.' Then indeed may we be assured that this Institution enjoys the smiles of a gracious Providence, and will be as others in our land,—the fruitful nursery of Christian patriots, of learned defenders of the faith, of able and eloquent ministers of the Gospel, as well as of those who shall adorn by their worth and talents all other professions of our land, and shed a mild lustre over the most private walks of life. Then will the most anxious Christian parents, and the most fearfully jealous Christian ministers, cherish it with fondness, as the favoured of God, and with confidence commit, as to a fostering mother, the sons whom they have dedicated to Heaven, and would have to be trained up in its holy nurture and admonition; and then will those pious youths who have been here advancing in all divine as well as human wisdom ever look back to these seats of science with delight, and reckon among the happiest and best of their days those spent within these consecrated walls."

At this discourse much offence was taken by some, and many misrepresentations went forth through the State. It was charged against it that, besides undertaking to interpret and apply the judgments of God in a way which had been most carefully avoided, a personal attack had been made on the Professors and Visitors of the University, and especially on its chief founder, whose opinions, having been published to the world, were known to be contrary to those expressed in the sermon. So extensively were these charges, with many colourings and exaggerations, spread abroad, that after due consideration the sermon was published, and the author had the happiness of learning that the effect of its publication was such as he desired. Many were astonished to find that any in a Christian land could object to its doctrine, or expect any other improvement of the occasion from a Christian minister. But it was long before the preacher could be forgiven by some within the walls of the University. Previous to that he had been freely invited to preach there, but for some years even some of his friends were afraid to propose it. We must, however, in justice say, that the opposition was not from Virginians, nor from Americans, but from foreigners, who were allowed to forbid a minister of Virginia to be heard in the University of Virginia. It was, however, the happiness of that minister to see, only a few years after, all the offensive features of his sermon adopted into the administration of the College, as far perhaps as is practicable under the circumstances of its existence as the common property of all denominations of Christians and all citizens of the State.

ARTICLE LII.

Parishes in Amherst, Nelson, Botetourt, Rockbridge, Greenbrier, and Montgomery.

IN 1761, Amherst county and Amherst parish were separated from Albemarle county and St. Anne's parish. In the year 1778, Amherst parish was divided and Lexington parish established. In the year 1780, the boundary-line was changed so as somewhat to reduce Lexington parish. The line, as settled in 1780, we presume is the same, or nearly the same, which now separates Nelson and Amherst. Amherst parish was left in that part which is now Nelson county. We have seen in our notice of the Rev. Mr. Rose, that he became minister of this region about 1745 or 1746, by being minister of all St. Anne's parish and Albemarle county, then extending over Amherst and Nelson; that he had four churches ordered by the vestry at one time,—two in what is now Albemarle, and two in what is now Amherst and Nelson. He was followed by the Rev. John Ramsey, who was minister in 1754 and also in 1758,—how much longer not known. In 1773-74-76 we find the Rev. Ichabod Camp minister of Lexington parish,—how long before 1773 not known. He lived at the glebe near New Glasgow, now in possession of Dr. Hite. The shell of the parsonage is still to be seen.

About the commencement of the war, Mr. Camp moved to Illinois, to a fort on the Wabash, and tradition says that he and his family were destroyed by the Indians. The first minister of Lexington parish, after its division from Amherst, was the Rev. John Buchanon, in the year 1780. The following is the entry in the vestry-book:—" The vestry, taking into consideration the distressed condition of the parish for want of an orthodox minister, elect Mr. J. Buchanon, a gentleman of fair character, &c." This is the same person who afterward ministered in Richmond. He was ordained in 1775, and had officiated acceptably elsewhere in Virginia. In the year 1788, the Rev. John W. Hole was elected. In the year 1789, the Rev. Charles Crawford, a native of Amherst, was ordained by Bishop Madison, and received as minister of this parish, and continued its minister until 1815, when, from great corpulency, age, and infirmities, he resigned.   Those who have retained the recollection of Mr. Crawford, and have knowledge of him otherwise, bear testimony to his excellency as a preacher and a Christian. The Rev. Silas Freeman succeeded him in 1823, and continued a few years.   The Rev. Charles Page followed him and laboured for many years in that and the adjoining parish of Amherst, in Nelson county.   The Revs. Nelson Sale, Stewart, Black, Caldwell, Walker, Caldwell again, and Martin, have followed in too rapid succession. The Rev. Mr. Nowlin is the present minister.

The churches in Lexington parish were—Pedlar's, near the mountains, where a new one was built some years since; Rucker's or St. Matthew's, some miles from the court-house; Maple Run Church, afterward moved to New Glasgow; and another called Bent Chapel, which was near James River.   This being burned down was never rebuilt.   The brick church now at New Glasgow was built by a general subscription, but chiefly of Episcopalians, and regularly assigned to them, but afterward claimed by others and forcibly entered by the Campbellites.   It was then bought, by the Episcopalians, of the executors of David Garland, to whom it legally belonged, being on his land, and was regularly consecrated as an Episcopal Church.   Another church of brick has within the last few years been built at the court-house of Amherst county. The following is the list of vestrymen of this parish from 1779:—

Richard Ballenger, Hugh Rose, Ambrose Rucker, Joseph Goodwin, Josiah Ellis, Richard Shelton, Richard Ogilsby, Benjamin Rucker, Wm. Ware, Henry Christian, John Christian, Charles Taliafero, Thomas Moore, Jos. Burras, W. S. Crawford, Nelson Crawford, Richard Powell, James Ware, James Franklin, Reuben Norvel, Thomas Crews, Richard Ellis, Thomas N. Eubank, William Shelton, John Coleman, Gabriel Penn, David Woodroof, James Dillard, Daniel Gaines, Samuel Higginbotham, Robert Christian, Roderick McCulloch, Samuel Meredith, John Wyatt, David Crawford, George Penn, Edward Carter, James Calloway, James Higginbotham, David Tinsley, Robert Walker, Henry Turner, John Eubank, James Ware, John McDaniel, Edward Winston, John Ellis, Arthur B. Davies, Cornelius Powell, Edmund Penn, David S. Garland, Dr. Paul Cabell, William H. McCulloch, Samuel M. Garland, Ralph C. Shelton, Zachariah D. Tinsley, Dr. H. L. Davies, James Thornton, William I. Cabell, William H. Johnson, John I. Ambler, Jr., Henry Loring, Valerius McGinnis, Whiting Davies, William R. Roane, Thomas Strange, James S. Pendleton, Captain J. Davies, Edward A. Cabell, Prosser Powell, William Waller, Wilkins Watson, A. B. Davies, Jr., B. B. Taliafero, Robert Warwick, Marshall Harris, D. H. Tapscott, George W. Christian, William Knight, Dr. William S. Claiborne, Lucas P. Thompson, Martin Tinsley, James Davies, William Shelton, James Rose, William Tucker, Edwin Shelton.

AMHERST PARISH, NELSON COUNTY.

We have seen that this was separated from Lexington in 1778. It is not known how many churches there were in it at that time, but certainly one at Rockfish Gap, near the mountain, and one near James River, in the neighbourhood of the Cabells. The Rev. Robert Rose, in his journal ending in the year 1751, often speaks of being at the houses of the Cabells and preaching in that neighbourhood, and doubtless a church must have been built there soon after, called Key's Church. About the year 1780, it is believed a Mr. Buchan was minister of that parish,—probably the same who was afterward in Stafford. In the year 1790 the Rev. Isaac Darneile appears on the journal of the Convention as minister of this parish. Of him I have spoken on a former occasion, as one who was always in pecuniary difficulties, who exchanged the pulpit for the bar, and, failing in that also, left his family behind, and, going to the South, spent some years there. In 1795 the Rev. William Crawford, brother or near relative of Mr. Charles Crawford, succeeded Mr. Darneile, preaching at Rockfish Key's, the old court-house, and Hat Creek. Mr. Crawford was, I believe, the last regular minister of this parish, until the Rev. Charles Page undertook the charge of it, in connection with that of Lexington, some years after the revival of the Church commenced. The Rev. Mr. King and Dr. Stephens, of Staunton, had performed some duties at Rockfish Gap Church before Mr. Page's more regular assumption of the charge of the parish. The Rev. Frederick Goodwin succeeded Mr. Page in this parish, and has continued to be its minister until the last year. The Rev. Mr. Martin is its present minister.*

As to the churches in the parish of Amherst and county of Nelson of more recent erection, there was, until a few years since, one called Calloway's Church, of whose date, however, I am unable to speak positively, but think it must have been at a much later date than the old ones which have long since passed away. This has been deserted of late years for two new brick houses,—the one called Trinity, near the residence (Oak Ridge) of old Mr. Rives, and built chiefly, if not entirely, by him, and the other at New Market, on the James River Canal, at the mouth of Tye River. The old church at Rockfish has also been removed to a more convenient place, not far off, and entirely renovated.

* The Rev. Cleland Nelson preceded Mr. Goodwin in this parish.

Amidst no little opposition, Captain John B. Coles and Mr. Martin, two fast friends of the Church, determined upon the effort for its removal and renewal, and invited all the neighbours—even the poorest—to meet at certain appointed days for its prostration, its removal and re-erection, and completely triumphed over all opposition and falsified all unfavourable prophecies. In another place I have stated that it has been for many years supplied with occasional services by ministers from Albemarle county.

THE FAMILY OF CABELLS.

Among the numerous families of Amherst and Nelson who were the active supporters of the Episcopal Church, the Roses and Cabells were most conspicuous. Of the Roses, the descendants of the Rev. Robert Rose, who died in 1751, leaving large estates to his four sons, we have already written in our sketches of the father in a previous article. Of the Cabells we will now make some mention, abridging our notice from the various accounts we have of them.

Dr. William Cabell, a surgeon of the British navy, emigrated to Virginia about the year 1720 or 1725, according to different accounts. It is said he owned twenty-five thousand acres of land on either side of Upper James River, in the counties of Nelson, Amherst, and Buckingham. He was one of the earliest vestrymen and wardens in the Church, as established in that part of Virginia, and was the intimate friend of the Rev. Robert Rose. Between the years 1740 and 1750 he appears as chiefly concerned in the contracts for the building of churches, &c. He had four sons,—William, Joseph, John, and Nicholas. William, the eldest, was the owner of the estate called Union Hill, in Nelson county, on James River. Mr. Grigsby has given a very glowing account of this mansion and the hospitality of its owner, and his great business-talents as a farmer, and in other respects comparing his house to Mount Vernon, except that it was larger, and himself to Washington, as to the management of his estate, and methodical accounts kept by him. He speaks of his association with Washington in all the great political bodies in Virginia previous to 1776, as well as in that year, and of his political career afterward, terminating in the adjournment of the Federal Convention. It remains for me to add, that before and after the death of his father, Dr. Cabell, he was also the active vestryman and churchwarden in the parish, the intimate friend of the Rev. Mr. Rose, who was often at his house. I have before me subscription-papers and contracts in which he is leader in all Church matters in the parish, especially after the Establishment was put down and it became necessary to raise a salary for the minister by private contributions. His son also, Mr. William Cabell, who was a representative in Congress from this district before his father's death, and in connection with his father, took part in the vestry-proceedings. Of his other sons I have no account. Of his daughters, one married Mr. Rives, the father of W. C. Rives and of a number of other sons and daughters; another married Judge Cabell; another the Rev. Mr. Legrand. The present Mayo Cabell, of Nelson, and Mrs. Bruce, of Richmond, are also descendants of Colonel Wm. Cabell. The second son of Dr. Cabell, father of the family, was Joseph, of whom all the information I have is, that he was also at various times in the House of Burgesses, and took part in the Revolution, and was the ancestor of General Cabell, of Danville, and of the Breckenridges of Virginia and Kentucky. Of the third son, John, I learn that he was in the Convention of 1775 and 1776, and was the father of the late Dr. George Cabell, of Lynchburg. Of the fourth son, Nicholas Cabell, of Liberty Hall, I find that he was both in the field and the Legislature, and was the father of the late Judge W. H. Cabell and Joseph C. Cabell. I have also papers showing that he was a vestryman of the church in this parish, and took a lively interest in its affairs. He was the collector of the subscriptions made to the ministers after the Revolution: to him Mr. Darneile applied in his difficulties, for relief, and both himself and his brother, Colonel Wm. Cabell, acted as friends to Mr. Darneile by advancing moneys for him. On a slip of paper before me I find that he also collected what was given to the Rev. Mr. Clay, while minister in Albemarle, for services rendered at Key's Church, in Nelson, but which Mr. Clay requested him to give to the poor of the parish.*

---

* The following additions to my account of the Cabells have been sent me by one of the family, and will, I am sure, prove interesting, not only to all of that wide-spread connection, but to many others.

"Dr. William Cabell came to Virginia either in 1723 or 1724. Colonel William Cabell, Sen. it was who once held twenty-five thousand acres of land in this region. His father may at one period have owned half so much. His object seemed to be rather to acquire that of the best and most durable quality for the use of his posterity, than to embrace a surface which could not be brought into use for a generation to come. He accordingly secured all the alluvial land in the Valley of James River, for more than twenty miles continuously, above this place, where he resided. Was not he also the Wm. Cabell whom Mr. Rose visited? I have some doubts whether Colonel Wm. Cabell (who was born in March, 1730) was settled at Union Hill

I have also a manuscript sermon preached by the Rev. Charles
O'Neale, then probably a minister of some neighbouring parish,

---

(or Colleton, as it was then called) before Mr. Rose's death. Two of the contracts
for building churches in Albemarle, which I sent you, were those spoken of by
Mr. Rose near the close of his diary, and probably left with Dr. Cabell for safe-
keeping.

"1. Of the sons of Dr. Cabell, the first and third—William and John—married respectively Margaret and Paulina, daughters of Colonel Samuel Jordan, who lived on
James River, in Buckingham, and near the Seven Islands. The former was accounted an able man and true patriot in his day, and was much respected in all the
relations of life. He had four sons, of whom three were somewhat distinguished
in the family. Samuel Jordan, the eldest,—who married Sarah, daughter of Colonel
John Syme, of Hanover,—was the member of Congress from this district from 1795
to 1803. He had risen to the rank of Lieutenant-Colonel in the Southern War, and
afterward served in the Legislature of the State, and in the Convention of 1789.
William, generally known as Colonel Wm. Cabell, Jr., also served in the latter scenes
of the war in this State, and was occasionally in the Legislature afterward. He
married Anne, daughter of Judge Paul Carrington, and was the father of Colonel
Edward A. Cabell, sometime of Amherst, now of Washington, D.C., of Mayo Cabell,
and of Mrs. Bruce, and others. Landon,—the third son,—a man of distinguished
talents and acquirements, but never in public life, married a daughter of Colonel
Hugh Rose, and was the father of Dr. R. Henry Cabell, now of Richmond. Colonel
Cabell's daughter Paulina had married Major Edmund Read, of Charlotte, (son of
Colonel Clement Read,) before she was married to Rev. Mr. Legrand.

"2. Colonel Joseph Cabell—who married a Miss Hopkins, of Amherst, (now Nelson,)—had but one son and several daughters. The son, who bore his own name,
married Pocahontas, daughter of Colonel Robert Bolling, of Chellowe, Buchanan,
and their descendants (of whom you have mentioned General Cabell) are numerous.
Colonel Joseph Cabell was the ancestor of the Breckenridges of Kentucky, and not
of Virginia. Thus, his daughter Mary married John Breckenridge, (elder son of
General James Breckenridge.) This gentleman, after a successful career at the
bar here, (he lived in Albemarle,) removed with George Nicholas to Kentucky,
of which territory they immediately became the leading citizens. When it was
erected into a State Mr. Breckenridge was sent to the Senate of the United States,
and at his death was Mr. Jefferson's Attorney-General. The eldest son of Mr.
Breckenridge (Joseph Cabell Breckenridge) was a rising statesman of Kentucky
at the time of his death. He married a daughter* of President Smith, of Princeton, and their son is now Vice-President of the United States. The three
younger sons of Mr. Breckenridge—John, Robert, and William—became distinguished Presbyterian clergymen. His daughter (Letitia) married first a son of
Mr. Senator Grayson, and second, General P. B. Porter, of New York, Mr. Adams's
Secretary of War. To return : Colonel Joseph Cabell had other daughters, of whom
Anne married Robert Carter, son of Carter Harrison, of Clifton, in Cumberland ; and Elizabeth married Colonel William J. Lewis, of Campbell, sometime member of Congress from that district. The major part of Colonel J. Cabell's descendants are now to be found in the West,—particularly in Kentucky and Missouri.

"3. Colonel John Cabell had several sons,—of whom Dr. George Cabell, of Lynch-

---

* Miss Caroline Smith, who, when the author of this work was at Princeton College, was a favourite
with the students by reason of her many interesting qualities.

afterward in Prince William, in the year 1794, on the occasion of the death of two of Mr. Nicholas Cabell's daughters, Hannah and Henningham, who died on the 7th and 8th of September of that year, aged the one eight and the other six years. In this sermon also we see the deficiency of the pulpit in that day. Once only is there allusion to Christ, when he says that " to those who lead a virtuous life, and die in the faith of Christ, the whole aspect of death is changed," while in the sermon, which is on resignation and preparation for death, he speaks of certain duties " to be performed in order to make us acceptable to God," and at the close of it says that "the best preparation for death is a virtuous temper and a good life. When once you are furnished with these qualifications, you may view it approaching toward you with a calm and constant mind, free from any timorous and unmanly solicitude." Nothing is said in the sermon about a new birth of the Spirit as a necessary qualification for heaven, of faith in Christ and repentance toward God as being the constant exercises of the true Christian, and from which any good works can flow. There are many very good things said about the vanity of earthly things and the duty of considering our latter end, but they are such things as are common to the Christian preacher and the pagan philosopher.

I might also speak of the Sheltons, Taliaferos, Thompsons, Ellises, Davises, Tinsleys, Garlands, and others, as having been fast friends of the Church in Amherst and Nelson, but refer to the list of vestrymen for the purpose of showing who were her persevering advocates.

There is one name on which I must dwell for a moment. Mr. William Waller, lately deceased, was perhaps inferior to none of the laity of Virginia in personal piety and hearty zeal for the

burg, was the eldest. His brother John, of the same place, was also a learned and successful physician.

" A third son—Frederick—succeeded to the family mansion on James River, opposite New Market, and his eldest son, of the same name, was several times a delegate from this county under the second Constitution, and the first Senator from this district under the present *régime*. A fourth son of Colonel John removed to Kentucky. One of his daughters married first her cousin Hector, and afterward Judge Daniel.

" 4. Colonel Nicholas Cabell embarked in the Revolutionary service so early as 1775, and several years afterward the Legislature appointed him to the command of one of the State Regiments; but it so happened, and much to his mortification, that he was never called into action. He served in the Senate for more than sixteen years from 1785. Of his four sons we have mentioned the first and third. The second was the father of Professor Cabell, of the University; the fourth of Francis Cabell, of Warminster."

Church, as well as for all that was amiable and excellent in private life. He was well known in our Conventions, which he delighted to attend, and acted as an efficient vestryman and lay reader for a long time. He has left a large family of children, who I trust will follow his good example.

One word is added concerning the family of Massies, in Nelson, not very far from Rockfish Church. It came at an early period from England, and settled in New Kent, where several in succession were vestrymen. Major Massie, of Nelson, after having served in the Revolution, moved from New Kent about the close of the war, and was a vestryman of the Church in Frederick county, with Colonel Burwell, Meade, and others. From thence he moved to Nelson, and lived in great seclusion the remainder of his days. He had three sons, of whom Dr. Thomas Massie, of Nelson, was the eldest.

COUNTIES AND PARISHES OF BOTETOURT, ROCKINGHAM, ROCK-BRIDGE, GREENBRIER, AND MONTGOMERY.

When Frederick county was first divided from Augusta, the latter was left with all of Western Virginia beyond the Alleghany Mountains, then extending to the Pacific Ocean, or, as it was sometimes said, to the "waters of the Mississippi."

In the year 1769, Botetourt was taken from Augusta, and also extended westward indefinitely. At a subsequent period Montgomery was taken from Botetourt. But in the year 1777, Rockingham, till then part of Augusta, and Rockbridge and Greenbrier, were cut off from Augusta, Botetourt, and Montgomery. In all of these, parishes were also established by Act of Assembly. What was done in them after this is unknown. In Rockingham, probably before its separation from Augusta, there were, as may be seen in our article on Augusta, two churches. In Rockbridge, when composed of parts of Augusta and Botetourt, there may have been a church or churches, but I have obtained no information of such. Before this period the Presbyterians had made settlements in this region, especially about Lexington. On none of our lists of clergy or records do we find any minister belonging to Rockbridge after its separation from Augusta and Botetourt. In Montgomery and Greenbrier parishes and counties, we presume there were none. In Botetourt parish, (for all the new parishes were called by the same name with the counties,) we find that the Rev. Adam Smith was the minister in the years 1774 and 1776. He was the father of Mr. Alexander Smith, sometimes written Smythe, of Wythe county, member of Congress, and General in the last war with England.

We know of no other but the Rev. Samuel Gray, who appears on the journal of 1796, and who died in the parish poor-house, the miserable victim of drink. In Fincastle there was an Episcopal church on the spot where the Presbyterian church now stands. A new church being built there, the Presbyterians worshipped in it, and were perhaps most active in its erection. By an Act of the Legislature, the lot of ground on which it stood was given to that denomination. It was not until the Rev. Mr. Cobbs commenced his labours in Bedford and extended his visits to Botetourt, that any hopes were raised, in the breasts of the Episcopalians in that county, of the establishment of the Church of their fathers and of their affection.

During the ministry of Mr. Gray, some of the descendants of Major Burwell, an old vestryman of the church in King William, had removed to the neighbourhood of Fincastle. General Breckenridge, and Watts, who had not forgotten the Church of their forefathers, were also there. Woodville, son of the old minister of Culpepper, one of the Taylors from Old Mount Airy, in the Northern Neck, Madison, son of Bishop Madison, and others who might be mentioned, were there to encourage the effort at establishing a church. And yet, on my first visit to that county after my consecration, only one solitary voice was heard in the responses of our service.

After some years the Rev. Dabney Wharton, from the neighbouring county, took Orders and entered on the work of resuscitating or rather establishing the Church there, and during his residence in the parish did much to effect it. The Rev. W. H. Pendleton succeeded him for some years, and, though removing for a time to another, has returned to a portion of his former field. He was succeeded by the Rev. Mr. McElroy, in 1847. The Rev. George Wilmer also spent some years there, first as minister to the whole parish, and then to a portion of it, which was formed into a distinct parish, now in the county of Roanoke. New churches have been erected in each portion,—one at Big Lick, in Roanoke, another at Fincastle, a third at Buchanon. The Rev. Mr. Baker has for some years been the minister of the two congregations in Fincastle and Buchanon. The new church at Buchanon deserves a word of special notice. It is chiefly the result of female enterprise. A lady well known in Virginia, who occasionally visited it in the summer season, fleeing from the sultry heat of Richmond, determined to effect it by collections, far and near, of only twelve and a half cents from each contributor, and by dint of perseverance, succeeded in the course of a few years,—at least, so far as to secure the object. A neat, well-filled brick church is now to be seen at Buchanon.

Although there was no church in Rockbridge county in former times, so far as I am informed, I must not omit to mention a most successful effort of later years. About the year 1839 or 1840, the Rev. William Bryant, a native of Virginia, and a graduate of West Point, who had left the army of his country to enter the army of the Lord and become one of the great company of preachers, was induced by his friend, and almost brother, as well as fellow-student at West Point, Colonel Smith, of the Military Institute at Lexington, to come and seek to establish an Episcopal church at that place. Difficult as the work seemed to be, and most doubtful the success of it, especially to one of so meek and quiet a spirit, and destitute of those popular talents in the pulpit so much called for in such positions, he nevertheless, in humble dependence on divine assistance, undertook the task and succeeded far beyond general expectation. With generous aids from other parts of the State, and active exertions on the part of the few friends in Lexington, a handsome brick church has been built and a respectable though still a small congregation been collected. The Rev. Mr. Bryant was succeeded by one of our present missionaries to China,—the Rev. Robert Nelson,—who, pursuing the same judicious course and putting forth the same efforts with his predecessor, carried on the work with the same success, until in the providence of God he was called to a distant field in which he had long desired to labour. The Rev. William N. Pendleton has now for some years been labouring as his successor.

Higher up the valley, in what was once Montgomery county and parish, but is now not only Montgomery, but Wythe, and Washington, and others, we cannot read or hear of any effort being made in behalf of establishing the Episcopal Church until within the last twenty years, when the Rev. Mr. Cofer was sent as missionary to Abingdon, in Washington county. Some years after his relinquishment of the station the Rev. James McCabe occupied it, and during his stay, I believe, a neat but very small brick church was put up. He was succeeded for two years by the Rev. Mr. Lee. It has now for some time been without a minister, though we hope for better times.

As emigration and natural increase of population shall follow the railroad up this narrow though fertile valley, and whenever the mountains on either side shall be cleared of their forests, we may

surely hope better things for our Church.   Already are there many
interesting families inheriting an attachment to the Church of their
fathers to be found along the great highway leading through this
part of Virginia and the West.   At Wytheville the indefatigable
efforts of a mother and daughter have raised a considerable sum of
money for the erection of a church.   The tongue hath spoken, the
pen hath written, and hands have laboured, in the cause, and none
of them in vain.   A most eligible sight, at great cost, has been
obtained, and perhaps great progress made in the erection of a
church.   Other openings, I am told by those who have made recent
missionary visits to this upper valley of Virginia, are likely to
present themselves.   The Rev. Frederick Goodwin has just settled
at Wytheville.

ARTICLE LIII.

St. George's Parish, Spottsylvania County.

I AM saved all trouble in the examination of records and documents, in order to the execution of this part of my work, by the full and interesting history of this parish from the pen of the Rev. Mr. Slaughter. His authorities are the old vestry-books and Henning's Statutes.

The county of Spottsylvania was established in 1720, being taken from the counties of Essex, King William, and King and Queen. It extended westward to *the river beyond the high mountains,*—the Shenandoah. The parish of St. George's was then commensurate with the county. In the year 1730, the parish was divided into St. George's and St. Mark's,—St. Mark's lying in the upper portion, which, in the year 1734, was made the county of Orange, and contained all that is now Orange, Madison, Culpepper, and Rappahannock. At the first establishment of Spottsylvania, in 1720, fifteen hundred pounds were appropriated by the House of Burgesses to a church, court-house, prison, pillory, and stocks. Governor Spottswood, after whom the county was named, established the seat of justice at Germanna, and there built a church, &c. In the year 1732, the seat of justice was, by Act of Assembly, removed to Fredericksburg, as a more convenient place; but, seventeen years after, the law was repealed as derogatory to his Majesty's prerogative to take from the Governor or Commander-in-Chief of this Colony his power and authority of removing or adjourning the courts because it might be inconvenient in a case of smallpox or other contagious disease. Fredericksburg was founded, by law, in the year 1727. Colonel Byrd, in his visit in the year 1732, says of it at this time, "Besides Colonel Willis, who is the top man of the place, there are only one merchant, a tailor, a smith, an ordinary-keeper, and a lady who acts both as a doctress and coffee-woman." A church was built in that year, (1732.) There had been a church near Fredericksburg in the year 1728, (as also one at Mattapony,) called the Mother-Church, besides that built at Germanna, by Governor Spottswood's order, at the first establishment of the county. Its first minister of whom we have any knowledge was the Rev. Theodosius Staige, whose name is found incorporated with the Davis family, of Albemarle, and with some others, I think. He continued until November, 1728. The Rev. Mr. De Butts, of Westmoreland, became a candidate for the parish; but the Rev. Rodham Kennor, having been recommended by the Governor, was accepted. He continued the minister for eighteen months, and then preached there once a fortnight for more than two years,—the Rev. Mr. Pearl occasionally officiating. The Rev. Mr. Kennor appears to have been a rolling stone,—passing from parish to parish,—and the vestry of St. George's were well pleased to part with him. In 1732, the Rev. Patrick Henry, uncle of the celebrated orator, and who was afterwards, and for a long time, minister of St. Paul's parish, Hanover, became the minister, and continued until April, 1734. Governor Gooch sent a Rev. Mr. Smith to the parish; but his preaching was so unacceptable that the vestry sent a deputation to inform the Governor that they could not accept him. . They also petitioned the Governor to allow the Rev. James Marye, who was the minister of the Huguenot settlement at Manakintown, in King William parish, then in Goochland, now in Powhatan, and who was willing to come, to leave his parish. He was accordingly inducted in October, 1735. During his ministry two chapels were built in the parish at places not now to be identified. Roger Dixon was allowed to have any pew in the church, except two already granted to Benjamin Grymes, provided he did not raise the pew higher than the other pews. In the year 1767, after a ministry of thirty-two years in this parish, Mr. Marye died, and was succeeded by his son, James Marye, who was born in Goochland, in 1731, was educated at William and Mary, and had been minister in Orange county. His father was one of the Huguenots who fled from France at the time of the persecutions of the Protestants in that country. He married a Miss Letitia Staige, of London, daughter of an English clergyman,—perhaps the one who was minister in Fredericksburg. Mr. Marye, Jr. continued the minister until 1780. He was the father of Mrs. Dunn, wife of the Rev. John Dunn, of Leesburg, and of Mrs. Yeamans Smith, of Fredericksburg. During his ministry a new church, near Burbridge's Bridge, was built, and was used as an Episcopal Church long after the Revolution, though now occupied by other denominations. The parish also was divided during his time, and Berkeley parish cut off from it. The parish was now vacant for seven years, at the end of which the Rev. Thomas Thornton was chosen its minister. Under his ministry and the voluntary system, which was of necessity adopted after the Establishment was put down, the congregation increased so as to require an addition to the church. This addition made it a cruciform church. It was, however, getting to be like an old garment with new cloth put upon its rent. During Mr. Thornton's ministry, General Washington, coming to Fredericksburg to visit his mother, attended, as usual, the Episcopal Church, which drew such a crowd that something gave way in the gallery, which produced great consternation in the attendants, who rushed out of it through the doors and windows. It, however, still lasted for a number of years. I was in it in the year 1811, but a more dark and cheerless place I have seldom seen. The rite of confirmation was first administered in this parish by Bishop Madison, in the year 1791, during the ministry of Mr. Thornton. Soon after this Mr. Thornton left the parish, and died at Dumfries. The following obituary, taken from a paper of that day, shows not only that he was a minister of that parish, but also the high esteem in which he was held:—

"Died, in Dumfries, on the 25th ultimo, in the 76th year of his age, the Rev. Thomas Thornton, late rector of this parish. He possessed steady faith, rational benevolence, and unaffected piety. With the dignity of the minister he associated the familiarity of the man, and was truly an ornament to human nature. In his sermons he was accurate and persuasive, more attentive to sense than to sound, to elevation of sentiment than to loftiness of style, expatiating on the evidences of Christianity when infidelity prevailed, and strongly urging the practice of Christian morality where vice predominated. His amiable qualities secured him universal respect, and his death is now the theme of universal lamentation."

A successor to Mr. Thornton was chosen in 1792, in a way most unusual in an Episcopal congregation, and contrary to her laws, except in the case of Christ Church, Norfolk, which is provided for by a special act. A notice was given in the old "Virginia Herald" inviting the subscribers to the Episcopal church to meet in the town-hall to elect a clergyman. On that occasion ninety-six votes were given for the Rev. Mr. Woodville, and thirty-four for the Rev. Thomas Davis. Mr. Woodville resigned the parish in 1793,—the year after his election,—and removed to St. Mark's, Culpepper, where he lived until his death, respected by all who knew him.

On the 6th of January, 1794, the people assembled in the market-house, and again, by a popular vote, unanimously elected the Rev. James Stephenson their minister. Mr. Stephenson resigned in 1805, on account of ill health. Mr. Stephenson married a Miss

Littlepage, a lady of fine intellectual endowments. He was the father of the Hon. Andrew Stephenson and Mr. Carter Stephenson, also of Mrs. Woodville.

In 1806, the Rev. Abner Waugh took charge of the parish, but was obliged to relinquish it by reason of ill health. Retiring to Hazlewood, where he soon died, he addressed the following letter to his friends in Fredericksburg:—

"Impressed with a high sense of their friendly regard and general attention to him during his residence and want of health among them, the Rev. Abner Waugh begs them to receive his acknowledgments. Loss of health, and consequently loss of power of being any longer useful, compelled him to relinquish his prospects in Fredericksburg. In bidding the citizens farewell, he wishes them, individually and generally, as much comfort, ease, and happiness in this life as may be consistent with a more exalted degree of happiness in the next."

In the year 1808, the Rev. Samuel Low succeeded Mr. Waugh. Mr. Low was a man of gigantic stature, stentorian lungs, and forbidding countenance. His powers of oratory were great. He had been, before his coming to Fredericksburg, preaching to crowds in Norfolk, Richmond, and elsewhere, on duelling and gambling, and other special topics. Some of these sermons were published. He was at that time living with a woman who was not his lawful wife, having deserted her who was his true wife and the mother of his children. It was some time before the news of this reached Fredericksburg, and when it did, he solemnly denied it in the pulpit. The fact being established beyond all doubt, he acknowledged it in a letter to the vestry, which is on record, and going to the North, obtained a divorce from his wife and married the other. The effect of all this must have been most disastrous to the Church.

In the year 1811, the Rev. Mr. Strebeck was chosen to fill the vacancy occasioned by the resignation of Mr. Low, but the Church was little benefited by the change. Such was the unhappy condition of the parish, that the people, in 1813, were glad to avail themselves of the services of their present minister, as lay reader, one year, I believe, before he was old enough to be admitted to Deacons' Orders.

As it has been a rule observed by me in these notices to avoid all praises or censures of the living, and in the fewest possible words refer to the acts and successes even of my oldest friends, therefore to Mr. Slaughter's account of the revival of the Church in this parish during the thirty-three years of Mr. McGuire's ministry, ending with his history of the parish, to which must now be added fourteen more, I refer my readers for a full view of the subject. Suffice it to say that, from that time, a succession of revivals, or rather a continued one, under faithful evangelical preaching, has added great numbers to the Church; that two new churches, each increasing in size and expense, have been called for; that several young ministers have issued from the parish,—among them the Rev. Launcelot Minor, whose remains are on the African shore, alongside of those of Mrs. Susan Savage, the devoted missionary, whose spiritual birthplace was St. George's Church, as Fredericksburg was that of her other nativity. Mr. McGuire and he who makes this allusion entered the ministry at a short interval apart, and cannot be long separated in leaving it behind, for another and we trust higher ministry, in the presence of our Redeemer.

Having done with the ministers and churches of St. George's parish, nothing remains but to present a list of the vestrymen of the same.

Vestrymen from 1725 to 1847.

Augustus Smith, William Grayson, John Waller, Thomas Chew, Geo. Wheatle, William Hansford, H. Sharpe, John Taliafero, Francis Thornton, Goodrich Lightfoot, Larkin Chew, Z. Lewis, Hon. John Robinson, Henry Beverley, Ambrose Grayson, Henry Beverley, Edward Hickman, John Chew, F. Taliafero, John Waller, Jr., Wm. Robinson, Rice Curtis, William Battaley, John Taliafero, Jr., Richard Tutt, John Thornton, Rice Curtis, Jr., William Waller, Edward Herndon, Robert Jackson, John Spottswood, Fielding Lewis, Joseph Brock, Roger Dixon, Richard Brook, Charles Lewis, Charles Carter, John Lewis, Charles Washington, William Dangerfield, Charles Dick, Joseph Jones, Edward Herndon, Thomas Fox, Lewis Willis, Thomas Colston, Thomas Minor, Michael Robinson, William Wood, James Tutt, Mann Page, George Thornton, Thomas Strachan, John Chew, John Steward, Thomas Crutcher, D. Branham, John Julian, J. W. Willis, James Lewis, G. Stubblefield, Benjamin Ballard, Thomas Sharpe, John Legg, Charles Mortimer, Chas. Urquart, Benjamin Day, Francis Thornton, Jr., George Weedon, Edward Carter, R. B. Chew, George French, W. S. Stone, John Herndon, Thos. Strachan, Edward Herndon, Beverley Stubblefield, John Welch, Edward Herndon, Jr., John Wright, William Stanard, William Lovell, Charles Gates, David Blair, Samuel Greenhow, Fontaine Maury, Elisha Hall, James Brown, William Taylor, John Chew, Hugh Mercer, Godlove Heiskell, Thomas Goodwin, William Smith, Robert Patton, David Henderson, David C. Ker, Jacob Kuhm, John Minor, Charles L. Carter, William I. Stone, Benjamin Botts, John Scott, John Lewis, Dabney Herndon, John Taliafero, Z. Lucas, Robert Wellford, James Smock, John Smith, Jr., William Bernard, G. W. B. Spooner, James Carmichael, Horace Marshall, Robert I. Chew, Francis Taliafero, Robert Lewis, Churchill Jones, Geo. Hamilton, John Mundell, Alexander F. Rose, R. Johnson, John Crump, Charles Austin, William A. Knox, John Gray, R. T. Thom, John Hart, William F. Gray, William Storke, F. J. Wyatt, John Metcalfe, John T. Lomax, H. O. Middleton, Larkin Johnson, George Rotchrock, Jr., Yeamans Smith, Thomas H. Hanson, Archibald Hart, W. M. Blackford, G. W. Bassett, Murray Forbes, E. H. Carmichael, Thomas F. Knox, R. B. Maury, John Coakley, James Cooke, R. C. L. Moncure, William Pollock, J. B. Ficklin.

BERKELEY PARISH, SPOTTSYLVANIA COUNTY.

This parish was taken from St. George's in March, 1769–70. The first minister was the Rev. James Stephenson, who was afterward the minister of St. George's. As he was ordained in London in 1768, and appears on the lists of 1773–74–76 as minister of Berkeley parish, it is more than probable that he was ordained expressly for this parish, and became its minister in 1769. He was, I believe, a citizen of Virginia, and an inhabitant of Fredericksburg, before his ordination. From the time that the Rev. Mr. Stephenson left it for Culpepper, previous to his removal to Williamsburg in 1794, we are unable to state who, if any, was the minister of Berkeley parish, until the year 1789, when the Rev. Hugh Coran Boggs appears on the journal of Convention. He was either ordained by some other English Bishop than the Bishop of London, or else by Bishop White, or some other American Bishop, since Bishop Madison was not consecrated until 1790. Mr. Boggs continued to be the minister of Berkeley parish until his death. Rev. Mr. Ward succeeded him in 1837. The Rev. Dabney Wharton, the present minister, succeeded to Mr. Ward in 1843. Two new churches have been built in this parish within the last year: one of them is near the court-house, and the other near the Louisa line.

ARTICLE LIV.

St. Mark's Parish, Culpepper County.

THIS parish was originally in Spottsylvania, when that was the frontier county, and was a part of St. George's parish. The vestry-book, from whence I derive my information concerning it, thus begins in 1730:—"In pursuance to an Act of the General Assembly holden at Williamsburg the 21st day of May, 1730, entitled An Act for dividing the parish of St. George, in the county of Spottsylvania, and that all the other parts of the said parish be known by the name of St. Mark: according to the said Act, the freeholders and housekeepers of the said parish of St. Mark did meet at the church at Germanna, in the said parish, on the 1st day of January, and there did elect and choose twelve of the most able and discreet persons of their parish to be vestrymen,—viz. : Goodrich Lightfoot, Henry Field, Francis Huntley, William Peyton, James Barber, (now Barbour,) Robert Slaughter, John Finlason, Francis Slaughter, Thomas Staunton, Benjamin Cave, Robert Green, Samuel Ball." Robert Slaughter and Francis Slaughter were the first churchwardens, William Peyton clerk, and William Peyton, William Philips, and John MacMath were continued lay readers at the several churches and chapels they formerly read at.

At the meeting of the vestry in March, 1731, the church at Germanna is ordered to be repaired and the roof tarred; the Fork Chapel and the Mountain Chapel ordered to be swept and kept clean. Three houses of worship are recognised as being in use before the division, that at Germanna being the church, the others the chapels. The church seems to have required repairs. This was doubtless the house built by Governor Spottswood for the German settlers, who, like the Huguenots on James River, had been patronized by Government and allowed certain immunities.* By this time, however, they had removed higher up the river, into what is now Madison county. Colonel Byrd, in his visit to General Spottswood in 1732, speaking of Germanna, says, "This famous

---

* Germanna was so called after this settlement by the Germans, as Spottsylvania was so called after Governor Spottswood.

town consists of Colonel Spottswood's enchanted castle on one side of the street and a baker's dozen of ruinous tenements on the other, where so many German families had dwelt some years ago, but are now removed some ten miles higher up the Fork of Rappahannock, to land of their own. There had also been a chapel about a bow-shot from the Colonel's house, at the end of an avenue of cherry-trees, but some pious people had lately burnt it down, with intent to have one built nearer to their own homes." Mr. Byrd's writings being full of such remarks, we may conclude that he does not always expect us to receive them as historical verities. No doubt the locality of the church was inconvenient, and many did not lament its destruction, as another would be built nearer to the body of the congregation.

Before we proceed further in the history of this parish, it may be well to state what information we have in relation to this German settlement which Governor Spottswood had cherished on his estate at Germanna, which estate, it is said, was only a part of a tract of forty-five thousand acres on which he worked a number of iron-ore furnaces. From the letter-book of the Venerable Society in England for Propagating the Gospel in Foreign Parts, we obtain the following document, headed—

CASE OF THE GERMAN FAMILIES IN THE YEAR 1720.

"The case of thirty-two Protestant German families settled in Virginia humbly showeth:—That twelve Protestant German families, consisting of about fifty persons, arrived April 17th, in Virginia, and were therein settled near the Rappahannock River. That in 1717 seventeen Protestant German families, consisting of about fourscore persons, came and set down near their countrymen. And many more, both German and Swiss families, are likely to come there and settle likewise. That for the enjoyment of the ministries of religion, there will be a necessity of building a small church in the place of their settlement, and of maintaining a minister, who shall catechize, read, and perform divine offices among them in the German tongue, which is the only language they do yet understand. That there went indeed with the first twelve German families one minister, named Henry Hœger, a very sober, honest man, of about seventy-five years of age; but he being likely to be past service in a short time, they have empowered Mr. Jacob Christophe Zollicoffer, of St. Gall, in Switzerland, to go into Europe and there to obtain, if possible, some contributions from pious and charitable Christians toward the building of their church, and bringing over with him a young German minister to assist the said Mr. Hœger in the ministry of religion, and to succeed him when he shall die; to get him ordained in England by the Right Rev. Lord-Bishop of London, and to bring over with him the Liturgy of the Church of England translated into High Dutch, which they are desirous to use in the public worship. But this new settlement consisting of but mean persons, being utterly unable of themselves both to build a church and to make up a salary sufficient to maintain such assisting minister, they humbly implore the countenance and encouragement of the Lord-Bishop of London and others, the Lords, the Bishops, as also the Venerable Society for the Propagation of the Gospel in Foreign Parts, that they would take their case under their pious consideration and grant their usual allowance for the support of a minister, and, if it may be, to contribute something toward the building of their church.

"And they shall ever pray that God may reward their beneficence both here and hereafter."

Whether they did succeed in their effort, and how long after this they continued at Germanna, and what was their history after their removal, we are not able to state. One thing we have ascertained from one of the oldest men now living in Culpepper,—that within his recollection, their descendants, when without a Lutheran minister, would come a long distance to receive the sacrament from an Episcopal minister at Buckrun Church, not many miles from Culpepper Court-House. It is very certain that at one time they had a large church, a flourishing congregation, a fine organ, and good music.

In passing on to our notice of the churches and ministers of St. Mark's, we cannot but express some surprise at not finding the name of General Spottswood among those of the vestry, although it is mentioned in the vestry-book, as he always appeared while Governor to be much interested in Church affairs. It may be that, as he lived on the outskirts of the parish, and the new church was now removed so far from him, he declined an active part in its concerns. In a few years after this he died. His widow and children continued to live at Germanna, and were within the pastoral charge of its ministers. We shall see hereafter that Mrs. Spottswood became the wife of one of them.

Previous to the year 1728, we ascertain that a Rev. Mr. Staige had officiated at Germanna, and after him a Rev. Rodham Kennor. Between the years 1731 and 1733 we find a Rev. Mr. De Butts and a Rev. Mr. Pruit often preaching in St. Mark's, but neither of them was elected. In May, 1733, the Rev. Mr. Beckett was regularly elected and continued minister until the year 1739.

In the year 1732, the vestry built a church at the Two Springs, on the Germanna Road, at the cost of thirty-six thousand-weight of tobacco. In the year 1633, the choice of a pew in the new church is offered to Colonel Spottswood. In the same year twenty-seven thousand pounds of tobacco are voted for building a new church in the Southwest Mountains; also, another, "twenty feet square, near Batley's Quarter, where David Cave be lay reader."

In the year 1735, a chapel is ordered between Shaw's Mountain and the Devil's Run. Ordered the same year "that the ministers preach as the law directs at every church and chapel."

In the year 1739 we find the following order:—"That the church-wardens agree with the Rev. Mr. McDaniel, if he please to serve the parish, and if not, some other minister, except Mr. Beckett." From something on the vestry-book a year or two before, there would seem to have been a serious cause of complaint against Mr. Beckett. In the year following—1740—the Rev. John Thompson comes, recommended by Governor Gooch, and is accepted. In this year also the parish of St. Mark, which was still in the county of Orange, was divided, and St. Thomas formed out of it. Mr. James Barber and William Cave being in the new parish of St. Thomas, Mr. William Triplett and William Russell were chosen in their room. Mr. John Catlett had been previously added to the vestry in place of one deceased. The estimate in which Mr. Thompson was held appears at once by the increased attention paid to the glebe-houses. In the year 1741, Mrs. Spottswood presents a velvet pulpit cloth and cushion to the church, and Goodrich Lightfoot is chosen vestry-man in place of Thomas Stanton, deceased. In 1742, a church was resolved on in Tenant's old field. In the year 1743, an addition of twenty-four feet square is ordered to the Fork Church. In 1746, Benjamin Roberts and Philip Clayton appear on the vestry. In the year 1747, Robert Slaughter, Jr. is appointed vestryman in place of W. Finlason, deceased, and William Green in place of Robert Green, deceased. In the year 1750, a chapel is ordered at the Little Fork, where an old chapel stood. In the year 1751, Abraham Field is on the vestry, also Thomas Slaughter in place of Robert Slaughter, Jr., who removed out of the parish, and James Pendleton in place of Samuel Ball, deceased. In 1744, large additions are made to the glebe-houses. In 1752, Bloomfield parish cut off from St. Mark's, and services at the court-house instead of at Tenant's Church. In 1752, Thomas Stubblefield and John Hackley on the vestry. In 1752, the site of the new chapel, which was ordered on the Little Fork, is changed to one in Freeman's old field, and to be called a church. In the same year,—1752,—a church ordered on Buckrun upon Colonel Spottswood's land, to cost fifty-four thousand pounds of tobacco. Some leaves being torn out, the next meeting of the vestry is in 1757,—Mr. Thompson still the minister. Nathaniel Pendleton and James Pendleton are each clerk of one of its churches. In 1758, Thomas Slaughter and Anthony Garnet elected vestrymen. In 1760, an addition ordered to the

Little Fork Church, thirty-two by twenty-two feet. William Williams vestryman in 1761. In the year 1763, William Ball vestryman in place of James Pendleton, deceased. Henry Field, Jr., in place of Henry Field, Sen., resigned. In the year 1764, the Rev. Mr. Thompson obtained leave to build a gallery in the church (that nearest Germanna) for the use of his family and friends. In the year 1766, Samuel Clayton vestryman in place of Philip Clayton, resigned. In 1768, Buckrun Church enlarged. In the year 1770, the old glebe sold to Samuel Henning, and Mr. Henning allowed to build a pew in the gallery of Buckrun Church. Cadwallader Slaughter chosen vestryman, and John Green in place of William Green, deceased. In the same year new glebe of three hundred acres bought of Francis Slaughter for one hundred and ninety-nine pounds and ten thousand-weight of tobacco. In 1771, Philip Pendleton appointed clerk of the vestry in place of William Peyton, deceased. He was also lay reader, as two others of the name had been, and others have been since elsewhere. In the same year French Strother and John Gray vestrymen, in place of Goodrich Lightfoot, resigned, and Henry Field, removed. Another addition to the Little Fork Church of the same dimensions with the last. In 1772, a glebe-house ordered, forty-eight feet long by thirty-two,—eight rooms,—for thirty-five thousand nine hundred weight of tobacco. In the midst of these preparations for the comfortable entertainment of the Rev. Mr. Thompson, his labours were ended by death, after a ministry of thirty-two years of uninterrupted harmony with his parishioners, and of laborious duty in a most extensive parish. Judging from the number of churches and chapels, and their frequent enlargement, and the benches we read of as placed at the doors, he must have been a most acceptable minister. His is one case added to a number which might be adduced, from the vestry-books, in proof that where the minister is faithful to his duty the people do not wish to exchange him. Some few exceptions doubtless there were. Of so exemplary a man as Mr. Thompson the reader will desire to know as much as can be furnished. Mr. Thompson was from Scotland, and took the degree of Master of Arts in the University of Edinburgh. On the 28th of October, 1739, he received Deacons' Orders in Duke Street Chapel, in the parish of Westminster, from the hands of Nicholas, the Bishop of St. David's. On the 4th of November of the same year, he received Priests' Orders from the same Bishop in the Chapel of St. James, within the palace royal of St. James of Westminster. On the following year we find him settled as minister in St. Mark's parish, where he continued until his death,—

knowing, as a minister, one only love. On the 9th of November, 1742, he married the widow of Governor Spottswood, who was one of his parishioners and living at Germanna. By this marriage he had two children, Ann Thompson, who was born at Germanna, in 1744, and married Mr. Francis Thornton, of Fall Hill, near Fredericksburg, at the early age of fifteen years, eight months. The other is Mr. William Thompson, of whom I have as yet received no certain information. In the year 1760, Mr. Thompson married a second wife, Miss Elizabeth Roots, by whom he had three children,—Mildred Thompson, John Thompson, and Philip Roots Thompson. The last married the daughter of old Mr. R. Slaughter, one of the vestrymen of that name in St. Mark's parish, and moved many years since to Kanawha, where his descendants for the last forty years have formed a little congregation of zealous Episcopalians.

But although Mr. Thompson was so good and amiable a man, and, as tradition informs us, one of the most imposing of men in his person, he did not easily succeed in securing his first wife, in consequence of the family pride of the children, which objected to the union of the widow of Governor Spottswood with a minister of the Gospel. Such was the opposition that, after an engagement, she begged to be released. This caused the following letter, which all must agree is a masterpiece of its kind. Its effect has already been told in the fact of their marriage in a few months. An entire reconciliation of all parties, however, was not effected until many years after, by the intervention of the Rev. Robert Rose, the friend and executor of Governor Spottswood, as I have said elsewhere.

Copy of a Letter from the Rev. John Thompson to Lady Spottswood.

"MADAM:—By diligently perusing your letter, I perceive there is a material argument, which I ought to have answered, upon which your strongest objection against completing my happiness would seem to depend, viz. : That you would incur ye censures of ye world for marrying a person of my station and character. By which I understand that you think it a diminution of your honour and ye dignity of your family to marry a person in ye station of a clergyman. Now, if I can make it appear that ye ministerial office is an employment in its nature ye most honourable, and in its effects ye most beneficial to mankind, I hope your objections will immediately vanish, y^t you will keep me no longer in suspense and misery, but consummate my happiness.

"I make no doubt, madam, but y^t you will readily grant y^t no man can be employed in any work more honourable than what immediately relates to ye King of kings and Lord of lords, and to ye salvation of souls, immortal in their nature, and redeemed by ye blood of the Son of God. The powers committed to their care cannot be exercised by ye greatest princes of earth; and it is ye same work in kind, and ye same in ye design of it, with y^t of ye blessed Angels, who are ministering spirits for those who shall be heirs of salvation.   It is ye same business y^t ye Son of God discharged when he condescended to dwell amongst men.   Which engages men in ye greatest acts of doing good, in turning sinners from ye errors of their ways, and, by all wise and prudent means, in gaining souls unto God.   And the faithful and diligent discharge of this holy function gives a title to ye highest degree of glory in the next world; for they y^t be wise shall shine as ye brightness of ye firmament, and they y^t turn many to righteousness as ye stars forever and ever.

"All nations, whether learned or ignorant, whether civil or barbarous, have agreed in this as a dictate of natural reason, to express their reverence for the Deity, and their affection to religion, by bestowing extraordinary privileges of honour upon such as administer in holy things, and by providing liberally for their maintenance.   And that the honour due to the holy function flows from ye law of nature appears from hence,—y^t in ye earliest times ye civil and sacred authority were united in ye same person. Thus Melchisedeck was King and Priest of Salem; and among ye Egyptians ye priesthood was joined with ye crown.   Y^e Greeks accounted ye priesthood of equal dignity with kingship, which is taken notice of by Aristotle in several places of his Politicks.   And among the Latins we have a testimony from Virgil y^t at ye same time Anias was both priest and king.   Nay, Moses himself, who was Prince of Israel, before Aaron was consecrated, officiated as priest in y^t solemn sacrifice by which ye covenant with Israel was confirmed.   And ye primitive Christians always expressed a mighty value and esteem for their clergy, as plainly appears from ecclesiastical history.   And even in our days, as bad as ye world is, those of ye clergy who live up to ye dignity of their profession are generally reverenced and esteemed by all religious and well-disposed men.

"From all which it evidently appears y^t in all ages and nations of ye world, whether Jews, Heathens, or Christians, great honour and dignity has been always conferred upon ye clergy.   And, therefore, dear madam, from hence you may infer how absurd and ridiculous those gentlemen's notions are who would fain persuade you y^t marrying with ye clergy you would derogate from ye honour and dignity of your family.   Whereas in strict reasoning the contrary thereof would rather appear, and y^t it would very much tend to support ye honour and dignity of it.   Of this I hope you will be better convinced when you consider the titles of honour and respect y^t are given to those who are invested with ye ministerial function as amply displayed in ye Scriptures.   Those invested with y^t character are called ye ministers of Christ, stewards of ye mysteries of God, to whom they have committed ye word of reconciliation, ye glory of Christ, ambassadors for Christ in Christ's stead, co-workers with him, angels of ye Churches.   And then it is moreover declared y^t whosoever despiseth them despiseth not man but God.   All which titles shew y^t upon many accounts they stand called, appropriated, and devoted to God himself.   And, therefore, if a gentleman of this sacred and honourable character should be married to a lady, though of ye greatest extraction and most excellent personal qualities, (which I am sensible you are endowed with,) it can be no disgrace to her nor her family, nor draw ye censures of ye world upon them for such an action.   And therefore, dear madam, your argument being refuted, you can no longer consistently refuse to consummate my happiness.   JOHN THOMPSON.

"May, 1742."

While we entirely agree with all that is written above as to the respectability of the ministry, we would caution against an ill use that is sometimes made of the principle advocated by Mr. Thompson. No matter how high the birth, how complete the education, of a lady, if she be truly pious, humble, and devoted to good works, she may be a suitable helpmate to a minister; but it is not often that one very delicately brought up in the higher walks of life can accommodate herself to the circumstances of many of the clergy. As to those who are born to large fortune, let the ministers of religion rather avoid than seek them as companions, taking warning from the many unhappy failures which have resulted from such experiments.

We now proceed with the history of the parish. After employing the Rev. Charles Woodmason for a short time, the vestry elected the Rev. Edward Jones, of Carolina, and had him inducted,—a thing of rare occurrence. In this year Mr. John Waugh is chosen vestryman. In the year 1773, it appearing that no convenient place, having water, could be found on the land purchased for a glebe, the vestry obtained one hundred more, at a cost of one hundred and fifty pounds, from Mr. Francis Slaughter. One of the churches being burned that year, the vestry determined to build one forty by sixty of wood, on Mr. Robert Freeman's or Peter Bowman's land. This order being reconsidered, it was resolved to build one eighty feet by thirty, of brick, on the land of Peter Bowman. In this year Captain Richard Yancey was vestryman in the place of Major John Green, who had entered the Continental service. In the year 1778, the vestry recommend subscriptions for paying the officers of the church. In the same year Biskett Davenport vestryman in place of William Williams, deceased. In February, 1780, Mr. Jones resigned the parish, and the vestry advertised it.* Mr. John Gray resigned his seat, Robert Pollard chosen vestryman. In April, 1780, the Rev. Mr. Stephenson was elected. The last meeting recorded in the vestry-book is in 1784. On the journal of the Convention in 1796, Mr. Stephenson appears as the minister of St. George's Church, Fredericksburg, and Mr. Woodville as from St. Mark's parish, they having changed places, as Mr. Woodville had been the minister of St. George's. Mr. Woodville had married the daughter of Mr. Stephenson, who was also the father of Mr. Andrew Stephenson, our late minister to England, and of Mr. Carter

---

* The Rev. Mr. Iredell also officiated for a time in this parish, but was a disgrace to the ministry.

Stephenson, who died some years since in Fredericksburg. With Mr. Woodville I became well acquainted soon after my entrance on the ministry, being often at his house (the glebe) in Culpepper, where he connected a school with the ministry, both of which he conducted in the most conscientious manner, being himself a man of unblemished character. His son James became a lawyer of distinction in Botetourt county, and his son Walker has for many years been supplying some parts of his father's old parish. With his wife and two daughters, Fanny and Sarah, I became intimately acquainted, and with purer spirits I do not expect to be acquainted on this side of heaven. The former has long since gone to her rest. The two latter—Fanny, who married Mr. Payne, and is the mother of a numerous offspring, and Sarah, who is unmarried, and lives with her—are residing in Mississippi. I often hear from them, and rejoice to know that they still love Virginia and the old Church of Virginia. I cannot take leave of old St. Mark's parish and vestry without a brief reference to those who once composed them,—the Spottswoods, Slaughters, Pendletons, Fields, Lightfoots, Barbers, Greens, Peytons, Caves, Balls, Williamses, Strothers, Knoxes, Stephenses, Watkinses, and others, who amidst all the adversities of the Church have been faithful to her. Others have followed in their path,—the Thompsons, Carters, Randolphs, Winstons, Mortons, Stringfellows, Cunninghams, Thoms, and others; but death, removals, and other circumstances, have sadly hindered her progress. Perhaps no part of Virginia has suffered more in this way than the county of Culpepper.

As I am writing of the past for the gratification and benefit of the present, and not of the present for the use of the future, I can despatch the remaining history of St. Marks in a few words. Soon after the resuscitation of the Church of Virginia commenced, a new church, called St. Stephen's, at Culpepper Court-House, was established within the bounds of St. Mark's parish, and the Rev. William Hawley appears on the journal during the years 1814 and 1815 as the minister. He laboured and preached zealously there and in Orange, and with much effect. He was followed by Mr. Herbert Marshall, who for some years laboured faithfully and successfully. In the year 1827, the Rev. George A. Smith commenced service and continued it for several years. The Rev. Annesley Stewart performed some duty there after Mr. Smith's removal.

The Rev. John Cole has now for a long term of years been minister in Culpepper. Previously to his coming a new church

had been built at Culpepper Court-House, and since his settlement
in the parish two new ones have been built on opposite sides of the
county, near each branch of the Rappahannock, while the old brick
church in Forke is still remaining.   A comfortable parsonage has
also been provided for the minister.

ARTICLE LV.

Orange County.—St. Thomas Parish.

[The Bishop is indebted for the following communication to the pen and labours of its present minister, the Rev. Mr. Earnest.]

THE county of Orange (embracing St. Mark's parish) was separated from Spottsylvania in the year 1734. It was "bounden southerly by the line of Hanover county, northerly by the grant of the Lord Fairfax, and westerly by the utmost limits of Virginia." In 1740, "for the convenience of the minister and the people," the parish of St. Mark's was divided. The southerly portion, including a part of what is now Madison county, was called St. Thomas parish, and its western limits were somewhat reduced. St. George's parish, Spottsylvania, of which St. Thomas was a part, had for its western boundary "the river beyond the high mountains:" the summit of the Blue Ridge being made the western limit of St. Thomas parish.

Before the days of the Revolution St. Thomas parish had within its limits three churches,—viz.: The Pine Stake Church, the Middle or Brick Church, and the Orange Church. The two former have disappeared entirely,—although both were standing and in tolerably good keeping within time of memory. The last named, and the oldest of the three, situated near Ruckersville, a small village about eighteen miles from Orange Court-House, in what is now the county of Green, is still standing, though it has long ceased to be used as a place of worship by an Episcopal congregation. It was for a long while in the occupancy of the Methodists. The old church, which is of wood, has undergone so many repairs since the time it was built, that it is thought, like the old frigate Constitution, little if any of the original timber is to be found in it. As I passed it some years since, for the first time, curiosity—rather I may say veneration for the ancient house of God—led me to stop and take a near view; but my heart was saddened to see this relic of former times so far gone into dilapidation as to be wholly unfit for the sacred purposes for which it was set apart. Here old Major Burton, a staunch patriot and as staunch a Churchman, who had served his country in the war of the Revolution, continued for a long while in the absence of the regular ministry to serve the church as a lay reader.

This church, though the oldest of these three Colonial churches, was not the first in point of time that was erected within this parish. The first church that was built in the parish was situated about ten miles northwest of Orange Court-House, on a portion of land now owned by Mr. Robert Brooking. The country adjacent was doubtless sacred ground with the aborigines long anterior to the discovery of America; for but a short distance from this "church in the wilderness," upon the right bank of the Rapidan River, is yet to be seen an ancient mound, or burial-place of the Indians. Here, as the waters of this rapid stream lave its banks, there are often exposed to view the bones of the mighty dead,—bones whose giant size indicate that a race of men hardy, athletic, and powerful once inhabited this fertile region.

At what period of time this first "Orange Church" was built, we have it not in our power exactly to verify. We have been told that it was frequented as a place of worship by some of the old settlers as early as 1723. Certain it is, that it was used as such in 1740,— the year in which St. Thomas was formed into a separate parish. The winter of this year was noted in this region for its exceedingly great severity. The degree of cold was so intense that several of the early planters determined on seeking a more genial climate farther south, and accordingly purchased lands in North Carolina. At that time an old Scotch minister of the Episcopal Church, whose name I have not been able to ascertain, but who it seems was fond of good cheer and a game of cards, officiated regularly at this church. He resided with Mr. Benjamin Cave, Sen., a first settler, whose residence was but a short distance from where the old church stood. Subsequently, as the settlements advanced westward, the old church was removed about eight miles distant to the place where its remains are still standing.

The Middle or Brick Church was situated about three miles southeast of Orange Court-House, on the old road leading to Fredericksburg, upon land owned originally by Mr. James Taylor, Sen., a first settler, and subsequently in possession of his grandson, Mr. Zachary Taylor, who was the grandfather of the late General Zachary Taylor, and is now owned by Mr. Erasmus Taylor. We have not been able to ascertain the year in which the church was built; but from certain private records in our possession we can assign the date of its erection somewhere between 1750 and 1758. This church, like the old Colonial churches generally, was well built and of durable materials. As late as 1806, time had made but little impression upon it. But what time failed to accomplish was reached by the unsparing hand of man. After the Church in Virginia was divested of her glebes, her houses of worship came to be regarded by the multitude as "common property." While her hand was against no man, every man's hand seemed to be against her. During or shortly before the last war with Great Britain the work of the church's destruction was begun. *Delenda est Carthago* seemed to be the watchword of the ruthless foe. They first commenced with the roof; this soon yielded to their onset; the rafters next gave way: the naked, massive walls resisted for a time their further onslaught, but, nothing daunted, they redoubled their forces and renewed the attack. The walls fell, and the triúmph of the invaders was complete, as they carried away as so many captives the vanquished, unresisting bricks. The altar-pieces, (the gift of Mr. Andrew Shepherd,) executed in gilt letters, and which long adorned the venerated chancel, were torn from their ancient resting-places, rent into fragments, and were afterward, though with no sacrilegious intent, attached as ornamental appendages to some articles of household furniture.

Amidst the general destruction of the property of the church, even the ancient Communion-plate, belonging to the parish, came to be regarded as *common property*. This plate, consisting of a massive silver cup and paten, with the name of the parish engraved thereupon, was, as we learn, the gift of a few pious communicants about a century since, among whom were Mrs. Frances Madison, grandmother of the President, and Mrs. James Taylor, mother of the late Mr. Robert Taylor, and Mrs. Balmaine. It has been only by the exercise of vigilance that this solitary remnant of the old church's property has been rescued and handed down in a state of perfect preservation, for the present use of St. Thomas's Church.

The time of the erection of the Pine Stake Church is, like that of the other two, involved in obscurity. It is probable that it was built about the same time as the Middle or Brick Church. It was situated near Mountain Run, about fifteen miles northeast of Orange Court-House, on lands originally taken up by Mr. Francis Taliafero, Sen. It continued to be used as a place of worship by an Episcopal congregation in the early part of the present century, and was standing at least as late as the year 1813. During the war of the Revolution a Mr. Leland, a Baptist preacher, who was a man of considerable notoriety in these parts at that period, applied to the vestry for the use of this church. The following letter from the *father* of President Madison, who was at the time a member of the vestry, written in a clear, bold hand, (the original of which we have in our possession,) answers his application, and at the same time throws no little light upon the rights and privileges of the Church as they stood at that time:—

"August 23, 1781.

"SIR:—For want of opportunity and leisure, I have delayed till now answering your letter relative to your preaching in the Pine Stake Church. When the vestry met I forgot to mention your request to them, as I promised you, till it broke up. I then informed the members present what you required of them; who, as the case was new and to them unprecedented, thought it had better remain as it then stood, lest the members of the church should be alarmed that their rights and privileges were in danger of being unjustifiably disposed of.

"I do not remember ever to have heard of your claiming a right to preach in the church till you mentioned in your letter of such a report. As to any right in Disenters to the church, you may see by the Act of Assembly made in the October Session in 1776, they are excluded. The Act, probably to satisfy the members, (as much as the nature of the case would admit of,) reserved to the use of the Church by law established the glebes, churches, books, plate, ornaments, donations, &c. Which, as hath been generally said, the Dissenters were well satisfied with, having in lieu thereof by the same authority gained a very important privilege,—the exemption from contributing to the support of an established Church and ministry, which they had long groaned under and complained of. On considering the case I make no doubt, sir, but your candour will readily excuse the vestry in not granting your petition.

"I am, sir, your humble servant,

"JAMES MADISON.

"Rev. Mr. LELAND."

At a later period, ministers of other denominations had free access to these old Colonial churches, and used and occupied them not so much by courtesy as of common right. The Old Orange Church was for a long while in the exclusive use of another denomination of Christians, and the Middle Church was for some time, as was also Walker's Church in Albemarle, alternately occupied by the Rev. Matthew Maury and the blind Presbyterian preacher. The latter came to this part of Virginia at a period of great depression in the Episcopal Church, and a house of worship was erected for him near Gordonsville, in this county, to which, however, he did not confine his ministrations. It was here, probably on his way from Albemarle to Orange Court, that Mr. Wirt was furnished with a theme which has given as much notoriety to himself as to the preacher. Before this Mr. Waddell laboured among his people in comparative obscurity. His fame as a preacher was little known, even in his own immediate vicinity, until after the appearance of Mr. Wirt's celebrated letter in the British Spy. His congregations, which previously had been very small, now became large to overflowing. Persons from a distance far beyond the usual limit of attendance upon divine worship in those days—some on foot, some on horseback, some in "every kind of conveyance"—flocked to hear the famous *blind preacher*. Without meaning to detract aught from his fame as a preacher, we have no doubt, if we may form an opinion from the representation of persons who knew him well and heard him often, that his discourse on the occasion referred to owes not a little of its surpassing beauty and effectiveness to the brilliant imagination and fine descriptive powers of the author of the British Spy.

Turning now from the old Colonial churches to the clergy who ministered in this parish in former times, we find ourselves, in the absence of vestry-books and other ancient records, somewhat at a loss to reproduce in exact chronological order their names and the period of their service. "The memory of man," and some private records in our possession, must furnish all the data upon which we can proceed in this regard. The old Scotch minister to whom we have already referred, who resided near and preached at the first Orange Church as early as 1740, is the first in the order of time of whom we can obtain any information; and even his name is passed into oblivion. In 1753, the name of the Rev. Mungo Marshall appears for the first time in connection with this parish, though it is probable he took charge of the same at an earlier period. He continued to reside here until the time of his death, which took place either in 1757 or 1758. We find it on record in the clerk's office of this county, that letters of administration upon his estate were taken out in the latter year. He was buried in the churchyard attached to the Old Brick Church, but for a long while no stone or other memento distinguished the place of his interment. At length, many years after his death, a connection of his bequeathed a certain sum, upon condition that his legatee was not to receive it until he had first placed a tombstone over the remains of the Rev. Mungo Marshall. In due time thereafter this was done. But it was not long permitted to designate the quiet resting-place of the dead. When the work of destruction commenced upon the church, the despoilers did not overlook the churchyard. The graves of the departed, and the monuments sacred to their memory, were not sacred in their eyes. The tombstones were borne off by their sacrilegious hands and appropriated to common and unhallowed uses. That which covered the remains of this man of God was used first to grind paints upon, and afterward served in a tannery for the purpose of dressing hides.

In 1760, we find the Rev. William Giberne officiating in this parish. Whether he was removed by death or otherwise we cannot ascertain; but his residence here was a brief one;* for at the close of the year 1761, the Rev. James Marye, Jr., having just entered into Orders, commenced his ministry in Orange. His first recorded official act to which we are able to refer was his preaching the funeral sermon of the paternal grandmother of President Madison. We find in the family record of her son (James Madison, Sen.) the following entry:—"Frances, wife of Ambrose Madison, departed this life October 25, 1761, and was interred the Sunday following, (at Montpelier in Orange.) Her funeral sermon was preached on Wednesday the 30th of December following, by the Rev. Mr. James Marye, Jr., on Revelations xiv. 13." Mr. Marye was a worthy exception to a class of clergy that obtained in Virginia in olden time. So far as we can learn, he was a man of evangelical views and sincere piety. We have seen a manuscript sermon of his on the religious training of children, which would do honour to the head and heart of any clergyman, and whose evangelical tone and spirit might well commend it to every pious parent and every enlightened Christian. He remained in charge of this parish about six years. Upon the death of his father, (the Rev. James Marye, Sen.,) who was the minister of St. George's parish, Spottsylvania, for thirty-one years, he was chosen to supply his place,—an unmistakable evidence of the high regard in which both father and son were held by the parishioners of St. George's. The Rev. Mr. Marye is the first minister in St. Thomas parish whose residence we can with any degree of certainty fix at the glebe. This farm, after passing through various hands since it ceased to be the property of the Church, is now by a singular coincidence in possession of one of his lineal descendants, Robert B. Marye, Esq.

The Rev. Thomas Martin succeeded Mr. Marye in 1767–68. He was a young man of merit. He came with his mother and sister to reside at the glebe; but his residence was of short duration. Death removed him from the scene of his labours and his usefulness not long after he entered upon the duties of the parish. He was followed by the Rev. John Barnett. His name occurs officially in 1771. But his connection with the parish was also of brief dura-

* He removed to Richmond county, Virginia.

tion, for in 1774 the Rev. John Wingate was the minister, and is the last of the ante-Revolutionary clergy whose name occurs. Whether he continued in charge of the parish during the war we have no means to verify; but circumstances justify the conclusion that, like some others of the old Colonial clergy, he surrendered his charge at the commencement of hostilities between the Colonies and the mother-country.

A period of sad depression dates from this time. For the long interval between 1774 and 1797, (twenty-three years,) the parish seems to be without a minister. The occasional services that were rendered by the Rev. Matthew Maury, of Albemarle, during the latter part of this interval, are, so far as we can see, the only ones performed by any clergyman. Mr. William Moore, a man of note in the parish at this time, a good old Churchman and an excellent reader, was generally called upon on funeral occasions to read the burial service. In the first Convention of the Church in Virginia, held in 1785, we find St. Thomas parish, though without a minister, not without a representative. Mr. Thomas Barbour (father of the late Governor and of the late Judge Barbour) appeared as the delegate. In the following year the parish is again represented by Mr. Barbour, in connection with Mr. William Moore. In 1790, Thomas Barbour and J. Daniel are the delegates. In 1793, the parish is again represented by Thomas Barbour. In 1797, we find the Rev. Charles O'Niel the clerical and William Moore the lay delegate. The Rev. Mr. O'Niel took charge of the parish in the latter year, and remained until 1800. He resided first near the Pine Stake Church, and preached at that church during his residence in Orange. He afterward removed to the upper part of the county, where, as well as at his former residence, he taught school in connection with his parochial duties. The late Judge Barbour was one of his pupils. Mr. O'Niel was an Irishman, and a man of ardent temperament and of ardent temper. We have often heard him spoken of by elderly persons, but more as a teacher than as a preacher. He was of that class of teachers that adopted not only the theory, but the practice also, of the old *régime*, as the best for the government of boys. Flogging was a main ingredient in the practice of his system. He had a summary method of reducing and gentling a refractory youth. Mounting him upon the back of an athletic negro man, whom he seems to have kept for the purpose, the culprit was pinioned hand and foot as in a vice, and, with the unsparing application of the rod to his defenceless back, was taught the lesson, if not the doctrine, of passive obedience. However his school may have flourished under his management, it seems his parish did not, for we look in vain for any fruits of his parochial labours. Another long interval now occurs in the history of the parish, without any one to take the regular oversight of its spiritual interests. The Rev. Matthew Maury again kindly extended his care to this neglected field, and performed occasional services in it at least as late as 1806. In 1809–11, we find the Rev. Hugh Coran Boggs, of Berkeley parish, Spottsylvania, devoting a portion of his time to Orange. He preached at the Pine Stake Church and also at the court-house. We have often heard it said, that when he preached at the latter place he was never known to use the Liturgy. This may have been owing to the difficulty he met with in procuring the responses. He may have rightly judged the *lex necessitatis* to be a "higher law" and of more stringent force than any canon or rubric to the contrary. From 1811 to 1815 the parish was again without a minister. In the latter year, the Rev. William Hawley, coming to reside at Culpepper Court-House, took charge of St. Thomas parish in connection with St. Stephen's Church, Culpepper. At the time he commenced his labours in Orange, the Episcopal Church had wellnigh died out in the county. But three or four communicants remained in all this region of country, and some of these were far advanced in age. So entirely had our time-honoured service gone into desuetude, that when Mr. Hawley first commenced its use it was listened to as a striking novelty. Under his ministry there began to appear the dawn of a brighter day for the Church. Several communicants were added; some of whom, in the providence of God, still remain with us. In the autumn of 1816, Bishop Moore made his first visitation of the parish, preached and administered the Lord's Supper, and also the rite of Confirmation, in the court-house. This was now our usual— nay, our only—place of worship. Referring to this visitation, the Bishop, in his report to the following Convention, says, "My labours commenced in the county of Orange, at which place I preached to a large and attentive auditory, celebrated the Lord's Supper, and administered the rite of Confirmation to a goodly number." The visit of the good Bishop, as well from its novelty as its effectiveness, was calculated to make, and did make, a great impression at the time. It was an event of unusual solemnity, and is still remembered with lively interest by some who were present. This was the first Episcopal visitation that had ever been made, and this the first time the rite of Confirmation had ever been administered, in the parish. Bishop Madison, it appears, was in the habit of visiting his relatives at Montpelier, socially, from time to time, but we learn from undoubted authority that he never visited the parish in his Episcopal capacity.   Among the "goodly number" confirmed by Bishop Moore on this occasion was the aged mother of President Madison.   She became a communicant at the age of twenty, and now at the age of fourscore and four she came forward to ratify her early baptismal vows.   Until that day an opportunity had never presented itself for the reception of this solemn and sacred rite.   The ministry of Mr. Hawley was evidently blessed during his connection with the parish; but the growing interest in religion and the Church which now became manifest was checked at this auspicious period by his removal in 1817 to another field of labour.   In 1820, the Rev. Herbert Marshall came to Culpepper and devoted some of his time to Orange.   This worthy young minister married the sister of the present Bishop of Kentucky.   The parish was very soon deprived of the benefit of his labours.   Death ended his usefulness not long after he came to this part of the diocese.   For about two years from 1823, the Rev. Frederick Hatch, of Albemarle, had the oversight of the congregation in Orange, officiating once a month at the court-house.   In the winter of 1826-27, the Rev. George A. Smith came to reside in Culpepper, and took charge of St. Thomas parish in connection with St. Mark's.   He continued in charge until 1830, and devoted two Sundays in the month to the congregation at Orange Court-House.   While it appears the attendance on divine service was good and the congregations attentive during the time he officiated here, yet at this period the interests of the parish were at a low ebb. In his report to Convention in 1828, Mr. Smith says, "There is no vestry in this parish, and the churches which existed there some years since have been destroyed."   A decided improvement, however, in the spiritual interests of the congregation took place under his ministry, and several communicants were added to the Church. In the early part of August, 1832, the Rev. William G. H. Jones, coming on a visit, was induced to take up his residence in Orange, and to undertake the pastoral care of the parish together with Walker's Church, in Albemarle.   Here he met with the Assistant-Bishop of the diocese, who had an appointment at Orange Court-House at that time.   This was a most auspicious period in the history of the parish.   There was found at the time of his coming a deep awakening in the hearts of many·on the subject of religion; and this interest was kept alive for some time thereafter.   The visit of Bishop Meade at the time was also most opportune, and was attended with the happiest effects. In his report to the following Convention he stated, "From Albemarle I proceeded to Orange Court-House, where I spent two days in ministering the word and ordinances to large and deeply-impressed assemblies; on the second day I administered the rite of Confirmation to seventeen persons, and the Holy Communion to more than twice that number. A spirit of earnest inquiry has been awakened among the people of that place, which will, I trust, lead to glorious results to themselves and their posterity." Of the communicants added on that occasion, Mr. Jones, in his first report from St. Thomas parish, says, "Five were added by Bishop Meade, and twelve by myself." An effort was now made to reorganize the parish. A vestry was elected—a body which had not existed in the parish for many years—and steps were shortly after taken for the building of a church. In 1833, a spacious and eligible lot in the village was selected, and a neat church-edifice of brick was commenced and completed the following year, at the cost of three thousand five hundred dollars. The Rev. Mr. Jones continued in Orange until the summer of 1840.

In January, 1841, the present minister took charge of the parish. Since that time there have been alternate seasons of prosperity and adversity in the congregation. Yet, in the face of some discouragements, both the communion and the congregation have steadily increased. Mr. Jones, in his last report to Convention from St. Thomas's Church, gave thirty-four as the number of communicants: the number now reaches ninety. In 1853, to accommodate the increasing congregation, the church-edifice was enlarged, and at the same time both the exterior and interior were much improved.

When we look back at the depressed state to which the parish was reduced, and compare it with what it now is, we cannot but exclaim, "What hath God wrought!" and to add, "Not unto us, O Lord, not unto us, but unto thy name, give glory." If we except the interval between 1797 and 1800, during which the Rev. Mr. O'Niel resided in Orange, the parish was without a resident minister from 1774 to 1832. Nowhere, during the long and dreary night through which the Church in Virginia was made to pass, was the darkness more distinctly visible than in Orange. With but three or four communicants left, and they far advanced in age,— with her substantial church-edifices, erected in Colonial times, utterly destroyed,—with the graves of her once honoured servants, who ministered at her altars, dismantled and insulted,—with her time-hallowed Liturgy, so dear to every true-hearted Churchman, gone into disuse and become a novelty in public worship,—with a parish without an organization and existing only in name, and with the place of litigation as the only place for the worship of Almighty God,—the destruction of the Church in Orange seemed wellnigh complete. But light was made to dawn upon her darkness. By the mercy of God she has risen again, phœnix-like, from her former ashes, and is now, in point of numbers, as it respects both her communion and her congregation, one of the largest of the rural parishes in Virginia.

During the darkest period of the parish, there were not wanting a few faithful witnesses. These were identified with the Church in the time of her prosperity and in the time of her adversity. They forsook her not because she was down-trodden and depressed; on the contrary, they loved her more the more she was afflicted, and clung to her like loving children to a devoted mother. If among God's ancient people the children were blest for their fathers' sake, so we may believe the Church in Orange was ultimately blest for the sake of these devoted servants of the living God. Among these we deem it proper to notice specially the names of several individuals, and we can do so now with the more propriety as we speak of the dead and not of the living. The individuals to whom we allude were the mother of President Madison, the mother of Governor and Judge Barbour, Mrs. Frances Burnley, and Mrs. Jane Howard,—the two last the sisters of Mrs. Lucy Balmaine, of Winchester. These were all bright ornaments of the religion which they professed, and the savour of their piety continues to the present day.

In the absence of vestry-books and other records, I am unable to furnish the names of the vestry prior to the reorganization of the parish in 1832. Since that time we find among the vestry the following:—

Charles P. Howard, Mann A. Page, Jeremiah Morton, James Shepherd, Peyton Grymes, Lewis B. Williams, Anthony Twyman, Robert T. Willis, Lawrence H. Taliafero, John Taliafero, Benjamin Franklin Taliafero, Jaqueline P. Taliafero, Uriel Terrill, Thomas T. Slaughter, John J. Ambler, John H. Lee, James H. Minor, William Bankhead, Peter T. Johnson, Thomas A. Robinson, and Horace D. Taliafero.

The principal families connected with the Church in Orange in Colonial times were the Barbours, Bells, Burtons, Campbells, Caves, Chews, Conways, Daniels, Madisons, Moores, Ruckers, Shepherds, Taylors, Taliaferos, and Whites. Mr. Richard White, who died some years since at the age of ninety, was the last communicant connected with the Old Orange Church. With comparatively few exceptions, the descendants of these respective families continued to retain their attachment to the Church of their fathers, and some of them are among its most worthy members.

The following letter has also been received from the same:—

"ORANGE COURT-HOUSE, March 7, 1857.

"RIGHT REV. AND DEAR SIR:—Since I wrote you some days since, a few items of interest in relation to this parish have come to my hands. A single leaf, and that somewhat mutilated, of the old vestry-book of St. Thomas parish, was found among the papers of one of my communicants who died last week, and has since been handed to me. From this I am able to ascertain who composed the vestry as far back as 1769. The record states:—'At a vestry held for St. Thomas parish, at the glebe, on Friday, the 1st day of September, 1769, present, Rev. Thomas Martin, Eras. Taylor, James Madison, Alexander Waugh, Francis Moore, William Bell, Rowland Thomas, Thomas Bell, Richard Barbour, William Moore.' The object of their meeting was to take into consideration the repairs necessary to be made to the house and other buildings connected with the glebe.

"From a private record kept at the time, I also learn that the congregation in Orange, in the year 1786, engaged the services of Mr. Waddell, the blind Presbyterian minister, to preach for them for two years. He officiated at the Brick Church. There was no Episcopal clergyman here at the time. It appears that forty pounds were subscribed for him, and it was expected the subscription would reach sixty pounds. The Rev. Mr. Balmaine was here occasionally at that period, addressing Miss Lucy Taylor, whom he married on the 31st day of October, 1786. He preached and administered the ordinances from time to time, both before and after his marriage. On one occasion, when Mr. Waddell preached, we observe he gave notice that he would preach and administer the Lord's Supper on the following Sunday.

"I have also ascertained that the Rev. Mr. O'Niel was in Orange in 1796. I stated he came in 1797. You will make this correction, and also add to the list of the families the Thomases and the Waughs.

"Yours very truly and affectionately, J. EARNEST."

ARTICLE LVI.

The Genealogy of the Madisons and Taylors—President Madison's religious character—Churches in Madison and Rappahannock.

THE following documents will give you the ancestry of President Madison. You may be aware that he married Mrs. Dolly Todd: her maiden name was Payne. She was, as I am informed, a Quakeress, and was born in the county of Hanover, but at the time of her marriage resided in Philadelphia. It was, if I mistake not, while he was a member of Congress, sitting at the time in Philadelphia, that he made her acquaintance. She was a lady of exceedingly attractive manners. During the latter years of her life she resided in Washington, and in her old age was baptized and became a member of St. John's Church in that city. Mr. Madison died without children. Mrs. Madison had one child, a son, by her former marriage.

I have thought it best to furnish you with a transcript from the record of James Madison, Sen., as it will give you some further information respecting the family. It was transcribed in great haste, and was intended only for my own eye.

A.—James Madison (the late President) is the eldest of twelve children—eight sons and four daughters—of whom but one brother and one sister are now living. He was born on the north bank of the Rappahannock, at Port Conway, opposite the town of Port Royal, on the 5th of March, 1751. His father's name was James, the son of Ambrose Madison and Frances Taylor. He lived to the age of seventy-eight years, and died in February, 1801. The father of Ambrose was John, the son of John Madison, who it appears took out, by a statement of a patent now in possession, certain lands on the shores of the Chesapeake, between North and York Rivers, in Glocester county, near Colonel Taylor's creek, in the year 1653,—6th Charles II.,—Richard Bennet, Governor and Captain-General of Virginia. The ancestors of Frances Taylor are traced one remove further back, and were residents of the same district of country. The name of his mother was Nelly Conway, descended from some of the early settlers. Her father, Francis, lived near Port Royal, in the county of Caroline, whose father, Edwin Conway, married Elizabeth Thompson. Her mother, Rebecca, was the daughter of E. Gaines and John Catlett, whose father, John, was born in Virginia and educated in England. He was killed by the Indians in defending the fort of Port Royal,—being a first settler. A great-aunt of his was likewise killed by the Indians lower down the river. It appears that all the ancestry just traced were natives of Virginia, and, it is believed, for the most part at least, if not altogether, of English descent. In both the paternal and maternal line of ancestry they were planters, and among the respectable though not the most opulent class.*

B.—*From the Record of James Madison, Sen., father of the President.*

Ambrose Madison was married to Frances Taylor, August 24, 1721.

Ambrose Madison was father of James Madison. Frances Taylor was sister of Erasmus Taylor and daughter of James Taylor.

James Madison, Sen. was born March 27, 1723, and was baptized April 21, and had for godfathers Thomas Madison and James Taylor, and for godmothers Martha Taylor and Elizabeth Penn.

Frances, wife of Ambrose Madison, departed this life October 25, 1761, and was interred the Sunday following at Montpelier in Orange. Her funeral sermon was preached on Wednesday, the 30th of December following, by the Rev. Mr. James Marye, Jr., on Revelation ch. 14, v. 13.

James Madison, Sen. was married to Nelly Conway, September 15, 1749.

The following are their children:—

James Madison, Jr., the President, was born on Tuesday night at 12 o'clock, being the last of the 5th and beginning of the 6th day of March, 1751, and was baptized by the Rev. Mr. Wm. Davis, March 31, and had for godfathers Mr. John Moore and Mr. Jonathan Gibson, and for godmothers Mrs. Rebecca Moore, Miss Judith, and Miss Elizabeth Catlett.

[James Madison, Jr. was born at Port Conway, in King George, and was baptized there,—his mother being on a visit there to her mother at the time of his birth.]

Frances Madison was born on Monday morning at 7 o'clock, June 18, 1753, and was baptized by the Rev. Mr. Mungo Marshall, July 1, and had for godfathers Mr. Taverner Beale and Mr. Erasmus Taylor, and for godmothers Miss Milly Taylor and Mrs. Frances Beale.

Ambrose Madison was born on Monday night between 9 and 10 o'clock, January 27, 1755, and was baptized by the Rev. Mungo Marshall, March 2, and had for godfathers Mr. James Coleman and Colonel George Taylor, and for godmothers Mrs. Jane Taylor and Alice Chew.

Catlett Madison was born on Friday morning at 3 o'clock, February 10, 1758, and was baptized by the Rev. Mr. James Maury, February 22, and had for godfathers Colonel Wm. Taliafero and Mr. Richard Beale, and for godmothers Mrs. Elizabeth Beale and Miss Milly Chew.

Nelly Madison (afterward Mrs. Hite) was born February 14, 1760, and was baptized March 6, by the Rev. Mr. Wm. Giberne, and had for godfathers Mr. Larken Chew and Mr. Wm. Moore, and for godmothers Miss Elizabeth Catlett and Miss Catharine Bowie. The said Nelly was born on Thursday morning just after daybreak.

William Madison was born May 1, 1762, baptized May 23, by the Rev. James Marie, Jr., and had for godfathers Mr. Wm. Moore and Mr. James Taylor, and for godmothers Miss Mary Willis and Miss Milly Chew. He was born on Saturday morning, about twenty-five minutes after 10 o'clock.

---

* These papers are copies from the originals loaned me by Mrs. L. H. Conway, niece of the late President Madison. They were found among his papers after the death of his wife. The original of this marked A. is believed to be in Mr. Madison's handwriting. The handwriting of the other is not known.

Sarah Madison, (Mrs. Thomas Macon,) born August 17, 1764, and was baptized September 15, by the Rev. James Marye, Jr., and had for godfathers Captain Richard Barbour and Mr. Andrew Shepherd, and for godmothers Mrs. Sarah Taylor and Miss Mary Conway. She was born forty-five minutes after 5 o'clock P.M., on Friday.

Elizabeth Madison was born February 19, 1768, half an hour after 12 o'clock, and was baptized February 22, by the Rev. Mr. Thomas Martin, and had for godfathers Major Zachariah Burnley and Captain Ambrose Powell, and for godmothers Miss Alice and Miss Milly Chew.

Reuben Madison was born September 19, 1771, between 5 and 6 o'clock in the evening, and was baptized November 10, by the Rev. Mr. John Barnett, and had for godfathers Mr. Thomas Barbour and Mr. James Chew, and for godmothers Miss Alice and Miss Milly Chew.

Frances Taylor Madison (afterward Mrs. Dr. Robert H. Rose) was born October 4, 1774, and was baptized October 30, by the Rev. Mr. John Wingate, and had for godfathers Mr. Thomas Bell and Mr. Richard Taylor, and for godmothers Miss Frances Taylor and Miss Elizabeth Taylor.

THE TAYLOR FAMILY.

The Taylors of Orange trace their ancestry back to James Taylor, of Carlisle, England. The time of his emigration to Virginia is not known. It appears he settled on the Chesapeake between the North and York Rivers, (Doc. A.) He died in 1698. He had several children,—one of whom (Mary) was the mother of Judge Edmund Pendleton. His son John (who married a Pendleton) is the ancestor of Colonel John Taylor, of Caroline. His son James took up lands in Orange, and was a first settler. He was the father of Frances, wife of Ambrose Madison and grandmother of the President. He had four sons,—James, George, Zachary, and Erasmus. From James are descended the Taylors of Kentucky. George had fourteen sons, seven of whom served in the Revolutionary War, and thirteen of whom held offices under Government at the same time. Some of his descendants are now residing in Orange, and are members of the Episcopal Church. Zachary had seven sons and three daughters. He was grandfather of General Zachary Taylor. The latter was born at Hare Forest, about four miles from Orange Court-House. Erasmus had two sons and five daughters,—viz.: John and Robert, Mildred, (married Wm. Morton,) Frances, (married —— Burnley,) Elizabeth, (married —— Glassel,) Lucy, (married the Rev. A. Balmaine,) Jane, (married Charles P. Howard.) John was father of the late Judge John Taylor, of Mississippi. Robert married Frances Pendleton, and from them are descended most of the Taylors now residing in Orange,—all of whom retain their attachment to the Church of their fathers.

PRESIDENT MADISON'S RELIGIOUS OPINIONS.

In the neighbourhood of Orange Court-House, at Montpelier, lived Mr. James Madison, once President of the United States, and relative of Bishop Madison. Having been often asked concerning his religious sentiments, I give the following, received from the Rev. Dr. Balmaine, who married his near relative, and by whom Mr. Madison himself was married. Mr. Madison was sent to Princeton College,—perhaps through fear of the skeptical principles then so prevalent at William and Mary. During his stay at Princeton a great revival took place, and it was believed that he partook of its spirit. On his return home he conducted family worship in his father's house. He soon after offered for the Legislature, and it was objected to him, by his opponents, that he was better suited to the pulpit than to the legislative hall. His religious feeling, however, seems to have been short-lived. His political associations with those of infidel principles, of whom there were many in his day, if they did not actually change his creed, yet subjected him to the general suspicion of it. This was confirmed in the minds of some by the active part he took in opposition to every thing like the support of churches by the Legislature, in opposition to Patrick Henry, Governor Page, Richard Henry Lee, and others. This, however, ought not to have been sufficient to fix the charge upon him, as George Mason and others, whose faith was not questioned, agreed with him in this policy. A reference to a memorial against any such act by Mr. Madison, at the request, it is affirmed, of some non-Episcopalians, will show his character and views. It is by far the ablest document which appears on that side of the question, and establishes his character for good temper as well as decision. It is drawn up on the supposition of the truth of Christianity. It must indeed have done this in order to be acceptable to those by whom it was solicited. Whatever may have been the private sentiments of Mr. Madison on the subject of religion, he was never known to declare any hostility to it. He always treated it with respect, attended public worship in his neighbourhood, invited ministers of religion to his house, had family prayers on such occasions, —though he did not kneel himself at prayers. Episcopal ministers often went there to see his aged and pious mother and administer the Holy Communion to her. I was never at Mr. Madison's but once, and then our conversation took such a turn—though not designed on my part—as to call forth some expressions and arguments which left the impression on my mind that his creed was not strictly regulated by the Bible. At his death, some years after this, his minister—the Rev. Mr. Jones—and some of his neighbours openly expressed their conviction, that, from his conversation and bearing during the latter years of his life, he must be considered as receiving the Christian system to be divine. As to the purity of his moral character, the amiableness of his disposition toward all, his tender affection to his mother and wife, kindness to his neighbours, and good treatment of his servants, there was never any question.

Among the many orations called forth by the death of Mr. Madison, there was one—now before me—by Mr. Philip Williams, of Winchester, Virginia. From this I select the following passages:—

" His parents were both pious, and instilled into his youthful mind the moral and religious principles which were the strong foundations of his future greatness. His father died before he was elevated to the Presidency, but his mother lived to see him advanced to that office, and enjoying all of worldly honours that the fondest mother's heart could wish. He received his classical education from Mr. Robertson, a Scotchman, who resided in King and Queen, and the Rev. Mr. Martin, an Episcopal clergyman, who lived for many years in his father's family. Under their instruction he prepared himself for college, and entered at Princeton in 1769. When he arrived at Princeton, he found that in his literary acquirements he was behind many of his juniors, and, with praiseworthy emulation, determined to learn twice as much each day as was usually acquired in that time. He persevered in his determination until he graduated on the last Wednesday in September, 1771. He continued at Princeton until 1772, from a desire to learn Hebrew and to extend his other studies under the superintendence of Dr. Witherspoon, then President of the College, to whom he was sincerely attached."

From his early training in pious principles, and from the testimony of his minister and others as to his later years, Mr. Williams expresses his conviction that Mr. Madison was an humble believer in Christianity. Mr. Williams, though a zealous Episcopalian, agrees with Madison in his opposition to the law advocated by Mr. Henry for the support of religion, and quotes the following passages with some others from his argument on the subject, introducing them with this statement:—

" The *free exercise* of religion was protected by the Bill of Rights; but there were many of our most distinguished men, who not only insisted upon the right of the Legislature, but urged the expediency of compelling every man to contribute to the support of some Church, but giving him the liberty to prescribe to which Church it should be paid. At the preceding session a bill for a general assessment 'for the support of Christian teachers,' upon this principle, was reported to the House. Its opponents, with the double view of enlightening the public mind and ascertaining more accurately the public will, succeeded in passing a resolution that the bill should be printed and submitted to the people, that it might be examined by them, and passed or rejected at the ensuing Legislature as they might dictate.

"Mr. Madison drew a memorial and remonstrance against the passing this bill, characterized by his usual mildness, good sense, and close reasoning, which was extensively circulated throughout the State, and doubtless contributed in a great degree to defeat the measure.

"This memorial was by many attributed to the pen of George Mason. While it admitted the divine origin of the Christian religion, and paid a just tribute to the purity of its doctrines, it showed clearly the impolicy and danger of any interference by the civil power with the subject of religion.

"This able paper is so little known that I must trespass upon your patience by some extracts from it:—

" 'The bill implies either that the civil authority is a competent judge of religious truth, or that it may employ religion as an engine of civil policy. The first is an arrogant pretension, falsified by the extraordinary opinions of rulers, in all ages and throughout the world; the second, an unhallowed perversion of the means of salvation. The establishment proposed by the bill is not requisite for the support of the Christian religion. To say that it is, is a contradiction to the Christian religion itself, for every page of it disavows a dependence on the power of this world; it is a contradiction to fact, for it is known that this religion both existed and flourished, not only without the support of human laws, but in spite of every opposition from them, and not only during the period of miraculous aid, but long after it had been left to its own evidence and the ordinary care of Providence.

" 'Experience testifies that ecclesiastical establishments, instead of maintaining the purity and efficacy of religion, have had a contrary operation.

" 'The establishment in question is not necessary for the support of civil government. What influence, in fact, have ecclesiastical establishments had on civil society? In some instances they have been seen to erect a spiritual tyranny on the ruins of the civil authority; in more instances have they been seen upholding the throne of political tyranny; in no instance have they been seen the guardians of the liberties of the people. Rulers who wished to subvert the public liberty may have found an established clergy convenient auxiliaries; a just government, instituted to secure and perpetuate it, needs them not. Such a government will be best supported by protecting every citizen in the enjoyment of his religion, with the same equal hand which protects his person and property, by neither invading the equal rights of any sect, nor suffering any sect to invade those of another. It will destroy that moderation and harmony which the forbearance of our law to intermeddle with religion has produced among its several sects. Torrents of blood have been spilt in the Old World by vain attempts of the secular arm to extinguish religious discord by proscribing all differences in religious opinion. Time has at length revealed the true remedy. Every relaxation of narrow and vigorous policy, whenever it has been tried, has been found to assuage the disease. The

American theatre has exhibited proofs that equal and complete liberty, if it does not wholly eradicate it, sufficiently destroys its malignant influence in the health and prosperity of the State. If, with the salutary effect of this system under our eyes, we begin to contract the bounds of religious freedom, we know no name that will too severely reproach our folly. At least, let warning be taken at the first-fruits of the threatened innovation. The very appearance of the bill has transformed that Christian forbearance, love, and charity, which of late mutually prevailed, into animosities and jealousies which may not soon be appeased. What mischief may not be dreaded should this enemy to the public quiet be armed with the force of law!

" 'The policy of the law is adverse to the diffusion of the light of Christianity. The first wish of those who enjoy this precious gift ought to be that it may be imparted to the whole race of mankind. Compare the number of those who have as yet received it with the number still remaining under the dominion of false religion, and how small is the former! Does the policy of the bill tend to lessen the disproportion? No; it at once discourages those who are strangers to the light of truth from coming into the regions of it, and countenances, by example, the nations who continue in darkness, in shutting out those who might convey it to them. Instead of levelling as far as possible every obstacle to the victorious progress of truth, the bill, with an ignoble and unchristian timidity, would circumscribe it with a wall of defence against the encroachment of error.

" 'Finally, the equal rights of every citizen to the free exercise of his religion, according to the dictates of his conscience, is held by the same tenure with all our other rights. If we recur to its origin, it is equally the gift of nature; if we weigh its importance, it cannot be less dear to us; if we consult the declaration of those rights which pertain to the good people of Virginia, as the basis and foundation of government, it is enumerated with equal solemnity, or rather with studied emphasis. Either, then, we must say that the will of the Legislature is the only measure of their authority, and that, in the plenitude of this authority, they may sweep away all our fundamental rights, or that they are bound to leave this particular right untouched and sacred; either we must say that they may control the freedom of the press, may abolish the trial by jury, may swallow up the executive and judiciary powers of the State,—nay, that they may annihilate our very right of suffrage and erect themselves into an independent and hereditary assembly; or we must say that they have no authority to enact into a law the bill under consideration.' "

THE CHURCHES IN MADISON AND RAPPAHANNOCK.

The following letter from the Rev. Mr. Leavell, the present minister of these counties, contains all that I have been able to collect concerning old Bloomfield parish:—

"DEAR BISHOP:—I have endeavoured to obtain all the information to be had respecting the old parish of Bloomfield,—embracing a section of country now known as Madison and Rappahannock. What I have gathered is from the recollections of the venerable Mrs. Sarah Lewis, now in her eighty-second year. Mrs. Lewis is descended from the Pendletons and Gaineses, of Culpepper, the Vauters, of Essex, and the Ruckers. From her I learn that there were two churches,—the brick church, called F. T., which stood near what is now known as the Slate Mills. It took its name from being near the starting-point of a survey of land taken up by Mr. Frank Thornton, who carved the initials of his name—F. T.—on an oak-tree near a spring, where his lines commenced. The other church was called South Church,—I presume from its relative situation, being almost due south, and about sixteen miles distant, and four miles below the present site of Madison Court-House. It was a frame building and stood on the land of Richard Vauters. Both buildings were old at the commencement of the Revolutionary War, and soon after, from causes common to the old churches and parishes in Virginia, went into slow decay. The first minister she recollects as officiating statedly in these churches was a Mr. Iodell, (or Iredell,) who was the incumbent in 1790 or 1792. He remained in the parish only a few years, when he was forced to leave it in consequence of heavy charges of immorality. He was succeeded by the Rev. Mr. O'Niel, an Irishman, who had charge of the parish for some years, in connection with the Old Pine Stake and Orange Churches. He was unmarried, and kept school near the Pine Stake Church, which stood near to Raccoon Ford, in Orange county. Mr. John Conway, of Madison, was a pupil of his, and relates some things which I may here mention, if you are not already weary of the evil report of old ministers. He played whist, and on one occasion lost a small piece of money, which the winner put in his purse, and whenever he had occasion to make change (he was a sheriff) would exhibit it, and refuse to part with it, because he had won it from the parson. He also took his julep regularly, and, to the undoing of one of his pupils, invited him to join him in the social glass. Still, he was considered as a sober man. Mr. O'Niel left these churches about the year 1800. After that the Rev. Mr. Woodville occasionally performed services there. After the parish became vacant, and the churches had gone to decay, the Lutheran minister, a Mr. Carpenter, officiated at the baptisms, marriages, and funerals of the Episcopal families. It was at the old Lutheran Church, near the court-house, that some of our first political men in Virginia, when candidates for Congress, held meetings and made speeches on Sundays, after the religious services. The same was also done in other places, under the sanction of Protestant ministers.

"The Episcopal families around the churches above mentioned were the Ruckers, Barbours, Beales, Keastleys, Lewises, Blafords, Vauters, Strothers, Thorntons, Burtons, Conways, Gipsons, Pannells, Gaineses.

"Since the resuscitation of the Church in Virginia, although a long time after the commencement of the same, efforts have been made to revive the Church in the old Bloomfield parish. A new brick church has been put up at Madison Court-House, and for a time there was a most encouraging prospect of a considerable congregation at that place; but emigration, the bane of so many other rising congregations in Virginia, has sadly reduced our numbers and disappointed our hopes.

"Since the first efforts in behalf of the churches in Madison, the following clergymen, ministers of the adjoining counties of Orange, Culpepper, and Rappahannock, have given a portion of their time and labours to Madison:—The Rev. Mr. Lamon, the Rev. Mr. Doughen, the Rev. Mr. Cole, the Rev. Mr. Brown, the Rev. Mr. Earnest, the Rev. Mr. Leavell.

" Of late years the county of Rappahannock has been formed, partly, I believe, from Madison, and a parish organized in the same. Through the zealous efforts of a few individuals, a neat brick church has been put up at Woodville, in that county. Previous to this the Rev. Mr. Brown spent some years in the parish, labouring there and in Madison. A few years since the Rev. W. H. Pendleton, of Leeds parish, Fauquier, rendered them regular though unfrequent services. For the last three years the Rev. Mr. Leavell has been dividing his time and labours equally between the two counties of Madison and Rappahannock.

ARTICLE LVII.

Northern Neck of Virginia.—Fairfax and Carter Families.

WE enter now on that most interesting portion of Virginia called
the Northern Neck, which, beginning on the Chesapeake Bay, lies
between the Potomac and Rappahannock Rivers, and crossing the
Blue Ridge, or passing through it, with the Potomac, at Harper's
Ferry, extends with that river to the heads thereof in the Alleghany
Mountains, and thence by a straight line crosses the North Mountain and Blue Ridge, at the head-waters of the Rappahannock. By
common consent this is admitted to be the most fertile part of
Virginia, and to abound in many advantages, whether we consider
the rich supply of fish and oysters in the rivers and creeks of the
tide-water portion of it and the rapid growth of its forests and
improvable character of its soil, or the fertility of the lands of the
valley, so much of which is evidently alluvial.

There were settlements at an early period on the rich banks of
the Potomac and Rappahannock by families of note, who took possession of those seats which originally belonged to warlike tribes
of Indians, which latter were forced to give way to the superior
prowess of the former. Of some of these families and their abodes
we shall have occasion to make mention in our progress along the
parishes lying upon the two rivers. It is not inconsistent with the
religious character and design of our work to begin with some
notice of that family to which the whole proprietorship of the
Northern Neck originally belonged, by a grant from the Crown,
especially as, both in England and in Virginia, so many of that
name have been attached to the Episcopal Church, and some of
whom have been bright ornaments of it.

In the corrupt and venal reign of Charles II., the whole State
of Virginia, except such parts as had been specially patented, was
made over for a time to Lord Culpepper. There was, of course, a
good pecuniary consideration given to the King for quitrents.
Lord Culpepper was not only the proprietary of the Colony, but
had the livings of all the parishes in his gift,—could bestow or
take away as he pleased. There was, however, too much of American feeling, even at that early period, to submit to such a mea-

sure. So heavy were the complaints, and so threatening the opposition, that the King withdrew the grant of proprietorship for the whole State, and restricted it with limitations to the Northern Neck, as above described. By intermarriage between the families of Culpepper and Fairfax, this part of the State came into possession of Thomas Fairfax, whose mother was daughter of Lord Culpepper, himself being the seventh Fairfax who had inherited the title of Lord Cameron. He it was who lived and died in the forests of old Frederick county, as we have stated in a former number, being one of the earliest vestrymen of the parish, an active magistrate, the patron of Washington, a friend of the poor, an eccentric but most upright man.

The family of Fairfax is a very ancient and respectable one, according to English history and family records. Within the last few years, four octavo volumes of the Fairfax history and correspondence have been published in England, a large portion of whose contents were accidentally discovered in an old box, supposed to contain tiles, in one of the old family seats. They had been secreted there during Cromwell's rebellion, or soon after, for safe-keeping, and lest they should fall into the hands of those who would make an ill use of them. Being in a box which, when opened, presented only tiles to the eye, they were supposed to be lost for the larger part of two centuries. Being furnished with a copy of these volumes, and having looked over them for the purpose of collecting any thing suitable to these pages, I present the following brief notices.

The Fairfaxes were of true Saxon origin, going back to the times of William the Conqueror. The name Fair-Fax meant Fair Hair. In the early history of the family an interesting fact is stated in old English verse,—viz.: that grandfather, son, and grandson, with their wives and children, lived in the same house at Bradford,—a village in England.

> " Under one roof they dwelt with their three wives,
> And at one table eat what God gives:
> Our times a sweeter harmony have not known:
> There are six persons, yet their hearts but one.
> In these three pairs Bradford may justly glory:
> What other place can parallel this story ?"

The above lines were written by the rector of Bradford, in 1647.

At the beginning of the Reformation, one of the Fairfaxes was so staunch a Catholic that he disinherited his eldest son for taking part in the sacking of Rome by the Protestants. The following extract from his will shows the character of his creed :—"First, I will and bequeath my soul to our Lord Jesus Christ, and to Lady Mary, his blessed mother." He leaves money to the poor, and also to fourteen poor persons with which to buy black gowns and torches for attendance at his funeral. In a few generations, however, after this, we find Romanism supplanted by as staunch a Protestantism. Thomas Fairfax, the first who had a peerage, and for which, besides many civil and military services, he had to pay fifteen hundred pounds to King James I. in his pecuniary difficulties, was a Protestant, and sympathized with Cromwell in his contest with Charles I. His son Ferdinand distinguished himself in Cromwell's army; and his grandson Thomas was the celebrated Lord Fairfax, one of the leaders in the rebel army.

The first Thomas, who purchased the title, had a brother named Edward, who signalized himself by translating "Tasso's Jerusalem Delivered" into a smooth English, before unknown. In a work on Demonology, he thus declares his religious belief and ecclesiastical position :—"I am, in religion, neither a fanatic Puritan nor superstitious Papist, but so settled in conscience, that I have the sure ground of God's word for all I believe, and the commendable ordinances of our English Church to approve all I practise."

The will of Ferdinando Fairfax, father of the great General in Cromwell's army, differs much from that of his Romish ancestor. Instead of commending his soul to Lady Mary, in conjunction with her son, his will runs thus :—"First, I commend my soul to their infinite Majesties, the Father, the Son, and the Holy Ghost,—the same God who hath with his manifold blessings been gracious to me in this world, and whose goodness, in his great mercy, I hope to enjoy in heaven. Next, I give my body to be buried, without much pomp or ceremony, in what place it shall please God to call me out of this sinful world; but, if with convenience it may be, I desire to be interred in the parish of Bolton Percy, near the body of my dear wife." A sensible and pious will, worthy of imitation.

This parish of Bolton Percy was one in which his brother, the Rev. Henry Fairfax, ministered. He appears to have been a truly pious man, and his wife to have been an helpmeet to him. Some interesting letters, written before and after their marriage, show them to have been well formed by nature and grace for the position which they chose in preference to all others. While the country was full of confusion and bloodshed, and his father, brother, and nephew were so actively engaged in revolutionary scenes, he quietly performed his duties as a parish minister, molesting none, and being unmolested by any. He had two sons: one of them, Bryan, was a scholar and author; another, Henry, was the fourth Lord Fairfax, inheriting the title from the great General, who had no son. His son, who was the grandson of the humble curate of Bolton Percy, was also inheritor of the title, and married the daughter of Lord Culpepper. Their son Thomas was the emigrant to America. At his death, his brother Robert, in England, inherited the title, who, dying without issue, bequeathed his estate to the Rev. Denny Martin, a relative of the family, who assumed the name of Fairfax. The title, however, descended to the Rev. Bryan Fairfax, minister of the Episcopal Church of Alexandria, who was the son of William Fairfax, of Belvoir, the friend of Washington, and manager of the estates of Lord Fairfax after the death of Robert Carter, *alias* King Carter, of Lancaster.

Before proceeding further with our brief notice of the Fairfax family in Virginia, I must add a word as to the celebrated General in Cromwell's army. Marrying into a Presbyterian family, and espousing a cause much patronized by that denomination, he inclined, for a time at least, to that persuasion. He appears to have been an upright and conscientious man. The language of his letters sometimes savours not a little of that which marked the communications of Cromwell; but his sincerity was never questioned, —which cannot be said of Cromwell, notwithstanding all the praises heaped upon him of late years. His great General (Fairfax) could not bring himself to pursue the ill-counselled, obstinate, and tyrannical Charles to the scaffold, but retired into private life until the time came to put an end to the troubles of the Commonwealth by the restoration of monarchy, in which he took an active part. He had an only child,—a daughter, who married the profligate Duke of Buckingham and led a suffering life. Her relative, Bryan Fairfax, the author, in writing of her, says, "She was an example of virtue and piety in a vicious age and debauched court;" adding, "David tells us, 'Men of high degree are a lie, (they promise and never perform,) and men of low degree are vanity,' (that is, have nothing to give.)"

Before leaving the English connections of this family, it may not be without interest to mention, that there appears to have been an intimate friendship between the Herberts and Fairfaxes in the mother-country, which may have laid the foundation of that which was established between some of them in this. The same may be said in relation to the many matrimonial connections between the Fairfaxes and Carys of Virginia. I meet with a notice of one occurring in England, which may have led to those in America. Coming back to Virginia, with my notices of this family, I take pleasure in recording the proofs of genuine piety in the Rev. Bryan Fairfax. On going to England to receive the title, and perhaps some property with it, he met with much trouble, delay, and mortification. The Earl of Buchan, General Washington's friend, addressed a letter of religious sympathy and condolence to him, to which he thus responds:—"I have the happiness to say with the Psalmist, in respect of God's dealings toward me, 'I know that of very faithfulness thou hast caused me to be troubled.'" I have also seen and published a sermon of his, in which the evangelical plan of salvation is most distinctly and happily set forth. He also married into the Cary family,—his marriage being one of five occurring between the families in the course of a few years. Mr. William Fairfax, of Belvoir, near Mount Vernon, the father of the Rev. Bryan Fairfax, had married one of the same. One of his daughters was married to General Washington's elder brother Lawrence, the owner of Mount Vernon, by which means it came to pass that there was such an intimacy between the General and the Fairfax family, and that matrimonial connections between the Washington and Fairfax families have been so multiplied.

I have thus unavoidably been led, in tracing the history of this family, to speak of titles and great possessions, which are now all gone and were of little worth while had.

Let me now address a few admonitory words to those who still bear the name, or in whose veins the blood of their ancestors continues to flow, and many of whom are still to be found in our State and land. I have adduced some interesting proofs of the Protestant, evangelical piety in a number of your ancestors. Show your estimate of a respectable ancestry, by faithfully copying their excellencies. Say not that you have Abraham for your father, said our Lord, for God is able to raise up children unto Abraham out of the stones of the earth. He bids them to do the works of Abraham in order to receive his favour. Your ancestry may, and will be, only a shame to you, except you copy what is worthy of imitation in their character and conduct. I especially ask your attention to one fact in the preceding account. In a few generations, as I have stated, three of your ancestors have chosen the sacred ministry as their profession, in preference to the army, the navy, or any other pursuit. Doubtless many others of their wide-spread relations have done the same. I counsel you, as you would regain far more than lost titles and lands, that you covet from the Lord in behalf of your sons the highest of all honours,—the privilege of seeking lost souls, and turning sinners to righteousness : then will they shine, not on the page of earthly history, but as "stars in the kingdom of God forever."

SKETCH OF THE CARTER FAMILY.

This may with propriety follow that of the Fairfaxes, as Mr. Robert Carter—called King Carter—was for a long time the agent and representative of the Culpepper and Fairfax families, and as his representatives have been so numerous and respectable in the Northern Neck.

The first of the family, so far as is known, settled in Upper Norfolk, now Nansemond county, and was a member of the House of Burgesses in 1649. In the year 1654, we find him a Burgess from Lancaster county, and Commander-in-chief of the forces sent against the Rappahannock Indians. He continued to be a member of the House of Burgesses for some years. Both himself and his eldest son John appear on the vestry-book as members of the vestry in the year 1666, the father having been acting in that capacity before,—how long not known. The father, who died in 1669, had previously built, by contract, the first church standing on the spot where Christ Church now is, and the vestry received it at the hands of his son John, in six months after the father's death. The name of John Carter, 1702, is still to be seen on an old dial-post of cedar, which was taken out of the ground, near the church-door, some years since, and placed under the pulpit in the present Christ Church. The first John Carter had three wives,—1st, Jane, the daughter of Morgan Glyn, by whom he had George and Eleanor; 2d, Ann, the daughter of Cleave Carter, probably of England; 3d, Sarah, the daughter of Gabriel Ludlowe, by whom he had Sarah. All these died before him, and he was buried with them, near the chancel, in the church which he built, and the tombstone from which we take the above covers them all, being still in the same position in the present church. He had also a son named Charles, of whom nothing is known. His son Robert was by his last wife, Sarah Ludlowe. The eldest son, John, married,—1st, Elizabeth Wormley, and 2d, a Miss Loyd, and had issue. Of this branch we have no account, and must confine ourselves to that of Robert, *alias* King Carter. He married twice :—first, a Miss Armistead; next, a widow Willis, daughter of Thomas Landon, of England. He had ten children by the two wives. Those of whom we have information were John, Elizabeth, Judith, Ann, Robert of Nomini, Charles, Landon of Sabine Hall, Mary, Lucy, and George. The eldest son, John, married Miss Hill, and was Secretary of State to the Colony, having to pay one thousand five hundred pounds sterling for the office. His daughter Elizabeth married, first Mr. Nathaniel Burwell, of Gloucester, and then Dr. George Nicholas, of Williamsburg. His daughter Judith married the first Mann Page, of Gloucester, and lived with him at Rosewell. His daughter Ann married Benjamin Harrison, of Berkeley. His son Robert married a Miss Bladen. His son Charles married first a Miss Walker, then a Miss Byrd, sister of Mr. Byrd, of Westover, lastly a Miss Taliafero. His son Landon, of Sabine Hall, married first Elizabeth, daughter of Mr. Wormley, of Rosegill, then Maria, a sister of Mr. Byrd, of Westover, then a Miss Beale. His youngest child, Lucy, married Henry Fitzhugh, of King George county. Thus we have disposed of the sons and daughters of Mr. Carter, of Corotoman, and their marriages. To attempt to do the same even with his grandchildren, much more with their descendants, would not merely exceed the bounds prescribed to such genealogies in these notices, but would require a small volume. Suffice it to say, that, besides intermarriages one with another, the family of Carter may be found intermingled, not only with those already mentioned, but with those of Moore, Lee, Berkeley, Champe, Skipwith, Braxton, Nelson, Waller, Randolph, Brown, Clayborne, Tasker, Churchill, Chiswell, Minor, Brooke, Thornton, Baylor, Grymes, Peck, Mitchell, Harris; and should we attempt to bring down the list to present times, it would contain others almost without limit. Out of the number of descendants, of whom both Church and State might well be proud, it would be invidious to select. So far as we have been able to judge by observation and learn by report, we may be permitted to say that there has been much of the amiable and the pious in the family, sometimes mixed with a portion of eccentricity in individuals of it. In Councillor Carter, of Nomini, the grandson of King Carter, this peculiarity was found in a large measure. Early in life his disposition was marked by a tendency to wit and humour. Afterward he was the grave Councillor, and always the generous philanthropist. At a later day he became scrupulous as to the holding of slaves, and manumitted great numbers. The subject of religion then engrossed his thoughts. Abandoning the religion of his fathers, he adopted the creed of the Baptists, and patronized their young preachers, having a chapel in his own house at Nomini. After a time he embraced the theory of Swedenborg, and at length died an unhappy death-dreading Papist. All the while he was a most benevolent and amiable man. I might mention many others, of both sexes, with whom I have had personal and intimate acquaintance, who have been beautiful specimens of piety, without the versatility and inconsistency of Mr. Carter, of Nomini. I was not acquainted with Mr. Charles Carter, of Shirley, though it has been my happiness to know many of his descendants and to love them for their work's sake. I find his name on the list of those few devoted friends of the Church who after the Revolution met together in Convention at Richmond, to rescue the things that remained and were ready to perish. I have, however, in the following letter, a better proof of his love to the Church and its ministers than any mere attendance on Conventions could furnish. It was addressed to his old friend and pastor, the Rev. Mr. Currie, of Lancaster, who was the faithful minister of Christ Church parish for fifty years. Anticipating his own death as well as that of Mr. Currie, as events which might occur before that of Mrs. Currie, he thus generously provides for her support during her remaining days. She did survive her husband a number of years, and doubtless enjoyed the bounty of Mr. Carter.

"Letter of Mr. Charles Carter, of Shirley, to the Rev. Mr. Currie, at the Glebe, Lancaster county, Virginia.

"SHIRLEY, May 12, 1790.

" MY DEAR FRIEND :—Your letters, the one by Mrs. Carter, and the other enclosing your amiable daughter's to that good lady, are both come safe to hand, and you may rest assured that nothing could give my family a greater pleasure than to hear and know from yourself—that is to say, to have it under your own signature—that you still enjoy a tolerable share of health; and your friend, Mrs. Ann Butler, [Mr. Carter's second wife,] begs leave to join with me in congratulating both you and Mrs. Currie upon being blessed, not only with dutiful, healthy, and robust children, but clever and sensible. We rejoice to hear it, and pray God they may prosper and become useful members of society.

" As you are of Caledonian race, you may yet outlive a Buckskin : should it so happen, my will has directed five hundred acres of my land at Nantypyron to be laid off for the use of Mrs. Currie for and during her natural life. In the mean time, no power that I know of can deprive you of your right to the glebe. Our best wishes attend you and yours, and believe me when I subscribe myself, dear sir,

" Your affectionate friend and servant,

"CHARLES CARTER."

Although Mr. Currie was a man who, judging from a sermon of his in my possession, put his trust in God for his fatherless children and widow when taken from them, yet it must have been truly comforting to know that this provision was made for them by a generous friend. The sermon is on the text, (Matthew vi. 34,) "Take no thought for to-morrow, for the morrow shall take thought for the things of itself. Sufficient unto the day is the evil thereof." It is a very sensible and pious discourse on the subject treated of, showing, among other things, the impropriety of all uneasy thoughts about our earthly condition, and is in some respects a "*conscio ad clerum*" one to poor clergymen. I find on the cover of it these words :—

"A sermon written by my father, which I have determined to read at least once a year.   "E. CURRIE.
"September 29, 1808."

In relation to the above act of generosity, on the part of Mr. Carter, to the widow and children of a worthy clergyman, though there be few who can follow his example in affording them the use of a farm of five hundred acres, yet there are many who can contribute something to their comfort; and the thought that there are many who will do it must be a great solace to the heart of a dying minister when taking leave of his fatherless ones and widow. It is thus that God fulfils his promise when he bids them leave their fatherless ones to him, and let their widows trust in him. And let me, in connection with this case, recommend to the pious charity of the living and dying members of our communion the two societies now established in our diocese,—the Society of the Widows and Orphans of Deceased Clergymen, and that for Disabled, Superannuated Poor Clergymen. They are both of them worthy of patronage.

Another instance of the charitable disposition of Mr. Carter is worthy of being mentioned and imitated.

Solomon in one of his Proverbs says, "He that withholdeth corn, the people shall curse him; but blessing shall be upon the head of him that selleth it." Here is an allusion to some covetous and hard-hearted persons, who, in a time of scarcity and suffering among the poor, hold up their corn for some high price and will not sell it. I have been told that, in a year of this kind, Mr. Carter sent a vessel full of corn down James River, disposing of it among the poor at a very reduced price, thus showing not only his charity, but his judgment in the disbursement of it. Let the rich throughout our land go and do likewise with all manner of goods which God hath given them in abundance, and of which others stand in need.

A few remarks concerning him who was called King Carter

seem to be called for, before we close our notice of this family. From the fact that such a title was bestowed on him, the idea has become prevalent in Virginia that he was not only of princely possessions, having numerous tenants and servants, and a splendid palace for his residence, but that, as a consequence of this, he was authoritative, lordly, and arbitrary in his bearing and conduct, moving as a king in the Colony. He ruled over the Colony for more than a year, until the arrival of Governor Gooch. I have in my possession copies of two of his letters during this period, concerning a suspected clergyman who was desirous of getting the parish of Wycomico, in Northumberland. They were addressed to Captain Charles Lee and Mr. Thomas Berry, churchwardens of the parish. They breathe a Christian spirit of moderation and yet of decision. There is nothing of a dictatorial temper about them, but only a desire to do his duty, in the absence of a Governor, and in reference to one when he should arrive. It is very certain that Mr. Carter and his family were very popular throughout the State. His daughters were married to the first men in Virginia, and his sons to the first ladies in Virginia. At his death a long Latin inscription, written by some ripe scholar, was placed on his tomb, in which the greatest virtues are assigned to him, and a sincere piety. The epitaph will be found in our next article, on Christ Church, Lancaster county.

ARTICLE LVIII.

Parishes in Lancaster County.

THE first mention which is made of Lancaster county in Henning's "Statutes at Large" (volume i., page 374) is in 1652, when it is represented in the House of Burgesses by Captain Henry Fleet and Mr. William Underwood. At that time, and for four years after, it included all that is now Lancaster, Middlesex, Essex, and Richmond counties. In 1656, the old county of Rappahannock was cut off from Lancaster, and contained what, in 1692, was divided into the two counties of Richmond and Essex,—Rappahannock being abolished. The county of Middlesex was not cut off from Lancaster until about 1664 or 1665, and, indeed, it is not mentioned in Henning until the year 1675, when a levy of twenty-five men from each of the counties of Lancaster and Middlesex is ordered for a garrison in Stafford county, to protect the frontiers against the Indians. We are enabled to approach very near to certainty, as to the time of the division, by reference to an old vestry-book of the church in Middlesex, beginning in 1664. In 1668 the vestry pass an order that a petition should be distributed among the people, praying the Assembly to ratify a former Act dividing Lancaster into two counties; from which it would seem that something was wanting to complete the division, though it must have been acted on, in some way, a year or two before. In the county of Lancaster, when including Middlesex, there were four parishes,—two on each side of the river. Those on the south side of the river were called Lancaster parish and Piankatank until, at an early period, they were merged in one and called Christ Church. Those on the north side were St. Mary's and Christ Church until, at a much later period, they were united in what is now Christ Church.

The vestry-book of Christ Church, Lancaster, before the union of the two parishes, commenced, I think, about the year 1654. I saw it for the first time about twenty years ago, and again three years after, I believe, and took extracts from it, some of which were published. Soon after this it disappeared, and, though carefully sought for since, can nowhere be found. For want of it we lose the names of the first vestrymen, (except those of the first John Carter and his sons John and Robert,) and some acts of the vestry, not remembered or written down by myself. I have recently been furnished with the vestry-book of St. Mary's parish, beginning in the year 1739, and continuing after its union with Christ Church, in 1752, until the war of the Revolution. But we still have to lament the loss of the proceedings of both parishes until 1739, and of Christ Church until 1752, except so far as I have retained in memory, and by print, the doings of the latter. Something more we have as to the names and acts of the vestry of Christ Church, by reason of the fact that, though the parishes were separate, they always employed the same minister, and met sometimes in what was called a general vestry,—that is, a meeting of both,—when their names are recorded.

We will first state such information as we have retained from the last records of Christ Church parish. About, as we believe, the year 1654, the name of John Carter, the father of that family, appears at the head of the vestry-lists, in a large, bold hand; then followed the name of the minister, which I do not recollect. The same may be said of his eldest son John, and his youngest son Robert, *alias* King Carter. Their names always preceded the minister's, and were written in a large, bold hand. This was one sign that they took the lead in the vestry,—even going before the minister. In all the other vestry-books I have seen, even in that of Middlesex, where, about the same time, baronets were in the vestries, as Chicheley and Skipwith, the minister's name was always first. The action of the vestry, doubtless under the influence of the Carters, seems to have been good in relation to the exercise of discipline on offenders. One instance is recorded where a fine of fifteen hundred-weight of tobacco is imposed on a man for swearing; but, upon his pleading poverty, it was afterward reduced to five hundred. Mr. Robert Carter had large possessions and numerous servants and tenants, as we have already said. Tradition has it that the congregation, which doubtless consisted chiefly of his dependants, did not enter the church, on Sunday, until the arrival of his coach, when all followed him and his family into it. Whether this be so or not, it is certain, from the agreement on the vestry-book when he built the church, that good provision was made for his tenants and servants, one-fourth of the building being secured for their use, besides a very large pew near the pulpit and chancel, which he prepared for his immediate family.

The following extract from my report to the Convention in the year 1838, after a visit to the parishes in the Northern Neck, will show what were the impressions made upon me by that venerable building,—impressions renewed and deepened by my subsequent visit :—

"My next appointment was at Christ Church, Lancaster, on the 23d of June. This was the day appointed by the Convention to be observed as a day of humiliation, fasting, and prayer, on account of the languor of the Church, and the sins and troubles of the nation. No temple of religion, and no spot in the diocese, could have been selected more in accordance with the solemn duty of that day, than the old and venerable church in which three of God's ministers were assembled. I preached a sermon adapted to the occasion, and then proposed that those who were minded to spend the day as the Church recommended should remain for some hours at that place, in suitable religious exercises. A goodly number complied with the invitation, and after the interval of perhaps an hour, which was spent in surveying the building and the tombs around this ancient house of God, another service was performed, and a second appropriate discourse was preached by the Rev. Mr. Nelson, the service having been performed by Mr. Francis McGuire, the present minister of the parish. The past history and present condition of this hallowed spot and temple deserve a more particular notice. This notice is derived from the memorials furnished by the house itself, the tombstones around and within, and the vestry-book of the parish, kept from the year 1654 to 1770, to which I had access.

"The present church was built on the site of an older one, which was completed in the year 1670, under the direction of Mr. John Carter, the first of that name, and the great ancestor of many bearing that name in Virginia. By the side of the chancel is a large marble slab, on which are the names of John Carter and his three wives, and several children, who all died before him and were buried in that spot.

"The church being too small for the increasing population, a larger one was meditated, and some change in its location talked of, when Mr. Robert Carter (since known by the name of King Carter) offered to build one at his own expense, saying that in consequence of his large possessions, increasing family, and number of tenants, he had intended for some time to build a larger one for the parish. The offer was cheerfully accepted, and the present house was completed about the time of Mr. Carter's death, —that is, about the year 1732,—and exhibits to this day one of the most striking monuments of the fidelity of ancient architecture to be seen in our land. Very few, if any, repairs have been put upon it: the original roof and shingles now cover the house, and have preserved in a state of perfection the beautiful arched ceilings, except in two places which have within a few years been a little discoloured by the rain, which found its way through the gutters where the shingles have decayed. The walls of the house are three feet thick, perfect and sound. The windows are large and strong, having probably two-thirds of the original glass in them. The pews are of the old fashion, high-backed, and very firm. A very large one near the altar, and opposite the pulpit, together with the whole north cross of the building, was especially reserved by Mr. Carter for the use of his family and dependants in all time to come.

"It deserves to be mentioned, that, in addition to the high backs which always concealed the family and prevented any of them from gazing around when sitting or kneeling, a railing of brass rods with damask curtains was put around the top of the pew, except the part opposite the pulpit, in order, it is supposed, to prevent the indulgence of curiosity when standing. These remained until a few years since, and parts of them may probably yet be found in the possession of neighbours or relatives. In further evidence of the fidelity with which the house was built, I would mention that the pavement of its aisles, which is of large freestone, is yet solid and smooth as though it were the work of yesterday. The old walnut Communion-table also stands firm and unimpaired, and not a round from the railing of the chancel is gone or even loosened. The old marble font, the largest and most beautiful I ever saw, is still there; and, what will scarce be credited, the old cedar dial-post, with the name of John Carter, 1702, and which was only removed a few years since from its station without the door, where it was planted in the ground, is still to be seen in its place of security under the pulpit. In such a house, surrounded by such memorials, it was delightful to read the word of God and the prayers of the Church from the old desk, to pronounce the commandments from the altar near which the two tables of the law, the creed, and Lord's prayer are still to be seen, in large and legible characters, and then to preach the words of eternal life from the high and lofty pulpit, which seemed, as it were, to be hung in the air. Peculiarly delightful it was to raise the voice in such utterances in a house whose sacred form and beautiful arches seemed to give force and music to the feeblest tongue beyond any other building in which I ever performed or heard the hallowed services of the sanctuary. The situation of this church, though low, and surrounded on two of its sides by woodland, with thick undergrowth, is not without its peculiar interest. A few acres of open land, with some very large trees, chiefly spreading walnuts, furnish ample room for the horses and vehicles of those who attend it. An old decayed brick wall, with a number of graves and tombstones around the house, adds no little solemnity to the scene. Among the latter, at the east end of the house, within a neat enclosure, recently put up, are to be seen the tombs of Robert Carter, the builder of the house, and of his two wives. These are probably the largest and richest and heaviest tombstones in our land. A long Latin inscription is to be seen on that of Mr. Carter. While the tomb of the husband is entire, those of the wives appear to have been riven by lightning, and are separating and falling to pieces. Such is the belief and testimony of the neighbours. It is pleasing to know that a considerable sum of money has been subscribed for repairing the roof, which requires a new covering, and for improving the interior of this remarkable building, and that a generous portion of it is contributed by some of the descendants of the original builder, or those connected with them, who, though residing at a distance from the spot, possess the land around it, and have given the best assurance to the remaining families of the church, that it shall ever be continued for its original and sacred purposes."

To the foregoing notices of Christ Church from my report to the Convention of 1838, I add the following from memory. Of the two days spent in this hallowed spot, the one following the day of humiliation was a dark and gloomy one,—the sky being overcast with heavy clouds, from which showers were descending upon the earth. To be in that old building, with only two-thirds of the glass in the windows, on such a day, had a peculiar interest in it to a soul at all inclined to the love of ancient things. The weather being mild, there was nothing to interrupt the indulgence of such a feeling. There was also something to encourage it, in the fact that an aged lady, (the descendant of Mr. Carter,) whose two nieces—the eldest daughters of Mr. Tomlin, who lived near at hand—had on the preceding day ratified their baptismal vows, desired on this occasion to do the same. I can never forget my feelings as I stood in the old chancel administering the rite, while only a few individuals, and they chiefly the descendants of the builder of the house, were here and there to be seen in the large double pews adjoining the pulpit and chancel. There was a circumstance which occurred at that time not unworthy to be mentioned, as showing that we of this day of progressive improvement are not in all things in advance of our fathers, but in some rather the contrary. I spent the night intervening between the two above-mentioned days at Mr. Tomlin's house, which was a new one scarcely finished, and, while lying in bed early in the morning and looking toward the ceiling, suddenly saw a large portion of the plastering giving way just above me, leaving only time to draw the covering over my head before it fell upon my body, and not without a slight bruise. I could not help then and often since instituting a comparison between the fidelity and durability of ancient and modern architecture. Here was the ceiling of a private house, not a year old, tumbling over me, and there was the heavy plastering of an old church, built one hundred and twenty or thirty years before, perfectly sound and impervious to rain, except in one or two small spots where it was a little discoloured underneath the gutter, where the shingles had decayed. Where is the house, built in these degenerate days of slight modern architecture, which may compare with Old Christ Church, either within or without? When a few years since it was repaired, as I in my report expressed the belief that it would be, the only repairs required were a new roof, (and but for the failure in the gutters that would have been unnecessary,) the renewal of the cornices, supplying the broken glass, and painting the pews, pulpit, &c. All the rest was in a most perfect state of soundness. The shingles, except in the decayed gutters, were so good that they were sold to the neighbours around, and will probably now last longer than many new ones just gotten from the woods,—having become hardened by age on the steep and taunt roofs from which the rains of more than a century rushed downward, not stopping for a moment to settle in the joints. That is one reason why all of the old roofs were more durable than the modern,—the fashionable taste for low or flat ones leading to their speedier decay. Another is the fact that in former days worms, so destructive now to timber, appear not to have abounded as at present, or else some method for drying and hardening all the materials used was adopted, which is now neglected. In taking off the roof of Old Christ Church for the purpose of renewing it, one secret of the durability of the plastering was discovered. Besides having mortar of the most tenacious kind and of the purest white, and laths much thicker and stronger than those now in use, and old English wrought nails,—our modern factories not then being known,—the mortar was not only pressed with a strong hand through the openings of the laths, but clinched on the other side by a trowel in the hand of one above, so as to be fast keyed and kept from falling.

In all respects the house appears to have been built in the most durable manner, but without any of the mere trinkets of architecture. The form and proportion of the house are also most excellent, and make a deep impression on the eye and mind of the beholder. Though the walls are three feet thick, yet such is their height and such the short distance between the windows and doors, and such the effect of the figure of the cross, that there is no appearance of heaviness about them. The roof or roofs are also very steep and high, and take the place of tower or steeple. A steeple or tower would indeed injure the whole aspect of the building.

For the repairing of this house we are indebted mainly to the liberality of two brothers,—Mr. Kelleys,—descendants of old Episcopalians of the Northern Neck. Not only did they furnish far the larger part of the fifteen hundred dollars required for it, but superintended most carefully the expenditure of the same. Their bodies lie side by side within a strong iron enclosure near the church. The eldest of the brothers has died within the last two years, leaving, among other bequests, two thousand dollars to our Theological Seminary and High School.

I am sure the reader will be pleased in having the following epitaphs added to the foregoing notices of Old Christ Church.

I.

This incription is to the north of the chancel, in the east end of the church :—

"Here lyeth buried y[e] body of John Carter, Esq., who died y[e] 10th of June, Anno Domini 1669; and also Jane, y[e] daughter of Mr. Morgan Glyn, and George her son, and Elenor Carter, and Ann, y[e] daughter of Mr. Cleave Carter, and Sarah, y[e] daughter of Mr. Gabriel Ludlow, and Sarah her daughter, which were all his wives successively, and died before him.

"'Blessed are y[e] dead which die in y[e] Lord; even soe, saith y[e] Spirit, for they rest from their labours, and their works do follow them.'"

II.

This inscription is in the centre of the church, at the intersection of the aisles:—

"Here lyeth the body of Mr. David Miles, who died the 29th of December, 1674, and in ye 40th year of his age.

"Hodie mihi, cras tibi."
(Mine to-day, yours to-morrow.)

III.

This tombstone is at the east end of the church:—

"H. S. E.

"Vir honorabilis Robertus Carter, Armiger, qui genus honestum dotibus eximiis et moribus antiquis illustravit. Collegium Gulielmi et Mariæ temporibus difficillimis propugnavit, Gubernator.

"Senatus Rogator et Quæstor sub serenissimis Principibus Gulielmo, Anna, Georgio Primo et Secundo.

"A publicis concilliis concillii per sexennium præses; plus anno Coloniæ Præfectus, cum regiam dignitatem et publicam libertatem æquali jure asseruit.

"Opibus amplissimis bene partis instructus, ædem hanc sacram, in Deum pietatis grande monumentum propriis sumptibus extruit. Locupletavit.

"In omnes quos humaniter excepit nec prodigus nec parcus hospes. Liberalitatem insignem testantur debita munifice remissa.

"Primo Juditham, Johannis Armistead, Armigeri, filiam; deinde Betty, generosa Landonorum stirpe oriundam, sibi connubio junctas habuit: e quibus prolem numerosam suscepit, in qua erudienda pecuniæ vim maximam insumpsit.

"Tandem honorum et dierum satur, cum omnia vitæ munera egregiæ præstitisset, obiit Pri. Non. Aug. An. Dom. 1732, æt. 69.

"Miseri solamen, viduæ præsiduum, orbi patrem, ademptum lugent."

EAST OF THE CHURCH.

IV.

"Here lyeth buried the body of Judith Carter, the wife of Robert Carter, Esq., and eldest daughter of the Hon. John Armistead, Esq., and Judith his wife. She departed this life the 23d day of February, Anno 1699, in the —— year of her age, and in the eleventh year of her marriage, having borne to her husband five children, four daughters and a son, two whereof, Sarah and Judith Carter, died before, and are buried near her. Piously she lived, and comfortably died, in the joyful assurance of a happy eternitie, leaving to her friends the sweet perfume of a good reputation."

EAST OF THE CHURCH, AND MUTILATED.

V.

"To the memory of Betty Carter, second wife of Robert Carter, Esq., youngest daughter of Thomas Landon, Esq., and Mary his wife, of Grednal, in the county of Hereford, the ancient seat of the family and place of her nativity. She bore to her husband ten children, five sons and five daughters, three of whom—Sarah, Betty, and Ludlow—died before her and are buried near her. She was a person of great and exemplary piety and charity in every relation wherein she stood: whether considered as a Christian, a wife, a mother, a mistress, a neighbour, or a friend, her conduct was equalled by few, excelled by none. She changed this life for a better on the 3d of July, 1710, in the 36th year of her age and 19th of her marriage. May her descendants make their mother's virtues and graces the pattern of their lives and actions!"

EAST OF THE CHURCH.

VI.

"Under this stone are the remains of Mary Carter, the affectionate wife of Charles Carter, of Corotoman, who died on the 30th of January, 1770, after a painful illness of three months, during which time she discovered a truly Christian fortitude, aged 34 years."

Mr. Carter moved to Shirly, on James River, in 1776, and married Ann Butler Moore,—his second wife.

The following translation of Mr. Robert Carter's epitaph may be a help to some of our readers :—

"Here lies buried Robert Carter, Esq., an honourable man, who by noble endowments and pure morals gave lustre to his gentle birth.

"Rector of William and Mary, he sustained that institution in its most trying times. He was Speaker of the House of Burgesses, and Treasurer under the most serene Princes William, Anne, George I. and II.

"Elected by the House its Speaker six years, and Governor of the Colony for more than a year, he upheld equally the regal dignity and the public freedom.

"Possessed of ample wealth, blamelessly acquired, he built and endowed, at his own expense, this sacred edifice,—a signal monument of his piety toward God. He furnished it richly.

"Entertaining his friends kindly, he was neither a prodigal nor a parsimonious host.

"His first wife was Judith, daughter of John Armistead, Esq.; his second Betty, a descendant of the noble family of Landons. By these wives he had many children, on whose education he expended large sums of money.

"At length, full of honours and of years, when he had well performed all the duties of an exemplary life, he departed from this world on the 4th day of August, in the 69th year of his age.

"The unhappy lament their lost comforter, the widows their lost protector, and the orphans their lost father."

MINISTERS OF THE PARISHES OF CHRIST CHURCH AND ST. MARY'S.

We have already stated that the same ministers served both parishes. Who the first minister or ministers were, we are unable to state; but upon the vestry-book, whose loss we lament, there was one whose name and history were too striking to be forgotten. His name was Andrew Jackson, and, for what cause we know not, some one wrote his name, and he made his mark, beneath the name of one of the John Carters. He was not Episcopally ordained, and this led to a correspondence between the vestry and one of the Governors of Virginia,—most probably Governor Nicholson,—at a time when an order came from England that the law requiring all holding livings in the Church to be Episcopally ordained should be enforced in Virginia. The vestry remonstrated earnestly with the Governor against its execution in the case of their minister, Mr. Jackson. They plead that he had been serving the parish faithfully for twenty-five years, that he was much esteemed and beloved, had brought up a large family of children, and laid up something for them from his industrious culture of the glebe, (then and now a good farm near the church,) and the people were very unwilling to part with him. They urged one argument very emphatically,—viz.: that, by reason of the inferiority of the quality of tobacco raised in the Northern Neck of Virginia, by comparison with that in many other parts, it being worth less by twopence per pound, the parish was not on an equal footing with a large number elsewhere in procuring suitable ministers, and that, therefore, they ought to be allowed to retain the one whom they had. What was the issue of the controversy either did not appear or is not recollected. My impression is that it took place early in the last century, and that he was succeeded by the Rev. John Bell, who was certainly the minister in 1713, and continued so until the year 1743, when, at his death, the Rev. David Currie succeeded, and continued until his death in 1792,—nearly fifty years. If such be the case, then were the people of Lancaster served for more than one hundred years by three ministers, who were esteemed and loved by them. In my previous account of the Carter family I have spoken more particularly of Mr. Currie, whose descendants are numerous and respectable and have adhered to the Church of their worthy ancestor. At the death of Mr. Currie, in 1791, the Rev. David Ball appears for one year on the list of our clerical delegates to the

Convention, and for one only. Whether he was of the large family of Balls belonging to Lancaster, or whence he came, or whither he went, I know not. He was followed by a Rev. Mr. Leland and a Rev. Mr. Page, each for a short time. Of each of these I shall speak in another place. In 1794, no clerical delegate appears; but there were two laymen,—Mr. Raleigh Downman and Mr. William Eustace. From the year 1796 to the year 1805, the Rev. Daniel McNaughton is on our list as minister of this parish. James Ball, Martin Shearman, and William Montague appear as lay delegates. In 1812, Raleigh Downman and J. M. Smith are lay delegates. In 1813, the Rev. Samuel Low is minister. Between him and his friends, and Mr. McNaughton, there was for some time a contest for the parish and the use of the churches. On one occasion Mr. Low had all the congregation in the church-yard, and preached from the seat behind a carriage, while Mr McNaughton had the pulpit and the empty pews within. They were both of them such unworthy characters, though in different ways, that we shall not waste time and words upon them. In the year 1824, the Rev. Ira Parker, an ignorant and incompetent minister, took charge of the parish, but soon left it for some other. After floating about for a few years, he adopted the system of Swedenborg, and was dismissed from the ministry. In the year 1832, the Rev. Ephraim Adams took charge of the parish and continued its minister for four years. He was a worthy man, but, by reason of some peculiarities, unfitted for much usefulness. In 1838, the Rev. Francis McGuire was its minister; and, in 1839, the Rev. Mr. Bryant, of whom we have spoken elsewhere, succeeded. In 1844 and 1845, the Rev. Mr. Richmond was its minister. In 1850 and 1851, the Rev. Mr. Nash. In 1853, its present minister, the Rev. Edmund Withers, took charge of it. Within the last few years a small church has been built at Kilmarnock, about four miles from Old Christ Church. It being more convenient to the majority of the people in that region than the old one, services are held there alternately. Although but few attend generally at the old and venerable one, by reason of its inconvenient location, yet at my recent visit to it, although there were other services near at hand, one hundred and seventy-five persons might be counted there on a Sabbath morning. It is somewhat remarkable that Kilmarnock is the very spot on which the vestry determined to build a new church nearly one hundred and fifty years ago, deeming it the most central and convenient place, when Mr. Carter offered to build one at his own expense, if allowed to locate it nearer to his residence at Corotoman. Tradition says that the bricks of which the church is built were brought from England. It is far more probable that it is true in this case than in most of the other houses, public or private, of which the same report has come down to us; for Mr. Carter, having so many vessels from England assigned to him, may, at little cost, have had English bricks put in as ballast, and then conveyed in flatboats up the creek, within a short distance of the place where the church stands. Piles of stones thus coming from England may yet be seen near the river-bank at Corotoman, there cast to prevent the waves from depredating on the bank near his house.

List of Vestrymen in St. Mary's Parish, before the union of the parishes, from 1739 to 1756, and of both parishes after the union.

William Bertrand, William Ball, Jr., Joseph Ball, Joseph Heale, Jos. Chinn, Martin Shearman, Raleigh Chinn, Richard Chichester, Jesse Ball, Robert Mitchell, Colonel Ball, Major Ball, (making five Balls in one vestry,) Joseph Carter, Thomas Chinn. In the year 1743, the following vestrymen from Christ Church met with the vestry of St. Mary's White Chapel,—viz.: Henry Carter, Henry Lawson, Mr. Edwards, Mr. Steptoe, Mr. Martin, Captain Tayloe, Colonel Conway, Thomas Lawson, John Steptoe, Mr. Pinkard. At this time six of each vestry are appointed to form a general vestry, and it is sometimes difficult to determine to which parish each one belongs. Hugh Bent, from Christ Church, James Ball, Jr., Dale Carter, Stephen Towles, George Payne, Merryman Payne, Richard Selden, Thomas Chinn, Solomon Ewell, John Fleet, William Dymer, Charles Carter, John Chinn, James Kiok, Thaddeus McCarty, Thomas Griffin, Thomas Lawson, Edwin Conway, William Montague, in place of Charles Carter, in 1776, Henry Towles, James Newby, William Sydnor, John Berryman, Colonel John Tayloe, James Brent, William Chewning, James Ball, Jr.

In 1786, Cyrus Griffin is appointed to attend the Episcopal Convention in Richmond, and James Ball to attend the examination of the Rev. Edward Jones at the court-house. For what purpose and of what character that examination was; is not certainly known, but it is believed to have been a kind of trial under a canon of Virginia. Thus ends the vestry-book.

WHITE CHAPEL CHURCH.

The first church was torn down. From the vestry-book it appears that the present was built in 1740. It was contracted for with Mr. James Jones. In that year Major James Ball and Mr. Joseph Ball are allowed to build a gallery in the church for their families, provided it be completed at the same time with the church, and finished in the same style with the west gallery. Leave is also granted to two of the Balls and two Mr. Burgesses to build an end-gallery on the same terms. The house was originally in the form of a cross. The two wings have been taken down, and it is now an oblong square.

In the early part of the last century the parishes must have been in a flourishing condition, so far as numbers and attendants go. In the year 1724, Mr. Bell, who had then been their minister for twelve years, informs the Bishop of London that there were three hundred families in it; that the churches were thronged; that almost all the white persons in the parish attended; that there were a great many negroes who neither understood his language, nor he theirs; that the old church was opened to them, and the word preached, and the sacraments administered with circumspection. He says at that time the two parishes were united in one, and called Trinity: but of this we read nothing, either in the Acts of Assembly or in the vestry-book.

Around Old White Chapel Church, under the venerable pines which enclose it on two sides, and near an old county road, lie a number of those strong, heavy tombstones which betoken a deep regard of the living for the dead. Almost all of them are inscribed with the name of Ball,—a name which so abounds in the vestry-book, the county, and the State. Through the attention of a friend I have a document of more ancient date than any tombstone inscription there. It is a description of the coat of arms of the family of Ball, brought to this country about the year 1650, by the first of the name who came to Virginia. The coat of arms has much that is bold about it, as a lion rampant, with a globe in his paw, and there is helmet and shield and vizor, and coat of mail, and other things betokening strength and courage; but none of these suit my work. There is, however, one thing which does. On the scroll which belongs to it are these words:—" *Cœlumque tueri.*" They were taken, of course, from these lines of Ovid:—

> " Pronaque cum spectant animalia cætera terram
> Os homini sublime dedit, *cœlumque tueri.*"

May it be a memento to all his posterity to look upward, and " seek the things which are above." On the back of the original copy of this armorial document are the following words, in a bold hand, such as was common in those days:—" The coat of arms of Colonel William Ball, who came from England with his family about the year 1650, and settled at the mouth of Corotoman River, in Lancaster county, Virginia, and died in 1669, leaving two sons, William and Joseph, and one daughter, Hannah, who married Daniel Fox. William left eight sons, (and one daughter,) five of whom have now (Anno Domini 1779) male issue. Joseph's male issue is extinct. General George Washington is his grandson, by his youngest daughter, Mary. Colonel Burgess Ball is the only child of Jeduthun, who was the third and youngest son of James, the third son of said William." On the tombstones around the church there is no inscription of the first William Ball or any of his children, but only of his grandchildren and other descendants. The first is over the grave of David Ball, seventh son of Captain William Ball, who was born in 1686. The others are the tomb-stones of Mildred Ball, Jeduthun Ball, Mary Ann Ball, daughter of the Rev. John Bertrand, of Jesse Ball, of Mary Ball, daughter of Edwin Conway, of James Ball, her husband, of William Ball, "who died in a steadfast faith in Christ and full hope of a joyful resurrection," of James Ball and Fanny, his wife, daughter of Raleigh, and Frances Downman, of Lettuce, third wife of James Ball, and daughter of Richard Lee, of Ditchley, of Colonel James Ball, of James Ball, second son of James and Mary.

P.S.—Since the above was written I have received a communication from a friend who has looked into the earliest records of Lancaster county, when Middlesex and Lancaster were one. They go back to 1650. A few years after this, in the absence of a vestry, the court appointed the Rev. Samuel Cole the minister of the whole county on both sides of the river. This is the same minister who appears on the vestry-book of Middlesex in the year 1664. The court also appointed churchwardens and sidesmen, as in the English Church, on both sides of the river. They were John Taylor, William Clapham, John Merryman, Edmund Lurin, George Kibble, and William Leech. Other names also appear on the records, as Thomas Powell, Cuthbert Powell, Edward Digges, W. Berkeley, Robert Chewning, Henry Corbyn, David Fox, John Washington, of Westmoreland. In the year 1661, a general vestry is formed, and Mr. John Carter, Henry Corbyn, David Fox, and William Leech, are appointed to take up subscriptions for the support of the minister. They were chosen from each side of the river. An instance is recorded at this early period of a man being fined five thousand pounds of tobacco by the court for profane swearing.

In the year 1685, we find John Chilton fined, and required to appear four times on his bended knees, and ask pardon each time, for a misdemeanour committed in their presence.

In the year 1699, we find that none are allowed to be teachers of youth except such as are commissioned by the Bishop of London, and, in the same year, that inquiries were ordered as to any religious meetings except those of the Established Church. These things were under the mild reign of the *amiable* Governor Nicholson. In the year 1727, we find presentments for being absent from church one month and two months, for swearing, for selling crawfish and posting accounts on Sunday.

In addition to the above, it may be stated that the county records, as well as vestry-books, show that the family of Balls was very active in promoting good things. At an early period of our history, it is stated that a measure was set on foot for educating a number of Virginia youths for the ministry, in order to a larger and better supply. It would appear from the county records that this measure originated, in 1729, with Mr. Joseph Ball, of Lancaster. The following is the entry :—

" A proposition of Joseph Ball, gentleman, in behalf of himself and the rest of the inhabitants of Virginia, directed to the Honourable the General Assembly, concerning the instructing a certain number of young gentlemen, Virginians born, in the study of divinity, at the county's charge, was this day presented in court by the said Joseph Ball, and on his prayer ordered to be certified to the General Assembly."

This Joseph Ball married a Miss Ravenscroft, of England, and settled in London as practitioner of law. He had only one daughter, Fanny, who married Raleigh Downman in 1750. Her children were Joseph Ball Downman, of Moratico, Fanny, who married Colonel James Ball, of Bewdley, and Mr. Raleigh W. Downman, of Belle-Isle. This Joseph Ball was the uncle of General Washington. I have before me two letters from him, the one addressed to his sister Mary, and the other to his nephew George Washington, from which I take the following passages. The first is to his sister, when her son was thinking of going to sea. It is dated Stratford-by-Bow, 19th of May, 1747 :—

" I understand that you are advised and have some thoughts of putting your son George to sea. I think he had better be put apprentice to a tinker, for a common sailor before the mast has by no means the common liberty of the subject; for they will press him from a ship where he has fifty shillings a month and make him take twenty-three, and cut and slash and use him like a negro, or rather like a dog. And, as to any considerable preferment in the navy, it is not to be expected, as there are always so many gaping for it here who have interest, and he has none. And if he should get to be master of a Virginia ship, (which it is very difficult to do,) a planter that has three or four hundred acres of land and three or four slaves, if he be industrious, may live more comfortably, and leave his family in better bread, than such a master of a ship can. . . . . He must not be too hasty to be rich, but go on gently and with patience, as things will naturally go. This method, without aiming at being a fine gentleman before his time, will carry a man more comfortably and surely through the world than going to sea, unless it be a great chance indeed. I pray God keep you and yours.

"Your loving brother,   JOSEPH BALL."

To his nephew he writes thus after Braddock's defeat:—

"STRATFORD, 5th of September, 1755.

"GOOD COUSIN :—It is a sensible pleasure to me to hear that you have behaved yourself with such a martial spirit, in all your engagements with the French, nigh Ohio. Go on as you have begun, and God prosper you. We have heard of General Braddock's defeat. Everybody blames his rash conduct. Everybody commends the courage of the Virginians and Carolina men, which is very agreeable to me. I desire you, as you may have opportunity, to give me a short account how you proceed. I am your mother's brother. I hope you will not deny my request. I heartily wish you good success, and am

"Your loving uncle,
"JOSEPH BALL"

"To MAJOR GEORGE WASHINGTON,
"At the Falls of Rappahannock, or elsewhere, in Virginia.

"Please direct for me at Stratford-by-Bow, nigh London."

A few words concerning a minister and church of another denomination will close my notices of Lancaster.

The county of Lancaster was the scene of the early labours of the Rev. Mr. Waddell, the blind Presbyterian preacher who is so feelingly described by Mr. Wirt, in the British Spy. At a time when disaffection toward the Established Church was spreading through Virginia, and great numbers were leaving it, Mr. Waddell, by his talents, zeal, and piety, gathered two congregations in this county. One of the churches was near the court-house. The graveyard, in its ruins, is the only relic of the establishment of that denomination in Lancaster county. About fifty years since, the church shared the same fate with those of the Establishment which have now passed away. The two acres of land on which it stood, and beneath which are the remains of numerous adherents to that denomination, has ever been regarded as sacred. A grove of oaks, sycamores, pines, and other trees shaded the hillocks and some tombstones which were spread over the surface of the earth, which was carpeted with a covering of green grass. It was, I am told, a favourite resort to the people of the village and country around,—to the young as a play-ground, to the old as a scene of contemplation. I recently visited the spot, but found it no longer a scene for the young or old, the gay or the grave. Nearly every tree was gone, having been, within a year or two, cut down and converted into cord-wood and sold to the steamboats. Nothing is now to be seen but stumps and piles of dead branches, which hide not only the hillock-graves, but the few tombstones which were once to be seen. Young cedars are everywhere putting forth their shoots, and in a few years it will be with this spot as with many like it in Virginia,—it must be so hidden from the view that it will be difficult for any ecclesiastical antiquary to discover the spot where Mr. Waddell once proclaimed the Gospel of Christ. Rumour says that, in the absence of any member of the Church near at hand, application was made to some Presbyterian ministers at a distance, and leave granted to do something to this interesting spot which has resulted in such utter desolation.

ARTICLE LIX.

Parishes in Northumberland County.—Wycomico and St. Stephen's.

NORTHUMBERLAND county, lying on the bay and the Great Potomac, was partially settled at an early period. In the year 1646, during the government of Sir William Berkeley, we find the following Act of Assembly:—"Whereas, the inhabitants of Chicawane, *alias* Northumberland, being members of this Colony, have not hitherto contributed toward the charges of the war, [with the Indians,] it is now thought fit that the said inhabitants do make payment of the *levy* according to such rates as are by this present Assembly assessed. . . . And in case the said inhabitants shall refuse or deny payment of the said levy, as above expressed, that, upon report thereof to the next Assembly, speedy course shall then be adopted to call them off from the said Plantation." It had in the previous year been allowed a Burgess, in Mr. John Matram. In the following year Mr. William Presley was the delegate. In the year 1648, we find the following Act:—"That the ninth Act of Assembly of 1647, for the reducing of the inhabitants of Chickcoun and other parts of the neck of land between Rappahannock and Potomacke Rivers be repealed, and that the said tract of land be hereafter called and known by the name of the county of Northumberland." In the year 1649, it is declared "that the inhabitants on the south side of the Potomacke [Potomac] shall be included, and are hereafter to be accounted within the county of Northumberland." In the year 1653, the bounds of Northumberland are reduced by the establishment of Westmoreland county, which was made to extend "from Matchoactoke River, where Mr. Cole lives, and so upward to the falls of the great river Potomacke above the Necostins town;" that is, above what is now Georgetown, in the District of Columbia. In the year 1673, the boundary-line between Lancaster and Northumberland is settled, according to an order of the Assembly, by Colonel John Washington, (the first settler, and great-grandfather of General Washington,) Captain John Lee, William Traveson, William Moseley, and R. Beverley. While we have the above Acts of Assembly in relation to its civil divisions, we find nothing as to its religious concerns. The establishment of a parish or parishes within its bounds is nowhere given us, excep) in two lists of the counties in the year 1754, when it is called St. Stephen's parish, with Mr. Thomas Smith for its minister, and in 1758, when it is called Wycomico, and has the Rev. John Leland as its minister. In the year 1776, it is said to have two parishes,—Wycomico and St. Stephen's,—Mr. John Leland the minister of the former, and the Rev. Benjamin Sebastion of the other. Mr. Leland was ordained by the Bishop of London in 1775, and Mr. Sebastion in 1766. It is, however, confidently affirmed to this day that there were two parishes, called Upper and Lower St. Stephen's, besides Wycomico, and that the glebes can be pointed out.

In the year 1785, we find the two parishes represented in the Convention,—Wycomico by the Rev. Mr. Leland, and as lay delegate T. Gaskins, St. Stephen's by the Rev. Thomas Davis, with Mr. Hudson Meuse as lay delegate. In the year 1786, Wycomico alone is represented by Mr. Leland and Mr. Gaskins. In 1787, Mr. Leland appears for the last time, with Mr. David Ball as lay delegate. In 1789, Mr. Oneriphorus Harvey is lay delegate from Wycomico, and in 1790, Mr. Isaac Besye. In that year the Rev. Thomas Davis represents St. Stephen's parish, and also in 1792. In 1795, the Rev. John Seward, with Abraham Beacham as lay delegate, represents St. Stephen's, while three lay delegates, Messrs. Hopkins, Hardy, and Hurst, represent Wycomico. In the year 1797, Thomas Gaskins and Thomas Hurst are lay delegates from Wycomico, and Mr. William Claughton from St. Stephen's. In 1799, the Rev. Mr. Seward still represents St. Stephen's, while William Davenport and Thomas Harvey are lay delegates for Wycomico. There being no Convention, or, if one, no records of it, until 1805, we are unable to say who ministered in Northumberland in the interim. In that year the Rev. Duncan McNaughton represented St. Stephen's, with John Hull as lay delegate. In the year 1812, the Rev. Samuel Low, with Thomas Gaskins as lay delegate, was in the Convention. Mr. Low was also there in 1813, accompanied by Mr. Joseph Ball. From that to the present time there has, I believe, been no regular minister belonging to either of the parishes of this county, though services have been rendered to them both by the ministers of Lancaster county.

Concerning the church in Wycomico parish, and which was called Wycomico Church, we have something to say from personal knowledge. Bishop Moore and myself both performed services in it, though to a small number of persons. The last time that Bishop Moore was in the desk, a piece of plastering from its high arched ceiling fell upon his head, which was protected by only a few gray hairs. Judging from the size of the house, there must, at the time of its erection, have been many attendants, for it was the largest of the old churches in Virginia of which I have any knowledge. It was built about the beginning of the Revolutionary War, when faithful architecture had already waned. After my last visit to it in 1837, I made the following communication to the ensuing Convention of 1838:—

"On Thursday, the 22d instant, I visited Northumberland Court-House in company with the Rev. Washington Nelson, and preached to a respectable congregation in the Reformed Methodist Church. But few Episcopal families are now to be found in this county. There were formerly three large brick churches in it, two of which are entirely gone, and the third will soon share their fate unless speedy means of prevention be adopted. The one yet remaining, called Wycomico Church, was built in the year 1771, not long before the Revolution, and the walls are still firm. The other part of the workmanship was so inferior to that of former times, that the vestry refused to receive it at the hands of the contractor. The roof is now falling in, and the ceiling has given way some years since. Each of the Bishops of Virginia have preached in this decaying house, though not without some apprehension. Its present condition is truly distressing. The doors and windows are gone. The fine bricks which case the windows and doors are gradually disappearing. Along the deserted aisles, and in the pews of this large cruciform church, measuring seventy-five feet in every direction, may now be seen the carriage, the wagon, the plow, the fishing-seine, barrels of tar and lime, lumber, and various implements of husbandry. The cattle have free admission to it, and the pavement of the aisles, and even the marble slab which covers the remains of one of the latest of its ministers, is covered with dirt and rubbish. The old bell which once summoned the neighbours to the house of God is lying in one of the pews near the falling pulpit. In the deserted chancel you look in vain for the Communion-table and the baptismal font, and there is too much reason to fear that these also are used for purposes far other than those to which they were originally consecrated and applied. Some steps have recently been taken toward the repair of this large and venerable building, but whether they will be continued and the work consummated is still doubtful."

At the end of twenty years it pains me to say that my faintest hopes have been more than disappointed, and my worst fears more than realized, since not only every vestige of the house is removed and its site enclosed and cultivated with an adjoining field, but I cannot learn that there is a single family or even individual in the parish still connected with or attached to the Church. The whole population is incorporated with other denominations. That worthy friend and member of our Church, Mr. Joseph Ball, of the old seat of Ditchley, was near enough to attend Wycomico, and in Romish days would have been regarded and called its patron saint. Some years after my last visit to this falling church, he placed in my hands a rich service of Communion-plate which belonged to it, saying, that as he was the only surviving friend of the old church, and utterly despaired of its revival, he wished me to take charge of it and let it be used in some other parish. This I did, on the condition that if the parish ever revived it should receive back again the property of its ancestry. The vessels are now used in the congregation and church at Millwood, in Clarke county, and the condition of their loan is recorded in the vestry-book of the parish. The following inscription will also show that its date and use were far anterior to the establishment of old Frederick parish, out of which the parish about Millwood has been carved.

They are as follows:—on the tankard, "The gift of Bartholomew Shriver, who died in 1720, and of Bartholomew his son, who died in 1727, for the use of the parish of Great Wycomico, in the county of Northumberland, 1728." The inscription on the plate is, "The gift of Reynard Delafiae to Quantico Church." We know of no Quantico Church but that which stood near Dumfries, in Prince William county, and suppose that this plate must once have belonged to it. There is no date to the inscription. The cup, as will be seen hereafter, was the gift of Hancock Lee, in 1711.

I sincerely wish that it were in my power to give as good an account of the remnant of the old church itself. The following extract from my report to the Convention of 1841 will tell the history of the disposal of the walls of Wycomico Church:—

"Having thus briefly stated my Episcopal duties in the Northern Neck, I must beg leave to advert to a circumstance which was particularly presented to my consideration while near the site of one of our old churches in the county of Northumberland, and which has been not a little misunderstood and even misrepresented in the public prints and on the floor of our Legislature. In the spring of 1840, I received a communication from Mr. Joseph Ball, an old and valued member of our Church in Northumberland, on the subject of the sale of the church in his neighbourhood. It was then just in that condition when, spoliation of the bricks having begun, it would become an object of plunder to all around and soon disappear. One of the neighbours, therefore, proposed to purchase it, and my consent was asked. I replied that I had no right whatever to dispose of it. Visiting that part of the State soon after, Mr. Ball informed me that a gentleman living near the church, and professing an attachment to it, declared that it distressed him to see the church thus treated; that in a short time not a brick would be left; that they would be used for hearths, chimneys, and such like purposes, all the country around; that, if Mr. Ball would consent, he would give five hundred dollars, either to rebuild it or to take it down,—the materials in the latter case being his own; that he had consulted a lawyer, who told him that the head of the Church could dispose of it. As Mr. Ball was an old warden of the parish and the only surviving member, the gentleman thought he might be regarded as the head; but, on being told that the Bishop was so regarded, it was referred to myself. In reply to the renewed proposal, I stated again that I had no right to sell it, and was unwilling to have any thing to do with it, as it might be misunderstood and misrepresented. On its being urged by Mr. Ball that a refusal to give such permission would only encourage great numbers to robbery, I at length said that, if he chose to sell it, I would receive the proceeds, and place them in the hands of the trustees of our Theological Seminary, to be returned should it ever be called for to build a church in its room. I was induced to do this partly by the consideration that our Convention had many years before passed a resolution calling upon persons having church-plate in vacant parishes to send it for safe-keeping to the Bishop of the Diocese, liable to be called for should the parishes ever be revived. Such property has been given into the hands of Bishop Moore and myself, and has been lent to other parishes on that condition. I accordingly, in writing, stated my assent to the sale of the walls of the church (nothing else remaining) for five hundred dollars, giving what right I might be thought to have. I looked upon the transaction as an affair between the person proposing it, Mr. Ball, and myself, as friends to religion and the Church, who were desirous to prevent a dishonourable use of the remains of a building not likely to be wanted again, and as an act which would be approved by all good and pious persons. After having paid one-half of the money, the purchaser refused the remainder, on the plea of its having been an improper sale. In order to prevent all future misunderstanding of this transaction, I have thought it best thus to place it among our records. The two hundred and fifty dollars which were paid were expended, I believe, on the Chapel attached to our Theological Seminary, and I hold myself personally responsible for its return whenever any competent authority shall claim it."

I am sorry to add that to this day the remaining two hundred and fifty dollars is unpaid. I trust that the descendants of the purchaser, even to the latest generation, will feel bound to Wycomico, even as the trustees of the Theological Seminary, for the part which has been used.

NOTICES OF THE LEE FAMILY IN VIRGINIA.

In the county of Northumberland and parish of Great Wycomico, and within sight of the Chesapeake Bay, there is an estate and mansion called Ditchley,—an English name of note,—which has probably from its first settlement, more than one hundred years ago, been the favourite resort of the ministers of the Episcopal Church. Its present owner is Mr. Flexmer Ball. His father, Mr. Joseph Ball, was one of the truest members of our Church. Of his ancestry we have just written in our last article. Many and pleasant have been the hours which, in company with some of the brethren, I have spent at Ditchley within the last thirty years. Ditchley is one of the old residences of the Lees. The mansion called Cobbs, where Colonel Richard Lee, the first of the family, lived for some time, was near to Ditchley, and has only very recently been removed to make place for another, although it must have been built two hundred years ago or more. The first settler, of whom more will hereafter be said, had many sons, of whom the seventh, Hancock Lee, built and lived at Ditchley. He was twice married,—first to a Miss Kendall, then to a Miss Allerton, by each of whom he had children, whose descendants are among us to this day. He died in 1729, as his tombstone in the family burying-ground at Ditchley shows to this day. Both of his wives are buried at the same place. That he was a patron of the church is shown by the fact that he presented a Communion-cup to the parish in 1711. In honour either of himself or father, or the whole family, the parish was then called Lee parish, as may be seen by the inscription on the cup. It was afterward called Wycomico. After the downfall of the parish, Mr. Joseph Ball placed this and other pieces into my hands for preservation, in hope that the day might come when the old Lee and more modern Wycomico parish might call for it again. It is now used in the church at Millwood, Clarke county, and the source whence it came and the pledge given are recorded in the vestry-book of the same, as has already been said.

The following account of the Lee family is copied from a manuscript in the handwriting of William Lee, dated London, September, 177–, the last figure not known, but just before the war, as is evident from the document itself. Its author was one of the six sons of Thomas Lee, so many of whom were active in the Revolution. It is somewhat doubtful whether in the early part of it Mr. Arthur Lee and William Lee, in London, were not as effective as Richard Henry Lee and Francis Lightfoot Lee in America. Mr. William Lee, author of the following sketch, was sheriff and alderman in the city of London, and subsequently commercial agent for Congress in Europe and their Commissioner at the Courts of Berlin and Vienna. He married a Miss Ludwell and left three children,—William Ludwell, of Greenspring, who is buried in the old churchyard at Jamestown, Portia, who married Mr. William Hodgson, and Cornelia, who married Mr. John Hopkins. The high character of Mr. Lee stamps a value on the following statement:—

" Richard Lee, of good family in Shropshire, and whose picture, I am told, is now at Cotton, near Bridgenorth, the seat of Lancelot Lee, Esq., some time in the reign of Charles I. went over to the Colony of Virginia as Secretary and one of the King's Privy Council, which last part will for shortness be called 'of the Council.' He was a man of good stature, comely visage, enterprising genius, a sound head, vigorous spirit, and generous nature. When he got to Virginia, which at that time was not much cultivated, he was so pleased with the country that he made large settlements there with the servants he carried over. After some years he returned to England, and gave all the lands he had taken up and settled at his expense to those servants he had fixed on them, some of whose descendants are now possessed of very considerable estates in that Colony. After staying some time in England, he returned to Virginia with a fresh band of adventurers.

" During the civil war here, Sir William Berkeley was the Governor of Virginia: he and Lee, both being loyalists, kept the Colony to its allegiance, so that after the death of Charles I. Cromwell was obliged to send some ships-of-war and soldiers to reduce the Colony, which not being able to do, a treaty was made with the Commonwealth of England, wherein Virginia was styled an independent dominion. This treaty was ratified here as made with a foreign power, upon which Sir William Berkeley (who was of the same family as the present Earl of Berkeley) was removed, and another Governor appointed in his room. When Charles II. was at Breda, Richard Lee came over from Virginia and went there to him to know if he could undertake to protect the Colony if they returned to their allegiance to him; but, finding no support could be obtained, he returned to Virginia and remained quiet until the death of Cromwell, when he, with the assistance of Sir William Berkeley, contrived to get Charles II. proclaimed there King of England, Scotland, France, Ireland, and Virginia two years before he was restored here, and Sir William Berkeley was reinstated as his Governor, in which station he continued until some time after the Restoration, when he came over, and died presently. It was in consequence of this step that the motto of the Virginia arms always till after the union was 'En dat Virginia quintam;' but since the union it was changed to 'En dat Virginia quartam;' that is, King of Great Britain, France, Ireland, and Virginia. Here, by-the-way, I cannot help remarking the extreme ingratitude of this Prince Charles II. Oliver Cromwell, to punish Virginia and some of the other parts of America for adhering to the royal cause, after he had got himself quite fixed in his supreme authority, both here and there, contrived the famous Navigation Act, upon a model he borrowed from the Dutch, by which the American Colonies were deprived of many of their ancient and valuable privileges: upon the Restoration, instead of repealing this Act, it was confirmed by the whole Legislature here; and to add to the ingratitude, at two other periods in his reign, taxes were imposed on American commodities under the pretext of regulations of trade, from which wicked source have flowed all the bitter waters that are now likely to overwhelm America or this country, and most probably will in the end be the ruin of both. But to return. This Richard Lee had several children. The two eldest—John and Richard—were educated at Oxford. John took his degree as doctor of physic, and returned to Virginia, and died before his father Richard. He was so clever and learned, that some great men offered to promote him to the highest dignities in the Church, if his father would let him stay in England; but this offer was refused, because the old gentleman was determined to fix all his children in Virginia. So firm was he in this purpose, that by his will he ordered an estate he had in England, (I think near Stratford-by-Bow in Middlesex,) at that time worth eight hundred or nine hundred pounds per annum, to be sold and the money to be divided among his children. He died and was buried in Virginia, leaving a numerous progeny, whose names I have chiefly forgot. His eldest son then living was Richard, who spent almost his whole life in study, and usually wrote his notes in Greek, Hebrew, or Latin,—many of which are now in Virginia; so that he neither improved nor diminished his paternal estate, though at that time he might with ease have acquired what would at this day produce a princely revenue. He was of the Council in Virginia, and also in other offices of honour and profit, though they yielded little to him. He married a Corbin or Corbyne, I think of Staffordshire: from this marriage he had and left behind him when he died in Virginia—which was some time after the Revolution [in England under William and Mary]—five sons,—Richard, Philip, Francis, Thomas, and Henry, and one daughter.* Richard settled in London as a Virginia merchant, in partnership with one Thomas Corbin, a brother of his mother: he married an heiress in England of the name of Silk, and by her left one son, George, and two daughters, Lettuce and Martha. All these three children went to Virginia and settled. George married a Wormly there, who died leaving one daughter; then he married a Fairfax—nearly related to Lord Fairfax, of Yorkshire—and died, leaving by his last marriage three sons that are now minors and are at school in England under the care of Mr. James Russul. Lettuce married a Corbin, and her sister married a Turberville: their eldest children intermarried, from which union George Lee Turberville, now at school at Winton College, is the eldest issue. Philip, the second son, went to Maryland, where he married and settled. He was of the Proprietor's Council, and died leaving a very numerous family, that are now branched out largely over the whole Province, and are in plentiful circumstances. The eldest son, Richard, is now a member of the Proprietor's Council. Francis, the third son, died a bachelor. Thomas, the fourth son, though with none but a common Virginia education, yet, having strong natural parts, long after he was a man he learned the languages without any assistance but his own genius, and became a tolerable adept in the Greek and Latin. He married a Ludwell, of whose genealogy I must give a short account, being maternally interested therein. The Ludwells, though the name is now extinct, are an old and honourable family of Somersetshire, England, the original of them many ages since coming from Germany. Philip Ludwell and John Ludwell, being brothers, and sons of a Miss Cottington, who was heiress of James Cottington, the next brother and heir to the famous Lord Francis Cottington, of whom a pretty full account may be seen in Lord Clarendon's History of the Rebellion, were in court favour after the restoration of Charles II. John was appointed Secretary, and was one of the Council in Virginia, where, I believe, he died without issue. Philip, the eldest brother, went to America Governor of Carolina, from whence he went to Virginia, and married the widow of Sir William Berkeley, by whom he had a daughter, (that married Colonel Parke, who was afterward the Governor of the Leeward Islands, in the

---

* The daughter married Mr. William Fitzhugh, of Eagle's Nest, King George county,—son of the first William Fitzhugh,—and was the mother of the late William Fitzhugh, of Chatham.

West Indies, and died in Antigua, the seat of his government,) and one son named Philip.

"After some time old Philip Ludwell returned to England, and died here. He was buried in Bow Church, near Stratford: his son Philip remained in Virginia, where his father had acquired a considerable estate, and married a Harrison, by whom he had two daughters,—Lucy, the eldest, married a Colonel Grymes, who was of the Council in Virginia, and Hannah, who married the before-mentioned Thomas Lee,—and one son, Philip. This Philip was, as his father had been, of the Council of Virginia. He married a Grymes, by whom he had several children,—most of whom died in their infancy; and in the year 1753 his wife died; in 1760 he came over to England for his health, and in the year 1767 he died here, when the male line of Ludwell became extinct. He left heiresses three daughters,—Hannah Philippa, Frances, and Lucy: the second is since dead unmarried. This Thomas Lee by his industry and parts acquired a considerable fortune; for, being a younger brother, with many children, his paternal estate was very small. He was also appointed of the Council; and, though he had very few acquaintances in England, he was so well known by his reputation, that upon his receiving a loss by fire, the late Queen Caroline sent him over a bountiful present out of her own privy purse. Upon the late Sir William Gooch's being recalled, who had been some time Governor of Virginia, he became President and Commander-in-chief in the Colony, in which station he continued for some time, until the King thought proper to appoint him Governor of the Colony; but he died before his commission got to him. He left by his marriage with Miss Ludwell six sons,—Philip Ludwell, Thomas Ludwell, Richard Henry, Francis Lightfoot, William, and Arthur,—and two daughters, all well provided for in point of fortune.

Here ends the manuscript of Mr. William Lee, of London; but we are enabled by another document to proceed further, though not justified by the bounds prescribed to our notices to pursue it in its details. Of the six sons of Thomas Lee, of Stratford, something must be said, or we should be justly condemned.

Philip Ludwell, the eldest, succeeded his father at Stratford, in Westmoreland. He married a Miss Steptoe, and left two daughters. Matilda, the eldest, married General Henry Lee, of the Revolution; and Flora married Mr. Ludwell Lee, of Loudoun. Thomas Ludwell settled in Stafford, and married a Miss Aylett. Richard Henry was educated in England, and returned in the nineteenth year of his age, and married first a Miss Aylett, and next a Mrs. Pinkard, who was a Miss Gaskins or Gascoigne. He took an active part in the Revolution. His life has been written by his grandson, Richard Henry Lee. Francis Lightfoot Lee also participated largely in the events of the Revolution, and was regarded as one of the ablest orators and statesmen of that period. He married a Miss Rebecca Tayloe, daughter of Colonel John Tayloe, of Richmond county. Of the fifth son, William, the sheriff and alderman of London, we have already given some account. Arthur, the sixth and youngest, as a scholar, a writer, a philosopher, a politician and diplomatist, was surpassed by none and equalled by few of his contemporaries. He studied physic in Edinburgh, where he took his degrees; but, disliking the profession, he studied law, and distinguished himself as a lawyer in England. The services rendered by him to his country as her minister at foreign courts were most valuable.

In the English document immediately preceding, nothing is said of one branch of the family,—viz.: Henry Lee, one of the brothers of Thomas Lee, of Stratford, and grandson of the first Lee. He married a Bland, and had several children. His son Richard was Squire Lee, of Lee Hall. His only daughter married a Fitzhugh. Henry, the third son, married a Miss Grymes, and left five sons and three daughters,—viz.: Henry, who was Colonel in the Revolution, Charles, Richard Bland, Theodoric, and Edmund; also, Mary, Lucy, and Anne. A numerous posterity has descended from these, among whom are some bright ornaments of the Church, the State, and the army. Mention is made in our English document of one of the family at an early period moving to Maryland and having numerous and influential descendants in that Province. I have reason to believe, from recent examinations into the records of different courts in the Northern Neck, that some of that branch returned to Virginia, and were for a long series of years clerks in the county of Essex. The following extract from a communication sent me by a competent person establishes the fact. "John Lee, clerk of Essex county, who succeeded Captain William Beverley, came from Maryland. His nephew, John Lee, who was a member of the House of Burgesses, succeeded him. At his death, his son Hancock Lee succeeded to the office. At the death of Hancock Lee, his son John Lee succeeded to it." Thus four of the name held the office of clerk in Essex in succession.

The family of Lees, in all its branches, so far as I know and believe, have always been Episcopal. I know of scarce an exception. I have been intimately acquainted with some most excellent specimens of true piety among them,—too many to be specified and dwelt upon. If tradition and history and published documents are to be relied on, the patriotic, laborious, self-sacrificing, and eloquent Richard Henry Lee, of the Revolution, must have deeply sympathized with Washington, and Peyton Randolph, and Pendleton, and Nicholas, and Henry, in their religious character and sentiments.

In looking over the two volumes containing the life and correspondence of Richard Henry Lee, of Chantilly, in Westmoreland, the reader cannot fail to ask himself the question, "Was there a man in the Union who did more in his own county and State and country, by action at home and correspondence abroad, to prepare the people of the United States for opposition to English usurpation, and the assertion of American independence? Was there a man in America who toiled and endured more than he, both in body and mind, in the American cause? Was there a man in the Legislature of Virginia, and in the Congress of the Union, who had the pen of a ready writer so continually in his hand, and to which so many public papers may be justly ascribed, and by whom so much hard work in committee-rooms was performed?" To him most justly was assigned the honourable but perilous duty of first moving in our American Congress "that these United Colonies are, and of right ought to be, free and independent States." Nor is it at all wonderful that one who was conversant with the plans and intentions of the English ministry should have declared that, in the event of the reduction of the Colonies, the delivery of General Washington and Richard Henry Lee would be demanded, in order to their execution as rebels. Although the great principles of morality and religion rest on infinitely higher ground than the opinion of the greatest and best of men, yet it is most gratifying to find them sustained in the writings and actions of such a man as Richard Henry Lee. Mr. Lee advocated private education as being better calculated for impressing the minds of the young "with a love of religion and virtue." His biographer says that he had early studied the evidences of the Christian religion, and had through life avowed his belief in its divine origin. He was a member of the Episcopal Church in full communion, and took a deep interest in its welfare. He proved the sincerity of what has been quoted from him, in favour of private education, by having a minister or candidate for the ministry in his family as private tutor. Mr. Balmaine was sent over to him by his brother Arthur, from London, as both a staunch friend of America and a pious man. I have often heard Mr. Balmaine speak in the highest terms of Mr. Lee as a Christian and a patriotic statesman. His attachment to the Church of his fathers was evinced by the interest he took in seeking to obtain consecration for our Bishops, immediately after the war, and when he was President of Congress. Twice were thanks returned to him by our General Convention for his services. Mr. Lee was a decided advocate of the appointment of public acts of supplication and thanksgiving to Almighty God in times of adversity and prosperity. When all was dark and lowering in our political horizon, and when it was proposed that, as one means of propitiating the favour of God, it should be recommended to the different States to take the most effectual means for the encouraging of religion and good morals, and for suppressing "theatrical entertainments, horse-racing, gaming, and such other diversions as are productive of idleness, dissipation, and a general depravity of manners," while some voted against the measure, Mr. Lee was found in company with the most pious men of the land in favour of it, and it was carried by a large majority. Again, when by the capture of Burgoyne's army the hearts of Americans were cheered, we find Mr. Lee one of a committee drafting a preamble and resolution, which is believed to be from his own pen, in the following pious strain:—"Forasmuch as it is the indispensable duty of all men to adore the superintending providence of Almighty God, to acknowledge with gratitude their obligation to him for benefits received, and to implore such further blessings as they stand in need of; and it having pleased him, in his abundant mercy, not only to continue to us the innumerable bounties of his common providence, but also to smile upon us in the prosecution of a just and necessary war for the independence and establishment of our unalienable rights and liberties; particularly in that he hath been pleased in so great a measure to prosper the means used for the support of our arms, and crown them with the most signal success: it is therefore recommended to the Legislature and executive powers of these States, to set apart Thursday, the eighteenth of December next, for solemn thanksgiving and praise; that with one heart and one voice the people may express the feelings of their hearts, and consecrate themselves to the service of their Divine Benefactor; and, together with their sincere acknowledgments and offerings, they may join the penitent confession of their manifold sins, whereby they have forfeited every favour, and their earnest and humble supplication that it may please God, through the merits of Jesus Christ, mercifully to forgive and blot them out of remembrance; that it may please God," &c.

Mr. Lee, though entirely opposed to any Church establishment, was, together with Henry, an advocate for a proposition to make every man contribute to the support of the Christian religion, as the only sure basis of private and public morality. In this, however, they failed. When the question about paying debts in depreciated currency came on, Mr. Lee evinced his high and honourable sense of morality in the earnest and eloquent opposition made to it. He declared that nothing so deeply distressed him as a proposition which he regarded as a violation of honesty and good faith among men, and said that it "would have been better to have remained the honest slaves of Britain, than dishonest freemen."*

Of the descendants of so great and good a man, I cannot refrain
from adding something.   His oldest son was Thomas Lee, whose
daughter Eleanor married Girard Alexander.   His second son was
Mr. Ludwell Lee, of Loudoun county, who was a worthy member
of our Church, and left children and grandchildren who have followed his example.   His daughter Mary married Colonel William
Augustin Washington, but died childless.   His daughter Hannah
married Mr. Corbin Washington, many of whose descendants have
been or are zealous members of the Church.   His daughter Harriet
married twice,—first Mr. George Turberville, and then the Rev. Mr.
Maffit, of the Presbyterian Church.   Many of their descendants,
whether of the Episcopal or Presbyterian Church, are characterized
by exemplary piety.   Sally married Edmund I. Lee, of Alexandria,
and has left a numerous posterity of children and grandchildren
and great-grandchildren, who belong to and love the Church of
their ancestors.   The Rev. William F. Lee was one of her sons.

Anne, the other daughter of R. H. Lee, married Charles Lee.
Her daughter Ann married General Walter Jones, and was the
mother of a numerous family of children, who love the religion and
Church of their ancestors.   Her daughter Catherine is one of our
missionaries in China.

NORTHUMBERLAND HOUSE.

On the Potomac, and within sight of the bay, are the remains
of an old graveyard, belonging to what has always gone by the
name of the "Northumberland House."   The place was originally
settled and a house built on it by a Mr. Presley, one of the earliest
settlers, who was murdered in it by his own servants.   It was
afterward owned by Mr. Presley Thornton, who lies buried there.
The following extract from the letter of a friend is worthy of insertion:—

"I have also, according to promise, visited the graveyard of old Northumberland House, and found the remains of but one tombstone.   This,
although erected of the heaviest materials, has been so much mutilated
by lightning and the waste of time, that nothing more can be deciphered
than that it was erected to the memory of Presley Thornton, who was
elected in early life to the House of Burgesses from the county of Northumberland, which office he held until 1760, when he was appointed one
of the Council of State for this Colony; and that he filled both offices
with great credit to himself and to the public emolument.   He departed

* I have ascertained, beyond a doubt, that he was buried at Chantilly, in the
yard or garden.

this life on the 8th of December, 1769, in the forty-eighth year of his age, having enjoyed all the chief honours of his country."

To this I add that, in the absence of the vestry-books and court-records, I find that at an early period the Lees, Presleys, Poy-thresses, Kenners, Thorntons, Newtons, &c. were the leading persons in Northumberland.

The assertion by Mr. Lee that Charles II. was proclaimed King in Virginia before he was received as such in England is a matter of dispute among historians. Beverley, our earliest, who published his work in 1705,—about forty-five years after the event is said to have occurred,—affirms it as a fact. Robertson, the historian, and Chalmers, another writer of that day, repeat the same. Burke, who published in 1805, agrees with the foregoing so far as to think that something of the kind took place, though not in a regular way. Dr. Hawks agrees with Beverley and his followers. Mr. Henning, in his Statutes at Large, compiled by order of the Virginia Assembly, and commenced in 1809, is of opinion that there is no foundation for any such supposition, and appeals to the entire absence of all notice of such proceeding in the documents of that period. Mr. Bancroft and Mr. Charles Campbell adopt the opinion of Mr. Henning. Of course, if it was an irregular, partial, or tumultuous act of individuals, as Mr. Burke supposes, we could not expect to see it among the recorded Acts of Assembly, as we do see the later and more formal acknowledgment of Charles II. It is not, however, a matter of sufficient importance to produce a Trojan war. It is scarcely probable that Mr. Lee is mistaken in the tradition that his ancestor was a zealous loyalist, and did, on his return to England, visit Charles at Breda and hold communion with him on the subject of his acknowledgment by Virginia, then having so many staunch Cavaliers in it, whatever uncertainty may rest upon the subsequent proceedings.

Since the foregoing article was written, I have received some further information concerning the first of the Lee family and his children, which is worthy of insertion. The will of the first Richard Lee, dated 1663, may be seen in Mr. Charles Campbell's History of Virginia, p. 157. From it I extract the following:—"I, Colonel Richard Lee, of Virginia, and lately of Stratford-Langton, in the county of Essex, Esquire, being bound out upon a voyage to Virginia aforesaid, and not knowing how it may please God to dispose of me in so long a voyage," &c. "First, I give and bequeath my soul to that good and gracious God that gave it me, and to my blessed Redeemer Jesus Christ, assuredly trusting in and by his meritorious death and passion to receive salvation, and my body to be disposed of, whether by sea or land, according to the opportunity of the place, not doubting but at the last day both body and soul shall be united and glorified." Here again we see the faith and the divinity of that day. He then directs that his wife and children, who it seems had not yet been to Virginia, should be sent there, except Francis, to whose option it was left. To his wife Anna he left Stratford-on-the-Potowmacke (to which he had removed from Cobbs) and Mock Necke, together with servants black and white, and other property during her life. To his son John he leaves his plantation called Matholic, with servants, &c. This is now the Mount Pleasant farm owned by Mr. Willowby Newton. To his son Richard he leaves his plantation called Paradise, and the servants there. To his son Francis he leaves his plantations called Paper-Maker's Neck and War Captain's Neck, with servants black and white. To his five younger children, William, Hancock, Betsy, Anne, and Charles, he leaves a plantation, including Bishop's Neck on the Potomac, four thousand acres on the Potomac, together with Stratford and Mock Neck at the death of their mother. To William he leaves his lands on the Maryland side; to Francis an interest in his two ships. He also leaves a fund for the better education in England of his two oldest sons, John and Richard.

Since writing the account of the marriages of Richard Henry, as given by his brother William Lee, I have received two communications, stating that one of his wives was a Miss Gaskins, so that, unless he was married three times, there must have been a mistake as to the name of one of those before mentioned.

THE CORBIN FAMILY.

The following account of the Corbin family may very properly be added to that of the Lees, on account of their early connection by marriage.

The vestry-books of Middlesex and King and Queen counties doubtless speak of some of the same persons mentioned in this genealogy.

Henry Corbin settled in the parish of Stratton Major, King and Queen, about the year 1650. One Nicholas Jernew obtained a patent for Peekatone, in the county of Westmoreland, dated 18th October, 1650, which he transferred to Henry Corbin, who had another patent issued in his own name, dated 26th of March, 1664. Henry Corbin had three children, of whom mention is made in the old papers in my possession. Thomas Corbin, one of his sons, must have died without male issue, as his brother Gawin Corbin, by his will, devises to his son Gawin Corbin "the land of my brother, the late Mr. Thomas Corbin." His eldest daughter, Letitia, married Richard Lee, second son of Colonel Richard Lee. Gawin Corbin, the other son of Henry Corbin, and once President of the Council, married a daughter of William Bassett, and left seven children,—three sons and four daughters. Jenny, one of his daughters, married a Mr. Bushrod; Joanna married Major Robert Tucker; Alice married Benjamin Needler, and the other a Mr. Allerton. His sons were—1st, Richard Corbin of Laneville, who married Miss Betty Tayloe, daughter of Colonel John Tayloe, (Carter Braxton married their oldest daughter;) 2d, John Corbin, of whose history I am ignorant, (the lands devised to him were chiefly in Maryland;) 3d, Gawin Corbin, once a member of the Council, and who married Hannah Lee, sister of Richard Henry Lee. Gawin Corbin, third grandson of Henry Corbin, left an only daughter, Martha, who married George Turberville. George Turberville left two sons,—viz.: Gawin Corbin Turberville, and Richard Lee Turberville. Gawin Corbin Turberville married a daughter of Colonel John Dangerfield, and left an only daughter, Mary, who married William F. Taliafero.

A friend has sent me the following record, which shows at how early a period that kind of dissipation which proved so destructive to Virginia made its appearance in the Northern Neck. "John Lee, Henry Corbin, Thomas Gerrard, and Isaac Allerton, entered into a compact, dated 30th of March, 1670, (recorded 27th March, 1774,) to build a banqueting-house at or near the corner of their respective lands."

ARTICLE LX.

Cople Parish, Westmoreland County.

WESTMORELAND county was cut off from Northumberland county in 1653, and extended along the Potomac as high as the Falls above Georgetown. In the years 1661–62 the two counties were temporarily reunited, because, by the removal of some leading persons, there was not a suitable number of civil and military gentlemen to constitute a proper commission in either of them alone. After some time Stafford was taken from Westmoreland, leaving it a small, narrow county lying on the Potomac, and only extending half-way across the neck toward the Rappahannock River. First Lancaster, then Rappahannock, and then Richmond counties, divided what is now Westmoreland. In time, all the land lying between the rivers was given to Westmoreland, and Cople parish occupied the lower part of the county and Washington the upper. We will begin with Cople parish.

The first minister we have on any of our lists is the Rev. Charles Rose, brother to the Rev. Robert Rose, of Essex. He appears on the earliest list we have,—that of 1754,—but from the diary of his brother we know that he was its minister some years before this. He was also minister in 1758. In the year 1773, the Rev. Thomas Smith was its minister, as he was in 1776. Either before or after him, we are informed that the Rev. Augustine Smith was its minister. We presume that they were relatives of the many respectable persons of that name in this and other counties around, but we have received no particular account of them. In the year 1799, the Rev. James Elliott was minister. Of him we hear nothing good from this or any other parish which he served. We hear of no other minister in Cople parish until the Rev. Washington Nelson took charge of it in connection with the parishes in Richmond county. He was succeeded in 1842 by the Rev. Mr. Ward. The Rev. Mr. Rumney succeeded him in 1849, and was succeeded by the Rev. Edward McGuire in 1850. He was followed by the Rev. William McGuire in 1852. The present minister, the Rev. Mr. Dashiel, took charge of it in 1854.

There were two churches in this parish,—one at Yeocomico River or Creek, from which it takes its name, Yeocomico; and another about ten miles off, on Nominy River or Creek, from which it also took the name of Nominy. The latter was destroyed by fire soon after our last war with England, but a new brick one has taken its place within the last few years. The plate belonging to this church was carried off by Admiral Cockburn and his party, when they were on a pillaging-expedition on the Potomac and its tributaries. The plate was kept on a plantation upon the banks of Nominy River, just opposite the church. The farm itself was called Nominy, and was then, and still is, owned by the Griffith family, relatives of the Bishop-elect of that name. The house was plundered and then burned. The other—Yeocomico Church—is still in good repair, but among the rudest and roughest of all the old brick churches. It was built in 1706. For the first time a new roof has, within a few years, been put upon it, and some internal changes been made in it. Although I think it might have been better done and made more complete, yet it would be difficult, and perhaps not desirable, to give a more modern aspect to it. The following extract from my report in 1838 may not be without interest to the reader:—

"On Monday I went, in company with Mr. Nelson, to Yeocomico Church, in Westmoreland, where I preached, and administered the rite of Confirmation to three persons.

"Yeocomico Church, so called after the river of that name, is one of the old churches, being built in the year 1706. The architecture is rough, but very strong, and the materials must have been of the best kind. Its figure is that of a cross, and, situated as it is, in a little recess from the main road, in the midst of some aged trees, and surrounded by an old brick wall which is fast mouldering away, it cannot fail to be an object of interest to one whose soul has any sympathy for such scenes. It has undergone but little repair since its first erection, and indeed has needed little. It is not known or believed that a single new shingle has ever been put upon the roof, and the pews and whole interior are the same. During the late war it was shamefully abused by the soldiers who were quartered in it while watching the movements of the British on the Potomac. The Communion-table was removed into the yard, where it served as a butcher's block, and was entirely defaced. Being of substantial materials, however, it admitted of a new face and polish, and is now restored to its former place, where it will answer, we trust, for a long time to come, the holy purposes for which it was originally designed. Nor was the baptismal font exempt from profanation. It was taken some miles from the church, and used as a vessel in which to prepare the excitements to ungodly mirth. This, however was not long permitted, for in the absence of every member of our own communion, none being left to do it, a venerable old man of the Presbyterian connection,* mortified at the dishonour done to religion,

---

* The name of this worthy old man is Murphy. He has now gone to his rest.

took pains to regain it and restore it to its former place. It is a large and beautiful marble font, and by its side I took my station while I heard the renewal of baptismal vows from the lips of those who were confirmed. The canvas on which the Ten Commandments, the Lord's Prayer, and the Creed were impressed was so torn by the soldiers that they could no longer be permitted to retain their place, and are now lying in fragments in one of the distant and unoccupied pews.

"It deserves to be mentioned that whatever repairs have been put upon this house were at the expense of the good man mentioned above, and a worthy gentleman of New York, a member of our communion, and whose matrimonial connection in the family often brought him to that part of Virginia. A large and excellent stove, which completely warmed the whole church, was a present from the latter, and on the desk and pulpit the Bible and Prayer-Book bear the name of J. Rogers, of New York."

It deserves to be stated that I have in my possession a contract with the vestry for the repairs of this church in 1773, at a cost of one hundred pounds, or five hundred dollars. In the agreement, various repairs within and without the house and in the walls around the yard are specified, but nothing is said about a new roof, which goes to establish the tradition that the present roof is the original one put upon the house in 1706.

THE McGUIRE FAMILY, BY THE PRESENT MINISTER OF COPLE PARISH.

For twenty years or more, prior to the pastorate of the Rev. Washington Nelson, this parish was without clerical services. In all that time there was nothing except the visitations of the Bishop to remind the people here that there was an Episcopal Church. And depressing as was such a state of things, and calculated as it was to break us down entirely, we were just as likely to have the same end brought about by the life and character of the man who had last been rector. I do not know whether this man resigned the parish, or died whilst in charge: be that as it may, his course was well calculated to disgust people and drive them from our services. Looking at the consequences which must naturally flow from such a connection, and from the long period in which there was entire absence of Episcopal ministrations, we cannot otherwise than wonder, whilst we thank God, as we now see our Church upon the same spot enjoying every promise of prosperity. Whilst, during the period referred to, there was nothing done by us, other Christian bodies were active; and, under all the influences which operated against us, it is not surprising that all or nearly all who had any affection for our Church should have lost their feelings of attachment and have sought comfort elsewhere. In truth, when Mr. Nelson came here the Episcopal Church had nearly *died out*. The only communicants he found were three old ladies in the humblest walks of life. An account of these pious and excellent people was published by Mr. Nelson, but I believe it must be out of print. Even, however, if there should be any copies of it in existence, their history is so remarkable that it will very well bear the mention here made. The name of these sisters was McGuire,—Miss Emily, Miss Mary, and a widow, Mrs. Davis. Two of them are still alive and still continue warmly attached to our Church, and are exerting a considerable influence in its favour among their acquaintances. The eldest of them—Miss Emily—died in August, 1855. I tried to obtain for myself a satisfactory account of how they became Episcopalians, and how they retained their love for the Church when every one else in the surrounding country deserted it. They said, in substance, that they had been educated by their mother, who was an Episcopalian, and brought up to love all our services. They were baptized by our ministry, and attended its preaching whenever they could. When their mother died she left them a large Prayer-Book, with the request that they would abide by its teachings; and, from affection for her as well as for the Church, they obeyed her word. They told how the Church had flourished in days gone by,—how it had been ridiculed when its clergy behaved badly,— and how the members had been shamed away from it, and how themselves still clung to it. I asked them how they got along during the many years there was no minister. "Why, sir," said Miss Emily, "whenever there was preaching at Westmoreland or Richmond Court-House, we would walk to it,—once in a while we would have this chance,—and when there was no preaching I would read the Lessons on Sunday to my sister and we would go through the morning service, and if any neighbours came in maybe I would read a sermon." Westmoreland Court-House is four miles from their residence and Richmond Court-House about twelve miles; and I have it certified by others that the statement of Miss Emily is true,—they have been known to walk to and from these places to attend our Church services in the coldest and hottest weather. I asked them if in that time they never attended the services of other denominations. "Well, sir," they said, "we did sometimes; they would be holding church all around us, and sometimes we would go; but it wasn't like home to us. We know they're good, but still we felt happier worshipping here in our own way."

The piety of these worthy people is even more remarkable than their attachment to their Church. They are very poor, but their uniform contentment and happiness is rarely to be met with. Upon one occasion whilst Miss Emily was alive, her sister Mary remarked that now in their old age they sometimes got right cold while walking to church in the winter. "But what of that, sister?" says Miss Emily; "why should we care for that?" "And I don't care for it," was the reply.

We have mentioned that Miss Emily died in August, 1855. She was very aged, and for some weeks previous to her decease was imbecile. It pleased God, however, not to let her depart in this state. The day before she died her reason returned, and she talked solemnly and impressively to those around her. She remained thus conscious almost up to the very moment of her death. Miss Mary and Mrs. Davis still attend their church and see the parish which once could number only themselves as its friends, now containing more than twenty families, about thirty communicants now living, and many evidences that it is still to flourish. May God help us to remember and cherish the poor!

To this it well deserves to be added, that during the entire intermission of services in this parish, these sisters were in the habit of going once in a year in a sail-boat to Alexandria in order to receive the Communion.

THE NEWTON FAMILY.

From a document of Mr. Willowby Newton, father of the present Willowby, and grandson of a Willowby Newton, I learn that at an early period four brothers emigrated to Virginia,—one of whom settled in Norfolk, another in Alexandria, one in Westmoreland, and one in Stafford; so that it is probable that all of the name in Virginia, and many out of it, are from the same stock. Richard Lee, of Lee Hall, in Westmoreland, not far from the ruins of the old burnt house, which was an ancient Lee establishment, married a Miss Poythress, of Prince George, who was a granddaughter of Richard Bland. After the death of Mr. Lee—commonly called Squire Lee—she married Mr. Willowby Newton, both of whom were vestrymen, as was John Newton, father of this Willowby, and son of the first Willowby. The name of Willowby was an ancient one about Norfolk, and intermarried with the Newtons.

At Bushfield, in this county, there is an inscription which gives us the origin of the name Bushrod, which is incorporated in many other names of Virginia:—

"Here lies the body of John Bushrod, Gentleman, son of Richard Bushrod, Gentleman, by Apphia his wife. He was born in Gloucester county, Virginia, the 30th of January, 1663.   He took for his wife Hannah, the daughter of William Keene, of Northumberland, and Elizabeth his wife, and by her left two sons and four daughters, and died the 6th of February, 1719, in the 56th year of his age."

At Wilmington, the family seat of the Newtons, we have also the following inscription:—

"Beneath this stone are deposited the remains of Mrs. Sarah Newton, daughter of George Eskridge, and late wife of Captain Willowby Newton, of Westmoreland county, who, after having justly established the character of a dutiful child, a faithful friend, an affectionate mother, and sincere Christian, departed this life on the 2d of December, 1753, in the 46th year of her age."

In the same graveyard is the tomb of Mrs. Elizabeth Oldham, wife of Colonel Samuel Oldham, who died in 1759, in her 72d year.

TOMBSTONES IN COPLE PARISH.

From a tombstone in the Burnt-House fields, at Mount Pleasant, Westmoreland county, where are yet to be seen the foundations of large buildings, are the following:—

"Hic conditur corpus Richardi Lee, Armigeri, nati in Virginia, filii Richardi Lee, generosi, et antiqua familia, in Merton-Regis, in comitatu Salopiensi, oriundi.

"In magistratum obeundo boni publici studiosissimi, in literis Græcis et Latinis et aliis humanioris literaturæ disciplinis versatissimi.

"Deo, quem, summa observantia semper coluit, animam tranquillus reddidit xii. mo. die Martii, anno MDCCXIV. ætat. LXVIII."

"Hic, juxta, situm est corpus Lætitiæ ejusdem uxoris fidæ, filiæ Henrici Corbyn, generosi, liberorum matris amantissimæ, pietate erga Deum, charitate erga egenos, benignitate erga omnes insignis.   Obiit Octob. die vi. MDCCVI. ætatis XLIX."

The first is thus translated:—

"Here lieth the body of Richard Lee, Esq., born in Virginia, son of Richard Lee, Gentleman, descended of an ancient family of Merton-Regis, in Shropshire.

"While he exercised the office of a magistrate he was a zealous promoter of the public good.   He was very skilful in the Greek and Latin languages and other parts of polite learning.   He quietly resigned his soul to God, whom he always devoutly worshipped, on the 12th day of March, in the year 1714, in the 68th year of his age."

The second is thus translated:—

"Near by is interred the body of Lettuce, his faithful wife, daughter of Henry Corbyn, Gentleman.   A most affectionate mother, she was also distinguished by piety toward God, charity to the poor, and kindness to all. She died on the 6th day of October, 1706, in the 49th year of her age."

VESTRYMEN OF COPLE PARISH.

Although no vestry-book of this parish has come down to us from which we might give a connected list of the vestrymen, yet we are glad to present to our readers the result of two elections which were held in this parish,—the one in 1755, and the other in 1785. Those chosen in 1755 were John Bushrod, Daniel Tibbs, Richard Lee, Benedict Middleton, Willowby Newton, Robert Middleton, George Lee, John Newton, Samuel Oldham, Robert Carter, Fleet Cox, James Steptoe. Those chosen in 1785—thirty years after—were Vincent Marmaduke, Jeremiah G. Bailey, John A. Washington, Samuel Rust, John Crabb, Richard Lee, George Garner, George Turberville, Patrick Sanford, John Rochester, Samuel Templeman.

CONTEST ABOUT YEOCOMICO CHURCH.

During the ministry of the Rev. Mr. Ward in Cople parish, a difficulty arose as to this church, and the question was carried before the Legislature. The following letter from Judge McComas shows his opinion on the subject. The action of the Legislature was in favour of the claim of the Episcopal Church :—

"RICHMOND, January 20, 1844.
"TO THE REV. WM. N. WARD.

" DEAR SIR :—You will remember that I objected sitting as a member of the Committee for Courts of Justice, whilst it was acting upon the petition in relation to Yeocomico Church, because I was a member of the Methodist Episcopal Church,'and understanding that it was the subject of dispute between that Church and the Episcopal Church; but at your instance I did sit, but, being chairman of the committee, its action made it unnecessary for me to vote. I take this mode, however, of saying that I perfectly agreed with the committee, and even desired to go further than the committee in this. I wished to pass a law giving to the Episcopal Church all churches that it is now in possession of, to which it had a right before the Revolutionary War. I think the construction given by the committee to the Act of 1802, or at least my construction of it, is, that the General Assembly claimed for the Commonwealth the right to all the real property held by that Church, but that Act expressly forbids the sale of the churches, &c. It is true, the proviso to that Act does not confer upon the churches the right of property in the houses, &c. But it intended to leave the possession and occupancy as it then existed; and, that possession and occupancy being in the Episcopal Church, it had a right to retain it until the Legislature should otherwise direct. I believe that the Committee was of the opinion that the Episcopal Church had a right to the use and occupancy of the church now in question : it certainly is my opinion. I hope my Methodist brethren will see the justness of the determination of the Committee, and with cheerfulness acquiesce in its decision.

"Yours very respectfully,

"DAVID McCOMAS."

The following letter from Mr. W. L. Rogers, of Princeton, New Jersey, will form an interesting supplement to what has been said about Old Yeocomico:—

"TO THE RIGHT REV. BISHOP MEADE.

"HONOURED SIR:—The Rev. Wm. Hanson, rector of Trinity Church in this place, a few days since handed me a number of the 'Southern Churchman' from Alexandria, dated the 27th of February, 1857. In it is an historical sketch, from your pen, of Cople parish, Westmoreland county, Virginia, and particularly of Yeocomico Church,—a spot ever near and dear to my memory. From a long and intimate acquaintance with its locality and history, I beg leave very respectfully to present the following facts. It was built in the year 1706, as an unmistakable record will show,—it being engraved in the solid wall over the front-door. It was called by that name after the adjacent river,—the Indian name being preserved. The Rev. Mr. Elliot was the last settled minister up to the year 1800, when he removed to Kentucky. From that time it was wholly unused and neglected as a place of worship until the Methodists occasionally met under the shadow of its ruin about the year 1814, and continued so to do, keeping alive the spark of vital piety, until the Rev. Mr. Nelson in 1834 took charge of it as a settled minister. During his ministration it was jointly used by the Episcopalians and Methodists in Christian harmony and good-will. He being succeeded by the Rev. Mr. Ward in 1842, the question of occupancy and right of possession was unhappily agitated, which led to a decision of the Legislature giving to the wardens and vestry of the Episcopal Church the exclusive right to its use and control. Thus it will be seen, for thirty-four years there had been no settled minister of our communion, or its sublime and beautiful service performed, except two or three times by occasional visits.

"The Mr. Murphy you allude to was a Scotch gentleman from Ayrshire, living at Ayrfield, half a mile distant from Old Yeocomico, whose estate, consisting of some thousands of acres, surrounded the church and burial-ground on all sides. He was a gentleman of intellectual culture, an honoured magistrate, and a Presbyterian of the 'Covenant' school; whose residence was the seat of hospitality and the home of the clergy, with a welcome to all 'who proclaimed the glad tidings, that published salvation, that saith unto Zion, Thy God reigneth.' The Mr. Rogers you kindly allude to is the unworthy writer of these lines and the following narrative. I am a citizen of New Jersey by birth and education, (not of New York, as you incidentally state.) In the spring of 1813, I joined the 36th Regiment of United States Infantry (Colonel Carberry) at Washington. In the fall of that year, I was detached by order of General Bloomfield to Sandy Point, Westmoreland county, Virginia, on the Potomac, with a company of men to watch the movements of the British fleet. In the spring of 1814, our quarters becoming uncomfortable, we sought out an encampment in what is called there the Forest or high ground. Among other places recommended to us by the late General Alexander Parker, we visited the ruins of Yeocomico Church. As soon as I saw it, I exclaimed, 'There is Kirk-Alloway,' (alluding of course to Burns's 'Tam O'Shanter.') Had it stood for the original picture as drawn by the humorous poet, it could not have more forcibly impressed me with awe and deep-abiding interest. Its form,—that of a cross,—its solitude, were strikingly impressive, for it stood in a dell where its silence was only disturbed by the passing breeze whispering through the pines and cedars and undergrowth which choked up the entrance. It was overshadowed also by ancient oaks stretching their gigantic arms, as it were, to guard the sacred relic from mouldering time and the desolating elements. Its doors were open, its windows broken, the roof partly decayed and fallen in, and, to complete its apparent hopeless fate, a pine-tree thirty or forty feet high was blown up by the roots and lay across the main structure. Its burial-ground, which is spacious, was enclosed by a costly, high brick wall, with narrow gateways,—symbolical perhaps of the 'narrow path,'—filled to its utmost capacity with broken tombstones and desolate graves overgrown with briers and shrubbery, showing that the 'rich and the poor there rested together, and the servant was indeed free from his master,'—alike unprotected and uncared-for. A ruin outside the wall, which was intended and once served as a vestry, had rotted down; the chimney, a strong brick one, alone standing,—a naked monument of better days. In an alcove of forest-trees a few yards distant flowed numerous springs of cool, delicious water. Indeed, it required no great stretch of imagination to fancy the midnight-scene so graphically described in Burns's Kirk-Alloway, and the race to cross the running stream (for one really flows across the main road, some hundred yards distant) where 'mare Meggie lost her tail.' With some difficulty I entered the porch, which was built of brick and formed the upper part of the cross, spacious and on a level with the ground,—its massive double doorway quite open, presenting within as hopeless a ruin as its exterior,—the roof rotted away at its angles, one of the galleries partly down, the girders rotted off and fallen upon the pews, and the wall in two places mouldered away by years of saturation from snow and rain. The remains of a large Bible still lay upon the desk. The font was gone,—which I was told was of marble, and now used for convivial purposes. The chancel, in the eastern arm of the cross, to the right of the pulpit, surmounted by a large Gothic window much broken, was still in tolerable preservation. In it was the Communion-table,—its frame antique, covered with a heavy walnut slab,—sound, but rough and soiled from exposure. Large frames, once covered with canvas exhibiting in distinct characters the Lord's Prayer, the Ten Commandments, and other texts of Scripture, hung upon the walls, now much defaced, mouldered, and torn. The aisles were paved with brick, and covered with abundant evidence of its being the resort of sheep and cattle running at large; and, to complete the evidence of its abandonment, the ceiling—which was of boards—was tenanted by squirrels, snakes, and scorpions. Indeed, we may truly say, 'All its hedges were broken down by the wild boar of the wilderness,' and there was no one to care for it. Besides, I was told, it was the terror of the neighbourhood, from being the resort of runaway negroes and wandering vagrants, added to the awe inseparably connected with the lonely, silent depository of the dead. In contemplating the scene before me, I felt a mysterious attachment to this relic of piety and early faith of our fathers,—not dreaming (being a stranger and a wanderer) at some future day I should be honoured and favoured by the commission to restore this temple, now in the dust, to the service of my Creator and Redeemer. We resolved at once to pitch our tents outside the wall : a fatigue-party was detailed to trim up the trees, cut down the undergrowth, and burn up the leaves and rubbish, to remove the tree which lay across the roof, to cleanse the church and repair it as far as practicable, to make it a safe depository for our stores and camp-equipage. This being done, we were presented with a shady grove, dry ground, and a most inviting and lovely prospect,—with an abundance of pure, delicious water at our feet, and a central position to make nightly detachments to guard the historic shores of old Potomac,—for there rest the remains of the Washingtons, the Lees, the Parkers, and many other gallant spirits of patriotic memory. As illustrative of the actual condition of the spot I am now describing, permit me to relate an original anecdote, which occurred a short time before my visit.

"Colonel Garner, an officer of the Revolution, lived three or four miles distant: passing the church late in the evening with a friend, they were overtaken by an angry cloud of wind and rain, accompanied by lightning and thunder. The colonel proposed taking shelter in the church, leading their horses in, which they could do without difficulty, as the porch and pavement of the aisles were on a level with the ground. To this his friend positively objected, declaring he would rather bear the pelting of the storm than pass an hour within its gloomy walls. He therefore put spurs to his horse for his home. Not so with the colonel: he was a brave man, not fearing hobgoblins or witches. He dismounted at the opening in the wall, where there had once been a gate. Taking the bridle-rein in his hand, he proceeded to thread his way through the bushes to the porch. He got inside, followed by his horse, and was just entering the church, when the unusual visit frightened a flock of sheep that had taken shelter there, who suddenly rushed to the door to make their escape. The charge took the colonel by surprise, knocked him down, routed his horse, and trampled him in the dust, (for it was not paved as it now is.) After the column had passed over him, he found in the 'mêlée' he had lost his hat, and was scratched and bruised about the face and hands. Nothing daunted, however, he groped his way into the church, and, being well acquainted with its internal arrangement, he took shelter in the pulpit, where he knew was a comfortable seat, and where he would be protected from the wet by the sounding-board, made of durable materials and still firmly attached to the wall. The storm was now raging without, lightning and thundering and raining, with a tempest of wind. After sitting for a time he fell asleep and did not awake until three or four in the morning. By this time the cloud had passed over, the stars were shining, and he was glad to extricate himself by a hasty retreat homeward. He found his discomfited horse taking his rest at the stable-door.

"Our happiness at this encampment, after some months, was unexpectedly broken up by the arrival of a vessel with an order to embark for St. Mary's, Maryland. We finished our military service by assisting in the defence of Fort McHenry, Baltimore. We had the satisfaction, however, of carrying with us the united testimony of the whole neighbourhood that not a chicken, an egg, or a vegetable, had been wrongfully taken by any one of the soldiers, nor an injury or an insult offered to any one. The church and its environs had been sacredly guarded, and we left it in a much better condition than we found it. But it was not so (as I afterward learned) by our successors, a company of militia from the upper country, who proved themselves to be a scourge to those they professedly came to protect, by robbery, violence, and destruction of private property. It was they 'who made a chopping-block of the Communion-table' and otherwise defaced the church. In ascribing it to the soldiers, be assured, sir, you have been led into an unintentional error. They served under a discipline paternal but strict, both as regards order and cleanliness. In the year 1820, being on a visit to Ayrfield, and seeing Old Yeocomico still a ruin, even more deplorable than when I left it, I proposed to Mr. Murphy to undertake its repair. To this he not only assented, but gave money, labour, and his personal service. The gentlemen of the neighbourhood subscribed cheerfully and liberally, and the work was pushed forward by employing suitable mechanics and importing from Alexandria lumber, shingles, paints, and seven or eight barrels of tar for the roof, which had not had a shingle put upon it since the year 1788, at which time, I heard Mr. Murphy say, the gentlemen of the surrounding estates were assessed to meet the expense. It is true as you state,—the font, 'a beautiful marble one,' as you describe it, had been taken away and used for unholy purposes, and by him restored; also, the plate, with a damask tablecloth and napkins marked 'Yeocomico Church' in the centre, had been safely kept at Lee Hall, and were gladly restored by the pious and excellent lady, the late Mrs. Sarah Newton, who at that time owned and occupied the mansion and estate. The first thing we did was to open a double gateway in front, with a wide gravel-walk up to the porch or apex of the cross, the pavement of which I laid with my own hands, none there being familiar with such work. If the narrow opening in the wall was symbolical of the 'narrow path,' the one we now opened was illustrative of 'free grace,'—a truth to which I feel myself indebted for a knowledge of salvation through the interceding blood of a crucified Redeemer. It is also true, as you state, I presented the church with a large stove and ample pipe to warm it thoroughly, it having stood for upward of a century without one. It is also true I had the great pleasure to place a Bible and Prayer-Book both on the desk and in the pulpit, and I rejoice to know the church is still protected and cared for,—although I have not seen it for more than twenty years. Permit me now, sir, in conclusion, to say I have frequently reflected with sorrow on the mysterious desolation of the ancient churches of Virginia, and can only account for it by the demoniac influence of the infidel theories and sentiments of the French Revolution, which at that time pervaded the public mind and had poisoned the very fountain of our better nature and sealed the best impulses of the human heart. These temples of the living God, these sacred monuments of the faith of our fathers and the religious care of the Provincial Government, were generally of lofty and commanding structure, of costly finish, and of the most durable materials,—such as in England have lasted for centuries. They stood in well-chosen positions, and under their shadow lay the remains of the kindred of large congregations, many of whom were the immediate descendants of holy men who had ministered at their altars; yet, most strange to say, not an arm was put forth to save, or an eye found to pity. 'Behold, therefore, saith the Lord, your house is left unto you desolate.'

"Be pleased to accept, reverend sir, my most respectful regard,

"WM. L. ROGERS.

"Princeton, New Jersey, March 20, 1857."

ARTICLE LXI.

Washington Parish, Westmoreland.

THIS name was doubtless given to it at an early period, and after the first of the Washingtons; though we see nothing of its first establishment in the Acts of Assembly. The Bishop of London sends a circular to its minister in 1723. The Rev. Laurence De Butts was its minister in that year, and had been for the three preceding years. The parish was thirty miles long and five wide, extending only half-way across the Neck at that time. There were two churches in it. He administered the Communion three times a year, and two quarts of wine had been used at one time. Mr. De Butts preached also, during the week, at St. Stephen's Church, Northumberland county, at Farnham Church, Richmond county, and in Cople parish, they all being vacant at that time. The glebe of four hundred and fifty acres was bequeathed to the parish for the better maintenance of a minister and schoolmaster, and the vestry gave it entirely to him on condition that he would provide one to teach reading, writing, and arithmetic, which he had done. What has become of this glebe we know not. We find in the old county records the name of another minister in Westmoreland, about this same time,—the Rev. Walter Jones. He may have ministered in some other parish, or been a private teacher, and been merely summoned as a witness. We have no record of any minister in Washington parish after this until the year 1754, when the Rev. Archibald Campbell appears on one of our lists.

Of him and his family I have something special to say. Our lists of clergy show him to have been the minister of Washington parish from the year 1754 to 1774,—a period of twenty years. During most of that time Round Hill Church (afterward in Hanover parish, King George county, by a change of the boundary-line in the two counties) was connected with Pope's Creek Church, in Washington parish, and Mr. Campbell was minister of those churches. I have something to say about the former of these churches which has a bearing on the date of Mr. Campbell's ministry and first coming to this country.

In my report, in the year 1838, of a visit to this region in the preceding year, I thus speak:—"In passing from Westmoreland to King George county, where my next appointment was made, the traveller may see, immediately on the roadside, the last vestiges of an old church called 'Round Hill Church.' A few broken bricks and a little elevation made by the mouldered ruins are all now left to say, Here once stood a church of the living God."

Within the last few months I spent a night at the hospitable house of Colonel Baber, near whose outer gate the old church stood. On learning that there was an old tombstone still to be seen among the ruins, I determined to search for it. In the morning, on our way to St. Paul's Church, Colonel Baber's son, Rev. Mr. Dashiel, and myself, dismounted and made our way to the spot through the thick pines and cedars with which it was overgrown. After considerable search we discovered the end of a large tombstone, the greater portion of which was covered over with the roots of trees, moss and leaves. After clearing away the two latter, we made out the inscription, as follows:—"Here lies Rebecca, the wife of the Rev. Archibald Campbell, minister of Washington parish, who died the 21st of March, 1754." "Here also lies Alexander, their child." Now, as it is well known that he had another son by the name of Alexander, an eminent lawyer of Virginia, the one buried beneath or near this stone may have been born and died some years before this, and so Mr. Campbell's ministry be carried back a number of years before 1754, his second son Alexander being born before that time. If this be so, and it be also true that the Rev. Mr. Campbell kept a school in Westmoreland,—as tradition says, and of which there is no doubt,—it may also be true, as tradition further reports, that General Washington and Thomas Marshall, father of the Chief-Justice, and perhaps Colonel Monroe and Mr. Madison, all of whom were born in this region, may at one time have been scholars of Mr. Campbell. General Washington was born in 1732, and until his sixteenth year was much in Westmoreland. It is only necessary that Mr. Campbell's ministry and school should have commenced five or six years before the death of his wife, to render this a probable thing. I introduce the report in order to elicit either confirmation or rejection. Of the history of this branch of the Campbells of Virginia I have obtained the following statement. Two brothers, Archibald and Alexander, emigrated to Virginia some time before the war. Archibald settled as a clergyman in Westmoreland, and Alexander as a merchant in Falmouth. At the breaking out of the war, Archibald took part with the Americans, with the Washingtons and Lees, his parishioners, while Alexander preferred the British side of the question, and returned to Scotland. The youngest son of Alexander was born in Glasgow, in 1777.*

---

* This youngest son was none other than the celebrated poet Thomas Campbell.

In a letter from a friend who is much interested and deeply versed in such matters, there is the following passage:—"Of the Campbells I can say nothing more than you have related at this moment, except perhaps that lawyer Campbell was a most eloquent man, and that Campbell, a brother of the poet, married a daughter of Patrick Henry. This I will inquire into. As Patrick Henry himself was descended on the mother's side from the stock of Robertson the historian, and is in that way a relative of Lord Brougham, so his descendants are connected with the poet Campbell, thus showing a connection between our great orator and one of the greatest politicians and one of the sweetest poets of the age."

The following extract from a letter of one of Mr. Campbell's grandsons throws additional light on the history of the family:—"I will now give you some facts that I have been able to gather in reference to him and his descendants. Parson Campbell came to Virginia previous to the year 1730. He resided at the glebe near Johnsville, in what was then Westmoreland but now King George county. He preached at Round Hill Church, and probably at Pope's Creek Church. A road leading a part of the way from the glebe to Round Hill Church still goes by the name of the Parson's Road. It was said to have been cut through the forest for Parson Campbell's use. Parson Campbell was twice married. His first wife died soon after her marriage. His second wife was a sister of the Rev. William Stuart, of King George County. By this marriage there were three sons,—Archibald, Alexander, and John: the two last-mentioned were distinguished lawyers. Archibald, my grandfather, left a daughter and two sons. Frederick, the elder son, was a lawyer. He inherited an entailed estate in Scotland, and died in Europe. Ferdinand, the second son, was formerly Professor of Mathematics in William and Mary College, and died near Philadelphia. Alexander was twice married, and left two daughters, one of whom died unmarried: the other is the wife of Judge Wayne, of the Supreme Court. John was also married twice, and left several children. Parson Campbell was from Scotland. He was related to the Stuart and Argyle families of that country, and was the uncle of Thomas Campbell the poet. In addition to the performance of his ministerial duties, he also taught a school. It is said that he had among his pupils Madison, Monroe, and Chief-Justice Marshall. The Rev. William Stuart studied theology under his direction. Parson Campbell died leaving a considerable estate."

The following letter, having been received since the foregoing was published in the "Southern Churchman," corrects some inaccuracies and furnishes additional information.

"BISHOP MEADE,   "NEWSTEAD, March 20, 1857.

"REV. AND DEAR SIR:—In perusing the brief sketch given by you of the Campbells of Virginia, my mother discovered some inaccuracies, which it gives us pleasure to correct as far as we can do so. She says that her grandfather (Archibald Campbell) married twice. Of the history of his first wife, whose name you saw on the tombstone at the Round Hill Church in King George, she knows very little, as she survived but a very short time after marriage, leaving no descendants. The second wife, who was her grandmother, was a Miss McCoy, daughter of William McCoy, who was the pastor of North Farnham parish, Richmond county, in the year 1754, but

The sons of Archibald were Archibald, Alexander, and John. Archibald inherited the property of his father in Westmoreland, consisting of two seats, the one called Pomona, the other Campbellton, at the last of which the father lived and kept his school. It is now the summer residence of Mr. Laurence Washington. The other sons, Alexander and John, were eminent lawyers. Alexander married a Miss Fitzhugh, of King George, who at his death married the Rev. Dr. Kollock, minister of churches in Princeton, New York, Charleston, (South Carolina,) and lastly in Savannah. An only daughter, by her first husband, married Judge Wayne, of the Supreme Court. The last son, John, was a lawyer in Westmoreland, and represented the county in the Legislature, and the parish in one of our Conventions. His daughters were Eliza, who married Mr. Leland; Emily, who married Robert Mayo; Sarah, who married Landon Berkeley; Louisa, who married John Mayo; and Octavia.

After the disappearance of Mr. Campbell from any of our re-

---

whose name you incorrectly spell, in your article on that parish, McKay. This William McCoy married a Miss Fitzhugh, of Marmion, King George,—a woman distinguished for her eminent piety,—and our grandmother was a daughter by that marriage. The school which you speak of was established after his last marriage, for the benefit of his own sons, Archibald and Alexander. My grandfather, who was John, being an infant at the period of his death, was baptized by him on his death-bed. My mother thinks she has heard that Chief-Justice Marshall, Mr. Madison, and Mr. Monroe, were taught by him, with her uncles Archibald and Alexander. She does not think that the school was established early enough to admit the belief of Colonel Marshall or General Washington's having been pupils of his. To the property acquired by my mother's grandfather in Virginia, he gave the name of Kirnan, after a family seat in Argyleshire, Scotland. Campbellton was the residence of my grandfather. Alexander married his cousin, Miss Fitzhugh, of Marmion, and had only one daughter by that marriage, whose name was Lucy: she lived in my grandfather's family until the period of her death, which occurred within a few years past. Mrs. Wayne was by a second marriage. The other brother, Archibald, married Miss Hughs, of Maryland, and had two sons and a daughter. The eldest son, Frederick, inherited a large entailed estate in the island of Bute, in Scotland, from the Stuarts, who intermarried with the Campbells, and he took the name of Frederick Campbell Stuart with the estate. The second son, Ferdinand, was Professor of Mathematics in William and Mary, under the administration of Drs. Smith and Wilmer. The daughter, Anna Campbell, married Dr. Tennant, an eminent physician of Port Royal: she died not many years since. Her children were Washington, who was a physician; Mercer, who married Miss Grymes, of King George; Susan, the first wife of Dr. John May, of Westmoreland; Maria, who married Thomas Hunter, of Fredericksburg; and Lucy, who married his brother, Taliafero Hunter. Mrs. Tennant lived and died a very consistent member of the Episcopal Church, and her children are all members of it. We give this information in compliance with your request that mistakes might be corrected.

"Yours very respectfully,   ELIZA C. LELAND."

cords, we have no account of any minister in Washington parish until the year 1785, when the Rev. Francis Wilson serves it for one year. In the year 1796, the Rev. John O'Donnell appears once in a Convention. We have none after this until the year 1822, when the Rev. Josiah Clapham appears in Convention, with Mr. John Campbell, son of the Rev. Mr. Campbell, as lay delegate. Mr. Clapham continued its minister for some years, performing his duties piously and faithfully, and with as much energy as his bodily infirmities would allow of. After a considerable interval, we find the parish again supplied by the services of the Rev. William McGuire, who served it in connection with Cople parish. Within a few years past, a new parish has been taken from Washington parish, by the name of Montross, in which a new church has been built, while another, by the name of St. Peter's, has been built at Oak Grove. We are much indebted to the labours of the Rev. William McGuire for both these new churches. The Rev. Mr. Tuttle was the minister of Washington parish for one year, since which time the Rev. Mr. Chesley has been settled there.

THE OLD CHURCHES IN WESTMORELAND.

There were three of these,—the Round Hill Church, Pope's Creek Church, and one at Leeds, on the Rappahannock. Pope's Creek Church lay immediately on the road from Westmoreland Court-House to King George. The following notice of it is taken from my report to the Convention of 1838 :—

"It was near to this church that General Washington was born. It was in this that he was baptized. Here it was that he received those early impressions of religion which, instead of being effaced by age, seemed to grow with his growth and strengthen with his strength. The proofs of this have been abundantly furnished in the 'Religious Opinions and Character of Washington,' by the Rev. Mr. McGuire, a work recently published, and for which the writer deserves the thanks of every friend of Washington, of religion, and of our country. I have said that this church is now in ruins, and I would add, that about twenty-six years ago, [1812,] when I was in Deacon's Orders, I remember to have been in it, with the Rev. Mr. Norris, an early and beloved associate in the ministry, at which time it was beginning to decay in the roof; but there was a large congregation, and twenty-eight children were brought forward for baptism. It was the first service which had been performed in it for a long time, and from that period it continued to decay, until a few years ago it was set on fire in order to prevent injury, from the falling of the roof, to the cattle which were accustomed to shelter there."

It ought to be added that so attached were the citizens of the county to this old building, that the excuse for its destruction by fire was not readily admitted. Indeed, so indignant were they, that it was brought before the grand jury and the court. The result, however, was the acquittal of the party. It has now been twenty years since the above-mentioned visit, and I have often within that time passed the same spot, at each time perceiving the disappearance of all that was old, and the rise and growth of what was new. Trees and shrubs have been growing up over and around the old site, rendering it more difficult each year to the passing traveller to find out where Old Pope's Creek Church once stood. I should not myself, in a recent visit, have been able to discover it, but for the aid of a friend who was with me. I could not but ask myself and that friend if it were not possible that a simple but durable monument—say a pillar a few feet high—could be placed on the roadside, with the name of Pope's Creek Church upon it, to inform posterity that on that spot stood the church of the Washingtons, the Lees, the Paynes, and others. It is said that the Legislature intends to have an enclosure around the birthplace of Washington and the burying-place of his ancestors, which are near at hand; and surely some individual or individuals would take pleasure in marking the spot where God was worshipped by so many, and where the remains of not a few were interred, although no tombstones have preserved their names. Among those whose bodies were deposited around this church is to be numbered the Hon. Thomas Lee, (the father of Richard Henry Lee and a noble band of brothers and sisters,) the owner of Stratford, for whom it was rebuilt by the Queen, after being consumed by fire, who held the first offices in the Colony under several Governors, and whose commission as Governor reached Virginia in 1756, just after his death. I take the following inscription from his tombstone, which I saw some years since, lying against the wall of the family vault at Stratford:—

"In memory of the Hon. Thomas Lee, whose body was buried at Pope's Creek Church, five miles above his country-seat, Stratford Hall, in 1756."

Of Mr. Lee some account has been given in the sketch of the Lee family in the article on Northumberland county.

LEEDS OR BRAY'S CHURCH.

This church stood on the Rappahannock, at the outskirts of the place called Leeds. It was of brick. The ruins of it are yet to be seen, apparently hanging on the bank of the river. It has undergone many changes of late years since it was deserted as a house of worship, having been used as a tavern, stable or barn, and been altered so as to suit the different purposes to which it has been applied.   Leeds was once a place of note in this part of Virginia. It was doubtless named, either by the Fairfaxes or Washingtons, after the town of Leeds, in Yorkshire, near which both of their ancestral families lived.   This in Virginia was a place of much trade in tobacco and other things.   Its shipping was very considerable at one time, and it gave the promise of being a town of no small importance, but, like many other such places in Virginia, as Dumfries, Colchester, Warren, Warminster, it failed to fulfil the expectations excited.   For one thing it deserves to retain a lasting place in the history of the American Revolution.   As Boston was the Northern, so Leeds may be called the Southern cradle of American Independence.   This was the place where, with Richard Henry Lee as their leader, the patriots of Westmoreland met, before any and all others, to enter their protest against the incipient steps of English usurpation.   At this place did they resolve to oppose the Stamp Act, nor allow any citizen of Westmoreland to deal in stamps.   This is a true part of the American history.

ROUND HILL CHURCH.

Of this we have said something in our mention of the Rev. Mr. Campbell.   In the following communication from my brother, Bishop Payne, of Africa, further notice of it will be found, together with interesting accounts of his own family.   One of these at my first visit to Pope's Creek Church promised one hundred dollars for its repairs,—a large sum for those times.

"In the summer of 1833, after leaving Williamsburg, I visited a great-uncle, Captain William Payne, a venerable old gentleman, (grandfather of Richard Payne, of Warrenton,) residing near Warrenton.   He was dressed in short pants, had served in the Revolution, and was a fine specimen of the old Virginia gentleman.   Finding me interested in the history of our family, he took down from his library a copy of Smith's History of Virginia, and in the index showed me the names of our ancestors to whom King James gave patents of land in Virginia.   They were Sir William Payne, John Payne, and Richard or Thomas, I forget which.   Sir William, he said, never came to America, but the other two brothers did.   One of these brothers, as I learned from him, and his daughter,—my cousin,—Mrs. Scott, of Fredericksburg, settled in the country about Lynchburg, and from him descended Mrs. Madin, (Polly Payne.)   The other—John Payne —settled between the Potomac and Rappahannock, probably in or near that which was to be the great city Leedstown.   My grandfather, John Payne, whom you saw, I think died when I was six or seven years old, but I recollect him distinctly as dressed in the old style, like Uncle William. His residence was at the old family-stead called, when I knew it, the Red House. It is immediately in the rear of Bunker's Hill, (Henry Taylor's place,) and three miles from Leedstown. His estates—subsequently divided between my father and his brothers, Daniel, George, and daughter Elizabeth—were on the Potomac and Rappahannock Rivers, and partly in Richmond county. My third great-uncle, Richard, whom I remember well, settled in Culpepper, and his descendants, (except one son, William,—Episcopalian,—who married old Parson Woodville's daughter, and removed to Columbus, Mississippi,) Methodists, are now to be found in Culpepper county.

"When in Alexandria, Mr. Dana showed me in the vestry-books of Christ Church the name of William Payne associated with George Washington; and one of the cross-streets in Alexandria, near the head of King, I noticed, still bears the name of 'Payne Street.' Learning that this family emigrated to the West, when in Lexington I made inquiries about them, and soon found multitudes of most respectable people in and about Lexington and Frankfort bearing this name. They are Presbyterians. Mr. Berkeley, the Episcopal minister, subsequently introduced me to Dr. Payne, of Lexington, who said at once, 'We are doubtless the same family,' and he and all his relatives about there were descended from Washington's contemporary and associate, William Payne, of Alexandria. He told me with a spirit of too much self-complacency—as I told him—that this was the same William Payne who knocked down General Washington in Alexandria for insulting him. But he replied quickly, "Oh, no! he was right. For General Washington the next day sent him an apology, instead of a challenge as his friends had anticipated.'

"Of the ecclesiastical and theological views of my father and grandfather I know but little. I think you told me that the latter gave you proof that he clung to 'the old Church' and eschewed all others. I am inclined to think, from circumstances which I can remember, that my father was like-minded. I found among his books 'The Theological Repertory,' with whose history you are familiar; and one of the few things that I can remember about him well was his holding long and late discussions with the Methodist ministers who in 1823–25 began to preach in the neighbourhood and occasionally to visit my father's house. My father was a teetotaller, very thoughtful,—I will hope, a religious man, though of this I cannot be certain. My mother, however, from my earliest recollection I know *was*, but she did not make a profession of religion until after my father's death, nor until my eldest sister (now dead) made a profession among the Methodists. This circumstance leads me to think my father's influence prevented my mother from uniting herself before with the Methodists,—though the only representative of the Episcopal Church in the neighbourhood was our poor friend, Mr. Clapham.

"The last baptism by a *Church parson* in our family was that of brother William. I infer it was one of the old sort, as his godfather was any thing but a pious man, and thought his duty to his godson quite performed after he had given him *a yoke of oxen*.

"I have said I was born in the White Oak Swamps about one mile from the Potomac. This was my father's residence for two or three years after his marriage, being convenient to his estate on the Potomac. But it proved so unhealthy that he purchased one of the old glebes in the Pine Forest, on t' ridge between the Potomac and Rappahannock, seven miles from the former, and three from the nearest point of the latter. Here eight of us were reared in most remarkable health. From this glebe to the Old Round Hill Church, or rather its remains,—for it was demolished before my earliest recollection,—there was in my childhood one of the most beautiful roads I ever saw. It led for several miles in a direction perfectly straight, under an avenue of beautiful oaks. It was called 'the Parson's Road,' and was no doubt the road by which the parsons travelled to the Round Hill Church. By-the-way, have you ever ascertained or written the history of this said Round Hill Church? It was situated on a beautiful and commanding knoll, near old Machodoc Meeting-House, which superseded it, and in which Mr. Clapham was wont to officiate before his removal from King George to Loudon.   But, as I have said, nothing of it but some fragments remained at the time of my earliest visits to the neighbourhood.

"I have given you all that occurs to me of my family history of interest. Should you wish to make further inquiries, I would refer you to my cousin, Mrs. Scott, of Fredericksburg, and through Cousin Richard Payne, of Warrenton, to his father and Mrs. Scott's eldest brother, Daniel Payne, who resides in the neighbourhood of Warrenton. He is called the Frenchman of our family, and should you ever meet with him you will find him very agreeable and fond of talking, and on no subject more than that about which I have been writing."

THE WASHINGTON FAMILY.

It is agreed on all hands that, about the year 1655, two brothers, John and Laurence Washington, came over to Virginia and settled in Westmoreland county. In all the histories which I have seen of the Washington family there is not another word said of Laurence Washington, except that he and his brother came together and settled at the same place. While the descendants of John Washington, in all their branches, are minutely described in genealogies and histories and biographies, doubtless in a great measure because the great Washington was one of them, Laurence Washington was forgotten and lost sight of as though he had never been. I have met with persons who could not trace their connection with General Washington or his first ancestors, yet were certain of some connection with the family, but never thought of inquiring whether their descent is not from the other brother. In a recent visit to Tappahannock, the county seat of Essex county, (where are the records of the old county of Rappahannock, which from 1653 to 1692 embraced all that lay on each side of the Rappahannock River for some miles up to the Falls above Fredericksburg,) in searching in an old record of wills, I found that of this same Laurence Washington. Although he may have settled near the Potomac with his brother John, he must have removed into Rappahannock county, for his will is there recorded. He may have done this without moving many miles from his brother, as Westmoreland county and Washington parish were only about five miles wide, and Rappahannock county and Littenburne parish were about the same width, the one lying on the Potomac, the other on the Rappahannock River. I have also obtained, by the help of a friend, the will of Mr. John Washington, which was recorded at Westmoreland Court-House, and whose original is still there in an old book of wills, though in a somewhat mutilated form. That they were the two brothers is evident from the fact that they mention each other in their wills. Both of the wills are made in the same year,—that of one on February 26, 1675; that of the other on September 27, 1675. The one is proved the 10th of January, 1677, and the other the 6th of January of the same year, at an interval of only four days, so that it is probable they died in a few days of each other. There is something so pious in the language of these wills, that I make no apology for introducing a portion of them. Without any means of ascertaining which was the elder of the two, we begin with the will of John Washington:—

"In the name of God, Amen. I, John Washington, of Washington parish, in the county of Westmoreland, in Virginia, gentleman, being of good and perfect memory, thanks be unto Almighty God for it, and calling to remembrance the uncertain state of this transitory life, that all flesh must yield unto death, do make, constitute, and ordain this my last will and testament and none other. And first, being heartily sorry, from the bottom of my heart, for my sins past, most humbly desiring forgiveness of the same from the Almighty God, my Saviour and Redeemer, in whom and by the merits of Jesus Christ I trust and believe assuredly to be saved, and to have full remission and forgiveness of all my sins, and that my soul with my body at the general resurrection shall rise again with joy."

Again he repeats the same sentiment, hoping "through the merits of Jesus Christ's death and passion to possess and inherit the kingdom of heaven prepared for his elect and chosen." He directs his body to be buried on the plantation upon which he lived, by the side of his wife and two children. He then proceeds to distribute his property, which he says it has pleased God to give him "far above his deserts." After dividing a number of landed estates between his second and surviving wife and his children,— John, Laurence, and Anne,—and also his property in England, he directs that a funeral sermon be preached and no other funeral kept, and that a tablet with the Ten Commandments be sent for to England and given to the church. I think, also, that he directs four thousand-weight of tobacco to be given to the minister, though of this I am not certain, some words being lost. He leaves one thousand pounds to his brother-in-law, Thomas Pope, and one thousand pounds and four thousand-weight of tobacco to his sister, who had come or was coming over to this country. He makes his wife and brother Laurence his executors. From the above it would seem that, great as were his military talents, being commander-in-chief in the Northern Neck, high as he stood in the Government, so that the parish was called after him, and large as was his property in England and America, he was also a sincerely pious man, and in his will emphatically testifies to those great Gospel principles which are so prominent in the Church of his fathers.

In the will of his brother Laurence there is the same spirit of piety. After the usual preamble, he says, "Imprimis: I give and bequeath my soul unto the hands of Almighty God, hoping and trusting, *through the mercy of Jesus Christ, my one Saviour and Redeemer, to receive full pardon and forgiveness of all my sins,* and my body to the earth, to be buried in comely and decent manner by my executor hereafter named: and for my worldly goods, I thus dispose of them." To his daughter Mary Washington (by a former wife in England) he bequeathed his whole estate in England, both real and personal, to be delivered immediately after his death, together with a ring and other articles. To his loving son John he left all his books and part of his plate, the other part to his daughter Ann, when they should be of age or marry. His lands are divided between his wife and the two children—John and Ann—by her. A farm called West Fales, which lay on the south side of the Rappahannock, which once belonged to Captain Alexander Fleming, and which came to him by his wife, was to be sold for his debts. It is probable that his second wife was a daughter of Captain Fleming. He leaves his wife executrix of the estate, but provides that in case of her death or neglect to be the guardian and overseer of his children, his loving brother John Washington and loving friend Thomas Hawkins should be. In a codicil written at the same time, he leaves that part of the land on which he then lived, and which came to him by marriage, to the sole disposal of his wife. It is probable, from the above, that he lived on the north side of the river, in what is now Westmoreland. From the foregoing particulars, some other than myself may be able to ascertain the maiden name of his wife, and who, if any, are the descendants of his three children, as it is more than probable they had descendants.

THE WASHINGTON FAMILY SEAT AND VAULT.

I recently paid a visit to the old family seat of the Washingtons, which is sometimes said to be on Pope's Creek, and sometimes on Bridge's Creek, near the Potomac. The farm lay between the two, which are about a mile apart, near their junction with the Potomac. The family mansion lies near Pope's Creek, and the vault where the dead were deposited near Bridge's Creek. The latter appears to have been favourable to a rich growth of cedars, and may have been chosen for this reason. Or it may be that one of the two brothers first settled there. The estate is still in the family, or in the possession of one intermarried with the family. Some years since it was owned by Mr. John Gray, of Travellers' Rest, near Fredericksburg, who either repaired one of the outhouses or a wing of the old one, or built a small house for his overseer out of the old materials. The brick chimney is all that remains of the Washington mansion,—the birthplace of General Washington,—except the broken bricks which are scattered about over the spot where it was built. The grandson of Mrs. General Washington, Mr. Custis, of Arlington, some years since placed a slab with a brief inscription on the spot, but it is now in fragments. I was happy to hear that a bill had passed one branch of our Legislature, appropriating a sum of money for enclosing this spot, as well as the vault in a neighbouring field nearly a mile off. I also visited that spot, which no one can look upon without distress and even disgust. The condition of all such vaults as were once common in some parts of Virginia, especially in the Northern Neck, must after the lapse of time be necessarily thus distressing and disgusting, like the sepulchres of old when filled "with rottenness and dead men's bones." The vault where so many of the Washington family are interred is in an open field and unenclosed. A small space around it is covered with grass, briers, shrubs, and a few small trees. Itself can only be distinguished by the top of the brick arch which rises a little above the surface. The cavity underneath has been very properly filled up with earth by Mr. Laurence Washington, one of its late proprietors, to prevent the bones of the dead being taken away by visitors, who had begun thus to pillage it. Not far from the vault there was a large slab lying on the ground, with the name of one of the family and two of his children. There were also fragments of another. It is to be hoped that the Legislature will resolve on putting a permanent enclosure around this also.

THE VAULT OF THE LEES AT STRATFORD, IN WESTMORELAND.

In the preceding sketch of the Lees, by Mr. William Lee, of London, there is mention made of a loss by fire sustained by his father, Thomas Lee, of Stratford, and of a present to him by Queen Caroline. This establishes the source from whence came the means of building the present most durable building at that place, which for the thickness of the walls and the excellency of its architecture is not surpassed, if equalled, by any in Virginia.* It has sometimes been called the Governor's House, probably because its owner and builder, Thomas Lee, was commissioned as Governor, though he did not live to act in that capacity. The cemetery was not built by him, as he was buried at Pope's Creek Church. I have been assured by Mrs. Eliza Turner, who was there at the time, that it was built by General Harry Lee. The cemetery is much larger than any other in the Northern Neck, consisting of several apartments or alcoves for different branches of the family. Instead of an arch over them there is a brick house, perhaps twenty feet square, covered in. A floor covers the cemetery. In the centre is a large trapdoor, through which you descend by a ladder to the apartments below. I went down into it some years since, when nothing was to be seen but the bones of the deceased, which were scattered over the dirt floor. I was informed that it had sometimes been filled with water, and that then the bones and skulls of the deceased might be seen floating upon the surface,—at any rate, if stirred up with a pole, as was sometimes done. The entrance to this house has of late years been almost prevented by a thick growth of young aspens and briers. I am happy to state that it is the purpose of the present proprietor to fill up the vault, take down the brick walls and convert them into a mound over the place, and on the top of the mound to have the tombstone of old Thomas Lee fixed in some immovable way.

Some mournful thoughts will force themselves upon us when considering the ruins of churches, of mansions, and of cemeteries, in Westmoreland. By reason of the worth, talents, and patriotism which once adorned it, it was called the Athens of Virginia. But how few of the descendants of those who once were its ornaments

---

* An American writer says there were once a hundred rooms in this house. A view of the engraving of it will show how untrue this is. Even including the basement and the large hall, there are not more, I think, than seventeen, and never were more. Another says there were one hundred stalls for horses in the stable,—almost equally untrue.

are now to be found in it! Chantilly, Mount Pleasant, Wakefield, are now no more. Stratford alone remains. Where now are the venerable churches? Pope's Creek, Round Hill, Nomini, Leeds, where are they? Yeocomico only survives the general wreck. Of the old men, mansions, churches, &c. we are tempted to say, "Fuit Illium, et ingens gloria Dardanidum;" and yet we rejoice to think that new ones have taken their places, in some respects better suited to present times and circumstances. Those who, in the general defection, have remained to the Church, are exerting themselves to repair the waste places; and we trust there awaits for Westmoreland a greater glory than the former.

ARTICLE LXII.

Farnham and Lunenburg Parishes, Richmond County.

To do justice to the history of this county and these parishes, we must go back to the time when they were a part of Rappahannock county and Littenburne parish,—which they were from the year 1653 to 1692,—when new counties and parishes were established. But where are the vestry-books or county records from whence to draw our facts? Of the former there are none. Some few of the latter are to be seen in Tappahannock, the county seat of Essex, where the archives of old Rappahannock county are preserved.

At my request, a worthy friend—most competent to the task—has searched these records, and though unable to specify who were the vestrymen of the parish, yet, in giving the following list of magistrates from 1680 to 1695, has doubtless furnished us with the names of far the greater part of the vestrymen, if not the whole of them, during that period. We cannot determine to which side of the river they belonged, as both the county and parish were on both sides. They are as follows:—Henry Aubrey, Major Henry Smith, Captain George Taylor, Mr. Thomas Harrison, Colonel John Stone, Colonel Leroy Griffin, Major Robinson, Colonel William Loyd, Captain Samuel Bloomfield, William Fauntleroy, Samuel Peachy, William Slaughter, Cadwallader Jones, Henry Williamson. My friend adds that " the character and habits of the early settlers, so far as can be ascertained from their wills and the records, indicate intelligence and a high state of morals for the times." This section appears to have been settled chiefly by those coming from the lower counties,—the names of the principal men being those of families in the lower country. There are some, however, whose names are rarely met with in other counties; and there is evidence that they originally settled here. They are such as Latane, Waring, Upshaw, Rowsee, Rennolds, Micou, Roy, Clements, Young.

To the labours of another friend, on the other side of the river, we are indebted for information gotten from the records of Richmond county after the year 1692, which can nowhere else be found, as we have no vestry-book of that county, except that of North Farnham parish, from the year 1787 to 1804. The first justices of the peace were Captain George Taylor, William Underwood, Captain William Barber, James Scott, Captain Alexander Swan. From that time to the Revolution, the principal families in the county were Stone, Glascock, Deane, Donaphun, Colston, Thornton, Travis, Peachy, Tayloe, Conway, Brockenbrough, Gwin, Tarplay, Downman, Slaughter, Parker, Sherlock, Davis, Robinson, Beale Smith, Woodbridge, Heale, Barrow, Taverner, Barber, Griffin, Fitzhugh, Fauntleroy, Gibson, Taliafero, Ingo, Bellfield, Tomlin, Grymes, Metcalf, Newton, Barnes, Sydnor, Jordan, Hornby, Hamilton, Carter, Mountjoy, Flood, Plummer, Beckwith. Of all these, my informant says, a very few have descendants in the county at this time who are called by these names.

According to the records of the court, he says, there were once three parishes in the county,—North Farnham, Lunenburg, and St. Mary's,—having separate ministers.

Of the three ministers mentioned on the records, from the year 1693 to 1742, the account is sad. The two first—John Burnet and John Alexander—were always in court, suing or being sued. The third—the Rev. Thomas Blewer—was presented by the grand jury as a common swearer. A particular account is drawn from the records of different families. From the votes on election-days, the Woodbridges and Fauntleroys appear to have been at one time the most popular. The Carters and Tayloes, of Sabine Hall and Mount Airy, were active and useful men. The Chinns first appear in 1713. "From Raleigh Chinn," he says, "descended those model males and females of that name who have served to give character to our county in modern times." The McCartys were an ancient family, springing from Daniel and Dennis McCarty, who are first mentioned in 1710.

Having furnished this general account of individuals and families from the court records, we proceed to give the information in our possession concerning each of the parishes separately.

First, of North Farnham. This was established in 1693, when Rappahannock county was stricken from the list of counties and Richmond and Essex erected in its stead, and South Farnham parish created in Essex. The first minister of this parish whom we have on our lists—though there were doubtless many before—is the Rev. William Mackay, who was there in 1754, and continued until 1774.* From his long continuance in the parish and the respectability of the people, we have grounds for believing that he was a worthy man,—although in a few years after his death, or departure from the parish, it seems to have been in the most deplorable condition, as we shall soon see. The Rev. John Leland, a worthy minister from Northumberland, officiated statedly in Farnham for some time after Mr. Mackay disappears. Then the Rev. Thomas Davis, from one of the parishes of Northumberland, gives them a portion of his time for two years. After this a considerable interval occurred in which there was no vestry,—several efforts at an election having failed. At length, a partial meeting having been had, the following address was prepared:—

"FRIENDS AND FELLOW PROTESTANT EPISCOPALIANS:—

"Permit us, surviving members of the late vestry of this parish, to address you and entreat you, for your own sakes as well as that of the rising generation, to come forward on this occasion. Although our church, from various causes, has been most woefully neglected for a season, we flatter ourselves that the time is at hand when the members thereof—of whom there are not a few—will throw off their lukewarmness and exert themselves in the cause of that profession of Christianity handed down to us by our forefathers, who—God rest their souls—left us a goodly fabric to assemble in and pay our devotions to the Almighty Creator and Preserver of the universe, as they had done,—although by our neglect it is mouldering into ruins. The first step toward a reform is the appointment of trustees; for, until that is done, our church must remain in that miserable condition we see it. There is now a probability of procuring a minister to perform divine service once a fortnight; but this cannot be done until there shall be persons authorized to meet and consult on the ways and means of affording him an adequate compensation for his services. Awaken, then, from this fatal supineness. Elect your trustees, and they, we doubt not, will make the necessary arrangements, in the accomplishment of which, aided by your hearty exertions and concurrence, our church will be restored to its former decency and rank as the temple of the living God.

"We are your Christian brethren and friends of true religion,

"BENJAMIN SMITH,	WILLIAM PEACHY,
"B. McCARTY,	JOHN SYDNOR,
"WALKER TOMLIN,	JOHN FAUNTLEROY,
"RICHARD BEALE,	SAMUEL HIPKINS."

Great pains were taken to circulate this; and yet on the appointed day less than thirty persons assembled, and half of these after two o'clock, and so there was no election.† Five or six of those present agreed to appoint Whit-Monday for another meeting, and

---

* It should probably be McKay, though it is written Mackay in our printed lists.
† This was probably less than the number hitherto required by law.

to get a neighbouring minister to preach on that day. This was successful, and they paid the minister four pounds ten shillings for coming.

The vestry direct Mr. William Peachy to write to Bishop Madison for a minister, to which the following answer was received :—

"WILLIAMSBURG, August 1, 1794.

"DEAR SIR :—It would afford me great pleasure, could I give you an assurance of being speedily supplied with a worthy minister. I sincerely regret the deserted situation of too many of our parishes, and lament the evils that must ensue. Finding that few persons, natives of this State, were desirous of qualifying themselves for the ministerial office, I have written to some of the Northern States, and have reason to expect several young clergymen who have been liberally educated, of unexceptionable moral character, and who, I flatter myself, will also be generally desirous of establishing an academy for the instruction of youth, wherever they may reside. Should they arrive, or should any other opportunity present itself of recommmending a worthy minister, I beg you to be assured, if your advertisement proves unsuccessful, that I shall pay due attention to the application of the worthy trustees of North Farnham.

"With great respect, I am, dear sir,
"Your most ob't servant,
"JAMES MADISON."

The Bishop, it seems, was as much troubled about getting a meeting of the Convention as the friends of the Church in Farnham had been to get an election of vestrymen. The following circular will too surely establish that :—

"WILLIAMSBURG, December 13, 1795.

"REVEREND SIR :—It is, no doubt, well known to you that the failure last May in holding a Convention at the time and place agreed upon was matter of deep regret to every sincere friend of our Church. To prevent, if possible, a similar calamity at the next stated time for holding Conventions, the deputies who met last May requested me to send circular letters to the different parishes, exhorting them to pay a stricter regard to one of the fundamental canons of the Church. I fulfil the duty with alacrity, because the necessity of regular Conventions is urged by considerations as obvious as they are weighty. I need not here enter into a detail of those considerations; but I will ask, at what time was the fostering care of the guardians—nay, of every member—of the Church more necessary than at this period? Who doth not know that indifference to her interests must inevitably inflict a mortal wound, over which the wise and the good may in vain weep, when they behold that wound baffling every effort to arrest its fatal progress? Who doth not know that irreligion and impiety sleep not whilst we slumber? Who doth not know that there are other enemies who laugh at our negligent supineness and deem it their victory?

"But, independent of these general considerations, there are matters of the first moment to our Church, which require the fullest representation at the ensuing Convention.　Those parishes which, faithful to their duty, have not failed on former occasions to send forward their deputies, as directed by the injunction of the Church, need no exhortation on this subject. The same laudable sentiments which have hitherto directed their conduct will doubtless continue to produce a similar effect.　But to those which have been neglectful in making the necessary appointment of deputies, and in supplying the means for their attendance, I address myself with peculiar solicitude.　Let me then, sir, through your agency, and, where there is no minister, let me through the agency of the churchwardens or vestry, exhort and entreat such parishes to be no longer unmindful of the interests of their Church,—no longer to be languid and indifferent in what concerns her essential welfare,—no longer to treat her injunctions with disrespect,— but, on the contrary, animated by a warm and laudable zeal, and satisfied how much the holy cause of religion must depend on wise and prudent exertions, let them evince, at the approaching Convention, that they will not abandon a Church which they cannot fail to love and to venerate so long as piety and virtue shall continue to maintain the least portion of influence in the hearts of men.　Permit me only to add, that I feel a confidence that this exhortation will not be disregarded, and that the next Convention, which is to be holden on the first Tuesday in May next, will manifest to the Church and to the world that the zeal of both clergy and laity remains unabated.　Such is the confidence and such the sincere prayer of　　　　　　　　　　　　Your brother in Christ,

"JAMES MADISON,

"*Bishop of the Prot. Epis. Church in Virginia.*"

In the year 1796, the vestry obtained the services of the Rev. George Young, for one Sunday in three, (the other two being engaged to the adjoining parish of Lunenburg,) agreeing to pay him the sum of two hundred and fifty dollars, besides the rent of the glebe.　In the year 1799, the Rev. John Seward offers his services one Sunday in three, and receives two hundred dollars with the glebe.　Here the vestry-book ends, except an entry of an election of vestrymen in 1802.

The following is a list of the vestrymen from 1787 to 1802:—

William Peachy, William Miskell, John Fauntleroy, John Sydnor, Leroy Peachy, Griffin Fauntleroy, Thaddeus Williams, J. Hammond, Benjamin Smith, Samuel Hipkins, Epaphroditus Sydnor, Jno. Smith, Walker Tomlin, Richard Beale, Bartholomew McCarty, David Williams, Ezekiel Levy, Charles Smith, Abner Dobyns, William McCarty, William Palmer, John G. Chinn, Vincent Branham, W. T. Colston, George Miskell, Peter Temple, J. M. Yerby.

If there were any other minister or ministers in this parish until the Rev. Washington Nelson, in 1835, took charge of it in connection with Lunenburg parish, of the same county, and Cople parish, Westmoreland, we have not been able to ascertain the fact.　Under Mr. Nelson's charge the Old Farnham Church was repaired at a cost of fourteen hundred dollars, and a new church built at the court-house, by the side of whose walls his body is interred. Mr. Nelson was succeeded in all his congregations by the Rev. William Ward. The Rev. Mr. Coffin succeeded him in Farnham and at the court-house, and continued about two years, resigning them both in the summer of 1856.

CHURCHES IN NORTH FARNHAM PARISH.

Besides the one now standing, there was another about half-way between it and the court-house, the foundation of which may yet be seen. It was probably deserted at the time that North Farnham Church was built; but when that was, cannot be discovered. We have mentioned that among the families once prominent in this parish—though now dispersed—were those of the Fauntleroys and Colstons. To each of these, within a few miles of Farnham Church, there were those unhappy receptacles of the dead, called vaults, which were so common from an early period in the Northern Neck. What the precise condition of the former is, we have not heard, though we believe a bad one. As to the latter, the following note, which I find among my papers, gives what I doubt not is a true account :—

"The burying-place of the Colston family is on the Rappahannock River, about seven miles from North Farnham Church. The vault is in a dilapidated condition. It was originally arched over with brick. A number of bones are exposed,—so much so, that with but little difficulty an entire human frame could be collected.

The following account of Old Farnham Church in my report to the Convention of 1838 will complete my notices of this parish:—

"My appointment next in order was at Farnham Church, which had recently been so much refitted, that on this account—because it is believed that none of the old churches were ever consecrated—it was on Tuesday, the 20th of June, set apart to the worship of God, according to the prescribed form. A considerable congregation assembled on the occasion, when I preached,—the service having been read by the Rev. Francis McGuire, and the deed of consecration by Mr. Nelson, the pastor of the congregation. This church was first built more than a hundred years ago, after the form of the cross, and in the best style of ancient architecture. Its situation is pleasant and interesting,—being immediately on the main county road leading from Richmond Court-House to Lancaster Court-House.

"What causes led to its early desertion, premature spoliation, and shameless profanation, I am unable to state; but it is said by the neighbours not to have been used for the last thirty or forty years. Thus deserted as a house of God, it became a prey to any and every spoiler.

An extensive brick wall which surrounded the church and guarded the graves of the dead was torn down and used for hearths, chimneys, and other purposes, all the county round.   The interior of the house soon sunk into decay and was carried piecemeal away.   For many years it was the common receptacle of every beast of the field and fowl of the air.   It was used as a granary, stable, a resort for hogs, and every thing that chose to shelter there.   Would that I could stop here! but I am too credibly informed that for years it was also used as a distillery of poisonous liquors; and that on the very spot where now the sacred pulpit stands, that vessel was placed in which the precious fruits of Heaven were concocted and evaporated into a fell poison, equally fatal to the souls and bodies of men; while the marble font was circulated from house to house, on every occasion of mirth and folly,—being used to prepare materials for feasting and drunkenness,—until at length it was found bruised, battered, and deeply sunk in the cellar of some deserted tavern.   But even that sacred vessel has been redeemed, and, having been carefully repaired, has resumed its place within the sacred enclosure.   Although the doors of the house had been enlarged, by tearing away the bricks, to make a passage for the wagons that conveyed the fruits that were to be distilled into the means of disease and death; although the windows were gone and the roof sunk into decay,—the walls only remaining,—yet were they so faithfully executed by the workmen of other days as to bid defiance to storms and tempests, and to stand not merely as monuments of the fidelity of ancient architecture, but as signals from Providence, held out to the pious and liberal to come forward and repair the desolation.   Nor have these signals been held out in vain to some fast friends of the Church of their fathers in the parish of North Farnham.   At an expense of fourteen hundred dollars, they have made Old Farnham one of the most agreeable, convenient, and beautiful churches in Virginia.   It should also be mentioned that the handsome desk, pulpit, and sounding-board now to be seen in Farnham Church were once in Christ Church, Baltimore, when the Rev. Mr. Johns officiated in the same.   They were a present from the minister and vestry of that church; and few events could give more pleasure to the congregation at Farnham than to see them again occupied by the former tenant, and to hear from his lips, if only one or two of those impressive appeals which have so often been heard from the same."

LUNENBURG PARISH, RICHMOND COUNTY.

The first information we have of this parish is from communications made to the Bishop of London by the Rev. Mr. Kay, its minister, between the years 1740 and 1750, as well as my memory serves me, not having the documents before me at this time.   A most painful and protracted controversy took place between him and a portion of his vestry,—especially Colonel Landon Carter.   Though the doors of the church were closed against Mr. Kay, such was the advocacy of him by a portion of the vestry and many of the people that he preached in the churchyard for some time.   The dispute appears to have been about the right of Mr. Kay to the parish in preference to another who was desired by some of the vestry and people. The cause was carried before the Governor and Council, and from thence to the higher court in England. The sympathy of the Commissary and the clergy appears to have been with Mr. Kay. How it was finally settled in the English courts does not appear, but we find Mr. Kay in Cumberland parish, Lunenburg county, in the year 1754.* In that year the Rev. Mr. Simpson becomes minister of Lunenburg parish, Richmond county. How long he continues, and whether any one intervenes between him and the Rev. William Giberne, who becomes the minister in 1762, is not known. The name and memory of Mr. Giberne have come down to our times with considerable celebrity. The first notice I have of him is in a letter to the Bishop of London, in which he inveighs with severity on some things in the Church of Virginia. On the Bishop of London's writing to Commissary Robinson concerning them, the Commissary denies the charge in its fulness, and says that it comes with ill grace from Mr. Giberne, who himself sets an ill example, being addicted to card-playing and other things unbecoming the clerical character.

All the accounts I have received of him correspond with this. He was a man of talents, of great wit and humour, and his home a pleasant place to the like-minded,—especially attractive to the young. He lived at the place now owned by the Brockenbrough family, near Richmond Court-House. He married a daughter of Moore Fauntleroy and Margaret Micou. Her father was Paul Micou, a Huguenot who fled from Nantes in 1711.† In the following communication from a friend in Richmond county there is more particular mention of Mr. Giberne, in connection with some interesting particulars about the two churches in Lunenburg parish.

" The church here, which I remember, was situated near the public road, near our court-house, and was surrounded by large and beautiful trees, affording a fine shade in summer to those visiting the church. The ground was enclosed by a brick wall, which was finally overthrown by the growing roots of a magnificent oak. Like most of the old churches in Virginia, it was built of brick, finished in the best manner, and cruciform in shape; the pulpit was very elevated, and placed on the south side at an

* In different vestry-books I find the name sometimes Kay and at others Key. There may have been ministers of both names.

† At the old Port Micou estate on the Rappahannock may still be seen the large, heavy, iron-stone or black marble tombstone of this Paul Micou, the first of the name who came into this country. By reason of its weight and the lightness of the soil, it sinks every few years somewhat beneath the earth, but is raised up again. The inscription is as follows:—" Here lies the body of Paul Micou, who departed this life the 23d of May, 1736, in the seventy-eighth year of his age."

angle near the centre of the building. The aisles were floored with large stones, square and smoothly dressed, and the pews with planks. They were high at the sides and panelled, and better suited for devotion than our churches at the present day. The church was claimed by an individual, when in ruins, and the materials from time to time removed and used for various domestic purposes.

"It was built, according to the recollection of an individual now living, in 1737, and he remembers to have seen the date marked in the mortar, 'Built in 1737.' This building remained until about 1813, when its walls were thrown down by the outward pressure of the roof, which had fallen from decay. The Rev. Isaac Wm. Giberne was the pastor of this church. He was an Englishman, and I think the nephew of the Bishop of Durham. I ascertained the fact from an inscription in an old Prayer-Book, which was in the possession of Mr. Giberne, and which after his death came into my hands. It had belonged to her Majesty Queen Anne, and was used by her in her private chapel: on her demise it was retained by her chaplain. The inscription further stated it was intended to be presented to the 'Bodleian Library,' in which the Prayer-Books of two of the crowned heads of England had been preserved.

"Mr. Giberne commenced his services in this church in January, 1762, as we learn from the parish register, and continued to officiate in this and the 'Upper Church,' as it was called, until incapacitated by age. He was a man of great goodness of heart and Christian benevolence, highly educated, well read, and extensively acquainted with the ancient and English classic writers.

"After an interval of some eight or ten years or more, Mr. Giberne was followed in his pastoral duties by the Rev. W. George Young, an Englishman, who, I believe, occupied the glebe in 1800 or 1802. I am unable to learn how long he continued, but he removed, and the glebe, like many others, was sold under an Act of Assembly.

"The silver vessels consisted of a massive silver tankard, goblet, and plate. These remained in the keeping of our family until sold by a decree of the Court. They were purchased by the late Colonel John Tayloe, of Mount Airy, and by him presented to St. John's Church, Washington.

"The principal families attached to the old church here were the Carters, Tayloes, Lees, (Colonel F. L. Lee, of Manakin,) Beckwiths, Neales, Garlands, Belfields, Brockenbroughs, Rusts, Balls, Tomlins, &c.

"The 'Upper Church,' as it was commonly called, situated in the upper part of this county, has been long a ruin, the spot marked only by the mounds of crumbling bricks. Mr. Giberne was the last minister who regularly officiated in it. The families chiefly belonging to its congregation were the Fauntleroys, Lees, Belfields, Beales, Mitchells, Jenningses, &c. It would be impossible to ascertain at this time, I presume, when this church was built.

"There was but one other church in 'old times' in the county of Richmond: it was Farnham Church, which continued in tolerable repair until after 1800. I think in 1802 there was regular service in this church by a Mr. Brockenbrough, a minister of the Church, a remarkably small man, as I recollect him, so diminutive that he required a block in the pulpit to stand on. He did not live at the glebe, but at Cedar Grove, the property of a Miss McCall, and kept a grammar-school there. After this time the church became dilapidated, and no service was performed in it; in truth, it was completely desecrated, and served as a shelter for cattle, hogs, and horses for many years. Its walls, however, were permitted to stand, and its magnificent oaks allowed to grace the place and to give their friendly shade to the weary traveller who halted at the neighbouring tavern to refresh himself and horse. When we look back on this period of infidelity and heathenism in this county, when the old churches were pulled down or permitted to fall to decay, when no religious instruction was to be found, no declaration of the Gospel but by an itinerant preacher, little calculated to awaken the slumbering people, we are led to wonder how the land escaped some signal mark of divine vengeance,—that some calamity had not overshadowed it to call its thoughtless and wicked inhabitants back to the Christian fold.

"I have never heard what became of the sacred vessels belonging to this church. The glebe was in the occupancy of Dr. Thomas Tarpley, a well-educated and highly-polished man; how it came into his possession I never knew,—probably by purchase at public sale."

After the Rev. Mr. Young, mentioned in the foregoing communication, I know of no minister until the Rev. Washington Nelson, in 1834 or 1835, who took charge of this parish in connection with those of North Farnham and Cople. At his death the Rev. Mr. Ward succeeded to all three of the parishes, and at his resignation, a young man, whose name I forget, was minister of Lunenburg for part of a year. He was succeeded by the Rev. Mr. Coffin for two years.

The most remarkable of the old seats in this parish, known to the writer, are those of Sabine Hall, belonging to the Carters, and of Mount Airy, belonging to the Tayloes. Having in a preceding article given some account of the Carter family, which has so abounded in the Northern Neck, I subjoin a brief genealogy of the Tayloes, who have appeared on our vestry-books in the Northern Neck from their first settlement to the present time.

THE TAYLOE FAMILY.

"William Tayloe, (probably Taylor at that day,) of London, emigrated to Virginia about 1650. He married Anne, a daughter of Henry Corbin, (who was settled in King and Queen county,) the ancestor of the Corbins. John Tayloe, son of William and Anne, married Mrs. Elizabeth Lyde, daughter of Major Gwyn, of Essex county. Their children were William, John, Betty, and Anne Corbin. The first died young. John was the founder of Mount Airy. Betty married Colonel Richard Corbin, grandson of Henry Corbin. Anne Corbin married Mann Page, of Mansfield, near Fredericksburg.

"The last-named John Tayloe, of Mount Airy, was a member of the Council of Virginia, before the War of the Revolution, and was re-elected with his colleague by the House of Burgesses during the progress of the war. He died suddenly on the 18th April, 1779, leaving a large family. He had twelve children, of whom eight daughters and one son survived him. His wife was Rebecca Plater, sister of the Honourable Governor

George Plater, of Maryland, whom he married in 1747. She died in 1787 Their eight daughters married,—1st, Elizabeth, to Governor Edward Lloyd, in 1767, of Maryland; 2d, Rebecca, to Francis Lightfoot Lee, the signer of the Declaration of Independence, in 1769; 3d, Eleanor, to Ralph Wormly, of Middlesex, in 1772; 4th, Anne Corbin, to Thomas Lomax, of Caroline, in 1773; 5th, Mary, to Mann Page, of Spottsylvania, in 1776; 6th, Catherine, to Landon Carter, of Richmond county, in 1780; 7th, Jane, to Robert Beverley, of Essex, in 1791; 8th, Sarah, to Colonel Wm. Augustine Washington, of Westmoreland, in 1799.

"John, son of the foregoing John and Rebecca, third of the name, was born in 1771, the only son in a family of twelve. In 1792 he married Anne, daughter of Governor Benjamin Ogle, of Maryland. He died in Washington in 1828. Their children were fifteen, of whom three died young, and eleven (six sons and five daughters) survived their father. Their mother died in 1855, at the unusual age of eighty-three. Five sons and three daughters have survived her. Their eldest son, John, entered the navy, and was distinguished in the battles of the Constitution with the Guerriere and with the Cyane and Levant. After the first action the State of Virginia presented him with a sword. He was captured in the Levant by a British squadron whilst lying at Port Praya, Cape de Verde Islands. He died in 1824 at Mount Airy, having resigned, shortly before, his rank of lieutenant in the navy, to which he was promoted soon after his first action. Benjamin Ogle Tayloe, the second son, resides in Washington. Three other sons—William, Edward, and George—reside in Virginia, and one in Alabama,—Henry Tayloe, an active member of the Church in that State. John Tayloe, a grandson, resides at Chatterton, in the county of King George."

From the earliest accounts of this family, they have been either warm friends of the Church, or in full communion with it. Many of the male members of the family have been active and liberal vestrymen.

ARTICLE LXIII.

Parishes in King George County.

KING GEORGE county was taken out of Richmond county in the year 1720, at which time Richmond county extended as far on one side of the Rappahannock as Essex did on the other, which was, I believe, near the Falls of the Rappahannock or Fredericksburg. It did not extend from the Rappahannock to the Potomac, as Westmoreland and King George now do, for Westmoreland and Stafford* extended along the Potomac, while Richmond and King George lay on the Rappahannock. Formerly there were two parishes in King George,—Hanover and Brunswick, lying along the Rappahannock, the latter reaching up to the falls at Fredericksburg, for we find Mr. W. Fitzhugh, of Chatham, opposite Fredericksburg, representing Brunswick parish in the Conventions of 1785 and 1786. In 1776, the boundaries of Stafford and King George were changed, and each of them made to extend from river to river, instead of being divided by a longitudinal line running east and west. At this time St. Paul's parish, and part of Overwharton, formerly in Stafford, were thrown into King George county, and that of Brunswick parish into Stafford. There are, therefore, now in King George, St. Paul's parish, on the Potomac side, and Hanover, chiefly on the Rappahannock. In the parish of Brunswick there was formerly a church some miles below Fredericksburg, whose ruins, or the traces of whose foundation, may yet, I am told, be seen.

---

* Stafford is first mentioned among the counties in 1666, in the following manner. It seems that, besides the private looms of weavers, there was required by Act of Assembly a public one in each county, with certain exceptions:—"Provided that the executing hereof in the counties of Rappahannock, Stafford, Westmoreland, and Northumberland, who, by the newness of their ground, pretend themselves incapable of making provision for the soon employment of a weaver, be respited for fowre years after the date hereof." From this Act we may see what was the state of the whole Northern Neck of Virginia in 1666, nearly sixty years after the first settlement of the Colony. It either was not, or pretended not to be, able to support one weaver at public expense. It is pleasing to think that there was a better state of things as to religion, and that there were several ministers in the district at the above-mentioned period.

There was also a church in Falmouth which belonged to this parish, and in which I have preached at an early day of my ministry.

In Hanover parish there were, from 1779 to 1796, two churches, —viz.: Strother's, between Port Conway and Oakenbrough, and Round Hill, under the charge of the ministers of the parish. Until the year 1777, Round Hill Church was in Washington parish, Westmoreland, but certain changes in the boundaries of King George and Westmoreland in that year threw Round Hill Church into King George county and Hanover parish. As we have but little to say of Hanover parish, we will say it at once. We cannot ascertain the precise time of its establishment. It was in existence in 1720, and probably established in that year, as King George was then cut off from Richmond county. In 1753, we find on one of our lists the name of William Davis as its rector. In the years 1773, 1774, and 1776, we find the Rev. William Davies. But in the mean time the Rev. Mr. Boucher was the minister of the parish for some years.

We have nothing on any of our lists, or in the vestry-book of this parish, concerning this distinguished man, and for the plain reason that we have no list or vestry-book covering the period of his ministry in Hanover parish. He was ordained for this parish in 1762, having been resident in Virginia since he was sixteen years of age, and probably in that part of Virginia. He was an intimate friend of General Washington, and, as has been stated in the article on Caroline county, dedicated a volume of sermons to Washington. He was selected by the General as a travelling-companion and guide to young Custis, son of Mrs. Washington, when it was contemplated that he should make the tour of Europe. The following extract from a letter of General Washington on the subject will at the same time explain the causes of the relinquishment of this plan, and show the amiableness and sound judgment displayed by him on the occasion. Mr. Boucher was the tutor to young Custis at Annapolis, in the year 1771, when the letter was written of which the following is an extract:—

"Upon the whole, it is impossible for me at this time to give a more decisive answer, however strongly inclined I may be to put you upon a certainty in this affair, than I have done; and I should think myself wanting in candour, if I concealed any circumstance from you which leads me to fear that there is a possibility, if not a probability, that the whole design may be totally defeated. Before I ever thought myself at liberty to encourage the plan, I judged it highly reasonable and necessary that his mother should be consulted. I laid your first letter and proposals before her, and desired that she would reflect well before she resolved, as an unsteady behaviour might be a disadvantage to you. Her determination was, that if it appeared to be his inclination to undertake this tour and it should be judged for his benefit, she would not oppose it, whatever pangs it might give her to part with him. To this declaration she still adheres, but in so faint a manner, that I think, with her fears and his indifference, it would soon be declared that he had no inclination to go. I do not say that this will be the case. I cannot speak positively; but, as this is the result of my own reflections on the matter, I thought it but fair to communicate it to you. Several causes have, I believe, concurred to make her view his departure, as the time approaches, with more reluctance than she expected. The unhappy situation of her daughter has in some degree fixed her eyes upon him as her only hope. To what I have already said, I can only add, that my warmest wishes are to see him prosecute a plan, at a proper period, which I may be sure will redound to his advantage, and that nothing shall be wanting on my part to aid and assist him."

It seems that Mr. Custis preferred an early marriage to a European tour, and so the matter ended.

We return from this digression to the other ministers of Hanover parish. We have a vestry-book beginning in 1779, which shows that in 1780 the Rev. Rodham Kennor (an old Virginia name) was chosen its minister. In 1785, he resigned and removed to his farm in Fauquier. The next year the Rev. John Low became its minister, and continued until 1796, when he was allowed to preside in the vestry till the end of the year, on condition that he would resign at that time, which he did in a letter recorded in the vestry-book. We know of no other minister being in this parish until its reorganization and the election of the Rev. Mr. Friend, who has recently left it. The following list of vestrymen from 1779 to 1796 will show who were the leading friends of the Church in that parish. Messrs. Piper, Woffendall, Kendall, Jett, Boon, Lovall, Marshall, Kirk, Conway, Washington, Bernard, Johnson, Dade, Stewart, Dishman, Flood, Oldham, Berry. Mr. Johnson was reader at Round Hill Church, and Mr. Thornby at Strother's. Two orders on the vestry-book serve to throw light on the manners of the parish. One directs Mr. Ashton to try to procure four locks for the glebe-house, evidently showing that there was difficulty and uncertainty about it. This speaks well for the honesty of the times, locks being so little used that they were hard to be gotten. The other is not so creditable to the temperance of the times and parish, as it directs that "forty pounds of tobacco be paid for two quarts of brandy for burying a poor woman,"—that is, for use at the funeral.

A few words will suffice for the history of the parish since the year 1796. Some years since, a number of families in the upper part of it—the Tayloes, Masons, Turners, &c.—united in building a neat brick church near the court-house, for which they secured the partial services of the Rev. Mr. Friend, by which means a very respectable congregation has been formed.   As stated above, Mr. Friend has recently resigned his charge.

Since writing the above, we have been indebted to the kindness and diligence of one or two friends for some further information concerning this parish, obtained from the old records of the court. In the years 1725, 1727, and 1737, the names of the Rev. Mr. Skaife, Mr. Edyard, and Mr. Mackay, appear on the record, though it is not known with what parishes they were connected.   The following were the names of vestrymen between the years 1723 and 1779:—John Grimsley, James Kay, William Strother, Rowland Thornton, Thomas Turner,* John Furguson, Jos. Strother, Maximilian Robinson, William Thornton, Joseph Murdock, Joseph Jones, George Tankersley, George Riding, Thomas Vivian, Isaac Arnold, Samuel Skinker, Harry Turner, Charles Carter, John Triplett, Thomas Jett, Thomas Hodges, Richard Payne, Thomas Berry, Horatio Dade, John Skinker, William Robinson, George Marshall, John Washington, Townsend Dade, Robert Stith, Henry Fitzhugh, Jr., Laurence Washington, Sen., John Pollard, William Fitzhugh, Laurence Ashton, Thomas Hood, William Newton, William Bruce, James Kenyon, John Taliafero, Joseph Jones, James Hunton, John Taliafero, Jr.   Whether all these belonged to Hanover parish I think doubtful.   In the year 1744, there is a suit in King George Court in the name of Henry Downs and Zachary Taylor, (doubtless the ancestor of our late President,) the churchwardens of St. Thomas's Church, Orange county.

---

* The families of Tayloes and Turners are the most ancient with which I am acquainted in the parish of Hanover. Of the former I have given some account in my article on Lunenburg parish, Richmond county. The first of the Turners was a physician who came to Virginia about 1650 or 1660, and settled in the very region now occupied by his descendants, on the banks of the Rappahannock, in Hanover parish. He left two sons, Harry and Thomas. The latter died young. Harry married the only surviving daughter of Mr. Nicholas Smith, of "Smith's Mount," in Westmoreland, by whom he became possessed of that estate, which he bequeathed to his posterity, and which has gone by the name of the seat of the Turner family. He and his wife Elizabeth are both buried there, as are also their parents. The tombstones still remain and testify of them. Mr. Harry Turner left only one son, Thomas, who married a daughter of Colonel William Fauntleroy, of Naylor's Hole, in Richmond county, about the year 1767, and left a family of eight children,—four sons and four daughters. The sons were Henry, Thomas, Richard, and George,— the descendants of whom, as well as of the daughters, are dispersed throughout the State; a number of them living in King George, where, as we have said, the first ancestors settled.

BRUNSWICK PARISH.

A short notice will suffice for Brunswick parish. This was also in existence in 1720. In 1754 and 1758, the Rev. Daniel McDonald was its minister. In the year 1786, we find the parish, or a portion of it, included in Stafford county. It was no doubt taken into it at the establishment of the new boundaries between it and King George, in the year 1776. I have already mentioned that there was a church a few miles from Fredericksburg, within the parish of Brunswick. It was called Muddy Creek Church, and about nine miles from Fredericksburg. Muddy Creek is now the boundary-line between King George and Stafford. At a later period, Lamb's Creek Church was the church of Brunswick parish. The stepping-stone at the door bears the date of 1782, but the church may have been built before that. From the records of the court we find that a Mr. Anthony Hainy was churchwarden in this parish as far back as 1734, and Mr. Charles Carter and John Champe in 1739. Mr. Charles Carter was also vestryman in 1750.

ST. PAUL'S PARISH, KING GEORGE COUNTY.

Our authority for the earlier part of the history of this parish is a vestry-book beginning in 1766, during the rectorship of the Rev. William Stuart, who, according to the Rev. Robert Rose, was a man of eloquence and popularity and high character.

There is also a register of the marriages, and of the births, baptisms, and deaths of both white and black. Much of it is torn out. Its first entry is in 1722. At that time, and long before, the Rev. David Stuart was the minister. He continued to be so until his death, in 1749, when he was succeeded by his son, William Stuart, who was probably his father's assistant for some time before his death. The son died in 1796. The earlier part of my mother's life was spent under his ministry, and I have often heard her speak in high praise of him. He was in bad health for some years before his death. The following is his letter of resignation:—

"To the Vestry of St. Paul's Parish.

"Gentlemen:—I have been curate of this parish upward of forty years. My own conscience bears me witness, and I trust my parishioners (though many of them have fallen asleep) will also witness, that until age and infirmities disabled me I always, so far as my infirmities would allow, faithfully discharged my duties as a minister of the Gospel. It has given me many hours of anxious concern that the services of the Church should be so long discontinued on my account. The spirit indeed is willing, but the flesh is weak. I therefore entreat the favour of you to provide me a successor as soon as you can, that divine service may be discontinued no longer; and at the end of the year the glebe shall be given up to him by your affectionate servant,

"WILLIAM STUART."

It is most probable that the father's term of service was equal to that of his son's; and if so, we should go back to near the beginning of the century with the ministry of the two,—and that would carry us to a period not far from that in which the first of the Fitzhughs—Mr. William Fitzhugh—of this region wrote to the Bishop of London urging him to send them a sober and pious minister. Mr. Fitzhugh lived at Bedford, in what is now King George but was then Westmoreland, and there was a church and graveyard near his residence (Bedford) on the Potomac. A second church was built near the present, and a few miles only from the first. Before closing our notice of Mr. William Stuart, I must extract from the record an entry which shows that, though he lived some years after his resignation, his zeal for the Church did not abate: though unable to preach, he was able and willing to give. When a subscription was raised for his successor, Mr. Parsons, (the Establishment being put down,) his name stands first on the list for ten pounds,—no other exceeding three. The voluntary system was then in its infancy, and only fifty-seven pounds were raised; but this was as much as the most of the parishes paid their ministers under the Establishment. Mr. Parsons was never admitted to Priests' Orders: for what reason I am unable to say. It is not wonderful that on this account the religious condition of the parish should have rapidly declined, and at his death, in 1808, was in so deplorable a state. The house of worship, which, at successive periods from the year 1766, had been begun, completed, and repaired, and become one of the best of the cruciform churches in Virginia, was permitted to fall into ruins,—except its well-built walls. In the year 1838, I gave the following account of a visit paid to it many years before :—

"On Thursday and Friday, services were performed in St. Paul's Church, King George county. I preached in the morning of each day, and Mr. Nelson and Mr. Friend in the afternoon. Here I baptized three children and confirmed two persons and administered the Communion. About twenty-six years ago, (in the year 1812 or 1813,) the Rev. Mr. Norris and myself visited this place together. St. Paul's was then in ruins. The roof was ready to fall; and not a window, door, pew, or timber remained below. Nevertheless, notice was given that we would preach there. A rude, temporary pulpit or stand was raised at one angle of the cross, and from that we performed service and addressed the people. On the night before the meeting a heavy rain had fallen, and the water was in small pools here and there where the floor once was, so that it was difficult to find a dry spot on which the attendants might stand. Such was its condition twenty-six years ago, and thus did it continue for some years after, until the Legislature granted leave to citizens of the county to convert it into an academy. This being done, it was used conjointly as a seminary of learning and place of worship. At length, the seminary being neglected, and the house useless for purposes of education, as well as inconvenient for public worship, the neighbours petitioned the Legislature to restore it to its rightful owners and original purposes; which being done, it was converted back again into a temple of God,—one part of it being divided into three small rooms for the residence of a minister, and the other part— three-fourths of the whole house—being handsomely fitted up for public worship. It is now one of the most convenient and delightful churches in Virginia."*

The following extract from the letters of a friend and relative in King George, (Dr. Abraham Hooe,) who has long faithfully served as vestryman of the parish, and who has carefully examined its records, will complete our notice of it:—

"At a meeting of the vestry on the 19th of January, 1797, the resignation was accepted by the following order:—'That the Rev. William Stuart having resigned as rector of St. Paul's parish, and having petitioned the vestry to appoint him a successor, we, the vestry of said parish, do receive the Rev. John Parsons to officiate as Deacon agreeably to the canons of the Protestant Episcopal Church.'

"Mr. Parsons survived until some time in 1808, as I learned. I suppose it was subsequent to his death that the church went into ruins. Then the glebes were sold, and the very life of the Church here seems to have gone out. During the interval between the death of Mr. Parsons and 1817, you and others would occasionally come and minister to our fathers and mothers, and afford them the opportunity of placing their dear children in covenant with their God; and I believe the late Dr. Keith, of the Seminary,—at that time a private tutor in the parish,—was in the habit of lay-reading within the ruins. But these ruins were not only used for occasional religious services; they were a resort (for shelter they furnished none) for the beasts of the field as well as for the soldiers of the camp, and furnished material for plunder to all the ruthless of the land. In mentioning the kindness of those who would come among us, I cannot omit to refer to that of the Rev. John McGuire, who had so often taken part in

---

* An old African woman, who, in her youth, had been brought to Virginia and piously brought up in some good family, near St. Paul's, and carried there every Sunday and taught to join in the service, became so attached to the place and mode of worship, that after the church was deserted of minister and people, and her fellow-servants were all going to other meetings and joining in other ways of praying, used regularly to go to the old place and sit upon one of the naked sleepers by herself, for some time every Sabbath. Upon being questioned and perhaps ridiculed for this, she said it did her more good to go to the old church and think over by herself the old prayers she was used to, than to go into any of the new ways.

those 'associations' which, though of course less frequent, at one time seemed to be looked for with almost the same regularity as the stated services of the Church, and with no less interest. On the 18th of May, 1816, a vestry was again organized, and Richard Stuart and Townshend S. Dade, son and grandson of the late rector, Mr. Stuart, were appointed delegates to the Convention to be held in Richmond, thus reorganizing the parish after an interval of so many years. The vestry elected consisted of Richard Stuart, Townshend S. Dade, Abraham B. Hooe, Langhorne Dade, John J. Stuart, William F. Grymes, Cadwallader I. Dade, and Charles Massey, Sen.; but not until the 11th of December, 1817, were the services of a minister obtained. Then the Rev. Joseph R. Andrews, also a private tutor in the neighbourhood, was elected as rector. This gentle and godly man officiated in the Academy and, I believe, at King George Court-House, as well as at Port Royal, for several years, when, feeling himself called to the work of missions, (honoured of Heaven,) he left his native land to find an early martyr's grave on the unfriendly shore of Africa, and I have the pleasant recollection of having helped him to pack his little all in my father's house.

"In 1822, the Rev. Josias Clapham was called to the charge of this parish, and his last official signature on the vestry-book bears date May 3, 1824. How long subsequently he may have continued in charge does not appear, and, being from home for several years about that time, I do not know myself. He, however, preached in Washington parish, Westmoreland county, and in a small meeting-house near Round Hill Church in this county, for some years afterward, when he removed to Halifax county, from which time his history is unknown to me further than to be able to say I am sure he has received the reward of the righteous, for he was a good man and a faithful and strict follower of his Lord and Master. Even the days just spoken of were days of destitution with us; but, as in the days of the ruins, so in those of our destitution, one and another minister of our Church would once and again come to preach the word to us; and none were more kind and true in so doing than the Rev. Charles Mann, now of this diocese, but then rector of William and Mary parish, just across the Potomac River, in Charles county, Maryland, the grateful recollection of which kindness can only cease with the lives of those of us who remember it.

"It was also customary in those days for the Methodists to have stated appointments to preach at the Academy, as did occasionally the Baptists and Presbyterians, up to the time of the Repeal Act restoring to us our church. On the 11th of January, 1828, the Rev. Edward W. Peet, now at Des Moines, Iowa, was chosen minister of the parish. He, I think, had been at first, in 1827, sent to us by the Diocesan Missionary Society, and, having been elected as above, he continued our minister until 1830, when he resigned, to take charge of St. John's Church, Richmond, and was succeeded by the Rev. Mr. Goldsmith, who was elected on the 20th of August of that year. It was mainly owing to the exertions of Mr. Peet that the restoration of the church to its former and rightful proprietors may be attributed, as was certainly the new roofing of Lamb's Creek, mentioned above. During his ministry there is reason to believe much interest in the cause of religion was awakened among us, and from that time on, the borders of the Church have been enlarged. The Rev. Mr. Goldsmith continued in charge of our parish and of Lamb's Creek united, most of the time until his resignation of the former in April, 1837; and it was during his ministry that the consecration of the church took place.   On the 22d of July following, the Rev. Charles Goodrich, Deacon, was chosen as rector of this and Lamb's Creek Churches, and entered on his duties on the 1st of October, 1837.   Of his services among us I need only say his praise is on all our lips, and the love of him fills all our hearts.   He left us at the end of a year for New Orleans, where he has been faithfully labouring in his Master's cause.   From October, 1838, to the fall of 1840, we were without the regular services of the Church. Repeated unavailing attempts were made to secure them, and in the mean time our kind and good neighbour, the Rev. William Friend, as he always has done in our need, would come among us and minister to us, as his convenience would allow or circumstances might require.   On the 26th of June, 1840, the Rev. John Martin, now of Maryland, was elected, and continued as minister of this parish and Washington parish, in Westmoreland, until July, 1844, when he resigned, and was succeeded by the Rev. Lewis Walke, Deacon. Difficulty in maintaining a minister in conjunction with other parishes having become manifest, it was determined to endeavour to do so ourselves, and Mr. Walke's services were obtained for our parish exclusively, and he continued to officiate for us most faithfully until the summer of 1848, when the parish was again vacant until the fall of 1851, when the Rev. B. B. Leacock took charge of it, and we were favoured with his valuable services for one year, when he resigned, owing to ill health, as well as with a view to a mission to Africa, and was succeeded by the Rev. Joseph A. Russell, our present rector.   Of the glebes I can only say they were sold after the death of the last incumbent, Mr. Parsons, and as much of the proceeds of the sales as was needful were appropriated as before referred to,—the remainder being now a fund in the hands of a board of school-commissioners for the county, to aid in a system of education established under a late Act of the Legislature.   The earliest notice of the plate of this parish is an entry on the vestry-book as follows:—' On the 4th day of June, 1802, the following articles of church-plate belonging to this parish,—viz.: one large silver can, a silver chalice and bread-plate,—were deposited in the care of Mr. John Parsons, the then incumbent.

"'Signed,   TOWNSEND DADE, *Warden.*'"

These same articles of plate are now in possession of the parish, and I am sure are familiar to you.   They had been, at some period prior to the above date, the gift of Colonel Henry Fitzhugh, of Stafford, in this county, as appears from the following inscription on each piece:—"Given by Henry Fitzhugh, of Stafford county, St. Paul's parish, Gent., for the use of your church."   There are also a large Bible and Prayer-Book belonging to the parish.   The first has the following inscription in gilt letters on the back:— "Given for the use of the church in St. Paul's parish, by the Rev. Wm. Stuart, rector of the same, 1762."   It is a Cambridge edition, appointed by his Majesty's special command to be read in churches, "*Cum privilegiis,*" and its dedication is, "To our most high and mighty Prince James, by the grace of God King of Great Britain, France, and Ireland, Defender of the Faith, the translators of the

Bible wish grace, mercy, and peace, *through our Lord Jesus Christ.*" The inscription on the Prayer-Book is, "Presented to St. Paul's Church, King George county, by Miss Jane S. Parke, 1831." Miss Parke was great grand-daughter to the Rev. William Stuart, the former rector.

P.S.—Since the foregoing was written, the Rev. Mr. Russell has left the parish, and the Rev. Mr. Stuart has taken his place.

The following is the list of vestrymen of this parish from the year 1720 to the present time:—

Richard Bernard, John Hooe, Richard Foote, Captain John Alexander, Captain Baldwin Dade, Colonel Henry Fitzhugh, Jerard Fowke, John Stith, Cadwallader Dade, John Stewart, John Alexander, Jr., Francis Thornton, John Washington, Thomas Pratt, Thomas Bunbury, (Thomas Stribling, reader,) Henry Fitzhugh, Jr., Wm. Fitzhugh, Wm. Fitzhugh, Jr., Samuel Washington, Laurence Washington, Townsend Dade, in the place of Samuel Washington, who removed in 1770; John Berryman, in 1771, in place of William Fitzhugh, removed out of the county; Robert Washington, Andrew Grant, Robert Stith, W. G. Stuart, William Hooe, Daniel Fitzhugh, Wm. Thornton, Wm. Stith, Henry Fitzhugh, Robert Yates, Wm. Stork, Wm. Quarles, Thomas Short, Benjamin Grymes, Thomas Washington, Rice W. Hooe, John B. Fitzhugh, John Waugh, Langhorne Dade, William Stone, Henry A. Ashton, Charles Stuart, J. K. Washington, Abraham B. Hooe, J. J. Stuart, William F. Grymes, Charles Massey, J. Queensbury, Robert Chesley, Needam Washington, Alexander Keech, Francis C. Fitzhugh, B. O. Tayloe, Thomas Smith, Dr. Robert Parsons, G. B. Alexander, Henry Mustin, Gustavus B. Alexander, Hezekiah Potts, T. L. Lomax, Jacob W. Stuart, Henry T. Washington, Drury B. Fitzhugh, Benjamin R. Grymes, John T. Washington, W. E. Stuart, M. Tenent.

AN ACCOUNT OF THE FITZHUGH FAMILY; ESPECIALLY OF THE FIRST ANCESTOR, WILLIAM FITZHUGH.

The Fitzhugh family is a very ancient and honourable one in England. Some of its members were high in office and favour during the fifteenth and sixteenth centuries. The name is a combination of the two names Fitz and Hugh. Sometimes one, sometimes the other, would precede, until at length they were united in Fitzhugh. The first who settled in this country was William Fitzhugh. His father was a lawyer in London, and himself of that profession. He settled in Westmoreland county, Virginia, when a young man, and married a Miss Tucker, of that county. He was born in the year 1650, and died in 1701. He left five sons,—William, Henry, Thomas, George, and John,—between whom, at his death, he divided 54,054 acres of land in King George, Stafford, and perhaps Essex. His sons and their descendants owned the seats called Eagle-nest and Bedford in King George, and Bellaire and Boscobel in Stafford. He had one daughter named Rosamond, who married Colonel Oberton, of Westmoreland, but died without issue. His son William married Miss Lee, of Westmoreland. Henry married Miss Cooke, of Gloucester. Thomas and George married daughters of Colonel George Mason, of Stafford, and John, Miss McCarty, of Westmoreland. From these have sprung all the families of Fitzhughs in Virginia, Maryland, and Western New York. The Rev. Robert Rose married Ann, the daughter of Henry Fitzhugh, of Eagle-nest, in the year 1740. She lived to the year 1789, surviving her husband thirty-five years. There are some things in the life and character of the father of this large family of Fitzhughs worthy to be mentioned for the benefit and satisfaction of his posterity. I draw them from his pious and carefully-written will, and from a large manuscript volume of his letters, a copy of which was some years since gotten from the library of Cambridge, Massachusetts, by one of his descendants, and which is now in the rooms of the Historical Society of Virginia.

It appears that he was, during the period that he exercised his profession, an eminent and most successful lawyer, and published in England a work on the laws of Virginia. He was much engaged in the management of land-causes for the great landholders, whether residing in England or America. He was counsellor for the celebrated Robert Beverley, the first of the name, and who was persecuted and imprisoned for too much independence. He transacted business for, and purchased lands from, Lord Culpepper, when he held a grant from King Charles for all Virginia. In all these transactions he appears to have acted with uprightness and without covetousness, for in his private letters to his friends he speaks of being neither in want nor abundance, but being content and happy; though before he died he acquired large tracts of lands at a cheap rate. The true cause of this was his being a sincere Christian. This appears from his letters to his mother and sister, to whom he remitted pecuniary assistance according to his ability, increasing it as his ability increased. The following brief letter to his mother in the year 1694 will exhibit his filial and pious disposition:—

"DEAR MOTHER:—I heartily condole with you in your present sickness and indisposition, which your age now every day contracts. God's grace will make you bear it patiently, to your comfort, his glory, and your ever-lasting salvation. I cannot enough thank you for the present of your choice Bible. The money that you say you had present occasion for 1 have ordered Mr. Cooper to enlarge, and you will see by his letter that it is doubled. Before I was ten years old, as I am sure you will remember, I looked upon this life here as but going to an inn, and no permanent being. By God's grace I continue the same good thoughts and notions, therefore am always prepared for my dissolution, which I can't be persuaded to prolong by a wish. Now, dear mother, if you should be necessitated for eight or ten pound extraordinary, please to apply to Mr. Cooper, and he upon sight of this letter will furnish it to you."

He adds a postcript to the letter, saying, "My sister died a true penitent of the Church of England."

His sister had come over to America at his instance some years before and married here, but died without children. Other letters to his mother, who it seems was much afflicted with some troubles, which are not mentioned, he writes in a very consoling manner, bidding her regard her sorrows as from Heaven, and thanks her for pious instruction of him. His habits were strictly temperate. In writing to a friend who was much afflicted with the gout, he tells him the secret of his freedom from it,—viz.: that he never was addicted to the orgies of Bacchus, or to the adoration of Ceres or Venus, never courted unlawful pleasures, avoided feasting and the surfeit thereof, and bids him tell the physician this.

Mr. Fitzhugh was not merely a moral man, but a sincerely religious man, beyond the measure of that day. He is not ashamed in one of his legal opinions to quote Scripture as the highest authority. He was a leading member of the Episcopal Church in his parish. Through him presents of Communion-plate and other things from English friends were made to the parish. Referring to the unworthiness of many of the ministers who came over from England, he communicated with his friends and with the Bishop of London, asking that *sober, reputable, and educated men* might be sent over instead of such as did come. All this appears from passages in his letters to England. But, were there none of these letters extant, the following extract from his will would testify to his sound and evangelical views of our blessed religion.

Extract from the will of Colonel William Fitzhugh, of Stafford county, Virginia, who died in October, 1701. He was the parent of the Fitzhugh family in Virginia, and the patentee of Ravensworth:—

"At a court held for Stafford county, December 10, 1701. Present her Majesty's Justices for said county.

"In the name of the Father, Son, and Holy Ghost, Trinity in Unity, Unity in Trinity, Three Persons and One God, blessed forever. Amen. I, William Fitzhugh, of Stafford county, in Virginia, being by God's grace bound for England, and knowing the frailty and uncertainty of men's lives, and being at present in perfect health and memory, do now ordain, constitute, and appoint this my last will and testament, revoking all other and former, or other wills, this 5th day of April, 1701.

"Imprimis: I recommend my soul into the hands of God, through the mediation and intercession of my blessed Saviour and Redeemer, hoping by the merits of his death to have my sins washed away in his blood, nailed to his cross, and buried in his grave, and by his merits and passion to obtain everlasting life; therefore, now do bequeath and dispose such estate as it hath pleased God to bestow in his mercy upon me, after this manner following,

"After they have disposed of my body to decent interment, without noise, feasting and drink, or tumult, which I not only leave to, but enjoin, my executors, hereafter named, to see decently performed.

"Item: I give and bequeath to my eldest son, William Fitzhugh, all these tracts of land following," &c. &c.

(Then follow the bequests to the various members of the family.)

It is evident that in the foregoing will there is much more than the usual formal recognition of a God and future state. Here is to be seen a true acknowledgment of the Holy Trinity, and an entire reliance on the merits of the Saviour's death and the cleansing of his blood, such as no orthodox divine could better express.

None can doubt but that the recorded sentiments and the consistent life of this father of a numerous family must have had its effect upon many of his posterity. I have known many, and heard of others, who imbibed his excellent spirit, and not in Virginia only, but in other States, to which they have emigrated. One there was, too well known to the writer of these lines, and to whom for Christian nurture and example he was too much indebted, ever to be forgotten. A beloved mother was a lineal descendant of this good man, born and nurtured on the soil which his economy and diligence had bequeathed to a numerous posterity. To her example and tuition, under God, am I indebted for having escaped the snares laid for the youth of our land and for having embraced the blessed religion of Christ. And if I may be permitted to single out one from the numerous families of the name, it must needs be that one which was nearest to me, and with which I have been most intimately acquainted from my childhood up. The name of Mr. William Fitzhugh, of Chatham, in the county of Stafford, as a perfect gentleman, as a most hospitable entertainer, and a true son of Virginia in her Councils, will not soon be forgotten. His name is not only on the journals of our civil Legislature, but may be seen on the ecclesiastical records of our Church, among those who were the last to give up her regular assemblies and the hope of her prosperity in her darkened days. Nor is it unlawful to proceed to some brief notice of the two children who survived him. His son, William

Henry Fitzhugh, my associate at college, entered life with as fair a prospect for honour and usefulness as any young man in Virginia. Twice only, I believe, did he appear in the legislative hall of our State, and once in a Convention of the same; but such a promise of political distinction was there given, that it could not but be felt that a few years would find him in the higher Councils of the land. It pleased Providence to interfere, and by a sudden and early death to remove him from this earthly scene. Before this decree of Heaven was executed, as if admonished of its coming, he had, after pleading by his pen and voice for the American Colonization Society, directed that all his slaves—amounting, I believe, to about two hundred—should be prepared for, and allowed to choose, Africa as their home.

But I must not lay down my pen, though the heart bleed at its further use, without the tribute of affection, of gratitude, and reverence to one who was to me as sister, mother, and faithful monitor. Mrs. Mary Custis, of Arlington, the wife of Mr. Washington Custis, grandson of Mrs. General Washington, was the daughter of Mr. William Fitzhugh, of Chatham. Scarcely is there a Christian lady in our land more honoured than she was, and none more loved and esteemed. For good sense, prudence, sincerity, benevolence, unaffected piety, disinterested zeal in every good work, deep humility and retiring modesty,—for all the virtues which adorn the wife, the mother, and the friend,—I never knew her superior. A husband yet lives to feel her loss. An only daughter, with a numerous family of children, also survive, to imitate, I trust, her blessed example.

ARTICLE LXIV.

Overwharton Parish, Stafford County.

I COME now to Overwharton parish in Stafford county. The county and parish take their names from the corresponding ones in England. Stafford county once extended up to the Blue Ridge Mountain. In the year 1730, Prince William county was formed from the "heads of King George and Stafford." Overwharton parish was also coextensive with Stafford before Prince William was taken off. In the same year,—1730,—Overwharton parish was divided and Hamilton parish taken off. Overwharton covered the narrow county of Stafford, and Hamilton the large county of Prince William before Fauquier, Fairfax, and Loudoun were taken away. Stafford, in its original dimensions, first appears as a county in 1666. When it was erected into a parish is not known,— but most probably about the same time. Its division in 1730 is the first mention of it. The Rev. Robert Rose in his account-book mentions the Rev. Alexander Scott as a minister in it in 1727; and it is well known that he was the minister of this parish for many years.* He came from Scotland,—being obliged to leave, it is supposed, after some unsuccessful rebellion. He never married. Having acquired considerable property, he invited his younger brother, the Rev. James Scott, to come over and inherit it. He had one estate in Stafford called Dipple, at which he lived. His

---

* The Rev. Alexander Scott was minister in this parish in 1724, and for thirteen years before, as appears from his report to the Bishop of London. Being then a frontier-county, its limits were not known ; but it was inhabited about eighty miles along the Potomac and from three to twenty miles in the interior. There were six hundred and fifty families, eighty to one hundred communicants, in attendance, one church, and several chapels. Glebe so inconvenient that he rented it out and bought one more convenient for himself. His church and chapels as full as they could hold.

Epitaph of Rev. Alexander Scott, who was buried at Dipple, his seat on the Potomac:—"Here lies the body of Rev. Alexander Scott, A.M., and presbyter of the Church of England, who lived near twenty-eight years minister of Overwharton parish, and died in the fifty-third year of his age,—he being born the 20th day of July, A.D. 1686, and departed this life the 1st day of April, 1738.

"Gaudia Nuncio Magna."

This is written upon his coat of arms, which is engraved upon his tomb.

brother came over, and after some time became the minister of the adjoining parish of Dettingen in Prince William, which was separated from Hamilton when Fauquier was taken from Prince William, and in which he ministered for thirty-seven years. Mr. Alexander Scott had as his assistant or curate, for a short time before his death, the Rev. Mr. Moncure, a Scotchman, but descendant of a Huguenot refugee who fled from France at the revocation of the Edict of Nantes. Mr. Moncure was the successor of Mr. Scott. In what year he entered on his duties I have been unable to ascertain, but his name is still to be seen painted on one of the panels of the gallery in Old Aquia Church, together with those of the vestry in 1757. The first church was burned in the year 1751. I here give the names of the minister and vestry as painted on the gallery in the year 1757, when it is supposed the second church was finished. John Moncure, minister. Peter Houseman, John Mercer, John Lee, Mott Donithan, Henry Tyler, William Mountjoy, Benjamin Strother, Thomas Fitzhugh, Peter Daniel, Traverse Cooke, John Fitzhugh, John Peyton, vestrymen. It is gratifying to know that the descendants of the above are, with probably but few exceptions, in some part of our State or land still attached to the Episcopal Church. Their names are a guarantee for their fidelity to the Church of their fathers. Of the minister, the Rev. J. Moncure, the following extract from a letter of one of his daughters, who married General—afterward Governor—Wood, of Virginia, will give a more interesting account than any which could possibly be collected from all other sources. It was written in the year 1820, to a female relative, the grand-daughter of the Rev. James Scott, who married a sister of the Rev. Mr. Moncure's wife, and daughter of Dr. Gustavus Brown, of Port Tobacco, Maryland:—

"I was only ten years old when I lost my dear father. He was a Scotchman descended from a French ancestor, who fled among the first Protestants who left France in consequence of the persecution that took place soon after the Reformation. He had an excellent education, and had made considerable progress in the study of medicine, when an invitation to seek an establishment in Virginia induced him to cross the Atlantic, and his first engagement was in Northumberland county, where he lived two years in a gentleman's family as private tutor. During that time, although teaching others, he was closely engaged in the study of divinity, and, at the commencement of the third year from his first arrival, returned to Great Britain and was ordained a minister of the then Established Church; came back to Virginia and engaged as curate to your great-uncle, Alexander Scott, who at that time was minister of Overwharton parish, in Stafford county, and resided at his seat of Dipple. Your uncle died a short time after, and my dear father succeeded him in his parish and resided at the glebe-house. Your grandfather, the Rev. James Scott, who inherited Dipple, continued there until he settled at Westwood, in Prince William. He was my father's dearest, kindest friend, and one of the best of men. Their intimacy brought my father and my mother acquainted, who was sister to your grandmother Scott. Old Dr. Gustavus Brown, of Maryland, my maternal grandfather, objected to the marriage of my father and mother. Although he thought highly of my father, he did not think him an eligible match for his daughter. He was poor, and very delicate in his health. Dr. Brown did not, however, forbid their union, and it accordingly took place. The old gentleman received them as visitors and visited them again, but would not pay down my mother's intended dowry until he saw how they could get along, and 'to let them see that they could not live on love without other sauce.'* I have often heard my dear mother relate the circumstances of her first housekeeping with tears of tender and delightful recollection. They went home from your grandpapa's, where they were married, with a slenderly-supplied purse and to an empty house,—except a few absolute necessaries from their kind friends. When thus arrived, they found some of my good father's parishioners there : one had brought some wood, another some fowls, a third some meal, and so on. One good neighbour would insist on washing for them, another would milk, and another would tend the garden; and they all delighted to serve their good minister and his wife. Notwithstanding these aids, my mother found much to initiate her into the habits of an industrious housewife, and my father into those of an active, practical farmer and gardener, which they never gave up. When the business of preparing their meal was over, a small writing-stand was their table, the stair-steps furnished one a seat, and a trunk the other. Often, when provisions were scarce, my father took his gun or his fishing-rod and with his dog sallied forth to provide their dinner, which, when he returned, his happy wife dressed; and often would she

---

* The opposition of Dr. Brown to the marriage of his eldest daughter with a poor clergyman does not seem to have been attended with the evils which he doubtless apprehended, for Mr. Moncure prospered both in temporal and spiritual things. He has numerous descendants who have also prospered, and many of them are living on the very lands bequeathed to them by their ancestor, who purchased them at a cheap rate during his ministry. They are also zealous friends of the Church wherever we hear of them. Dr. Brown had many other daughters, four of whom followed the example of their eldest sister and married clergymen of the Episcopal Church. The Rev. James Scott, of Dettingen parish, Prince William, married one, who is the maternal ancestor of numerous families in Virginia of whom we shall soon speak. The Rev. Mr. Campbell and the Rev. Mr. Hopkins and the Rev Samuel Claggett, of Maryland, (doubtless a relative, perhaps a brother, of Bishop Claggett,) married the fifth, so that the family of Browns were thoroughly identified with the Episcopal Church and ministry.

Epitaph of Mrs. Frances Brown, who was buried at Dipple, the seat of the Rev. Alexander Scott, on the Potomac :—"Here lyeth the body of Frances, the wife of Dr. Gustavus Brown, of Charles county, Maryland. By her he had twelve children, of whom one son and seven daughters survived her. She was a daughter of Mr. Gerard Fowke, late of Maryland, and descended from the Fowkes of Gunster Hall, in Staffordshire, England. She was born February the 2d, 1691, and died, much lamented, on the 8th of November, 1744, in the fifty-fourth year of her age."

accompany him a-fishing or fowling, for she said that they were too poor to have full employment in domestic business. Though destitute of every luxury, they had a small, well-chosen library which my father had collected while a student and tutor. This was their evening's regale. While my mother worked with her needle he read to her. This mode of enjoyment pleasantly brought round the close of the first year. When the minister's salary was paid they were now comparatively rich. My dearest father exchanged his shabby black coat for a new one, and the next year was affluent. By this time the neighbouring gentry found out the value of their minister and his wife, and contended for their society by soliciting visits and making them presents of many comforts. Frequently these grandees would come in their splendid equipages to spend a day at the glebe, and bring every thing requisite to prevent trouble or expense to its owners,—merely for the enjoyment of the society of the humble inhabitants of this humble dwelling. In the lapse of a few years, by frugality and industry in the management of a good salary, these dear parents became quite easy in their circumstances. My father purchased a large tract of land on the river Potomac. He settled this principally by tenants; but on the most beautiful eminence that I ever beheld, he built a good house, and soon improved it into a very sweet establishment. Here I was born : my brother and two sisters, considerably my seniors, were born at the glebe. My brother, who was intended for the Church, had a private tutor in the house. This man attended also to my two sisters, who previously to his residence in the family were under the care of an Englishman, who lived in the house, but also kept a public school under my father's direction about a mile from his house. Unhappily for me, I was the youngest, and very sickly. My father and mother would not allow me to be compelled to attend to my books or my needle, and to both I had a decided aversion, unless voluntarily resorted to as an amusement. In this I was indulged. I would sometimes read a lesson to my sister or the housekeeper, or, if their authority was resisted, I was called to my mother's side. All this amounted to my being an ignorant child at my father's death, which was a death-stroke to my dearest mother. The incurable grief into which it plunged her could scarcely be a matter of surprise, when the uncommonly tender affection which united them is considered. They were rather more than middle-aged when I was first old enough to remember them; yet I well recollect their inseparable and undeviating association. They were rarely seen asunder. My mother was an active walker and a good rider. Whenever she could do so, she accompanied him in his pastoral visits,—a faithful white servant attending in her absence from home. They walked hand in hand, and often rode hand in hand,—were both uncommonly fond of the cultivation of flowers, fruits, and rare plants. They watched the opening buds together,—together admired the beauty of the full-blown blossoms, and gathered the ripening fruit or seed. While he wrote or read, she worked near his table,—which always occupied the pleasantest place in their chamber, where he chose to study, often laying down his pen to read and comment on an impressive passage. Frequently, when our evening repast was over, (if the family were together,) some book, amusing and instructive, was read aloud by my dear father, and those of the children or their young associates who could not be silent were sent to bed after evening worship,—which always took place immediately after supper. Under the void which this sad separation occasioned, my poor mother's spirits sunk and never rallied. The first six or eight months were spent in a dark, secluded chamber, distant from that formerly occupied. The management of the family devolved on my brother and second sister. My eldest married two or three years previous to this period. I was left pretty much to my own management. The education of my brother and sister was so far finished that they not only held what they had acquired, but continued to improve; but alas, poor me! I as usual refused every thing like study, but became, unfortunately, immoderately fond of books. The key of the library was now within my power, and the few romances it contained were devoured. Poetry and a botanical work with plates came next. This gave me a useless, superficial knowledge of what might have been useful, but what in this indigested way was far otherwise. The Tattler, Guardian, and Spectator were the only works I read which contained beneficial instruction; and of these I only read the amusing papers; and, taking the beautiful and sublime allegories which abound with moral instruction in a literal sense, I read them as amusing tales. This kind of reading made up a pernicious mass of chaotic matter that darkened while it seemed to enlighten my mind, and I soon became romantic and exceedingly ridiculous,—turned the branches of trees together and called them a bower, and fancied I could write poetry, and many other silly things. My dear mother suffered greatly toward the close of her life with a cancer: for this she visited the medicinal springs, and I was chosen to attend her. It was a crowded and gay scene for me, who had lived almost entirely in seclusion. I did not mix in its gayest circle; yet it was of service to me, as it gave me the first view of real life that ever I had. My beloved parent was not desirous of confining me; but I rejoice at the recollection that I very seldom could be prevailed on to leave her. There I first became the favourite and devoted friend of your most excellent mother. Forgive the vanity of this boast, my dear cousin, but I cannot help observing that she afterward told me that it was the manner in which I discharged this duty that won her esteem and love. At this place I first met with General Wood, who visited me soon after my return home, and became my husband four years after."

The time of Mr. Moncure's death is seen from the following letter from that true patriot and statesman, Mr. George Mason, of Gunston, Fairfax county, Virginia. As he signs himself the kinsman of Mrs. Moncure, the relationship must have come from connection between the Browns, of Maryland, and Masons. Dr. Brown came to this country from Scotland in 1708, and married in Maryland.

"GUNSTON, 12th March, 1764.

"DEAR MADAM:—I have your letter by Peter yesterday, and the day before I had one from Mr. Scott, who sent up Gustin Brown on purpose with it. I entirely agree with Mr. Scott in preferring a funeral sermon at Aquia Church, without any invitation to the house. Mr. Moncure's character and general acquaintance will draw together much company, besides a great part of his parishioners, and I am sure you are not in a condition to bear such a scene; and it would be very inconvenient for a number of people to come so far from church in the afternoon after the sermon. As Mr. Moncure did not desire to be buried in any particular place, and as it is usual to bury clergymen in their own churches, I think the corpse being deposited in the church where he had so long preached is both decent and proper, and it is probable, could he have chosen himself, he would have preferred it.   Mr. Scott writes to me that it is intended Mr. Green shall preach the funeral sermon on the 20th of this month, if fair; if not, the next fair day; and I shall write to Mr. Green to-morrow to that purpose, and inform him that you expect Mrs. Green and him at your house on the day before; and, if God grants me strength sufficient either to ride on horseback or in a chair, I will certainly attend to pay the last duty to the memory of my friend; but I am really so weak at present that I can't walk without crutches and very little with them, and have never been out of the house but once or twice, and then, though I stayed but two or three minutes at a time, it gave me such a cold as greatly to increase my disorder.   Mr. Green has lately been very sick, and was not able to attend his church yesterday, (which I did not know when I wrote to Mr. Scott:) if he should not recover soon, so as to be able to come down, I will inform you or Mr. Scott in time, that some other clergyman may be applied to.

"I beseech you, dear madam, not to give way to melancholy reflections, or to think that you are without friends.   I know nobody that has reason to expect more, and those that will not be friends to you and your children now Mr. Moncure is gone were not friends to him when he was living, let their professions be what they would.   If, therefore, you should find any such, you have no cause to lament the loss, for such friendship is not worth anybody's concern.

"I am very glad to hear that Mr. Scott purposes to apply for Overwharton parish.   It will be a great comfort to you and your sister to be so near one another, and I know the goodness of Mr. Scott's heart so well, that I am sure he will take a pleasure in doing you every good office in his power, and I had much rather he should succeed Mr. Moncure than any other person.   I hope you will not impute my not visiting you to any coldness or disrespect.   It gives me great concern that I am not able to see you.   You may depend upon my coming down as soon as my disorder will permit, and I hope you know me too well to need any assurance that I shall gladly embrace all opportunities of testifying my regard to my deceased friend by doing every good office in my power to his family.

"I am, with my wife's kindest respects and my own, dear madam, your most affectionate kinsman,   GEORGE MASON."

As to the successor of Mr. Moncure in this parish, it is probable that the Rev. Mr. Green, mentioned in the above letter, took his place in 1764.   It is certain that Mr. Scott did not.   In the years 1774 and 1776 the Rev. Clement Brooke was minister.   After the Revolution, in the Convention of 1785, called for organizing the diocese and considering the question of a general confederation of Episcopalians throughout the Union, we find the Rev. Robert Buchan the minister of Overwharton parish, and the Rev. Mr. Thornton of Brunswick parish, which had been taken from King George and given to Stafford when St. Paul's was taken from Stafford and given to King George.   The lay delegates at that Convention were Mr. Charles Carter, representing Overwharton parish, and Mr. William Fitzhugh, of Chatham, representing Brunswick parish, which lay on the Rappahannock and reached to Hanover parish in King George. In the year 1786 we find Mr. Fitzhugh again representing Brunswick parish; and this is the last notice we have of the Church in Stafford until some years after the revival of Conventions. In the year 1819, the Rev. Thomas Allen, the present devoted missionary to the poor in Philadelphia, took charge of this parish and laboured hard for its resuscitation, preaching alternately at Dumfries and Aquia Churches. At a subsequent period the Rev. Mr. Prestman, afterward of New Castle, Delaware, gave all his energies to the work of its revival. The labours of both were of some avail to preserve it from utter extinction, but not to raise it to any thing like prosperity. The Rev. Mr. Johnson also made some ineffectual efforts in its behalf as a missionary. In the year 1838, I visited Old Aquia Church as Assistant-Bishop. It stands upon a high eminence, not very far from the main road from Alexandria to Fredericksburg. It was a melancholy sight to behold the vacant space around the house, which in other days had been filled with horses and carriages and footmen, now overgrown with trees and bushes, the limbs of the green cedars not only casting their shadows but resting their arms on the dingy walls and thrusting them through the broken windows, thus giving an air of pensiveness and gloom to the whole scene. The very pathway up the commanding eminence on which it stood was filled with young trees, while the arms of the older ones so embraced each other over it that it was difficult to ascend. The church had a noble exterior, being a high two-story house, of the figure of the cross. On its top was an observatory, which you reached by a flight of stairs leading from the gallery, and from which the Potomac and Rappahannock Rivers, which are not far distant from each other, and much of the surrounding country, might be seen. Not a great way off, on another eminence, there might be seen the high, tottering walls of the Old Potomac Church, one of the largest in Virginia, and long before this time a deserted one. The soldiers during the last war with England, when English vessels were in the Potomac, had quartered in it; and it was said to have been sometimes used as a nursery for caterpillars, a manufactory of silk having been set up almost at its doors. The worshippers in it had disappeared from the country long before it ceased to be a fit place for prayer. But there is hope even now for the once desolated region about which we have been speaking. At my visit to Old Aquia Church in the year 1837, to which I allude, I baptized five of the children of the present Judge Moncure, in the venerable old building in which his first ancestor had preached and so many of his other relatives had worshipped. He had been saving them for that house and that day. I visited once more, during the last spring, that interesting spot. Had I been suddenly dropped down upon it, I should not have recognised the place or building. The trees and brushwood and rubbish had been cleared away. The light of heaven had been let in upon the once gloomy sanctuary. At the expense of eighteen hundred dollars, (almost all of it contributed by the descendants of Mr. Moncure,) the house had been repaired within, without, and above. The dingy walls were painted white and looked new and fresh, and to me it appeared one of the best and most imposing temples in our land. The congregation was a good one. The descendants of Mr. Moncure, still bearing his name, formed a large portion. I was told that all those whom I had baptized eighteen years ago (some of whom, of course, were not babes at the time) were there and meant to make it their home. The country, which seemed some time since as if it were about to be deserted of its inhabitants by reason of sickness and worn-out fields, is putting on a new aspect. Agriculture is improving. A better population is establishing itself in the county, and at the end of a century there is an encouraging prospect that a good society and an Episcopal congregation will be again seen around and within Old Aquia Church. The Rev. Mr. Wall is now their minister.

The Hon. Judge Daniel, of the Supreme Court, has been kind enough to supply me with the following letter, which, with the accompanying extracts from the county records, will be an important addition to my notices of this parish:—

"WASHINGTON, November 12, 1855.

" DEAR SIR:—In reply to your inquiries concerning the Old Potomac Church and its neighbourhood, I give you the following statement, founded in part upon tradition and partly upon my own recollection. My maternal grandfather, John Moncure, a native of Scotland, was the regular minister both of Aquia and Potomac Churches. He was succeeded in the ministry in these churches by a clergyman named Brooke, who removed to the State of Maryland. The Rev. Mr. Buchan succeeded him: he was tutor in my father's family, and educated John Thompson Mason, General Mason, of Georgetown, Judge Nicholas Fitzhugh, and many others. Going back to a period somewhat remote in enumerating those who lived in the vicinity of Potomac Church, I will mention my great-grandfather, Rowleigh Travers, one of the most extensive landed proprietors in that section of the country, and who married Hannah Ball, half-sister of Mary Ball, the mother of General George Washington. From Rowleigh Travers and Hannah Ball descended two daughters, Elizabeth and Sarah Travers: the former married a man named Cooke, and the latter my grandfather,

Peter Daniel. To Peter and Sarah Daniel was born an only son,—Travers Daniel, my father,—who married Frances Moncure, my mother, the daughter of the Rev. John Moncure and Frances Brown, daughter of Dr. Gustavus Brown, of Maryland. The nearest and the coterminous neighbour of my father was John Mercer, of Marlborough, a native of Ireland, a distinguished lawyer; the compiler of 'Mercer's Abridgment of the Virginia Laws;' the father of Colonel George Mercer, an officer in the British service, and who died in England about the commencement of the Revolution; the father also of Judge James Mercer, father of Charles F. Mercer, of John Francis Mercer, who in my boyhood resided at Marlborough, in Stafford, and was afterward Governor of Maryland; of Robert Mercer, who lived and died in Fredericksburg; of Ann Mercer, who married Samuel Selden, of Selvington, Stafford; of Maria Mercer, who married Richard Brooke, of King William, father of General George M. Brooke; and of another daughter, whose name is not recollected,—the wife of Muscoe Garnett and mother of the late James M. Garnett.

Proceeding according to contiguity were Elijah Threlheld, John Hedgeman, who married a daughter of Parson Spencer Grayson, of Prince William; Thomas Mountjoy, William Mountjoy, and John Mountjoy, the last-mentioned of whom emigrated to Kentucky, having sold his farm to Mr. John T. Brooke, the brother of the late Judge Francis T. Brooke, and who married Ann Cary Selden, daughter of Ann Mercer and grand-daughter of John Mercer. Next in the progression was the residence of John Brown, who married Hannah Cooke, daughter of Elizabeth Travers and grand-daughter of Hannah Ball, wife of Rowleigh Travers. Next was the glebe, the residence of the Rev. Robert Buchan. Adjoining this was the residence, (in the immediate vicinity of the church,) called Berry Hill, of Colonel Thomas Ludwell Lee, who possessed another plantation, on the opposite side of Potomac Creek, called Bellevue. The son of the gentleman last named, and bearing the same name, removed to London. Of his daughters, one married Daniel Carroll Brent, of Richland, Stafford, and the other Dr. John Dalrymple Orr, of Prince William. Next to Berry Hill was the plantation of John Withers, on the stream forming the head of Potomac Creek. Crossing this stream were those of John James, Thomas Fitzhugh, of Boscobel, Major Henry Fitzhugh, of Belle Air, Samuel Selden, of Selvington, the husband of Ann Mercer, and lastly, Belle Plaine, the estate of Gaury Waugh, and, after his death, of his sons, George Lee Waugh and Robert Waugh. I have thus, sir, without much attention to system or style, attempted a compliance with your request, and shall be gratified if the attempt should prove either serviceable or gratifying. I would remark that the enumeration given you, limited to a space of some eight or ten miles square, comprises none but substantial people, some of them deemed wealthy in their day, several of them persons of education, polish, and refinement.

"With great respect, yours,   P. V. DANIEL."

The present clerk of Stafford county (Mr. Conway) has also been kind enough to search through the old records, going back to the year 1664, for such things as may answer my purpose. Among the items furnished is the presentment, in the year 1693, by Richard Gipson, of George and Robert Brent as being Popish recusants.

He calls upon the court to insist upon their taking the test-oath in order to the practice of law. That oath is abjuration of transubstantiation. The court sustains the presentment and requires them to take the oath; but they refuse, and appeal to the General Court in Williamsburg. What was the issue we know not, but believe that they were leading men at the bar after that. One of them was associated in the practice with the first William Fitzhugh, and one of them joint sponsor with the first George Mason at the baptism of an Indian boy whom they had taken prisoner.

We find also presentments for swearing, for pitching and playing on the Sabbath, for not attending church. The fines were five to ten shillings, to be paid to the churchwardens for the poor of the parish. To the great kindness and diligence of Mr. Conway I am indebted for a list of the justices from the year 1664 to 1857. Of course it is a long list. I shall only select the surnames of those most familiar to our ears:—

Williams, Alexander, Mason in great numbers, Osburn, Fitzhugh in great numbers, Buckner, Thompson, Withers, Maddocks, Massey, Anderson, Waugh, West, Hoe, Washington in great numbers, Sumner, Jameson, Dade, Harrison, Storkey, Broadwater, Linton, Berryman, Farrow, Thornton, McCarty, Triplett, Grigsby, French, Aubrey, Hedgeman, Markam, Lee, Carter, Brent, Fowke, Bernard, Foote, Doniphan, Peyton in numbers, Grant, Daniel in numbers, Scott, Walker, Waller, Chapman, Mercer, Strother, Stewart, Stith, Seldon, Moncure, Bronaugh, Edrington, James, Adie, Brown, Banks, Mountjoy, Hewett, Vowles, Morson, Hood, Nicholas, Eustace, Ficklin, Richards, Botts, Wallace, Fox, Brooke, Bristoe, Lewis, Lane, Seddon, Tolson, Voss, Crutcher, Forbes, Skinker, Rose, Beale, Grayson, Hill, Cooke, Norman, Briggs, Morton, Bowen, Kendall, Conway, Green, Benson, Chinn, Browne, Stone, Irvine, Slaughter, O'Bannon, Harding, Hickerson, Clift.

We must not in our minds confine all these to Stafford as it now is, but think of its original dimensions.

ARTICLE LXV.

Dettingen Parish, Prince William County.

THIS was taken out of Hamilton parish, which, in 1745, covered all of what is now Prince William and Fauquier. It is supposed to have been named after a town in Germany, called Dettingen, near which the English gained a victory in the year 1743,—two years before. The parish register having been destroyed in the Clerk's office in Fauquier, as we shall hereafter see, we have no record of the parish of Dettingen previous to the year 1745. All that I can learn is that the Rev. Mr. Keith, the grandfather of Chief-Justice Marshall, was the minister of Hamilton parish previous to the division, and continued to be the minister of that part called Hamilton after the division. My information concerning Dettingen parish is derived from a vestry-book in the Clerk's office of Prince William, commenced in the year 1745 and continued to the year 1785. It commences with the following test, signed by the vestry:—"We do declare that we do believe there is not any transubstantiation in the Sacrament of the Lord's Supper, or in the elements of bread and wine, at or after the consecration thereof by any person whatsoever." It would seem that the above was the only test subscribed in this parish, showing that there was at this time some peculiar fear and detestation of Popery, it being about the time of the last efforts in England in behalf of the Pretender. Although a form of the subscription of vestrymen was prescribed by Act of the Assembly, which was generally used, the vestries did not always conform to it, but adopted several different ones, as we shall show hereafter. The first minister of this parish after its separation from Hamilton was the Rev. James Scott, of whom we have already spoken as coming over to this country by the invitation of his elder brother, Mr. Alexander Scott, minister of the adjoining parish of Overwharton, in Stafford. How long Mr. James Scott had been in America is not known. The following resolution of the vestry shows that he was living in Stafford at the time of his election, and also the probability that he

was married at that time.* "Ordered, that the Rev. James Scott
be received into this parish on condition of his moving into it as
soon as a glebe and house is prepared." The following letters
from Governor Gooch and Commissary Dawson speak well in his
behalf.

"WILLIAMSBURG, April 26, 1745.

"GENTLEMEN :—As your parish is at present unfurnished with a minister, I recommend to your approbation and choice the Rev. Mr. Scott,
who, in my opinion, is a man of discretion, understanding, and integrity,
and in every way qualified to discharge the sacred office to your satisfaction. I am your affectionate friend and humble servant,

"WILLIAM GOOCH."

FROM THE COMMISSARY.

"GENTLEMEN :—I hope and believe that your parish will be worthily
supplied by the Rev. Mr. James Scott. His merit having been long known
to you, I need not dwell upon it. That you may be greatly benefited by
his good life and doctrine, and mutually happy with each other, and all
the souls committed to his charge may be saved, is the daily prayer of,

"Gentlemen, your most affectionate, humble servant,

"WILLIAM DAWSON.

"WILLIAM AND MARY COLLEGE, April 26, 1745."

In the above letter, Mr. Scott is said to have been long known
to the vestry of Dettingen parish. It is supposed that he was for
some years assistant or curate to his brother Alexander Scott in

---

* The Rev. James Scott, who married Sarah Brown, had several sons and daugh-
ters,—viz. : James Scott, (the father of Alexander Scott, Mrs. Dr. Horner, and Mrs.
Brown, of Fauquier,) the Rev. John Scott, (father of the late Judge Scott, of
Fauquier, and Mrs. Peyton, of Gordonsdale ; of a daughter, who first married Mr.
Y. Peyton, then Mr. Charles Lee, and lastly, Mr. Glassell,)—Gustavus, (the father
of Robert and John Scott, and Mrs. Rankin.) One of the daughters of Rev. James
Scott married Judge Bullett, father of Judge Bullett, of Maryland, and of Mr.
Alexander Bullett, an eminent lawyer of Louisville, Kentucky, who has left a num-
ber of descendants. Another married Colonel Blackburn, of Rippon Lodge, not
very far from Dumfries, father of Mr. Thomas Blackburn, who married Miss Sin-
clair ; and of Richard Blackburn, father of Mrs. Jane and Polly Washington, of
Jefferson county, Miss Christian Blackburn, and Miss Judy Blackburn, now Mrs.
Alexander, of King George. Colonel Blackburn, of Rippon Lodge, was also the
father of Mrs. Washington, of Mount Vernon, wife of Judge Washington, and of
Mrs. Henry Turner, of Jefferson county, Virginia. Mrs. Blackburn, mentioned above,
was long known, loved, and revered, as one of the most exemplary members of our
Church in the parish of Wickliff, in old Frederick county. From my first entrance
on the ministry, the house of Mrs. Blackburn was my frequent resort. I have
never known a family of children and servants more faithfully regulated by Christian
principles than was hers, and by herself, for she was a widow at an early age. She
left three children, who are members of the Episcopal Church, and who seek to
follow her example in the regulation of their household. One of the daughters of
the Rev. James Scott married Dr. Brown, of Alexandria, who was at one time
General Washington's family physician.

Stafford, and was succeeded in that station by the Rev. Mr. Moncure.
A glebe was purchased for Mr. Scott on Quantico Creek, which
runs up the Potomac to Dumfries. It consisted of four hundred
acres of land, and was bought of Mr. Thomas Harrison, for one
hundred and thirty-five pounds sterling. So far as I have ascertained, but few of the glebes cost that much, and when rented out,
as they often were, seldom brought more than twenty or thirty
pounds. Mr. Scott continued the minister of that parish until his
death in 1782, being minister of the parish for thirty-seven years.
He lived most of the time at his own estate of Westwood, the gift,
it is believed, of his brother. Before we proceed to make mention
of his successors in office, there are some things worthy of notice,
in relation to the parish, which had better be disposed of in this
place. There were two churches in the parish, between which the
services of the minister were equally divided. One of them was
very near Dumfries, the other near the two streams Broad Run and
Slater Run, and sometimes called by either name. At the time of
the division of the parish, there was an old and indifferent one
near Dumfries, which, in the year 1752, was sold for fifteen hundred-
weight of tobacco, and a new one costing one hundred thousand-
weight was ordered. The contractor for it was a Mr. Waite, ancestor to the worthy member and lay reader of our Church in
Winchester, Mr. Obed Waite. The church at Broad Run was also
contracted for in 1752. Both were of brick, and very substantial
ones. It has not been many years since the roof and walls of the
latter fell to the ground. Some remnant of the ruins of the former
may perhaps be seen near Dumfries at this time. I have often
seen them, when more abundant, in my travels through that region.
Dumfries itself, once the mart of that part of Virginia, the scene
of gayety and fashion, the abode of wealthy merchants from Scotland, who named it after a city of that name in the mother-country,
is now in ruins, almost as complete as those of the old church.
Quantico Creek, through which the trade from Europe came, is now
filled up, while the pines have covered the spot where the church
once stood near its banks. Desolation reigns around. The old
court-house was fitted up some thirty-five or forty years ago for
worship, but that has long since been abandoned for want of worshippers. A few years since I spent a night in the neighbourhood,
in a worthy Baptist family, and, while conversing on the past, the
lady of the family mentioned that she had in her possession some
things belonging to the old church, which she would be glad to put
into my hands, as she wished to be clear of them. After hunting for

some time amid the rubbish of the top-shelf of an old cupboard standing in the room, she brought out two small, old, well-worn pieces of church-plate, supposed to be those once used in the Old Quantico Church. I still have them in my possession, to bestow on some poor parish which will not be too proud to use them. There were galleries in the church at Broad Run, one of which was allowed to be put up by Mr. Thomas Harrison, provided it was done so as not to incommode any of the pews below it. The others were put up by the vestry and sold. The pews below were all common, though doubtless taken possession of by different families, as is usual in England. The old English custom (beginning with the Royal family in St. George's Church at Windsor) of appropriating the galleries to the rich and noble was soon followed in Virginia, and, as we shall see hereafter, the old aristocratic families could with difficulty be brought down from their high lofts in the old churches, even after they became uncomfortable and almost dangerous. I find an entry on this vestry-book concerning payment to the sextons of these churches for making fires, which is the first of the only two instances I have met with, and I am in doubt whether the payment was for fire in the churches or vestry-rooms in the yard; for I have never seen where provision was made for fires in any of the old churches, either by open chimneys or stoves, if indeed stoves were then known in the land. It was the same case in the old churches in England, and still is in cathedrals to this day, and it is no wonder that the latter are so cold, damp, and comfortless. Very few, if any, of the country churches, even in New England, were warmed by stoves when I travelled through it in the year 1819. In this respect I think we have certainly improved on the customs of our fathers. I think that in some other respects we have advanced in liberality. Nothing was done gratuitously by any member of the church. The lay readers were always paid one thousand or twelve hundred weight of tobacco. Clerks received about the same. No liberal gentleman gave his wine for the Communion, as in latter days, but always charged for it. The annual cost at each of the churches in this parish was four pounds for twelve bottles of wine. One thing has struck me, in all the indentures required of those to whom orphan or illegitimate children were bound by the vestry, as speaking well for the times. The masters were required to teach those who were bound to them "the art and mystery of some trade," to "instruct them in the principles of the Christian religion." Sometimes the catechism, Lord's prayer, creed, and Commandments are specified, as also the doctrines of the Episcopal Church. On the part of those bound, they must "obey their masters, keep his secrets, not leave his house night or day without leave, not embezzle his goods or suffer others to do it, not play at cards, dice, or any other unlawful game, or frequent taverns or tippling-houses." Whether these promises were faithfully complied with or not, we are unable to say. We shall see hereafter that, by the laws of the Assembly, the very same things were forbidden the clergy,—viz.: cards, dice, and other unlawful games; also taverns and tippling-houses and such places: but they were disregarded by many. It is, however, a matter of rejoicing to see such testimonies to good morals by those in authority, and by legislative acts, even though contradicted by the conduct of those who bear them. In the most corrupt ages of the Christian Church the most wholesome laws are to be found and the best forms of religion have been used. That God who has kept the Bible pure through so many ages of darkness and corruption has also, by civil and ecclesiastical legislatures and rulers, preserved and handed down many most faithful expositions of its moral code. Some faithful ones there have been in every age who have obeyed these laws. I doubt not but there were some ministers in the darkest age of the Church in Virginia who obeyed her canons, and some masters and mistresses who fulfilled pledges to orphans and poor unfortunates.

I now return to the history of the ministers of Dettingen parish. At the death of Mr. James Scott, his son, the Rev. John Scott, was chosen minister. His ministry was of short duration. He resigned the following year on account of ill health, and died soon after. There are some painful circumstances in the history of this minister; and, as they have been misrepresented and made worse than they really were, it is due to himself and posterity to make a correct statement. Even in that there is much not only to be regretted, but utterly condemned,—the spirit of the times affording no excuse which should for a moment be entertained. From a letter in my possession, I think it probable he was set apart for the ministry in early youth. At the age of eighteen, however, he was engaged in an affair which showed that he was ill qualified for it at that time,— being destitute of all godliness,—however changed he may have been afterward. He conceived that his father and himself had been insulted and injured by the misrepresentations of one who, according to report, was a most unworthy and dangerous man, and that it was his duty to seek reparation by a resort to arms. He accordingly determined to challenge, and applied to Mr. Bullett, his brother-in-law, to be with him in the contest.   Mr. Bullett dissuaded him from the challenge in a letter, which I have in my possession, and which contains some of the many unanswerable arguments against duelling.   Failing in his effort, he attends him to the place of combat,—the end of Old Quantico Church, where the father of young Scott had so often read the words of Jehovah from Mount Sinai, "Thou shalt do no murder."   The result was, that the second, who had warned against the act, and who, it was supposed, had gone in the hope of preventing the contest, was so treated by the challenged man on the ground as to engage in a contest with him, in which the other was slain.   He was tried and unanimously acquitted by the court upon the ground of self-defence.   Mr. Scott was obliged to fly the country, and, with his younger brother, Gustavus, went to Scotland.   I take the following account of him while in Scotland, and after his return, from a letter written by one of his descendants:—

"Immediately after the trial and acquittal of Mr. Bullett, my grandfather and his younger brother, Gustavus, left this country for Scotland. Soon after their arrival in Scotland they entered King's College, old Aberdeen, where they finished their education.   My grandfather, who seems to have taken life by storm, married, while a student of King's College, Elizabeth, daughter of Thomas Gordon, one of the professors.   He was afterward ordained by the Bishop of London.   It was during his residence in Scotland that my grandfather formed an acquaintance (which ripened into a friendship) with Sir Robert Eden, an English or Scotch baronet.   When Sir Robert was appointed Governor of Maryland, he invited my grandfather to Annapolis, promising to appoint him his chaplain, and to use his influence to obtain for him the rich parish of Eversham. My grandfather readily accepted so advantageous an offer, and soon after sailed for America, leaving his infant son, Robert Eden Scott, (who it was feared could not bear a three months' voyage,) with his maternal relatives. Upon his return to America, he proceeded to Annapolis, was appointed chaplain to the Governor, and pastor of the parish of Eversham.   He resided in Maryland until the war between the Colonies and the mother-country broke out.   An Englishman in principle, he adhered to the royal cause, and, taking too active a part in politics, became obnoxious to the Revolutionary party,—into whose hands the government had passed,— and was banished one hundred miles from tide-water.   Compelled to leave Maryland, he sold his property there for Continental money, and returned to Virginia, intending to return to Scotland as soon as he could make the necessary arrangements.   While making those arrangements he resided on his plantation, which he called Gordonsdale, after the name of his wife. His health soon after failing, he was advised to try the waters of Bath, in Berkeley county, Virginia.   On his return from Bath he stopped at the residence of General Wood, who had married his cousin, Miss Moncure,— died there, and was buried under the pulpit of the old Episcopal church in Winchester.   Whether he was pastor of any parish in Fauquier, I am unable to say; but, as he did not long survive his banishment from Maryland, I am inclined to think he never received such an appointment.* My grandfather, as the Bishop has no doubt heard, was a man of fine talents and remarkable eloquence, as well as the handsomest man of his day. His gayety and wit caused his society to be much sought after, and, from all that I have heard, rather unfitted him for his sacred profession. After his death, my grandmother, who had been summoned to Winchester to receive his expiring adieu, returned to Gordonsdale. The distracted condition of the country (the Revolutionary War was then at its height) compelled her to relinquish all hope of a return to her native country. She continued to reside at Gordonsdale, devoting herself to the education of her children,—a task for which she was eminently fitted, since she had received a college education. She lived to see her children grown and settled in life, and died lamented. Several years before her death she had the pleasure of welcoming to Virginia her eldest son, Robert Eden Scott, and, although twenty-one years had elapsed since she had left him an infant in Scotland, she recognised him immediately. During his visit to Virginia he received the office of a professorship in King's College, old Aberdeen, where he had received his education and his maternal ancestors had held professorships for three hundred years. He returned to Scotland, was made professor of mathematics, married a daughter of Sir William Forbes, and died young and childless.''

To the above notice of Mr. Scott I add a report, which is not improbable, that, at the time he was summoned before the Council at Annapolis to give an account of his anti-American principles, Robert Goodloe Harper, then a young lawyer, was called in to examine him, and ever afterward spoke of him as the most talented man with whom he had ever engaged in controversy. After the resignation of the Rev. John Scott in 1784, the Rev. Spence Grayson was chosen minister. How long he continued such we do not know; nor can we say any thing concerning him or his ministry,—though our impression is that he was a worthy man. The vestry-records end with the year 1785. At the last meeting vestrymen were elected under the new organization of the Church, a delegate appointed to the Convention, and an order made to raise funds for the support of the minister,—as nothing now remained but the glebe, which was of little value. Although an order was passed that the records of the vestry should be handed over by the old clerk to the clerk of the new vestry, it fell into the hands of the overseers of the poor; and, some blank leaves being left in the vestry-book, the proceedings of the latter body were for a few years recorded on them. In this way it happened that the vestry-book came into the possession of the court. I have petitioned the court to have it sent for safe-keeping to our fireproof library at the

---

* In this the writer is mistaken, as the vestry-book shows that he was minister in Dettingen parish nearly two years.

Theological Seminary of the Episcopal Church near Alexandria, to which, I hope, many such documents will be transmitted. We have no certain accounts of any successor to Mr. Grayson; but it is confidently believed that the Rev. Thomas Harrison was the minister for some years after Mr. Grayson's death, as his name appears in the list of the overseers of the poor from 1792 to 1802, when it disappears, and when he either probably died or resigned. I have been unable to obtain any reliable accounts of Mr. Harrison. His name is nowhere to be seen on any of the lists of the clergy which I have. My old friend, Mr. Samuel Slaughter, of Culpepper, (now eighty-eight years of age,) told me, during the last summer, that he went to school to him in Culpepper when he was minister of Bloomfield parish, and that he afterward moved over to Prince William. He was the father of a numerous offspring of sons and daughters, who became scattered over the land. The late Mr. Phil. Harrison, of Richmond, was one of his sons, who are said to have been nine in number. I became acquainted with one of the families many years since near Dumfries. Its members were then preparing to move to the South. On the first page of the vestry-book of Dettingen parish, I find a leaf taken from the old Overwharton vestry-book and fastened to the latter,—doubtless by Mr. Harrison,—in which there is the following genealogy, taken from the parish record of St. Margaret's, Westminster, and certified by Richard Gibson, London :—

"Burr Harrison, of Chappawamsic, born in England, son of Cuthbert Harrison, baptized in the parish of St. Margaret's, Westminster, 28th December, 1637. His son Thomas born in 1665; grandson Burr born May 21, 1699; great-grandson Thomas born 3d of March, 1723; his sister Jane the 9th of December, 1726; his sister Seth the 30th of November, 1729."

This last Thomas Harrison was, I suppose, the minister. There was doubtless an intermarriage between the Powells, of Loudon county, and the Harrisons, of Prince William, from which it comes that the names Cuthbert and Burr are so often to be found in these families. Whether all of the above were born in England, or some of them in this country, I am unable to say. There was a Thomas Harrison belonging to Broad Run Church, in Dettingen parish, long before the Rev. Mr. Harrison appears in the parish, and may have been his father. After the death of the Rev. Mr. Harrison, the Rev. Mr. O'Neal officiated for a short time. He died after I entered the ministry; but I never met with him. No clerical delegate, and only one lay delegate,—Mr. Jesse Ewell,—ever appears in the Conventions of Virginia from Dettingen parish.   It only remains that I mention, for the satisfaction of their posterity, the lay readers and vestrymen of this old parish during the fifty years of which the records testify.   At Broad Run we find the names of John Bryant, William Peyton, Joseph Sherman, James Gray, George Carter.   At Quantico Church, Mr. Thomas Machem or Mitchem, John Peyton, Jeremiah Moore, lay readers.   The following are the names of the vestrymen of this parish during the fifty years of its recorded proceedings :—Peyton, Rearser, Butler, Deskin, Linton, Renno, Blackburn, Furguson, Ewell, Seale, Grayson, Baxter, Whetlige, Fouchee, Rust, Roussan, Crump, Frogg, Harrison, Wright, Bullett, Wickliffe, Bell, Copedge, Thornton, Elsey, Betty, Eustace, Blackwell, Waggener, Nisbett, Kennor, Tibbs, Triplett, Carr, Lee, Baylis, Buchanon, Bennett, Hoe, Alexander, Fitzhugh, Kincheloe, Washington, Guatkin, M'Millon.   The names of Adie and Tompkins are mentioned as men of uprightness, to whom the vestry and minister referred some important matters of difference for decision.   The Lees, Peytons, Blackburns, and Ewells appear to have been most numerous and prominent in the vestries.

After a failure of all efforts for the resuscitation of the Church in Dumfries, our attention was directed to the other parts of the parish of Dettingen.   The Rev. Mr. Steel, beginning in 1822, laboured for some years with partial success, and built a small church in the centre of the parish.   The Rev. Mr. Slaughter followed him in 1835, and preached with more success at Brentsville—the new county seat—and at Hay-Market.   The Rev. Mr. Skull succeeded Mr. Slaughter at the same places.   The Rev. Mr. Towles has now for many years been faithfully and acceptably serving the parish. A new and excellent stone church has been built at Brentsville; and the old court-house at Hay-Market has been purchased and converted into a handsome and convenient temple of religion.   A race-course once adjoined the court-house, and in preaching there in former days I have, on a Sabbath, seen from the court-house bench, on which I stood, the horses in training for the sport which was at hand.   Those times have, I trust, passed away forever.

ARTICLE LXVI.

Hamilton and Leeds Parishes, Fauquier County.

AFTER the division of the former parish of Hamilton into Dettingen and Hamilton, in the year 1745, the Rev. Mr. Keith continued to be minister in Hamilton. How long he had been minister of the whole parish is not known; neither have I been able to ascertain how long he continued to be minister of Hamilton parish after the division, only that in 1758 the Rev. Joseph Brunskill was the minister. The vestry-book, which could have informed us, was placed in the Clerk's office, and there torn up, page after page, by the clerks or others, for the purpose of lighting cigars or pipes. Of the Rev. Mr. Keith and his descendants I have not been able to obtain all the information I desire and hope for. From all that I can learn, he was a worthy man. He was a native of Scotland. Being involved in the rebellion in favour of the Pretender, he was forced to fly his country, and came to Virginia. Returning to England for Orders, he was then settled in Hamilton parish, and performed the duties of his office there for a long time,—probably until 1757 or 1758. A daughter of his married Colonel Thomas Marshall, of Oakhill, Fauquier, the seat of the Marshalls to this day. He was the father of the late Chief-Justice. Both father and son were in the Revolutionary Army, and fought together at the battle of Monmouth. Another of Mr. Keith's children was the Clerk of Frederick county, Virginia, who so long and faithfully performed the duties of that office. The descendants of Mr. Keith are numerous. They are also devoted members of the Episcopal Church. After the division of the parish of Hamilton, Mr. Keith served, until his death, all that region now embraced in Fauquier county, as it was not until 1769 that Leeds parish was cut off. I am unable to ascertain how many churches there were then in that part now making the parish of Leeds. I can only speak of the two in that which is now Hamilton,—namely, Elk Run and Turkey Run Churches, both of which I have often seen, and in one of which I have preached. Elk Run Church was about fifteen miles, I think, below Fauquier Court-House, on the road to Fredericksburg, upon a small stream from which it took its name. It was a substantial brick church,—cruciform, I believe. I am not certain that the roof was on it when I first saw it, in 1811. Its walls continued for many years after this, and I saw them gradually disappear during my annual visits to the Conventions. The other was called the Turkey Run Church, and was situated about a mile below Fauquier Court-House. It was an old frame church, which, after the erection of one at the court-house, was carried away and converted into a barn, and is still used as such. It was here I first met with Bishop Moore, after his arrival in Virginia in 1815. His preaching was very melting. I saw an old Episcopalian wiping the tears from his eyes during the sermon, but, on speaking to him afterward about the Bishop's preaching, was surprised to hear him say that the Bishop was nothing but a Methodist, so different was his style and manner from what had hitherto been common in Episcopal pulpits. The Bishop confirmed fifty persons at that time, the most of whom came forward in ignorance of the proper qualifications for this rite, or of the nature of true religion. Such was the case with many other congregations at the Bishop's earlier visits, some of which had no ministers, and others new ones, so that due precautions could not be easily taken to prevent unsuitable persons from coming forward. It injured the Church and the Bishop not a little for some time. He once told me that he really feared to hold a Confirmation in a new place, lest some unworthy candidates should come forward. Of the ministers who succeeded Mr. Keith, but little is known. In the year 1758, the Rev. Joseph Brunskill was the minister.* In the year 1774, the Rev. James

---

* Since writing the article on Hamilton parish, I have learnt something concerning the Rev. Mr. Brunskill which deserves to be noticed, especially as it is connected with the question of discipline in the Colonial Church. He was a notorious evil-liver, being given to intemperance and other vices. His vestry complained of him to Governor Dinwiddie, who summoned him and his accusers, with their witnesses, to Williamsburg. They appeared before the Governor and Council, Commissary Dawson being one of the Council. Being found guilty, the Governor ordered the vestry to dismiss him and choose another minister. On his return to the parish, Mr. Brunskill posted the Governor and Council on the church-door, and perhaps elsewhere, declaring that they had no jurisdiction in the case, and adding in the same notice a canon of the English Church, whereby none but a Bishop could pass sentence on a clergyman. The justification of the Governor was, that, although none but a Bishop could absolutely deprive of Orders, yet the Governor, as supreme ruler in Virginia, and representing the Crown, which was chief in Church and State in England, had a right and was bound to exercise some discipline and prevent such dishonour to religion, and that, as ministers were tried before the civil courts in England, so Mr. Brunskill had been tried before the Governor and Council, which was the supreme court in Virginia. Commissary Dawson entertained some doubt as to the canonical regularity of the proceeding, but in a letter to the Bishop of London justified it on the ground of necessity.

Craig is minister.   After Mr. Craig, I hear of the Rev. Mr. Kennor, from Hanover parish, King George, and the Rev. Mr. Iredell, from Culpepper, as living in the parish and preaching,—neither of whom was very creditable to the Church.   In the year 1805, the Rev. Mr. O'Neale and Mr. Charles Marshall appear as delegates in the Convention, as minister and lay delegate.   Mr. O'Neale taught school in Warrenton for some years, and then removed to Dumfries, and died since I entered the ministry.   Most prostrate was the condition of the parish in the year 1812 or 1813, when I first visited it.   There was no house of worship at Warrenton belonging to any denomination, and the old Turkey Run Church was inconvenient, so that the service was held in the court-house.   Notice being given that I would preach at three or four o'clock on a certain day during the session of the court, a large crowd assembled from the country around to hear a young Virginia Episcopalian.   It so happened that a very important case detained the court beyond the appointed hour of worship.   The people, however, gradually filled the house and hemmed in the lawyers.   The ladies ascended the bench on which judges and magistrates sat, and enclosed the judge, until at length the business of the court was obliged to stop, and neither judge nor lawyers could escape.   The house being completely filled, I was sent for, and, being unable to pass through the crowd, was raised up through the window and put into the sheriff's box, from which I preached.

About this time, the Episcopalians and Presbyterians proposed to build a church in conjunction.   It was commenced, and a wall was put up and a roof completed.   Some difficulty arising between the partners, as is generally the case, the Episcopalians determined to build one for themselves, without relinquishing their claim on the unfinished one.   Accordingly, a frame building was put up and consecrated as an Episcopal Church.   This was used until within a few years.   A still better one of brick now receives the increasing congregation, under its faithful and zealous minister, the Rev. Mr. Norton, whose father and myself became candidates for the ministry at the same time.   His lot was cast in Western New York, though by birth a Virginian.   He still lives, a venerable though disabled minister.

LEEDS PARISH, FAUQUIER.

This parish, as we have seen already, was taken out of Hamilton in the year 1769.   The first and only minister, before the Rev. Mr. Lemmon took charge of it in 1816, was the Rev. James Thomson, from Scotland, born near Glasgow, in the year 1739, and who died in February, 1812. He came to this country in 1767 or 1768. He lived at first in the family of Colonel Thomas Marshall, of Oakhill, and instructed his sons, John Marshall, afterward Chief-Justice, James Marshall, and others. In 1769, he went to England for Orders. On his return, he married Miss Mary Ann Farrow, sister of the late Nimrod Farrow, of Leeds Manor, and settled at the glebe, near Salem, where he had a school, to which some of the sons of Mr. Thomas Marshall were sent to him again. Mr. Thomson, at the coming on of the Revolution, partook largely of the spirit which animated Colonel Marshall and his son, the Chief-Justice. In a sermon preached at the time of the first difficulties at Boston, he thus speaks:—

"You have all heard before now of the measures taken by the British Parliament to deprive his Majesty's subjects of these Colonies of their just and legal rights, by imposing several taxes upon them destructive of their liberties as British subjects. And to enforce those acts they have for some time blocked up the harbour of the city of Boston with ships-of-war, and overawed the inhabitants by British troops. By which illegal steps, the people in general have endured great hardships by being deprived of their trade, and the poor reduced to great want. It is therefore incumbent upon every one of us, as men and Christians, cheerfully to contribute according to our ability toward their relief. And as we know not how soon their case may be our own, I would likewise recommend to you to contribute something toward supplying the country with arms and ammunition, that if we be attacked we may be in a posture of defence. And I make no doubt that what you bestow in this manner will be employed in the use you intend it for. If you want to be better informed with respect to the Acts which have been passed with a view to impose illegal taxes upon us and deprive us of our liberties, I shall refer you to the gentlemen of the committee for this county, who will satisfy you on that head."

Mr. Thomson, from the memoranda on a number of sermons or fragments of sermons I have seen, seemed to have been punctual in preaching in four churches,—Taylor's Church, not very far from Warrenton, Goose Creek Church, near Salem, Old Bull Run Church, whose location I cannot specify, and Piper's Church, in Leeds Manor, not one of which are now standing. They were, I suppose, all badly-built wooden churches, which soon came to ruin. I never saw Mr. Thomson, though he lived in a neighbouring parish and did not die until the year after I entered the ministry. From an examination of some of his sermons, or parts of sermons, I should say that they were marked by more taste and talent than most of those which have been submitted to my perusal. But the Episcopal Church from various causes failed, and almost disappeared, under his ministry. Other denominations took possession of the ground which was once entirely ours.

My nearness to Leeds parish, and its position being such that I must pass through it on my numerous visits to other parts of Virginia, caused me to preach more frequently there than in any of the surrounding parishes. Mr. Thomas Marshall, eldest son of the Chief-Justice, lived at the old homestead of the Marshalls, Oakhill, on the road to Warrington and Fredericksburg. He was one of my earliest and dearest Christian friends. He became a communicant at an early period. He often begged that, in any efforts I might make for the promotion of religion, which required pecuniary aid, I would consider him as ready to afford it. Mr. Thomas Ambler, a nephew of Judge Marshall, and an old school-mate of my early years, lived in the same neighbourhood. Cool Spring Meeting-house lay between them. At this I often preached, and it was the place where Mr. Lemmon officiated until perhaps the close of his labours in that parish. The Marshalls and Amblers continued to settle in this neighbourhood, until they have become two small congregations, or rather important parts of two congregations. The children of my esteemed friend, Mr. Thomas Marshall, six in number, settled in sight of each other, on the estate of their father, and are all living.* The Peytons, Turners, Beverleys, Hendersons, and others, descendants of Episcopal families, still adhere to the old Church, and are active in seeking its resuscitation. In the year 1816, the Rev. George Lemmon, of Baltimore, who graduated at Princeton College a year or two before me, took charge of both Hamilton and Leeds parishes, and continued to be the minister, with the exception of a few years spent in Hagerstown, Maryland, until his death. In my report to the Convention of 1847, I find the following notice of him:—

" In the death of the Rev. Mr. Lemmon, the Church has parted with one who had grown old and gray in her service, having devoted all his strength of body and mind to the promotion of her welfare. He who now addresses you has lost his earliest and oldest brother in the ministry. Our acquaintance, our friendship, our choice of the ministry, are all of the same date, and reach back to forty years save one. During all this period we have been living in the most intimate communion of soul. A sounder theologian, a more true-hearted minister, a more sincere Christian, I have never known."

Never was there a minister more esteemed and beloved by his

---

* Mr. Marshall was killed by the falling of a brick upon his head in Baltimore, on his way to Philadelphia to see his father, who died there a few days after.

people of all ages and characters. His preaching-talents were not attractive, on account of the harshness of his voice, but he was faithful to the truth, and understood how to present it experimentally to the people. His *forte* was in private intercourse as a pastor and gentleman. Though strict in his views of fashionable amusements, in which the young are apt to delight, yet so tender, courteous, and loving was he, that the young were ever pleased with his company and conversation. It is delightful to hear him spoken of to this day by his old parishioners. His health was very imperfect for many years, and his ministrations very irregular; yet such was the attachment of his people in both congregations, that they bore it almost without complaining. The active friends of the Church and Mr. Lemmon were Colonel Randolph, of Easternview, (who was always sure to be at the minister's house on the first day of each year with his subscription of one hundred dollars,) the Horners, the Bells, the Withers, Smiths, Paines, Edmonds, Hendersons, Fitzhughs, Digges, and others, in Hamilton parish, and the Marshalls, Amblers, Scotts, Adamses, Carters, Chunns, and others, in Leeds parish. In Hamilton parish Mr. Lemmon was succeeded by the present rector, the Rev. Mr. Norton, in the year 1847, under whose ministry the congregation has greatly increased, and by whose enterprise, aided by the zeal of some untiring ladies, a new church has been built at the cost of seven or eight thousand dollars. I have mentioned before that Judge Marshall had no hope of the revival of the Church in Virginia, though contributing liberally to the efforts made for it. He lived to see himself mistaken, and to unite with his children and grandchildren in the services of our resuscitated Church in the very place of his nativity and amid the scenes of his early life. In my frequent visits to Coolspring and Oakhill, I often met with him, as I had done at my father's house, and other places in Frederick, in more boyish days. Though not a communicant, he was the sincere friend to religion and the Episcopal Church. I can never forget how he would prostrate his tall form before the rude low benches, without backs, at Coolspring Meeting-House, in the midst of his children and grandchildren and his old neighbours. In Richmond he always set an example to the gentlemen of the same conformity, though many of them did not follow it. At the building of the Monumental Church he was much incommoded by the narrowness of the pews, which partook too much of the modern fashion. Not finding room enough for his whole body within the pew, he used to take his seat nearest the door of his pew, and, throwing it open, let his legs stretch a little into the aisle. This I have seen with my own eyes. He was a most conscientious man in regard to some things which others might regard as too trivial to be observed. It was my privilege more than once to travel with him between Fauquier and Fredericksburg, when we were both going to the lower country. On one occasion, the roads being in their worst condition, when we came to that most miry part called the "Black Jack," we found that the travellers through it had taken a nearer and better road through a plantation. The fence being down, or very low, I was proceeding to pass over, but he said we had better go round, although each step was a plunge, adding that it was his duty, as one in office, to be very particular in regard to such things. As to some other matters, however, he was not so particular. Although myself never much given to dress or equipage, yet I was not at all ashamed to compare with him during these travels, whether as to clothing, horse, saddle, or bridle. Servant he had none. Federalist as he was in politics, in his manners and habits he was truly republican. Would that all republicans were like him in this respect! He was fond of agriculture, and to gratify himself, and for the sake of exercise, he purchased a small farm a few miles from Richmond, to which he often went. On one of my visits to Richmond, being in a street near his house, between daybreak and sunrise one morning, I met him on horseback, with a bag of clover-seed lying before him, which he was carrying to his farm, it being the time of sowing such seed. But the most interesting and striking feature in the domestic character of this truly great and good man was the tender and assiduous attentions paid to his afflicted companion. Mrs. Marshall was nervous in the extreme. The least noise was sometimes agony to her whole frame, and his perpetual endeavour was to keep the house and yard and outhouses as free as possible from the slightest cause of distressing her; walking himself at times about the house and yard without shoes. On one occasion, when she was in her most distressing state, the town authorities of Richmond manifested their great respect for him, and sympathy for her, by having either the town-clock or town-bell muffled. I am sure that every Virginian will excuse this digression.*

---

* The strength as well as tenderness of Judge Marshall's attachment to Mrs. Marshall will appear from the following affecting tribute to her memory, written by himself, December 25, 1832:—

"This day of joy and festivity to the whole Christian world is, to my sad heart, the anniversary of the keenest affliction which humanity can sustain. While all

I have nothing more to say of Leeds parish, but that during the few years of Mr. Lemmon's stay at Hagerstown, the Rev. Mr.

---

around is gladness, my mind dwells on the silent tomb, and cherishes the remembrance of the beloved object which it contains.

"On the 25th of December, 1831, it was the will of Heaven to take to itself the companion who had sweetened the choicest part of my life, had rendered toil a pleasure, had partaken of all my feelings, and was enthroned in the inmost recess of my heart. Never can I cease to feel the loss and to deplore it. Grief for her is too sacred ever to be profaned on this day, which shall be, during my existence, marked by a recollection of her virtues.

"On the 3d of January, 1783, I was united by the holiest bonds to the woman I adored. From the moment of our union to that of our separation, I never ceased to thank Heaven for this its best gift. Not a moment passed in which I did not consider her as a blessing from which the chief happiness of my life was derived. This never-dying sentiment, originating in love, was cherished by a long and close observation of as amiable and estimable qualities as ever adorned the female bosom. To a person which in youth was very attractive, to manners uncommonly pleasing, she added a fine understanding, and the sweetest temper which can accompany a just and modest sense of what was due to herself. She was educated with a profound reverence for religion, which she preserved to her last moments. This sentiment, among her earliest and deepest impressions, gave a colouring to her whole life. Hers was the religion taught by the Saviour of man. She was a firm believer in the faith inculcated by the Church (Episcopal) in which she was bred.

"I have lost her, and with her have lost the solace of my life! Yet she remains still the companion of my retired hours, still occupies my inmost bosom. When alone and unemployed, my mind still recurs to her. More than a thousand times since the 25th of December, 1831, have I repeated to myself the beautiful lines written by General Burgoyne, under a similar affliction, substituting 'Mary' for 'Anna:'—

" 'Encompass'd in an angel's frame,
        An angel's virtues lay;
Too soon did Heaven assert its claim
        And take its own away !
My Mary's worth, my Mary's charms,
        Can never more return !
What now shall fill these widow'd arms ?
        Ah me ! my Mary's urn !
        Ah me ! ah me ! my Mary's urn !' "

As to the religious opinions of Judge Marshall, the following extract from a letter of the Rev. Mr. Norwood may be entirely relied on :—

"I have read some remarks of yours in regard to Chief-Justice Marshall, which have suggested to me to communicate to you the following facts, which may be useful should you again publish any thing in relation to his religious opinions. I often visited Mrs. General Harvey during her last illness. From her I received this statement. She was much with her father during the last months of his life, and told me that the reason why he never communed was, that he was a Unitarian in opinion, though he never joined their society. He told her that he believed in the truth of the Christian revelation, but not in the divinity of Christ; therefore he could not commune in the Episcopal Church. But during the last months of his life he read Keith on Prophecy, where our Saviour's divinity is incidentally treated, and was

Barnes took his place both in Leeds and Hamilton, and that after Mr. Lemmon's death the Rev. Mr. Slaughter officiated in Leeds parish in conjunction with Upperville and Middleburg. At Mr. Slaughter's resignation of the charge, the Rev. Wm. H. Pendleton became the minister, and so continued until the year 1854. The present minister is the Rev. Mr. Callaway. The parish has recently been subdivided. There are two new churches under the care of the Rev. Mr. Shields, in the part recently cut off, and one in the other under the care of Mr. Callaway. An excellent parsonage is now being built.

---

convinced by his work, and the fuller investigation to which it led, of the supreme divinity of the Saviour. He determined to apply for admission to the Communion of our Church,—objected to commune in private, because he thought it his duty to make a public confession of the Saviour,—and, while waiting for improved health to enable him to go to the church for that purpose, he grew worse and died, without ever communing. Mrs. Harvey was a lady of the strictest probity, the most humble piety, and of a clear discriminating mind, and her statement, the substance of which I give you accurately, (having reduced it to writing,) may be entirely relied on.

"I remember to have heard Bishop Moore repeatedly express his surprise (when speaking of Judge Marshall) that, though he was so punctual in his attendance at church, and reproved Mr. ——, and Mr. ——, and Mr. ——, when they were absent, and knelt during the prayers and responded fervently, yet he never communed. The reason was that which he gave to his daughter, Mrs. Harvey. She said he died an humble, penitent believer in Christ, according to the orthodox creed of the Church.

"Very truly, your friend and brother in Christ,   WM. NORWOOD.

"P.S.—Another fact, illustrating the lasting influence of maternal instruction, was mentioned by Mrs. Harvey. Her father told her that he never went to bed without concluding his prayer with those which his mother taught him when a child,—viz.: the Lord's Prayer and the prayer beginning, 'Now I lay me down to sleep.' "

ARTICLE LXVII.

Truro Parish, Fairfax County.

FAIRFAX county was separated from Prince William in the year 1742, and at first embraced Loudon county. The whole of this was covered with Truro parish.* In 1749, Cameron parish was cut off from it, and was afterward in Loudon, when that county was separated from Fairfax in 1757. The parish of Truro was again divided in the year 1764. In the years 1754, 1758, and 1764, I have evidence that the Rev. Chas. Green was the minister of Truro parish, and probably lived in the neighbourhood of Gunston, the seat of the Mason family, near which stood the old church which was superseded by Pohick or Mount Vernon Church. Mr. George Mason makes mention of him in a letter dated 1764. I think it probable General Washington also mentions the same person as visiting Mount Vernon in 1760, when Mrs. Washington was sick. How long he may have been the minister after 1764, I cannot ascertain. He was succeeded by the Rev. Lee Massey, either in or before the year 1767, as that is the date of one of his sermons preached at the Old Pohick Church. He was also in the parish as minister in the year 1785, as I find from the date of a sermon preached at the present Pohick Church, which was built during his ministry, of which I possess the proof. How long he ministered after this, I am unable to say. Mr. Massey was a lawyer previous to his engaging in the ministry, and was ordained by the Bishop of London

---

* A curious circumstance in relation to the first movements of this parish is recorded in the fifth volume of Henning, pp. 274-275. The Act of Assembly is as follows:—" Whereas, it is represented to this Assembly, that divers of the inhabitants of the parish of Truro, in the county of Fairfax, do now and for several years past have acted as vestrymen of the said parish, although many of them were never lawfully chosen or qualified; that several pretending to act as vestrymen are not able to read or write, and, under a colour of being lawfully chosen, have taken upon themselves to hold vestries, and imposed many hardships on the inhabitants of the said parish: for remedy thereof be it enacted," &c. The Act proceeds to order a new election, though ratifying the levies of the pretended vestry. As Laurence Washington, the elder brother of the General, William Fairfax, George Mason, and his father, of Gunston, and others of character and education, were then in the parish, and soon after were vestrymen, we presume that the condemned act was done in some other part of the county.

for Virginia in 1766.   His sermons evince talent and are sound in
doctrine, but, like most of that day, want evangelical life and
spirit, and would never rouse lost sinners to a sense of their condition.   He was a man of great wit and humour, the indulgence
of which was the fault of many of the clergy of that day.   The
following account of a dispute between himself and his vestry
has been sent me, and illustrates his character.   The clerk whom
Mr. Massey had selected was unacceptable to the vestry, and in order
to get rid of him they give him no salary or a very small one.   Mr.
Massey complaining, the vestry met and passed two resolutions :—
1st. That the minister had a right to choose his clerk; 2d. That
the vestry had a right to fix his salary.   In a letter to the vestry
Mr. Massey descanted on these resolutions with severity, and thus
concluded :—" And now, gentlemen, as to the knowing ones among
you,—and I admit there are such,—I would say, ' *humanum est
errare;*' and, as to the rest of you, '*ne sutor ultra crepidam.*' "
Mr. Massey was a native of King George.   His mother was an
Alexander.   He lived to his eighty-sixth year, and died in 1814.
He had, however, ceased from the ministry for many years before his
death.   The old families had left the neighbourhood or the Church.
General Washington, at the close of the war, had fully connected
himself with Christ Church, Alexandria, and Pohick was deserted
or only attended occasionally by some ministers of whom I shall
presently speak.   Before taking leave of Mr. Massey, I will adduce
the proof that was mentioned that Mount Vernon or Pohick Church
was built during his ministry, and not at the much earlier date as
supposed by some.   A friend has furnished me the following statement :—

" The date of its erection is inscribed on and near the head of one of the
columns forming part of the ornamental work of the chancel, in the following manner :—' 1773.   W. B., sculptor.' "

The date is also further established by a deed recorded in the
county court, of which I have a copy.   It is a deed from the vestry
of a pew in the church to Mr. Massey and his successors.

" A deed from the vestry of Truro parish, in the county of Fairfax, to
wit :—George Washington, Geo. Mason, Daniel McCarty, Alexander Henderson, Thomas Ellzey, Thomas Withers Coffer, Peter Waggener, Thomas
Ford, Martin Cockburn, William Triplett, William Payne, Jr., John Barry,
John Gunnell, and Thomas Triplett, to Lee Massey, dated 25th of February, 1774, recite that, whereas, in the new church lately built near
Pohick, the vestry have set apart one of the pews,—viz.: the one next

the pulpit, on the east side thereof, and adjoining the north front wall of the church, for the use of the said Lee Massey, (now rector,) of the said parish, and his successors.

"Teste,   ALFRED MOSS."

We have in this document not only a witness to the age of the present Pohick Church, but a list of the vestrymen of that day. We have seen a printed list of the vestry of Truro and Fairfax parishes in the year 1765,—just after the division,—in which are some other names belonging to the neighbourhood of Pohick,—as George Wm. Fairfax, Edward Blackburn, William Lynton, William Gardiner, &c. It comes from a leaf, it is said, of the old Pohick vestry-book, which has by some means gotten into the Historical Society of New York. Of the vestry-book itself I can hear no tidings. In the year 1785, I find the name of George Washington, in his own handwriting,—not as a vestryman, but as a pew-holder and subscriber,—in the vestry-book of Christ Church, Alexandria. After this he seldom, if ever, attended at Pohick.

It will be expected that I should say something concerning the tradition as to the part which Washington took in the location of Pohick Church. The following account is probably the correct one. The Old Pohick Church was a frame building, and occupied a site on the south side of Pohick Run, and about two miles from the present, which is on the north side of the run. When it was no longer fit for use, it is said the parishioners were called together to determine on the locality of the new church, when George Mason, the compatriot of Washington, and senior vestryman, advocated the old site, pleading that it was the house in which their fathers worshipped, and that the graves of many were around it, while Washington and others advocated a more central and convenient one. The question was left unsettled and another meeting for its decision appointed. Meanwhile Washington surveyed the neighbourhood, and marked the houses and distances on a well-drawn map, and, when the day of decision arrived, met all the arguments of his opponent by presenting this paper, and thus carried his point. In place of any description of this house in its past or present condition, I offer the following report of a visit made to it in 1837:—

"My next visit was to Pohick Church, in the vicinity of Mount Vernon, the seat of General Washington. I designed to perform service there on Saturday as well as Sunday, but through some mistake no notice was given for the former day. The weather indeed was such as to prevent the assembling of any but those who prize such occasions so much as to be deterred only by very strong considerations. It was still raining when I approached the house, and found no one there. The wide-open doors invited me to enter,—as they do invite, day and night, through the year, not only the passing traveller, but every beast of the field and fowl of the air. These latter, however, seem to have reverenced the house of God, since few marks of their pollution are to be seen throughout it. The interior of the house, having been well built, is still good. The chancel, Communion-table, and tables of the law, &c. are still there and in good order. The roof only is decaying; and at the time I was there the rain was dropping on these sacred places and on other parts of the house. On the doors of the pews, in gilt letters, are still to be seen the names of the principal families which once occupied them. How could I, while for at least an hour traversing those long aisles, entering the sacred chancel, ascending the lofty pulpit, forbear to ask, And is this the house of God which was built by the Washingtons, the Masons, the McCartys, the Grahams, the Lewises, the Fairfaxes?—the house in which they used to worship the God of our fathers according to the venerable forms of the Episcopal Church,—and some of whose names are yet to be seen on the doors of those now deserted pews? Is this also destined to moulder piecemeal away, or, when some signal is given, to become the prey of spoilers, and to be carried hither and thither and applied to every purpose under heaven?

"Surely patriotism, or reverence for the greatest of patriots, if not religion, might be effectually appealed to in behalf of this one temple of God. The particular location of it is to be ascribed to Washington, who, being an active member of the vestry when it was under consideration and in dispute where it should be placed, carefully surveyed the whole parish, and, drawing an accurate and handsome map of it with his own hand, showed clearly where the claims of justice and the interests of religion required its erection."

"It was to this church that Washington for some years regularly repaired, at a distance of six or seven miles, never permitting any company to prevent the regular observance of the Lord's day. And shall it now be permitted to sink into ruin for want of a few hundred dollars to arrest the decay already begun? The families which once worshipped there are indeed nearly all gone, and those who remain are not competent to its complete repair. But there are immortal beings around it, and not far distant from it, who might be forever blessed by the word faithfully preached therein.

"The poor shall never fail out of any land, and to them the Gospel ought to be preached.

"For some years past one of the students in our Theological Seminary has acted as lay reader in it, and occasionally a professor has added his services. Within the last year the Rev. Mr. Johnson, residing in the neighbourhood, has performed more frequent duties there.

"On the day following the one which has given rise to the above, I preached to a very considerable congregation in this old church, one-third of which was made up of coloured persons. The sacrament was then administered to twenty persons. If I should ever be permitted to visit this house again, it must be under circumstances far more cheering, or far more gloomy, than those which attended my recent visit."

I am happy to say that this report led the Rev. Mr. Johnson to its use, in a circular, by means of which he raised fifteen hundred dollars, with which a new roof and ceiling and other repairs were put on it, by which it has been preserved from decay and fitted for such occasional services as are performed there. A friend, who has recently visited it, informs me that many of the doors of the pews are gone. Those of George Washington and George Mason are not to be found,—perhaps borne away as relics. Those of George William Fairfax, Martin Cockburn, Daniel McCarty, William Payne, and the rector's, are still standing and their names legible. Of Martin Cockburn and Mrs. Cockburn, intimate friends of George Mason, we have heard a high character for piety and benevolence. Mr. Cockburn was from the West Indies, and Mrs. Cockburn was a Miss Bronaugh, a relative of the Masons, of Gunston. They left no children to inherit and perpetuate their virtues and graces. The family of Mason has long adhered to Old Gunston, near which was the Old Pohick. The following account, from one of the family, will be interesting to its members and friends. The first of the family who came to Virginia was Colonel George Mason, who was a member of the British Parliament in the reign of Charles the First. In Parliament he opposed with great eloquence the arbitrary measures of the King, but when the civil war commenced he drew his sword on the side of the King and was an officer in Charles the Second's army, and commanded a regiment of horse. When the King's army was defeated at Worcester by Oliver Cromwell in 1651, he disguised himself, and was concealed by some peasants until he got an opportunity to embark for America. He had considerable possessions in Staffordshire, (though the family was of old a Warwickshire one,) where he was born and generally lived; all of which were lost. A younger brother embarked with him, and they arrived and landed in Norfolk, Virginia. The younger brother, William, married and died at or near Norfolk. He left a son, who went to Boston and settled. His female descendants married among the Thoroughgoods, and that family was for a long time in Princess Anne,—perhaps may be now. Colonel George Mason went up the Potomac and settled at Accotink, near Pasbytanzy, where he died and was buried. He called the county

Stafford, after his native county in England. Such at least is the probable conjecture. This is the George Mason who, in another place, we have spoken of as being, with his wife and Colonel Brent, sponsor in baptism for a young Indian chief whom they took prisoner in Maryland. Our notice was taken from one of the early Tracts, republished by Peter Force, and which is ascribed to Mr. Mason himself. The Mason family intermarried with the Brents, Fitzhughs, and Thompsons at an early period, and afterward with the McCartys, Bronaughs, Grahams, and many others.

Of one branch of this family, in connection with another old family of Virginia, I have something to say. There was at Hampton, in Elizabeth City county, an old Episcopal family by the name of Westwood. A daughter of one member of it, Elizabeth Westwood, married a Mr. Wallace. At his death she married John Thompson Mason, who settled at Chappawamsic, in Stafford county. She was the mother of Mr. Temple Mason, of Loudoun, and other children, among whom was a daughter named Euphan, who married Mr. Bailey Washington, of Stafford. At the death of her husband, Mr. Washington, she married Mr. Brent, and lived and died at Park Gate, in Prince William county. She had many children. Among them was a daughter, who married first Mr. McCrae, then Mr. Storke, of Fredericksburg. Her daughter Euphan married Mr. Roy, of Matthews. This is mentioned as introductory to some extracts from a few letters of old Mrs. Mason to her son, Temple Mason, of Leesburg, showing the earnest desire she had for the religious welfare of her children. From a letter of her grand-daughter, Mrs. Storke, I learn that she was living at the time of her death at Dumfries, in Prince William county. She was one of those old-fashioned Virginia ladies who, like Mrs. General Washington and Solomon's model of a lady, not only superintended the labours of her servants, but worked with her own hands. This she did until within a few days of her death. But her soul was much more actively engaged with God. While it was possible, she bent her knees daily before God, even when it was thought improper to attempt it. Among her last words were the following:—"*Certainly, certainly*, I can see no other way than that of Christ crucified." "Christ is my all in all."

Let the following sentences, from a letter to her son Temple in 1816, sink deep into the hearts of all her descendants. After exhorting him earnestly to attend at once to personal religion, by reading the Scriptures, and prayer, and attendance on public worship, she thus concludes:—

"Have no work done on the Sabbath more than is necessary to be done. Have your victuals cooked on Saturday. Give your poor slaves who work in the field, Saturday to sell what they make, that they may have it in their power to go to worship on Sunday. Attend to your dear children. Bring them up in the fear of the Lord. He requires it of you to teach them their prayers. Set them an example, by having family worship for them and your servants. Pray for faith: it is the gift of God. He will hear our prayers, if we ask in faith. Oh that the Lord Almighty and my blessed Saviour may awaken you and open the eyes of your understanding, while you are reading these lines, and bring you to consider what will make for your everlasting salvation. Oh, if you did but know what your aged mother feels for you and the rest of her children and grandchildren, how much she implores the mercy of God with daily fervent prayer, that he would of his great love and pity convert you all," &c.

In two other letters, one of them dated in 1818, she writes in the same earnest strain. One of them to her son Temple, whom she addresses, "My dear child," thus concludes:—"O my blessed God, of thy great mercy, grant, while you are reading these lines, that you may consider and turn and seek him and find him. Oh, what a joy it would give your aged mother to hear or see that you were converted!"

That the prayers of this aged woman were heard in behalf of one of her grandchildren, all who knew Mrs. Henry Magill, of Leesburg, will be ready to believe.

Among the families which belonged to Pohick Church was that of Mr. Lawrence Lewis, the nephew of General Washington, the son of his sister Betty, who married Mr. Lewis. Mr. Lawrence Lewis married Miss Custis, the grand-daughter of Mrs. Washington. In many of the pictures of the Washington family she may be seen, as a girl, in a groupe with the General, Mrs. Washington, and her brother Washington Parke Custis. There were two other full-sisters, who married Mr. Law and Mr. Peter. Mrs. Custis, the widow of Mr. Washington's son, married again. Her second husband was Dr. David Steuart, first of Hope Park, and then of Ossian Hall, Fairfax county. He was the son and grandson of the two Mr. Steuarts who were ministers in King George for so long a period. They had a numerous offspring. The residence of Mr Lawrence Lewis was a few miles only from Mount Vernon, and was called Woodlawn. After the desertion of Pohick they also attended in Alexandria, and some time after the establishment of St. Paul's congregation, and the settlement of Dr. Wilmer in it, they united themselves to it, and were much esteemed by Dr. Wilmer, as he was by them. After some years they removed to an estate near Berryville, in what was then Frederick, now Clarke county. Mr. Lewis was one of the most amiable of men by nature, and became a sincere Christian, and a communicant of our Church. His person was tall and commanding, and his face full of benignity, as was his whole character. I wish some of our friends at a distance could have seen him in the position I once beheld him in the church at Berryville, when I was administering the Holy Communion. Some of his servants were members of the church in that place, and on that day one of them came up after the white members had communed. It so happened that Mr. Lewis himself had not communed, but came up and knelt by the side of his servant, feeling no doubt that one God made them and one Saviour redeemed them. Mrs. Lewis was also a zealous member of the Church, a lady of fine mind and education, and very popular in her manners. Like her grandmother, she knew the use of her hands, and few ladies in the land did more with them for all Church and charitable purposes, even to the last days of a long life. They had three children. Their son, Lorenzo, married a Miss Coxe, of Philadelphia, and settled on the estate in Clarke, but died some years since. The two daughters married, the one Mr. Conrad, of New Orleans, and the other Mr. Butler, of Mississippi or Louisiana. A numerous posterity is descending from them.*

---

* The Lewis family of Eastern Virginia is of Welsh origin. Their ancestor, General Robert Lewis, (whose name is favourably mentioned in English history,) came from Wales to Gloucester county, Virginia, in the latter part of the seventeenth century, and there lived and died. His son Robert, who also lived and died in Gloucester, had three sons,—Fielding, John, and Charles. Of the two last I have received no account. Mr. Fielding Lewis, of Wyanoke, Charles City county, was doubtless a descendant of one of them. Colonel Fielding Lewis, son of the second Robert, removed to Fredericksburg early in life, was a merchant of high standing and wealth, a vestryman, magistrate, and burgess, and during the Revolution, being a genuine patriot, superintended the manufacture of arms in the neighbourhood. He was twice married. His first wife was the cousin and his second the sister of General Washington. One child only, out of three by his first wife, lived to any considerable age. His name was John. He moved to Kentucky, and left a posterity there. The children of Colonel Lewis by his second wife, Betty Washington, were six,—Fielding, George, Elizabeth, Lawrence, Robert, and Howell. Fielding died in Fairfax county, leaving descendants. Elizabeth married Mr. Charles Carter, and was one of the most interesting and exemplary of Christians. George was captain in Baylor's regiment, and commander of General Washington's life-guard. In his arms General Mercer expired on the field of battle at Princeton. Toward the close of the war he married and settled near Berryville in Old Frederick, and took an interest in the affairs of the Church in that parish. After some years he removed to Fredericksburg, and from thence to King George, dying at his seat, Marmion, in 1821. He enjoyed the highest confidence of General Washington, being sent by him on a secret expedition of great importance to Canada. Mr.

There were other families who belonged to this parish and church, but I am not possessed of information to enable me to speak of them as I could wish. The Chichesters, the Footes and Tripletts, were, I am told, the last to leave it. The following letter from my friend, General Henderson, of Washington, gives some notice of his father, Alexander Henderson, who was one of the vestry of Pohick Church who signed the deed of a pew to Rev. Mr. Massey:—

"WASHINGTON, 5th of February, 1857.

"MY DEAR SIR:—I received yours this morning. My father, Alexander Henderson, came to this country from Scotland in the year 1756, and settled first as a merchant in Colchester. During the Revolutionary War he retired to a farm in Fairfax county to avoid the possibility of falling into the hands of the English, as he had taken a decided part on the side of freedom against the mother-country. About 1787 or 1788 he removed to Dumfries. He died in the latter part of 1815, leaving six sons and four daughters, all grown. John, Alexander, and James emigrated to Western Virginia, and settled as farmers in Wood county. Richard and Thomas were known to you, the former living in Leesburg and the latter for the last twenty years being in the medical department of the army. James and myself are the only surviving sons. Two of my sisters—Mrs. Anne Henderson and Mrs. Margaret Wallace—are still alive. My sisters Jane and Mary died many years ago. The latter married Mr. Inman Horner, of Warrenton. All the members of the family have been, with scarce an exception, steady Episcopalians."

Of Mr. Richard Henderson, of Leesburg, Dr. Thomas Henderson, and the sisters, I need not speak to the inhabitants of Leesburg and Warrenton, where they were so well known as the props of our Church. The author of the letter from which I have extracted has long been a communicant and active vestryman of the Church in Washington.

I have said that after the Revolution, when General Washington changed his attendance from Pohick to Alexandria, and others left the parish, regular services ceased in that part of the county. Mr. Massey either relinquished services because none attended, or from some other cause, although he lived many years after. The Rev.

_____

Lawrence Lewis, of whom we have spoken above, was aid to General Morgan, in his expedition to the West to quell the insurrection in Pennsylvania. Mr. Robert Lewis, the fourth son of Colonel Fielding Lewis, was the private secretary of General Washington during a part of his Presidential term. In the year 1791, he took up his residence in Fredericksburg, where as private citizen, as mayor of the town, and as a communicant of the Episcopal Church, he was universally esteemed and beloved. His daughter Judith married the Rev. E. C. McGuire, who has so long been the minister of the Episcopal Church in Fredericksburg. Mr. Howell, the fifth and last son of Colonel Fielding Lewis, moved to Kanawha county, where some of his posterity still reside.

Mr. Weems, in his books, announces himself as the rector of this parish after this period. If some may, by comparison, be called "nature's noblemen," he might surely have been pronounced one of "nature's oddities." Whether in private or public, in prayers or preaching, it was impossible that either the young or old, the grave or the gay, could keep their risible faculties from violent agitation. To suppose him to have been a kind of private chaplain to such a man as Washington, as has been the impression of some, is the greatest of incongruities. But I wish to do him ample justice. Although his name never appears on the journals of any of our Conventions, and cannot be found on the lists of those ordained for Virginia or Maryland by the Bishop of London, so that a doubt has been entertained whether he ever was ordained a minister of our Church, yet I have ascertained that to be a fact. We presume that he was from Maryland, as there are or were persons of that name there, who were said to be his relatives. We will give him credit for much benevolence, much of what Sterne called the milk of human kindness, and of which Mr. Weems delighted to speak in his sermons and writings. In proof of our disposition to do him ample justice, we present the following account of his boyhood in Maryland, which has been given us by one who knew him :—

" In his youth Mr. Weems was an inmate of the family of Mr. Jenifer, of Charles county, Maryland. They confided in him as a boy of principle, and had no doubt as to his uprightness and morality until about his fourteenth year. When at that age he was seen to leave the house every evening after tea and to be often away until late at night. The family began to be afraid that he was getting into corrupt habits, and, notwithstanding his assurance that he would do nothing that would render him unworthy of their esteem and friendship, they felt uneasy. He scorned the idea of abusing their confidence, but, as he persisted in the practice of going away, at length they determined to find out what was the cause of it. Accordingly one night a plan was laid by which he was tracked. After pursuing his trail for some distance into the pines, they came to an old hut, in which was young Weems, surrounded by the bareheaded, barefooted, and half-clad children of the neighbourhood, whom he had been in the habit of thus gathering around him at night, in order to give them instruction."

I acknowledge that he was in the habit of having the servant, assembled in private houses, where he would spend the night, and would recite a portion of Scripture, for he never read it out of the book, and perhaps say something to them, or in the prayer about them, but then it was in such a way as only to produce merriment. This I have experienced in my own family and at my mother's, and have heard others testify to the same. I do not think he could have long even pretended to be the rector of any parish. From my earliest knowledge of him he was a travelling bookseller for Mr. Matthew Carey, of Philadelphia, visiting all the States south of Pennsylvania, and perhaps some north of it, in a little wagon, with his fiddle as a constant companion to amuse himself and others. If he would pray with the servants at night in their owners' houses, he would play the fiddle for them on the roadside by day. One instance of his good-nature is well attested. At the old tavern in Caroline county, Virginia, called the White Chimneys, Mr. Weems and some strolling players or puppet-showmen met together one night. A notice of some exhibition had been given, and the neighbours had assembled to witness it. A fiddle was necessary to the full performance, and that was wanting. Mr. Weems supplied the deficiency.

He was of a very enlarged charity in all respects. Though calling himself an Episcopal minister, he knew no distinction of Churches. He preached in every pulpit to which he could gain access, and where he could recommend his books. His books were of all kinds. Mr. Carey, his employer, was a Roman Catholic, but dealt in all manner of books. On an election or court-day at Fairfax Court-House, I once, in passing to or from the upper country, found Mr. Weems, with a bookcaseful for sale, in the portico of the tavern. On looking at them I saw Paine's "Age of Reason," and, taking it into my hand, turned to him, and asked if it was possible that he could sell such a book. He immediately took out the Bishop of Llandaff's answer, and said, "Behold the antidote. The bane and antidote are both before you." He carried this spurious charity into his sermons. In my own pulpit at the old chapel, in my absence, it being my Sunday in Winchester, he extolled Tom Paine and one or more noted infidels in America, and said if their ghosts could return to the earth they would be shocked to hear the falsehoods which were told of them. I was present the following day, when my mother charged him with what she had heard of his sermon, and well remember that even he was confused and speechless. Some of Mr. Weems's pamphlets on drunkenness and gambling would be most admirable in their effects, but for the fact that you know not what to believe of the narrative. There are passages of deep pathos and great eloquence in them. His histories of Washington and Marion are very popular, but the same must be said of them. You know not how much of fiction there is in them. That of Washington has probably gone through more editions than all others, and has been read by more persons than those of Marshall, Ramsey,

Bancroft, and Irving, put together. To conclude,—all the while that Mr. Weems was thus travelling over the land, an object of amusement to so many, and of profit to Mr. Carey, he was transmitting support to his interesting and pious family, at or near Dumfries, who, if I am rightly informed, were attached to the Methodist Church. If in this, or any thing else which I have written, any mistake has been made, I should be glad to receive its correction.

There were three other ministers who occasionally preached at Pohick, and visited Mount Vernon after the death of General and Mrs. Washington, of whom a few words must be said. But, before these few are said, it is proper to speak of the change which took place at Mount Vernon by the death of its illustrious owners. It is well known that Judge Bushrod Washington, the son of General Washington's brother John, inherited Mount Vernon. He was in full communion with the Church when I first became acquainted with him in 1812, having no doubt united himself with it in Philadelphia under Bishop White, while attending the Supreme Court in that place. I know that he was intimate with Bishop White and highly esteemed him. Judge Washington attended one or more of our earliest Conventions in Richmond and was a punctual member of the Standing Committee from that time until his death. He married into the family of Blackburns, of Ripon Lodge, not many miles from Dumfries, and perhaps twelve from Mount Vernon. The first Richard Blackburn of whom our vestry-books speak married a daughter of the Rev. James Scott, of Dumfries. His son was, I believe, the father of Mrs. Bushrod Washington, Mrs. Henry Turner, of Jefferson, Mr. Richard and Thomas Blackburn. The family at Ripon Lodge had long been the main support of the church at Dumfries and Centreville, and their house the resort of the clergy. I have before me a paper drawn up in 1812 for the support of the Rev. Charles O'Neill. The first and highest subscriber is Mr. Thomas Blackburn, who was, I believe, the husband of our excellent friend Mrs. Blackburn, who lived near Berryville for many of the last years of her life. His subscription is fifty dollars. The next highest is that of a Mr. Edmund Denny, twenty-five dollars. The next Dr. Humphrey Peake, for twenty dollars. All the rest much less. Old Mrs. Blackburn, with her four grand-daughters,—Jane, Polly, Christian, and Judy Blackburn,—daughters of Mr. Richard Blackburn, were much at Mount Vernon. I became acquainted with them during the years 1812 and 1813, while I was ministering in Alexandria. They were the first-fruits of my ministry in that place, and very dear to me. Two of them—Jane and Polly—married nephews of Judge Washington, and settled in Jefferson. One of them—Judy—married Mr. Gustavus Alexander, of King George, and the fourth—Christian—died unmarried. By my intimacy with these four most estimable ladies and with Mrs. Blackburn and her sister, Mrs. Taylor, I have from time to time become acquainted with the state of things at Ripon Lodge and Mount Vernon as to the clergy. The Rev. Mr. Kemp and the Rev. Mr. Moscrope occasionally officiated at Dumfries and Pohick, and perhaps at Centreville, for the want of those who were better. But in order to conceal the shame of the clergy from the younger ones, and to prevent their loss of attachment to religion and the Church, the elder ones had sometimes to hurry them away to bed or take them away from the presence of these ministers when indulging too freely in the intoxicating cup. The doctrine of total abstinence in families, of banishing wine and spirits from the cellar and the table, was not thought of then in the best of families. If the minister chose it, he must drink. The third and last minister, and who died, I think, in 1813, was the Rev. Charles O'Neill, who was an improvement on the two last. The families at Mount Vernon and Ripon Lodge were fond of him. He always spent his Christmas at Mount Vernon, and on those occasions was dressed in a full suit of velvet, which General Washington had left behind, and which had been given to Mr. O'Neill. But as General Washington was tall and well proportioned in all his parts, and Mr. O'Neill was peculiarly formed, being of uncommon length of body and brevity of legs, it was difficult to make the clothes of the one, even though altered, sit well upon the other.*

---

* In speaking of Mount Vernon, it might be expected that I should say something of this venerable house and beautiful place, and the Washington vault, and that I should have an appropriate pictorial representation of the same; but, as they are to be read of and their similitudes seen in so many books, I shall refer my readers to those books. There was, however, one object of interest belonging to General Washington, concerning which I have a special right to speak,—viz.: his old English coach, in which himself and Mrs. Washington not only rode in Fairfax county, but travelled through the length and breadth of our land. So faithfully was it executed that, at the conclusion of this long journey, its builder, who came over with it and settled in Alexandria, was proud to be told by the General that not a nail or screw had failed. It so happened, in a way I need not state, that this coach came into my hands about fifteen years after the death of General Washington. In the course of time, from disuse, it being too heavy for these latter days, it began to decay and give way. Becoming an object of desire to those who delight in relics, I caused it to be taken to pieces and distributed among the admiring friends of Washington who visited my house, and also among a number of female associations for benevolent

I am happy to be able to add to this article the following extracts from two letters of my old college friend, Colonel Stoddert, of Wycomico House, Maryland, concerning his grandfather, the Rev. Lee Massey:—

"My grandfather I remember well. He died in 1814, at the age of eighty-six, a rare instance of physical and mental vigour for so advanced an age. He was the friend and companion of Washington from early youth, and the legal adviser and friend of George Mason. He commenced life a lawyer,—having pursued his studies in the office of George Johnston, Esq., than whom an abler lawyer was not to be found in the Northern Neck of Virginia. He married the daughter of Mr. Johnston, and began his professional career with every prospect of success, but retired when a young man, because his 'conscience would not suffer him to make the worse appear the better reason,' and to uphold wrong against right. He tried to follow in the lead of Chancellor Wythe, to examine cases placed in his care and to accept the good and reject the bad. It proved a failure, and he withdrew from practice. He was afterward appointed a judge, but declined it as taking him too much from his family. He recommended to me to read law, but earnestly opposed my pursuing it as a vocation. He often said Mr. Wythe was the only ' honest lawyer he ever knew.'

"General Washington, Mr. Mason, Fairfax, McCarty, ——, Chichester, and others urged him to study divinity and become their pastor. He yielded to their counsels and was ordained in London,—Beilby Porteus, Lord-Bishop of London, assisting in the ordination. I have heard him speak of the high oratorical powers of Dr. Dodd, who then preached in the Queen's Chapel, and describe the personal appearance of George III. and his Queen. He witnessed the performances of the famous Garrick, and thought he deserved the high fame he had won. All the clergy of the Church of England then attended the theatre. The loss of his fore-teeth impairing his speech was the cause of his ceasing to preach. He then studied medicine as a means of relieving the poor, and announced that he would practise without charge. He said he was soon sent for by all classes, and he had to withdraw altogether and confine his medical aid to giving advice and medicine at his office ; and, of course, with few exceptions, his advice was given only in cases of children brought to him. His conversation was rich with anecdotes and reminiscences of the distinguished men of Virginia, and of social customs and manners before the Revolution. He had read deeply the great volume of human nature, and was a good judge of character. He loved virtue, and hated vice intensely, and perhaps had too little compassion for the weaknesses and infirmities of our nature. His social intercourse was influenced greatly and visibly by the moral character of the men he was brought into contact

and religious objects, which associations, at their fairs and on other occasions, made a large profit by converting the fragments into walking-sticks, picture-frames, and snuff-boxes. About two-thirds of one of the wheels thus produced one hundred and forty dollars. There can be no doubt but that at its dissolution it yielded more to the cause of charity than it did to its builder at its first erection. Besides other mementos of it, I have in my study, in the form of a sofa, the hind-seat, on which the General and his lady were wont to sit.

with. His manner was an index to his opinions of those he was with in this respect; and often he would admonish persons of their vices. His integrity and honour were of the highest order, and he detested all meanness and double-dealing with his whole heart. No advantage of position, or fortune, or official distinction, saved the profligate or unjust and oppressive from his open and strong denunciation; and no man had at his command a more ready wit and biting sarcasm. But goodness of life and character—though clothed in rags and despised of men—commanded not only his sympathy but open respect. From these traits, I have often heard my excellent mother express her fears that her father looked too much to good works; but my opinion is that the Christian's faith only could have produced and preserved so high a standard of morality and so keen a sense of moral duty. My grandfather was possessed of high powers of mind, and they had been well developed and cultivated. He was a ripe Latin scholar, and familiar with all the best English writers. He was remarkable for conciseness of style and condensation of matter in composition. He admired a plain and nervous as much as he disliked a florid and diffuse style: the more of the old Saxon and the less of French or Latin and Greek derivatives the better. Addison and Swift pleased him as much as Dr. Johnson displeased in this particular. He met death without fear: his last words were, 'The great mystery will soon be solved and all made plain.'

" In person he was six feet high and finely proportioned: his eyes were a deep blue, and expressive to the last, and his nose and mouth well shaped. I have often fancied that in his youth he must have possessed much manly beauty. He made his mark on his age and generation, for many traditions are preserved of him and his sayings.

" With sincere esteem and regard, yours truly,

"J. T. STODDERT.

"P.S.—In the burial-ground of one of the Episcopal churches first erected in Maryland, near the site of St. Mary's City, is a beautiful monument of Italian marble erected to the memory of the Rev. Lee Massey, by his parishioners, 'as a testimony of their grateful affection for the memory of their much-loved pastor.' It was placed there not many years after the settlement of the Colony, and is now in excellent preservation. This divine, who died in his youth, but not before he had deeply stamped his image on the heart and minds of his charge, was the uncle of my grandfather.

" The memory of the devoted zeal and piety of this young clergyman may have had its influence in determining my grandfather to enter the ministry. This, however, is mere speculation. J. T. S."

The following extract is from a second letter in answer to further inquiries:—

" In answer to your note of the 14th instant, this day received, I state that my grandfather was married three times. His first wife (my grandmother) was the daughter of George Johnston, Esq., a distinguished lawyer residing at Alexandria, with whom my grandfather read law, and who drew the resolutions against the Stamp Act,* which were moved, at his

* In ascribing the authorship of the resolutions, offered by Mr. Henry, to his distinguished ancestor, Mr. Johnston, I think it probable my friend, Mr. Stoddert, is

instance, by Patrick Henry in the Virginia Legislature in 1765. Mr. Johnston always claimed the credit of being the first man who discovered the great but hidden powers of that unrivalled orator. He had great difficulty in persuading Mr. Henry that he was the only man who was fitted to make such a speech as suited the occasion,—which would electrify the State and rouse the people to resistance. His own powers, being only argumentative, would fail to produce such an effect. Such is the history of this bold and effective movement, which, in the language of Mr. Jefferson, 'gave the first blow to the ball of Revolution.' His son George was a member of General Washington's military family as aid and confidential secretary. When ill-health compelled him to retire, Washington looked to the same family to find his successor, and selected Colonel Robert Hanson Harrison—son-in-law of Mr. Johnston, and then a practising lawyer in Alexandria, though a native of Maryland—for this delicate trust. This gentleman would have declined the appointment but for the influence of my grandfather, whose whole heart was in the struggle, and who removed the only difficulty by agreeing to receive his two orphan-daughters in his family on the footing of his own children. Colonel Harrison, after the war, returned to Maryland and was made Chief-Justice of the General Court. On the organization of the Supreme Court, President Washington selected him as one of the Associate Justices,—an appointment at first declined, as it would separate him from his daughters, whose education he was conducting, but accepted on an appeal to his duty by his old military chief, who said 'he must select by his own knowledge the officers to insure success to the new government.' He died at Bladensburg on his way to Philadelphia to take his seat on the bench. These things show the many links in the chain of friendship which bound together the hero and patriot of Mount Vernon and his pastor and early associate.

"The second wife of my grandfather was a Miss Burwell, who died nine months after marriage. She was a lady of rare excellence, and my grandfather often dwelt on her memory with the tenderest affection. His last marriage was with Miss Bronaugh, of Prince William county, by whom he had two children,—a son, who was an officer in the navy and was drowned at Norfolk, and Mrs. Triplett. I think it probable her mother was a sister of Colonel George Mason, though I cannot state it as a fact.*

---

mistaken. Mr. Wirt, in his life of Mr. Henry, says that he left the original of these resolutions, drawn on the blank leaf of an old law-book, with his will, to be opened by his executors. A copy of that original is framed, and may be seen at Red Hill, one of his places of residence in Charlotte county, and now owned by his son, John Henry. Mr. Wirt says that Mr. Henry, after having prepared the resolutions, showed them to two members of the House only,—Mr. John Fleming, of Cumberland, and George Johnston, of Fairfax. Mr. Wirt alludes to a report of the day, that they were drawn by Mr. Johnston, but says that it was unfounded. He speaks of Mr. Johnston, however, in the highest terms. The religious reflections of Mr. Henry, attached to the copy of the resolutions left behind him, are worthy of insertion in this place. As to the effects of our independence he says, "Whether it will prove a blessing or a curse will depend upon the use our people make of the blessings which a gracious God hath bestowed upon us. If they are wise, they will be great and happy. If they are of a contrary character, they will be miserable. Righteousness alone can exalt them as a nation. Reader, whoever thou art, remember this, and in thy sphere practise virtue thyself, and encourage it in others.   P. HENRY."

* She was a first-cousin of George Mason.

The Masons claimed Aunt Nancy as a cousin, and I do not know how else the relationship could originate. George Mason, the eldest son of Colonel George, married a first-cousin of my grandfather, as did Thomas Mason, a younger son. Martin Cockburn—the uncle of Admiral Cockburn, a native of Jamaica, whither his father had removed from Scotland—married a sister of this last lady. He was a fine scholar and polished gentleman and good Christian. He, a youth of eighteen years, was travelling with Dr. Cockburn in this country, when he met with Miss Bronaugh. The father objected on the score of their youth, but said if his son wished it at the age of twenty-one years, he would cheerfully assent; but the absence of three years was to intervene. Martin was faithful and constant to his first love and returned. A new difficulty then sprung up : the lady would not go to Jamaica, and the gentleman had to come to Virginia. He purchased a residence near Colonel Mason's, (an adjoining farm,) and a few miles from my grandfather, where both husband and wife lived to an advanced age. I have often heard my grandfather say that they were the only couple, he believed, who had lived fifty years together without one word, look, or act to disturb their harmony for a moment. Such was said to be the fact in their case. The courteous and affectionate attentions which each paid to the other impressed my mind when a child, and are now present to my recollection with vivid distinctness. Nothing but the gentle teachings of Him who taught as man never taught could have wrought so beautiful a picture of conjugal love, forbearance, and peace."

It should be stated that the old church, called Payne's Church, near the railroad, and a few miles from Fairfax Court-House, as well as the new one at the court-house, are both in Truro parish.

ARTICLE LXVIII.

The Religious Character of Washington.

AN interesting question in relation to Washington will now be considered,—viz.: What are the proofs of his personal piety? This work is already done to my hands by the Rev. E. C. McGuire, of Fredericksburg, from whose careful and faithful volume on the "Religious Opinions and Character of Washington" I select the following particulars. He was the child of pious parents and ancestors, was baptized in his second month,—Mr. Beverley Whiting and Captain Christopher Brooks godfathers, and Mrs. Mildred Gregory godmother,—at a time when care was taken to instruct the children in our holy religion, according to the Scriptures as set forth in the standards of the Episcopal Church. Until he had passed his eleventh year he enjoyed the superintending care of both parents, and after that of his mother and uncle. It is also believed that, besides the instructions of the parish sexton and Mr. Williams, he also sat under the ministry of the Rev. Archibald Campbell, and perhaps was for a time at his school in Washington parish, Westmoreland county. While with his mother in Fredericksburg, there can be no doubt of his receiving pious instruction from her and her minister, the Rev. Mr. Marye. While at school, he was remarkable for his abhorrence of the practice of fighting among the boys, and, if unable to prevent a contest, would inform the teacher of the design. When about thirteen years of age he drew up a number of resolutions, taken from books, or the result of his own reflections. Among them is the following:—"When you speak of God or his attributes, let it be seriously, in reverence." "Labour to keep alive in your breast that little spark of celestial fire called conscience." At the age of fifteen his filial piety was remarkably displayed in relinquishing an earnest desire to enter the navy, just when about to embark, out of a tender regard to his mother's wishes. The religious sentiments of his mother and of himself were drawn from the Bible and, Prayer-Book, and next to them, from the "Contemplations, Moral and Divine, of Sir Matthew Hale," judging from the great use which seems to have been made of this book by both of them; and in no uninspired book do we find a purer and more elevated Christianity.* Should it be said that, notwithstanding his early religious education and some indications of youthful piety, he may have fallen into the irreligion and skepticism of the age, and should proofs of his sincere belief of Christianity, as a divine revelation, be asked for, we will proceed to furnish them. At a time when so many of the chief men in France and America, and even some in England, were renouncing the Christian faith, and when he was tempted to be silent at least on the subject, in his public addresses, he seems to have taken special pains to let his sentiments be known, and to impress them upon the nation, in opposition to the skepticism of the age,—a skepticism which was sought by some leading men to be propagated with great zeal among the youth of Virginia.

In his address to the Governors of the States, dated at Head-Quarters, June, 1783, when about to surrender up his military command, speaking of the many blessings of the land, he says, *"And, above all, the pure and benign light of revelation."* He also speaks of *"that humility and pacific temper of mind which were the characteristics of the divine Author of our blessed religion."*

In his farewell address to the people of the United States, on leaving the Presidential chair, he again introduces the same subject:—*" Of all the dispositions and habits which lead to political prosperity, religion and morality are indispensable supports. A volume could not trace all their connections with private and public felicity."* He warns against the attempt to separate them, and to think that *"national morality can prevail to the exclusion of religious principles."*

No candid man can read these and other expressions, in the public addresses of Washington, without acknowledging that, as though he were the great high-priest of the nation, availing himself of his position and of the confidence reposed in him, he was raising his warning voice against that infidelity which was desolating France and threatening our own land. That Washington was regarded throughout America, both among our military and political men, as a sincere believer in Christianity, as then received among us, and a devout man, is as clear as any fact in our history. Judge Marshall, the personal friend, the military and political associate, of Washington, says, *" He was a sincere believer in the Christian faith, and a truly devout man."* Judge Boudinot, who knew him

---

* The book appears to have been much used, and has many pencil-marks in it, noting choice passages.

well during and after the Revolution, testifies to the same.   General Henry Lee, who served under him during the war, and afterward in the civil department, and who was chosen by Congress to deliver his funeral oration, says, in that oration, "First in war, first in peace, and first in the hearts of his countrymen, he was second to none in the endearing scenes of private life.   *Pious*, just, humane, temperate, and sincere,—uniform, dignified, and commanding,—his example was edifying to all around him, as were the effects of that example lasting."   Sermons and orations by divines and statesmen were delivered all over the land at the death of Washington. A large volume of such was published.   I have seen and read them, and the religious character of Washington was a most prominent feature in them; and for this there must have been some good cause.   Let the following extracts suffice.   Mr. Sewell, of New Hampshire, says:—

"To crown all these moral virtues, he had the deepest sense of religion impressed on his heart,—the true foundation-stone of all the moral virtues. He constantly attended the public worship of God on the Lord's day, was a communicant at His table, and by his devout and solemn deportment inspired every beholder with some portion of that awe and reverence for the Supreme Being, of which he felt so large a portion.   For my own part, I trust I shall never lose the impression made on my own mind in beholding in this house of prayer the venerable hero, the victorious leader of our hosts, bending in humble adoration to the God of armies and great Captain of our salvation.   Hard and unfeeling, indeed, must that heart be that could sustain the sight unmoved, or its owner depart unsoftened and unedified.   Let the deist reflect on this, and remember that Washington, the saviour of his country, did not disdain to acknowledge and adore a greater Saviour, whom deists and infidels affect to slight and despise."

Thus spake New Hampshire.   What says South Carolina? David Ramsay, the historian, says:—

"Washington was the friend of morality and religion; steadily attended on public worship; encouraged and strengthened the hands of the clergy. In all his public acts he made the most respectful mention of Providence, and, in a word, carried the spirit of piety with him, both in his private life and public administration.   He was far from being one of those *minute philosophers* who think that death is an *eternal sleep*, or of those who, trusting to the sufficiency of human reason, discard the light of divine revelation."

Mr. J. Biglow, of Boston, says:—

"In Washington religion was a steady principle of action.   After the surrender of Cornwallis he ascribes the glory to God, and orders, 'That divine service shall be performed to-morrow in the different brigades and divisions, and recommends that all the troops not on duty do assist at it with a serious deportment and that sensibility of heart which the recollection of the surprising and particular interposition of Providence in our favour claims.'"

To the foregoing I will only add, that Major William Jackson, aid-de-camp to Washington, in his address, speaks of the "milder radiance of religion and morality 'as shining in his character,' and of his being beloved and admired by the holy ministers of religion;" and that Captain Dunham of the Revolution, in his oration, says of him, "A friend to our holy religion, he was ever guided by its pious doctrines. He had embraced the tenets of the Episcopal Church; yet his charity, unbounded as his immortal mind, led him equally to respect every denomination of the followers of Jesus." The Rev. Mr. Kirkland, of Boston, says, "The virtues of our departed friend were crowned with piety. *He is known to have been habitually devout.*" We conclude with the testimony of our own Devereux Jarratt, of Virginia, whom none will suspect of flattery or low views of religion:—

"Washington was a professor of Christianity and a member of the Protestant Episcopal Church. He always acknowledged the superintendence of Divine Providence, and from his inimitable writings we find him a warm advocate for a sound morality founded on the principles of religion, the only basis on which it can stand. Nor did I ever meet with the most distant insinuation that his private life was not a comment on his admired page."

Nor was the belief of his piety confined to America. The Rev. Thomas Wilson, the pious son of the pious Bishop Wilson, of Sodor and Mann, thought he could make no more suitable present to General Washington than his father's family Bible in three volumes, with notes, and a folio volume of his father's works. The former was left by the will of General Washington to his friend the Rev. Bryan Fairfax, minister of Christ Church, Alexandria; the latter is, I presume, still in the Arlington library. From the latter I selected, forty-six years ago, a small volume of private and family prayers, as I have elsewhere stated.

If more certain proofs of personal piety in Washington be required than these general impressions and declarations of his co-evals and compatriots, founded on their observation of his public conduct, and derived from his public addresses, we proceed to furnish them. They will be taken from the testimony of those whose intimacy with his domestic habits enable them to judge, and from his own diary. As to his private devotions, of course the same kind of testimony is not to be expected as that which attests his public observances. It may most positively be affirmed, that the impression on the minds of his family was, that when on each night he regularly took his candle and went to his study at nine o'clock and remained there until ten, it was for the purpose of reading the Scriptures and prayer. It is affirmed by more than one that he has been seen there on his knees and also been heard at his prayers. In like manner it is believed, that when at five o'clock each morning, winter and summer, he went to that same study, a portion of time was then spent in the same way. It is also well known that it was the impression in the army that Washington, either in his tent or in his room, practised the same thing. One testifies to having seen him on more than one occasion thus engaged on his bended knees. It is firmly believed that when in crowded lodgings at Valley Forge, where every thing was unfavourable to private devotions, his frequent visits to a neighbouring wood were for this purpose. It is also a fact well known to the family that, when prevented from public worship, he used to read the Scriptures and other books with Mrs. Washington in her chamber.

That there was a devotional spirit in Washington, a belief in the virtue of prayer, leading to private supplication, is also rendered most probable by his conduct as an officer in seeking to have public prayer for his soldiers, and even conducting them himself in the absence of a minister.

At twenty-two years of age, when heading an expedition against the Indians, he was in the habit of having prayer in the camp at Fort Necessity, at the Great Meadows, in the Alleghany Mountains. His friend and neighbour, Mr. William Fairfax, of Belvoir, a few miles from Mount Vernon, and whose daughter, Lawrence, the elder brother of George Washington, married, thus writes to him while at the Great Meadows, and in the letter evinces not only his own pious disposition, but his confidence in that of the youthful Washington:—"I will not doubt your having public prayer in the camp, especially when the Indian families are your guests, that they, seeing your plain manner of worship, may have their curiosity to be informed why we do not use the ceremonies of the French, which, being well explained to their understandings, will more and more dispose them to receive our baptism and unite in strict bonds of cordial friendship."

In the year 1755, Washington was the volunteer aid-de-camp to General Braddock, and, though in danger of pursuit by the Indians, he did, on the night after the memorable defeat, in the absence of a chaplain, himself perform the last funeral rites over the body of Braddock, a soldier holding the candle or lighted torch while the solemn words were read. For several successive years Washington was engaged in a trying contest with the Indians, and during a considerable portion of that time—according to the testimony of one of his aids, Colonel B. Temple, of King William county— he frequently, on the Sabbath, performed divine service, reading the Scriptures and praying with them when no chaplain could be had. It was during this period that a sharp correspondence was carried on between Washington and Dinwiddie, the latter being offended at the persevering importunity of the former that a chaplain might be allowed his army. At the recall of Dinwiddie, Washington addressed the following letter to the President of the Council, who was chief in the Colony until the arrival of Governor Fauquier, saying, "The last Assembly, in their Supply Bill, provided for a chaplain to our regiment. On this subject I had often, without any success, applied to Governor Dinwiddie. I now flatter myself that your honour will be pleased to appoint a sober, serious man for this duty. Common decency, sir, in a camp, calls for the services of a divine, which ought not to be dispensed with, although the world may think us void of religion and incapable of good instructions."

In the year 1759 Colonel Washington was married, and until the Revolution lived at Mount Vernon. That he was interested in the affairs of the Church at this time is evident from what we have said as to the part he acted in relation to the building of Pohick Church. The Rev. Lee Massey was the minister during part of this time. His testimony was, "I never knew so constant an attendant at church as Washington. His behaviour in the house of God was ever so reverential that it produced the happiest effects on my congregation and greatly assisted me in my pulpit labours. No company ever kept him from church."

In the year 1774 he was sent as a Burgess to Williamsburg. It was at that time that a day of fasting and prayer was appointed in view of the approaching difficulties with England. The following entry in his diary shows his conduct on that occasion:—"June 1st, Wednesday. Went to church and fasted all day." In September of that year he was in Philadelphia, a member of the first Congress. In his diary he speaks of going, during the three first Sabbaths, three times to Episcopal churches, once to the Quaker, once to the Presbyterian, and once to the Roman Catholic. He was a member of Congress again the next year, and then chosen commander-in-chief of our army. On the day after assuming its command he issued the following order:—"The General requires and expects of all officers and soldiers, not engaged on actual duty, a punctual attendance on divine service, to implore the blessings of Heaven upon the means used for our safety and defence." On the 15th of May, 1776, Congress having appointed a day of humiliation, the following order is given:—"The General commands all officers and soldiers to pay strict obedience to the order of the Continental Congress, that by their unfeigned and pious observance of their religious duties they may incline the Lord and giver of victory to prosper our arms." The situation of the army not admitting the regular service every Sunday, he requires the chaplains to meet together and agree on some method of performing it at other times, and make it known to him. Such was Washington as head of the army.

As President of the United States his conduct exhibited the same faith in and reverence for religion. Not only did he regularly attend divine service in the Church of his fathers and of his choice, but he let it be understood that he would receive no visits on the Sabbath. The only exception to this was an occasional visit, in the latter part of the day, from his old friend, the Speaker of the House of Representatives, Colonel Trumbull, who was confessedly one of the most pious men of the age, and who would not have sought the company of an irreligious man on the Sabbath, even though that man were President of the United States. On the subject of a strict observance of the Sabbath, we might have mentioned other proofs of it, occurring before his being elevated to the chief command of the army or first Presidency in the Republic. His private diary shows it in various places. Let one suffice. On a certain occasion he was informed on Saturday evening that the smallpox was among his servants in the valley. He set out the next morning to visit them, but notes in his diary, "Took church on the way," thus combining duty to the poor and to his God.

His condemnation of the prevailing vices of the day deserves also to be mentioned in proof that he understood Christianity as being that "grace of God which hath appeared unto all men, teaching us that, denying ungodliness and worldly lusts, we should live soberly, righteously, and godly in this present evil world."

Not only was he addicted to no kind of intemperance, scarcely ever tasting ardent spirits or exceeding two glasses of wine,—which was equal to total abstinence in our day,—and not using tobacco in any shape, but he used his authority in the army to the utmost to put down swearing, games of chance, and drinking, and irregularities of every other kind. Whilst at Fort Cumberland in 1757, we find the following order:—"Colonel Washington has observed that the men of his regiment are very profane and reprobate. He takes this opportunity to inform them of his great displeasure at such practices, and assures them that if they do not leave them off they shall be severely punished. The officers are desired, if they hear any man swear, or make use of an oath or execration, to order the offender twenty-five lashes immediately, without a court-martial. For the second offence he shall be punished more severely." The day after General Washington took command of the American army he issued orders to the troops, from which we take the following:—"The General most earnestly requires and expects a due observance of those articles of war which prohibit profane cursing, swearing, and drunkenness," and soon after issued the following order:—

"All officers, non-commissioned officers, and soldiers are positively forbid playing at cards and other games of chance. At this time of public distress men may find enough to do in the service of their God and their country, without abandoning themselves to vice and immorality." Again, we find in August of that year an order in these remarkable words:—"The General is sorry to be informed that the foolish and wicked practice of profane cursing and swearing—a vice hitherto little known in the American army—is growing into fashion. He hopes the officers will, by example as well as influence, endeavour to check it; and that both they and the men will reflect that we can have little hope of the blessing of Heaven on our arms, if we insult it by our own folly and impiety: added to this, it is a vice so mean and low, without any temptation, that every man of sense and character detests and despises it." And is this the man of whom some have reported that he was addicted to this very disgusting vice, only saying that he did it most gracefully and swore like an angel? *Credat Judæus Apella.* It has also been attempted by some to introduce greater variety into the character of Washington, and bring him down to the common level, by representing him as passionately fond not merely of the chase and much addicted to it, but also of the dance, the ballroom, and the theatre. On what ground does this rest? His fondness for the chase is associated with that of Lord Fairfax, during the time that he lived at Mount Vernon and his lordship at Belvoir, the seat of his relation, William Fairfax, a few miles off. But how long did this sporting-intimacy continue? Washington came to Mount Vernon in his sixteenth year. Lord Fairfax came to Virginia at that time, and young Washington for a few months sometimes attended him in hunting, but not neglecting his mathematical studies and surveying, which recommended him to Lord Fairfax as a suitable agent in the valley.   At the beginning of his seventeenth year, Washington came over the Blue Ridge on duty,— laborious duty.   Lord Fairfax, after visiting England, settled at Greenway Court.   His house was only the occasional abode of Washington during the two years in which he was surveying and dividing the immense landed possessions of Lord Fairfax, and also acting as public surveyor in all Western Virginia.   What time was left him to waste in the sports of the chase ?   From the age of nineteen he was faithfully and painfully serving his country in the field of battle, except when on his voyage to the West Indies with a sick brother.   During the period between his marriage and the Revolution, he was a most diligent farmer at Mount Vernon,— sometimes visiting his plantations in Jefferson, and acting as Burgess in Virginia and Delegate to the earlier American Congresses. What time, I ask, for the sports of the field ?   What do we find, in his diary, of dogs and kennels and the chase ?   We do not say that he may never have thus exercised himself at a time and in a country where game and forests abounded and it was less a waste of time than at other periods and other places : but how different must have been the pursuit with Washington from that of the idlers of his day ?*   And as to his admiration of the theatre and his delighting in its ludicrous and indelicate exhibitions, does it seem probable

---

* In proof of how little dependence is to be placed on assertions of this kind, I quote a passage from the life of General Muhlenberg.   While a minister at Woodstock, in what is now in Shenandoah county, in the Valley, he was among the first to join Revolutionary movements in 1774.   It is said that he " corresponded extensively with the prominent Whigs of the Colony, and with two of whom—Washington and Henry—he was on terms of personal intimacy.   With the former he had frequently hunted deer among the mountains of his district ; and it is said that, fond as Washington was of the rifle and skilled in its use, on trial he found himself inferior to the Pennsylvanian."   Now, Mr. Muhlenberg did not come to the Valley until twenty years after Washington had left the service of Lord Fairfax, and fourteen years after he had been settled at Mount Vernon as a farmer.   Mr. Muhlenberg came to Virginia in the fall of 1772, and in the summer of 1774 he was— though a clergyman—in the House of Burgesses and Convention with Washington and Henry, and there, in all human probability, commenced their acquaintance and subsequent correspondence.   As for Washington's frequently hunting deer with him in the mountains of Shenandoah, during the short time Mr. Muhlenberg was there, preceding their meeting in Williamsburg, it is a most improbable conjecture. Washington was, during that time, busy with his farm at Mount Vernon and as a Delegate to the House of Burgesses.   He visited his estates in Jefferson occasionally, but I believe there was nothing to draw him to the mountains of Shenandoah.

that the grave and dignified Washington, with all the cares of the army and afterward of the state pressing upon him, should have found time for such entertainments? In a letter to the President of Congress, dated New York, April, 1776, he thus writes:—"I give in to no kind of amusements myself, and consequently those about me [alluding to his aids] can have none." On the 12th of October, 1778, the following preamble and resolutions were adopted by the American Congress:—"Whereas, true religion and good morals are the only solid foundation of public liberty and happiness, Therefore, resolved, that it be, and is hereby, recommended to the several States to take the most effectual measures for the encouragement thereof, and for suppressing *theatrical entertainments, horse-racing, gaming, and such other diversions as are productive of idleness, dissipation, and a general depravity of manners.*" Is it probable that Washington, at the head of the army, then calling upon his officers and soldiers to abandon their oaths and drinking and games of chance, in obedience to military laws and lest they should offend God and lose his favour, would himself despise and disobey this solemn call of Congress, and that too when the names of Adams and Gerry, Sherman and Ellsworth, Morris and Dean, Lee and Smith, of Virginia, Laurence and Mathews, of South Carolina, were on the list of those who voted for it, and so few were against it?

As to Washington's passionate fondness for the dance, if Cicero thought it an unbecoming exercise for any Roman citizen, as beneath the dignity of any who were admitted to the citizenship of that great republic, how unlikely that our great Washington—even if feeling no religious objection to this childish amusement—should be still a child and delight himself in such frivolous things! May we not rather suppose him to have felt and said, with a great man in Israel when tempted to leave the work of the Lord—the building of his house on Mount Zion—and come down to some meeting in one of the villages of the plain, "*I am doing a great work, so that I cannot come down*"? Let not the sons and daughters of idleness, vanity, and pleasure seek to find a sanction for their favourite amusements in the example of Washington,—even though in a dark age and under peculiar circumstances he may at times have lent himself to some of them.

I come now to speak of that feature in Washington's religious character which must most forcibly strike every reader of his public and private communications,—his firm reliance on a special Providence, as distinguished from that philosophic belief in Providence which is little better than atheism. In a letter to his brother, John

A. Washington, written a few days after Braddock's defeat, he says, "By the all-powerful dispensations of Providence, I have been protected beyond all human probability or expectation; for I had four bullets through my coat and two horses shot under me,—yet escaped unhurt,—although death was levelling my companions on every side of me." In his entrance on the contest with England, he thus writes to General Gage:—"May that God to whom you appeal judge between America and you! Under his providence, those who influenced the councils of America, and all the other inhabitants of the Colonies, at the hazard of their lives, are determined to hand down to posterity those just and invaluable privileges which they received from their ancestors." In a letter to his friend, Joseph Reed, in 1776, under some great trials in relation to his supplies, he writes, "How it will end, God in his great goodness will direct. I am thankful for his protection to this time." In his address to the General Assembly of Massachusetts, after the evacuation of Boston without blood, he ascribes it "to the interposition of that Providence which has manifestly appeared in our behalf through the whole of this important struggle." Speaking of the expectation of a bloody battle, he says, in a letter to his brother John, "It is to be hoped that, if our cause be just,—as I do most religiously believe it to be,—the same Providence which has in so many instances appeared for us will still go on to afford its aid." In view of an expected attack from the combined forces of the enemy he thus calls on his soldiers:—"The fate of unborn millions will now depend, *under God*, on the courage and conduct of this army. Let us rely upon the goodness of the cause, and *the aid of the Supreme Being, in whose hand victory is, to animate and encourage us to noble actions.*" After the surrender of Burgoyne's army, he writes to his brother John, "I most devoutly congratulate my country and every well-wisher to the cause on this signal stroke of Providence." In the year 1778, just after the battle of Monmouth, he writes to his brother, that all would have been lost "had not that bountiful Providence, which has never failed us in the hour of distress, enabled me to form a regiment or two of those who were retreating in the face of the enemy and under their fire." To General Nelson, in that same year, in taking a retrospect of the vicissitudes of the war, he says, "The hand of Providence is so conspicuous in all this, that he must be worse than an infidel that lacks faith, and more than wicked that has not gratitude enough to acknowledge his obligations." In a letter to Benjamin Harrison, in 1778, he writes, "Providence has heretofore taken care of us when all other means seemed to be departing from us." To General Armstrong, in 1781, he writes, "Our affairs are brought to a perilous crisis, that the hand of Providence may be *more conspicuous in our deliverance.* The many remarkable interpositions of the Divine government in the hours of our deepest distress and darkness have been too luminous to suffer me to doubt the issue of the present contest." The foregoing are only a few out of the many passages which pervade all the private letters and public communications of Washington touching a special Providence. Is it too much to say that the communications of no king, ruler, general, or statesman in Christendom ever so abounded in expressions of pious dependence on God? There was an habitual reliance on God which must have been connected with habitual prayer to God. Nor can we forbear to institute a comparison between the language of trust in Providence, as seen in the letters and orders of Washington, and those of Cromwell. Who for a moment questions the sincerity and deep feeling of Washington in all he writes? Who does not sometimes suspect at least the hypocrisy of Cromwell and revolt at his cant? Who does not see and feel that, while Washington was all for his country and his God, Cromwell was sometimes seeking his own?

On one other subject in connection with the religious character of Washington I must ask the attention of the reader. Washington in word and deed condemned duelling. Nearly all our great men have done it by word, but, if they have not recommended it by deed, have been afraid to say that they might not so do, either by giving or receiving a challenge. When a young man in Alexandria and an officer in the army, a quarrel ensued on an election-day, in which he used strong and offensive language to one who, with a stick, prostrated him to the ground. On the following day he sought an interview with his antagonist, when it was fully expected that another rencounter or the preliminaries for one would take place. Instead of this, Captain Washington, conscious of being in fault, declared that the interview was sought in order to acknowledge it. Here was true greatness of soul. Here was the true courage of the Christian, breathed into the soul by the Spirit of God. God was training up the spirit of Washington for all the subsequent trials and duties of life. In the army he of course discouraged and prevented this most foolish and wicked practice. M. Lafayette, in a chivalrous spirit, wished to revenge some supposed insult to his country on an Englishman who offered it, and asked leave of Washington to send a challenge. Washington conducted the matter with consummate skill,—and, while fully resolved not to permit it, chose rather by a grave irony to laugh him out of it. What an example was thus set to the gentlemen and officers and public functionaries of America! How does Washington tower above those who, while acknowledging that the practice is indefensible by any laws of God or man, and utterly opposed to them, and condemned by common sense and true honour and humanity, yet, in a most inconsistent and cowardly manner declare that, nevertheless, such is their apprehension of public opinion, they might be induced to engage in this murderous act! To receive a blow, be felled to the earth before a crowd, and then ask pardon for having provoked the blow, must surely be considered in a young officer as an act of moral courage which is prompted by the Spirit of God.

One question only remains to be settled:—Was Washington a communicant of the Church? That he was, might be reasonably inferred from the indication of youthful piety, his religious, his ministerial offices at the head of his regiment, the active part taken in the concerns of the parish, his habits of devotion, his regular attendance at church, his conscientious observance of the Sabbath, his strict fasting on appointed days. It is also believed that he was a communicant, from the testimony of the Rev. Lee Massey, as handed down through his family, and also of others which have come down to us. The testimony which has often been adduced to prove that, during the war, he did commune on a certain Sabbath in a Presbyterian church at Morristown, New Jersey, ought to be enough to satisfy a reasonable man of the fact. Add to these the declaration of so many, in the sermons and orations at the time of his death. But still it has been made a question, and it may be well to consider on what ground. It is certainly a fact, that for a certain period of time during his Presidential term, while the Congress was held in Philadelphia, he did not commune. This fact rests on the authority of Bishop White, under whose ministry the President sat, and who was on the most intimate terms with himself and Mrs. Washington. I will relate what the Bishop told myself and others in relation to it. During the session or sessions of Congress held in Philadelphia, General Washington was, with his family, a regular attendant at one of the churches under the care of Bishop White and his assistants. On Communion-days, when the congregation was dismissed, (except the portion which communed,) the General left the church, until a certain Sabbath on which Dr. Abercrombie, in his sermon, spoke of the impropriety of turning our backs on the Lord's table,—that is, neglecting to commune,—from which time General Washington came no more on Communion-days. Bishop

White supposes that the General understood the "words turning our backs on the Lord's table" in a somewhat different sense than was designed by the preacher; that he supposed it was intended to censure those who left the church at the time of its administration, and, in order not to seem to be disrespectful to that ordinance, thought it better not to be present at all on such occasions. It is needless to attempt to conjecture what may have been the reason of this tempo-rary (as we hope it was) suspension of the act of communicating. A regard for historic truth has led to the mention of this subject. The question as to his ever having been a communicant has been raised on this fact, as stated by Bishop White, and we have thought it best to give the narrative as we heard it from the lips of the Bishop himself. It has been asked why he did not, in the dying hour, send for some minister and receive the emblems of a Saviour's death. The same might be asked of thousands of pious communi-cants who do not regard the sacrament as indispensable to a happy death and glorious eternity, as some Romanists do. Moreover, the short and painful illness of Washington would have forbidden it. But his death was not without proofs of a gracious state. He told to surrounding friends that it had no terrors for him,—that all was well. The Bible was on his bed: he closed his own eyes, and, folding his arms over his breast, expired in peace.

ARTICLE LXIX.

Fairfax Parish, Fairfax County.

THE town of Alexandria was at first called Hunting Creek Warehouse, sometimes Bell Haven, and consisted of a small establishment at that place. Its growth was encouraged by successive Acts of the Legislature, establishing semi-annual fairs and granting certain privileges to those who attended them. In the year 1762, it was enlarged by the laying off of numerous lots on the higher ground, belonging to Dade, West, and the Alexanders, after which it improved rapidly, so that at the close of the last or beginning of the present century its population was ten thousand, and its commerce greater than it now is. So promising was it at the close of the war, that its claims were weighed in the balance with those of Washington as the seat of the National Government. It is thought that, but for the unwillingness of Washington to seem partial to Virginia, Alexandria would have been the chosen spot, and that on the first range of hills overlooking the town the public buildings would have been erected. Whether there had been any public worship or church at Alexandria previous to this enlargement of it, and the great impulse thus given to it, does not appear from the vestry-book, though it is believed that there was. But soon after this, in the year 1764, Fairfax parish is established, and measures taken for the promotion of the Church in this place. The vestry-book commences in 1765. At that time there were two churches in the new parish of Fairfax,—one at the Falls, called, as the present one is, Little Falls Church; the position of the other—the Lower Church—is not known. It may have been an old one at Alexandria.

Among the first acts of the vestry was the repairing of the two old churches in the parish, at a cost of more than thirty-two thousand pounds of tobacco. In the year 1766, it is determined to build two new churches,—one at the Little Falls, very near the old one, and one in Alexandria, to contain twenty-four hundred square feet, and to be high-pitched so as to admit of galleries. Mr. James Wrenn agrees to build the former, and Mr. James Parsons the other, for about six hundred pounds each. A most particular contract is made for them. The mortar is to have two-thirds of lime and one of sand,—the very reverse of the proportion at this day, and which accounts for the greater durability of ancient walls. The shingles were to be of the best cypress or juniper, and three-quarters of an inch thick, instead of our present half-inch ones. Mr. Parsons was allowed to add ten feet to the upper part of the church on his own account, and to pay himself by their sale, on certain conditions. He commenced his work, but was unable to finish it. It lingered for some years, until, in 1772, Mr. John Carlisle undertakes it, and completes it in 1773. The ten pews are now sold, and General Washington, though having just been engaged in the erection of Mount Vernon Church, which was finished the same year, and having a pew therein, gives the highest price for one in Christ Church, which was occupied by him and his family during his life, and has been by some of his name and family ever since. The gallery was not put up until the year 1787, at which time the pews were balloted for. The steeple is of modern construction. A gallery never was erected in the Little Falls Church. The following notice of my visit to this church in 1827 will tell something of its history:—

"The exercises of the Seminary being over, I next directed my steps to the Falls Church, so called from its vicinity to one of the falls on the Potomac River. It is about eight miles from Alexandria, and the same from Georgetown. It is a large oblong brick building, and, like that near Mount Vernon, has two rows of windows, being doubtless designed for galleries all around, though none were ever put there. It was deserted as a house of worship by Episcopalians about forty years ago. About that period, for the first, and it is believed for the last time, it was visited by Bishop Madison. Since then it has been used by any who were disposed to occupy it as a place of worship; and, the doors and windows being open, itself standing on the common highway, it has been entered at pleasure by travellers on the road and animals of every kind. Some years since, the attention of the professors of our Seminary, and of some of the students, was drawn toward it, and occasional services performed there. This led to its partial repair. The most successful effort in its behalf was made by one of those devoted youths who has given himself to Africa. Young Mr. Minor, of Fredericksburg, (then a student at the Seminary,) undertook the task of lay reader in this place, and by his untiring zeal and most affectionate manners soon collected a large Sunday-school, in the conduct of which he was aided by some of his fellow-students of kindred spirit. In losing Mr. Minor (when he went to Africa) the parents and children thought they had lost their all; but Providence raised up others, and doubtless will continue to raise up as many as are needed. Our Seminary will surely furnish the supply that is called for. The house of which we are speaking has recently been more thoroughly repaired, and is now, as to outward appearance, strength, and comfort, one of our most desirable temples of religion, bidding fair to survive successive generations of those unworthy structures which are continually rising up and falling down throughout our land.   On Saturday and Sunday, assisted by several of our ministers, I performed pastoral and episcopal duties in this church.   On the latter day, in the midst of an overflowing congregation, I confirmed six persons and administered the Holy Communion.   On the evening of this day, I visited an interesting school of young ladies at Mr. Henry Fairfax's, and sought to make some improvement of my visit by addressing a discourse especially to the young ones."

Mr. Henry Fairfax was the grandson of the Rev. Bryan Fairfax, of whom we shall soon speak as the minister of this church.   He inherited the generous and disinterested spirit of his grandfather. It was chiefly at his expense that the church was repaired, and by his liberality the minister supported, when another than the professors was employed.   Being a graduate of West Point, he felt that he owed his country a debt, which could only be discharged by engaging in the late Mexican war, and, in opposition to the wishes and judgment of his friends and relatives, raised a company for that purpose; but scarcely had he reached the scene of action before he fell a victim to the climate, leaving a devoted family and congregation to feel and mourn his loss.

While on the subject of churches, it may be as well to mention that at a more recent date a neat frame church has been built at Fairfax Court-House, under the auspices of the Rev. Mr. Lockwood, who for some years officiated there as well as at the Falls Church.   The Rev. Templeman Brown had officiated at the Falls Church and at the court-house for some time before Mr. Lockwood's ministry, and has again been serving them for a number of years, since Mr. Lockwood's relinquishment.

We proceed now to such notices as we possess of the ministers of Fairfax parish.   For these we are indebted to the vestry-records. The Rev. Townshend Dade was ordained for this parish by the Bishop of London in 1765, and entered upon his duties in the following year or perhaps sooner.   It is more than probable that he was the son of Mr. Townshend Dade, who appears on the list of the first vestry, or of Mr. Baldwin Dade, who was a vestryman at a later date, and owner in part of the land on which Alexandria was built. We are sorry to be unable to make a favourable report of the Rev. Mr. Dade.   In the year 1768, the vestry discuss the question of examining into some alleged misconduct of his, and decide against it, five members entering their dissent from the decision.   In the year 1777, a committee is appointed to wait upon him to know why he neglects his congregation.   Some months after, the committee is enlarged and directed to take further steps.   The result was his resignation and relinquishment of the glebe and rectory. In the same year the Rev. Spence Grayson is a candidate for the parish, but the Rev. Mr. West, probably from Maryland, is preferred. He continues until February of 1779, and resigns. The Rev. David Griffith, then chaplain in the army, and formerly minister of Shelburne parish, and well known to the people, is elected, though he does not appear on the vestry-book as minister until October, 1780. He continued to be its minister until his death in 1789. Of him we shall speak more fully after our brief notice of the succession of the ministers of this parish. The Rev. Bryan Fairfax succeeded him in 1790. He was ordained deacon in 1786 by Bishop Seabury. Mr. Bryan Fairfax had been a vestryman of the parish and delegate to the Virginia Conventions for some time before this. Whether it was that his health was delicate from the first, or whatever was the cause, he wished an assistant in the parish, and the vestry passed an order allowing him to invite the Rev. Mason Locke Weems, or any one else whom he might choose, to act as such. Mr. Fairfax made a very different selection, and called the Rev. Bernard Page, giving to him all the emoluments of the parish. Mr. Page was very decidedly of the then rising evangelical school in the Church of England, and a very zealous preacher of its doctrines. I doubt not but that Mr. Fairfax sympathized with the principles of that school. In a sermon of his which I have published, he sets forth the doctrine of salvation by grace through faith in Christ in such a way as was not common in that day. In the year 1792, he resigns his charge in a letter stating his reasons, which is not entered on the record, though the most flattering letter of the vestry, regretting their loss of him, is. I am not aware how long he lived after this. His residence during the latter years of his life was at a place called Mount Eagle, a short distance beyond the Hunting Creek Bridge. He was the father of the late Ferdinando Fairfax and Thomas Fairfax, the latter of whom inherited his empty title of Lord Fairfax, also of the late Mrs. Charles Catlett, by a second marriage. I am not aware of other children, though there may have been. I have, in another place, stated that he endeavoured to dissuade his friend and neighbour, General Washington, from the war with England. The General, in his letter to him, deals most gently and respectfully with him. He was the son of his old friend and neighbour, George William Fairfax, of Belvoir, and the brother of the wife of Lawrence Washington, elder brother of the General. The Rev. Mr. Fairfax acted with such prudence, if he did not see cause to change his sentiments, as not to forfeit the friendship of Washington and of the patriots in Fairfax parish, but was, as we have seen, chosen to be their minister. He has left behind him many worthy adherents to our Church, though some few have varied from it. At the resignation of Mr. Fairfax the Rev. Thomas Davis was chosen. He continued its minister until 1806, when he removed to Hungar's parish, on the Eastern Shore, where he died. Mr. Davis had ministered in various places throughout Virginia, and, though a man of temperate habits and correct life by comparison with too many of our clergy, was not calculated by his preaching or conversation to promote the spiritual welfare of any people. He was succeeded by the Rev. Mr. Gibson, of Maryland. Previous to his removal to Alexandria, and while the church was vacant, the vestry invited the Rev. Mr. McQuerr a Scotch minister of the Presbyterian Church, who was then principal of the Washington Academy in Alexandria, to officiate for them. With the character and habits of Mr. McQuerr I became acquainted through my old teacher, Mr. Wiley, who was educated at that school. They were nothing better than those of many of the old Episcopal clergy. I am happy, however, to say that more than twenty years after this, on one of my journeys to the South, I heard of him as a most pious and exemplary minister of that communion in the State of Georgia, a zealous advocate of the Temperance and Colonization societies and of every good work, and highly esteemed by all. He lived to a great age, persevering to the last. There is something sad in the history of the Rev. Mr. Gibson, but it must be told for the benefit of others. He began well, preached zealously, was praised and flattered to his undoing. He gave offence to some by a rather harsh way of saying true things. This was complained of, and perhaps harsh things said in return. These were communicated to him by a few of those false friends who think to ingratiate themselves with their minister by communicating to him what ought to be concealed. This exasperated a temper naturally excitable. Under the influence of this, he suddenly and unexpectedly, from the pulpit, resigned his charge. The vestry were divided as to the acceptance of it, but the majority were in favour of it. When too late he apologized, and wished to retract. Parties were formed, and the result was another congregation under his auspices. But, as will be seen when I come to speak of that congregation, he did not continue long with it, but returned to Maryland, where, after a short time, he was dismissed for intemperance. There was reason to fear that the habit had commenced in Alexandria, under the too popular pretext of using ardent spirits privately as a medicine. He afterward united with the Methodist Church and ministered in it. Let the clergy learn from his fate to beware of false friends who inform them what their enemies say of them, and to eschew alcohol, even as a medicine, unless prescribed by a temperate physician and as a mere temporary expedient imperiously called for.

In the following year, 1810, the Rev. Mr. Barclay, who came to this country from the West Indies, was chosen. Bishop Clagett, of Maryland, certified to his character for the last six years, during which he had been ministering in Maryland; but in April of 1811 a wife, whom he had deserted, followed him from the West Indies, and he resigned his charge in Alexandria and has been heard of no more since.

Under these circumstances, the writer of these sad notices, having been ordained by Bishop Madison in the spring of that year, at the age of twenty-one, was induced to take the charge of Christ Church in October, 1811, in conjunction with his charge in Frederick, visiting the latter once a month. For some account of his ministry at that time and place he refers to the second article in this series.

At the close of that brief term of service, extending only to eighteen months, the Rev. Oliver Norris took charge of Christ Church. Mr. Norris was of Quaker descent, but, occasionally attending the services of St. Peter's Church, Baltimore, during the ministry of Mr. Dashiel, first became convinced of sin, then of his need of a Saviour, and then of the excellency of our service to build up a convert in the true faith and practice of a Christian. He has often detailed to me the circumstances of his conversion. He first ministered at Elk Ridge and near Bladensburg, in Maryland, and then came to Virginia. He was an affectionate pastor and faithful preacher of the Gospel, very dear to his people, and esteemed in the Church of Virginia. Being called upon to preach his funeral sermon, and the same being published by the vestry, I am able to present the following passage on one trait in his ministerial character :—

"May I not, fearless of contradiction, ask this congregation if there be one among them who has not experienced many evidences of his pastoral fidelity and tenderness? Who has ever complained of neglect there, where a people are so apt to complain? What individual so poor or so obscure but has received a full share of his pastoral kindness? Which of you, rich or poor, did he ever meet, but affection beamed from his eye and spoke from his lips, and was felt in the warm pressure of his affectionate hand? Which of you ever left (though but for a season) his pastoral care, but he was with you to bid a kind farewell and commend you to the care of Heaven, and when you returned was he not the first to meet and welcome you back again? Which of you was ever sick, but he was soon at your side, ready to comfort you, pray with you, entreat you to take it in good part as the dispensation of God, and, if there was need, to be your tender nurse? Which of you was ever in any distress of soul, body, or estate, but he was the first to condole with you and endeavour to make some spiritual improvement of your affliction? Which of his people departing this life, but he was with them, exhorting to due preparation, and strengthening them for the conflict with the last enemy and great adversary? Once more, let me ask which of your dear little children but has received his kind attentions, heard from his lips some words of counsel suited to their age, and which should be remembered and treasured up in their hearts?"

After the death of Mr. Norris, in the summer of 1825, efforts were made to obtain the services of the Rev. John Johns, then in Fredericktown, Maryland, and of the Rev. Mr. Cobbs, of Bedford county, Virginia, and on the failure of these applications the Rev. Mr. Keith was induced to add the duties of a pastor and preacher to those of professor. He continued this, with some interruption, for the greater part of three years, when the Rev. Geo. Griswold, son of Bishop Griswold, became pastor in 1828. On account of ill health he resigned the following year, to the deep regret of the congregation. The Rev. J. P. McGuire followed for one year, and, unable through weakness of his eyes to make the necessary preparation for the pulpit, resigned the charge. The Rev. Mr. Mann succeeded, and, after continuing for three years, accepted an agency for the Seminary. The Rev. Mr. Dana, its present minister, then took charge of the church.

THE REV. DAVID GRIFFITH.

Concerning the Rev. David Griffith we have something more particular to record. He was born in the city of New York, and educated, partly in that place and partly in England, for the medical profession. After taking his degree in London, he returned to America and entered on his profession in the interior of New York about the year 1763. Determined to enter the ministry of the Episcopal Church, he went to London in the year 1770, and was ordained by Bishop Terrick, August the 19th of that year, and returned as missionary to Gloucester county, New Jersey. He could not have continued there long; for, in the close of the next year, he accepts the charge of Shelburne parish, Loudoun county, Virginia. Governor Johnson, of New York, was very anxious to obtain his services in that State, where he was regarded as a "man of uncommon merit." The Governor of Virginia, also,—either from personal knowledge or report,—recommends him very highly to

Shelburne parish. He continued in it until May, 1776, when—being an American not only by birth but in heart—he entered the service as chaplain to the 3d Virginia Regiment. In this service he continued until some time in the year 1780. He appears as the minister of Christ Church, Alexandria, during that year,—though he was elected the previous year. He is represented as a man of good size and fine appearance and pleasing manners, and as enjoying the confidence of General Washington and the army. Tradition says that, on the night before the battle of Monmouth, he sought an interview with General Washington, and, in the presence of his aids, bade him beware of General Charles Lee, though he was not at liberty to give his reasons or authority. When Lee unnecessarily and ingloriously retreated on the field of Monmouth, and almost lost America the battle, there were those who believed that he wished only to diminish the reputation of Washington and receive the supreme command to himself. We only give this as tradition. From the year 1780 to his death, in 1789, Mr. Griffith was the much-esteemed pastor of Christ Church, Alexandria, and that called Little Falls, higher up on the Potomac. During the greater part of this time General Washington was his parishioner—having a pew in Christ Church—and Mr. Griffith was a welcome visitor at Mount Vernon. Mr. Griffith was not merely attentive to his duty as a parish minister, but, in the dark and distressing days of the Episcopal Church in Virginia and in the other States, took a deep interest in the measures proposed for her welfare. When a number of the clergy from the Northern States met—of their own motion, in New York, in October, 1784—to consult about those measures, Mr. Griffith appeared of his own accord from Virginia. But before that time, I have letters to and from him, showing that he was earnestly engaged in correspondence, both North and South, with a view to promoting both State and General Conventions, as the instruments of saving the Church from ruin. The following letters which passed between himself and Dr. Buchanon of Richmond will show how deplorable was the condition of things in Virginia at this time, and also establish the fact that Dr. Griffith was the first mover of the proposition to have a Convention in Virginia after the war. I have also a letter in August, 1784, from the Rev. Mr. West, dated from Baltimore, in which he delivers a message from Dr. Smith, of Philadelphia, to Mr. Griffith, showing his estimate of the latter in relation to this movement. It is probable that this Mr. West was the same who preceded Mr. Griffith in Alexandria, as he speaks of being there.

The following letter of Dr. Griffith to Dr. Buchanon, of Richmond, must have been written in the fall of 1783, before any meeting of Episcopalians, in any part of the land, had occurred with a similar object. Dr. Buchanon's reply was not until the February following, except so far as a verbal message went :—

" DEAR SIR :—You may recollect the conversation we had when I had the pleasure of seeing you at Richmond; that we mutually lamented the declining state of the Church of England in this country, and the pitiable situation of her clergy,—especially those whose circumstances are not sufficiently independent to place them beyond the reach of want. I am satisfied our Church has yet a very great number of powerful friends who are disposed to give it encouragement and support, and who wish to see some plan in agitation for effecting a business so important, and at this time so very necessary. It is (and very justly) matter of astonishment to many, that those whose more immediate duty it is to look to the concerns of their religious society should show so much indifference and indolence as the Church and clergy do, while the leaders of almost every other denomination are labouring with the greatest assiduity to increase their influence, and, by open attacks and subtle machinations, endeavouring to lessen that of every other society,—particularly the Church to which you and I have the honour to belong, in whose destruction they all (Quakers and Methodists excepted) seem to agree perfectly, however they may differ in other points. Against these it behooves us to be cautious. But, unless the clergy act conjointly and agreeably to some well-regulated plan, the ruin of our Church is inevitable without the malevolence of her enemies. Considering her present situation and circumstances,—without ordination, without government, without support, unprotected by the laws, and yet labouring under injurious restrictions from laws which yet exist,—these things considered, her destruction is sure as fate, unless some mode is adopted for her preservation. Her friends, by suffering her to continue in her present state of embarrassment, as effectually work her destruction as her avowed enemies could do by their most successful contrivances.

" In the late contest for a stake of the last importance to this country, it would have been imprudent to enter on a regulation of ecclesiastical affairs, or to attempt any thing that might interrupt that union which was so necessary for our mutual security and preservation. But that time, God be thanked, is happily over, and those reasons no longer exist. It seems to be high time for those whom it concerns to be engaged in the important business of regulating the affairs of the Church. I have been for some time in the hope that some of my brethren near the seat of government would have set on foot this necessary business; and my reason for addressing you at this time is to be informed whether any thing of the kind is begun or intended,—the time when, the place where, and manner how,—and, if nothing of the kind should be yet determined upon, to request of you, as your situation renders it noway inconvenient, to undertake to promote a Convention of the clergy for that purpose. I shall also presume to offer my advice. In order that the measures agreed on may be generally acceptable to the clergy and no objection remain to impede their future execution, it will be necessary to have as numerous a meeting as possible. I would recommend to have the clergy summoned to this Convention both by public notice and private information; for, as the Virginia newspapers seldom come into this and several other quarters, perhaps the end would be best answered by sending printed circular letters to all quarters of the State : if circular letters were not sent, many of the clergy might not have timely notice. I would recommend this Convention to be called on the authority of the few clergy contiguous to the seat of government,—the notices to be signed by the whole of them, or one as chairman. I would advise the notices to be couched in general terms, to avoid, as much as possible, assigning reasons for it, especially such as may alarm the Dissenters and rouse them into opposition. The time for sending and publishing these notices should be near three months before the intended Convention, that the clergy might with certainty be informed of it and be prepared to leave their homes. As Richmond is near the centre of the State, I think it is the properest place to hold the Convention at. The time for holding the Convention I would recommend to be about the 20th of April next. It will be impossible to have any thing like a full meeting in the winter season ; and, about the season I have mentioned, the weather is generally fine for travelling and the roads settled. Besides, our plans should be agreed upon previous to the session of Assembly, as we must necessarily have recourse to it for the repeal of those existing laws which made a part of the old Establishment, and which, while they do exist, must prove ruinous to the Church in spite of any regulations the clergy may adopt. I have not the pleasure of knowing Mr. Blagrove, chaplain to the House of Assembly, but I think his name, or yours, or both, would not appear improperly at the bottom of the notices, or any thing that will answer the purpose. If the above proposal should be adopted, I shall be much obliged to you for informing me of it as soon as it is determined on. Please direct to me at Alexandria, either by post or some private hand. If a meeting is likely to take place, it would not perhaps be amiss if yourself and our brethren in your neighbourhood were to digest some plan for the consideration of the Convention. If it was well considered by sensible men what regulations were wanting and what reform necessary, it would save abundance of time. If I have timely notice, I will cheerfully devote all the spare time I have to this service. And if the Convention is resolved on, I will engage to send the notices to all the clergy in the Northern Neck above Falmouth, if the copies or a form are sent me in time. You may remember that when I had the pleasure of seeing you I expressed a wish that a coalition might take place between us and the Dissenters : it is still my most earnest wish, but I am now satisfied it is a vain one : and I think our Church has no chance of preserving any of its ancient and excellent forms of worship, but from the united zeal and efforts of her clergy. I think it is this alone that can preserve her very existence. I am, &c.

"DAVID GRIFFITH."

The following is Dr. Buchanon's answer:—

"DEAR SIR :—I received your letter, favoured by Mr. Fairfax, which reminded me of a conversation which passed between us respecting the low state of the Church whereof we are members, and in which you make inquiry whether any thing has been attempted by any of its clergy to raise it from its distressed situation, and inform me that reflections have been thrown out against them for their remissness and want of zeal in an affair of so much consequence. In order to remedy these evils, you propose a plan for convening the clergy in the month of April next, to the end that some form of ecclesiastical government might be established, particularly a mode of ordination; and that an application might be made to the Assembly for redress of grievances and a legal support.

"As I had nothing of consequence to write you by Mr. Fairfax, I desired him verbally to acquaint you that your brethren in this neighbourhood had done nothing to forward the re-establishment of our Church: indeed, they seemed to despair of any thing being done effectually without its originating in the Assembly. I showed them your letter: they approved highly of your zeal, but were by no means sanguine in the result of a convocation. It was agreed among us that we should meet on some day most convenient for Mr. Leigh, who lived the greatest distance from this city,* to take into further consideration the subject of your letter. Thus matters stood until the 29th of December, when Mr. Selden received a letter from the above gentleman,—a copy whereof is herein enclosed that you may have a full view of the argument he offers against your plan of a convocation. For my own part, before I was favoured with your ideas I was firmly of opinion that the reformation should first take place in the Legislature;—that, if they thought public religion essential not only to the good order but to the very existence of government, it behooved them to make a legal provision for its teachers, and to raise them from that state of indigence and dependence which, I will not scruple to say, they themselves were the cause of; otherwise they cannot reasonably expect that religion will flourish in a country where its ministers are reduced to a state of beggary and contempt. I remember, in a conversation at Wilton,† on this very subject, a Mr. Douglass, lately from England, expressed his surprise that the clergy of our Church had never presented a memorial to the House respecting the state of religion; in which he was joined by the Speaker of the Senate. I gave my opinion as above, and further added, that such an application would give the alarm to the Sectaries, who would, no doubt, throw every obstruction in the way, if not render totally abortive every measure we should adopt. The present Governor thought my argument had weight, and said that it was a reproach on Government that they had done nothing in support of religion. I am apt to think that some who are no well-wishers to our persuasion had got intelligence of our design; for, soon after Mr. Fairfax's appearance here, some scurrilous publications appeared in the papers concerning the importation of clergy at forty or fifty pounds a head, according to certain qualifications specified, and other stuff to that purpose. I am told that a petition was last session preferred to the House, representing the fatal decline of religion, and of consequence the great depravity of morals resulting from it, and praying that the House would take into their most serious consideration a subject of so much importance. Some were for putting it off 'to a more convenient season,' but Mr. Henry thought it of too much moment to be deferred to another session. Notwithstanding this, the matter was dropped, and when it will be resumed I know not. At the beginning of the session, you would think that most of the House, from their speeches without-doors, were for doing something effectual; but they no sooner get involved in secular matters, than the idea of religion is obliterated from their minds.

"You observe Mr. Leigh expresses a willingness to meet us at any appointed time, to put into execution the plan you propose, or, if we think

---

* The Rev. William Leigh, of Chesterfield.
† A seat of the Randolphs, near Richmond.

proper, he allows us to put his name down to any notification to our brethren.

"As we have been so long undetermined, nothing, I think, can be done this winter. Should business, or your inclinations, lead you to this city in April, pray send me previous notice of it, that I may inform some of the gentlemen in this neighbourhood. Your presence may rouse us from our lethargy; and for my own part, if you should think a memorial to the House expedient, I will give it my hearty concurrence, or any other plan you may adopt.

"I am, dear sir, with real esteem

" Your most obedient servant,

" JOHN BUCHANON.

"RICHMOND, February 2, 1784."

Nothing could better exhibit the true condition of things in Virginia than this correspondence. Dr. Buchanon acknowledges that the clergy had brought this ruin upon themselves by their own misconduct. Guilt-stricken, they were afraid and ashamed to come forward boldly and call upon the Legislature to do something for the cause of religion and morals, which were both declining. It never seemed to enter into the thoughts of some, as a possibility, to do any thing on the voluntary principle, independent of the State, so accustomed were they to the old English system. Whether any such meeting as that proposed by Dr. Griffith ever took place, I have not the means of ascertaining. In the winter of 1785, the Legislature incorporated the Episcopal Church, tendering the same privilege to others, and in the preamble states that it was done at the petition of the Episcopal clergy. How many united in it, and whether it was done at a general meeting called for the purpose, I know not. In May of that year, 1785, the first Convention of clerical and lay deputies met in Richmond, under the Act of incorporation. Mr. Griffith, being there, was appointed a delegate to the General Convention in Philadelphia that fall. The second Virginia Convention was held in May, 1786, when the Rev. Dr. Griffith was chosen Bishop, by a vote of thirty-two members. Dr. Bracken received ten, and Mr. Samuel Shield seven. An assessment was made upon the parishes for funds to bear the expenses of his visit to England for consecration; but such was the depressed condition of the Church, that a sufficiency was not raised, either in that year or the two succeeding ones. In May, 1789, Mr. Griffith resigned his claim upon the office, and in the summer of that year died at the house of Bishop White, while attending the General Convention. At the following Convention, the Rev. James Madison was chosen Bishop by a vote of forty-five,—the Rev. Samuel Shield having nine. To the shame of the Church of Virginia, in that day be it said, sufficient funds were not raised for Bishop Madison's consecration. A part was drawn from his private resources, and that worthy man, Graham Franks, of London, of whom we have before spoken as the warm friend of the Church of Virginia, and whose wife lies buried in old York graveyard, contributed five guineas toward it.

List of the Vestrymen.

John West, Wm. Payne, Jr., Wm. Adams, John Dalton, Thomas Wren, Edward Duling, Daniel French, Thomas Shaw, Townshend Dade, Richard Sanford, Charles Broadwater, Edward Blackburn, James Wren, Henry Gunnel, John West, Jr., Richard Conway, Henry Darne, John Hunter, Charles Alexander, Presley Cox, Wm. Chapman, Townshend Hooe, Wm. Herbert, Thomas Triplett, George Gilpin, Wm. Browne, Bryan Fairfax, Robert Powell, Wm. Syles, David Stewart, John Courts, Wm. Hunter, Roger West, John Jackson, Benjamin Harris, Lewis Hipkins, George Gilpin, Nicholas Fitzhugh, Robert T. Hooe, Baldwin Dade, Philip R. Fendall, James P. Nicholls, Ludwell Lee, Wm. Fitzhugh, George Taylor, John Roberts, George Deneale, Daniel McClean, H. Smoot, John Tinker, Edmund I. Lee, Charles Simms, Charles Alexander, Jr., John Tucker, James Kieth, Wm. S. Moore, Cuthbert Powell, John Muncaster, Jonah Thompson, Thomas Swann, Tristam Dalton, Augustin J. Smith, William Hodgson, Anthony Crease, Richard M. Scott, Francis Adams, Wm. H. Fitzhugh, James Kieth, Jr., James H. Hooe, Craven Thompson, Thomas Semmes, Horatio Clagget, Noblet Herbert, Newton Keene, John Roberts, Bernard Hooe, Wm. Herbert, Peyton Thompson, John Lloyd, J. J. Frobell, Wm. Fowle, J. A. Washington, James Atkinson, J. H. Crease, W. C. Page, Edward Latham, R. H. Claggett, W. F. Alexander, Daniel Minor, George Johnson, Guy Atkinson, Cassius F. Lee, Solomon Masters, Wm. Morgan, Richard C. Mason, George Fletcher, James Irwin, J. Grubb, General John Mason.

The following names, not in the old vestry-book, have been furnished me:—

Louis A. Cazenove, William W. Hoxton, William L. Powell, Edgar Snowden, Edward C. Fletcher, William G. Cazenove, Henry C. Neale, John J. Lloyd, Reuben Johnston, Charles H. Lee, William C. Yeaton, Richard C. Smith, Thomas C. Atkinson, Lawrence B. Taylor, Henry W. Vandegrift, John Crockford, Douglass R. Semmes.

Concerning two of the above-mentioned vestrymen I may be permitted to say a few words. Mr. George Taylor and Edmund I. Lee were churchwardens when I took charge of Christ Church in 1811, and so continued until the removal of one by a change of residence, and the other by death, after a long term of service. They were both of them members of the Standing Committee during the same period. I think I knew them well, and knew them to be sincere Christians, and useful, punctual business-men. Mr. Taylor, l think, nearly reached his century of years, his step still elastic and form erect and countenance fine and temper unruffled,—walking between Washington and Alexandria without weariness almost to the last, and lifting up a distinct voice in the utterance of those prayers in which he delighted,—dying, as he had lived, in the faith of the Gospel. Mr. Lee generally attended on State Conventions, and sometimes the General Convention. He was a man of great decision and perseverance in what he deemed right,—obstinate, some of us thought, even to a fault, when we differed from him. There was no compromise at all in him, with any thing which he thought wrong. He was as fearless as Julius Cæsar. On a certain Sabbath, while I was performing service in Christ Church, a certain person in the gallery disturbed myself and the congregation by undue vociferation in the responses, and also at the opening of the sermon. I paused, and requested him to desist, and was proceeding, but Mr. Lee, who was near him, arose and asked me to suspend the sermon. Walking toward the offender, he told him that he must leave the house. As he approached to enforce it, the person raised a loaded whip and struck at him. Mr. Lee, nothing moved, took him by the arms and led him out of the house, and deposited him in the town jail. When mayor of the town, he was a terror to evil-doers. Ascertaining that there was much gambling going on among the gentlemen of the place, and some of the principal ones, he took effective measures for their discovery, brought between thirty and forty before the court, and had them fined. The prosecuting attorney was his particular friend, and was slightly implicated in the evil practice; but he did not spare him. Nor did he wish to be spared, but, coming forward and paying his fine, then did his duty with all the rest. Mr. Lee was of course not a popular man, nor did he seek or care to be, but did his duty entirely regardless of all others. He kept our Conventions in good order, by always insisting upon the observance of rules of which the clergy are not always mindful. He was the great advocate of our Bishops' fund, and defended it from all invasions. I not only knew Mr. Lee from my youth up, but I saw him in his last moments, and heard him with the truest humility speak of himself as a poor sinner, whose only hope was in Christ. And can I speak of him without remembering that meek and holy woman to whom he was so long a most affectionate husband? She was the daughter of that Christian patriot, Richard Henry Lee. For more than thirty years she was gradually dying of consumption, and yet in such a way as to admit of the exhibition of all her Christian graces in the various relations of life.   By universal consent, she was one of the purest specimens of humanity sanctified by the grace of God.

P.S.—It was in this parish that the question of the right of the Church to the glebes, which had been determined against the Church in the Virginia courts, was reconsidered.   Being brought before the Supreme Court, the former decision was reversed, so far as the glebe in Fairfax parish was concerned.   The opinion of the court, which was drawn up by Judge Story, of Massachusetts, may be seen in the Appendix.

From Sparks's Life of Washington.

"After the French War, while in retirement at Mount Vernon, Washington took a lively interest in Church affairs, regularly attending public worship, and being at different times a vestryman in two parishes.

"The following list of votes for vestrymen in Fairfax parish and Truro parish is copied from a paper in Washington's handwriting, and shows that he was chosen a vestryman in each of those parishes.   How long he continued in that station, I have no means of determining.   The place of worship in Fairfax parish was at Alexandria; in Truro parish, at Pohick; the former ten, the latter seven, miles from Mount Vernon."

Vestry chosen for Fairfax parish, 28th March, 1765, with the number of votes for each.

John West	340	George Johnston	254
Charles Alexander	309	Townshend Dade	252
William Payne	304	Richard Sandford	247
John Dalton	281	William Adams	244
George Washington	274	John Posey	222
Charles Broadwater	260	Daniel French	221

Vestry chosen for Truro parish, 22d July, 1765, with the number of votes for each.

George Mason	282	Alexander Henderson	231
Edward Payne	277	William Gardner	218
George Washington	259	Tomison Ellzey	209
John Posey	259	Thomas W. Coffer	189
Daniel McCarty	246	William Lynton	172
George William Fairfax	235	Thomas Ford	170

ARTICLE LXX.

St. Paul's Church, Alexandria and Cameron and Shelburne Parishes, Loudon County.

WE have already said that St. Paul's Church grew out of a difference between the Rev. Mr. Gibson and the congregation of Christ Church, in 1809. There were worthy persons in the vestry and congregation who thought that Mr. Gibson's apology for the manner in which he resigned his charge ought to have been accepted, and that he should have been allowed to withdraw his resignation and continue his ministry. The majority of the vestry thought otherwise, and that it would be better to let the connection be dissolved. Some of the vestry and of the congregation thought that the harshness of manner and language sometimes apparent in his discourses proceeded from an honest zeal, which made him speak very differently from the tame way and courteous strain of the old clergy, and therefore determined to form a new congregation. They accordingly purchased a small vacant church belonging to the Presbyterian denomination, and commenced services in it. On the 23d of January, 1810, a vestry was organized, consisting of Daniel McLean, Lawrence Hooff, James B. Nicholls, Mark Butts, Nathaniel C. Hunter, John Young, Joseph Thomas, Adam Lynn, Joseph Thornton, John Hooff, Thomas West Peyton, to whom at different times, until the year 1832, have been added Charles Page, Thomas Moore, Augustin Newton, Ferdinand Mastellar, John Gird, Lawrence Lewis, Humphrey Peake, W. C. Gardiner, James Entwisle, Isaac Cannell, Christopher Neale, George Johnson, Norman Fitzhugh, Silas Reed, Lewis A. Cazenove, Benjamin I. Fendall, Bernard Hooe, Charles Koones, William Fowle, Lewis Hooff, Anthony McLean, Geo. U. Smoot, William H. Fowle, James Green, Dr. Isaac Winston, Francis L. Smith, Stephen Shinn, David Funsten, Orlando Fairfax, Silas Reed, George Brent, Bernard Hooe, &c.

MINISTERS OF ST. PAUL'S CHURCH.

The Rev. Mr. Gibson resigned in the month of September, 1811. In the following February the Rev. Wm. Wilmer entered upon the charge and continued in it until the 19th of October, 1826, when he accepted the Presidency of William and Mary College. During his ministry the old church was enlarged and the present church built, and the congregation increased manifold. Of Dr. Wilmer I have already spoken in one of the articles on Williamsburg. I will only add that the congregation could not have been supplied with one better calculated to build it up, whether we consider his zeal, prudence, or ability for the work, in private or public. During his residence in Virginia he was always sent to the General Convention, and when there chosen to preside over its deliberations. With his pen he defended Protestantism against Romanism, and moderate views of the Church and Sacraments against certain extravagant ones which were at that early period finding their way among us. At the resignation of Mr. Wilmer, the Rev. William Jackson was chosen, but did not enter upon his duties until February, 1827. Most acceptably and usefully did he labour in this congregation, until his resignation in June, 1832, when he accepted a call to St. Stephen's Church, New York. He left St. Paul's and the diocese of Virginia with the deep regrets of all who knew his amiable character, heard his excellent sermons, and had opportunity to appreciate his great worth. The Rev. James T. Johnson was then elected, and entered upon his duties in the fall of 1833, and continues the minister until the present time, 1857.

I find one or two things on the records of this parish which are worthy of insertion. Bishop Madison was applied to to consecrate the first St. Paul's Church, but declined on account of collegiate duties, and requested Bishop Claggett to perform the office, which was done promptly and much to the gratification of all. An instance of liberality deserves also to be inserted. The first St. Paul's Church was bought on credit for the sum of three thousand five hundred dollars. In the year 1813, Mr. Daniel McLean, one of the vestry, paid the amount and made a deed to the vestry for it. The second church so exceeded the first in size and expense as to cost twenty-six thousand dollars.

CAMERON AND SHELBURNE PARISHES.

Cameron parish was cut off from Truro parish in 1749, and until 1769 included Shelburne parish. A few words will suffice for all the information I have to communicate concerning it. In the year 1758 the Rev. John Andrews was its minister; whether before or after this, or how long, is not known. Whether he was the minister who was subsequently the professor at Williamsburg, and after the war discontinued the ministry and moved to Philadelphia, is not known. He was ordained in 1749, and the Rev. Archibald Avens, who probably succeeded him in Cameron parish, in 1767. In the years 1773, 1774, and 1776, the Rev. Spence Grayson was the minister; whether before or after, or how long, not known. We hear nothing of this parish after the Revolution. There was a church in it near the Gumspring, the traces of which are yet to be seen. There was, I think, another not far from the junction of the roads from Georgetown and Alexandria to Leesburg.

In addition to this brief notice of Cameron and Shelburne parishes, we are able to furnish the following facts concerning the latter, taken from an old vestry-book, or rather fragment of one, commencing in 1771 and ending in 1806. On the 10th of April, in the year 1771, the churchwardens—John Lewis and Thomas Shore— are directed to employ some minister to perform divine service once in every three months during pleasure, and that the preference be given to the Rev. Mr. Scott, and that the minister employed do preach at Leesburg and the other chapel (called the Mountain Chapel) in the parish, as also at some convenient place near the gap of the Short Hill, to be fixed on by the churchwardens. On the 27th of July of that year, at the meeting of the vestry, it appears that the Rev. Archibald Avens, who was no doubt the minister in the parish of Cameron in the year 1769, two years before, when Shelburne was cut off from it, and who was living in the part which was assigned to Cameron, had moved into Shelburne and claimed to be its minister. This the vestry resisted, and advertised for a minister in the Virginia Gazette. In the month of August of the same year we find the following entry:—

" Mr. William Leigh, a student of William and Mary College, having been warmly recommended to this vestry by the president, masters, and professors of said college, as a young man of sound learning, unfeigned piety, and unexceptionable morals, we do hereby undertake and agree to receive him as minister of this parish, provided it should continue vacant till he returns from Great Britain in Holy Orders, unless he should by some misconduct forfeit the good opinion we entertain of him."

At a meeting in November of the same year, five thousand three hundred and twelve pounds of tobacco were levied for the Rev. James Scott, who had been officiating for them. He was doubtless the minister of Prince William parish, of whom we have formerly written, and who had been engaged to visit this parish during the last six months.

In the next month we find the Rev. David Griffith elected and unanimously recommended to the Governor for induction, which was a striking proof of their confidence in him. Five thousand-weight of tobacco were added to his salary in place of a glebe,—there being none at that time. Mr. Griffith continued their minister until May, 1776. During that year he engaged in the Revolutionary struggle as chaplain. There is no record of any meeting of the vestry after May the 22d, 1776, until April 27, 1779. In 1780 the vestry advertise for a minister. From 1776 to 1792 the vestry was unable to obtain a minister. Indeed, it was impossible to collect any thing for that purpose. The glebe which had been purchased for Mr. Griffith was rented out during that time for a very small sum. In the year 1794 the Rev. Alexander Jones is minister for one year on a salary of fifty pounds. In 1796 the Rev. Alexander McFarlan becomes the minister, on the written condition that he may be removed at any time according to the canons of the Church of Virginia. He engaged to preach two Sundays at Leesburg, one at the Pot-House, and one at Middleburg. In the year 1801, Mr. McFarlan, in a letter to the vestry, resigns the parish and gives up the glebe, on the express condition that they choose the Rev. John Dunn as his successor. The vestry accept his resignation, adding that they have no regard to his conditions, which he had no right to make. They, however, elect Mr. Dunn, who was their worthy minister until his death in 1827. He was ordained Priest by Bishop Madison. Mr. Dunn was suddenly seized with paralysis while performing service in Middleburg, and died in Leesburg shortly after.

I was called to witness his happy, triumphant death, and after some time to make an improvement of both his life and death in a funeral discourse, which was published. Had I a copy of it, I would make use of some parts of it in order to convey to my readers the impressions then resting on my own mind and on that of the community concerning this excellent man. The text was, "Behold an Israelite indeed, in whom there is no guile." And seldom has it ever been so true of any of the frail children of men. He was in all things a most sincere and upright man, "speaking the truth from his heart." He was a man of a most humble and contented mind. He lived on his glebe, and, though not much of a farmer, and a very easy master to the few servants belonging to himself or Mrs. Dunn, lived on its proceeds, receiving little or nothing else, until perhaps the last few years of his life. I can never forget his words or looks when, walking about his premises, he told me that he had nothing to wish for more; that he had corn enough in his granary to last until Christmas, and some hay, and was out of debt; "and what do I want more?" he emphatically asked. Mr. Dunn was a man of sound views of religion and an honest preacher of them. From the time of the first efforts for the revival of religion in Virginia until his death, he was a member of the Standing Committee of the diocese and punctual in his attendance, though living at some distance from the place where its meetings were held.

He was succeeded by the Rev. Thomas Jackson, who continued for three years to fill the place with ability and great acceptableness. The Rev. Mr. Cutler then spent a year in the parish, and, at the end of that time, removed to his present charge in Brooklyn, New York.

The Rev. George Adie took charge of it in 1832, and continued in it until his death, in 1856,—being its faithful, laborious, and beloved minister for nearly twenty-four years,—and has been succeeded by the Rev. Mr. Caldwell. Mr. Adie, for many years connected with his charge at Leesburg regular though infrequent services at Upperville, Middleburg, and Aldie. He also acted as chaplain to the female school at Belmont, a few miles from Leesburg, kept by Miss Margaret Mercer. For a faithful and deeply-interesting account of this remarkable woman we must refer our readers to the little volume by Dr. Caspar Morris, of Philadelphia, than which there are few biographies more just, more edifying, or more pleasing. Miss Mercer still lives in the memories and affections of her numerous pupils, who are scattered over the land. For some years the Sunday afternoon services of Mr. Adie were held in the large hall at Belmont; but, as there were many poor in the neighbourhood, Miss Mercer, at her own expense, put up a neat little chapel a short distance from the house, for their benefit. I have spent some interesting seasons in this house of God, preaching and administering Confirmation. Miss Mercer was then and there to be seen in her highest glory and happiness, in the midst of her pupils and the poor. At her death, a tomb was erected in the churchyard by a general contribution from her pupils, with the following inscription:—

"Sacred to the memory of Margaret Mercer, born July 1, 1791; died September 17, 1846. Her remains repose beneath the chancel of this church, built by her own self-denying labours. This monument is erected by her pupils, as a testimony of their admiration of her elevated Christian character, and of their gratitude for her invaluable instructions."

The history of the churches in Shelburne parish, as seen on the vestry-book, is amusing. For some years before the war, the record states that various places were determined upon and then abandoned, various plans agreed upon and then changed. Twice was it ordered that a church be built at a place belonging to George William Fairfax, once on the land of Colonel Tayloe, then at the fork of the road leading to Noland's Ferry; sometimes it was to be of wood, then of stone, sometimes of one size, then of another. I am unable to designate either of the places. The war came upon them while thus divided in sentiment, and settled the question in favour of none. It was not until the second war with England that an Episcopal church was begun in Leesburg, on its present site. Services were held by Mr. Dunn in the old Presbyterian church in Leesburg, and the free church in Middleburg.

A few words concerning the old glebe in this parish will not be without interest to the present generation. About the year 1772, a tract of land containing four hundred and sixty-five acres, on the North Fork of Goose Creek, was purchased, and, soon after, a house put upon it. When Mr. Dunn became minister, in 1801, an effort was made by the overseers of the poor to sell it, but it was effectually resisted at law. At the death of Mr. Dunn, in 1827, the overseers of the poor again proceeded to sell it. The vestry was divided in opinion as to the course to be pursued. Four of them—Dr. W. C. Selden, Dr. Henry Claggett, Mr. Fayette Ball, and George M. Chichester—were in favour of resisting it; the other eight thought it best to let it share the fate of all the others. It was accordingly sold. The purchaser lived in Maryland; and, of course, the matter might be brought before the Supreme Court as a last resort, should the courts of Virginia decide against the Church's claim. The minority of four, encouraged by the decision of the Supreme Court in the case of the Fairfax glebe, determined to engage in a lawsuit for it. It was first brought in Winchester, and decided against the Church. It was then carried to the Court of Appeals, in Richmond, and, during its lingering progress there, three out of four of the vestrymen who engaged in it died, and the fourth was persuaded to withdraw it.

List of the Vestrymen of Shelburne Parish from the year 1771 *to* 1806.

William Smith, Thomas Lewis, James Hamilton, Francis Peyton, Josias Clapham, Levin Powell, John Lewis, Thomas Ousley, Thos. Shore, Thompson Mason, Stephen Donaldson, Craven Peyton, Colonel Wm. Bronaugh, Colonel John Alexander, Joshua Gore, Thos. Respass, Jos. Combs, Colonel Symon Triplett, Thomas Kenner, J. Daniel, Benjamin Grayson, Joseph Lane, Stephen Thompson Mason, Matthew Rust, Wilson C. Selden, Chas. Bennett, A. B. T. Mason, William Bronaugh, Jr., W. H. Powell, William

Jones, Thomas Fouch, William Fouke, Dr. Thomas Simm, Burr Powell, Peter B. Whiting, Jas. Leith, William Chilton, Charles Fenton Mercer.

The vestry-book from the year 1806 to this present time having been mislaid or lost, a friend has sent me from recollection the following list of vestrymen in addition to the above :—

W. C. Selden, Henry Claggett, Richard H. Henderson, W. T. T. Mason, Fayette Ball, G. M. Chichester, Jno. I. Harding, William Ellzey, Lewis Berkeley, B. Maulsby, C. Douglass, W. H. Gray, Dr. J. Gray, W. A. Powell, George Lee, J. P. Smart, H. Saunders, A. Belt, C. Powell, C. Hempstone, John Wildman, S. K. Jackson, B. W. Harrison, H. T. Harrison, I. Orr, Thomas H. Claggett.

THE POWELL FAMILY.

I have not been able to ascertain any thing very certain concerning the family of Powells which appears on the records of the Church in Loudon county.   The name of Powell is a very ancient one on the civil records of Virginia.   Cuthbert Powell was contemporary in Lancaster county with the first John Carter. Indeed, the name is found on one or more of the earliest lists of adventurers to Virginia.   Colonel Powell, of Loudon,—father of Messrs. Leven, Burr, Cuthbert, Alfred Powell, and their sisters,—married a near relative of the Rev. Mr. Harrison, of Dumfries, of whose ancestors some account, taken from the record of Westminster parish, England, was given in our sketch of Dettingen parish.   Colonel Powell was once a member of Congress from his district.   With his widow I was acquainted in the earlier years of my ministry.   She was one whose fidelity to the Church no adversity could shake.   When all others were deserting it, she continued steadfast.   A minister of another denomination was once conversing with her on the subject of his own and her Church, and said that there was but little difference between them,—that they were like twin-sisters.   Whether she suspected him of some design at proselyting or not, I cannot say, but she very decidedly replied, "It might be so, but that she greatly preferred one of the sisters to the other."   She was old-fashioned in all her ways,—in her dress, her home, her furniture, and domestic occupations.   She lived in a plain house, a little back of the main and indeed only street in Middleburg.   On one of my journeys to Alexandria, while stopping on a summer's afternoon at that place, I walked over to her abode, and found her busily engaged at her wheel, spinning tow or flax, on what was called the small wheel in those days, in contradistinction to that on which wool and cotton were spun, and which was called the large wheel.

The march of improvement has left both sorts far behind, and with them much honest, domestic industry and substantial clothing.

One word concerning my old friend, Mr. Lewis Berkeley, of Aldie. We were school-boys together. He was descended from the old family of Berkeleys in Middlesex, which lived at Barnelms, on the Pyankatank, and which was the last to leave the county, after having been a main prop to the Church for more than one hundred and fifty years. Mr. Lewis Berkeley married a daughter of Mr. William Noland, an old member of the Legislature from Loudon, in days long since passed away. Mr. Noland signalized himself by his zealous advocacy of the law against duelling. So just and sensible was his speech on the subject, that it was soon introduced into the school-books or collection of pieces for school-boys, and still holds its place. Mr. Berkeley, his excellent wife, and Mr. and Mrs. Noland, were for a long term of years the pious, consistent, active, and liberal supporters of the Episcopal Church in Loudon, whether the services were at Aldie, Middleburg, or even twelve miles off, at Leesburg, at which latter place they often attended.

ARTICLE LXXI.

Parishes in Frederick County.

IN our last communication we had reached the Blue Ridge,—the great dividing-line between Eastern and Western Virginia. We now ascend that beautiful range of mountains, and look down on the wide and extensive valley which lies between it and those numerous ones which hide the great Alleghany from our view. I believe it is generally admitted that this valley is not only the most fertile and desirable portion of the State, but also the most picturesque and beautiful. But it is not our province to descant on such themes. We may, however, be permitted to declare our assent to the hypothesis of Mr. Jefferson and others, that it was once a great lake or sea, which emptied itself through the channel formed by the force of the waters at Harper's Ferry, leaving immense prairies behind to be covered in due time with heavy forests, some of which our eyes now behold, while most of them have been felled by the hands of our forefathers.*

Such a country could not but attract the attention of hardy and adventurous farmers. The first who entered it were from Pennsylvania. Crossing the Potomac at what is now called Shepherdstown, but at first and for a considerable time Mecklenburg,—doubtless after some town or place in Germany,—they there made a settlement. From thence emigration proceeded on toward Winchester, Stephensburg, or Newtown, Woodstock, &c. Joist Hite, the ancestor of all the Hites, was the first to make a settlement north of Winchester, with sixteen families. This was in the year 1732. His

---

* It is a true tradition, I believe, that one of the Carters, who at an early period took up or purchased a large tract of land in old Frederick, including all that which now belongs to the Burwell family, and extending beyond and along the Opequon and its barren hills and stunted trees, offered to one of his sons the choice of an equal portion of that upon the Opequon and of that fertile prairie lying between it and the Shenandoah River, and that the former was preferred because of the timber, which was visible, though of so indifferent a character. That the lower and richer lands of this part of the valley were once prairie in the days of our forefathers is generally admitted. Old Mr. Isaac Hite, of Bellgrove, now deceased, informed me that his father often spoke of the land about the White Post as being, in his day, covered with a thicket of saplings.

descendants of that name became active members of, or friends of, the Episcopal Church. Soon after this, Presbyterians of Scotch and Irish descent began to settle in the valley. In the year 1738, a number from Pennsylvania, wishing to add themselves to those already settled, sent, through the synod of Pennsylvania, a deputation to Governor Gooch, of Virginia, "asking all liberty of conscience and of worshipping God agreeably to the principles of their education." They professed the utmost loyalty to the King, and promised "the most dutiful submission to the government which is placed over them." The Governor assured them of his favour, and that no interruption should be given to their ministers, if they should "conform themselves to the rules prescribed by the Act of Toleration in England." It was the same principle which had been acted on before this time in Virginia, and continued to be to the end of the Colonial Establishment. Under that law, any number of persons, of whatsoever name, might ask for and should receive a license for some place of meeting where they might worship after their own way. Even during the preceding century, the first of our settlements in Virginia, the Germans on the Rappahannock and the French Huguenots on James River had not only been tolerated, but allowed special favours, such as grants of lands and freedom from taxes, until of their own accord they applied to be admitted into union with the Established Church under Episcopal ministers,—finding it difficult to procure any of their own. Other denominations also were allowed licenses for places of worship,— whether private or public houses,—provided they sought and used them in compliance with the true intent of the law. In the case of President Davies, about the middle of the last century,—which we have considered when speaking of the parish in Hanover,—seven places of worship were licensed for him before the Governor declared that he was exceeding the bounds prescribed by the spirit and intent of the law.

With these general observations we proceed to the history of the parish of Frederick. The materials are furnished by the Acts of Assembly dating back to the year 1738, to the records of the court beginning in 1744, and to the old vestry-book going back to the year 1764, and some papers of an earlier date.

In the year 1738, the Assembly, in consideration of the increasing number of settlers in the valley, determined to cut off two new counties and parishes—West Augusta and Frederick—from Orange county and parish, which latter then took in all Western Virginia. The county and parish of Frederick embraced all that is now Shenandoah, with a part of Page, Warren, Clarke, Frederick, Jefferson, Berkeley, and Hampshire. Augusta had all the rest to the utmost limits of Virginia, wherever they were,—the contest with France as to the boundaries not being then settled. The execution of the Act, however, was postponed until it should be made to appear that there were inhabitants enough for the appointment of justices of the peace, &c. In the year 1744, the vestry and court of Frederick county were organized and in action. Of the vestry, nothing more is heard after its organization, except the appointment of processioners in 1747, until the year 1752, when an Act of Assembly was passed dissolving it and ordering a new election, on the ground that it had raised more than fifteen hundred pounds for building a number of churches which were unfinished and in a ruinous condition. As the churches of that day and in this region were log-houses, costing only from thirty to forty or fifty pounds, there must have been much misspending of money. Who those vestrymen were does not appear. Those chosen in their place were the following:—Thomas Lord Fairfax, Isaac Perkins, Gabriel Jones, John Hite, Thomas Swearingen, Charles Buck, Robert Lemmon, John Lindsey, John Ashby, James Cromley, Lewis Neil. Thomas Bryan Martin, the nephew and one of the heirs of Lord Fairfax, does not ever appear as vestryman, but seems to have been an active magistrate, and to have taken a considerable part in completing McCoy's Chapel, on the road from Winchester to Front Royal, in the neighbourhood of the McCoys and Cunningham Chapel, which stood near the spot where what has been long called the Old Chapel—near the Burwell burial-ground—still stands. Mr. Edward McGuire also appears as a magistrate, but not as vestryman,—he being of the Romish Church. He was the ancestor of many worthy ministers and members of the Protestant Episcopal Church of Virginia.

Having mentioned Lord Fairfax as the first on the list of that most respectable body of vestrymen given above, and who also gave the land on which the church in Winchester stood, and under which he was buried, it is but right that we should add a few words as to himself and his numerous and most estimable relatives now scattered through this and other States.

The first of the Fairfaxes who came to this country, and who settled in Westmoreland, and then on an estate near Mount Vernon, called Belvoir, was Mr. William Fairfax, a scholar, a soldier and civilian. The latter character he exhibited as President of the Council of Virginia,—the station next to that of Governor. By two marriages he had five children,—George William, Thomas, William, Bryan, and Hannah. George William married a Miss Cary, of Virginia, but left the county before the Revolutionary War. Thomas and William died, the one in the English navy and the other in the army. Bryan took Orders in the Episcopal Church, and was for some years minister of Christ's Church, Alexandria. Hannah married Warner Washington, of Fairfield, a near relative of George Washington, and was a worthy member of our Church, leaving two sons and three daughters behind. Two of her daughters—Mrs. Milton (who was previously Mrs. Nelson) and Mrs. Whiting—were long and well known to me as among the best of women. Of their mother I have often heard Mr. Balmaine speak in the highest terms.* The elder William Fairfax was the manager of the estates of his kinsman, Lord Thomas Fairfax, the owner of all the lands in the Northern Neck of Virginia, which he inherited from his mother, the daughter of Lord Culpepper, and which were bounded by the Rappahannock and Potomac, extending to the head-waters of each, the one beginning in the Blue Ridge, the other in the Alleghany Mountains. Lord Fairfax was a man of the most perfect English education, Oxford being his Alma Mater. He was a member of that club of which Addison was the head, and to whose pens we are indebted for that immortal work, the Spectator. He was early and deeply disappointed in love, which gave a turn to his character and habits, and prepared him for seclusion in the wilds of America. In 1749, he visited his estates in Virginia, and was so much pleased with the country that he determined to settle here. During that visit he became acquainted with, and attached to, young George Washington, then only sixteen years of age. The affection was returned on the part of Washington, and he readily accepted the proposition of Lord Fairfax to become surveyor of all his lands. Lord Fairfax returned for a short time to England, while Washing-

---

* In proof of the zeal of Mrs. Hannah Washington, of Fairfield, in the cause of religion and the Church, I might adduce a brief correspondence between herself and Mr. George Lewis, who lived at the place afterward owned by Mr. Milton, on the subject of securing the services of Mr. Balmaine in the year 1787, when steps were taken to build what has always been called The Chapel. Mrs. Washington, whose example has been followed by many good ladies in Virginia since, took an active part in some Church matters, and wrote to Mr. Lewis, proposing that, inasmuch as at least a year must elapse before the chapel could be finished, the neighbours on both sides of Battletown should unite in renting a house of a Mr. McMahon, at Traphill, for divine service, and promises to send *her carpenters* to fit it up for the purpose. To this Mr. Lewis readily assents, and the plan was adopted. The house was pointed out to me between forty and fifty years ago.

ton immediately repaired to his work in the valley, making his head-quarters at Greenway Court. Washington continued for two or three years in the service of Lord Fairfax, and as public surveyor for Western Virginia. At the death of Lord Fairfax, in 1781, being ninety-two years of age, the title fell to his only surviving brother, Robert, in England, and at his death, which occurred soon after, to the Rev. Bryan Fairfax, the nearest kinsman. It deserves to be mentioned of Lord Fairfax, that, titled as he was, and rich, he never failed to perform his duty as a citizen and neighbour, but, besides acting as Keeper of the Rolls for Frederick, was uniform in his attendance at Winchester, twelve miles off, as one of the magistrates of the county. The poor around him cultivated some of his lands, and received all the benefits of the same.*

To McCoy's and Cunningham's Chapel are to be added two on the north and south branches of Shenandoah, whose location cannot now be ascertained, one in Winchester, one at Bunker's Hill, called Morgan's Chapel, of which we shall speak more fully hereafter, perhaps one called Wood's Chapel, between Winchester and Charlestown, and one at Shepherdstown, then called Mecklenburg Chapel. All these were probably begun, and some of them sufficiently completed for use, between the years 1740 and 1750. In 1768, Mr. Van Swearingen received one hundred and forty-eight pounds for completing a new church at Mecklenburg, now Shepherdstown. In the year 1768, Isaac Hite was directed to contract for a church at Leith's—place not known—for forty-nine pounds. In the year 1774, a church was ordered to be built near Cedar Creek for one hundred pounds; whether executed or not, I cannot tell. In the year 1772, it was resolved to build a church, costing two hundred and fifty-two pounds, at Carney's Spring, near Berryville, on land given by Mr. Charles Smith, which was afterward increased to four hundred and forty-nine pounds, and a contract made with Mr. John Neville, father of General Neville, and some of the materials collected on the spot. In the following year it was determined to build it at Cunningham's

---

* In proof of the needlessness of great landed or other possessions, let me mention the end of all Lord Fairfax's earthly property. His nephew, Colonel Martin, was his heir. In the year 1794, his estate in lands was nine thousand seven hundred acres. My father's farm lay beside it. I have a letter from my father in that year to Mr. Charles Carter, of Shirly, on James River, who, it seems, thought of moving to Frederick, urging him to purchase it, as Colonel Martin had determined to sell. The price asked was forty shillings per acre, Virginia currency. The whole Northern Neck of Virginia, computed at many millions of acres, is thus reduced to less than ten thousand.

Chapel, two acres of ground being given by Colonel Hugh Nelson, of York, the then owner of the Burwell tract, and the materials moved there. Again it was resolved to build at Carney's Spring, and the materials removed a second time. The result of the controversy was that no such church was ever built, though the money was in hand. The war soon came on, and at the end of it the funds were delivered into the hands of the overseers of the poor. In the year 1762, a new stone church was contracted for in Winchester,—the same which was afterward sold in order to build the present church.

Having thus brought down the history of the church-buildings to the time of the Revolution, we will now give a list of the lay readers and vestrymen from the year 1764, when the vestry-book commences, merely premising that the county and parish of Frederick were in 1769 divided into the counties of Dunmore, afterward changed to Shenandoah, Frederick, and Berkeley, and into the parishes of Beckford, Frederick, and Norbone.

Names of the vestrymen from the year 1764 until the year 1780, when no more meetings of the vestry take place until 1785:—Isaac Hite, John Hite, John Greenleaf, Thomas Rutherford, James Keith, John Neville, Charles Smith, James Wood, Jacob Hite, Thomas Wadlington, Burr Harrison, Thomas Swearingen, Van Swearingen, Angus McDonald, Philip Bush, Frederick Conrad, George Rice, Alexander White, James Barnett, Marquis Calmes, John McDonald, Edward Snickers, Warner Washington, Joseph Holmes, Benjamin Sedwick, Edmund Taylor, John Smith, Samuel Dowdal. Of these, Philip Bush and some others, in consequence of some unknown difficulties, resigned in the year 1774, though all of them resumed their seats except Mr. Bush. Lord Fairfax in the year 1775 made a deed to Mr. Bush, Frederick Conrad, and others, for the lot on which the Lutheran church stood, though Mr. Conrad continued as vestryman until the year 1780, when the vestries were all dissolved by Act of Assembly. James Wood, who was both clerk and vestryman, resigned in 1777 and entered the army. He rose to the rank of General, and was afterward Governor of the State, and represented the parish two years in Convention while Governor. James Barnett resigned in 1773 and joined the Baptists.

The lay readers during all this period, at the different chapels, were John Ruddell, James Barnett, John Barns, Henry Nelson, James Graham, Henry Frencham, Morgan Morgan, John James, William Dobson, William Howard, John Lloyd.

THE MINISTERS OF FREDERICK PARISH.

The Rev. Mr. Gordon was the first; when his ministry commenced and ended, not known. The Rev. Mr. Meldrum comes next, and continues until 1765. Between him and the vestry a long law-suit was carried on, which terminated in his favour. The vestry applied to the Legislature for relief, and obtained it. Mr. Sebastian was recommended by the vestry to the Bishop of London for Orders in 1766, and became their minister, but after two years removed to Northumberland county. The Rev. Mr. Thruston became the minister in 1768, binding himself to preach at seven places scattered over the large parish of Frederick, Shepherdstown being one of them. Mr. Thruston was a native of Gloucester, where the name still abounds, and was captain of the militia in that county. The vestry of Petsworth parish, in Gloucester, recommended him for Orders, and he was their minister for some years before coming to Frederick. He laid down the ministry and entered the army in 1777. After the war he lived at Mount Zion, in Frederick. In his latter days he removed to the neighbourhood of New Orleans, and, it is said, was preparing to take some part in defending that place against the British when they were defeated by General Jackson. He was the father of the late Judge Thruston, of the District of Columbia, and the ancestor of many respectable families in Virginia and elsewhere. From the time of Colonel Thruston's resignation in 1777 to the year 1785, there was no minister, so far as we can ascertain. In the year 1785, a vestry was elected, consisting of Colonel R. K. Meade, George F. Norton, churchwardens, John Thruston, Edward Smith, Raleigh Colston, Girard Briscoe, John Milton, Robert Wood, Major Thomas Massey. By this vestry the Rev. Alexander Balmaine was chosen minister. He had been chaplain in the army of the Revolution, in which a number of the above-mentioned vestrymen had served. Mr. Balmaine was born in Scotland, in the neighbourhood of Edinburgh, in the year 1740, was educated at St. Andrews with a view to the Presbyterian ministry, but relinquished the design. Himself and his brother, who was a lawyer, were warm friends of the Colonists in the Stamp Act difficulties, and became so obnoxious on that account to the loyalists about Edinburgh, that they thought it best to try their fortunes elsewhere, and moved to London, where they became acquainted with Mr. Arthur Lee, who recommended Mr. Balmaine to the family of Richard Henry Lee, as private tutor. While there, he prepared for the ministry of the Episcopal Church, and upon receiving Orders became rector of Augusta parish, then extending to the Ohio River, and including, it is believed, Pittsburg itself, for he paid several visits to the Episcopalians in that place. When our difficulties commenced with England, true to his principles adopted in Scotland, he took an early and active part, was chairman of the Committee of Safety in Augusta, and drafted the resolution adopted by that committee. Soon after this, he entered the Virginia line as chaplain, and continued so until the very close of the war. Mr. Balmaine was the rector of the parish of Frederick until his death. I was his assistant during a number of the last years of his life.

ARTICLE LXXII.

Parishes in Frederick County.—No. 2.

AFTER the death of Mr. Balmaine, the Rev. Mr. Bryan officiated for a time at Winchester, Bunker's Hill, and Wickliffe, in the capacity of assistant to myself, for a few years. He was followed by the Rev. Mr. Robertson as assistant in Winchester alone. After a few years he resigned and went on a mission to Greece. In the year 1827, Christ Church, Winchester, was organized into a separate parish, to be called the parish of Frederick, Winchester, with the Rev. J. E. Jackson, minister. Mr. Jackson was one of three worthy brothers of most respectable parentage in Tutbury, England, all of whom ministered in the Church of Virginia and elsewhere in this country. The Rev. J. E. Jackson was the father of the Rev. William Jackson, who recently died so enviable a death in Norfolk. He was a most diligent and faithful pastor, preaching the true doctrines of the Gospel. Under his careful supervision the present excellent church and parsonage were built. In 1842, he resigned and moved to Kentucky. He was succeeded in 1842 by the Rev. Mr. Rooker, who resigned in 1847. Its present rector, the Rev. Cornelius Walker, succeeded Mr. Rooker. In May, 1834, another division of Frederick parish took place, when Wickliffe, including Berryville, was organized. The Rev. Mr. Jackson had been my assistant in that part of the parish for two years before this. The Rev. Mr. Rice had preceded him in that capacity. The Rev. Mr. Shiraz followed Mr. Jackson. Its next was the Rev. Richard Wilmer, who was succeeded by the Rev. Mr. Peterkin. Its present, the Rev. Mr. Whittle. This parish has recently been subdivided, and the Rev. Mr. Powell, who was disappointed during the last year in going to China, is the minister of that part which includes Wickliffe Church. Another offshoot was also made from Frederick parish many years since, in the neighbourhood of Middletown, where a parish was organized and a neat brick church built in the village, under the auspices of the late Strother Jones, the families of Hites, and others. It has had mainly to depend on the occasional services of the ministers in Winchester. The Rev. Mr. Bryant and the Rev. Mr. Irish were each for some time settled among them, and in none of our congregations have more zeal and liberality been displayed, according to numbers and means.

Having thus spoken of the five different divisions of Frederick parish, after itself had been reduced by Acts of Assembly, I proceed to mention the new churches built since the Revolution, in addition to those at Winchester and Middletown, already alluded to. Among the first things done by the vestry of Frederick, after its reorganization in 1787, was the adoption of measures for the building of a stone chapel where it was designed to erect that one which failed, through the disagreement of the people and vestry, just before the Revolution,—viz.: where that called Cunningham's Chapel stood. The land having now come into possession of Colonel Nathaniel Burwell, the same two acres for a church and burying-ground, which were offered by Colonel Hugh Nelson before the war, were now given by Colonel Burwell, and the present stone chapel ordered to be built in 1790. At what time it was completed does not appear, but probably in the same year. After the revival of our Church in Virginia commenced, a stone church was built at Wickliffe, Mr. Tredwell Smith and General Thomas Parker being the most active agents. A strenuous effort was made to have it a free church, which I earnestly opposed, and offered to insure from elsewhere as much as was pledged by other than Episcopalians. It was ascertained that not more than fifty dollars, out of the two or three thousand dollars which it cost, would be subscribed by other than Episcopalians, and the plan was dropped. This church was badly executed, and after a time the present excellent one of brick was built under the superintendence of Mr. Jaqueline Smith, and in a great measure at his expense. The ground on which it stood had been given by the family of Williams, who, with their ancestors in the Northern Neck of Virginia, had ever been staunch friends of the Church. After some years the church at Berryville was built on ground given by Mr. John Taylor, who owned the farm of which it was a part. The building of this church was delayed for some years by the attempt to have it placed on some basis which would make it common to all denominations. Effort after effort was made to effect it on this plan, without success. At length, when the friends of the scheme acknowledged its failure, I addressed the congregation in favour of an Episcopal church, and succeeded at once. In the year 1834, it was found that the old chapel was too small and inconvenient for the increasing congregation, and it was therefore determined to erect another and larger one, in a more central and convenient place, in the vicinity of Millwood, on ground given by Mr. George Burwell, of Carter Hall. Such, however, was the attachment of many to the old chapel that funds for the latter could not be obtained, except on condition of alternate services at the chapel. From year to year these services became less frequent, until at length they are now reduced to an annual pilgrimage, on some summer Sabbath, to this old and much-loved spot, except when services are held for the servants, or death summons the neighbours to add one more to the tenants of the graveyard.*

My remarks on the old parish of Frederick, and some of its branches, will be brought to a close by a brief reference to a spot of all others most sacred to many now living as the depository of all that was mortal of those most dear to us,—the burying-ground which lies at the foot of the hill on which still stands the old stone chapel. Ever since its appropriation to this purpose, it has been the graveyard of rich and poor, bond and free, those who lived near it, and the stranger from afar who died near it. It is called the Burwell graveyard, not merely because the land was given by one of that name, but because it is the resting-place of a far greater number bearing that name than any other. It has recently been enlarged and a portion of it divided into lots and the whole enclosed with a strong stone wall. The vestry have also proposed the raising and vesting in stock the sum of one thousand dollars for the perpetual preservation of it and the old chapel which overlooks it. Both of them stand in the immediate angle of two public and much-frequented roads, and the passing traveller may see old and venerable trees overshadowing many tombs, younger ones of perpetual verdure more recently planted, green hillocks, covered with grass and ivy, high headstones and large marble slabs, marking the place of interment and designating the names of those whose remains are beneath, and now and then a pillar, either for young or old, rising above the other memorials. To this place, for more than sixty years, have I been travelling, either borne in the arms of others, or as a mourner, or as officiating minister. To it, at no

---

* The following are the names of the vestrymen of Frederick parish before the division of it took place. It would be too tedious to enumerate all those belonging to the subdivisions down to the present time. In addition to those already mentioned as composing the first vestry after the war, in 1787, are the following:— John Woodcock, John Peyton, Edward Smith, Thomas Byrd, Isaac Hite, Jr., Nathaniel Burwell, Warner Washington, Jr., John Page, General Thomas Parker, Robert Page, Matthew Page, Philip Nelson, Robert Carter Burwell, Fairfax Washington, Henry St. George Tucker, Alfred Powell, George Norris, Philip Burwell, G. R. Thompson, Nathaniel Burwell, Jr., Obed Waite, Dabney Carr, Joseph Baldwin, Richard Briarly, Daniel Lee, William B. Page, John W. Page, Strother Jones.

distant day, I expect to be carried, and from it I hope to see arise the bodies of some of the truest saints of the Lord, unto whom, in the adjoining.temple, I was privileged to preach the blessed Gospel of our Lord and Saviour Jesus Christ.

A brief notice of the family of Burwells, so many of whom lie buried there, and of one other individual mentioned in the vestry-book as the friend and defender of the Church, and whose body was interred among his relatives, is all that I shall further say in connection with this spot. The early genealogy of this family I take from Henning's Statutes at Large, Campbell's History of Virginia, and the tombstones at Carter's Creek, in the county of Gloucester. The first of the name in this country was Major Lewis Burwell, of Carter's Creek, in Gloucester county, Virginia, who died in 1658. His wife was a Miss Higginson, whose father signalized himself in the wars with the Indians. He had two sons,—Nathaniel and Lewis. Nathaniel married a daughter of Robert Carter, commonly called King Carter, by whom he had three sons and one daughter. The daughter was named Elizabeth, and married President Nelson. His sons were Lewis, Carter, and Robert Carter. Lewis was either father or grandfather of that Lewis Burwell who was President of the Council in 1750. Carter married Lucy, the daughter of John Grymes, and settled at the Grove, near Williamsburg. He was the father of Colonel Nathaniel Burwell, who moved to Frederick and built Carter Hall. The third son, Robert Carter, settled in Isle of Wight, and was the father of Nathaniel Burwell, of that county, and of Fanny, the first wife of Governor Page. His son Nathaniel was the father of Robert Carter Burwell, who moved to Frederick, of Mrs. Philip Nelson, and of their three sisters, Jane, Fanny, and Ariana, who died unmarried, and lie with their brother in the Burwell graveyard. The second son of the first of the Burwells was, as we have stated, Major Lewis Burwell. His first wife was Abigail Smith, heiress of Nathaniel Bacon, who was for many years President of the Council, and near relatives of Bacon the rebel. Hence the name of Bacon, in the Burwell family. By this marriage, he had four sons and six daughters. His second wife was the widow of the Hon. William Cole, and came from Nansemond county, by whom he had two sons and three daughters. He died in the year 1710, leaving only three sons out of the six, and six daughters out of the nine. He lived at King's Mill, or somewhere near, either in York county or James City. His son Lewis built a large house at King's Mill and improved the place at great expense, also purchased other lands around, and a tract in the Isle of Wight; on account of which, in 1736, he obtained leave of the Assembly to dock the entail of a tract of land in King William and dispose of it. Of his numerous descendants, and of those of the other branches, we can only say that we find them settled in King William, Lancaster, Nansemond, Isle of Wight, and then moving to Frederick, Berkeley, Botetourt, Richmond City, and other places. The father of those settled in Botetourt we read of as an active member of the vestry in King William. Wherever they have gone, they have retained their attachment to the Church of their fathers, and some have entered its ministry.

I shall be excused for adding to the above a piece of family history connected with that of a high public functionary of Old Colonial Virginia, which may serve to cast some light on the state of society and of the Church at the close of the first century of our settlement. The second Lewis Burwell, as we have seen, had nine daughters, one of whom completely upset what little reason there was in Governor Nicholson of famous memory. He became most passionately attached to her, and demanded her of her parents in royal style. Neither she, her parents, or the other members of the family, were disposed to comply. He became furious, and for years persisted in his design and claim. All around him felt the effects of his rage. The father, brothers, Commissary Blair, and the Rev. Mr. Fowace, minister of some parish near Williamsburg, were the special objects of his threatened vengeance. To the young lady he threatened the life of her father and brothers if she did not yield to his suit. This caused a friend of his in England to write a letter of remonstrance, in which he says, "It is not here as in some barbarous countries, where the tender lady is dragged into the Sultan's arms, just reeking with the blood of her nearest relatives, and yet she must strangely dissemble her aversion." To Commissary Blair he declared that "he would cut the throats of three men if the lady should marry any other but himself,—viz.: the bridegroom, the officiating minister, and the justice who issued the license." The Rev. Mr. Fowace, in a letter to the Lord-Commissioners in England, complains, among other things, of being assaulted by Governor Nicholson one evening on his return from a visit to the family, (the Major being sick,) and ordered never again to go to this house without leave from himself. It seemed that the Governor was jealous of him. Besides abusive language and other indignities, he pulled

off the minister's hat, as being disrespectful to him even on horseback. Such was the conduct of the Governor to him in this and
other respects that the Council and some of the clergy united in a
petition to the Crown for his removal, which was granted. All this
and much more is on record in the archives of Lambeth Palace,
copies of which are before me. What was the subsequent history
of the young lady who, like another Helen, was the innocent cause
of so much strife, is not told. Even her Christian name is not
given. I need not say that if a Governor of Virginia under our free
system should assume such royal airs, the case would be much more
speedily and easily disposed of by the lady, the parents, and the
minister.

I promised to conclude this article with some mention of a gentleman whose name was on the vestry-book and whose body was
interred in the old graveyard. That person was Mr. Edmund
Randolph, a distinguished lawyer of Virginia, who was often employed by the vestries as their counsellor. Such was the case with
the vestry of Frederick parish. Mr. Edmund Randolph was the
son of Mr. John Randolph, once Attorney-General of the State, but
who, at the breaking out of the war, preferred the royal to the republican cause, and went to England with his family. His office
was given to his patriotic son Edmund Randolph, who figured so
largely, as the defender of his country, in the councils of the
State and of the nation, and the zealous supporter of the Church
against all which he believed to be assaults upon her rights. Young
Edmund Randolph was adopted by his uncle Peyton (who had
no children,) and espoused the same side, both as to the Church
and State, with the uncle, and was for a time the Secretary of State
under General Washington. He was educated at Williamsburg,
soon after Mr. Jefferson, Governor Page, and other distinguished
men of Virginia. It was a period of growing infidelity at that
college, and Mr. Randolph was for a time somewhat tinctured with
it, as he himself told me toward the close of his life. I can never
forget the manner in which he described the effect of a little flattery
from one of the leaders of the new school, for some doubts expressed
by him as to the truth of Christianity or of some of its doctrines.
That leader patted him on the head, calling him a promising youth
for the utterance of so independent a thought. The pressure of
that hand, he said, was felt for a long time afterward. But he
happily escaped the infidelity which soon deluged the State, and
joined Mr. Peyton Randolph, Robert C. Nicholas, Judge Pendle-

ton, Governor Page, and others, in defending the Church and religion. He was not only engaged by different vestries in special cases, as in the parish of Frederick, but was counsel for the whole Church in that great question of the constitutionality of the law which took away the Church property, and which was lost to the Church by the sudden death of Judge Pendleton. Mr. Randolph informed me that he had read that opinion and decision which was drawn by Judge Pendleton, the President of the court, and, as I think, that it was among his papers. Since his death I have repeatedly inquired for it, but was informed that neither among his papers nor those of Judge Pendleton was it to be found. It has always been said that the document was in the pocket of Judge Pendleton when he was suddenly struck dead on the morning of the day on which it was to have been used. The latter days of Mr. Randolph's life were spent chiefly at his son-in-law's, Mr. Bennett Taylor's, of Frederick county. I saw him during this period, and conversed with him on religious subjects, in which he seemed to take a deep interest. McKnight's Commentary on the Epistles came out about this time, and Mr. Randolph, who had probably never been much conversant with such books, became passionately fond of it, and sometimes talked of preparing and publishing some selections from it, or an abridgment of it, that others might enjoy the pleasure he had experienced in some of its elucidations of Scripture, which seemed to him, to use his own language, like a new revelation on some dark points. Mr. Randolph died at Carter Hall, the seat of Colonel Nathaniel Burwell, of Frederick county, and lies buried in the old graveyard by the side of Mrs. Taylor and her husband. I close by referring in anticipation to a topic which at some later stage of this work I purpose to notice more fully. I have said above that the time of Mr. Randolph's residence at William and Mary was one of growing infidelity. I was not aware until lately that infidelity was of so recent an origin in Virginia. In the year 1723 the Bishop of London addressed a circular to all the clergy of Virginia, with a view of ascertaining the state of religion in all the parishes. Among the questions was the following:—Are there any infidels in your parish? Invariably the reply was, none but the Indians and negroes. An infidel among those who had been brought up in the Christian faith was an unhappy being not then known in Virginia. The great deep of the French Revolution had not then begun to be broken up. Even France was not then infidel. I could scarce believe those uniform responses of the clergy of Virginia, registered as they are in the archives of our Mother-Church, and copies of which are before me, until I came to another record of a somewhat later date, which tells of the introduction of the first infidel book which came over to Virginia. It was entitled, "A Plain Instruction." The fact is communicated to the authorities in England, by a letter or letters from the authorities here, as a most dreadful one.

ARTICLE LXXIII.

Norbourne Parish, Berkeley County.--No. 1.

THIS parish and county were, by Act of Assembly, taken from Frederick in the year 1769,—just after the completion of the church at Mecklenburg, or Shepherdstown, under the superintendence of Mr. Van Swearingen. A small church had previously stood probably on the same spot. By his will in 1776, the father of Mr. Abraham Shepherd—Mr. Thomas Shepherd—directed his executor to deed "a lot of two acres on which the English church stood." A third was erected on that lot many years since, and has been enlarged of late years to its present dimensions. A new, larger, and more excellent one in all respects is now far advanced. Without detracting from the praise due to many who have contributed funds and efforts to the last two churches, we must ascribe the first of them chiefly to the zeal, perseverance, and liberality of that true friend of the Church in her darkest days, Mr. Abraham Shepherd, and its enlargement to the generous donation of eight hundred dollars by his pious widow; and the erection of the fourth to the gift of three thousand dollars by one of his sons, while other members of the family, and the parishioners generally, have not been wanting in their contributions. To an excellent parsonage for the minister they also contributed; but the holy woman, the aged mother, excelled them and all others,—contributing not less than one thousand dollars to it. From the year 1813 to the time of her death, in 1852, when she had reached her ninety-second year, I knew her well. It was good to hear her speak from the abundance of her heart on the subject which interested her most. Out of the Bible first, and then out of the writings of Hervey, Newton, and others of the evangelical school of the Church of England, she drew her views of doctrinal and practical piety. It so happened that several of those ministers under whose teachings she sat were of that class, having for a time been followers of Lady Huntingdon, Wesley, and Whitefield, but who drew back from their path when they were about to turn aside from the old way of the Church of England. She was most faithful in the use of all the means appointed of God in his Church for "the perfecting of his saints,"—in prayer private and public, in the participation of the Lord's Supper, in the strict observance of the Lord's Day, in fasting and alms, in simplicity and cheapness of apparel, in self-denial that she might have to give to the poor and good objects. She was conscientious even to scrupulousness. Her sons delighted in fine cattle, and, at great expense and with great care, became possessed of some of the finest in the land, and sold the young ones at high prices. She has often told me that she could not be reconciled to their asking and receiving such enormous prices for poor little lambs and calves; and she took care to be in no way partakers with them. Much more might I say, but prefer directing my reader to the excellent and just picture of her character given in a funeral-sermon by the Rev. Mr. Andrews, her minister.

Having thus referred to the first establishment of the Church at Shepherdstown, I proceed to notice its next settlement in the parish of Norbourne, at Charlestown, in what is now Jefferson county. It took its name from Mr. Charles Washington,—one of the brothers of General Washington,—who settled on some of the fine land taken up or purchased by the latter during the period when he was public surveyor. His house still stands in the suburbs of the village. Others of the family soon moved to this neighbourhood, and for the last forty years have formed a considerable portion of the flourishing congregation now surrounding the county-seat of Jefferson. The venerable walls of an Episcopal church, built of stone, in the form of a T, are still to be seen a short distance from Charlestown. Various conjectures have been offered as to the age of this house. I have recently made particular inquiry on the spot, of some of the oldest inhabitants, and have no doubt that it was erected soon after the division of the parish from Frederick, in 1769, and not many years before the war. As Washington had large possessions in this neighbourhood, and was often there, none can doubt but that he was a contributor to its erection and had often worshipped within its walls. Under the ministry of the Rev. Mr. Allen, a new brick church was erected on the site of the present one. That becoming too small to hold the congregation, another, much larger and more expensive, was put up under the ministry of the Rev. Mr. Jones. Scarcely was it consecrated and begun to be used, before it was consumed by fire, owing to some negligence or defect about the furnace. To the praise of the congregation be it recorded, a third was immediately erected on the same spot, which now stands, and I hope will long stand, a monument of what may be done by zeal and enterprise.

As to the ministers who officiated in Norbourne parish at an early date, we have but little information. From a list of ministers licensed for the Plantations by the Bishops of London in 1745 and onward, I find that the Rev. Daniel Sturges was licensed for Norbourne parish, in 1771,—two years after its separation from Frederick,—and tradition speaks well of him. In 1786, he was succeeded by the Rev. Mr. Veasy, of whom a venerable old lady in Charlestown—Mrs. Brown—speaks as a man who faithfully performed his duty in preaching and catechizing, as she was the subject of both. He was succeeded by the Rev. Mr. Wilson, of whom I can learn nothing. In the year 1795, the Rev. Bernard Page was minister. Of him I have often heard old Mrs. Shepherd speak as one of the evangelical school,—deeply pious, zealous, and far beyond the ministerial standard of that day. He had been previously an assistant minister to the Rev. Bryan Fairfax, in Christ Church, Alexandria. From Shepherdstown he went to the lower part of Virginia, but soon died from the effects of the climate. Mr. Page was succeeded by the Rev. Mr. Heath, who was minister in 1800, and died in the parish. Mr. Heath was a follower of Mr. Wesley, and came over to this country under his auspices, to preside over a female institution in Maryland, as appears by a letter to him from Mr. Wesley, which I have seen. He, I presume, like many others, refused to separate from the Episcopal Church when the secession took place. The Rev. Emanuel Wilmer succeeded him, and was in the parish about the years 1806 and 1807. The Rev. Mr. Price had been occasionally preaching in this parish, especially at Martinsburg and Shepherdstown, when I first visited them about the year 1812 or 1813.

Having treated of the churches about Shepherdstown and Charlestown, and the ministrations in Norbourne parish generally, I shall now give an account of the churches in Martinsburg and the vicinity, with some notice of certain laymen whose names are worthy of a place in these sketches. The first church built at Martinsburg, and which stood in the suburbs of the town, was erected chiefly at the cost and under the superintendence of Mr. Philip Pendleton,—father of the present Mr. P. Pendleton, of that place. He was a zealous Churchman, and, so far as we know and believe, a good Christian. He had a brother,—Mr. William Pendleton,—who lived some miles off, and who, for a number of years during the almost entire destitution of ministers, acted as a lay reader in Martinsburg and at the church in Hedgesville,—the latter having been built chiefly by himself and Mr. Raleigh Colston. Of the latter we have already spoken as vestryman near the old chapel in Frederick. The families of Hedges, Coxes, and Robinsons also took part in it. As it is a part of our plan to introduce brief notices of some of the old families of the Church, and as there is mention of the name of Pendleton, a name belonging to so many true friends of the Episcopal Church of Virginia and elsewhere, we shall devote a short space to a notice of the family. That notice shall be chiefly taken from a brief autobiography of Judge Pendleton, President of the Court of Appeals, and from a genealogy by the same, —both executed not long before his death. From these we learn that about the year 1674 there came from England to Virginia two brothers,—Nathaniel, a minister, and Philip, a teacher. The former died without issue. The latter left three sons and four daughters. The two younger sons married and had children, but of them there is no certain account. The four daughters married Messrs. Clayton, Vass, Taylor, and Thomas,—leaving numerous descendants. The eldest son married, at the age of eighteen, Mary Taylor, who was only thirteen. Their sons were James, Philip, Nathaniel, and Edmund,—the latter being the President of the Court of Appeals. Their daughters were Isabella and Mary, who married William and James Gaines, from one of whom the late General Gaines was descended. The sons all married and left children, except Edmund, the Judge, who first married Miss Roy, having one child, who died, and next Miss Pollard, who had none, and who lived to the age of ninety. The descendants of the above-mentioned grandchildren of the first Pendleton have intermarried with the Taylors, Pollards, Roys, Gaineses, Lewises, Pages, Nelsons, Harts, Richards, Taliaferos, Turners, Shepherds, Carters, Kemps, Palmers, Dandridges, Cooks, and others unknown to me, and who now exist in thousands throughout Virginia and elsewhere. I shall only particularize the line of those above mentioned in the parish of Berkeley. Nathaniel Pendleton—grandson of the first of the name and brother of Judge Pendleton—lived in Culpepper and had four sons,—Henry, Nathaniel, William, and Philip. Henry was put in business in Falmouth or Fredericksburg, but, not liking it, and his father not consenting to its relinquishment, ran away and became a great man in South Carolina,—having the Pendleton district of that State called by his name. Nathaniel studied law,—went first to Georgia, then to New York, where he became the intimate friend of General Hamilton, and was the father of the late member of Congress from Cincinnati. William was the faithful lay reader in Berkeley, whose son followed his example, and whose grandson is the Rev. William

H. Pendleton, of Virginia. Philip—the last of the four sons—was the father of the present Philip Pendleton, of Martinsburg, and the late Edmund Pendleton, of Maryland, and of Mrs. Cook and Dandridge. The Rev. William N. Pendleton, of Virginia, belongs to a different branch of the same family,—his mother being the daughter of Colonel Hugh Nelson, of Yorktown. It would be inexcusable in me not to record something more particular of one member of this large and respectable family,—viz.: Mr. Edmund Pendleton, President of the Court of Appeals. He was born in Caroline county, and brought up in the clerk's office of that county. At an early age he was clerk of the vestry, and the little which he received for that office was spent in books, which he diligently read. At twenty years of age he was licensed to practise law. In a few years we find him in the General Court. He was in the House of Burgesses in the beginning of the war,—taking a leading part in all its incipient steps. He was also in the first Congress. After this, and until his death, he was Judge and President of the Court of Appeals. Thus he says, (in that brief autobiography from which I have taken the above,) "Without any classical education, without patrimony, without what is called the influence of family connection, and without solicitation, I have attained the highest offices of my country." His following words deserve to be written in letters of gold:—"I have often contemplated it as a rare and extraordinary instance, and pathetically exclaimed, "Not unto me, not unto me, O Lord, but unto thy name, be the praise!'" I cannot refrain from adding the following words, written by himself, in the year 1801, at the bottom of a genealogical tree of the family drawn by his own hand:—"I have never had curiosity (or, more properly, pride) enough to search the Herald's Office or otherwise inquire into the antiquity of my family in England, though I have always supposed the two brothers who came here were what they call there of a good family, fallen to decay,—since they were well educated, and came the one as a minister, the other as a schoolmaster: however, I have had pleasure in hearing uniformly that my grandfather and his immediate descendants were very respectable for their piety and moral virtue,—a character preserved in the family to a degree scarcely to be expected in one so numerous. My mother was among the best of women, and her family highly respectable." The elevation to which Judge Pendleton attained by diligence and moral worth,—the latter resulting from true piety,— without the advantages of birth, education, and fortune, affords great encouragement to the young men of our land to imitate his noble example. He did not despise such advantages, but he considered the blessing of God on honest industry and the having of moral and religious ancestors as infinitely better. He did not, in a proud spirit, boast of his own achievements, saying,—

> "Nam genus et proavos, et quæ non fecimus ipsi,
>   Vix ea nostra voco,"—

but humbly ascribed all merit and success to God.

Of a renowned and wealthy ancestry we have no reason to be proud: for a pious one we ought to be thankful to God; for he has promised his mercy to thousands descended from such. To be descended from a Lord Nelson or a George IV., a Cromwell or a Bonaparte, with all their honours and offices, while their characters were stained with crimes of deepest dye, is not to be coveted; but to be descended from such virtuous and religious patriots as were some of those who achieved the independence of America, is a lawful gratification, though we have no reason to be proud of or to value ourselves on account of that. If at any time we are tempted to think highly of ourselves at the thought of worthy ancestors, it would be well to remember that, by going a little further back, we may find ourselves in company with some of the most ignoble and base of the human family. We should, indeed, ever bear in mind that all of us must trace our origin to two most notorious transgressors who were driven into evil from one of the richest and most beautiful lands on earth. Such exiles are we, their descendants, to this day, before that God with whom not only a thousand days, but a thousand generations, are but as one.

Having said thus much of a family two of whose members—Mr. William Pendleton and his son—contributed so much as lay readers to the sustaining the Church at Hedgesville, I should be inexcusable not to make some record of the character and services of one of the most honest and upright specimens of humanity, in the person of Colonel Edward Colston, in the same neighbourhood, who also was a most efficient lay reader, as well as promoter of every good work in the parish and in the diocese. Whether we view him as a member of the parish, of the diocese, or General Convention, or the State Legislature, or Congress, as husband, father, master, neighbour, or friend, he was the same open, manly, consistent person. You always knew where to find him on every question. As was said by one of General Hamilton, "he carried his heart in his hand, and every one might see it." Though through life often pressed in his pecuniary affairs,—but this no fault of his own,—he made a conscience of setting apart a due portion to the cause of religion and charity. On one occasion, when he had lost a most valuable mill by fire, before I could condole with him on the event, he enclosed to me a share of bank-stock worth seventy-five dollars, requesting me to apply it to some good object, and saying that perhaps he had withholden something which was due to other objects besides his family, and God had taken away from him a portion of what was put in his hands as a steward, considering him unworthy of the trust. I may also appeal to all his neighbours, if in his intercourse with them he did not display the same simplicity and friendliness which so remarkably characterized his uncle, Judge Marshall, and his venerable mother, who was a softened image of that uncle both in person and character. I might also speak of other worthy persons in that interesting parish among the Robinsons, Hedges, and Coxes, who contributed after a time to build the present larger church at Hedgesville, and one not far off on Back Creek; but I must hasten to the more particular mention of one in whom they are all deeply interested, as having been even more than an ordinary minister to their fathers and mothers.

ARTICLE LXXIV.

Norbourne Parish, Berkeley County.—No. 2.

IN a previous article I spoke of Morgan's Chapel, in old Frederick county and parish, and of Morgan Morgan as lay reader there and elsewhere. The site of that chapel is near the dividing-line between Frederick and Berkeley, and the family of Morgans has always been round about it. The foundation of the old chapel may still be seen in the graveyard, though two churches have since been built within a few paces of it. The following family sketch is taken from a pamphlet published many years since by the Rev. Benjamin Allen, and is so much better than any thing from my pen, that I shall make no apology for borrowing it:—

"MORGAN MORGAN.

"It is but justice to departed piety to hold up to the view of survivors its beauty and its value. Affection to the living also prompts us to depict the character of the Christian dead, in order that their holy examples may light others the way to happiness and peace. Actuated by these motives, we present our readers with an obituary of Morgan Morgan, a man by many of them respected and beloved already. Colonel Morgan Morgan, the father of him we propose to notice, was a native of Wales, whence he emigrated in early life to the then Province of Pennsylvania. There he married, and there his first son was born, in the year of our Lord 1715. Thence, about the year 1726, he removed to Virginia, to the place where his descendants now reside, in the county of Berkeley. He there erected the first cabin built on the Virginia side of the Potomac, between the Blue Ridge and the North Mountains. Of course the country was a wilderness, the dwelling-place of bears, wolves, and Indians. But in this wilderness did he find the God of the Christians present, for here, in the spirit of the patriarchs, did he wait upon Him, and here did he experience His providential care.

"In or about the year 1740, he—associated, as we are informed, with Dr. John Briscoe and Mr. —— Hite—erected the first Episcopal Church in the valley, at what is now called Mill Creek, or Bunker's Hill. In that building he had the satisfaction of seeing his son, Morgan Morgan, (who was born to him March 20, 1737,) perform the service of the Church as lay reader at the early age of sixteen. With the religious education of this son he appears to have taken peculiar care. He took him with him in his usual visits to the sick and dying. At seventeen, he induced him to act as clerk to the Rev. Mr. Meldrum, then rector of the parish at Winchester. He lived a pattern of piety and good citizenship until the advanced age of seventy-eight, when, under the roof of his son Morgan, he breathed his spirit into the hands of his Creator. The close of his life was spent in close communion with his God, in fitting himself for the change at hand, and in impressing the precious Gospel on the minds of his descendants. When on the bed of death, so anxious was he for the pious walk of his children, that he thus expressed himself:—'I hoped I should have lived to see Morgan's children old enough to say their catechism and read the word of God; but I must depart.' One of his expressions, uttered with the greatest humility, was, 'Lord Jesus, open the gates of heaven and let me in.' He fell asleep in that Jesus, leaving on the countenance of death the smile of the triumphant soul. He died the 1st of November, 1766.

"The mantle of the father was caught by the son. Morgan Morgan, the subject of our present notice, lived also a pattern of piety. He served his fellow-citizens in various public capacities. He officiated as clerk for the successive rectors of the parish, and as lay reader when there was no rector. He was the friend of the needy, and the comforter of the afflicted. Was any one sick with so contagious a disorder that their neighbours fled from them with alarm, Morgan Morgan was ready to attend their house of suffering, and to watch over their bed. In public ministrations, he officiated chiefly in his immediate neighbourhood, until within a few years of the close of his life, when, in consequence of the destitute state of the country generally, he was often called far from home to perform the religious duties proper for a layman. At length, from the frequency of those calls, he gave himself entirely to the work of a labourer in the vineyard. While the Church to which he belonged exists in this land, his labours will be remembered with gratitude. In a dark day, when desolation and death seemed brooding over her interests, he commenced a career of active exertion, which revived the attachment of her friends and kept her from descending to the dust. Though encumbered with the weight of years, and but a layman, he, by constant exhortation and incessant labours of love, through the blessing of God, impressed the minds of many of the young with the truths of the Gospel, and revived the spirit of piety generally in the land. Through Jefferson and Berkeley, and part of Frederick, Hampshire, and Maryland, his labours extended. He visited alike the mansions of the rich and the cottages of the poor,—everywhere acting in the spirit of a crucified Master. To the prosperous he was the messenger of warning,—to the afflicted, of consolation. Many are there now living, who can testify to his faithfulness; many are there, we trust, in heaven, who have hailed him as their spiritual father. His course through this country may be traced by the fruits of his labour,—fruits that still arise to call him blessed. He died, as he had lived, in the faith of his Redeemer. He was buried at the Mill Creek Church, which was named, after him, Morgan's Chapel."

Mr. Morgan died in the year 1797. An excellent sermon was preached on the occasion by Dr. Balmaine, of Winchester. He does ample justice to his personal piety, his active zeal, and his evangelical views, as displayed in the sermons which he read. To the latter I can testify. I have a large number of the sermons which he used as lay reader, and have read not a few of them. They are faithful, and deeply experimental. He has evidently compiled some of them from various authors, and adapted them to the occasions on which they were preached. By the notes on the outside leaf, they appear to have been preached at funerals, in private houses, on thanksgiving-days, on the first opening of Morgan's Chapel, and other special subjects. Had all the sermons preached in Virginia, from its first settlement, been like these, and all the ministers and readers been like Morgan Morgan, the history of the Church of Virginia would have been different from that which truth now requires it to be. So well calculated was he for the ministry, and so esteemed by the people whom he served, that they united in a letter of recommendation to some Bishop, (supposed to be Bishop Madison, not long before Mr. Morgan's death,) begging that he might be ordained as their pastor, notwithstanding his deficiency in human learning. The paper lies before me, and is very strong in his praise. His age, infirmities, and the distance to be travelled, prevented his application. The effect of his example and ministrations has been felt to this day, where his services were more frequent, and are to be seen especially among his own descendants, who have been among the chief supporters of the church at Mill Creek, or Bunker's Hill. At my last visit there, a few months since, the congregation was called to mourn the sudden death of one of his grandsons, William G. Morgan, who had followed the pious example of his father, grandfather, and great-grandfather. I mention, as one of the effects of Morgan Morgan's example and exhortations upon his descendants and neighbours, that when Mr. Allen first visited the neighbourhood he found no difficulty, though twenty years after the death of this good man, in raising a large catechetical class, among whom were full-grown young men and women, repeating the Church catechism and hearing it explained. This my eyes have seen, in a public tavern at Bunker's Hill, the old church being unfit for use.

Having thus brought the history of the ministers and churches of Norbourne parish to the time when, by God's blessing, a new order of things commenced, I now proceed to make mention of the chief instrument by which the revival was effected. On Christmas eve, in the year 1814, a little after dark, there entered into my house a gentleman who introduced himself to me as Mr. Allen, from New York, with letters of introduction from Bishop Moore and Dr. Wilmer, certifying that he was a candidate for Orders, and wished employment in the valley as a lay-reader. Although the roads were in their worst condition, much rain having fallen, he had in two short days walked from Alexandria to my house, about sixty miles.   Carrying him with me to the Old Chapel the next day, we met with Mr. Beverley Whiting and his sister, Miss Betsy, from Jefferson county, who had, as they and others near them afterward did, come about fifteen miles to church through bad roads.   Into their hands I consigned Mr. Allen, on a horse which I had lent him.   In just two weeks he returned in high spirits.   He had itinerated through the whole of Jefferson and Berkeley counties, found out all the principal families who were still attached to the Church, established at least twelve places for service, and received a kind invitation from Mr. Whiting and his sister to bring his little family to their house and make it a home for the present.   To Alexandria he immediately returned, where his wife and infant were, and without delay, in a spell of bitter cold weather in the month of January, brought them up in a road-wagon of Mr. Whiting's, on its return from Alexandria, to which it had carried a load of flour.   Mr. Whiting's was his home for a considerable time,—for years indeed ; and even after a parsonage was provided his visits to that abode of hospitality were frequent and long.   From this time until the year 1821, with feeble health, the pressure of debt upon him, a growing family, he perhaps rode as great a distance, preached as often, studied his Bible as much, and prepared as many things for the press, as any man of his day.   No one had a better opportunity than myself of knowing this, for I had often to go the rounds with him, doing more duty from necessity than I ever did before or have done since.   Sleeping in the room with him, often I have seen him watch the morning light with his little Bible, and reading it when others were sleeping.   I have travelled with him, and seen that Bible, or some other book, in his hand on horseback, and during any little spare time in private hours busy with his pen in preparing something for the press.   While thus itinerating in these counties, and also in the adjoining county in Maryland, he was conducting a little paper called the "Layman's Magazine," and actually abridged and published the History of the Reformation, by Burnet, in a small volume, and compiled a history of the whole Church in two octavo volumes.   All this he did while, like an honest man, he was paying his debts out of a small salary and the scanty profits of these publications, if indeed there were any.   For nine years he thus laboured, contracting his sphere, though not his diligence, by the introduction of one or two ministers into some of the numerous places he had taken in charge, when he was called to St. Paul's Church, Philadelphia, being the next choice to Bishop McIlvaine.   His labours in such a congregation and city were of course not diminished.   He again issued a religious magazine, and engaged in every plan for promoting Sunday-schools, infant-schools, Bible-classes, missionary societies, and all such things, being especially interested in Bishop Chase's college in Ohio. His house was the Bishop's home. The increase of Episcopal churches in Philadelphia soon attracted his mind. At a time when a narrow and selfish policy kept ministers and vestries in a state of fear and trembling whenever a new church was talked of, lest its establishment might somewhat interfere with their monopoly, his large soul, disdaining all petty considerations, determined on at least one other church, under the patronage of St. Paul's. Mr. Bedell was about leaving North Carolina, and wished some situation in the North. Mr. Allen, learning this, immediately determined to secure him for Philadelphia, and proposed it to a few friends. Alarmed at the thought of such a great work, they shrunk back from it; but Mr. Allen persevered and succeeded, and St. Andrew's Church was the result. While Mr. Bedell was collecting the congregation and the house was rising up, Mr. Allen insisted that he should use St. Paul's during a part of each Sabbath. Some of his people and friends were alarmed, and predicted that the popularity of Bedell would ruin Mr. Allen's prospects, and diminish, if not destroy, St. Paul's congregation. But nothing of this kind moved such a man. His reply was, "Let me decrease, so the Church increases." By God's blessing on such a Christian course, both increased, though Mr. Allen's pulpit-talents were only of the moderate order. At length, under the pressure of mental and bodily labour, his health so failed that a voyage to Europe was resorted to. But it was only used by him on his way to England, in England, and on his return, as an occasion for greater efforts in his Master's cause and for the souls of men. Providence found work for him in a foreign land, and gave him favour with the most zealous of the Christian philanthropists in England. It may be safely affirmed that, within the same short period, no minister from this country had ever attracted more attention, and had, and zealously used, more opportunities of promoting the welfare of all religious and benevolent societies, than Mr. Allen. Even the Society of Quakers felt the influence of his zeal in behalf of Sunday-schools, and to this day speak of him as "that wonderful man." After these dying labours, which were like the last notes of the swan, he returned toward America in a vessel which, by contrary winds, was detained nearly one hundred days on the deep, the crew suffering for provisions. Mr. Allen's grave was the great deep, as though no narrow sepulchre was fit for one of so large a soul.

We now draw to a close these notices of what was once Berkeley county and Norbourne parish, but which in the year 1801 became Berkeley and Jefferson counties, and in time has been divided into six parishes,—those around Charlestown, Harper's Ferry, Shepherdstown, Martinsburg, Bunker's Hill, and Smithfield. The Rev. B. B. Smith, now Bishop of Kentucky, succeeded Mr. Allen in the congregations at Charlestown and Shepherdstown, and continued to serve them most acceptably for nearly two years. The Rev. Alexander Jones succeeded in 1823, and for fifteen years served the same congregations, at the end of which time he confined his services to the congregation at Charlestown. The Rev. Mr. Morrison took his place at Shepherdstown and continued for two years, and was succeeded by the present rector, the Rev. Mr. Andrews. Dr. Jones continued in Charlestown until his removal to Richmond a few years since. During his long ministry in that parish the congregation steadily increased, until it became one of the largest of our country parishes, and two noble churches were erected, the first having been consumed by fire, as we have said before. Mr. Jones was followed in Charlestown by the Rev. Dudley Tyng, and he was succeeded by its present rector, the Rev. Charles Ambler.

The small number of Episcopalians at Harper's Ferry had, from the time of Mr. Allen, been occasionally—sometimes regularly— visited by the ministers at Charlestown and Shepherdstown, until a few years since, when the church now standing on an imposing eminence was built. During its erection, and with much attention on his part, the Rev. Horace Stringfellow, Jr., was its minister. To him succeeded for a time the Rev. Mr. Wilcoxon. The congregation at Martinsburg, after being organized and for a time supplied by Mr. Allen, was put in charge of the Rev. Mr. Horrell, who continued for several years, and was succeeded in 1819 by the Rev. Enoch Lowe. The Rev. Mr. Lippitt succeeded him. The Rev. Dr. Brooke, now of Ohio, the Rev. James Tyng, the Rev. Mr. Johnson, the Rev. Mr. Taliafero, the Rev. James Chisholm, the Rev. D. F. Sprigg, and the present minister, the Rev. Richard Davis, have successively for the last thirty years supplied the two congregations at Martinsburg and Hedgesville. The church at Bunker's Hill, or Morgan's Chapel, has been for the most part supplied by the ministers from Martinsburg and Winchester, but of late years has united with the congregations of Smithfield and Leetown, each about five miles off. The Rev. Mr. Brown was the first who had charge of these three in conjunction, who, after some years, was succeeded by the Rev. Mr. Callaway. The Rev. Mr.

Grammer has just taken charge of them.   In Smithfield and Lee-town two excellent churches have recently been erected, the former by the zeal and liberality of a very few ladies and gentlemen, and the latter at the expense of the Rev. Lewis Balch, of Baltimore, with the aid of some of his people in the church of St. Bartholo-mew, of New York, while he ministered to them.   It being the birthplace or early home of some of his ancestors, and the present residence of his parents, Mr. Balch has sought to confer upon it an honour far higher than the proudest and most expensive monument. There is a circumstance peculiar to this neighbourhood which de-serves a record.   Not only was the property and the residence of General Charles Lee, of Revolutionary memory, from whom it took its name, in sight of the church, but not far distant were the estates of General Gates, General Stephens, and General Darke, all of them officers in the American army.   It was meet that a Christian church should tower above the abode of such a wretched blasphemer as General Lee.   The following extract from his will declares the character of him who once enviously sought to de-throne Washington from the confidence of the nation, and to have the chief command of the American army conferred on himself, who wellnigh lost us the victory on the field of Monmouth, and who ingloriously terminated his days, a selfish celibate, in the midst of dogs for his most familiar friends, and an enemy to God and man :—

"I desire most earnestly that I may not be buried in any church or churchyard, or within a mile of any Presbyterian or Anabaptist meeting-house, for since I have resided in this country I have kept so much bad company when living, that I do not choose to continue it when dead.   I recommend my soul to the Creator of all worlds and all creatures, who must, from his visible attributes, be indifferent to their modes of worship or creeds, whether Christians, Mahometans, or Jews, whether instilled by education or taken up by reflection, whether more or less absurd, as a weak mortal can no more be answerable for his persuasions, notions, or even skepticism in religion, than for the colour of his skin."

Extracted from his will, recorded in the court of Berkeley county.

ARTICLE LXXV.

Parishes in Hampshire and Shenandoah Counties.

HAVING disposed of Berkeley county, I come to Hampshire, which was formed into a county and parish in the year 1753. I perceive how the parish of Hampshire was divided and one established in Hardy in 1785, but of the ministers and churches of the same I have but little to say. In the year 1771 the Rev. Mr. Ogilvie, and in the year 1772 the Rev. Mr. Manning and the Rev. Mr. Kenner, were all ordained, in England, for Hampshire. Mr. Manning alone ever reached there,—the others settling in parishes below the Ridge. About the year 1812, or 1813, I remember to have seen a Rev. Mr. Reynolds, who said that he was the minister in Hampshire and Hardy. No churches, I expect, were ever built in these counties until those I am about to mention. The Rev. Norman Nash, a friend of Mr. Allen, desired to become a candidate for Orders in Virginia, and be ordained without the knowledge of the languages. To this Bishop Moore objected. Mr. Nash strongly declared his conviction that he was called of God and moved by the Holy Ghost to the work, but that he was advancing in years, and, having never studied the ancient languages, it must be a long time before he could be prepared for the ministry, if a knowledge of these were requisite; that he might die before that period arrived, and that if God should inquire of him why he had not obeyed his orders, he could only say that Bishop Moore would not let him, until he had studied Latin and Greek. Without entering into the merits of the question between him and the Bishop, suffice it to say that the latter yielded. Mr. Nash was ordained for the county of Hampshire, where the ancient languages were but little known and not much required. Hampshire may be truly called the hill-country of Virginia,—not surpassed in high hills and deep valleys by that of Judea itself. In one of its deep narrow valleys, and on its hill-sides, a few families of plain people had settled, who retained a strong attachment to the Church while all around had forsaken her as the Babylon of prophecy. There was added to them one which had emigrated from Scotland, with all the Scottish prejudices against the Church; but the father of the family, on his way to these Western hills, had met with some of Bishop Hobart's works, and become a thorough convert to his views of Episcopacy and the Church.   The old man was also a great reader of Scripture, and spent many of his latter years in writing a full paraphrase of large portions of it,—even of the prophetical books.   At his death he bequeathed them to Dr. Balmaine and myself for publication, if we deemed them worthy.   A box of considerable size was full of these manuscripts, in very close, small hand.   We were, of course, afraid to venture on so great an undertaking.   Into this hilly region did the Rev. Mr. Nash enter, and never did man labour more faithfully than he did.   It might have been said of him, if he could not say it of himself,—

> "Si Pergama dextra defendi possent,
>   Etiam hac defensa fuissent;"

for he was well suited to the work and place.   Having spent his earlier days in mechanical pursuits, he diligently employed his skill in helping to erect and complete two log churches,—working with his own hands in various ways.   When completed, he used every proper effort to fill them with Episcopal worshippers, and, for a time, did in a measure succeed.   But there are some winds and tides against which even the power of steam proves ineffectual, and there are some places and societies where the excellencies of our Church system and service cannot avail against violent and long-established prejudices, even though the Gospel be faithfully preached in connection with it.   Such was the case in relation to this part of Virginia, where not only Norman Nash laboured zealously and preached faithfully, but where his nephew,—Mr. Sylvester Nash,—who succeeded him, did the same, and where other ministers have lent their aid, and Bishops have not failed in their peculiar offices. Bishop Moore visited these churches several times.   Mr. Sylvester Nash not only officiated for some years at these log churches, but, by much solicitation and perseverance, succeeded in building a neat brick church in Romney, the county seat of Hampshire, where materials more abounded and the prospects for a time were more flourishing, but he was not encouraged to make a permanent abode there.   The Rev. Mr. Hedges also made a few ineffectual efforts after the resignation of Mr. Nash, and, within a few years past, the Rev. Mr. Irish repeated the same, with the same result.   Since this last effort, the church has been consumed by fire.   In the many changes which are continually going on in society, we will not despair of seeing her old bare walls clothed again with garments of praise, and a crown once more on her head.

I come now—if not in the order of time, yet of geography—to the county of Shenandoah,—originally called after Lord Dunmore, but changed to its present title by reason of the conduct of Dunmore, which made his name so hateful to Virginia. The parish was named Beckford. All this region was settled by Germans and Swedes. Hence it was that a Swedish congregation was here collected, and that the Rev. Peter Muhlenburg—son of the Rev. Mr. Muhlenburg, father of the Lutheran Church in America—was sent to take charge of it. A brief sketch of his history is necessary to the proper understanding of his settlement at Woodstock, the county seat of Shenandoah. He was born in the village of Trappe, in Pennsylvania, in the year 1747, and baptized John Peter Gabriel Muhlenburg. His father emigrated from Germany in 1742, and became the founder of the Lutheran Church in this country,—living at first, and for some years, in Philadelphia, then moving to Montgomery county, Pennsylvania, and thence back again to Philadelphia. His son was early destined in his father's mind and purpose to the ministry, and educated with a view to the same. In the year 1763, Peter, then sixteen years of age, and his two brothers,—Frederick and Henry,—were sent to Halle, in Germany, for their education. Before this time, his father had begun to fear that Peter's disposition and habits were not suited to the ministry. In writing to a friend, to whose care he consigned him, he says:—

"My son Peter has, alas, enjoyed but little of my care and control, on account of my extensive official duties; but he has had no evil example from his parents, and many reproofs and counsels. His chief fault and bad inclination has been his fondness for hunting and fishing. But if our most reverend fathers at Halle observe any tendency to vice, I humbly beg that they will send him to a well-disciplined garrison-town under the name of Peter Weiser, before he causes much trouble or complaint. There he may obey the drum, if he will not follow the Spirit of God. My prayers will follow him, and if his soul only is saved,—be he in what condition he may,—I shall be content. I well know what Satan wishes for me and mine."

I take the following account of him, until his settlement in Virginia, from his life, written by Mr. Henry Muhlenburg, who was either his brother or some near relative:—

"These anticipations were soon realized. Perhaps the young Americans were looked upon as demi-savages by their German fellow-students, and perhaps Peter's disposition was too fiery to submit to the strict discipline of a German school,—at that time strict even to the verge of cruelty. Be that as it may,—whether caused by one or the other reason, or by a combination of both,—Peter was continually in trouble. Things went on from bad to worse, until some time in the year 1764, upon the occasion of a public procession in the presence of the heads of the University, some insult was offered to him by his tutor, which his hot temper would not brook, and it was revenged upon the spot by a blow.

"This outrage rendered his expulsion inevitable. He did not, however, wait for its official notification, but, collecting his little property, fled from the University. A regiment of dragoons was passing through the town, in which, upon the spur of the moment, he enlisted, little thinking that his father had recommended that very remedy to cool his hot blood. Although not eighteen, he was tall and well proportioned, and so desirable a recruit was readily accepted. He thus left the University, little caring what became of him, so rejoiced was he in being freed from what he deemed the tyranny of rectors and proctors.

"The precise length of time he remained with this regiment, the writer has no means of ascertaining. He must, however, have fully upheld the character he had gained at the University, as appears from the following anecdote connected with this regiment, related by himself, and still preserved as a family tradition. Ten or eleven years after, the battle of Brandywine was fought. In that action General Muhlenburg commanded a brigade of Virginians, which, with Weedon's, was thrown forward, at the close of that hard-fought day, to repel the victorious advance of the enemy and give time to our shattered columns to retreat. The struggle was at the point of the bayonet, and it so happened that this very regiment dismounted was one of those opposed to Muhlenburg's command. The General, mounted on a white horse, tall and commanding in his figure, was very conspicuous at the head of his men leading on the long line of Continentals : when the contending parties came near enough to be recognised, many of the older soldiers (German enlistments being for life) remembered their former comrade, and the cry ran along their astonished ranks, '*Hier kommt teufel Piet!*' (Here comes devil Pete!) Finally he was freed from the obligations he had so rashly assumed, in the following manner. A colonel in the British army, whose name is unfortunately forgotten, was leaving Hanover, where he held some official appointment, for America. He had been, prior to this, long stationed in that country, was a frequent visitor at the house of Dr. Muhlenburg, and knew the family and Peter well. On his journey he happened to pass through the town in which this regiment was then quartered, and, to his utter surprise, recognised his young American acquaintance among its soldiers. He sought him out, and learned the cause of his present position, after which, by representing the matter in its true light, as a boyish student's freak, and certifying to the respectability of his family, he easily procured his discharge. Peter took leave of his comrades and accompanied his kind friend to America, where he arrived some time in the year 1766. This interposition was probably the most fortunate event of his life ; for, although his family would sooner or later have procured his discharge, yet, from the rarity of intercourse and length of time necessarily occupied, he might have remained there a year or two longer and become utterly disqualified for any other pursuits. As it was, the occurrence had a beneficial effect upon his character and disposition, rendering him more tractable, although most probably the taste for military life here acquired influenced his whole future career.

"His father, who, as we may well conceive, had suffered much anxiety on account of his son, in his joy at the lost being found, received him with open arms, and granted him forgiveness for, and oblivion of, the past.

For some time Peter remained at home, his father personally superintending the completion of his education.

"It was now time for him to turn his thoughts to the selection of a profession, and, had his own wishes only been consulted, he would doubtless have chosen the army; but his father very earnestly desired that the Church which he had founded in America should be supported and sustained by the efforts of his sons. The uniform kindness which his many youthful follies had met with at his father's hands inclined him to yield to his wishes; and accordingly he commenced the study of theology, under his father's directions.

"Early in the year 1768, he was ordained a minister of the Evangelical Lutheran Church, according to the rules and discipline of that sect, and on the 12th of May was appointed assistant rector of Zion's and St. Paul's Churches, in New Jersey. These congregations, commonly known as the Valley Churches, were situated at New Germantown and Bedminster, in Hunterdon and Somerset counties. On the 5th of February in the ensuing year, he commenced officiating, and remained in that capacity for several years.

"Retaining his strong partiality for hunting and fishing, (the bad inclinations referred to earlier by his father,) he become thoroughly acquainted with that part of the country,—a knowledge which, during the long stay of the army at Morristown and its subsequent operations in New Jersey, became of great value. While situated in New Jersey, his marriage with Anne Barbara Meyer took place, the ceremony being performed on the 6th of November, 1770.

"For some years prior to this, the German inhabitants of the Middle States commenced emigrating in considerable numbers to Virginia, settling principally in the Valley of the Blue Ridge. These German settlements gradually became large, particularly those in Dunmore; and, being Lutheran, a congregation was formed at Woodstock, the seat of justice for that county. This congregation desired a pastor, and accordingly application was made to Dr. Muhlenberg to appoint one, with the request that his son might be assigned to that situation. Some difficulties, however, presented themselves. In order to meet the peculiar laws of the Colony of Virginia on the subject of Church establishment, these Germans had organized themselves as members of the Swedish branch of the Lutheran Church, there being no difference between that and the German, save in point of form only. Some congregations of the former existed at this very time in Pennsylvania, and were in close connection with the Lutheran Church proper. The Swedish Church, at the Reformation, differed from the German in retaining its Bishops, and their discipline required that pastors should be ordained and consecrated by a Bishop. This had not been done in Mr. Muhlenberg's case, who had been ordained by his father in accordance with the rules and discipline of the German Lutheran Church. Another obstacle arose from the union of Church and State in Virginia, where the Church of England was established by law, and, in order that the rector might enforce the payment of tithes, it was necessary that he should have been ordained by a Bishop of the English Church, in which case he came under the provisions of the law, although not a member of the Established Church. To meet these difficulties, it was deemed necessary that Mr. Muhlenberg should be ordained anew, according to the discipline prescribed by the Swedish Lutheran Church. Accordingly, he resigned his charge in New Jersey, and made preparation for a voyage to

England to receive Episcopal ordination, any properly-consecrated Protestant Bishop being competent for that purpose. He sailed from Philadelphia for London on the 2d of March, 1772, and arrived at Dover on the 10th of the following month. During this journey, Mr. Muhlenburg kept a daily journal, now in the writer's possession, which is in many parts highly interesting; but space forbids any extracts being here made. From this journal, however, we learn that, if any scruples did exist in his mind with respect to his profession at the time of his entering upon the study of it, they were now entirely removed, and he seems to have been fully impressed with the serious nature of the duties he had assumed, and to have brought to their discharge a spirit of pure and humble Christianity."

His biographer informs us that his stay in London was brief, and that he was ordained at the same time with a Mr. Braidfoot and Mr. White, the latter being afterward Bishop of Pennsylvania. He further adds, that the disputes between the mother-country were just commencing to be of intense bitterness, when Mr. Muhlenburg removed with his family from Pennsylvania to take charge of his congregation in Virginia. Arriving among them in the fall of 1772, sufficient time was given him, before the breaking out of hostilities, to become extensively acquainted throughout the valley. With Washington and Henry he was soon on terms of personal intimacy, for in June, 1774, he was with them in the House of Burgesses, being sent as representative by the people of his county. This friendship had afterward much weight in determining Mr. Muhlenburg to enter the army. Dunmore county, afterward Shenandoah, under the controlling influence of Mr. Muhlenburg, was one of the first to step forward in opposition to British usurpation. At the first meeting of its citizens he was chosen moderator, and one of the committee of correspondence. Although still a minister, he was sent to the House of Burgesses and Convention again and again, and with all his zeal supported Mr. Henry in the boldest measures he proposed. His character became so well known that in 1775 he was elected Colonel of the 8th regiment, without any other knowledge of military matters than he had acquired when a truant youth in Germany. Washington and Henry both urged his appointment, for they had doubtless seen in which direction his talents moved. His was the first regiment completed on the field. His biographer endorses the tradition of his last sermon, which concluded with the words that there was " a time for all things; a time to fight, and that time had now come." The sermon finished, he pronounced the benediction. A breathless silence brooded over the congregation. Deliberately pulling off the gown which had thus far covered his martial figure, he stood before them a girded warrior, and, descending from the pulpit, ordered the drums at the church-door to beat for recruits. From all the foregoing, we must conclude that though he was doubtless conscientious and respectable, for that day at least, as a minister, yet he still loved his juvenile sports of hunting and fishing too much to excel in the duties of the sacred office, and that he had never ceased to be more of the soldier than the divine.

"Quo semel est imbuta, recens, servabit odorem,
Testa diu."

Of the subsequent history of that Swedish Episcopal congregation in Woodstock I have as yet been unable to obtain any accurate information. Some time after the revival of the Episcopal Church in Virginia, an effort was made by General Steenbergen, the Arthurs, Blackfords, and Allens, to establish it in their neighbourhood, and I paid them several visits; but the effort failed. The same was done more than once by some friends of the Church at Woodstock, headed by Mr. Williams, the old and much-esteemed clerk of the county and staunch member of the Church; but with like success.

I cannot take leave of this county and parish without a brief notice of one remarkable locality in it. In the very centre of Mr. Muhlenburg's parish, and only a few miles from his residence at Woodstock, commence the mountains, almost touching each other at first, and running parallel, so as to form a valley between. After running some distance, they unite in one, which is called the Massamatti Mountain. The valley between is called Powell's Fort, and contains some thousands of acres. The mountains on either side are called the East and West Fort Mountains. The entrance to this valley is through a narrow defile, along which a small but bold stream runs out into the surrounding country, with high, steep mountains on each side, as if some convulsion of nature had opened a passage for the waters. If the whole Valley of Virginia was once a lake, emptying itself at Harper's Ferry, this may be regarded as a lake within a lake, the smaller emptying itself into the larger through this narrow passway, and both of them sending their waters through Harper's Ferry and the Potomac into the great Atlantic. Washington and Muhlenburg had doubtless often been within and around this place, and the military eye of each may have been caught by it, as one of the strongest of nature's fortifications. In one of the darkest and gloomiest seasons of the Revolution, when even the soul of a Washington began to fear the stability of his fellow-citizens, they may have communed together about this, as the last retreat of their diminished and retreating forces. Certain it is that Washington once referred to it as the place to which he should conduct his wasted remnant, there to call the God of nature to its defence, and bid defiance to the British army; thus hoping to arouse his countrymen to renewed and more vigorous efforts for liberty and independence. I can never look at, (for it is, on a clear day, in sight of my own residence,) pass by, or read of this spot, and recollect that proposal of Washington, without remembering the Edom of Scripture,—the strong city, as it is called; for, if travellers and historians be true, there is a strong resemblance between them, as to their entrance, their valley, and high surrounding mountains. The loose stones almost overhanging this narrow pass, and covering the nearly-perpendicular sides of other parts of the mountains, would have furnished weapons of defence to a few brave men sufficient to overwhelm thousands of assailing foes.

ARTICLE LXXVI.

Parishes in Augusta and Rockingham Counties.

WE come now to that part of the valley which was the first seen by the white man. In the year 1714, Governor Spottswood and his gallant band of Cavaliers, with their attendants, ascended the Blue Ridge, at Rockfish Gap, in Albemarle county, and became the delighted beholders of the rich and beautiful valley below.* Carving the name of his King on one of the highest rocks of the mountain, while one of his followers did the same with the Governor's on another, they returned to Williamsburg,—the young gentry being established into an order, and dubbed "Knights of the Horse-Shoe,"—each having a small miniature golden horseshoe presented to him by their enterprising leader. They were followed, after some years, by hardy and daring adventurers, who settled in the valley,—driving back the Indians still farther westward. It was not, however, until the year 1738, that it, together with old Frederick, was separated from Orange,—which was until then the frontier-county, extending to the Pacific Ocean, and one hundred miles into it, according to a charter given by King James to the London Company for Virginia,—whose dimensions were four hundred miles wide on the Atlantic, and of the same width from sea to sea, with all the islands in both seas within one hundred miles from the shores thereof. Such was old Virginia when Illinois, embracing all beyond the Ohio River, was, in 1778, made one of her counties. Such was old Virginia until, by various acts and charters of the Crown and her own liberality, she was restricted to her present boundaries. Augusta, in the year 1738, became the frontier-county, and was therefore called West Augusta. All that I could say about the parish of Augusta is so much better said in the following extracts, taken from a sermon at the opening of the new church in Staunton, a few weeks since, by the Rev. Mr. Castleman, its present minister, that no apology is needed for using it:

"The county of Augusta was organized in 1738. Its boundaries extended from the line of old Frederick on the north, along the summit of

---

* Some think that he crossed at a gap lower down the valley,—near the headwaters of the Rappahannock.

the Blue Ridge Mountain indefinitely to the south and west. Its parish was known as the parish of Augusta, and filled up the circuit of the illimitably-extended territory of the county. The first election that was ever held in the county was the election of the vestry. This was in the year 1746, and resulted in the choice of James Patton, John Buchanon, John Madison, Patrick Hays, John Christian, Colonel John Buchanon, Robert Alexander, Thomas Gordon, James Lochart, John Archer, John Matthews, and John Smith. These were among the most prominent and influential men of the county. From the records which remain of their various meetings and deliberations for the general good, we cannot doubt that they were men of intelligence, good moral character, and fidelity in the trusts committed to them.

"On the 6th of April, 1747, they assembled, for the first time after their organization, to elect a minister to break to them the bread of life. Having received letters from Governor Gooch commending the Rev. John Hindman as an able and worthy minister of the Gospel, they unanimously chose him as their spiritual instructor. He entered immediately into the duties of his pastoral office,—the first minister of the Church of England who ever set foot on Augusta soil and preached the glad tidings of Christ among the mountains of this wild home of the Indian. Owing to the sparseness of the population and inability of the people to build a church, Mr. Hindman was obliged to preach and administer the sacraments in the courthouse and in private houses in different parts of the parish during the whole of his ministry here."

In the year 1747, the vestry determined to purchase a glebe near Leper's old plantation, and build a house; also, a church on the plantation of Daniel Harris. Nothing of either now remains. The glebe was sold and the proceeds vested in the academy at Staunton. Mr. Hindman was minister for about three years. Nothing is known of his ministry or of his death.

"On the 6th of August, 1750, the vestry met and empowered its wardens —James Lochart and John Madison—to employ any minister they might think fit to serve them in the Lord. And on the 16th of October, 1752, the following letter was presented to the vestry from Governor Dinwiddie:—

"'GENTLEMEN:—The Rev. John Jones has been recommended to me by many of good repute and undoubted credit as a worthy and learned divine. As such I recommend him to you, gentlemen, to be your pastor,— not doubting but his conduct will be such as will entitle him to your favour by promoting peace and cultivating morality in the parish. Your receiving him to be your pastor will be very agreeable to

"'Your very humble servant,

"'ROBERT DINWIDDIE.'

"Just one month after the reading of this letter, Mr. Jones was unanimously received into the parish and assigned a salary of fifty pounds per annum for his services and twenty pounds per annum for board, until the glebe-buildings were improved and put in order for his occupancy.

"Between 1756 and 1759, John Matthews, Samson Archer, Robert Breckenridge, and Israel Christian, were added to the vestry.

"On the 20th of May, 1760, it was unanimously resolved to erect a church-building in the town of Staunton, forty feet by twenty-five. It stood partly on the spot now occupied by the new church, just completed, the foundation of its southern wall being covered by the northern wall of the present building.

"Either the infirmities of age, or enfeebled health, had so worn upon the constitution of Mr. Jones as to render him unequal to the duties of his office. He therefore called a meeting of the vestry and advised the employment of a curate, and offered to relinquish one-half of his salary (which by this time had been increased to two hundred pounds) toward his support. In obedience to his wishes, the vestry procured the services of the Rev. Adam Smith, who entered upon his duties as curate in the spring of 1772. Of Mr. Smith's character and usefulness as a preacher, or in what way his connection with the parish was severed, we have no information. He did not, however, remain longer than one year. On the 9th of November, 1773, the Rev. Alexander Balmaine was unanimously chosen to fill his place. From this time onward, we hear no more of Mr. Jones. Though the history which remains of his labours as a preacher and pastor is exceedingly meagre and unsatisfactory,—confined almost entirely to his meetings with the vestry and to the records which he kept as its clerk,—we cannot but revere his memory as a devout and faithful minister of God. The only substantial and valuable relic of him which remains to us is the old worn and defaced Bible which is constantly used in our pulpit.

"How long, precisely, Mr. Balmaine remained in the parish, we are not informed. The time was drawing near which tried men's souls. The spirit of '76 began to swell and agitate the American breast. Of this spirit Mr. Balmaine seems to have partaken in no small degree. The following proceedings of a meeting of the freeholders of Augusta county, held at Staunton on the 22d of February, 1775, will throw no little light on his character as a patriot :—

" 'After due notice given to the freeholders of Augusta county to meet in Staunton, for the purpose of electing delegates to represent them in Colony Convention, at the town of Richmond, on the 20th day of March, the freeholders of said county thought proper to refer the choice of their delegates to the judgment of the committee, who, thus authorized by the general voice of the people, met at the court-house, on the 22d of February, and unanimously chose Mr. Thomas Lewis and Captain Samuel McDowell to represent them in the ensuing Convention.

" 'Instructions were then ordered to be drawn up by the Rev. Alexander Balmaine, Mr. Samson Matthews, Captain Alexander McClanahan, Mr. Michael Bowyer, Mr. William Lewis, and Captain George Matthews, or any three of them, and delivered to the delegates thus chosen, which are as follows :—

" 'To Mr. Thomas Lewis and Captain Samuel McDowell. The committee of Augusta county, pursuant to the trust reposed in them by the freeholders of the same, have chosen you to represent them in Colony Convention, proposed to be held in Richmond on the 2d of March instant. They desire that you may consider the people of Augusta county as impressed with just sentiments of loyalty and allegiance to his Majesty King George, whose title to the imperial crown of Great Britain rests on no other foundation than the liberty, and whose glory is inseparable from the happiness, of all his subjects. We have also respect for the parent State, which respect is founded on religion, on law, and on the genuine principles of the Constitution. On these principles do we earnestly desire to see harmony and a good understanding restored between Great Britain and America.

" 'Many of us and our forefathers left our native land and explored this once-savage wilderness to enjoy the free exercise of the rights of conscience and of human nature. These rights we are fully resolved, with our lives and fortunes, inviolably to preserve; nor will we surrender such inestimable blessings, the purchase of toil and danger, to any Ministry, to any Parliament, or any body of men upon earth, by whom we are not represented, and in whose decisions, therefore, we have no voice.

" 'We desire you to tender, in the most respectful terms, our grateful acknowledgments to the late worthy delegates of this Colony for their wise, spirited, and patriotic exertions in the General Congress, and to assure them that we will uniformly and religiously adhere to their resolutions providently and graciously formed for their country's good.

" 'Fully convinced that the safety and happiness of America depend, next to the blessing of Almighty God, on the unanimity and wisdom of her country, we doubt not you will on your parts comply with the recommendations of the late Continental Congress, by appointing delegates from this Colony to meet in Philadelphia on the 10th of May next, unless American grievances be redressed before that time. And so we are determined to maintain unimpaired that liberty which is the gift of Heaven to the subjects of Britain's empire, and will most cordially join our countrymen in such measures as may be deemed wise and necessary to secure and perpetuate the ancient, just, and legal rights of this Colony and all British America.

" 'Placing our ultimate trust in the Supreme Disposer of every event, without whose gracious interposition the wisest schemes may fail of success, we desire you to move the Convention that some day, which may appear to them most convenient, be set apart for imploring the blessing of Almighty God on such plans as human wisdom and integrity may think necessary to adopt for preserving America happy, virtuous, and free.'

"In obedience to these instructions, the following letter was addressed :—

" 'To the Hon. Peyton Randolph, Esq., President, Richard Henry Lee, George Washington, Patrick Henry, Richard Bland, Benjamin Harrison, and Edmund Randolph, Esqrs., Delegates from this Colony to the General Congress.

" 'GENTLEMEN :—We have it in command from the freeholders of Augusta county, by their committee, held on the 22d February, to present you with the grateful acknowledgments of thanks for the prudent, virtuous, and noble exertions of the faculties with which Heaven has endowed you in the cause of liberty and of every thing that man ought to hold sacred, at the late General Congress,—a conduct so nobly interesting that it must command the applause not only from this but succeeding ages. May that sacred flame that has illuminated your minds and influenced your conduct in projecting and concurring in so many salutary determinations for the preservation of American liberty ever continue to direct your conduct to the latest period of your lives! May the bright example be fairly transcribed on the hearts and reduced into practice by every Virginian, by every American! May our hearts be open to receive, and our arms strong to defend, that liberty and freedom, the gift of Heaven, now being banished from its latest retreat in Europe! Here let it be hospitably entertained in every breast, here let it take deep root and flourish in everlasting bloom, that under its benign influence the virtuously free may enjoy secure repose and stand forth the scourge and terror of tyranny and tyrants of every order and denomination, till time shall be no more.

" 'Be pleased, gentlemen, to accept of their grateful sense of your important services and of their ardent prayers for the best interests of this once happy country. And vouchsafe, gentlemen, to accept of the same from your most humble servants, THOMAS LEWIS,
SAMUEL McDOWELL,
Delegates.'

" 'To Thomas Lewis and Samuel McDowell, Esqrs. :—

" ' GENTLEMEN :—Be pleased to transmit to the respectable freeholders of Augusta county our sincere thanks for their affectionate address approving our conduct in the late Continental Congress. It gives us the greatest pleasure to find that our honest endeavours to serve our country on this arduous and important occasion have met their approbation,—a reward fully adequate to our warmest wishes; and the assurances from the brave and spirited people of Augusta that their hearts and hands shall be devoted to the support of the measures adopted, or hereafter to be taken, by the Congress for the preservation of American liberty, give us the highest satisfaction, and must afford pleasure to every friend of the just rights of mankind. We cannot conclude without acknowledgments to you, gentlemen, for the polite manner in which you have communicated to us the sentiments of your worthy constituents, and are their and your obedient, humble servants, PEYTON RANDOLPH,
PATRICK HENRY,
RICHARD HENRY LEE,
RICHARD BLAND,
GEORGE WASHINGTON
BENJAMIN HARRISON,
EDMUND PENDLETON.'

" The letter of instruction which called forth this correspondence between the delegates from Augusta and these distinguished statesmen and patriots is drawn up in a style so free and easy that we cannot doubt it was written by one accustomed to the pen of composition. It breathes so much of the spirit of true piety, and of humble dependence on the God of nations, that we cannot doubt it was the production of a pious man and a minister of God. This man must have been Mr. Balmaine. In this we are still further sustained by the fact that Mr. Balmaine was the chairman of the committee appointed to draw it up, and that, while the other members were prominent and influential men in the county, they were yet plain farmers and by no means accustomed to that diplomatic style which characterizes the letter.

" March 20, 1775, just one month after these letters were drawn up, the Convention met in the Old Church in Richmond. There it will be seen, by reference to Wirt's Life of Patrick Henry, pp. 132–136, that all the objects desired to be attained by them were adopted, and there the great speech of Patrick Henry, which seemed to set in motion the great ball of the Revolution, was made.

" From this time Mr. Balmaine laid aside his peaceful vestments as a minister of God, and went into the army as chaplain in defence of his country."

The foregoing documents, it is believed, have never been published in any history or newspaper, and are therefore, as well as on account of their intrinsic merits, here inserted.   Nor are they inconsistent with the character of these notices, since a minister and laymen of the Episcopal Church are so prominent in them.

" From the commencement of the Revolution onward, until the year 1781, the doors of the venerable old church in Staunton remained closed. We have no information that its solemn silence was ever broken by the voice of any public speaker.   In that year, however, a portion of the British army, under the command of Tarleton, drove the Legislature from its place of meeting in Richmond, first to Charlottesville, and thence to this place. And here they held their counsels in the old church, and here the proposition was made to create a "dictator."   Here they remained in session undisturbed for about sixteen days, and adjourned to meet in Richmond in October following.

"About the year 1788 the rectorship of the old church was in the hands of a Mr. Chambers.   Who he was, or how long he remained in the parish, we are nowhere informed.   Tradition says that, after a short residence in this place, he removed to Kentucky.

" Years rolled on, in which a long interval occurred in the rectorship of the parish. At length the few friends who had been left from the desolations of the Revolution, and from the withering odium which had fallen on the Church because of its connection with the British Crown, began to lift up their heads and to look round with a cautious and timid eye for some one to minister to them in holy things.   At length a good old man, moving in the humbler spheres of life, remarkable for nothing but his consistent and inoffensive piety, presented himself as willing to serve them in the capacity of God's minister.   He had long been a member of the Methodist Church, and had there imbibed that spirit of feeling and ardent religion which seemed so peculiarly to characterize that body of Christians in those dreary days of our Church. Notwithstanding Mr. King's (for that was his name) roughness of manners, his meagre education, his simplicity of intellect, and his humble profession as a steam-doctor, he was taken in hand by a few friends of the Church, and pushed forward in his laudable efforts. He was sent off, with letters of commendation from Judge Archibald Stuart and the Hon. John H. Peyton, to Bishop Madison, who ordained him Deacon and sent him back to read the services and sermons to the little desolate flock in Staunton. His ministry began in the year 1811 and closed with his death in 1819. That was a long and cheerless day for the Church here.   No evidence can be found that she then had a single communicant besides the simple-hearted old Deacon to kneel at her altar. So unpopular was her cause that none but those whose principles were as true and unbending as steel would venture openly to avow themselves her friends.   An eye-witness of the scene told me that on the occasion of the first service after Mr. King's return from Williamsburg, the small congregation, the feeble and disjointed response, the dampening dreariness of the church, with its old high-back pews, and the long, singsong, drawling tones in which the new deacon attempted to read the service and one of Blair's Sermons, presented a solemn ludicrousness he never before or since witnessed. The congregation, numbering not a dozen, left the church dispirited and ashamed, almost resolved never to repeat the experiment. Mr.

King died here, esteemed by all who knew him for his humble zeal and simple-hearted piety.

"On the 1st of January, 1820, the Rev. Daniel Stephens, D.D., visited the parish, and remained until the following Easter. On Easter Monday, the congregation assembled, and elected Vincent Tapp, Chapman Johnson, John H. Peyton, Briscoe G. Baldwin, Dabney Cosby, William Young, Erasmus Stribling, Levi L. Stevenson, Jacob Fackler, Alexander McCausland, Armstead M. Mosby, and Nicholas C. Kinney. This vestry immediately assembled, and passed resolutions highly commendatory of the preaching and living of Dr. Stephens, unanimously electing him as their rector. These were the props and the pillars of the Church in its darkest and most trying day. Dr. Stephens laboured and preached with a zeal and devotion which secured for him the confidence and love of the great mass of his congregation. Under his ministry, the Church was somewhat revived, and the hearts of its friends cheered. At a Convention held in Staunton in May, 1824, the number of communicants reported was fifteen.

"In 1827, Dr. Stephens removed to the Far West, where he died but a few years since. His ministry was followed in 1831 by the Rev. Ebenezer Boyden. In the early part of Mr. Boyden's ministry, the venerable old church was torn down, and a new one erected near its site. The latter was ready for use on the 23d of July, 1831. Mr. Boyden continued in the parish, with high credit and universal acceptability to his congregation, until January, 1833, when he resigned for another field in the West.

"Next came the Rev. Wm. G. Jackson, who preached with success and acceptability in the parish for several years. He was succeeded by the Rev. Frederick D. Goodwin, who continued until 1843, and removed to Nelson county, leaving sixty-two communicants."

The present rector entered on his duties in August, 1843. For some years past, the desirableness of a new church had been felt, and various plans proposed and efforts made in its behalf, the minister being very anxious for it.

"At length, about three years ago, an interesting little boy, on whose head scarce five summer suns had shone, stood at the window of his mother's chamber, just as the sun was going down, holding something thoughtfully in his hand. Observing his seriousness, his mother said to him, 'What are you thinking about, my son? What are you looking at so earnestly?' It was a new gold dollar, which his father had given him. His answer was, 'Mother, I am thinking of giving my gold dollar to Mr. Castleman, to build a new church I have heard him say he would like to have.' The mother encouraged the thought, and said, 'Well, my son, do give it. God will bless you for it.' Accordingly, that dollar was wrapped in a small paper, with the written request that I would receive it for that object. This little event cheered my heart, and caused me to resolve at once to move forward with the enterprise. The result is a beautiful church, seventy-three feet six inches by forty-six feet six inches in the clear, thirty feet high, with a tower of eighty feet, and capable of accommodating comfortably six hundred and fifty persons."

The following communication from General Samuel Lewis, of Port Republic, Rockingham county, is a suitable sequel to the foregoing:—

"Rockingham parish, Rockingham county, was formed from a part of Augusta in the year 1776. In that portion of Augusta now constituting the county and parish of Rockingham, there were two chapels of the Established Church. One was situated about four miles west of Harrisonburg, near the present village of Dayton. The families of Smith and Harrison, with others of the early settlers in that neighbourhood, were of the Church of England. The other chapel was situated about five miles north of Port Republic, on the road from that place to Harrisonburg. The early settlers on the Shenandoah River near Port Republic were generally of English descent, and belonged to the Established Church. John Madison, (Clerk of Augusta county, the father of Bishop Madison,) Gabriel Jones, (the most distinguished lawyer of his day in the valley,) and Thomas Lewis, (who for many years represented Augusta county in the House of Burgesses, and was one of the earliest advocates of American independence,) had married sisters, (Misses Strother, of Stafford county,) and were among the earliest settlers in that neighbourhood. Peachy R. Gilmer, John Mackall, of Maryland, and others, soon after settled among them. These families were all of the Church of England. The Rev. Alexander Balmaine for several years officiated at these two chapels, and spent much of his time with his parishioners on the Shenandoah.

" The old chapel near Dayton (a framed wooden building) remained standing until within the last twenty or thirty years. During and after the war of the Revolution, the services of the Church were discontinued; and, after the rise of Methodism in this county, most of the families who had formerly worshipped there became Methodists, and this chapel was used for many years as a Methodist meeting-house. The property on which it stood, after a lapse of years, fell into the hands of a Tunker* family: its use as a place of worship had been abandoned by the Methodists, and it was finally used as a barn by its Tunker proprietor. But few of the descendants of the original worshippers at this chapel now reside in its neighbourhood, and but one of them, within the knowledge of the writer of this sketch, retains any attachment to the Church of their ancestors.

" The descendants of the Church-of-England settlers in the neighbourhood of Port Republic are many of them now members of the Protestant Episcopal Church, but very few of them remain in the neighbourhood. One of the sons of Thomas Lewis—the late Charles Lewis, Esq.—inherited, and lived, and died upon, the paternal estate. He ever retained his attachment to the Church, and several of his descendants are now communicants in the church at Port Republic."

Among those descendants is the author of the foregoing communication, General Samuel Lewis, so often the delegate, not only to our Diocesan but to our General Conventions. I knew his ex-

---

* A sect of German Christians.

cellent father, Mr. Charles Lewis, well. A truer friend to the Church when friends were few, a more perfect gentleman, and a worthier citizen, could not be found. I also knew that venerable old lady, Mrs. Gabriel Jones. The first visit ever paid to that parish was in company with her grandson, Mr. Strother Jones, of Frederick, when we saw her in her old age, rejoicing in the prospect of the resuscitation of the Church of her love. Her large old Prayer-Book is still in the hands of one of her descendants. Her husband, Mr. Gabriel Jones, was for a long time so prominent at the bar in the valley, that he was called "The Lawyer." His name is on the vestry-book of Frederick parish as council for the Church in one of her suits.

THE LEWIS FAMILY.

Augusta is undoubtedly the county in which something should be said of this name, as John Lewis, the father of the numerous families of Lewises in Western Virginia, was the great Augusta pioneer in 1720. Whether this family, and other families in Virginia of the same name, are allied by reason of a common origin in a foreign land, cannot positively be affirmed; but the sameness of family names, and oftentimes resemblance of personal appearance and character, are such that many have inferred a common origin. Such was the expressed opinion of the late Benjamin Watkins Leigh, as of others. Mr. John Lewis, of Augusta, came from the county of Dublin, in Ireland, about the year 1720,—his eldest son, Thomas, being born there in 1718: some ascribe a Welsh origin, and others a Huguenot, to the family. His eldest son, Thomas, was a vestryman of the early Church in Augusta, and one of the first delegates to one of the first Conventions in Virginia after our troubles began. His library was well stored with old English theological books; and such was his attachment to the Episcopal Church, that in his will he requested that his friend and brother-in-law, old Peachy Gilmer, should read the burial-service of the Prayer-Book over his remains, there being no minister in the parish at that time. At one time he was in correspondence with the Rev. Mr. Boucher in reference to Augusta parish. He was the father of the Charles Lewis spoken of above, and grandfather of the present General Lewis, of Port Republic. There were three other sons of the first John Lewis. The second was Andrew Lewis, the hero of Point Pleasant. ' The third was William, who was also a vestryman in Augusta, and afterward settled at the Sweet

Springs.   The fourth was Charles, who was killed by the Indians in the battle of Point Pleasant.   Such is the information I received from one of the family, who speak of only four sons.   Howe in his book on Virginia, and Charles Campbell after him, speak of two others.   They say that all six of the brothers, under the command of Samuel, the oldest, were with Washington at Braddock's defeat.

ARTICLE LXXVII.

Churches in Western Virginia.—St. Paul's and St. John's, Brooke County.

WE introduce our notices of the churches in Western Virginia by the following passage from a sketch of Western Virginia, by the Rev. Dr. Doddridge, whose ministry will be duly noticed:—

" The Episcopal Church, which ought to have been foremost in gathering their scattered flocks, have been the last and done the least of any Christian community in the evangelical work. Taking the Western country in its whole extent, at least one-half of its population was originally of Episcopalian parentage; but, for want of a ministry of their own, they have associated with other communities. They had no alternative but that of changing their profession or living and dying without the ordinances of religion. It can be no subject of regret that those ordinances were placed within their reach by other hands, whilst they were withheld by those by whom, as a matter of right and duty, they ought to have been given. One single *chorepiscopus*, or suffragan Bishop, of a faithful spirit, who, twenty years ago, should have ' ordained them elders in every place' where they were needed, would have been the instrument of forming Episcopal congregations over a great extent of country, and which, by this time, would have become large, numerous, and respectable; but the opportunity was neglected, and the consequent loss to this Church is irreparable.

"So total a neglect of the spiritual interests of so many valuable people, for so great a length of time, by a ministry so near at hand, is a singular and unprecedented fact in ecclesiastical history, the like of which never occurred before.

" It seems to me that if the twentieth part of their number of Christian people of any other community had been placed in Siberia, and dependent on any other ecclesiastical authority in this country, that that authority would have reached them many years ago with the ministration of the Gospel. With the earliest and most numerous Episcopacy in America, not one of the Eastern Bishops has yet crossed the Alleghany Mountains, although the dioceses of two of them comprehended large tracts of country on the western side of the mountains. It is hoped that the future diligence of this community will make up in some degree for the negligence of the past.

"There is still an immense void in this country, which it is their duty to fill up. From their respectability, on the ground of antiquity, among the Reformed Churches, the science of their patriarchs, who have been the lights of the world,—from their number and great resources even in America,—she ought to hasten to fulfil the just expectations of her own people as well as those of other communities, in contributing her full share to the science, piety, and civilization of our country.

"From the whole of our ecclesiastical history, it appears that, with the exception of the Episcopal Church, all our religious communities have done well for their country."

Without questioning the perfect sincerity and honest zeal of Dr. Doddridge in this severe criticism, or desiring to apologize for what was blameworthy in the Episcopal Church in regard to the West, we think that truth and justice require some modification of the sentence. We cannot assent to the fact that one-half of the Western population was originally of Episcopal parentage. We must remember that even Maryland had a large proportion of Romanists, as well as other Protestant denominations besides the Episcopal. North of this there was scarce any Episcopalians from the first settlement of the country. A short time before the war, Bishop White was the only Episcopal minister in Pennsylvania. The emigrants from all the Northern States, beginning with Pennsylvania, were not of Episcopal parentage. Although Episcopalians abounded from the first in Virginia and the Carolinas, yet it should be remembered that, of the emigrants to the West, immense numbers— far the larger part—had renounced the Episcopal Church before their removal, and only carried with them bitter hatred toward it. I am satisfied that not a tenth part of those who have left the Eastern for the Western States were Episcopalian at their removal: perhaps a much smaller proportion would be a correct estimate. Soon after the issue of Dr. Doddridge's book,—perhaps forty years ago,—I prepared something on this subject and offered it for publication.

Owing to various circumstances in her history, the Episcopal Church may be regarded as the last of all the Churches in our land which began the work of evangelizing. Her race only commenced after the Revolution. All that was done before proved but a hinderance to her. All other denominations were in active operation long before, and were so prejudiced against her as not to be willing to have her as a co-worker with them. Instead, therefore, of the advantages possessed by the Episcopal Church for establishing herself in the West being greater than those of other Churches, they were less, whether we consider the Bishops and clergy at her command, or the difficulty of the work to be done, by reason of existing prejudices. Justice to the memory of our fathers requires this statement. That of Dr. Doddridge has often been quoted without due consideration.

We must, however, do the justice to Dr. Doddridge to say that, if we had had many such laborious ministers as himself, the West would have been far better supplied with Episcopal churches and ministrations than it has been. And yet truth requires us to admit, what will soon appear, that even his zealous labours have not been followed by all the results which we could desire, by reason of the numerous opposing influences with which he and the Church had to contend. Nothing that I could draw from any documents or record, or from living witnesses, could so interest the reader as the following sketch of Dr. Doddridge's life and labours, from the pen of a friend, and I therefore adopt it :—

"The following article, with some slight alterations, was sent to me as a friend of the late Rev. Dr. Doddridge, by the Hon. Thomas Scott, of Chillicothe. The writer was among the early settlers of the Northwest Territory,—was Secretary to the Convention which framed the Constitution of the State of Ohio, and has since held important and responsible offices under its government. He is now far advanced in life, and employs a still vigorous intellect in throwing together for publication his reminiscences of early associations and bygone days. D.

"*Reminiscences of the first Minister of the Protestant Episcopal Church who adventured into the Wilderness Regions of Western Virginia and Eastern Ohio,—the late Rev. Dr. Joseph Doddridge, of Wellsburg, Brooke County, Virginia.*

"Presuming that but few of the present members of the Episcopal Church in the now flourishing diocese in this State are aware that it was owing, in a great measure, to the early labours and indefatigable exertions of the individual above named that an Episcopate was obtained in Ohio, we feel persuaded that a few brief reminiscences connected with his self-denying and persevering efforts for the establishment in the West of the Church of his fathers will not be unacceptable at the present period : indeed, as the early and intimate friend of this pioneer-herald of the Cross in our Western borders, we deem it but a measure of justice to the memory of a man who, for a series of years, laboured in the good cause single-handed and almost without remuneration. We shall, however, only advert to his labours in general, not having at hand the data to enable us to do so in detail.

"My first acquaintance with the subject of this notice commenced in 1788, in Hampshire county, Virginia. He was then about nineteen years of age, and a successful and highly-esteemed labourer among the Wesleyan Methodists, in connection with whom he continued several years. Being recalled from his field of labour to the paternal mansion, in Western Pennsylvania, by the sudden decease of his father, in consequence of which event the younger members of the family—of whom he was the eldest— were placed in circumstances requiring for a time his personal supervision, the youthful itinerant felt it to be his duty to resign his charge, and, in conformity with the last wish of his deceased parent,—who had appointed him the executor of his will,—to apply himself to the settlement of his estate.

"This accomplished, he found himself in possession of sufficient means to enable him to prosecute his education, which as yet was limited, owing to the few facilities for obtaining one afforded by their wilderness location.

"Accompanied by his younger and only brother, Philip,—who subsequently became eminent in Virginia as a lawyer and legislator, dying, while a member of Congress, in Washington City, in 1833,—he entered Jefferson Academy, Canonsburg, Pennsylvania, they being among the first students at that pioneer literary institution, in what was at that period, in the transmontane States, denominated the 'Far West.'

"The Wesleyans having now laid aside the Prayer-Book or ritual enjoined to be used on occasions of public worship by the founder of their society, the Rev. John Wesley,—a formula which Dr. Doddridge's judgment sanctioned as being not only beautifully appropriate but highly edifying,—he did not therefore resume his connection with them after his return from college, but diligently applied himself to an examination of the claims of the Protestant Episcopal Church, of which his parents had been members prior to their removal to the West. Suffice it to say, this examination resulted in a determination to offer himself a candidate for Orders in that Church. Early in the year 1792, he received ordination at the hands of the Right Rev. William White, of Philadelphia, soon after which he located temporarily in Western Pennsylvania, but in the course of a few years settled permanently in Charlestown, now Wellsburg, in Brooke county, Virginia.

"At this early period of the settlement of the country, the greater portion of the population of Western Virginia and Pennsylvania consisted of emigrants from Maryland and Virginia, where many of them had been attached to the Mother-Church; hence the advent of a preacher of their own denomination was hailed by them as an auspicious event, filling their hearts with gladness. He was everywhere greeted with kindness, cheered and encouraged in his labours by the presence of large and attentive congregations; albeit in most places where they assembled for public worship their only canopy was the umbrageous trees of the unbroken forest, whose solemn silence was, for the time-being, rendered vocal by their devotions.

"During the year 1793, I occasionally attended the ministrations of this zealous advocate for the cause of Christ, at West Liberty, then the seat of justice for Ohio county, Virginia, and the residence of many respectable and influential families. At this place divine service was held in the court-house. Although still a young man, Dr. Doddridge was an able minister of the New Covenant. When preaching, there was nothing either in his language or manner that savoured of pedantry or awkwardness; yet he did not possess that easy graceful action which is often met with in speakers in every other respect his inferiors; but this apparent defect was more than compensated by the arrangement of his subject, the purity of his style, the selection and appropriateness of his figures, and the substance of his discourses. He was always listened to with pleasure and edification, commanding the attention of his hearers not so much by brilliant flights of imagination and rhetorical flourishes, as by the solidity of his arguments and his lucid exhibition of the important truths which he presented for their deliberate consideration.

"In person he was tall and well proportioned, walking very erect. He possessed fine colloquial powers, was social, an agreeable companion, and highly esteemed by those who knew him on account of his plain, unostentatious manners, courteous demeanour, and rigid devotion to duty.

"The first Episcopal church in Western Virginia, if I remember rightly, called St. John's, was erected in 1792–93, in a country parish, a few miles distant from the residence of Dr. Doddridge, whose pastoral connections with it, I have been informed, continued for nearly thirty years, when declining health compelled him to dissolve it. At no great distance from St. John's, and occupied by the same pastor, another edifice, also in Virginia, was erected at a very early period, the name of which I cannot now recollect.

"In the course of a few years after he took up his abode in Virginia, many families reared in the Episcopal Church removed from the older States and settled west of the Ohio River, where they were as sheep in a wilderness without a shepherd. To those of them within a convenient distance from his residence he made frequent visitations, holding service in temples not made with hands but by the Great Architect of nature.

"We have been credibly informed that Dr. Doddridge was the first Christian minister who proclaimed the Gospel of salvation in the now flourishing town of Steubenville, in this State, and that some years previous to the close of the last century he officiated there monthly, the place at that time containing but a few log cabins and a portion of 'Fort Steuben.'

"The parish of St. James, on Cross Creek, in Jefferson county, was early formed by him, and was for many years under his pastoral charge. At St. Clairsville, Belmont county, he had a congregation and church, the pulpit of which he occupied from time to time until another pastor could be obtained. Occasionally his missionary excursions included Morristown, Cambridge, and Zanesville.

"In the autumn of 1815, this untiring apostle of the Church, with a view of preparing the way for future missionaries, made a tour through part of Ohio, coming as far west as this city,—Chillicothe,—preaching in the intermediate towns and ascertaining where Episcopal services would be acceptable. He was, I think, the first regularly-ordained clergyman of that Church who officiated in our place, which he did several times during his stay among us.

"In Virginia at a very early period he held religious services at Charlestown, Grave Creek, and Wheeling. At the latter place was quite a number of Episcopalians, whom he frequently visited, keeping them together until the arrival of that pious and devoted servant of God, the Rev. John Armstrong, their first resident pastor.

"From the time of his ordination, he made it a practice to visit and preach wherever he could find a few who desired to be instructed in the faith of their fathers. These efforts to collect and keep within the fold of the Church the scattered sheep of the flock imposed upon him the necessity of traversing a wide extent of country, which, being but sparsely settled, was poorly provided with roads; consequently, all his journeys had to be performed on horseback.

"In labours this Christian minister was most abundant, sustained under their performance by the approbation of his own conscience and the long-deferred hope that the time was not far distant when Episcopalians in the Atlantic States—to whom, through letters to several of their Bishops and otherwise, he made request and earnest appeals in behalf of a field already white for the harvest—would awake from their apathy to a lively consciousness of the imperative duty of making the long-neglected West a theatre for missionary exertion.

"Some years subsequent to his entrance into the ministry of the Protestant Episcopal Church, he found it necessary, in order to meet the wants of an increasing family, to combine with his clerical profession one that would be more lucrative in a new and sparsely-settled country : he accordingly studied medicine, completing his course under Dr. Benjamin Rush, in the Medical Institute of Philadelphia.   To the avails of the latter profession he was mainly indebted for means to rear and educate a large family of children.

"His life was one of close application and incessant toil; but his health eventually failed, and an asthmatic disease, with which in his later years he was sorely afflicted, in a great measure impaired his ability for usefulness.   In the fall of 1824 he attended a Convention of his Church holden in this city, but he appeared greatly enfeebled.   In the course of the succeeding summer, he spent some weeks here in the family of a beloved sister, Mrs. N. Reeves, hoping, though vainly, that a cessation from labour, change of air and scene, would in some measure renovate his exhausted energies.   During this period the friendship of our youthful days and the remembrance of former years revived.   He often visited me at my own domicile, where we held free converse and communion together, and I found him the same cheerful, agreeable companion as in days 'lang syne.' Nothing ever occurred to mar our friendly intercourse or to diminish our kindly regards for each other.   But he is taken from our midst; his disencumbered spirit has been called to its reward by the Great Head of the Church.

"Finding that neither travelling nor rest availed to arrest the progress of disease, my friend returned to his home and family in Virginia, as he emphatically said, 'to die among his own people.'   He lingered in much bodily affliction till November, 1826, when, strong in the faith which he had preached, in the fifty-eighth year of his age, his sufferings were terminated by death, to him a most welcome messenger.

"Of the published writings of the Rev. Dr. Doddridge, his 'Notes on the Settlement and Indian Wars, together with a View of the State of Society, Manners, Customs, &c., of the Early Settlers of the Western Country,' is the principal.

"This graphic picture of pioneer scenes, manners, customs, and events, is peculiarly interesting as well as valuable on account of its fidelity,—it being the result of the writer's personal experience and observation.   The work was undertaken by its author not only for the purpose of preserving the facts therein recorded, but also with a view of enabling those who come after him properly to estimate the advantages of position in a civilized and refined state of society, by contrasting them with those possessed by their forefathers in the Western regions.   THOMAS SCOTT.

"CHILLICOTHE, ROSS COUNTY, OHIO, June 25, 1855."

To the foregoing we add a few things which we received from those who knew him as the minister in Brooke county.   He preached at four places in that county, two of which are now occupied by Presbyterians and Methodists.   The other two were Wellsburg and the neighbourhood where St. John's Church now stands. Although he was followed by that most zealous and popular man, the Rev. Mr. Armstrong, still it was found impracticable to sustain congregations in all of them.   Dr. Doddridge died in the year

1826, in his fifty-eighth year. He was buried in a vault under his own house, near Wellsburg, but afterward removed to a public burying-ground.

The Rev. Mr. Armstrong, from Wheeling, preached much and zealously to the congregations after Dr. Doddridge's death, as did also his son at a subsequent period. The Rev. Mr. Wheat, of Wheeling, who was the immediate successor of the elder Armstrong, also laboured for them. After some time, the Rev. Mr. Skull was sent as a missionary to Brooke county. He was followed by the Rev. Mr. Harrison in the same capacity. The Revs. Mr. Goodwin, Hyland, and Tompkins followed in succession. The Rev. Mr. Christian is the present minister. During the intervals of ministerial supply, which have been very considerable, the Rev. Dr. Morse, of Steubenville, Ohio, has most kindly and laboriously served the people of St. John's, for which he is most justly very dear to them. Three churches have been put up in St. John's parish on the same site,—the first of log, the second of framework, and the last of brick,—the last being consecrated in 1850. There has always been a considerable congregation at St. John's, and I have ever been delighted to find myself in the midst of that plain, unpretending, hospitable, and zealous congregation of people, devoted to the true principles of the Gospel and worship of our Church.

In Wellsburg, which is about seven miles from St. John's, on the Ohio River, the congregation is small. They have a neat brick church, which was built some years since, almost entirely at the expense of two brothers, John and Danford Brown. The former has gone to his rest. The latter still lives and hopes for better times to the church of his affections.

To these notices of the Church in Brooke county, I subjoin an extract from a pamphlet which I had occasion to publish some years since, when the question of forming a separate diocese in Western Virginia was considered. In discussing it I was led to consider the real condition of that part of the State, which unfitted it for the support of a separate organization at that time. The following is, I believe, a true account of it:—

"Those who would see the main causes of the feeble condition of the Episcopal Church in Western Virginia, and of the difficulties in the way of its speedy progress, under any helps that can be brought to bear upon it, must consider the history of Western Virginia, and the peculiarity of her condition, by comparison with other portions of our land, similar as to soil and position. Take, for instance, Ohio and Western Pennsylvania, lying on two sides of Western Virginia. While the latter (Western Virginia) is more hilly and mountainous, and less attractive on that account to the emigrant, she has also had other obstacles to settlement and improvement, which have left her far behind the former two. In the first place, the unsettled condition of her land-titles continues to this day to present most serious difficulties in the way of sale to those who would form such materials as might be moulded into Episcopal congregations. Another obstacle to the settlement of Western Virginia is the fact of its being part of a slave-holding State. This has prevented immense numbers from the North from choosing this as their home, while, on the other hand, the fact of the contiguity of Western Virginia to the free States, furnishing a facility for the escape of slaves, has prevented Eastern Virginians from settling there. Episcopal families for a long period of time have in great numbers been passing by or through Western Virginia, and have formed the basis of churches in the South or Southwest. Comparatively few have settled in Western Virginia. The few are indeed the chief materials out of which our churches are composed. The causes above-mentioned have mainly produced the immense difference between the present condition of Ohio, Western Pennsylvania, and Western Virginia. While the two former have their forests cleared, their lands well cultivated and covered with comfortable dwellings and farm-houses,—while they abound in flourishing villages and even large towns, and churches and schools and colleges,—it is quite otherwise with the latter. A large proportion of her high hills and mountains are still covered with dense forests. Her villages and towns are few and small,—some not increasing at all, others but slowly. Immense bodies of her lands are owned by non-residents, being only inhabited by those who have no inducements to improve them, and who only seek to gain, during their uncertain residence, just what is necessary for the sustenance of life. On my recent visit, I passed through four tracts of fifty thousand acres each, owned by four different individuals, who were non-residents. These, I am told, are only a few of many large unimproved tracts: hundreds of thousands of acres can be bought at the low price of from twenty-five cents (perhaps less) to one dollar per acre, and of good land too, which will one day, though a distant one, be covered with flocks and herds. Of course, as villages and towns in the interior are for the most part sustained by the surrounding country, if this be uncultivated, or does not flourish, those cannot increase greatly. That Western Virginia has, on her surface and within her bosom, the materials of great wealth and improvement, none can doubt. I have ever believed and said that at some future day she would be one of the most interesting and desirable portions of our country. The improvements in the roads, already made from Winchester, Staunton, and other places, to the Ohio River, have done something for the comfort of the traveller and the improvement of the country; but it is only necessary to travel these roads in order to see in how wild and uncultivated a condition large portions of Western Virginia still are; while those who traverse it on horseback, by the cross-routes, will see a far more rugged state of things. The Baltimore and Ohio Railroad will do much for certain portions of Western Virginia; and the Central Railroad, if pursued, as we trust it may be, will do much for some other portions. There will also be a general, though it cannot be a rapid, improvement throughout the greater part of this region. Still, however, the causes mentioned above will continue for a long time to operate. The slave-holder from Eastern Virginia and elsewhere will not choose this increasingly-unsafe position for his slave-property. The Northern man, who still cherishes strong opposition to slavery, will not come where it exists, nor would he be welcomed there; for in no part of Virginia is the opposition stronger to any thing savouring of abolitionism. Still, it is our duty, as I have often said privately, publicly, and officially, not only diligently to cultivate the places already opened to us, tend the little flocks already gathered, search for wandering sheep among the hills and mountains, but be ever ready to occupy any new positions, such as Fairmont and Fellowsville, which shall from time to time present themselves. If we cannot do all that we would, let us do all that we can. But it is best to think soberly, and not deceive ourselves with false calculations. Even Western Pennsylvania, though having more ministers and churches than Western Virginia, has but few by comparison with her agricultural and other improvements, and by comparison with Ohio and other parts of our country. The cause of this may be found chiefly in the character of the population which first took possession of it, and still holds possession, and which was and is averse to the Episcopal Church. The same may be said of the population of Western Virginia. Though for the most part of a different kind from that which first established itself in Western Pennsylvania, it was not and is not favourable material for the Episcopal Church, as past experience has shown. Western Virginia was doubtless settled chiefly from Eastern Virginia. Those who moved from the valley were not Episcopalians, for it is well known that the Germans and Scotch-Irish took possession of the valley at an early period, and that the Episcopal Church had scarcely an existence there until a very late period. Those who emigrated from Eastern Virginia were chiefly of that class who had deserted the Episcopal Church and been engaged in a violent hostility to it, and carried with them and transmitted to their children nothing but prejudice against it,—which prejudice has been cherished ever since by their religious teachers. But, even if such prejudice has not been, so many generations have since grown up in utter ignorance of our Church, that in the great body of the people of Western Virginia there is no tendency to it, but the reverse. That the service of our Church is most admirably adapted to the edification of the poor and labouring man, I firmly believe and often delight to affirm; but the difficulties in the way of getting such to make trial of it are so great, by reason of their partiality to other denominations, and various other circumstances, that hitherto all the efforts to induce them so to do, whether in Virginia or elsewhere, have been of little avail."

ARTICLE LXXVIII.

Churches in Wheeling, Fairmont, Clarksburg, Weston, Buchanon.

THE Rev. Joseph Doddridge was the first Episcopal minister, it is believed, who officiated in Wheeling. Residing in Wellsburg, he occasionally visited the few Episcopal families then in Wheeling; but there was no organization until the 11th of May, 1819. This is to be ascribed to a visit of Bishop Chase, at whose instance it doubtless took place. The organization was with the title of "St. Matthew's Church, Wheeling." The persons composing the first association were as follows:—John Armstrong, Jr., W. T. Good, W. Gray, T. H. Armstrong, Joshua Morton, J. Good, W. Perrine, Richard Simms, P. Ray, J. C. Williams, Josiah Chapline, J. Wilson, Jr., W. Chapline, Jr., P. Bier, S. Scovill, T. M. Cowles, C. D. Knox, J. M. Smith, R. C. Thompson, Moses Shepherd, Moses W. Chapline, H. Thornbury, John Eoff, Samuel Chamberlain. A vestry being appointed, we find that the Rev. John Armstrong, from Maryland, was chosen the first minister. In the year 1821, Mr. Noah Zane presented a lot for an Episcopal church. On the 9th of May, 1821, the corner-stone of St. Matthew's Church was laid by the order of Masons,—the Rev. Mr. Armstrong delivering a sermon and the Rev. Dr. Doddridge an oration. In the fall of that year it was ready for divine service. Mr. Armstrong's labours continued for seven years, at the end of which time he died and was buried in the church. He was an honest, zealous, laborious, and faithful minister. At the building of the new church his remains were removed to it and now rest beneath its chancel. His son—the Rev. William Armstrong—was elected to fill the vacancy, but declined, and recommended the Rev. Thomas Wheat, who was chosen. In 1832, the Rev. Mr. Wheat resigned, and the Rev. Wm. Armstrong, being again elected, became the minister of St. Matthew's Church. The congregation so increased under his care that it became necessary to build a larger house. The present one was consecrated by myself on the 26th of October, 1837. In the year 1849, the question of dividing the diocese of Virginia having been agitated in the western part of the State, and being brought before the vestry, it was decided by a unanimous vote to be inexpedient. In the year 1853, the Rev.

Mr. Perkins was appointed assistant to the Rev. Mr. Armstrong. In the following year Mr. Armstrong resigned. The vestry and congregation were so unwilling to part with one who had faithfully served them for nearly one-quarter of a century, that earnest efforts were made to prevent his removal from Wheeling or the vicinity; and, had he consented, provision would have been made for his support without the performance of the usual ministerial services; but he felt it his duty to return and spend his remaining days in a small parish in Maryland, which he had served during the first thirteen years of his ministry The Rev. Mr. Perkins was therefore chosen as his successor, and still continues to be the pastor of St. Matthew's Church.

List of the Vestrymen of St. Matthew's Church.

John Good, Richard Simms, Wm. Chapline, Jr., S. Scovill, J. C. Williams, Noah Zane, W. Chapline, Sen , Alexander Caldwell, Josiah Chapline, Eli B. Swearingen, Moses Shepherd, Richard Lane, Peter Garnall, Patrick Roy, Joseph Caldwell, Jas. Tanner, Edmund I. Lee, Jr., Dr. Morton, W. H. Heiskell, John F. Clark, Major Good, Z. B. Curtis, F. Bassett, John Robinson, W. T. Selby, H. D. Brown, W. B. Atterbury, C. T. Strong, Alexander T. Laidley, Morgan Nelson, Samuel Neil, Alfred Richardson, A. P. Woods, Alexander Caldwell, J. L. Newby, J. R. Greer, W. K. Linsay, George Armstrong, S. Brady, R. C. Bonham, G. C. Tingle, M. C. Good.

Of the high respectability of the above body of vestrymen, under whose guardianship the Episcopal Church in Wheeling has so eminently flourished, the citizens of Wheeling, during the term of their service, would, I doubt not, bear a strong and willing testimony. Some of them were, and others still are, personally known to me. Of those who were known to me on earth, and whom I hope to know again in a higher sphere, and who are specially noticed and honoured on the records, I may be permitted to mention the names of Judge Caldwell and Richard Simms. The latter I knew from the year 1820 to the time of his death,—a few years since,—and knew him always as the same active, useful vestryman, and consistent Christian. He helped to build the first church in Wheeling, when it was in the midst of the woods. He loved, like David, to be a doorkeeper in the house of the Lord, though from first to last he was the chief churchwarden. Providence permitted him to experience great reverses during his earthly pilgrimage, but, through grace, he knew how to abound and how to suffer need. One thing he did not know, and that was to be idle and dependent. When, in extreme old age, he was deprived of all earthly property, but when both the church and the town would have felt honoured in making provision for him, he could not endure the thought of being unemployed, but obtained the place of toll-keeper on the great turnpike-road from east to west, a few miles from Wheeling, and there, with his old and excellent companion, who yet survives him, spent the evening of his days,—still turning the curse into a blessing, and by the sweat of his brow making an honest livelihood. Mr. Simms was a native of Maryland, moved to Wheeling in 1816, was married by Dr. Doddridge, died in Triadelphia in March, 1854. His remains were brought to Wheeling, and into the church, and from thence to the East Wheeling Cemetery. Judge Caldwell was a man of high character and standing in every position in society, but above all was an humble Christian. Whenever the Holy Communion is administered, the pastor and the people partake of the emblems of the Saviour's body and blood from a rich service of plate, costing, according to the vestry-book, the sum of three hundred dollars, a present from Mr. Joseph Caldwell, the brother of Judge Caldwell.

ST. JOHN'S CHURCH, EAST WHEELING.

The following account of it has been furnished me by one who is fully acquainted with its history. St. John's parish, Wheeling, was organized in the year of our Lord 1849. Previous to that time St. Matthew's parish embraced the whole of the city of Wheeling, and was the only Episcopal church in Ohio county.

The location of the church-building was at an inconvenient distance from the residences of a portion of the congregation. This, together with the rapid increase of the population and business of the city, demanded the formation of a new parish. Moved by these considerations, and an earnest desire to extend the influence and benefits of the Church, the Rev. William Armstrong, rector of St. Matthew's Church, on the 31st of July, 1849, called a meeting of his vestry for the purpose of considering the propriety and expediency of erecting a church and forming another congregation in the southern part of the city. The vestry, in pursuance of said call, met on the second day of August, 1849. The following are the proceedings of the vestry at said meeting, so far as they relate to a division of the parish:—

"The petition of Robert C. Woods and others upon the subject of a new parish being the first business before the meeting, Mr. Brady offered the following paper:—'A communication from Robert C. Woods, Beverley M. Eoff, and Henry Tallant,—committee,—was presented and read, signifying that the necessary means had been raised for the support of a minister of the Protestant Episcopal Church in a new parish which it is proposed to organize within the city, and asking the assent of the rector, wardens, and vestry of this church to such organization.' Whereupon it was unanimously ordered, that the assent desired be and the same is hereby cordially given, and that the new parish embrace within its limits all south of Wheeling Creek.

"*Resolved*, Moreover, that this vestry would humbly invoke God's blessing upon the organization contemplated in the communication this day submitted."

Having obtained the consent of 'the vestry of St. Matthew's Church, and being favoured with the hearty support and sympathy of the respected and beloved rector, the committee promptly called a meeting of such of the citizens of South Wheeling as were favourable to the formation of a parish of the Church in that part of the city. At the meeting so called, the rector of St. Matthew's Church was present, and, in remarks appropriate and impressive, explained the object of the meeting. After which, suitable measures were adopted for the complete organization of the new parish, and prc vision made for the erection of a building for the services of the Church.

On the 6th of August, 1849, the Rev. Jas. D. McCabe was invited to take charge of the parish as rector thereof, which invitation was accepted on the 24th of the following month. The rector-elect did not, however, enter upon the duties of his office until January, 1850.

On the 8th of February, 1850, the building erected by the congregation was sufficiently near completion to be used, and the pulpit was, for the first time, occupied on that day by the Rev. Mr. Armstrong. The services were conducted by the rector, assisted by the Rev. William L. Hyland. The organization of the parish was sanctioned and confirmed by the Convention of the Diocese of Virginia, in May, 1850, as "St. John's Parish, Wheeling." The church-edifice—which had been erected and completed by the congregation—was consecrated to the service of Almighty God, by the Rt. Rev. John Johns, Assistant Bishop of Virginia, on the 1st of November, 1850.

The Rev. Dr. McCabe laboured profitably and acceptably to the congregation until the 8th of January, 1856, when he removed to Baltimore, as associate rector of St. Paul's Church, in that city.

The following is part of the proceedings of the vestry of St. John's parish at the meeting called to act upon the resignation of the rectorship of the parish by the Rev. Dr. McCabe. This resolution was adopted unanimously, and heartily concurred in by every member of the congregation :—

" *Resolved*, That the Rev. James D. McCabe, D.D., has by courtesy and kindness, by purity of life and doctrine, and by the faithful discharge of duties pertaining to his holy office, secured the love and confidence of his people."

The Rev. George K. Warner was elected rector of the parish in January, 1856, and took charge of the congregation on the 16th of March following. St. John's parish was established upon the free-seat system, which has been found to work satisfactorily. The rector's salary is provided for by the voluntary subscription of the members. The incidental expenses, &c. are met by weekly collections at the Sunday morning services. The parish has a commodious and convenient dwelling-house, erected in 1855 expressly for the use of the rector.

St. John's parish has at this time (February, 1857) eighty-six communicants. The Sunday-school connected with the parish is in a flourishing condition, and, under the judicious care and management of the rector, proves an important auxiliary to the Church.

I must add to the above, for the encouragement of others to go and do likewise, that the rectory mentioned above, and which cost three or four thousand dollars, was at the sole expense of a very few zealous individuals. May they be rewarded for it by always having a faithful minister of God to occupy it!

THE CHURCH IN CLARKSBURG.

The first missionary movement in our diocese was in behalf of Western Virginia, by the association in the valley, composed of the ministers in Frederick, Jefferson, and Berkeley, in the early part of the ministry of the Rev. Benjamin Allen, Mr. Bryan, B. B. Smith, Enoch Lowe, and the author of these pages. The first missionary sent into Western Virginia was the Rev. Wm. F. Lee, and the first point to which he went was Clarksburg and the next Morgantown. In each of these places he preached repeatedly and acceptably and did his duty faithfully as a pioneer and explorer. He was soon followed by his relative,—the Rev. Charles Henry Page,—who imitated his example in all things. The first effort of a more permanent character was made by the Rev. Mr. Ward. In a letter from a friend in Clarksburg, he thus speaks of this effort:—"Mr. Ward came here in the fall of 1834 or 1835. At first he was the inmate of the family of Mr. Trapnall, a firm friend of the Church. Mr. Trapnall dying, Mr. Ward abode the remainder of his time with Mr. Richard Despard, a devoted friend of the Church from the old country. I have been informed that Mr. Ward succeeded in awakening considerable interest among the friends of the Church,—that his Sabbath-school was flourishing, and his public services well sustained." The same friend continues :—"Mr. Ward was succeeded by the Rev. Mr. McMechin, about the year 1840. He had previously been in the Methodist ministry. You are well acquainted with the course pursued by him and with the unhappy termination of his ministry." The foregoing remark requires explanation. Other records of the Church have already made it, but, for the benefit of young ministers, it deserves a place here. Mr. McMechin, though of an ancient Episcopal family, had united himself with the Methodist communion and ministry. During the few years of his continuance in this Society he was much esteemed. He then entered the Episcopal Church and ministry. After a short stay in Parkersburg, he commenced the duties of the latter under very favourable auspices in Clarksburg. At his own cost he provided a house which should answer the double purpose of school-room and place of worship. In this place he preached on the Sabbath and instructed young females during the week,—deriving his support chiefly if not entirely from the latter. His pulpit-addresses were very acceptable. Numbers attended his ministry. His sermons seemed about to be blessed in the conversion of many, and there was a reasonable probability that most if not all of them would be united to our Church. In several successive letters he communicated to me the joyful intelligence, and the confident expectation of a large class of candidates for Confirmation when I should next visit Clarksburg, which was to be after a few months. Before that time arrived, however, I perceived a change in the tone of his letters. He was less confident that many would be ready for Confirmation,—was afraid that he would be disappointed in a number who had promised well. At length my visit was made. On my arrival, he gave me the following honest account of the whole matter. After having for some time earnestly preached the Gospel of salvation to those who attended his ministry, and having reason to believe that a number were prepared to make an open profession of religion, and to do it after our manner and in connection with our Church, he determined to make the latter sure by a series of discourses on the ministry, the Sacraments, the Liturgy, and the rite of Confirmation. I do not know what particular position he took in regard to these, but the effect, he told me, was to reduce his congregation from Sabbath to Sabbath, so that, by the time the series was over, a mere handful were left him. Meanwhile the pulpits of other denominations were denouncing him and the Church, and tracts and books against Confirmation and our peculiarities were gotten up and put in circulation through the place, so that when I reached Clarksburg there was but one individual who would dare to appear for Confirmation, and sickness prevented the attendance of that one. Nor did the calamity end here; for, not long after, Mr. McMechin himself returned, under the influence of excited feelings, to the Methodist communion as a lay member. It is, however, proper to state that when that excitement passed away he resumed his place in the bosom of the Episcopal Church, but, of course, only as a lay member,—having been displaced from our ministry. Let young ministers in new parishes learn a lesson from the foregoing statement, and old ones even in old parishes not despise it.

The letter of my correspondent continues by saying that "after Mr. McMechin abandoned the ministry, the Rev. Thomas Smith, of Parkersburg, gave the little flock such pastoral care as his distant residence allowed. He called the friends of the Church together, proposed and caused to be adopted articles of confederation, and had a regular vestry elected. Until the services of a regular minister were secured, he paid them several visits,—riding on horseback the distance of eighty-five miles to supply their spiritual necessities. The Rev. Mr. Kinsolving was the next settled minister. He officiated regularly at Clarksburg and Weston, and occasionally at Morgantown. He remained about a year, and was not only acceptable to his own people, but popular with all classes. The Rev. Mr. Tompkins succeeded him at Weston, and preached occasionally at Clarksburg,—perhaps once a month,—as well as at other places." To this communication I add that in the year 1852, the Rev. Robert A. Castleman went to Clarksburg, and was soon after joined by the Rev. James Page, who, between them, supplied Clarksburg, Weston, Fairmont, Morgantown, and Buchanon, for one year, when the former confined his services to Clarksburg and Fairmont, and the latter to Weston and Buchanon. During the residence of the Rev. Mr. Tompkins in Weston, and chiefly by his exertions, an Episcopal church has been built in that place. During the ministry of Mr. Castleman, one has been built in Clarksburg and one purchased and repaired at Fairmont. To his efforts in Clarksburg and his solicitation abroad, we are indebted for the excellent house now standing in Clarksburg. A few zealous friends in Fairmont are entitled to praise for what they have done. Although our efforts have thus far failed in Morgantown, I cannot pass it by without

FAMILIES OF VIRGINIA. 343

mention of the pleasant visits made to that place, and the hospitable
reception given me by those worthy members of our Church,—Mr.
John Rogers and Mr. Guy Allen. Could the zeal and liberality of two
individuals have sufficed for the establishment of the Episcopal Church
in Morgantown, theirs would have done it. I have nothing more
to add but that Mr. Castleman is about to leave Clarksburg, and
the Rev. Mr. Smyth, a Deacon, is officiating in Weston.

ARTICLE LXXIX.

Churches in Kanawha, Ravenswood, Parkersburg and the neighbourhood, New Martinsville, and Moundsville.

STILL pursuing the order in which efforts have been made for the establishment of the Episcopal Church in Western Virginia, we proceed to speak of the churches in Kanawha. The Rev. Messrs. Lee and Page, our first missionaries, extended their visits to Kanawha, and by the way of Point Pleasant ascended the Ohio, stopping at Parkersburg. The visit of Mr. Page led to his settlement in Kanawha, and during the time of his residence there he officiated in Charleston, at Coalsmouth, and Point Pleasant. A good beginning was made by Mr. Page, and, if circumstances had not made him feel it his duty to seek another field of labour after a few years, it is thought that the Church in that county would have greatly benefited by his labours. He was succeeded, after a number of years, by the Rev. Frederick D. Goodwin, who laboured amidst many difficulties for two years and then removed to another field. The Rev. Mr. Martin followed Mr. Goodwin, and laboured at Charleston and Coalsmouth. He was succeeded by the Rev. Mr. Craik, now of Louisville, who laboured among them for some years. Mr. Whittle and Mr. Ward were the next ministers. Mr. Ward was followed by the Rev. R. T. Brown, who, after a few years, was obliged, on account of his failing voice, to relinquish the charge. The Rev. Thompson L. Smith is the present minister.

There is an excellent brick church in Charleston, whose history deserves a special notice. When I first visited Kanawha, there were only two communicants in our Church in Charleston,—Mrs. Colonel Lovell and Mrs. Quarrier. There were some few other ladies, who by birth or education were attached to the Episcopal Church, and some few gentlemen who laughingly advocated it in preference to others. There was no Episcopal Church, and the idea of building one seemed preposterous. Some two or three ládies, however, determined upon a trial,—their husbands, fathers, and brothers making sport of it. They used their tongues, their hands, their pens, and raised in one year about a hundred dollars, which afforded amusement to the gentlemen. The ladies, with characteristic good-humour, patience, and perseverance, endured it all, putting their earnings in the bank, and proceeded in their work. The next year doubled their collections, which were also put at interest. How many years were thus spent, and what was the increase of each year, I cannot say; but this I know, that after many years of patient perseverence, and the accumulation of a very considerable sum, the gentlemen found that the ladies could not be laughed out of their determination, and, some of them having also come to better thoughts on the subject of religion, it was resolved to accept the large amount now in hand, and add to it as much as was necessary to build a church costing four or five thousand dollars.

OLD MRS. QUARRIER.

I mentioned that at one time there were only two communicants in our Church at Charleston,—Mrs. Lovell and Mrs. Quarrier. The latter died in the year 1852, full of years, and ready to depart and be with Christ. As Mrs. Quarrier, beyond any other individual, may be considered the mother of the Church in Western Virginia, by reason of her age, her holy life, and numerous posterity, who in different places have zealously promoted it, I must give a brief genealogical sketch of the same. Mr. Alexander Quarrier was born in Scotland in the year 1746. He removed to America in his twenty-ninth year, and, settling in Philadelphia and marrying, lived there twelve years, when he removed to Richmond. His wife dying, he contracted a second marriage with Miss Sally Burns. He left Richmond in 1811, and removed to Kanawha, where he died at the advanced age of eighty-two. By his first marriage he had six children,—Harriet, Eliza, Margaret, Helen, Alexander, and Betsy. By his second wife he had seven children, —William, James, Gustavus, Monroe, Archibald, Fanny, and Virginia. Being unable to state the marriages and localities, &c. of all of them, I shall mention none. The members of the Church in different parts of Western Virginia know how much it has been indebted to them.

THE CHURCH IN THE SALINES.

About six miles above Charleston, in the midst of the celebrated salt-works, there is a considerable population and several churches. One of them belongs to the Episcopalians. When I was last there, it had been deserted for a time on account of its bad construction, with a view either to its repair or the building of another. The minister at Charleston gives a portion of his time and labours to this place.

THE CHURCH AT COALSMOUTH.

About twelve miles from Charleston, and lower down, the river Coal enters into the Kanawha. At this place a number of Episcopal families settled themselves from thirty to sixty years ago. They attracted the attention of our first ministers in Kanawha, and shared their labours. Among those families was that of Mr. Philip Thompson, of Culpepper, son of the Rev. Mr. Thompson, of St. Mark's parish, of whom we have given so good an account in our article on Culpepper. His family, now reduced in numbers by death and dispersion, have contributed largely to the support of this congregation. The venerable mother, daughter of old Mr. Robert Slaughter, of Culpepper, was loved and esteemed by all who knew her, as one of the humblest and most devoted members of the Church in Virginia. I have always felt my own sense of the divine power and excellency of religion strengthened by every visit made to her abode. She exchanged it some years since for a better one above.

The following communication from Mr. Francis Thompson, who has long been a lay reader of the Church, contains every thing of importance in relation to the congregation at Coalsmouth:—

"COALS, February 24, 1857.

"RIGHT REVEREND AND DEAR SIR :—I hasten to give you an imperfect account of the history of the Church in this neighbourhood; and, as there are no records to refer to, I shall have to rely on an imperfect memory. Morris Hudson, Elizabeth his wife, and their six children, nearly all married, removed to this neighbourhood from Botetourt county, Virginia, in 1797, and were probably the first Episcopalians that settled in this neighbourhood. They were both communicants of the Church. They came to Virginia originally from Lancaster county, Pennsylvania, and were members of Bangor Church,—an old church erected before the Revolution. They removed to Botetourt county, in this State, during Bishop Madison's time. The old patriarch, then in his eightieth year, (being uncertain whether he had been confirmed in childhood,) received the rite of Confirmation at your hands, on your first visit to this county, together with several of his children. Some of their descendants still continue true to the faith of their fathers, whilst others have wandered into other folds. The next Episcopalians who settled here were my father's family, with whose history you are well acquainted. They removed here in 1817. My father died in 1837, in the seventieth year of his age. My mother died the 8th of March, 1852, in the seventy-fifth year of her age.

"The first clergyman who visited us was the Rev. Mr. Page, who came as a missionary, and was afterwards the pastor of the congregation in this neighbourhood, and officiated generally throughout the county. He laboured zealously for several years, and, I have no doubt, accomplished much good. Had he remained, I think the Church would have been established here on a firm foundation. I do not recollect the precise time of his coming or leaving. The little brick church on the hill was erected in 1825, (chiefly by old Mr. Hudson.) I think the Rev. Mr. Page preached in it for some years. This church was used until 1835, when it was burned.

"The first vestry was P. R. Thompson, Davis Hudson, Jesse Hudson, and others whose names I have forgotten. After Mr. Page left, we were for some time without a minister, and the Methodists and Presbyterians came in and gathered up the sheaves already bound by him, as many baptized by him connected themselves with those Churches. The Rev. F. D. Goodwin succeeded Mr. Page, and continued about two years. I think he came in 1830 or 1831, and was followed by the Rev. Mr. Martin in 1833, who remained in the county about five years, and gave place to Mr. Craik, who preached for us occasionally for several years. Old Mr. West had charge of this parish part of a year during Mr. Craik's ministry in Charleston. After Mr. West left us, Mr. Craik still continued to preach for us, until the spring of 1845, when the Rev. F. B. Nash was called to this parish. He continued to labour zealously for several years. During his ministry St. Mark's Church was built on a part of the lot given by my father for a church and parsonage. The parsonage was built for Mr. Martin, but was never occupied by a minister until Mr. Nash came. St. Mark's Church was built in 1846, and shortly afterward St. John's in the Valley. The congregation in Quay's Valley was first gathered by Mr. Craik, and an old still-house converted into a place of worship. I think he started a subscription-paper for St. John's before he left. There are several communicants still living near this church, though they have never had any services since Mr. Nash left, with the exception of one or two sermons from Mr. Henderson, who continued here a short time. I was licensed as a lay reader about thirty-two years ago, and have continued to officiate in that capacity and as superintendent of the Sunday-school up to this time. Our school last summer, and as long as the weather permitted during the fall, was quite a flourishing one, numbering more than forty scholars. We shall resume it on next Sunday, if the weather continues good. I remain, dear sir, your attached friend, F. THOMPSON."

List of Persons who have acted as Vestrymen, (from memory.)

P. R. Thompson, Sen., Davis Hudson, Jesse Hudson, John Lewis, P. R. Thompson, Jr., John P. Turner, Alexander Bradford, Dr. John Thompson, Robert Simms, George Rogers, Alfred A. Thornton, Benjamin S. Thompson, George W. Thornton, Francis Thompson.

We have no other church besides these on the Kanawha River, though our ministers have had stations at the court-house in a neighbouring county and at Buffalo in Kanawha county. At Point Pleasant, besides the occasional visits of the Rev. Mr. Craik and Mr. Henderson, the Rev. James Goodwin laboured several years in the hope of building a church and raising up a congregation, but was disappointed. Various circumstances have prevented the establishment of a flourishing village on that most beautiful of all the sites on the Ohio and Kanawha Rivers, which, by their junction there, concur to make it as convenient for trade as it is memorable for the bloody battle with the Indians in which the family of Lewis so signalized itself,—some of whose descendants still live upon the spot and adhere to the Church of their ancestors.

BRUCE CHAPEL.

About twelve miles below Point Pleasant, on Mercer's Bottom, a large and fertile tract of land, once owned by Charles Fenton Mercer, we have a comfortable brick building called Bruce Chapel, erected during the ministry of the Rev. James Goodwin, and so named because of the large contribution made to it by Mrs. Eliza Bruce, now of Richmond, and whose liberality to so many other objects is well known throughout Virginia. The chapel is in the neighbourhood of the Moores, Beales, General Steenbergen, and others whose names I cannot now recall.

THE CHURCH AT RAVENSWOOD.

Ravenswood is a small village on the Ohio River, built on land taken up by General Washington, (who never made a mistake as to the quality of soil,) and left to some of the Ashton family of King George, with whom the Washington family was connected. Mr. Henry Fitzhugh, formerly of Fauquier, marrying a descendant of the Ashtons, became possessed of a part of this estate, and settled on it with a large family of children. At his expense a neat little chapel has been put up at Ravenswood, and when ministerial services were not to be had one of his sons has officiated as lay reader. The Rev. Mr. Tompkins has now for the last two years been residing there, discharging the duties of a teacher and minister at the same time. Services are also held at the court-house of that county.

Since the above was penned, I have received a communication which states that the ladies, by their zeal and diligence, raised one hundred and fifty dollars for the furnishing of the chapel, and that some contributions were made by individuals other than the family above mentioned, in the neighbourhood, and in Wheeling and Cincinnati, though not to a large amount. Contributions of labour were also made by some of the neighbours. The Rev. Mr. Wheeler was the minister for two years from the year 1842. The Rev. Messrs. Martin and Craik and Brown, of Charleston, the Rev. Mr. Goodwin, of Point Pleasant, the Rev. Messrs. Smith and Perkins, of Parkersburg, the Rev. Mr. Hyland, of Moundsville, and Drs. Armstrong and McCabe, of Wheeling, have all rendered acceptable services at

Ravenswood. The vestrymen have been Mr. Henry Fitzhugh, Dr. John Armstrong, Thomas Atkinson, W. S. Holmes, D. M. Barr, Burdett Fitzhugh, Henry Fitzhugh, Jr., R. H. Dickenson, James R. Mays, George H. Fitzhugh, T. D. Noussey, J. Beckwith, Thomas Kirk, D. Frost, I. J. C. Davenport, H. Harpold, James Beatty.

THE CHURCHES IN PARKERSBURG AND THE VICINITY.

Parkersburg was one of the places visited by our first missionaries,—the Rev. Messrs. Lee and Page. The Rev. Mr. Goodwin, also, either before or after his settlement in Kanawha, paid an acceptable visit to the people of that place. The Rev. Mr. McMechin, soon after his ordination, spent a year or more in attempting to raise up a congregation there. In the year 1843, the Rev. Thomas Smith was elected its minister and the church was regularly organized, and in the following year was admitted into union with the Convention of Virginia. Mr. Smith immediately commenced, with his accustomed enterprise, to raise funds for building a church, and was sufficiently successful in securing enough to provide a small and plain church; but, as is too often the case in the progress of such a work, the views of those engaged in it were enlarged, both as to the size of the building and the style of its execution, so that the completion of it was delayed for some years. It is a well-built and handsome brick church, and stands on ground presented to the vestry by J. F. Snodgrass, late member of Congress from that district. For a large portion of the funds for its erection, and for much of the superintendence of the work, the congregation is indebted to General J. J. Jackson, of Parkersburg. Mr. Smith died in 1847, and was buried beneath the vestibule of the church, at his own request, the reason being assigned that, as he felt himself to be a poor sinner, he wished to be trampled under the feet of all who entered the house. In the same year the Rev. Mr. Perkins was chosen, who entered on his duties in the month of October. In the year 1853, Mr. Perkins resigned the charge, since which time it has been vacant. During Mr. Perkins's term of service two other churches have been built in connection with Parkersburg,—one about fifteen or twenty miles above it, on Cow Creek, and another about ten or twelve miles below it, at Bellville. The latter was built almost entirely by Mr. Wells, on whose land and near whose house it stands. Mr. Perkins used occasionally to officiate at each of these places.

The following is the list of the vestrymen of this parish:—John Taylor, J. G. Stringer, Dr. D. Creel, A. L. Kinnaird, J. M. Littleboy, Sen., J. F. Snodgrass, J. R. Murdock, W. S. Gardiner, David B. Spencer, J. J. Jackson, Beverley Smith, W. P. Rathbone, Dr. Farmin, E. D. Safford, C. J. Meale, Isaac Morris, W. H. Morehead, G. B. Neale, J. J. Dickenson, W. H. Laurence, W. H. Small, J. J. Neale, J. H. Adams, E. F. De Selding.

CHURCH IN WETZEL COUNTY.

A church at New Martinsville, in this county, was partly built some years since, under the auspices of the Rev. James McCabe and the Rev. Mr. Hyland, and supplied for some time with services by the same. I have no list of the vestrymen of this parish, which was called Wetzel parish after the name of the county.

CHURCH AT MOUNDSVILLE.

Within twelve miles of Wheeling, on the Ohio River, is to be seen one of the largest of those Indian mounds which are to be found in our Western world. It gives the name to the place. In the time of the elder Mr. Armstrong, there were some families belonging to our Church in and around it, which were visited by him, and to whom with the other people of the place he preached. The passage of the Baltimore and Ohio Railroad through it, and the establishment of a large depôt at it, has increased the population so much that an Episcopal church was erected here some years since, and the Rev. Mr. Hyland has, in connection with a school, performed the duties of a minister in it.

The following is a list of the vestrymen of the parish:—Colonel John Thompson, Isaac Hoge, E. H. Caldwell, W. S. Lane, O. S. Hock, G. W. Bruce, William Collins, General G. Jones.

From the foregoing notices of the Church in Western Virginia, it will be perceived that our "beginning is small." May some future historian, when all its resources have been developed, have the pleasure of recording that "its latter end has greatly increased"!

ARTICLE LXXX.

Recollections of the Episcopal Church in this Country during the last Fifty Years.

HAVING thus disposed of the Church of Virginia, I purpose in the present to record some things in relation to the General Church which have come under my observation, and in which I have taken some part. As I introduced the notices of the Virginia Church with some preliminary remarks on its previous history, so would I offer a few thoughts as to the earlier history and character of the American Church generally, before entering on the particular narrative to which this article is devoted. And, as I was forced by a regard to historic truth to acknowledge that at no time from its first establishment was the moral and religious condition of the Church in Virginia even tolerably good, so am I also, by the same consideration, obliged to admit much that was defective in relation to other parts of the American Episcopal Church. More especially was this the case in regard to Maryland, which bore a strong resemblance to Virginia in more respects than one. The character of her early population resembled that of Virginia, in having more of the aristocracy than was to be found in some other parts of the English territory in this country. Slavery also was introduced at an early period, and served to strengthen that feature in her character. She, like Virginia, was also put under a regular establishment,—though not at so early a period. She had her Governors and Commissaries, who acted as substitutes for the Bishop in ecclesiastical matters. Neither Maryland nor Virginia were under the patronage of the Society for Propagating the Gospel in Foreign Parts, as other portions of America were. The history of those other portions, by comparison with those of Virginia and Maryland, establishes the fact beyond contradiction, that the selection of missionaries by that Society was generally better than the supply coming to Virginia and Maryland through the Bishop of London, or some other channel. The reader is referred to Dr. Hawks's faithful and laborious History of the Church in Maryland for proof of this in relation to that diocese. I adduce only one testimony besides, and that from the well-known Dr. Chandler, of our American Church. After a visit to the Eastern Shore of Maryland, about the year 1753, he addressed a letter to the Bishop of London, in which, after speaking in high terms of the laity of that part of the State, he adds, "The general character of the clergy, I am sorry to say, is wretchedly bad. It is readily confessed, that there are some in the Province whose behaviour is unexceptionable and exemplary; but their number seems to be very small in comparison,—they appearing here and there, like lights shining in a dark place. It would really, my lord, make the ears of a sober heathen tingle to hear the stories that were told me by many serious persons of several clergymen in the neighbourhood of the parish where I visited; but I still hope that some abatement may be fairly made on account of the prejudices of those who related them." My own recollection of statements made by faithful witnesses forty-five years ago, as to a number of the old clergy of Maryland, accords with the above. I have but little knowledge from any source of the few Episcopal clergy north of Maryland. They were not more than eighty in number when the War of the Revolution began. As to foreign importation of clergymen, Bishop White (who was once the only Episcopal minister in Pennsylvania) justly remarks, "It could not be the channel of a respectable and permanent supply." Nevertheless, as they nearly all of them depended chiefly for their support on the aid of the above-mentioned Society, it is to be believed that pains were taken to select the best which could be obtained from the English Church at that time, and to require the best recommendations in behalf of those who were natives of America. That there were mistakes none can doubt.*

The history of the missionaries of that Society in South Carolina, as given by one of her sons, (the Rev. Mr. Dalcho,) informs us of some who, on account of their evil character, were soon complained

---

* That some of the followers of Laud came over to Virginia after his fall, is evident from what Sir William Berkeley says in his memorable protest against much preaching and the establishment of a printing-press and schools in the Colony. He speaks in praise of some ministers who came out soon after Laud's death, and very slightingly of the rest, saying that, "if they would only pray more and preach less, he would like to see them better paid." As for free schools and a printing-press, he thanked God there were none in the Colony, and trusted there would be none for a hundred years to come, as he considered them fruitful nurseries of heresy and rebellion. No doubt Sir William sympathized with Laud in many things. He was as much disposed to high-handed measures in the management of the Colony as Laud was in England. Cromwell's rebellion in England and Bacon's rebellion in Virginia may be, in a great measure, traced to the arbitrary spirit and conduct of the Archbishop and Governor.

of, and either recalled or dismissed from the service. The congregations, indeed, became very cautious how they received the missionaries. They delayed institutions, as in Virginia, until satisfied of their good character by sufficient trial. The Society sometimes complained that too long a trial was required. Still, I doubt not that their general character for morals and piety was much superior to that of the imported clergy of Maryland and Virginia. But now a most important inquiry must be made, in order to form a correct estimate of the religion of the Colonial Churches. It is this :—What was the type of the theology—the substance and style of the preaching—of the ministers of that day? What doctrines were insisted on with emphasis from the pulpit? How did the preaching of that day accord with the doctrines of the apostles and the reformers on the subject of human depravity, and of Christ as the sinner's "all in all"? How did the sermons compare with our homilies on the misery or sinfulness of man, on justification, on the new birth, &c.? It will surely be admitted to be a fair way of deciding this question to ascertain what was the theology and preaching in England during the time when our supply was greatest from the Mother-Church. The clergy coming over to us must have borne a strong resemblance in their theology and style of sermonizing, and in other respects, to the great body of those left behind ; only that we are obliged to admit the probability of what was so generally declared in all the documents and histories of the times,—namely, that, with some honourable exceptions, they were inferior in character. In making this inquiry, we shall not go back to the few who came out during the reign of James I. We will pass over those few who came to America in the days of Laud, who, intent on establishing high Episcopal and Sacramentarian views and on putting down all dissent, neglected (as some of his own admirers admit) most shamefully the religious condition of the Colonies.*

---

* Dr. Coke, the Methodist Bishop, who from his office and his extensive travels throughout England and America had a good opportunity to form a correct judgment, says, not only of those who absconded at the American Revolution, but of those who remained, that, " Fallen as the ministers of the Establishment in England generally are, they are incomparably to be preferred before the clergy of America." (See his Life of Samuel Drew, p. 145.) The Bishop of London wrote a letter to Dr. Doddridge, in the year 1751, concerning a communication from the Rev. Mr. Davies, in which, while he endeavours to defend the American clergy against the wholesale charges brought against them, he is forced to make the following acknowledgment :— " Of those who are sent from hence, a great part are the Scotch or Irish, who can get no employment at home, and enter on the service more out of necessity than choice ; some others are willing to go abroad to retrieve either lost fortunes or lost character "

We pass over also the times of the Commonwealth and of the two succeeding reigns, and come down to that of William and Mary,—the time of the greatest influx of ministers to America,—the time of Tillotson and Burnet, and the formation of the two great societies for extending the Church,—the Christian Knowledge Society and the Propagation Society, which began their work within two years of each other under the direction of kindred spirits,—the one in 1698, the other in 1700. The history of those times shows that Romanism and Calvinism were equally eschewed. Let the sermons and tracts of that day be compared with those of the Calvinistic preaching in the time of Elizabeth and the semi-Romanistic ones in the days of Laud, and a marked difference will be seen. But there may also be seen as marked a difference between the sermons of Tillotson and others of his stamp, and those of the earlier Reformers, as well as those of a later period, which have been denominated Evangelical. The age of Tillotson and Burnet may be called the age of reasoning, of liberalism, of comprehension. Tillotson and Burnet were great and good and pious men,—practical and useful men. Their views of the Church, ministry, and Sacraments were conservative. Their charity was truly Christian. And yet it must be admitted that they stood at the beginning of a new school, differing from any going before, and destined soon to degenerate into something which they did not design. The sermons of Tillotson are masterpieces of reasoning on all theological subjects,—are a body of divinity to students; but then they are not addressed to the hearts and consciences of sinners so as to awaken them to cry, "What must we do to be saved?" They do not present Christ in all his fulness to the soul with that earnest application which the true evangelical preacher does. Burnet also admitted that he wished to lower the doctrine of the article "On Justification by Faith" somewhat,—though by no means to make it approach the Sacramental view, but rather the contrary. The followers of such men soon began to substitute reasoning, natural religion, and morality for the Gospel. They did not deny the evangelical system, but they did not preach it as they ought to have done, and the pulpit, of course, lost its power. There were but few sermons published

The Bishop on this and other accounts was anxious to have Bishops sent to America, that they might exercise discipline over the clergy coming from England, and ordain natives for the Church. Had all the ministers of Dissenting Churches in America been as liberal as Mr. Davies, Bishops would probably have been sent at an early period, and much evil been prevented. Mr. Davies, in his letter to the Bishop of London, expresses himself most favourably of the measure.

in that day. At any rate, Tillotson's so far exceeded all others in many respects, that they were the sermons of the Church. In the Church of Virginia none appear to have been used by the lay readers but Tillotson's. In many old vestry-books I have met with, a sufficient number of his sermons were ordered to supply the lay readers; and there were probably two lay readers to each clergyman in the diocese. They were indeed better and longer than the brief and most unimpressive sermons of the clergy, (judging from a number of the latter which I have read,) but still they are not calculated to rouse lost sinners to a sense of their condition and lead them to a Saviour, notwithstanding all that is so excellent in them. Tillotson's sermons, abridged into moral essays and dry reasonings on the doctrines of religion, were, I fear, the general type of sermonizing among the clergy who came over to America for the last seventy or eighty years before the War of the Revolution.

I fear that many of the publications of the Christian Knowledge Society were somewhat wanting in that pressing of evangelical principles upon the hearts and consciences of men in the way that has been found so effective to their conversion since the days of Venn, Newton, Simeon, and others. Soon after entering the ministry, I was desirous to publish a volume of sermons and tracts for servants, and, being unable to find any such in this country, I addressed a letter to Mr. Wilberforce, the warm friend of the negro race, and made known to him my wishes,—not without acknowledging my indebtedness to his book, under God, for much of that which I considered a true view of our holy religion. In reply, he sent me all the tracts of the Christian Knowledge Society,—perhaps all that then had been published in England for the poor. I confess I was disappointed in them; not that they had any of that false doctrine which, at a later period, was surreptitiously introduced into some of them by altering certain words, but that they did not press with sufficient force and earnestness certain truths upon the minds of the poor.

About this time my attention was called to some sermons of the Rev. Mr. Bacon, a minister of our Church in Maryland, addressed expressly to masters and servants. They were preached and published in 1743. Their style is plain and forcible, and all that is said is well said; but still there is the deficiency of the age in them. They do not present Christ to men as poor lost sinners, in the way they ought to do. They recognise the doctrine and declare it in few words, but do not emphasize and press it. They were the best I could get, however, and I published them. In an abridgment of two of them afterward, I sought to supply this deficiency. Let me add, that I think there may seem this same error in one of the directions for the conduct and preaching of the first missionaries of this Society when sent to South Carolina. The directions, with this one exception, are most wise and pious. Nothing could be better. The defective passage, as I think, is this:—"That, in instructing heathens and infidels, they begin with the principles of natural religion, appealing to their reason and conscience, and thence proceed to show the necessity of revelation," &c. Now, this is precisely the method attempted at first by the Moravian missionaries in the North, and which they found so fruitless, and therefore abandoned, choosing the more evangelical one with success.* (See Dalcho's History of the Episcopal Church in South Carolina, p. 46.) The fault of the Tillotson school was too much reasoning,—too much appeal to natural religion, which, though, like Butler's Analogy, it might be very effective with some for a certain purpose, could not answer for the multitudes. Had our Lord preached thus, the common people would not have heard him gladly. Nor would the wise and mighty have been converted by the Apostles, if such had been their preaching. In what I have said of the successors of the Tillotson school, there has been of late a general agreement of our divines, whether called High or Low Churchmen, all admitting that the moralizing system will not avail, though differing much as to other things. I would not be misunderstood on this subject. I do not deny to Tillotson most admirable method and valuable matter in his sermons; for I have read many of them with great pleasure, and not, I hope, without profit. But I must regard him and his imitators as false models of preaching, as comparatively ignoring the deep corruption of human nature, so that God in his good providence saw fit to raise up not only the Whitefields and Wesleys, who took an erratic course, but the Venns, the Newtons, and the Simeons in the bosom of the Church, to preach a simpler and fuller Gospel to the millions of lost ones in our mother-country. This failing to set forth the desperate wickedness of the human heart, calling for a Saviour,

---

* Bishop Horsley, in his charge of 1790, exposes the plan of beginning with natural religion, affirming that the difficulty of understanding the principles of natural religion is as great as that of understanding revealed; that the true way is to preach the plain Gospel of redemption to sinners, as that which God has provided for them, and look up to him to open the hearts of the hearers to receive what he has sent them. Such has been the experience of all who preach to the benighted heathen, or to the poorest and most illiterate in Christian lands.

a new birth, has, from my first entrance on the ministry, seemed to me the great defect of our old clergy. I remember to have preached before one of the oldest, most venerable and eminent of them, on the text, "The carnal mind is enmity toward God," and in the sermon to have quoted many of those Scriptures which represent us as "hating God," "being his enemies in our minds," "being children of the devil," and having quite grieved him by it. He said that he did not like such a mode of preaching. It was in vain that I adduced Scripture as my warrant and example. He did not like it. And yet I was not wont to speak the doctrine harshly, but tenderly and in pity.

Having presented this general view of the American Church, let me proceed to mention some things which will show that I have, from an early period, had opportunity of forming a correct estimate of some things occurring within it during the last forty or fifty years. At the age of seventeen I went to Princeton College. In going from and returning to Virginia during my collegiate course, I became a temporary inmate in the hospitable house of Dr. Abercrombie, the associate minister with Bishop White in the churches under his care. Several of the sisters of Mrs. Abercrombie, having lived for a long time in the family of one of my uncles of Virginia and received much kindness from him, became the means of my introduction to this very kind and agreeable household. The daughters were most interesting young women. On Good Friday, 1807, I heard Dr. Abercrombie, who was regarded as one of the pulpit orators of the day, preach on the Passion of Christ. A strong impression was made on my mind and memory by his action in the pulpit, as well as by his language. After describing some of the sufferings of Christ, he came to the crucifixion, and, erecting his tall form to the highest point, he stretched out his arms in a horizontal direction, and, standing motionless for a time, presented the figure of a cross. I have never entered St. Peter's since, without having the scene renewed. Nor has the impression made by the kindness of himself and family ever been effaced. At the close of my collegiate course, I formed some acquaintance with the Rev. Dr. Beasley, associate minister with Dr. Hobart in Trinity Church, New York; and with Dr. Montgomery, of Grace Church, New York. That acquaintance was increased into considerable intimacy afterward with Dr. Beasley, while he lived both in Baltimore and Philadelphia, and with Dr. Montgomery in the latter place, whom I often saw, for many years, at my home in the family of old Commodore Dale, that good man and true Christian, who married Dr. Montgomery's aunt. From these two ministers I necessarily learned many things about the Church of that day. In the year 1811, I was ordained, and soon after received from Bishop Hobart, by the hand of his old college friend, Charles Fenton Mercer, of Virginia, a large assortment of books, tracts, and pamphlets, most of them written by himself, on points of controversy with other denominations, and on some matters of internal trouble in the diocese of New York, and also some Episcopal devotional works. I read them all, and remember to have sympathized with him in his personal difficulties. I admired the ability displayed by him in his contest with Dr. Mason, and entirely agreed with him in his argument for the Apostolic origin of Episcopacy, though unable to follow when he proceeded to claim exclusive divine right for it. By means of these publications, I became tolerably well acquainted with the politics of the Church, and under circumstances quite favourable to an impartial judgment. About six years after this, (and before I attended any General Convention, though twice elected, being prevented by unavoidable circumstances,) I went on a painful errand to the South, bearing to its milder climate a sick and, as the result proved, a dying wife. During my stay in Charleston, South Carolina, myself and wife received every kind attention which brother ministers and Christian ladies could have shown us. It was during the last year of good Bishop Dehon's life, whose praise was on every tongue. Dr. Gadsden was then in the laborious discharge of his duties to bond and free. I saw him in the place of his greatest honour,—in the Sunday-school, teaching the coloured ones, both old and young. I preached in several of the churches in Charleston. In one of them—either St. Philip's or St. Michael's—I witnessed what surely would have gladdened the heart of the most prejudiced opponent of slavery. I saw what I was told were the last fruits of the labours of the old missionaries of the Society for Propagating the Gospel in Foreign Parts,—old negro men and women with some of their children sitting on benches along the side-aisles, and around the chancel and near the pulpit, which was advanced some distance into the middle aisle.* Spec-

---

* The structure of this building was nearly the same with that of most of the old large English churches, which is, I believe, the best that can be. The chancel is against the wall, behind the pulpit, that being advanced some distance into the middle aisle, which is always large enough to admit of benches for the poor. The poor also sit around the chancel, on the place where the communicants kneel, and on chairs and stools between that and the pulpit, and on the stair-steps leading up

tacles aided their aged vision, and, with Prayer-Books in their hands, they read the responses aloud in the midst of their owners. The missionaries were not prevented from teaching them to read, but rather encouraged so to do. Nor have masters and mistresses ever been prevented from doing it themselves, or having it done at home; though public schools are forbidden. On the contrary, there have, I believe, always been more well-instructed and intelligent coloured persons, bond and free, in Charleston than in any other city in the Union. I had occasion, two years after this, to take the gauge and dimensions of the condition of the coloured people in all the Atlantic States, and think that I am qualified to judge on the subject.

It was at this time that I became acquainted with Dr. Percy, and his excellent son-in-law, the Rev. Mr. Campbell, of South Carolina; both of whom agreed in their views of experimental piety, and that mode of presenting the Gospel to men for which we are pleading. Dr. Percy was a bold, impressive, and faithful preacher of the doctrines of grace. He was one of those who, under the auspices of Lady Huntington, felt called on to preach an almost-forgotten Gospel in England, though in a somewhat irregular way. He was a graduate of Oxford, and was ordained by an English Bishop in 1767. He came over to America as one of Lady Huntington's preachers. Here he took part with the Revolutionists, and preached to the American troops. At the fall of Charleston, he was ordered by Colonel Balfour to desist from preaching, on pain of confinement. When Lady Huntington in her old age proposed to secede from the Church of England, and wished Dr. Percy to ordain some preachers for her, he positively and indignantly refused, and then connected himself more closely with the Episcopal Church. In 1805, he became assistant minister in St. Philip's and St. Michael's Churches, Charleston, South Carolina. A few years after this, St. Paul's Church in that city was built for him. He died in the year 1817. Dr. Gadsden preached his funeral-sermon in St. Philip's Church, at the request of the Bible Society, of which he had been

---

to the pulpit. A door at the upper part of the church allows an easy ingress and egress to the poor. The minister is thus more in the midst of his people, and has them all so near to him that he can see their countenances and be seen and heard by them much better than on the more modern plan, where the preacher is either thrown against the wall, perhaps in a recess, or else is on one side of the congregation, before some little *quasi* pulpit where, what with the high-pitched roof and great distance of the congregation, the voice is almost lost.

President. Although Dr. Percy was honoured by the Church in Carolina, and was President of the Standing Committee, yet I could perceive there was a marked difference in his views on some points and those of the other clergy with whom I associated. His views are presented in two pamphlets which he published while officiating in St. Philip's and St. Michael's, and which he presented to me. One, on the Episcopal Church, sets forth her claims in such a manner that no sound Churchman could question his attachment to her, and yet no reasonable Non-Episcopalian complain. In the other we have a portrait at large of the true evangelical preacher in life and doctrine. One or two extracts from the latter of these will serve to confirm my views of the state of the Church at that time. He says, in his Introduction, "That real religion at the present period is at the lowest possible ebb, in most of our Churches, will hardly be denied by any serious and reflecting mind, who understands *what the religion of Christ is, and what Christianity was intended to do for mankind.*" He declares that all great and general declensions of religion, whether in principle or practice, begin at the Sanctuary or Church of God; and therefore he calls upon all the clergy to examine themselves, both as to their lives and preaching, and see whether they are not much in fault. He quotes Bishop Horsley as condemning the preaching of that day, saying to his clergy "that too many have continued so long preaching in the smooth and fashionable strain of dry ethics and mere moral suasion, instead of preaching the pure doctrines of the Reformation, that they had wellnigh preached pure Christian morality out of the world." Dr. Percy speaks very impressively of the duty of ministers "having their own hearts savingly converted unto God," as they hoped to be instruments of saving others. The whole pamphlet is worthy of perusal. I cannot, however, leave this topic without adverting to and correcting an error into which many have fallen in tracing the evangelical movement of the Church of England to the school of Whitefield and Wesley, with which Dr. Percy was for a time connected. Although God made much use for good of these zealous and fearless men, as all acknowledge, yet the great work of evangelical reformation in the English Church commenced in a different line, and at an earlier period, at Cambridge and London, and elsewhere, and has ever continued distinct. We begin our line with the Venns, Newtons, Romaines, Legh Richmonds, and bring it down through the Simeons, Cecils, Pratts, Gisbornes, Wilberforces, the Thorntons, Hannah Mores, and others. These were never associated with the Huntington school, but ever continued most true and faithful members of the English Church. There have been those both in England and in America who have sought to disparage the evangelical cause by identifying it with those who left the English Church; and many have been deceived by the misrepresentation. I remember that Mr. John Randolph could hardly be convinced by me that Mr. Wilberforce, Mr. Perceval, and Miss Hannah More were not regular members of the Methodist Church in England. His prejudices were quite strong against them on this account. In my earlier days there were many such persons. We in this country also were esteemed or spoken of little otherwise. By many we were considered as in no sense Churchmen, but rather intruders into the ministry of the Episcopal Church, having some sinister end in view. The wish has been often expressed that such would go to their place, —that is, to some other denomination with which they sympathized, —just as some of us have wished that Tractarians would go to their place, the Church of Rome. Which of us had the better right so to speak, let history declare. Hundreds of Tractarians have gone from the Church of England and America to Rome. Who of us have gone to Geneva? I doubt not but many were very sincere in their hard thoughts and hard speeches of us; but so was Paul in his denunciation of Christians. Even Bishop White has been declared (and it has often and recently been in print) to have denounced us in very strong and offensive language; which I shall believe when affirmed on sufficient authority. But if true, it only proves the justice of our complaint as to the manner in which we have been dealt with; for if the amiable Bishop White, with his moderate Church views, could thus speak, what might not others have said? Bishop Hobart issued a Pastoral entitled "The High-Churchman Vindicated," in which he not only boasts of the name and principles of High-Churchmen, predicting that they will one day prevail and be honoured universally, but makes some comparisons between them and Low-Churchmen which are not only invidious, but such as only party feelings (of which we did not profess to be free) could have induced him to make. I should not have adverted to this, but that this Pastoral and another on the Principles of a Churchman have been republished by the Protestant Episcopal Society of New York, bound up in its volumes, and transmitted to posterity. In one of them, those who rank the distinctive principles of the Church, for which he pleads, among the non-essentials of religion, are declared to be guilty of *treachery to their Church and to their Master*. It is well known that Low-Churchmen do not consider those things in which the Episcopal Church differs from orthodox denominations as among the essentials of religion, though they do regard them as important,—some of them very important. Of course they are among the non-essentials, nothing being essential in religion but what is necessary to salvation.

I now proceed to show how, in the providence of God, I was further led into circumstances very favourable to an accurate acquaintance with the General Church in this country, and to a just estimate of persons and things on both sides. Having taken an early and lively interest in the American Colonization Society, and written something in its behalf, I was induced, in the year 1819, to devote myself for some time to the formation of auxiliary societies throughout the United States, the collection of funds, and the selection of the first colonists. This led me to visit all the principal towns, from Milledgeville, in Georgia, to Portland, in Maine. As in duty bound, and by choice led, I invoked the aid of the ministers of all denominations, and especially of my own, without distinction of party. For visiting the former I was honoured with a printed pamphlet by one "Sopater of Berea," addressed to Bishop Moore, advising him to recall me to Virginia and to my duties at home. While I received much kindness from ministers of all denominations, I experienced still more from those of the Episcopal Church. Let me mention some of them:—The clergy of Savannah, Georgia; Bishop Bowen and the clergy of Charleston; the Rev. Mr. Lance, of Georgetown, South Carolina; the Rev. Mr. Bedell, then living in Fayetteville, North Carolina; Bishop Kemp, Dr. Beasley, and Dr. Henshaw, of Baltimore; Bishop White, (at whose house I was kindly entertained for three weeks while engaged in selecting colonists,) and Drs. Muhlenberg, Boyd, and Montgomery, of Philadelphia; Drs. Milnor, Lyell, and B. T. Onderdonk, of New York; Dr. Croswell, of New Haven; Dr. Wainwright, of Hartford; Dr. Crocker, of Providence; Drs. Eaton and Gardiner,* of Boston; Mr. Carlisle, of Salem; Dr. Morse, of Newburyport; Dr. Burroughs, of Portsmouth, New Hampshire; and Mr. Tenbroeck, of Portland, in Maine. One of the most pleasing impressions made on my mind by that visit, and which I have ever delighted to recall and speak of, resulted from the uniform hospitality and kindness experienced from one end of our land to the other. Whenever, since that time, I

---

* While in Boston, the corner-stone of St. Paul's Church was laid, and I then became acquainted with Bishop Griswold, Dr. Jarvis, and other clergy. Dr. Gardiner delivered a severe lecture on Unitarianism, standing on the corner-stone of the new church along one of the streets of Boston.

have heard any thing like a comparison instituted between different portions of our country in this respect, I have entered my protest against it. Circumstances render hospitality more easy to the rich in the South, by reason of their numerous servants and large estates; but, according to the means possessed, the hospitality is the same everywhere. It is, indeed, the most universal good feature in the character of man. When Mr. Pickering, at Salem, (my father's old friend and comrade in the Revolution,) cleaned my boots at daylight in the morning, and at a later period Bishop Griswold, in Boston, did the same, I felt that no greater hospitality could be shown me by the richest layman or Bishop of the South. All sectional prejudices I have ever endeavoured to discourage. Although I am aware of the advantage of having natives of the soil to be ministers in Virginia, yet do I always condemn any disposition to object to worthy ministers, come from whence they may. Virginia has reaped much advantage from ministers coming from most distant parts. Taking warning from the unhappy dissensions of other denominations on one painful subject, may our Church be at peace and prove one bond of union to the land! In advocating the claims of the Colonization Society from Northern pulpits, I always commended it for this, that, however we might differ as to the subject of slavery, we might all agree touching this mode of benefiting the African race; and there has been a very general and happy agreement.

It being evident that I must have gained some considerable share of information concerning the Church from the places thus visited and the persons seen and conversed with, I proceed to mention a few things which resulted from this visit.

INTRODUCTION OF MORE HYMNS INTO THE PRAYER-BOOK.

To my surprise, I found that there was a liberty taken in regard to hymns in public worship to which I had not been accustomed. Not only were there voluntaries before and after service, with words chosen by the choir or minister at pleasure, but there were several hymn-books in use not known to the Church, as, for instance, in Savannah, Georgia, and in Trinity Church, Boston. I saw also a few printed hymns for some special occasion at Dr. Moore's Church in Newburyport, Massachusetts. This struck me very forcibly, having been from a child accustomed only to those in the Prayer-Book; nor did it strike me very favourably.* I was not aware at

---

* Before the revival of the Church in Virginia, Dr. Buchanon, of Richmond, had also a collection of his own; probably one of the English collections.

that time that a variety of hymn-books was allowed in the English Church, and I knew that each denomination in this country deemed it best to have its own selection. Being conscious, however, that we were stinted in hymns, whether for public, social, or private use, and that many psalms were badly versified or unsuited for Christian worship, I introduced a motion at the General Convention of 1823, for additional hymns and a revision and selection of the metrical psalms, and had the honour of being placed at the head of the Committee of the Lower House. I urged the measure by stating the diversity which I had witnessed a few years before, and plead for such an increase of hymns and selection of psalms as would answer all the purposes of private, social, and public worship. Dr. Jarvis supported the resolution, and, I think, seconded it, though maintaining that there was a perfect liberty here, as in England, to have a variety of selections, as the hymns and psalms formed no integral part of the Prayer-Book, but were only an appendage, not subject to rubrics. The joint committee of both Houses, being appointed, met during the interval between that and the next General Convention. Dr. Muhlenberg, one of the Committee, selected, prepared, and published a volume of hymns for the use of the Committee, many of which were adopted. Dr. Onderdonk, afterward Bishop of Pennsylvania, also prepared a number of paraphrases of Scripture, some of which were also introduced into our collection. Severe strictures having from time to time been passed upon our work, I beg leave to offer a few remarks upon them. In the first place, I affirm that none but those who engage in the work of selecting hymns have any idea of the difficulty of the work. Dr. Muhlenberg had collected hymn-books from all over England and America, and brought a large basketful of them to the meeting. They covered the table around which the Committee sat. I recollect the remark with which he introduced them,—that he had no idea, when he undertook the work, what a mass of bad poetry and false sentiment was to be found in the hymn-books of the different denominations of England and America, and how difficult it was to get a good selection. The Committee found it so in the progress of their examination. The various and strange tastes which sought to be gratified in the selection formed another difficulty. I remember that one of the first classical scholars of the Church, and an excellent divine, proposed a great favourite to the Committee, expressing a most earnest desire for its admission, and there was every disposition to gratify him; but the hymn was so entirely unsuitable that no one could think of adopting it. Another instance may be mentioned. At this time the delegation from South Carolina came around to the General Convention by sea, and it was thought desirable, by one, at least, of their delegation, to have a hymn suited to their case while on the ocean. Accordingly, one had been prepared, and was put into my hands. The first line of it read thus:—

"O thou epithet-exhausting ocean!"

I need not say that it found no support in the Committee, being even more objectionable than one which may be found in some hymn-books, and which it was wished to have in ours, namely, "The Star of the East." Each partook too much of the character of pagan worship. The selection which has been made, we think, does not deserve the criticisms which have been unsparingly passed upon it. When we read the names of such men as White, Hobart, Professor Turner, Dr. Muhlenberg, and Mr. Francis Key, as members of the Committee, we might surely expect something more deserving of praise than censure. The selection has been highly esteemed by many good judges. When in England, at the house of Mr. Bickersteth, who had them, I was pleased to hear him say that it was either the very best, or among the best, he had ever seen; and he lived in the midst of hundreds, and had himself selected one for his own parish. Among the objections made to some of the hymns of our selection, I have been amused to hear the following,—namely, that we had altered the poetry of the authors of them. Now, it happens that one of the rules adopted by the Committee was, to give the preference to the original when it could be ascertained, except when there was some very sufficient reason. When a hymn was proposed, the original was called for. Certain changes complained of were actual returns to the originals from the versions in common use, whose compiler had altered them.

As to the desire expressed by some for an increase of hymns, I confess I cannot feel the force of it, being convinced that a smaller number frequently used, whether in private or public, is likely to produce the greater effect. I do not mean to condemn selections for Sunday-schools, and perhaps for some social meetings, but am still decidedly in favour of one book of hymns and psalms, as in the American Church, rather than the unbounded liberty of the English Church, where so many hundreds, I believe, are in use.

PUBLIC BAPTISM AND PIOUS SPONSORS ADVOCATED.

In my intercourse with many ministers and churches I discovered that there were very low notions and practices as to the administration of baptism and the qualification of sponsors, little or no regard being paid to the rubric, though so express as to the public performance of it, and sponsors being admitted without any reference to their pious qualities. My friend, Mr. Francis S. Key, and myself had often mourned over the profanation of this sacrament in Virginia and Maryland, where, in its private performance, even ungodly boys and girls had been sometimes admitted as sponsors. We were both of us on the Committee on the State of the Church, and there introduced, after a proper preamble, the following resolution to be acted on by the House:—" *Resolved*, That it is the opinion of this General Convention that the ordinance of baptism ought, in all possible cases, to be administered in public, and that when necessity requires it to be administered in private, then the office for private baptism should be used, and the infant and sponsors should be afterward required to appear in Church and to conform to the rubric in that respect, and that the Right Reverend the Bishops be respectfully requested to call the attention of the clergy to this subject, and to enjoin upon them a particular care in requiring proper qualifications in those who are admitted as sponsors." We were surprised to find ourselves opposed by those who held the highest views of the efficiency of baptism, and who ought on that account to have desired to see it most highly honoured in the performance. After considerable discussion, the following substitute was adopted:—"The House of Clerical and Lay Deputies, reverting to the notices of private baptism in some of the preceding statements, (the report from Virginia called special attention to it,) respectfully request the House of Bishops to insert in the pastoral letter, solicited by this House, their opinion and advice on the subject of the existing custom of administering private baptism without a great and reasonable cause, and of using in private the public office; and also on the proper qualification of sponsors." The difference between our resolution and its substitute is obvious and great. The resolution expressed a positive and strong opinion on the part of the clergy and laity that certain evils existed, and ought to be corrected, requesting the Bishops to warn against them in their pastoral letter. The substitute expressed no opinion on the part of the House, but placed it all in the hands of the Bishops, merely requesting their opinion and advice on the subject. It was then (for certain reasons) more customary for those in the majority to throw every thing into the hands of the Bishops, and those who doubted the propriety of such a course were regarded as wanting in respect for Bishops, and no Churchmen.* As some of us feared, the opinion of the House of Bishops was not such as we desired. It was regarded as rather apologizing for than condemning the violation of rubrics in relation to baptism, though admitting the duty and importance of public baptism and of pious sponsors. It is due to Bishop White, the supposed author of the pastoral, to say,

---

* A great change took place in this respect in after-years. It was particularly manifested at the time of the lengthened discussion in the Lower House on the question of Bishop McIlvaine's consecration. The Bishops, by a majority of one, were in favour of declaring the Diocese of Ohio vacant, and proceeding to the consecration of Bishop McIlvaine. After waiting the decision of the other House for nearly two weeks, the question was taken and the action of the Bishops sent down. It being understood by some, that the communication of the House of Bishops was in favour of consecration, a strong and successful opposition was made to its being read, on the ground that it was improper that the sentiments of the Bishops should be allowed to have any influence on the opinions of the members of the other House. Ten years before that, indeed, when my consecration was the subject of discussion for one week in the Lower House, on the alleged ground of a condition annexed to it by the Diocese of Virginia, it was well known that the Bishops, with one exception, (Bishop Ravenscroft,) were in favour of consecration, with a certain protest against the condition; but still the opposition was strong for one week. In both of these cases, the votes generally were too clearly marked by party distinction not to induce the belief that such distinctions had their influence. The same might be said in a somewhat lesser degree of the opposition made to the consecration of other Bishops since the above. It has so happened that the difficulties as to consecration have always occurred in regard to those of one party in the Church,— that of the minority. Some candid men of the majority have admitted that party feeling must have had a controlling influence. Should those who have in times past been in the minority ever become predominant, it is hoped that they will not follow the example which has been set. A most striking instance of the above-mentioned change in relation to the asking the opinion of Bishops, or requesting that they give advice in their pastorals on some disputed subject, may be found in the opposition made to a proposed request that the Bishops would notice the Tractarian heresies in the pastoral of 1844.

Hitherto, the Bishops, either by request or without it, had delivered their opinions and warnings freely on various disputed subjects, but when it was wished that they should warn the Church against these dangerous doctrines and practices, whose effects have been so pernicious to the Church, a most violent and successful opposition was made. As a matter of fact or history only do I allude to these things, among others, as worthy of remembrance and capable of being turned to some good use. I am not anxious to make the Bishops dictators to the other House, or to throw undue power into their hands. As to the pastoral letters, so far from desiring to make them discuss and settle doctrines, I have been most decided in opinion, for some years past, that they had better be omitted altogether, or something quite different be adopted in their place.

that not very long after this he became satisfied that more decisive measures ought to be adopted, and gave notice in all the three churches under his care, that henceforth there should be no more private baptisms in those churches, except for such cases as the rubric justified. In speaking to me on the subject soon after this order, he made this significant remark:—that if the parents had so little respect for the ordinance that they would not bring their children to the church, it only proved that the baptism would be of very little service to them, thereby showing that he regarded the chief efficacy thereof to depend on the view the parents took of it, and the use they made of it in the education of their children. One remark I beg leave to make as to the qualification of sponsors. Some ministers question their right to interfere as to the qualification of sponsors, in the absence of a positive statute. Are they then forbidden to exclude infidels, blasphemers, and most abandoned persons? If permitted and bound to require proper qualifications in adults coming to baptism, in candidates desiring Confirmation and the Communion, does not consistency require that they avert from the Church the shame of such an abuse of the sacred office of sponsors as sometimes occurs? The circumstance which determined my mind more resolutely than ever against private baptism and improper sponsors was the fact, that not long before this effort in the General Convention I consented to baptize a child in private, and during the ceremony discovered, to my deep concern, that the father, who had the child in his arms, and was acting as sponsor, was in a state of intoxication. I have during my ministry found it a comparatively easy task to prevent any but communicants presenting themselves as sponsors. By preaching on the subject, and showing its great inconsistency, I have generally prevented such applications, and when they have been made, I have never failed to convince the persons thus applying of the impropriety of the step proposed, by going over with them the baptismal service, and appealing to their own consciences and judgments. Rarely, if ever, has it happened that I was unable to receive into the visible Church any child, where parents desired it, no matter how unsuitable they were to become sponsors, as there could, by a short delay and a little trouble, be found some one communicant who would perform the part. I have on some few occasions acted as sponsor myself, making of course some changes in the service.

PROPOSED ALTERATION IN THE THIRTY-FIFTH CANON.

Another subject came up in this Convention worthy of some notice. It was the meaning and design of the thirty-fifth canon, which relates to the officiating of those not ministers of our Church in the houses of worship belonging to our communion. On my visit to Newburyport the preceding year, I spent several days in the hospitable family of the Rev. Dr. Morse, Episcopal minister in that place. So far from condemning me for preaching in the pulpits of other denominations on the subject I had in hand, as "Sopater of Berea," and perhaps some others, had done, he informed me that only on the preceding Sabbath he had a most respectable minister of the Presbyterian denomination in his pulpit, and justified the act. At the succeeding General Convention, in the year 1820, to my surprise, he brought forward a proposition to repeal the thirty-fifth canon, which seemed to forbid what he had done, and which he also alleged might be construed so as to forbid lay reading in our churches. His proposition was referred to a committee, which reported unfavourably. It was nevertheless carried. Being sent to the House of Bishops for concurrence, it was there negatived. A committee of conference was proposed and agreed to, and I was one of the committee. On a meeting of the joint committee, it was urged, by those who were in favour of its being rescinded, that our Bishops and ministers, in seeking to build up our Church in many places where we had no houses of worship, were often allowed the use of those of other denominations, and it would be unbecoming in us to seek or accept such favours without being willing to grant similar ones. The meeting, however, broke up without any agreement. On that or the following day I dined with Bishop Hobart at a Mr. Smith's, of Philadelphia, and just before dinner the Bishop took me aside and read me something which he thought would satisfy all parties. It is the same which may be seen on page 58 of the Journal of the Convention of 1820. It is as follows:—

"The Bishops have found by experience that such ministers, [those not of our Church,] in many instances, preaching in our churches and to our congregations, avail themselves of such opportunities to inveigh against the principles of our communion; and in some instances have endeavoured to obtain a common right with us to our property. It is therefore not from want of charity to worthy persons dissenting from us, but for the maintenance of such charity, and to avoid collision, that we declare our non-concurrence. The Bishops further declare their opinion concerning the thirty-fifth canon as it now stands, that it does not prohibit the officiating of pious and respectable persons as lay readers in our churches, in cases of necessity and expediency; *nor the lending of any church to any respectable congregation on any occasion of emergency."*

It will be seen that in the foregoing exposition of the Bishops there is no exclusive offensive reason assigned for their non-concurrence, but one which all candid persons must admit to be good, —which indeed all denominations act upon, according to circumstances. It is not said that no other ministers but ours have a right to preach, and that none but ours must enter Episcopal pulpits, but that, to promote charity, to prevent collision, it is best that they be opened only to our own, except when justifying causes exist. That we have suffered at times in the way complained of, in permitting the too free use of our churches, is a fact too well known to us in Virginia, as elsewhere. I have on more than one occasion advised the refusal of our churches, when there was no reasonable cause for the loan of them. Against the uniting in free and common churches I have protested from my first entrance on the ministry, and have on various occasions been instrumental in substituting Episcopal churches for such. Of course, it is for the ministers and vestries to apply the reasoning and advice of the Bishops, and decide when it is proper to open our churches to others. There is not much cause to fear the excessive hospitality of our own or other denominations in this respect; for all are so multiplying houses of worship through the land that there is little need of it. The jealousy of sects is also a sufficient safeguard against excess. Let me add, in conclusion, that this was an old canon of the English Church, adopted, like many others, into our code. Its title in England, and for many years in our own land, was, "Concerning the officiating of strangers, &c." It was designed to prevent strolling impostors from getting into our pulpits, and therefore their regular credentials were required to be shown to the vestries and ministers. Had it been originally framed to prevent all non-Episcopalian ministers from being admitted into Episcopal pulpits, it would surely have been declared in some plain, honest way, and the word "strangers" not have been used, for that would have been most inapplicable to some worthy ministers of other denominations living in the same town or parish, and well known. For many years the same title was used in the American Church. In the Convention of 1808, a committee was appointed (of which Dr. Hobart was one) to revise the canons. The title of the old canon, and nothing else, was altered, and perhaps without discussion or observation. Bishop Hobart was a good expositor of the design of the change, and of the construction to be put upon it. It is to be regretted that any alteration took place in the title. The Church has sustained injury by it in the increased prejudice produced by the construction put upon it by some too zealous friends and some too bitter foes,—namely, that the Episcopal Church hereby denies the right of any other minister to preach the Gospel, which is inconsistent with the exposition given of it by the House of Bishops. Without any such canon, all the ministers and trustees of other denominations guard their churches against intruders, and lend them out when it is deemed expedient. For various reasons, ours will always be yet more particular, even without law.

THE GENERAL THEOLOGICAL SEMINARY.

The General Theological Seminary was first established in New York in the year 1817, then removed to New Haven, as a more suitable place. Jacob Sherred, of New York, bequeathed a large sum to a seminary within the State. A question arose as to the construction of the will. Bishop Hobart maintained that the bequest properly belonged to New York, and that he had established a seminary there to inherit and apply it. Others thought somewhat differently. A General Convention was called in October, 1821, to settle the question. After much discussion, it was resolved that the seminary should be restored to New York on certain terms, and with a new constitution,—placing it, as many thought, too much in the power of the Bishop and diocese of New York. In Bishop White's Memoirs of the Episcopal Church in America, the following account is given of this transaction. Speaking of the committee to whom the subject was referred, he says, " All the members of the committee concurred in giving praise to Judge Cameron, of North Carolina, for the ability and good-temper manifested by him in the progress of the business; and the same were again displayed by him when it came before the House of Clerical and Lay Deputies. However, it did not pass without opposition, which was almost entirely confined to the clerical and lay gentlemen of Virginia, with whom it is a favourite idea to establish a theological professorshiᵖ in the College of William and Mary." I endorse all that is here said of Judge Cameron. I knew his venerable father,—one of the best of our old Virginia clergymen. I think I knew the son well. I heard him, during the time of his first love, tell what God had done for his soul, under the ministry of Dr. Bedell, while in North Carolina. He said, " If I have experienced a change in my soul,

I know that it was done by God's Spirit. That Spirit began the work, not I." He had no sympathy with certain views of religion, even then too prevalent. He did not desire the seminary to be placed at New York. He thought the terms forced upon the Church were hard; but they were the best that could be obtained, and the good-temper displayed by him was in submitting to them and counselling others to do so. I remember his speech well, and conversed freely with him in private. The question he believed to be between a General Seminary in New York, under the partial influence of the whole Church besides, or a Diocesan Seminary in New York, with Sherred's legacy and all the wealth and power and numbers of that State,—able to overwhelm a General Seminary elsewhere without funds. He believed, or at least hoped, that the evil of the undue influence of New York in the General Seminary, under the constitution as agreed upon by the committee, would be chiefly at the beginning, and would be decreasing every year. In glowing prophetic vision, he saw the Church extending itself over the land; new dioceses rising up in every part and rapidly filling themselves with ministers and churches,—sending their funds to the treasury of the General Seminary, and, on their account, as well as on account of the ministers, having the right to regulate the seminary; by which means the power of the General Church would be increasing, and that of New York proportionally decreasing. This he said to comfort those of us who feared the overwhelming influence of New York. I remember well how he applied the prophetic words of the patriarch Jacob, that "*the sceptre should not depart from Judah until Shiloh come; and unto him should be the gathering of the nations.*" I do not say that the scriptural application was correct, but his meaning was plain. The dioceses were to be the gathering together of the nations to take the sceptre from New York in the management of the General Seminary. Bishop White also intimates that the opposition from Virginia proceeded from "a favourite idea with us to establish a theological professorship in William and Mary College." We ought to have been better acquainted with our views, motives, and reasons than any one else. We were then struggling on with our effort at Williamsburg, faint, yet pursuing, with Dr. Keith and one student, and scarce any funds. We knew not but Virginia might have to depend on some General Seminary. It was not a selfish attachment to Virginia alone —a desire for the aggrandizement of ourselves or the destruction of others—which prompted what we said and did. Not knowing how soon we might have to rely on a general institution, we wished it placed under more favourable auspices for the promotion of what we believed to be sound views of the Gospel and the Church, than it would be in New York. The writer of these lines recollects his thoughts, and almost his very words, when he dared to lift up his voice even in opposition to Judge Cameron. Whether Judge Cameron, with all his purity of motive and strength of mind and practical wisdom, was in this instance right, or those so greatly his inferiors in all respects, let subsequent events and the present controlling influence of New York in the conduct of the General Seminary declare. The sceptre has not yet departed from Judah; Shiloh has not yet come. The gathering together of the nations (dioceses) has not yet been, and never will be. It was even formally proposed, some years since, by the Bishop of Western New York, to give it up entirely into the hands of New York, and let the several sums contributed from other dioceses be returned to them.

"Rusticus expectat dum defluat amnis, et ille."
"Labitur, et labetur, in omne volubilis œvum."

PROPOSAL BY THE HOUSE OF BISHOPS, IN THE YEAR 1826, TO MAKE SOME CHANGES IN THE SERVICE.

In my second article it was stated that Bishop Hobart acknowledged that there were some delinquents as to the use of the ante-Communion service in New York, as well as in Virginia, Maryland, or elsewhere, and that the discovery of this fact had something to do with his proposed changes.. I had a few years before—perhaps at the General Convention, 1823—told him that some of his clergy, chiefly in Western New York, were not more regular than some others in the Church. This, at the time, he could not assent to; but, at the opening of the Convention of 1826, he took me aside and said that, on inquiry, he had found that I was correct, and that he meant to propose something which he thought would satisfy all parties and produce a happy uniformity throughout the Church. His plan was soon proposed to and adopted by the other Bishops, and, being sent down to the Lower House, was, after some discussion, adopted by it, and spread before the Church for rejection or ratification by the ensuing General Convention. By this proposal, the Litany might be omitted, except on special occasions.* One or more of the Psalms might be selected and read by the minister in place of the morning or evening portions. The lesson might be

---

* This was withdrawn before the vote was taken in the Lower House.

abridged by the minister, only so that not less than fourteen verses be retained. The ante-Communion service was to be read on every Sabbath. A change was to be made in the preface to the Confirmation service and in one of the prayers of the same. By the latter, the vexed question of baptismal regeneration was to be settled, and settled at the lowest point,—namely, that of a mere change of state or conditional title to salvation,—in opposition to certain views which the Bishops said were imputed to the Church and injurious to it. This proposal was unanimously adopted by all the Bishops present. Bishop Moore, being absent, was much dissatisfied with it, and, at the next Convention in Virginia, most earnestly invoked a protest of the diocese against it. But for this appeal and a tender regard for the feelings of the Bishop, I believe that the Church in Virginia would, by its silence at least, have consented to the action of the General Convention,—although none of us were satisfied with some things in it. I took occasion at another Convention, where the delegates to the General Convention were directed to vote against the proposed changes, to declare my continued conviction that the action of the General Convention had been, on the whole, calculated to do good, though I meant not to oppose what had been determined on in the Convention of Virginia. The adoption of the changes would have effected much of what seems now so generally desired. Had the change proposed, whereby the meaning of baptismal regeneration was fixed at its lowest point, been adopted, there would have been, by anticipation, a protest of the whole Church against all that flood of error in relation to the effects of baptism of infants which has been since brought in by the Tractarian heresy. I would not, however, be understood as endorsing Bishop Hobart's mode of explaining our baptismal service, as I believe another is more consistent with the whole tenor of our services, of which the hypothetical theory, or the judgment of charity, is the way for their true understanding. The lead which Virginia took in opposition to the measure was followed by some other Conventions ; and, as it failed to give general satisfaction, Bishop Hobart proposed its withdrawal, and it was accordingly withdrawn, and the obligation to use the ante-Communion service on every Sabbath was left to rest on its former doubtful foundation. The Bishops had indeed expressed their opinion that it was obligatory, but it was of course only an opinion, wanting the force of law, as the General Convention had never adopted it. Nor did the Bishops claim more for it.

THE EPISCOPAL SUNDAY-SCHOOL UNION.

This was established at the General Convention of 1826. Nothing of its formation appears on the journal, for it was not even proposed to the House. It was the wish of some to make it an institution of the Convention, and such a proposition was talked of; but the whole history of the action of the General Convention was against it. On more than one occasion, individuals had applied to the Convention or to the House of Bishops to adopt or recommend certain Church-books, but were refused on the ground that the General Convention was formed for other purposes, and that the precedent would be bad. In that very year,—1826,—the Rev. Mr. Barlow brought forward a scheme for a Church book-establishment, and was permitted to occupy many hours in the explanation and advocacy of it. The following resolution was adopted in regard to it :—"*Resolved*, As the opinion of this House, that, without entering at all into the merits of the plan noticed in the report of the committee, it is inexpedient to legislate on the subject." On another occasion an effort was made to form a General Education Society under the patronage of the General Convention. This also, after being considered for some time, was postponed, and never resumed. In truth, the only institutions which have been brought under the General Convention are the General Seminary and the Missionary Society ; and whether they give any encouragement for the trial of others, all may judge for themselves. The Episcopal Sunday-School Union was therefore, as has since been publicly and formally admitted by itself, a voluntary institution. Several attempts were made, at different General Conventions, to have it enrolled and recognised among the general institutions of the Church; but they failed,—the Convention being reminded that it was only a voluntary society. The determination of the Church not to embarrass itself and produce discord, by adopting any such institution, was further manifested by the failure of an effort made in 1847 by Bishop Henshaw, who proposed to have a committee of both Houses to prepare a few catechetical books for the children of the Church, with a view to uniformity and harmony. It was opposed by Bishops Delancy, Whittingham, Hopkins, and myself. After a discussion during a part of several days, the question being taken, the mover of the resolution was the only one who voted for it.

There was, however, from the time of its formation a general disposition to encourage the Episcopal Sunday-School Union as a voluntary society. The American Sunday-School Union and the American Tract Societies were noble institutions, and furnished many excellent and suitable works for individuals, families, and Sunday-schools; but they could not supply certain books setting forth the peculiarities of the different denominations in connection with the Gospel. It was therefore desirable that Episcopalians as well as others should have some organization for supplying such. It was distinctly understood, at the establishment of ours in 1826, that it should assume no party character, but be conducted on liberal comprehensive principles, setting forth only those common truths about which Episcopalians are agreed,—which platform has been repeatedly declared since then. Accordingly, the diocese of Virginia, at the first Convention after its organization, earnestly recommended it to the patronage of the Episcopalians of the State. A few months only, however, had elapsed, when some of its publications contained sentiments very different from what was expected, and which were calculated to dissatisfy many of us. I immediately wrote to the chief manager of it,—the present Bishop of Maryland,—making complaints. In reply, I was assured that the greatest pains should be taken in the future to avoid giving offence; that the book most objected to should be withdrawn from circulation; and that henceforth books favouring both parties in the Church should be published. I did not question the sincerity of the promise and intention, but saw the impracticability of the plan proposed. Thus disappointed, I did not take any particular concern in the operation of the Society after that. I only saw that from time to time some things came out which were criticized, and which I could not approve, though there were many good little books published for children, chiefly from the pens of pious writers in England. At length, when Tractarian publications began to multiply in our own and Mother-Church, the character of the issues of this Society became more and more tinctured with the false doctrines of that school. Complaints became so numerous and heavy, that in the summer of 1846, when a number of Bishops were in New York at the annual meeting of the General Missionary Society, the Executive Committee of the Union was convened, and the complaints stated. An order was then passed that a set of all the books of the Society should be sent to each Bishop for examination. On receiving and examining those sent to myself, I found so much to object to, that the duty was felt to spread the same before the Church. This was done in an octavo pamphlet of more than sixty pages. For so doing I received much severe censure from the press and elsewhere. My charges were pronounced to be false. The books were declared to be worthy of all praise, and to have no unsound doctrine in them. The Church was solemnly and repeatedly called on to sustain it just as it was. Seeing that there was no promise or hope of amendment, a number of those who believed that better books and tracts might be procured determined to form another voluntary Society, in which those who agreed in sentiment might with more harmony and efficiency benefit the Church by the press, and resist that torrent of evil which was pouring itself over our own and Mother-Church. Wherefore a number of Bishops, clergy, and laity, who met together at the Convention of 1847, in New York, united in forming what is called the Evangelical Knowledge Society. For so doing they have been stigmatized by many of the friends of the other Society as the promoters of division, schism, and discord, and as slandering that Society, whose publications were still defended as sound and useful. God has nevertheless been pleased to bless our efforts and to extend the sphere of our operations beyond our first hopes. Under these circumstances, at the last General Convention, a most unexpected and extraordinary call was made upon us to cease from our work and unite with the elder Society under a somewhat new organization, which disavowed all former claims by its friends of being other than a voluntary society, and made fresh pledges of the avoidance of all which could offend any sincere and pious Episcopalian. Had the regular officers and members of this Society, after due consideration, formally proposed to those of the Evangelical Knowledge Society a conference for the purpose of inquiring whether there might not be a union of effort on some liberal basis, and, having agreed on the same, called upon the Church generally to sustain such a union, there would have been something worthy the name of compromise, though I do not believe such union practicable or likely to satisfy long. Or had the managers of the elder Society been content to discard such of their books as were at length found to be unworthy, and made, even on the ground of expediency, certain changes in others, and resolved on the most comprehensive and conciliatory mode of action for the future, and left the other Society to do its own work in its own way, there would have been nothing to complain of. All must have desired to see the work of reformation go on. But instead of this, as though it were the only Society having a right to exist, having resolved on certain changes and certain promises, and forgetful of past failures, it calls upon all the clergy and congregations of the Church to rally around its banner, and it only, under pain of being regarded as wanting in true attachment to the Church and devoid of Christian charity. If such is not the position which the old Society (under an altered name) has assumed toward the Evangelical Knowledge Society, consisting of a large number of Bishops, clergy, and laity of the Church, I have mistaken the movement. So have I understood the language of its managers, its committees, and its active friends, as spoken throughout the land. As to the probability of success in making it answer all the wants of the whole Church, it is not in place to discuss the question. It is sufficient to say that the Evangelical Knowledge Society has seen no cause to relinquish its work. That work is not the division of the Church, (as has been falsely charged upon it,) either as designed or as the natural or probable consequence. On the contrary, the best method of preventing division is to allow a reasonable liberty of thought and action. By attempting hermetically to seal the minds and lips of men, there may be a swelling and an explosion. In our Mother-Church, different societies, having the same great object in view, but using somewhat different means, are not considered as interfering with the unity and welfare of the Church. Many there are, among both clergy and laity, who actively co-operate with different societies. I sincerely hope that both of our Societies may be worthy of such general patronage.

THE DOMESTIC AND FOREIGN MISSIONARY SOCIETY OF THE CHURCH.

Our Church was too tardy in this noble enterprise, especially as to the foreign department. The first impulse given to us was the tender of some pecuniary help from the Church Missionary Society of our mother-country, if we would enter upon the work. The missionary character and tendency of the Colonization Society did much to excite our Church to action. The plea for Africa was a pathetic one, addressing itself to all hearts. But it was not heard at once by all. Even after our first efforts in behalf of that unhappy land, I heard an old and respectable clergyman of our Church, preaching at one of our General Conventions, designate the foreign missionary effort as a wild crusade, and another of high standing express the opinion that the foreign missionary work was for other denominations, and the domestic for Episcopalians. In three years after, however, I heard the latter plead zealously for the foreign missionary cause. An effort for preparing coloured missionaries for Africa was made at Hartford under the patronage of Bishop Brownell and Dr. Wainwright, but, from various causes, it proved of but little avail. The efforts of our Virginia Seminary commenced with preparing Mr. and Mrs. Hill for the Greek mission, and have ever since been successfully continued. The missionary work went on gradually increasing on its first platform until the year 1835. Some of its friends then thought that its labours and funds might more rapidly increase if some changes in its organization were effected. It was proposed to place it more entirely under the patronage and direction of the General Convention; to constitute the whole Church, consisting of every baptized person and child, the Society; to declare the whole world to be but one field, forbidding the distinction of foreign and domestic, or so arranging it that no dissensions should arise in the management of them. I was not at the opening of this General Convention, being detained several days in Virginia. All things were agreed upon before my arrival between some of those who, from their location and other circumstances, took a more active part in the conduct of the Society. On reaching Philadelphia, a number of those brethren whose lead I was always ready to follow in regard to such matters, and some of whom are yet alive, informed me that a most happy agreement had taken place among the active friends of missions, that all party distinctions were to be done away, and that, in proof of the liberal feeling toward those of our way of thinking—that one Bishop should be chosen for China and two for the domestic field—one of the latter, together with the former, should be such as we would designate. Of course this was very acceptable to one who had never professed to be indifferent to the distinctions which prevailed in the Church. It seemed to promise well. On conversing with that wise and good man, Bishop Griswold, I found that he was not at all carried away with the new plan; that he would rather it should assume more than less of the voluntary system, referring to the two successful Societies in England,—the Church Missionary Society and the Society for Propagating the Gospel,—which had always acted on the voluntary principle. When the proposed changes came before the whole Society for discussion, there was, I thought, a disposition on the part of some to underrate the character and success of the old organization, and I took the liberty to object to such strictures, and to refer to what it had done, and especially to the great increase of its funds for the last year or two, at the same time declaring my intention to act with those who understood the operation of the Society better than myself. All things were settled on the new platform, and some of us continued until the last night of the Convention under the pleasing expectation of having two missionary Bishops of our own choice; but it so happened that two of the other side were chosen for the domestic field, and the election of one for the foreign field was indefinitely postponed. This, among other things, may help to account for the fact that some of us are rather fearful of what are called compromises.

Though thus disappointed, we determined to support the new organization. In many addresses throughout Virginia, I advocated the peculiarities of it,—even as though it had commended itself entirely to my own choice and judgment. The Society under the new organization has certainly not succeeded as well as was expected by some. An impulse was given to it by the first extraordinary efforts made in its behalf, and its funds increased for a time; but, as they were already on the increase, it is impossible to say whether, with the same exertions, the increase under the old system might not have been even greater. Certain it is, that the annual increase soon began to decline, and that the advocates for the new arrangement were disappointed. The friends of missions have long mourned the want of zeal and liberality of the Church toward them. The domestic department especially has languished. The Constantinople mission dragged heavily for some years, then stopped altogether for want of men, means, and success. The Greek mission, being in a measure self-supporting, has sustained itself well. Those of China and Africa alone seemed to draw forth missionaries and support, and even these have done it in a degree most disproportioned to the importance of the object and the wealth of the Church. At the last General Convention, the causes of failure were inquired into, especially with a view to some change in the management of the domestic department, which was in a very languishing condition. A night was appointed for the consideration of the subject. Through some mistake on my part as to the place of meeting, I was not present. I had intended, if present and opportunity offered, to have stated my own candid convictions as to the main causes of the deficiencies complained of. I should have referred to the notorious fact, that the domestic department was unpopular with a large portion of those entitled Low-Churchmen, whose funds were given reluctantly, while many on the other side were far from being liberal to either department. I heard it said by at least two of the Bishops, ranging on the other side, that it would be necessary to place both departments in the hands of Low-Churchmen, in order to draw forth funds from the people. That confidence was wanting in the other portion was evident from the fact, that a voluntary society had been formed in Philadelphia for the disposal of its funds on such missionaries as it might select. The committee of the General Society was also changed, and some of well-known Low-Church views were put on it, in the hope of inspiring confidence and raising funds. Some effect has certainly been produced by this measure, though, unless other causes of failure be removed, the effect may be only temporary. Had a similar course been pursued in the election of Missionary Bishops at the reorganization in 1835, according to the supposed understanding of some, and as was most reasonable, that liberal policy might have attached a larger number of one portion of the Church to it, have received more funds, and have had some effect as to the kind of missionaries employed. But, in connection with this, there had been other causes in operation. I had never been disposed to ascribe to the domestic committee a desire or willingness to send unsuitable persons or men of extravagant views to the domestic field, in preference to others. It was not their province, indeed, to select where there were Bishops. The Bishops received certain sums of money, and nominated the missionaries on whom it was to be expended. The committee must, indeed, approve; but all must see that when a Bishop makes his selection the committee can scarce object, except in some most notorious case. Whatever be the cause, the fact is not to be questioned, that the reputation of the Society has suffered from the reported character of many of her missionaries. Their very reports, in the "Spirit of Missions," were often very unsatisfactory on several accounts. To hearts imbued with evangelic feeling there was nothing to interest,— the mere externals of religion being dwelt upon, and even those not prospering. Their evil report came back to the Eastern States through various channels. Although there were doubtless a considerable number of worthy men among them, yet I have from time to time met with clergymen and laymen who were to be relied on, who, from their own observation, have declared that, as to very many of them, we must have different men and of different views in the Western field, or our Church could never prosper. From Virginia many individuals and families have gone to various parts of the West, and from these, through their friends and relatives at home, I have heard much that was unfavourable. The great want of the Church, therefore, is not merely more missionaries, but more of the best kind,—evangelists in the truest sense of the word,—men of sense to eschew all follies and novelties, and men of self-denial and toil and with as much experience as possible. For such men must the Church pray and labour as she hopes for success. Many have withheld their funds from this Society, because not knowing unto whose support they might be given, and what false views of the Gospel and the Church they might be made to promote. I confess that such has been my case for many years. At first, and for some time, I gave my annual contributions to domestic missions, hoping the best; but such were the accounts received in various ways, and such the most unsatisfactory reports of some of the missionaries, that I could not continue them with a good conscience.

Still, I avoided all public declaration of my difficulties, and never attempted to interfere with the conduct of others in regard to it. Though hoping that the time would come when, under favourable auspices, some voluntary society might by general consent be formed, I have hitherto discouraged all suggestions or proposals, either public or private, which looked toward a new society antagonistic to that already established. In the Episcopal Missionary Society for the West, established a few years since in Philadelphia, I was pleased to see an organization which, while paying all due respect to the General Society, came as near as circumstances would allow to such an institution as will afford a channel for the conveyance of funds to those missionaries, and those only, who are believed by the donors to be calculated to disseminate the true doctrines of the Gospel and the Church. While it continues to fulfil the end and design of its formation, I shall gladly contribute to its support. I shall also rejoice to know that, by the blessing of God in turning the hearts of many right-minded and zealous young men to the ministry, our General Society may have such numbers of suitable ones at its command that no just cause for complaint may hereafter arise.

THE MEMORIAL AND COMMISSION OF BISHOPS.

At the last General Convention, a memorial from sundry presbyters, of all shades of opinion and from various parts of our land, on the subject of bettering the condition and extending the operations of the Church, was sent into the House of Bishops, which, together with the action thereon, has excited so much attention and called forth so much discussion that it deserves some notice in connection with the topics referred to in this article. As some of my brother-Bishops have, in addresses to their Conventions, declared their sentiments in relation to it, and Conventions also have had it under consideration, I shall be excused for a brief expression of my own views, especially as they have been misunderstood. Most suddenly and unexpectedly was this document introduced into the House of Bishops. I had never heard of it until it was read to the House. There were passages in it which seemed either unintelligible, or most likely to be misunderstood to the injury of the cause sought to be promoted by it. I asked for a second reading of it, but my difficulties were not removed. I asked for an explanation of the difficult passages, but none could be given. I suggested a reference of the paper to its authors and signers for explanation or modification, as I foresaw and predicted that such would be called for, and the Bishops expected to give an account of themselves if they accepted it and complied with its prayer. Not seeing my way clear in favour of the motion, after speaking freely concerning it, sometimes playfully, sometimes seriously, I united with a few others in voting against its being submitted to a commission. That I was not wrong in my apprehension as to the construction which might be put on some very undefined and latitudinarian expressions in the memorial, has been proved by the views since presented in an exposition of the same by the chief mover of it. Notwithstanding all the excellent things in that exposition, I have no hesitation in saying, as to its main feature, that, had such been the understanding of the plan, the Bishops would not have committed themselves to the consideration of the memorial without some modification of its language. Although voting against it, and wondering much at some things said in its behalf, I have never questioned the sincerity and purity of the motives of those presenting it or of those encouraging it, and have ever taken pains to declare my belief that no evil, and some good, would result from the movement. In proof of my favourable disposition toward it, when the questions of the commission, addressed to all the Bishops and clergy, came out, I made a response and offered some suggestions. I did not dream that the communication would ever see the light; but, inasmuch as some of my brethren in the Episcopacy have presented their views to the public, I here subjoin my own brief and imperfect one. I may also add, that the favourable notice of the memorial and commission by the last Virginia Convention met my entire approbation,—having been previously consulted on the subject.

"*To the Bishops appointed to consider the Memorial of the Rev. Dr. Muhlenberg and others.*

"DEAR BRETHREN:—I have received your circular asking communications on the important subject submitted to your consideration, and offer the following suggestions as coming within the terms of your commission:—

"1st. It has ever appeared to me that the Church does not make the most profitable use of the Psalms. One-half of our congregations—perhaps a much larger part—have only one service on the Sabbath, and therefore never hear one-half of the Psalms, in which half are some of the most edifying, while the other half, being read according to the days of the month on which the Sabbath falls, are read unequally. Would it not be better to have the whole of them (with the exception of such as are not so suitable for Christian worship) arranged in selections, according to the different topics of prayer, praise, penitence, &c., and according to the seasons and days which the Church celebrates, making some fifty or sixty in number, and leaving it to the minister to choose out of them as he may think best, except when they belong to a particular day or season? Would not that be better than the present plan, or than that of Bishops White, Hobart, and others,—namely, letting the minister select for himself one or more psalms at pleasure? Might not also some of the longer and less important lessons be abridged, as was proposed by the above-mentioned Bishops?

"2d. It has always appeared to me that the service on Communion-days was too long. Inasmuch as the prayers in the Communion-service contain nearly all that is in the Litany, and are therefore a repetition, I suggest that the Litany be omitted. I would substitute for it, and for the prayer for all conditions of men in the morning service, the prayer for the whole state of Christ's Church militant, and use it in the morning service in place of the prayer for all conditions of men. This prayer for the Church militant comes to us from primitive times, and was called the short or shorter Litany. This arrangement would supersede the necessity of one of the changes of posture in the Communion-service, which are thought by many to be too numerous.

"3d. The service on ordination-occasions is felt by Bishops, clergy, and people to be oppressive and injurious. The service peculiar to the ordination is most solemn and impressive, and its effect should not be weakened by the addition of so much of that which is used every Sabbath. I would suggest the omission of the Litany and Commandments on that occasion.

"4th. I would suggest that the same method which our forefathers adopted, in relation to a clause in the Apostles' Creed and to the form of ordination, be applied to the declaration of regeneration and being born of the Spirit after baptism. In the Creed we are allowed to omit the words, 'He descended into hell,' or use some others. In the ordination of ministers two forms are allowed, according to the option of the Bishop. Why not the same privilege of omission granted to the minister in baptizing, or the use of another prayer which might be prepared? I am persuaded that nothing would contribute more to peace among ourselves, and to the removing of prejudice from the minds of those who belong to other denominations and the community at large, than such an arrangement. It would be in entire accordance with what now seems to be generally admitted,—namely, that a considerable latitude of opinion as to the meaning of certain expressions in the baptismal service is allowed. If it be allowed, why enforce on all the use of the words which, by their sound, seem to convey a meaning which is repudiated by so many? I have long known that a painful difficulty is felt in the use of these passages, not by one portion of our ministers and people, but by a number who differ from such on other points. I believe that public baptism would be much more common but for the reluctance to use these expressions before so many who do not understand or approve them. Many parents, I believe, are prejudiced against the baptism of their children and put it off on account of these words and their supposed meaning. I believe that nothing stands more in the way of converts from other denominations, and especially such of their ministers as are worth having, than the required use of these words in our baptismal service. A slight alteration in the preface to our Confirmation-service, or rather another preface, to be used at the pleasure of the Bishop, would also be desirable.

"As I fear my brethren will be wearied with many and lengthy communications, I omit other suggestions of less importance, (in relation to the service,) and sincerely commend them to the direction of the Great Head of the Church.

"Your friend and brother, WILLIAM MEADE."

It will be perceived that in the above nothing like a complete scheme was attempted. That was not even thought of. I only offered a few unconnected suggestions for those who were appointed to draw up some regular plan for the consideration of the Church. As to the substance of them, they are less in amount than the changes proposed by the Bishops in 1826, and therefore, as an individual, I may shelter myself behind them from any charge of presumption or desire of change. I voted for those proposed by the Bishops and House of Delegates in 1826, believing it to be better to settle by law any thing which might be regarded as a serious departure from the order of our service, rather than leave it to individual discretion, though always maintaining that, as to smaller matters, there must ever be room left for the exercise of a sound discretion, and that even as to greater ones occasions must arise justifying a departure from them, on the principle that God loves mercy more than sacrifice, and that laws were made for men and not men for laws. I believe that some wholesome change may be made in the arrangements of the services, which, so far from interfering with their original use and design, will be conformable with the same. I trust that in a wise and conservative spirit such arrangements will be made. It was not for the purpose of encouraging an unlimited license in the use of the service that I opposed the Commission, nor do I believe that it is for such a purpose that some still contend against it, as has been sometimes intimated. I believe that there is now a disposition on the part of many who have hitherto been most strenuous for rubrical exactness and lengthened services to make more changes and relaxations than I ever practised, countenanced, or now desire. The omission of the ante-Communion service, except on Communion-days, was in truth almost all that distinguished some who were deemed irregular from the most strictly rubrical according to their understanding of rubrics. I am, however, willing for other arrangements more in accordance with the original plan and use of our varied services. In relation to the suggestion in my letter as to the omission of certain parts of our baptismal service after the rite is performed, I do not know that any others have made the same to the Committee, but I know full well that there are many, and they not of one party only, who feel the desirableness of it. It ought to be much less objectionable than that of Bishop Hobart, which was agreed to by the whole House of Bishops and by a large majority of the other House in the year 1826. That proposed to repudiate all high views of baptismal regeneration, as doing injustice and injury to the Church, and to establish the lowest theory—namely, a mere change of state and conditional title to salvation—as the doctrine of the Church. This only proposes to omit the use of certain parts following after the baptism, and not at all essential to its completeness, and about whose meaning there ever have been disputes in the Church, from the times of the fathers to the present moment, and will be perhaps to the end of the world. It leaves every one to form his own opinion as to the efficiency of the rite, drawing it of course from Scripture,—the only authoritative source, if, indeed, he believes that Scripture speaks on the subject,—or else to be content to remain in ignorance and only perform the duties enjoined by the ordinance. It only forbears to define and to render thanks for something of which we can have no certain knowledge. It will leave the service a purely devotional and scriptural one, to which none can object, which will not perplex or distress the consciences of either parents, sponsors, congregation, or minister, and will relieve the Church from much misunderstanding and censure on the part of many who hear it. I am well aware that in some of the confessions of other Reformed Churches there may be found expressions of the same kind, which of course are liable to a similar objection; but there is this difference, that in their case the expressions are locked up in books that are seldom seen. They are not used in the public administration of baptism; not put in the form of positive thanksgivings for a spiritual regeneration certainly received at a given moment and through a certain act, and are therefore not the occasion of such unhappy disputation. It is the great shame and reproach of Christendom that so much strife and bitterness have ever been about those things which lie beyond the reach and above the range of the human mind, and that the clergy especially should be the most curious and anxious to be wise above what is written and should puzzle their poor people with such questions. The disputes about the Divine decrees and the effects of baptism on the condition and the souls of unconscious infants are of this kind. How numerous and how contradictory and extravagant the theories as to the latter! How intolerant the feelings and speeches and conduct of some toward those who differ from them! Is it not time that these should cease? Could there be a better way of beginning it than by cutting off the continually-recurring occasions of bringing it before the minds and consciences of men? The Church has adopted this plan in relation to a clause in the Apostles' Creed and in the service for the ordination of priests, and has left some other things optional with the minister. Might not the same method be adopted with happy effect in relation to the interminable dispute about baptismal regeneration? None of the various expositions would then be either affirmed or condemned in the service. I am persuaded that though there always might be differences,—great differences, requiring to be discussed, false doctrines concerning it requiring to be exposed,—yet the omission of any thing like defining or seeming to render thanks for an effect certainly produced would greatly diminish controversy and be a solemn testimony on the part of the Church against the attempt to be wise above what is written. I confess I shall have little confidence in the existence or strength of a spirit of compromise in the Church for the sake of unity and peace, if there be not a willingness merely to omit a few words, about whose meaning there are such various opinions, and which no one can hold to be essential to the ordinance. To be baptized with water in the name of the Father, Son, and Holy Ghost is commanded and required. That the word should accompany it, and prayer be offered up for God's blessing, is manifestly proper; but that we should undertake to define the effect produced, and render thanks for it, is nowhere enjoined. The addition is the work of man, and has been a great unhappiness to the Church. Should any be disposed to think or say that some of us are desirous to dispose of some words in the service which interfere with our views of regeneration, I can most conscientiously say that such is not my case. As I understand the service, and believe it ought to be understood, after having examined all that has been written on the subject, it expresses my own convictions on the subject of baptism; but there are peculiarities and difficulties in the mode of presenting the subject, and in the terms used, which require continual explanations and defences, that perplex and injure the cause. It is therefore maintained that the omission of these words, which are the causes of almost all the controversy, would promote the peace and welfare of the Church; which words, it is again affirmed, are not at all necessary to the right performance of baptism. It is complete without them.

CONCLUDING REMARKS.

If I may be allowed to express an opinion as to the present state and prospects of our Church, I should say that some are now as much disposed to undervalue her efficacy for good, even without the proposed changes, as many were formerly to overrate it. Very soon after my entrance on the ministry, I read a sermon by one of our most distinguished Bishops on those words of the Psalmist,—"Walk about Zion; mark well her bulwarks; consider her palaces," &c. They were applied to our Church in this country, and her praises highly spoken. It was confidently affirmed that she must greatly prevail over others by reason of her divine organization and many excellencies. The same glorious things were continually spoken of her by such as claimed to be her true sons; and those who did not firmly believe that she must outstrip, or perhaps overwhelm, all others, were considered as wanting faith in the promises of God to his Church, and a hearty zeal in her behalf. Just at this time I met with a sermon, on the same text and in the very same style, by one of the oldest and most respectable Baptist ministers in Virginia, showing that the Baptist Church was so clearly the true Apostolic Church—of course after God's own heart—that it must carry every thing before it; that the signs of the times could not be mistaken. Shortly after this I went to the West, and heard of an eminent Presbyterian minister who was preaching from place to place a sermon, or series of sermons, if not from the same text, yet on the same subject, in which he declared his firm conviction that his Church was, as to her constitution, doctrine, and discipline, so scriptural and so suited to the genius of our government that in twenty years the whole land would embrace it. At this time also a favourite song with many Methodists was,—

"The Methodists are gaining ground;
The devil's kingdom's tumbling down;
Hallelujah! Hallelujah!"

Doubtless all these were most sincere in their belief that what they earnestly desired would surely come to pass. Forty years have since elapsed, and no one of them has taken the place of the other. On the contrary, all of them have, by God's blessing, done much good on the different theatres assigned them, are still doing good, and will do more good. Moreover, they have sustained very much the same relation to each other as to numbers and success. All of them have had their trials, their declensions, their reverses, which should make them humble, and cause them to refrain from taunts and reproaches, rather remembering the admonition that

"Brethren in calamity should love."

I believe that there are very few now to be found who would venture the prophecy that their own denomination must soon swallow up all others. Our own Church has not been favoured with the same abundant opportunities of preaching the Gospel to the poor, (except on Southern plantations,) while she has enjoyed greater opportunities of presenting it with acceptableness to the wealthy and educated. Nor have her evangelical Liturgy and the faithful preaching of many of her ministers been unblessed in the behalf of such. Sadly has she been afflicted for the last fifteen years with the hankerings of some of her ministers and people after Rome. Their apostasy has indeed been most mortifying, and is well calculated to punish her for much vain boasting, and to lead to a more chastened estimate of her character and mission. She has certainly lost much in the confidence of the community, and given to her enemies, both in the Church and the world, occasion for increased opposition and condemnation. It is needless to close our eyes on this most notorious fact. It will be wisdom, honesty, and good policy to acknowledge it freely. Sins must be confessed as well as forsaken, in order to be fully forgiven and their evil consequences prevented.

We must also adopt the most effectual means for recovering what has been lost. It is most encouraging to know that all of God's favour has not been lost. On the contrary, never has the Gospel been more faithfully and earnestly preached by greater numbers of our ministers in England and America than during our recent fiery trial. Though the enemy came in like a flood, the Spirit of the Lord, speaking from thousands of pulpits, has lifted up the standard of truth against him. The heretical movement has been arrested, and now stands, covered with shame and confusion, seeking to find out some object on which to lay the blame of its own mischievous proceedings.

Together with many who are guiltless of the evil sought to be removed, some of those who have contributed to it are now proposing certain changes in the mode of the Church's worship, in order to regain what is lost and press forward in the duty assigned us by God. It is believed that an abridgment of the usual worship, by a partial separation of services once distinct, will remove one stumbling-block out of the way of the Church's popularity, and I hope that it may be found practicable to do so. But whether the service be longer or shorter, if ministers preach the Gospel faithfully and perform all other duties piously and zealously, great will be the effect. Numbers will be added to the Lord of such as shall be saved. Too many instances of a true conversion and most exalted piety are to be found in our own and Mother-Church to allow of a doubt on this point. The great want of the Church is more pious and zealous ministers, who understand and preach the Gospel. Let them be sons of the Church,—not converts, except they be young,—not proselytes from other ministries. It is not reasonable to expect many useful and acceptable ones from the pulpits of other denominations. All experience is against it. If respectable, influential, and happy in the places of their birth, training, and ministry, it will not often happen that either conscience, choice, or judgment will induce them to leave their old associations. Most honourable exceptions there are. I have known such,—have laid my hands on such, and highly esteem them. But, at the same time, I have ever made it my boast, that if in any thing I have done good service to the Church, it has been in dissuading from our ministry those who would have gladly entered it, but who, like too many others, might have done us evil instead of good,—might either have been drones in our hive, or else have taken our ministry on the way to Rome. When I have heard it boasted that hundreds have left other ministries, drawn by the superior and exclusive claims of ours, and have known who and what too many of these were, I have mourned over the fact instead of rejoicing at it, and regarded it as the judgment of Heaven upon us for urging, to an extreme which neither Scripture nor our Protestant fathers nor our standards justify, the exclusive claims of the Episcopal ordination. At the same time, when I have heard some of other denominations declare that none but the unworthy ever leave them, I could not forbear the hint that there must be something most defective in the training of their ministers, when they have so many unworthy ones to spare.

The great complaint of those who desire some change is, that our Church does not, as at present administered, operate on the masses,—especially that we have so few of the very poor in our congregations, although some have laboured very faithfully to this end. It ought certainly to be regarded as a great unhappiness and defect to be without a due admixture of such. Ministers ought to covet the poor for their congregations, and seek them by all proper means. They should do it for their own sakes, and for that of the rich of their flock, as well as for the benefit of the poor. The presence of the poor will help them to preach the Gospel in a plainer and more effective way,—will exercise all their ministerial graces,—will call forth the alms of their parishioners the more abundantly. Our services, rightly understood and used, are admirably adapted to the poor and ignorant. It is deeply to be lamented that so much prejudice exists in the minds of the great mass of the American people against our Church and her peculiarities, so that thus far but little success has attended even the most zealous efforts of some who have devoted themselves to the work. Various circumstances connected with our political and religious history have contributed to this. With all the republicanism of our country, there is as much of social and religious prejudice, caste, and division among us as in any nation of Christendom, although it differs considerably in some of its modes. Political and religious demagogues are continually fostering it in order to promote their ends. Religious associations are hard to be broken. "Can a people forsake their gods?" may be asked now in relation to the religious sects of our country, as formerly concerning the sects in pagan lands. Two or three denominations among us have absorbed almost all of the poorer classes, and claim them as their birthright. To induce even a few of such to unite with us is attended with great difficulty, for against no denomination of Christians are their prejudices so strong as against our own. Still, let us endeavour to allure as many as possible of the more neglected ones into our fold, and tend them well. If any modifications of our system can adapt it the better for this purpose, most assuredly let it be done. In ordaining men for the purpose, however, let us beware of lowering our standard too much. Our Lord and the Apostles, who preached so well to the poor, were filled with all knowledge by the Spirit. All other denominations are raising their standard of ministerial qualification. Some expressions have been used among us which have excited fears that we were about to err in this respect. I have no such fears myself. At any rate, I am confident that a few mistakes in ordaining ignorant and unsuitable men would soon correct the error.

I have thus in a most imperfect manner completed my recollection of such things in the diocese of Virginia and in the General Church as seemed most worthy of being recorded. I had thought, in view of death, to leave behind me some such notices; but it may be better to have been surprised into this earlier statement, so that if I have fallen into any mistakes I may have the opportunity of correcting them, as I should be grieved to misrepresent even in the slightest degree the Church of my affections, or any member of it.

APPENDIX.

No. I.

A COPY OF THE JOURNAL OF THE PROCEEDINGS OF THE CONVENTION HELD AT THE COLLEGE OF WILLIAM AND MARY, IN THE CITY OF WILLIAMSBURG, IN APRIL, 1719.

AT a Convention of the Clergy of Virginia, begun on Wednesday, the eighth day of April, 1719, in the College of William and Mary, in the city of Williamsburg, Mr. Commissary Blair called over a list of the clergymen of this Colony, and the following members answered to their names:—

Mr. Selater, Mr. Guy Smith, Mr. Lewis Latane, Mr. Thomas Sharpe, Mr. Hugh Jones, Mr. Andrew Thomson, Mr. Ralph Bowker, Mr. Cargill, Mr. George Robinson, Mr. Monroe, Mr. Eml. Jones, Mr. Bar. Yates, Mr. Wm. Finney, Mr. John Shaife, Mr. Alex. Scott, Mr. John Worden, Mr. Benj. Pownal, Mr. Wm. Brodie, Mr. John Bagge, Mr. Fran. Mylne, Mr. Brunskill, Mr. Fountaine, Mr. Geo. Seagood, Mr. James Robertson, Mr. James Falconer.

Absent.

Mr. Alex. Forbes, Mr. John Bell, Mr. Giles Rainsford, Mr. James Breghin, Mr. John Span, Mr. Owen Jones, Mr. John Prince, Mr. James Tenant, (out of the country,) Mr. Daniel Taylor, (excused by letter,) Mr. Saml. Bernard, (sick,) Mr. James Cleck, (sick,) Mr. Wm. Black.

Then Mr. Commissary Blair read two letters from the Lord-Bishop of London, our Diocesan, one to himself, and another to Reverend the Clergy of Virginia, and recommended the particulars of them, which letters are as followeth,—viz. :

To the Rev. Mr. Blair, Commissary of Virginia.

DEAR BROTHER:—You will find in the enclosed the reason I have for writing it, and will, I doubt not, agree in opinion with me that it cannot but be useful to put the clergy under you in mind of their duty, even if there should be no failing, much more if there be any. I therefore desire you to communicate this letter to them, and to use all proper means to redress any deviations from our rules, considering that both you and I are to be answerable if we neglect our duty in that part.

393

I have wrote to the Governor, and entreated him to give you all proper countenance and assistance in these matters, and am persuaded he will be ready so to do upon any application you may have occasion to make him.

I should be glad to hear from you what vacant churches are in your parts, to the end I may use my best endeavours to procure you a supply.

I am, sir,

Your assured friend and brother,

FULHAM, August 6, 1718.   JOHN LONDON.

To the Reverend the Clergy of Virginia.

REVEREND BRETHREN:—It is always a joy to me to hear of the good success of your ministerial labours, and no less a grief to hear of any defaults and irregularities among you; to which disadvantageous reports I am not forward to give credit, finding that wrong representations are frequently made. Some occasions have been given to apprehend, there may have been faults and miscarriages in the life and conversation of some among you, which I trust are corrected; and that the grace of God, and a sense of duty you owe to Him, his Church, and to yourselves, will so rule in your hearts, as that I shall no more hear any thing to the disadvantage of any of you upon that head. Nevertheless, I cannot but give you notice, that I have information of some irregularities, which, if practised, will need very much to be redressed; and I cannot but hope, if such things there be, you will not be unwilling to do your part, as I think it a duty to do mine by this advisement.

Whether any ministers be settled among you who have not a license from my predecessor or myself, I must leave to the inquiry of your Governor, who is instructed in that case, and will, I believe, upon notice given, be ready to act accordingly, as also in reference to institutions and inductions. At least I must hope, that, by this case and yours, none will be suffered to officiate in the public worship of God, or perform any ministerial offices of religion, but such only as are Episcopally ordained; and from all such I cannot but expect a regular conformity to the established Liturgy, from which none of us can depart without violating that solemn promise we made at our ordination.

I have desired Mr. Commissary to communicate this to you, and, as I hope he will use all fitting earnestness in pressing the observation of these things, so I doubt not he will be able to procure a redress for those or any other disorders in the worship of God, when the same shall come to his knowledge.

I am, reverend brethren,

Your affectionate brother and assured friend,

JOHN LONDON.

FULHAM, August 6, 1718.

Then the Convention received a letter from the Honourable the Governor, directed to the clergy, which'was read, and with it a copy of a letter from the Governor to the vestry of St. Anne, in Essex, which was read also, which letters are as followeth, viz. :—

REVEREND GENTLEMEN :—You are now come hither at your Commissary's desire, that he might have the easier opportunity to communicate to you a letter from your Right Reverend Diocesan. And seeing his Lordship has been pleased to make mention of me in that letter, taking notice that I have instructions to act in reference to institutions and inductions, and that he must leave to my inquiry whether any ministers be settled among you who have not license from him or his predecessor, and as his Lordship seems to rely on my care as well as yours, that none may be suffered to officiate in the public worship of God, or perform any ministerial offices of religion, but such only as are Episcopally ordained, I ought not to be silent on this occasion, and thereupon must remark to you, that the very person whom his Lordship expects should use all fitting earnestness in pressing the observations of these things is he whom I take to be the least observer thereof himself. For none more eminently than Mr. Commissary Blair sets at naught those instructions which your Diocesan leaves you to be guided by, with respect to institutions and inductions; he denying by his practice as well as discourses that the King's Government has the right to collate ministers to ecclesiastical benefices within this Colony; for, when the church which he now supplies became void by the death of the former incumbent, his solicitation for the same was solely to the vestry, without his ever making the least application to me for my collation, notwithstanding it was my own parish church; and I cannot but complain of his deserting the cause of the Church in general, and striving to put it on such a foot as must deprive the clergy of that reasonable security which, I think, they ought to have with regard to their livings.

As to the disorders in the worship of God, which are pointed at in the said letter, it appears as if my Lord of London knew not that this Commissary is more apt to countenance than redress the same; for I myself have seen him present in the church while a layman (his clerk) has read the divine service to the congregation, he himself vouchsafing to perform no more of the ministerial office than to pronounce the absolution, preach, and dismiss with the blessing. I have also seen him present in the church-yard while the same clerk has performed the funeral-service at the grave. And I remember when he was for having the churchwardens provide lay readers, who should on Sundays read to their congregations some printed sermons; and so far he declared in Council his approbation thereof, that such practice had like to have had the sanction of the Government, had I not withstood it as destructive to the Establishment of the Church.

Those and many other instances that might be given induce me to believe that a reformation of what has chiefly (as I apprehend) given occasion to your Diocesan's letter will not be pressed very heartily upon you by your Commissary, especially if he made no such solemn promise at his ordination as his Lordship reminds you all of: wherefore I judge it to be the more incumbent upon the several members now in this Convention diligently to inquire of the disorders which your Diocesan takes notice of, and earnestly to apply yourselves to proper means for redressing them.

As to any faults and miscarriages in the life and conversation of some among you, which your Diocesan likewise touches upon, I trust your Commissary will use all fitting earnestness in pressing the reformation of such manners as may give offence and bring scandal upon your holy profession; and I have so good an opinion of the present body of the clergy, that I do not in the least doubt of a very general concurrence to censure and admonish any one of your fraternity here whom you shall know to have erred in either his doctrine or manners. For my part, I hope, after so many years' experience of my conduct in this Government, there is little need to express in words my disposition toward the Church; and I cannot suppose that any one of you doubts of my real inclination to support the interest thereof, or that I am otherwise than, reverend gentlemen,

Your very affectionate and assured humble servant,
A. SPOTTSWOOD.

WILLIAMSBURG, April 8, 1719.

To the vestry of St. Anne, in Essex, September 3, 1718.

GENTLEMEN:—Though the hurry of public business, wherein I was engaged, did not allow me time immediately to answer your letter of the 1st of August, yet I told Mr. Short on his going hence, on the 5th of that month, that you might expect my answer in a few days; and if he has done me justice he has informed you that I advised your forbearing, in the mean time, to run too rashly into the measures I perceived you were inclining to; assuring him my intentions are to make you easy, if possible, in relation to your minister. But, whether that advice was imparted to you or not, it is plain, by your proceedings of the 8th of the same month, that you resolved not to accept of it, seeing you immediately discarded Mr. Bagge and sent down Mr. Rainsford with a pretended presentation of induction. As soon as that came into my hands, I observed it expressly contrary to a late opinion of the Council, whereby it is declared that the right of supplying vacant benefices is claimed by the King, and by his Majesty's commission given to the Governor; and for that reason I let Mr. Rainsford know that before I could admit of such a presentation it was necessary for me to have likewise the advice of the Council thereon. But, not content to wait their resolution, I understand you have taken upon you the power of induction, as well as that of presentation, by giving Mr. Rainsford possession of the pulpit, and excluding the person I appointed to officiate. I have, according to my promise, taken the advice of my Council upon your pretended presentation, and here send it enclosed, by which you will find that the Board is clearly of opinion that I should not receive such presentation:

so that if you are the patrons (as you suppose) you may as soon as you please bring a "*quare impedit*" to try your title; and then it will appear whether the King's clerk or yours has the most rightful possession of this church. In the mean time I think it necessary to forewarn you to be cautious how you dispose of the profits of your parish, lest you pay it in your own wrong.

Should I end my letter here, it might be imagined that I am as willing as you to keep up contention; but, as I am rather desirous to prevail with you by reason than to convince you at your own expense, I think it necessary to exhort you to some just terms of accommodation: but I must tell you, that this is not to be accomplished by the interposition of such faithless deputies as Mr. Short, your late messenger hither; for if upon his return he reported what I have seen attested under Mr. Winston's hand, he ought to be excluded all human conversation; for I do assure you that no such discourse happened between Short and me as he has related, neither did Mr. Bagge ever solicit me to turn out any one of your vestry, nor did I ever receive such a proposal from any man else, except Mr. Rainsford, who in a letter last year did importune me to remove one of your vestry, whom he terms a Judas among the number of the twelve Bishops of St. Anne's, but, because I never pretended to intermeddle in the choice or removal of vestries, I never answered his letter. By the same hands it is like you received such another piece of news,—to wit: that Mr. Commissary Blair advised your insisting on your right, for that you had the law, and the major part of the Council is on your side. I have taxed Mr. Commissary with this, and he has publicly denied it, and even given it under his hand that he never did such a thing; but, if he did, the enclosed proceedings of the Council (wherein he joined) will convince you how much he was mistaken. Another thing, which perhaps may have given you a fallacious assurance, is, that the vestry of James City were taking the same measures with you to dispute the King's authority; but, to undeceive you on that point, that vestry has thought fit to drop the dispute, and the person they pretended to fix in their parish has been fain to supplicate me to put him into some other benefice.

Having thus endeavoured to remove the impression which false rumors and public insinuations may have made on you, I shall in the next place remind you of some particulars which probably some of you have forgot and others perhaps have never come to the knowledge of. In the year 1712, Mr. Bagge was so much in the esteem of your parish that, though he had then the care of another, he was the only person you would think of to supply yours, and you represented him to me as a sober man, a good preacher, and of a life and conversation blameless; when I yielded to supply your parish by collating Mr. Edwards, the only objection to Mr. Bagge was his non-residence in your parish; when, upon Mr. Edwards's decease, I was willing to prefer Mr. Bagge to that vacancy, you then only objected against him his not being in Priests' Orders; and when, in order to his qualifying himself for the care of your parish, he undertook a voyage to England, you gave him a very ample testimonial of his pious and laudable life and doctrine, all which are yet extant, under the hands of those who now so violently oppose him. It was on the testimony of your vestry that your Diocesan,—the Bishop of London,—after having admitted Mr. Bagge into Priests' Orders, recommended him to me that he might be collated into that parish where he had gained so good a reputation; and who could imagine he would not be acceptable to a people who had given such encomiums of his life and doctrine, after he had taken such pains to remove the only thing that could be objected to him? And what opinion your Bishop will have of men who, without any new experience of Mr. Bagge's behaviour, act so inconsistent with themselves, I leave you to judge.

That I may the better prevail with you to reflect in time upon what you are going about, I shall plainly lay before you the power by which I act, leaving you to judge whether I ought to give up a right so well founded both on law and reason: As the King is the sovereign of these plantations, so he is vested with the right of patronage of all ecclesiastical benefices, unless when it appears that he has by apt words granted the same away to private subjects.

That his Majesty doth claim the right here in Virginia appears by the commission under the broad seal, whereby his Majesty gives his Governor full power and authority to collate any person or persons to any churches or chapels, or any other ecclesiastical benefices, as often as any of them shall become void, (which power is also expressly excepted out of the Bishop of London's patent as Bishop of the Plantations;) and in his Majesty's instructions the Governor is particularly directed as to the qualifications of the persons so to be collated by him, and enjoined to cause all persons not so qualified to be removed, and immediately to supply the vacancies, without giving notice to the vestries, which is always done in England (in the case of deprivation) where there is a patron. This shows that the King acknowledges no other patron but himself. But, besides this commission, there is a further and very early evidence of the King's not looking on the law you hinge on to give the vestries any right of patronage: it is a lease made by King Charles II., to the Lords Arlington and Culpepper, of the whole Territory of Virginia for thirty-one years, wherein, among other things, there is this remarkable grant,—viz: "And we do further give and grant to the Lord Henry Earle of Arlington, and Thomas, Lord Culpepper, that they shall, for and during the said term of thirty-one years, be sole and absolute patrons of all the churches and chapels already built, or shall hereafter be built, within the said Territory," &c. Now, this grant being made in 1672, just ten years after the law for inducting of ministers passed here, is it to be supposed that the King's Counsel-at-law, who prepared the grant, and the Lord-Chancellor, who put the great seal to it, would have suffered it to pass had they judged it incompatible with a law of the Colony so lately enacted, when it must have been fresh in memory, especially considering that the Lord-Chancellor was always one of the Committee for Foreign Plantations? And the then Government, Council, and House of Burgesses, though they sent home agents to remonstrate against this law, did not plead that this grant of the patronage of churches was repugnant to the right of the vestries; neither could the agents prevail to get the grant set aside, though they were particularly charged to endeavour it. If you consider Sir Edward Northey's opinion, (which I find mentioned in your letter,) it is plain he never had the King's right under consideration; nor doth he at all determine that the vestries are the undoubted patrons; but, after he had cited the several laws relating to the churches, he declared that the right of advowson must be determined by the laws of England, (there being no law of this country that gives any further direction therein,) and the whole scope of his arguments thereafter is only to show what is the practice in England, where there are such undoubted patrons; which is but supposing what the King has not yet yielded in this country, seeing he still claims the right of supplying the vacancies of all ecclesiastical benefices, as the Council hath declared to be the true meaning of his Majesty's commission and instructions.

Lastly, I shall set forth to you the reasonableness of believing that the King looks upon the right of disposing of the benefices here as still vested in the Crown.

Every minister sent here is denominated one of the King's Chaplains, employed in his Majesty's service abroad, and as such receives twenty pounds out of his treasury to defray the charge of his passage. If any of the King's ships are coming hither, those ministers have the passage and provision gratis. The Bishop of London recommends them to the Government to be preferred to some ecclesiastical living. But they bring no recommendation to any vestry as patrons of the churches; nor doth either the King or the Bishop direct or desire the Governor to intercede with the patrons of the churches to bestow on such ministers the vacant livings in their gift. Now, to what purpose is the King at so much expense to send over clergymen to the Plantations, if they are to starve here till a lay patron thinks fit to present them? To what purpose doth the Bishop recommend them to the Government, if he has no preferment to bestow? To what purpose do they bring the Bishop's testimonial and license to preach, if their qualifications are to be again tried by a vestry here, and they to depend on popular humour for their livings? Can it be supposed that the Governor's instructions, prepared by the Board of Trade, (who are well acquainted with all the laws of this country,) and afterward read and approved of in Council, where the King's learned judges are present, should enjoin the Governor, upon the removal of a minister, immediately to supply the vacancy without waiting the six months' lapse, and should not rather direct him to follow the practices of England by giving timely notice to the patron to present another clerk, if their Lordships had any imagination that the law of Virginia gave the right of patronage to the vestries? Whatever wild notions some people may entertain of his Majesty's ministers intrusted with the inspection of the Plantations, I am confident they would never advise his Majesty to enjoin any thing repugnant to law; and therefore, till the King thinks fit to alter my commission and instructions, I hope I cannot be blamed for not giving up a right which his Majesty has intrusted me with, unless it be otherwise determined by due course of law, to which I shall be as ready as any man to submit; and I doubt not you will allow me to be a fair adversary in so fully informing you beforehand of the merits of the cause I am to defend. However, you have it in your power to bring this dispute between us to an accommodation; and I do again assure you that I shall be ready on my part to show myself an indulgent Governor, and, in order to make you easy, to yield what I can without betraying my trust to my master.

The said letter being read, a motion was made that the Commissary be desired to print his sermon preached this day before the members of the Convention, at the parish church of Bruton, in the city of Williamsburg. Mr. Commissary answered that he had never yet appeared in print; but, if the members of the Convention wished it, he would transmit a true copy of it to the Lord-Bishop of London; and it was desired accordingly.

Resolved unanimously that the Governor be addressed.

Then a committee of the seven members following was appointed to prepare the address,—viz.: Mr. Emanuel Jones, Mr. Hugh Jones, Mr. George Robertson, Mr. Skaife, Mr. Seagood, Mr. Brodie, and Mr. Yates,— and return it to the House by to-morrow morning, nine o'clock.

Ordered, That the Convention be adjourned to that hour.

THURSDAY, April 9, 1719.

Mr. Brodie, one of the committee that was appointed to draw up an address to the Governor, being absent by reason of sickness, the rest of the said committee—viz.: Mr. Emanuel Jones, Mr. Hugh Jones, Mr. George Robertson, Mr. Skaife, Mr. Seagood, and Mr. Yates—appeared, and Mr. Emanuel Jones in their name delivered it in; which, being read and examined paragraph by paragraph, passed without amendment, and is as followeth, viz:—

To the Hon. Alexander Spottswood, his Majesty's Lieutenant-Governor and Commander-in-Chief of this Colony.

May it please your Honour, should we, the clergy of his Majesty's Province of Virginia assembled in Convention, (who have, with the utmost indignation and resentment, heard your Honour affronted and abused by a few prejudiced men,) be silent upon this occasion, we should appear ungrateful in both capacities as ministers and subjects. Therefore, with grateful hearts we now express our deep sense of your just and wise government,—a government that has raised this Colony to a flourishing condition by exercising over it no other authority but that wherein its happiness and liberty consist, and which nothing but the groundless suspicions and unreasonable jealousies of the eager and violent can render liable to exception. Your Honour is happy to us rather than to yourself, in that you are perpetually toiling for the public, constantly doing good to many, whilst you do injury to none.

We approach you, therefore, not only as our Governor, but as a common good, and think we cannot better declare our love to this country than in our hearty wishes and fervent prayers that you may long, very long, preside over it, which we assure you are the sincere desires of your Honour's very much obliged and most humble servants.

WILLIAM AND MARY COLLEGE, April 9, 1719.

The Convention next took the Lord-Bishop of London's letter into consideration, which being again read and considered paragraph by paragraph, the first question that was put by Mr. Commissary was, Whether any of the members present knew of any person who officiated in this country as a minister without license from our present Diocesan or his predecessor? and the whole House declared they knew of none. The next question upon it was, Whether any of the members present knew of any minister that officiated in the Colony without Episcopal ordination? to which the following members answered they knew of none,—viz.: Mr. Monroe, Mr. Mylne, Mr. Smith, Mr. Fountaine, Mr. Brunskill, Mr. Sharpe, Mr. George Robertson, Mr. Finney, Mr. James Robertson, Mr. Thomson, Mr. Cargill.

The following members were doubtful whether Commissary Blair had Episcopal ordination or not,—viz.: Mr. Skaife, Mr. Latane, Mr. Yates, Mr. Bagge, Mr. Emanuel Jones, Mr. Bowker, Mr. Seagood, Mr. Scott, Mr. Hugh Jones, Mr. Falkoner, Mr. Downal, and Mr. Worden. Mr. Selater suspended his judgment. The next question was, Whether any member knew of any minister who did not conform punctually to the rules of the Established Church?

It was owned that there were many rules which were not observed by any of them, because of the circumstances of the country.

Ordered, That it be an instruction to the committee that shall be appointed to answer the Lord-Bishop of London's letter, that they set forth the particulars wherein at present they cannot help being deficient in the discharge of their function, and that his Lordship's directions be requested therein, and that they inform him that none of the members refuse to conform to the rubrics and canons to the utmost of their power.

The next thing inquired into was the irregularity of the lives of the clergy.

To which it was answered, that no member had any personal knowledge of the irregularity of any clergyman's life in this Colony.

Whereupon it was ordered, that it be an instruction to said committee modestly to vindicate the lives of the clergy from the aspersions (thrown on them by former informations to his Lordship) of faults and miscarriages in the lives of some among them.

Ordered, That it be an instruction to the committee to inform his Lordship that visitations have been attempted by Mr. Commissary, but have been found very difficult, and that his Lordship's directions be desired in that matter.

The next things in his Lordship's letter taken into consideration were institutions and inductions.

Upon which the question was put, Whether, in order to the redress of the grievances we labour under with reference to them, the difficulties which render our livings and circumstances precarious should not, in the said answer, be represented to his Lordship?

It passed in the affirmative.

Ordered, That the said committee be instructed accordingly; and that they let his Lordship know that, whenever the Governor has been applied to, he has been always ready to redress us in this matter to the utmost of his power.

Ordered, That the committee to be appointed to draw up the representation and answer to his Lordship's letter consist of seven members. Then the House named Mr. Commissary, Mr. Bagge, Mr. Hugh Jones, Mr. Cargill, Mr. Mylne, Mr. Finney, and Mr. Pownal to be that committee.

Ordered, That the committee meet this evening at six o'clock.

Resolved, That the address be presented to the Governor.

Ordered, That the committee that prepared it attend him to know when he will be pleased to be waited upon therewith. Then the Convention adjourned to 9 o'clock to-morrow.

FRIDAY MORNING, April 10.

Mr. Selater and Mr. Smith being absent when the House was called over, Mr. Bagge moved that no member should be allowed to be absent from the Convention without leave, which was seconded and ordered.

Mr. Yates moved that when the committee was engaged in drawing the answer to the Bishop of London's letter, a copy of the proceedings of the Convention should be laid before the rest of the members to inspect them, in order to reducing the same into a regular journal, which was seconded and granted.

Mr. Emanuel Jones reported that the committee which prepared the address had waited on the Governor to know when he would be pleased to be waited on by the House to present the same, and, his Honour having signified his pleasure that he would receive it at seven of the clock in the evening, the members accordingly presented it him, who was pleased to receive it very graciously, and to return an answer that he thanked us for our kind address, and that we should always find him willing and ready to promote the interest of the Church and clergy of this Colony, and assured us that we should not only have his protection but affection.

Mr. Bagge moved that the several letters, together with the address mentioned in the minutes, be inserted in the fair transcript of them in their proper places.

The committee desiring more time to finish the representation and answer to the Bishop of London's letter, the Convention adjourned till six of the clock in the evening.

Accordingly, the House meeting at that hour, the committee appointed to prepare the said representation and answer delivered in the same, which was read, and considered paragraph by paragraph.

The 1st paragraph being read, ordered that it pass.

And 2d paragraph being read, it passed unanimously.

And the 3d, it likewise passed unanimously.

And the 4th, ordered that it pass.

And the 5th, it passed unanimously.

And the 6th, ordered that it pass.

And the 7th, it passed unanimously.

And the 8th, it passed unanimously.

And the 9th, ordered that it pass.

And the 10th, ordered that it pass.

And the 11th, ordered that it pass.

And the 12th, ordered that it pass.

And the 13th, it passed unanimously.

Accordingly, the whole passed, which is as followeth,—viz.:

MAY IT PLEASE YOUR LORDSHIP :—

We, your Lordship's dutiful sons and servants, the clergy of Virginia, being, in obedience to your Lordship's monitory letter, in Convention duly assembled, and having in the fear of God impartially considered the import and contents thereof, beg leave to return your Lordship the following answer and representation.

We are extremely sensible of your Lordship's tender care of us in reminding us of our duty, and of the prudent manner of it, in that you have not been forward to give credit to disadvantageous reports concerning the clergy of this Colony, but have given us this opportunity of answering for ourselves, which we humbly and gratefully accept, and make use of with all sincerity.

We find, upon examination, that there is no minister among us who has not license from your Lordship or your predecessor.

We are fully satisfied that we all of us are Episcopally ordained, except Mr. Commissary, of whose ordination a major part doubt,—a true account of which he has promised to transmit to your Lordship, together with the journal of this Convention.

We must confess the circumstances of this Colony are such that, in many respects, they will not permit us to perform that regular conformity to the established Liturgy as otherwise we would willingly observe and our duty requires; particularly we beg leave to inform your Lordship, that the parishes are so large, the inhabitants so dispersed, and so distant from the church, (some twenty, thirty, forty miles and upward,) that throughout this whole country we have divine service but once every Sunday, and but one sermon; and, for the same reason, the people neglect and refuse to bring their dead to be buried in the churchyards, and seldom send for the minister to perform the office, but make use of a layman for that purpose,— alleging for reasons the extremity of heat in summer, and the great distance from the habitation of the minister. Also, that people observe no holy days except those of Christmas-day and Good Friday,—being unwilling to leave their daily labour; and you are well satisfied that we are obliged to administer the Sacrament of the Lord's Supper to persons who are not confirmed.

We must confess that we have some laws of the Colony which might favour us in the discharge of our sacred function; but, should they be put in execution, the defect or obscurity of others would expose us to the greatest difficulties; for which cause we are obliged to baptize, and church women, marry and bury, at private houses, administer the Lord's Supper to a single sick person, perform in church the office of both Sacraments without the decent habits and proper ornaments and vessels which our established Liturgy requires.

We have inquired into the irregularities among us which were intimated to your Lordship, and we have discovered none such to our personal knowledge, but observe that the lives of the clergy and laity are much improved of late years.

We deplore the unhappy precariousness of our circumstances, to which many of the afore-mentioned deviations from the established Liturgy are to be attributed, and beg to lay them in the most pressing manner before your Lordship for your advice and direction.

The people in general are adverse to the induction of the clergy,—the want of which exposes us to the great oppression of the vestries, who act often arbitrarily, lessening and denying us our lawful salaries,—the opinion of the Attorney-General being that we are incapable of taking the benefit of the law to oblige them to do justice, without that necessary qualification, or a compact.

Our Governor, who is, under God, our chief support here, has never been wanting to us in redressing our grievances to the utmost of his power, and would willingly act in our favour with respect to institutions and inductions, according to the King's patent and instructions; but he imputes the opposition he meets with in this affair to some of the Council, and particularly to Mr. Commissary, whom he also accuses of some other irregularities, as your Lordship, by his Honour's letter to us and by another to the vestry of the parish of St. Anne, in Essex, may perceive, and which we most humbly and earnestly pray your Lordship to interpose your advice and assistance.

Visitations have been attempted by Mr. Commissary; but he met with so many difficulties, from the churchwardens refusing to take the oath of a churchwarden or to make presentments, and from the general aversion of the people to every thing that looks like a spiritual court, that little has been done.

Could your Lordship procure any thing that might tend to the promotion of religion and the knowledge of the clergy or laity of this dominion from the Venerable Societies for Propagating the Gospel in Foreign Parts, and for the Propagation of Christian Knowledge, we assure your Lordship that we will use our utmost endeavours in the right application of any such charitable favours, and shall gratefully esteem it a signal instance of goodness from you and them.

We return our most hearty thanks for your Lordship's admonitions and advice, and, begging your Episcopal benediction, take leave to subscribe ourselves,   My Lord,

Your Lordship's most dutiful sons
and most humble servants.

COLLEGE OF WILLIAM AND MARY, AT WILLIAMS-
   BURG, VIRGINIA, April 10, 1719.

The members of the Convention having desired Mr. Commissary to sign the said letter and representation, he refused the same. Ordered it be entered accordingly. Mr. Hugh Jones moved that the members of the Convention sign the said letter and representation.

Ordered, That it be signed; and it was signed accordingly.

Ordered, That Mr. Commissary, Mr. Hugh Jones, Mr. Seagood, Mr. Bagge, or any two of them, examine the journal of this Convention, and transmit two copies, one to the Bishop of London, and one to the Governor, attested by them.

Then Mr. Commissary asked whether the members had any thing more to prepare, &c. It being answered in the negative, he dissolved the Convention.

(A true copy.)   JAMES BLAIR,
                                      HUGH JONES.

Mr. Commissary's Speech to the Convention, April 8, 1719.

REVEREND BRETHREN:—As in my letter for calling you together at this time I acquainted you that it was in pursuance of the directions of our Right Reverend Diocesan, my Lord-Bishop of London, I shall first read to you his Lordship's letter about it to myself, and his letter to the clergy of this country, which he has desired me to communicate to you; and then I shall (as I find my Lord expects of me) endeavour to resume the particulars and press the observation of them with all fitting earnestness.

Then, having read both these letters, he went on thus:—

Brethren, it is plain that the ground of this admonition is an information my Lord-Bishop has received of some irregularities among us that need very much to be redressed. I wish the informers, whoever they are, before they had given our worthy Diocesan this trouble and uneasiness, had first made known their complaint to me, who have the honour to be deputed by his Lordship for that purpose; and then, by your concurrent advice, matters might have been redressed among ourselves, without exposing us to his Lordship's suspicions, or bringing us under the character of a clergy guilty of several irregularities. As in secular affairs no man carries a cause from this country to England till it has been first tried in our Virginia courts, and, if any one is dissatisfied with their sentence, in weighty causes there lies an appeal for England, it is most regular that it should be so too in spiritual affairs. It would be too great a burden for my Lord-Bishop of London to be troubled in "prima instantia" with all the irregularities of the numerous clergy under him, especially in the remote Plantations, where he can't have the parties before him, or be sufficiently informed of the circumstances or the facts, the witnesses living at so great distance. But this piece of justice, which was not designed us by the informers, my Lord of London himself, out of his great prudence and unbiassed justice, has done us. He tells us that he "is not forward to give credit to disadvantageous reports, finding that wrong representations are not unfrequently made," and perhaps never more frequently than now. And therefore his Lordship has reduced this complaint into the right method; that is, he has given you and me notice of it; and, like a good Bishop, he stirs us up to do our parts toward redressing any irregularities that may be among us.

And, seeing our Diocesan has been so just and kind as not to proceed to censure upon this private information, but has left both the inquiry into the truth of the information and the redressing the irregularities, in great measure, to ourselves, let me with all earnestness exhort you to discharge a good conscience in this matter, and to speak freely, if ye know any that officiates as minister of any parish in this country, without license from my Lord-Bishop of London or his predecessor; if you know any among us who has not had Episcopal ordination; if you know any who does not comply with the established Liturgy; and, lastly, if you know any that are scandalous in their lives and conversation. These are the chief things pointed at with relation to our duty in my Lord's monitory letter. There is one word added concerning institutions and inductions, intimating that the Governor will be ready, upon notice given, to act accordingly, if any minister is settled among us who has not a license from the present Bishop of London or his predecessor, as also in reference to institutions and inductions. As to this of institutions and inductions, I say, I do not so well apprehend what is required of us in them. They are in the Governor's hands, who does not fail to institute and induct when presentations are duly made. But for want of these the clergy of this country have been upon a very precarious footing. Many endeavours have been made to procure a remedy for this evil, and, in the revival of the laws about sixteen or seventeen years ago, particular care was taken of it; but it miscarried in that Assembly which was in Governor Nott's time, when the great body of the revisal passed.

The common remedy in England is for the ordinary to take the benefit of the lapse, which is not so easy in this country, for want of men in Orders who are unprovided. And, indeed, this makes it much harder, too, on their side who are to present, if they are strictly limited to the six months, as in England,—there being no vacant ministers here for our vacant parishes. In the year 1703, Governor Nicholson had the opinion of Sir Edward Northey—then Attorney-General—as to the business of presentations and inductions. He gave his opinion that the right of presentation by our laws was in the parishioners, and the right of the lapse in the Governor; only, he added, that if the parishioners have never presented, they may have a reasonable time to present a minister. But, if they will not present,—being required so to do,—the Governor may, in their default, collate a minister.

These are the subjects of my Lord of London's letter and of our consultations, which, I think, we must go upon in the first place, and then, if any one has any thing further to propose, it will be time to consider it. Our consultations will be much shortened if we proceed regularly and with Christian temper, and speak on at once, without heat, or passion, or partiality, and without breaking in one upon another.

There is one thing more I have to recommend,—namely, a unanimity and brotherly love among ourselves, which will be a great ornament of our profession and a great mutual support to our interest.

I need not put you in mind that there are now many censorious eyes upon us, and therefore we must be very circumspect in our behaviour: prudence, gravity, sobriety and modesty, and moderation, are great ornaments of our profession at all times. I hope we shall leave a good character behind us in this place, that the very adversaries may have nothing to reprehend in our example or conduct, and so God, of his infinite mercy, accompany all our consultations with his blessing, and direct them to his glory and the welfare of that part of the Church in which we are more particularly concerned.

HISTORICAL REMARKS FOR THE BETTER UNDERSTANDING OF THE PROCEEDINGS OF THE CONVENTION OF THE CLERGY AT WILLIAMSBURG, IN APRIL, 1719.

Before the Convention was called, great pains were taken to prepossess the clergy in favour of the Governor by getting them to sign addresses of encomiums upon him, in which there was usually some reflection against the House of Burgesses that sent home a complaint against him to his Majesty, so that, without condemning themselves, it could not be expected they would act otherwise in relation to him than they did at the Convention. To make way for these addresses, it was confidently given out, and most industriously spread all over the country, that Mr. Commissary and three more were turned out of the Council, and that the address of the House of Burgesses was refused to be received, because it came not through the hands of the Governor; both which proved otherwise.

On the day of the Convention, the Commissary and clergy waited on the Governor at his house; and, the Commissary asking if he had any commands for the Convention, he said he would signify what he had to say in a letter.

While Mr. Commissary was yet giving his charge, and was come to that part of it which gives an account of Sir Edward Northey's opinion,—viz.: "In the year 1703, Governor Nicholson had the opinion of Sir Edward Northey, then Attorney-General, as to the business of presentations and inductions. He gave his opinion that " the right of presentation by our laws was in the parishioners, and the right of the lapse was with the Governor." Here Mr. Emanuel Jones interrupted him, crying out that it was a mistake; it was not the parishioners, but the vestry. "I have right to know it," said he, "for I brought in that opinion." Mr. Commissary answered, "Sir, you ought not to interrupt me : I have Sir Edward Northey's opinion here, and I'll show you presently that it is right quoted;" and accordingly produced it, and satisfied the whole Convention that he had right quoted it.

Immediately after the Commissary's charge, and before any other business was entered upon, Mr. William Robinson, Clerk of the Council, being sent by the Governor, desired admittance, and presented a letter from the Governor, directed to the reverend the clergy of Virginia in Convention at Williamsburg, and then withdrew. This letter, being all an invective against Mr. Commissary, contributed very much to the ill-temper of the Convention. There was such a confused noise upon it, that for a considerable space no one could be heard. When that confusion was a little over, so that he could be heard, Mr. Commissary said he was very unhappy to be under the frowns of the Governor, but was so conscious of his innocency, that, if they would have patience to hear him, he would ask no time, but would immediately answer all the accusations of that letter. And, beginning, as the letter does, with the business of collations, while he was showing the law and practice of the country and the opinion of the late Bishop of London and of Sir Edward Northey, by which he had always governed himself, another confused clamour arose, that they were not proper judges of these things, and therefore desired him to desist, and send his answer to the Governor's letter in writing to my Lord-Bishop of London; to which he acquiesced.

Then Mr. Hugh Jones and some others, faulting the doctrine of Mr. Commissary's sermon preached before them that day, desired Mr. Commissary to print it. He, excusing himself as never having appeared in print, said if they had any objections against it he was ready to answer them, or, if they desired it, he would transmit a true copy of it to my Lord-Bishop of London; and accordingly they insisted upon this last, and he promised to do it.

Then it was moved that an address be made to the Governor. Mr. Commissary and some others put them in mind that it was more proper, and would look better upon the minutes, to begin with the principal business they were called upon,—viz.: The answer to my Lord of London's letter. But, this being overruled, a committee was appointed to draw the said address. Some moved that Mr. Commissary might be one of this committee to help prepare the said address; but this was opposed by the greater part.

Then Mr. Commissary and some others moved that it might be considered whether it was not proper to give directions to the committee concerning the manner of the said address, particularly that they should abstain from intermeddling with those unhappy differences of State that were between the Governor and the House of Burgesses; and that they should confine themselves to what was more proper for the clergy,—namely, the thanking the Governor for his protection of the Church. If they drew a handsome address to this purpose, it was said, we should all unanimously join in it, which would do him more service than if they drew any thing which we could not all unanimously sign. But this motion was overruled and the committee left to themselves without any limitation.

THURSDAY, April 9.

Mr. Emanuel Jones delivered in the address to the Governor, which, being read and examined paragraph by paragraph, passed without amendment.

Though it was carried by a majority of the Convention that this address should pass without amendment, there was a very great debate on the subject-matter of it. They were put in mind that those prejudiced men by whom they said his Honour was affronted and abused were the body of the representatives of the country,—the House of Burgesses; that they had made a public complaint of the Governor, which now lies before the King; that it did not belong to our province either to prejudice his Majesty or to decide the points in difference between the Governor and the House of Burgesses; that, if we were ever so desirous to justify the Governor, we were not in a capacity to do it, the matters in difference being entirely out of our cognizance. The House of Burgesses complain that their privileges are encroached upon: is that a fit subject for us to determine? They complain of a great sum of money taken without order and spent about the Governor's house and gardens: they had the account before them, whereas if we say any thing upon that subject we must speak without book. And so of the forfeiture of lands and the Burgesses' salaries and some other things complained of, of which we are very incapable judges. They were likewise told that the duty of mediation of peace did much better become us than the espousing of any party; that we should thereby incur the displeasure of a great many gentlemen of our own parishes; that we should create to ourselves lasting uneasiness; and that a time might come when the House of Burgesses might think fit to call those to account that put such public affronts on them, as we heard the House of Commons in Ireland did those that counter-addressed in the case of Sir Constantine Phips.

When none of all this prevailed, but the address was carried by vote, the Commissary, and seven more that were against addressing in that form, desired that they might enter the reasons of their dissent. But this was wholly refused.

While this business was in debating, Mr. Robertson brought a letter from the Governor to the Commissary, requiring the perusal of his sermon preached yesterday before the Convention. The style of it is so particular that Mr. Commissary thought fit to set it down verbatim, which follows:—

SIR:—In your sermon preached yesterday before me, upon occasion of the Convention of the clergy, you thought fitting to advance such principles with respect to Government that I judge I should not discharge the duty I owe to my Prince if I failed to take notice thereof; and lest I might, upon one cursory hearing, misapprehend some positions you then laid down, I desire you will favour me now with a more deliberate perusal of the sermon in writing; and your immediate compliance with this request will be the only means to satisfy, sir, your most humble servant,

A. SPOTTSWOOD.

WILLIAMSBURG, April 9, 1719.

Upon this, he immediately sent the sermon, hoping the Governor would either rest satisfied, or, by the help of his friends of the clergy, form his objections and give him an opportunity of answering them. He heard no more of it, only understands he took a copy.

Upon the question of Mr. Commissary's Episcopal ordination, of twenty-four that were present besides Mr. Commissary himself, twelve voted that they were doubtful of his Episcopal ordination, eleven that they had no doubt about it, and one that he suspended his judgment. The reasons of those who were doubtful were, first, that they knew not the hand in which the certificate was written subscribed Jo. Edenburgen. To which it was answered, that they could not have a better proof, that fell within their knowledge, than the late Bishop of London's license under his hand and seal. Second, it was objected that the certificate was not in the usual English form, nor any seal annexed to it. To which it was answered that a certificate from a Scotch Bishop of any one being a minister in his diocese, in the Order of Presbyter, is a sufficient proof of the matter of fact, though it is not in the English form; and that, being taken for such thirty-four years ago by the late Bishop of London, (and the late Lord Effingham, Governor of Virginia,) to whom both his ministry in Scotland and the test for which he suffered were at that time well known, it ought not now to be called in question. Third, Mr. Hugh Jones objected to the word Presbyter in that certificate,—that it should have been Priest. But this objection was ridiculed by most of themselves, since in the English certificates of Priests' Orders they are said to be promoted "Ad Sacrum Presbyteratus Ordinem."

In answer to the question whether they knew of any minister in this Colony that did not punctually conform to the rules of the Established Church, there is no more set down in the minutes but that it was owned there were several rules which were not observed by any of them because of the circumstances of the country. But upon this Mr. Commissary urged that my Lord-Bishop of London had been certainly informed of great deviations from the Liturgy, and therefore that if any of the informers were then present they would acquaint us with what they had observed of this kind, that it might be certified, and told them they must expect he would acquaint my Lord with it if they had nothing to say. Upon this Mr. Hugh Jones said something to this purpose:—That he was desired by my Lord of London to give his Lordship some account of the state of this Church, and that accordingly he had given an account of some things in which Mr. Commissary did not observe the rubric. He instanced in the clerk's publishing the banns and some other things in church. For by the laws of this country all proclamations and many laws are published in Church, and, the clerks commonly keeping the register, the usual way is for them to publish the banns and give a certificate of it to the minister. He complained too of Mr. Ingles, his taking upon him in his school to make exhortations to his schoolboys, alleging that he should only teach them the Church Catechism. The whole Convention, judging these things frivolous, commended Mr. Ingles (who is a sober, good man, and master of arts) for giving good instructions to his boys concerning their morals; and as for some other things of small variation from the rubric, they found none but such as the different circumstances of the country from those of England necessarily engaged us in, which are more particularly mentioned in the clergy's answer to my Lord of London's letter.

In the evening of this day, after the Convention was adjourned, eight ministers, who, for the reasons above mentioned, did not join in the address which the major part prepared for the Governor, agreed upon one of their own, both to show their duty to him and their moderation with relation to the public differences in the country. It was as follows:—

To the Hon. Alexander Spottswood, his Majesty's Lieutenant-Governor and Commander-in-Chief of the Colony.

May it please your Honour, it is with no small concern we humbly represent to your Honour that we could not join with the rest of our brethren in one uniform address, being unwilling to determine between persons and things which, as we apprehend, were not properly under our cognizance nor within our province. Nevertheless, we think it our duty to return our most hearty thanks for the continuance of your Honour's protection to the Church and clergy of this country. We have no doubt of your Honour's ready concurrence in any present methods that can be offered for our support and encouragement. And seeing your Honour is well apprized of all our circumstances, without any further information from us, we desire to leave it with yourself to consider of the best ways and means to remedy what wants redress in the precariousness of our circumstances, whether by execution of the laws in being, or the contrivance of new ones, to answer better the circumstances of the Church and clergy and people of this country as in your wisdom you shall think fit.

It is far from our thoughts to add any thing to the uneasiness of your circumstances from other hands, being extremely concerned at the unhappy differences in the country. As we heartily wish a better understanding, we shall not fail by our prayers and endeavours in our station to procure it as far as in us lies. And in the mean time, committing you to God's conduct and direction, we take leave to subscribe ourselves, sir, your Honour's most obedient and most humble servants,

> JAMES BLAIR, *Com'y,*
> JAMES SELATER,
> JOHN CARGILL,
> PETER FOUNTAINE,
> JOHN BRUNSKILL,
> GAY SMITH,
> JNO. MONRO,
> FRANCIS MYLNE.

WILLIAM AND MARY COLLEGE, April 9, 1719.

And then they went to his house to present it. But he, having first perused it by himself, at last refused to receive it, called it a libel, and gave it back to Mr. Commissary.

FRIDAY, April 10.

There is nothing to be remarked upon this day's proceedings but that some objections were made to a few things in the clergy's answer to my Lord of London's letter, upon the amendment of which all the clergy declared their readiness to sign it. These objections were,--1st. The slur it casts upon Mr. Commissary's ordination. 2d. The unfair representation, or insinuation, at least, as if some of the Council, and particularly Mr. Commissary, obstructed the Governor's acting in favour of the clergy in the point of institutions and inductions. It is true they do not take it upon themselves to say this, but lay it upon the Governor, and say that he imputes the opposition "he meets with in this affair to some of the Council, and particularly to Mr. Commissary, whom he also accuses of some other irregularities, as your Lordship, by his Honour's letter to us and another to the vestry of the parish of St. Anne's, may perceive, both which, together with Mr. Commissary's answer, we doubt not your Lordship will receive, and in which we most humbly and earnestly pray your Lordship to interpose your Lordship's advice and assistance." Though this was the least they could do without directly incurring the Governor's displeasure, there were several who said they knew the Council and the Commissary had been such constant friends to the clergy that they would have no hand in putting this slight upon them, as if they opposed their institutions and inductions. 3d. That it lays the blame upon our laws that we are obliged to baptize, church women, marry, and bury, at private houses, &c., whereas it is not by our laws these things are occasioned, but partly by our precariousness, (the Governor never making use of the lapse,) and partly by the exceeding largeness of the parishes and other inconvenient circumstances of the country.

Immediately before dissolving the Convention, Mr. Hugh Jones moved something to this effect,—that, in regard a major part doubted of Mr. Commissary's Orders, the Governor should be required to suspend him from officiating as a minister of this country, and the Bishop desired to send another Commissary. This proposal was with a general voice exploded and cried out upon, and they asked him if he was not ashamed to offer any such thing. When nobody backed his motion, he desired it might be entered on the minutes. But the whole Convention rejected it with great indignation.

The above account, consisting of ten pages, is a true narrative, to the best of our remembrance.

JAMES BLAIR,
JNO. MONRO.

An Answer to the Accusation contained in the Governor's Letter to the Convention, which Letter is to be seen in Journal of the Proceedings of the said Convention.

ACCUSATION.

For none more eminently than Commissary Blair sets at naught those instructions which your Diocesan leaves you to be guided by, with respect to institutions and inductions,—he denying by his practices, as well as discourses, that the King's Governor has the right to collate ministers to ecclesiastical benefices within this Colony; for when the church he now supplies became void by the death of the former incumbent, his solicitation to the same was solely to the vestry, without his ever making the least application to me for my collation, notwithstanding it was my own parish church.

ANSWER.

As this accusation is here worded, the design of it is plainly to induce your Lordship to believe that I oppose the King's instructions and deny the Governor the power of collation, and that I was inducted into my parish without him. But none of all these do in the least touch and explain the true state of the difference betwixt his opinion and mine in this matter, which I must therefore beg leave more clearly to unfold to your Lordship.

The sole question as to this affair is, What is to be meant by collation as in the Governor's instructions?—whether such a power as the King has to bestow livings of which he himself is the patron? or such a power as the Bishop has to collate to livings that fall into his hands by lapse? He claims it in the first sense; I have always understood it in the second, for the following reasons. It has been the constant practice in this country that whatever ministers we have had inducted have had first a presentation from the vestries, who, by law here, act in the name of the parishioners. And before this gentleman's time, it was never known that ever a Governor refused to induct upon any such presentations, or gave collation and institution without it. 2d. By a law of this country, entitled Ministers to be Inducted, after it has spoken of a minister's producing a testimonial of his ordination, and his subscribing to be conformable to the orders and constitutions of the Church of England and the laws there established, follow immediately these words:—" Upon which the Governor is hereby re(~ested to induct the said minister into any parish that shall make presentation o. .im." And from these words it has been always understood here that the parish had the presentation and the Governor the induction. For, as to the word *requested*, they think, and he grants, it doth not alter the case when applied to the Governor,—that being the usual form in which our laws express his duty, and not by the more authoritative words of enacting, commanding, or requiring, as they do other people's. 3d. The parishes here are at the charge of founding the churches, the glebes, and the salaries. 4th. Governor Nicholson consulted Sir Edward Northey, the late Attorney-General, as to all this affair,—being desirous (as I thought) to remedy the precariousness of the clergy, who, except a very few, have no inductions. And Sir Edward was altogether of this opinion, as your Lordship will see by a copy of it, which I herewith transmit. Governor Nicholson sent copies of that opinion to the several vestries of this country, and threatened if they did not present that he would take the benefit of the lapse : the very threatening procured presentations, and consequently inductions, for some ministers. And had the Governor collated and inducted upon the lapse,—nay, had he made but one or two examples of it,— all this grievance might have been redressed long ago. But he only threatened, and never once collated upon lapse; so that the precariousness is as much fixed as ever. 5th. Having often discoursed with your Lordship's predecessor and written to him on this subject, I never found he had any other notion of collation by the Governor but that it was to be upon lapse. And the great difficulty started in those days to that scheme was, that the country complained six months was too short a time for them to supply their vacancies in,—there being no ministers to be had here who were not already provided. For remedy of which, in the last revisal of our laws, a law was provided in which two years (if I remember right) were allowed the parishes to supply their vacancies. This law, about fifteen years ago, was under consideration of the Council of Trade. My Lord-Bishop of London was that day present at the Board, and I, being then in London, was desired to attend. After full debate upon it, the law was approved of, and my Lord of London was very well satisfied. But after all it miscarried here in this country. Our Assembly could not agree about it, and so it fell. Sure, if either the Bishop or the Council of Trade had had any notion of this right of patronage which the Governor claims, (and his commission and instructions are the same now they were then,) having so ready a remedy for the precariousness of the clergy, they needed not to have made these extraordinary concessions. 6th. The Governor's new method would destroy all benefit of lapse; whereas, if the presentation is in the parish and the lapse in the Governor, we have the ordinary check upon the patron, as in England and other Christian Churches, which is a very valuable security. 7th. Collations for benefices, together with licenses for marriage and probates of wills,—being three things pertaining to the ecclesiastical jurisdiction, but expressly excepted out of it and by the King's instructions given to the Governor,—seems to be a good argument that, in the point of collations, the Governor acts only as ordinary, and consequently either institutes upon presentation or collates by lapse, but not as original patron.

These are the reasons which have induced me to think collations are to be interpreted in another sense than the Governor has lately fixed on them. I say lately; for I do not remember that he fell upon this notion above three or four years ago, which makes me astonished at the censure he gives of me for not applying to him for his collation. There are two wrong things here insinuated. One is, as if the Governor at that time had claimed (as he now does) the right of collating to the living as patron before it lapsed; whereas this pretension was, by four or five years, of a later date,—my coming to this parish being at Christmas, 1710,—and no-body at that time having ever questioned the vestry's right of choosing a minister when the parish was fairly void,—as it was here, by the death of my predecessor, Mr. Solomon Wheatly. As soon as I was elected by the vestry, I immediately acquainted the Governor, and he said he was very glad of it. And I do assure your Lordship he nor no one else at that time faulted this as being then, and long afterward, the common practice of the country. If a Governor ever interposed in such cases in those days, it was only by recommendation to the vestries, but never by way of collation, which he now begins to claim. The other thing which I take to be here insinuated is as if, upon the vestry's presentation of me, I had, in contempt of his authority and right to give collation, never applied to him for it. This, I confess, would have been a great contempt, and such one as never any minister in this country was guilty of. For, as soon as we can get a presentation from the vestry, we never fail to apply to the Governor for induction, as readily as any clerk in England applies to the Bishop with his presentation. But this is the unhappiness of our precarious circumstances in this country,—that the vestries are such enemies to induction that they will give no presentations, and our Governors have been so unwilling to disoblige the parishes that they have never taken the benefit of the lapse; so that the ministers generally officiate upon the election of the vestry, without presentation or induction. As this is the case of about nine or ten of our ministers, (for some four or five are inducted,) your Lordship will easily perceive that, as matters then stood, without a presentation it was in vain for me to apply to the Governor for collation or induction. But I thought it became me, in good manner, to wait on the Governor and to acquaint him with what was done : he signified his great satisfaction, and did not in the least fault any thing in the conduct of the matter. We were then, and for many years afterward, in perfect friendship; though now all things that are capable of any ill aspect are mustered up to make a crime where never any before was so much as pretended.

ACCUSATION.

And I cannot but complain of his deserting the cause of the Church in general, and striving to put it on such a foot as must deprive the clergy of that reasonable security which I think they ought to have with regard to their livings.

ANSWER.

It passes my skill to find out the defects of this method. If the Governor would give the parishes warning to present in a reasonable time, and, in case of failure, to make use of the lapse, it would remedy the precariousness of the clergy as well as the other, and would have this advantage,—that it would be much more easily applied, and a minister would have more of the love of his parishioners ; whereas, the other way will involve him in a lawsuit to defend his title ; and if we should at any time have a Governor that has little regard to the Church or religion, he may keep the parish void as long as he pleases,—there being no lapse ever incurred by that scheme.

ACCUSATION.

As to the disorders in the worship of God which are pointed at in the said letter, it appears as if my Lord of London knew not that his Commissary is more apt to countenance than redress the same; for I myself have seen him present in church while a layman—his clerk—has read the divine service in the congregation,—he himself vouchsafing to perform no more of his ministerial office than to pronounce the absolution, preach, and dismiss the congregation.

ANSWER.

It is well known that I do constantly, while I enjoy my health, read the whole divine service myself. And if the Governor has at any time seen it otherwise, it has been when I have been so weakened with sickness that I was not able to go through the whole service and preach too. If it be thought an irregularity that on such a case I made use of a laic, it is to be considered that this is a country where there is not one clergyman to be had on such an occasion,—they being all employed at the same time in their own far-distant parishes,—and that the country is so used to this practice, that long before I knew it, by the fifth law in the printed book, entitled Ministers to Provide Readers, it is enacted "That where there is not a minister to officiate every Sunday, the parish shall make choice of a grave and sober person of good life and conversation to read divine service every intervening Sunday at the parish church, when the minister preacheth at any other place." But I constantly read prayers myself, unless disabled or weakened by sickness.

ACCUSATION.

I have often seen him present at the churchyard, while the said clerk has performed the funeral-service at the grave.

ANSWER.

Here it is insinuated as if I had been at the funeral when the clerk performed the funeral-service at the grave. I can aver that my constant practice is otherwise. What might occasion it that one time—whether that I had not been spoken to, or that I was hoarse, or that I passed through the churchyard accidentally while the clerk was in the funeral-service, and I did not think fit to interrupt him—I can't tell, except the circumstances of the fact were explained. But it is a common thing all over the country—what through want of ministers, what by their great distance and the heat of the weather and the smelling of the corpse—both to bury at other places than churchyards and to employ laics to read the funeral-service,—which, till our circumstances and laws are altered, we know not how to redress.

ACCUSATION.

And I remember when he was for having the churchwardens provide lay readers, who should on Sundays read to their congregations some printed sermons; and so far he declared in Council his approbation thereof, that such practice had like to have had the sanction of the Government, had I not withstood it as destructive to the establishment of the Church.

ANSWER.

The Governor's memory must in this matter have exceedingly failed him, when he represents this of lay readers either as a new project—for (as I quoted above) there is a law of the country for it, duly put in practice when there is no minister to officiate—or as a project of mine.   The thing I would have rectified in it was, that I understood that readers took upon them to read what sermons they thought fit, and I was for their reading only the homilies.   This meeting with some opposition, (for it was alleged, if nothing but the homilies were read, the people would not come to Church,) it was, with the Governor's consent, accommodated thus:—that where there was a minister in the parish, the minister should direct what sermons the reader should read at the distant church or chapel, and where there was no minister the Commissary should do it.   But for the horrid innuendo this part of my accusation is capable of—as if ministers were hereby intended to be laid aside and lay readers set up in their places, and so the establishment of the Church destroyed—there was never any such thing thought of, far less argued, in Council.   I have upon all occasions acquainted your Lordship and your predecessor when vacancies fell by the death of the minister, and pressed for a speedy supply; and whenever they came in they were immediately provided with parishes, if the Governor himself did not delay them.

ACCUSATION.

These and many other instances that might be given, which induce me to believe that a reformation of what has chiefly (as I apprehend) given occasion to your Diocesan's letter, will not be pressed very heartily by your Commissary, especially if he made no such solemn promise at his ordination as his Bishop reminds you all of.   Wherefore I judge it to be more incumbent upon the several members now in Convention diligently to inquire of the disorders which your Diocesan takes notice of, and earnestly to apply yourselves to proper means for redressing them.

ANSWER.

Whether I did heartily press reformation in pursuance of your Lordship's letter, your Lordship will more readily apprehend from the copy of my speech to the Convention, than from these hard prognostications of it.   And though, by means of this letter of the Governor's and other more clandestine prepossessions, they were sufficiently inflamed, your Lordship will observe that, instead of accusing me of any irregularities, when I put the question, Whether any of them knew of any that did not punctually conform to the established Liturgy, they answered only that there were several things that were not observed by any, by reason of the circumstances of the country, which particulars were ordered to be mentioned by the committee appointed to answer your Lordship's letter, and that your Lordship's directions be requested therein.   But the worst innuendo of all is a doubt here suggested, and more industriously circulated in his private insinuations,— at least in the insinuations of his emissaries,—as if I never had Episcopal ordination.   The Governor, indeed, words it somewhat doubtfully. "Especially (says he) if he made no such promise at his ordination as his Bishop reminds you all of." He was satisfied before that I was ordained with Episcopal ordination in Scotland. The doubt he here suggests is concerning the form of that ordination,—whether it had any such stipulation as the English form has. I had told him that I was ordained by the very same English book of ordination,—as indeed I was. But, if he could not believe that,—having it only from my own testimony,—he might have remembered that I showed him my license under the hand and seal of your Lordship's predecessor, in which, among other things, is certified that I promised to conform to the Liturgy of the Church of England as by law established; so that there was no occasion for throwing out this reflection.

These are the accusations I am charged with in that letter: the sum of which is,—1st. A difference of opinion about presentation, which I own, and have given your Lordship my reasons for it; which yet I humbly submit to your more mature judgment. 2d. Some few irregularities as to the Liturgy, which were owing partly to sickness and weakness disabling me at that time to perform the whole service, and partly to the circumstances of the country, which will not admit of exact conformity as in England. This will be more fully explained in the clergy's answer to your Lordship's letter.

But that all this heat and anger should break out now, when the pretended causes were the same all along,—both during his nine years' government and all his predecessors', from the first seating of the country,—everybody here observes is owing to his late resentments because I could not go along with him in several late innovations, which have given such distaste to the country that our House of Burgesses have complained of them to his Majesty. Had he taken the advice of the Council, he might have made himself and the country easy. But he is so wedded to his own notions that there is no quarter for them that go not into them. He is now endeavouring to remove several gentleman of the Council of the most unblemished characters. But, his resentment having more ways to reach me than any of the rest, he has exerted himself to the utmost of his endeavours both to ruin me with the College and my parish and your Lordship. But your Lordship's backwardness to discard an old servant without some crime proved against him, and the clearness of my title to be president of the College by the charter, and the love of my parishioners, give him great uneasiness,—though my interest is a very unequal match for his. The fair, candid way with which your Lordship has used me, notwithstanding the vast pains he has taken to supplant me with your Lordship, has laid me under great obligations of gratitude, and the highest esteem of your Lordship's candour and justice.

I doubt not there are many other things laid to my charge which I have never heard of, and therefore cannot answer at this distance. But, if your Lordship will give me leave to come home, I hope I shall be able to clear myself of all imputations to your Lordship, as I had the good fortune to do formerly in the like case to your Lordship's predecessor, who sifted all those matters to the bottom.

I hope your Lordship will pardon all this trouble. God forgive them who have occasioned it. I am only on the defensive. The equity of my judge gives me great boldness,—knowing that I have endeavoured to keep a good conscience, and that whereinsoever I have erred I am ready to submit to your Lordship's judgment, and to correct whatever you think amiss in my conduct. Being, with all sincerity, my Lord,

Your Lordship's most

Obliged and humble servant,

JAMES BLAIR.

No. II.

EXTRACTS FROM A PAMPHLET REPORTING THE PROCEEDINGS OF A JUBILEE AT JAMESTOWN IN COMMEMORATION OF THE SECOND CENTENNARY ANNIVERSARY OF THE SETTLEMENT OF VIRGINIA, MAY 13, 1807.

DUE notice having been given of the intended celebration, the preparations commenced on the 10th. A packet, a sloop and schooner had arrived before the 12th, with bands of musicians and a company of artillery and cannon, and with a number of visitors.

On the 12th, the beach began to assume the appearance of a regular encampment, from the erection of tents for the sale of various articles; and the scene was agreeably diversified by groups of beautiful women who were every moment passing from the main into the island. It was not unusual to see groups of pilgrims stealing away from the throng and bustle of preparation, from the wild revelry of joy and the enthusiasm of satisfied and rapturous exultation, to saunter among the ruins, and converse in fancy among the tombs with the illustrious dead whose virtues and achievements had furnished the motives for their assemblage. It was in the highest degree interesting and edifying to trace the effects produced upon the minds and faces of the spectators by the view of these venerable remains of other times. The eye, in surveying the ruin of the church-steeple garlanded to its summit with irregular festoons of smilax and ivy, carried back the mind to the interesting incidents and events of the first settlers.

A crowd of pilgrims were discovered on their hands and knees within the churchyard, removing the dust and rubbish from the mouldering and mutilated tombs, and exploring with anxious though patient curiosity the almost effaced characters which affection and piety had sketched there in the vain expectation that they would be immortal. Whilst engaged in these pious and interesting offices, a pleasing melancholy insensibly stole over the mind; the grosser passions of our nature, the dull pursuits of the world, were forgotten, whilst each for a moment by the witchery of fancy imagined himself in the presence of those gallant and venerable spirits that once animated and informed the mortal tenants of those graves.

As it were by general consent, the discovery of the oldest stone became an object of general emulation, and, in the course of the examination, the results, as they seemed to be successful, were triumphantly announced. Not even the searchers of gold-mines, whose mania is so deservedly ridiculed and censured by Smith and our other historians, could have exceeded the zeal and patience with which the pilgrims of 1807 examined every character or fragment that promised to throw light on the character of their fathers and the antiquities of their nation.

Beyond 1682, nothing legible could be traced; but, from the freshness of the marble bearing this date, contrasted with the surrounding masses of mutilated and mouldering decay, it was the general impression that this stone was comparatively young.

Among the group of objects calculated to excite reflection on such an occasion, it was impossible to avoid noticing the growth of a sycamore,* whose germ had been inscrutably deposited between the fissure of two massy tombs, whose growth was gradually but certainly effecting their demolition. In vain did a brawny wreath of the poisoned oak, having first wound itself round the sycamore, grasp the trembling marbles for the purpose of averting their fall. The sycamore was a lever that incessantly propelled them from their centres, and it was obvious that nothing but its death could save them from falling without the line of the base. To a reflecting mind every incident is fruitful. This seemed to be a struggle between life and death; and, what may appear extraordinary, it was the general wish that death should come off victorious in the contest.

On the 13th, the dawn was ushered in by a cannon: a second announced the first faint etchings of the sun on the edge of the horizon. During the night, several vessels had arrived, and the eye rested with pleasure on the spectacle of thirty-two sail at anchor in the cove, boats plying incessantly off and on from the shore, groups of beautiful women every moment making their appearance, crowds flocking in and from every part of the adjacent country, and the Powhatan evolving in silent majesty his flood, margined as far as the eye could reach with cultivated plantations and gay villas.

About 11 o'clock, the long-deserted shores of Jamestown witnessed a spectacle equally picturesque and impressive. It was no longer the mournful image and gloomy silence of depopulation. Thirty-two vessels graced the ancient harbour; upward of four hundred ladies embellished the scene, which became every moment more animated by the increasing con-

---

* Platanus Occidentalis.

course of citizens, and upon which the presence of the military, and a band of music of Captain Nestle and his company of artillerists from Norfolk, reflected no small lustre.

At 12 o'clock, in consequence of arrangements previously agreed upon by the joint committees from Norfolk, Portsmouth, Petersburg, and Williamsburg, a procession marched to the ruins of the old church-steeple and the lugubrious group of tombstones contiguous to those ruins. The order of the procession was as follows:—

1. Bishop Madison, and the orators of the day.
2. The deputies from Norfolk, Portsmouth, Petersburg, and Williamsburg.
3. The ladies.
4. Band of music.
5. Artillery.
6. A cannon-ball weighing five cwt., supported by eight men.*
7. Citizens at large.

During the procession, several tunes of a solemn nature were struck by the music, and cannons fired at proper intervals. Upon reaching the ruins, the venerable Bishop of Virginia ascended a tombstone, and, in that affecting, pathetic manner which characterizes all his religious effusions, poured out a prayer strongly expressive of the national gratitude for that peculiar protection which the Deity has been pleased to bestow on the feeble but auspicious germ planted two hundred years ago in the wilderness,—a germ from which a State has sprung up now highly prosperous and flourishing. Here two sentiments equally dear to the human heart, and equally powerful,—religion and patriotism,—united their influence; and that influence was irresistibly felt: pious tears were seen hanging on many a cheek furrowed by age or adorned with youthful bloom.

BISHOP MADISON'S PRAYER.

O God! Parent Almighty, who, though unseen, upholdest this ponderous ball, and, breathing through the immensity of space, fillest with stupendous life all which it inhabit; Spirit invisible, God of our forefathers, to thee we raise the voice of praise and thanksgiving; oh, hear us, and deign to accept this our imperfect homage. Thou great and glorious Being, who, according to the plans of thy wisdom, didst first inspire our forefathers with the elevated idea of seeking an asylum for man in this Western world; thou, who badest the terrors of death to retire from their hearts, the remorseless billows of the deep to be at rest, and the horrors of the howling wilderness no longer to alarm, oh, hear, and, on this eventful day, suffer us to pour forth, from the fulness of our souls, the tide of reverential affection, of joy, and of gratitude; suffer us, the descendants and the heirs of

---

* This ball was originally brought over for the purpose of awing the aborigines.

those mighty men whose footsteps, under thy gracious providence, here were first impressed to approach thy divine Majesty, to declare the wondrous things which thou hast done for us, and to implore thy continued protection.

Assembled in thy sight, we now prostrate ourselves before thee, upon that ground which thou, O God, didst choose whereupon to rest the wearied feet of our progenitors. Twice one hundred times hath this earth, in obedience to thy command, performed its faithful revolution around the fountain of light, since thy providential goodness was here testified by our ancestors with heartfelt songs of gratitude and praise. The stream of time hath swept before thee the generations which since have arisen and passed away; but we, upon whom this day hath fallen, will rejoice in thy presence, and, with a sincere and ardent gratitude, will recall to vivid memory thy former and thy present mercies.

Hallowed be the place where thou didst particularly manifest thy goodness to our forefathers, and where the heavenly plan for spreading wide the blessings of social rights first beamed forth. It was here, O God, it was on this chosen ground, that thou didst first lay the sure foundations of political happiness. Here didst thou say to our forefathers, who, under thy guidance, had defied the perils of an untried ocean, "Here fix your abode; here shall the great work of political salvation commence; here I will strike deep the roots of an everlasting empire, where justice and liberty and peace shall flourish in immortal vigour, to the glory of my name and the happiness of man. Here ye shall sleep; but your sons and your daughters shall possess the land which stretcheth wide before you; shall convert the wilderness and solitary place into fields smiling with plenty; shall, in ages yet to come, exceed the sands upon the sea-shore in number; shall, when two hundred years are accomplished, here resort, here recall to mind your valour and your sufferings, and here, touched with a lively sense of the blessings vouchsafed to them, they shall exalt and adore my name, and acknowledge that the mightiness of my arm and the overshadowing of my Spirit hath done those great and excellent things for them."

Such, O God, was thy will. To thy servants now before thee has been given the high boon of living to see the light of that day, and of acknowledging that thy promises are as steadfast as the everlasting hills. To us has been given the triumph which this day affords. It was thy providence which reared the tender plant that here took root, and which nourished it with the dews of heaven until its branches have cast their shade from ocean to ocean. It was thy providence, gracious Benefactor of man, which awoke in our breasts a just sense of the inappreciable value of our rights, and infused that indomitable spirit which effected a revolution the most important in the annals of time, and which led to the establishment of civil governments throughout this rising empire upon the broad and firm basis of equal laws. It was thy providence which inspired that wisdom which hath guarded us against the horrors of war, and which, amidst the dread convulsions that agitate the Old World, hath still irradiated this thy chosen land with the blessings of peace. To thee, O God, we ascribe, as is most due, that never-ceasing current of national prosperity which has daily increased, and which, under thy auspices, we trust, will continue to increase, until its waters, spreading throughout every region of the earth, shall gladden, with their salubrious streams, nations which are now the victims of ambition, and thence diffuse peace and good-will among the whole family of mankind.

Continue, gracious Benefactor, thy mercies toward us. Oh, teach us ever to love and to reverence thy name; teach us that the God of virtue can love only virtue; teach us that it is thou only, the first Source of happiness, who can secure it to the human race. Impress upon our hearts an ardent love for thy holy religion : may its pure and sublime morality be to us the rule of all duties: may it guard us against the debasing in-fluence of licentiousness and vice, and inspire the people of these United States with those inflexible virtues which republics demand: may the love of our country and obedience to law be the dignified characteristic of citizens : may they never forget that, without religion, morality dies; and that, without morality, republics are swept from before thee with the besom of destruction.

Bless all the constituted authorities, and so rule their hearts and strengthen their hands that they may drive from among us all manner of vice.

Give prosperity to the different seminaries of learning; increase true knowledge, and infix upon the hearts of the rising generation a just sense of the duties which they owe to themselves, to their fellow-creatures, and to their God.

Finally, O God, pardon our offences, and deign to hear our imperfect prayer, for the sake of thy Son, our Saviour, Jesus Christ.*

The prayer being over, the citizens repaired to a lawn in front of the principal house on the peninsula, for the purpose of hearing the orations and poems prepared for the day. Mr. B. G. Baldwin, from Winchester, then a student at William and Mary,—afterward Judge Baldwin, of Staunton,—spoke first. He was followed by Mr. John Madison, also a student from the upper country. The speeches were creditable to the

---

* While we approve the patriotic sentiments of this prayer, we cannot but lament the absence of that without which no prayer can be acceptable to God,—the spirit of penitence, of true Christian humility. It was the fault of the age. Let any one, after reading this prayer, turn back to the beginning of our work, and read that sent over with our early colonists to be used, not by a Bishop or other minister, but by the officers on guard in behalf of themselves and soldiers: let him compare the two together, and he will see the difference between the theology of 1607 and 1807.

patriotism and talents of these young men. Then followed two odes, by Mr. C. B. Blanchard, of Norfolk, and Mr. Le Roy Anderson, of Williamsburg, which were interesting to the assembly.

Two days and nights were spent in these and other exercises of a different character. After feasting and mirth on the island, which continued two days and nights, the scene was transferred to Williamsburg, where another day and night was spent in like manner,—very unlike the manner of the first days of our forefathers on the island, whose first act was the solemn celebration of the Lord's Supper.

No. III.

Origin of the Names of Parishes.

[The following was furnished at my request by my friend, Mr. Hugh Blair Grigsby, of Norfolk, to whom I am indebted for many other things in the foregoing articles.]

My Dear Sir :—Your letter of the 18th was received last evening, and I hasten to reply at once to your interrogatories.

1. Augusta.—So called from the Princess Augusta, wife of Frederick, Prince of Wales, who was the eldest son of George II., but died before his father. The county of Augusta was created in 1738, and Frederick in the same year, and were thus named after the Prince and Princess of Wales.

2. Dale.—This is a fancy name, probably applied from the local propriety of the name,—probably from Dale Manor in England, from which some of the vestry may have emigrated; just as George Mason the first called the county of Stafford from Stafford in England. (See note to George Mason's Life in Virginia. Convention of 1776.) Thomas Dale was High-Marshal of Virginia in 1611.

3. Beckford.—The name of a place in England, and a common name of persons; but I know not its application here. By-the-way, its true meaning is *bec fort*, (a strong beak.)

4. South Farnham.—Farnham is the name of a town in Surrey, England, in which the Bishop of Winchester has a castle. Its products are hops and corn. It is on the banks of the Wey.

5. Truro.—This is the name of a borough in Cornwall, England, and is the shipping-port of the tin and copper ore found in its vicinity. Probably there were mines in the vicinity of Truro parish, in Virginia, or some of its people came from Truro.

6. Fincastle.—The name of this parish was taken from the county of Fincastle, which was so called after the country-seat of Lord Botetourt, in England. Fincastle county was taken from Botetourt in 1774. In Oc-

tober, 1776, the county of Fincastle was divided into Kentucky, Washington, and Montgomery,—the name of Fincastle having been dropped. The town of Fincastle, however, which had been incorporated in 1772, retained the name.

7. PETSWORTH.—The true name is Petworth, and is the name of a town in Surrey, England, which contains a church in which the Percys were buried. If the parish were created before 1630, it was doubtless so called in honour of Percy, who was for a short time Governor of Virginia, and was of the noble house of Northumberland. A likeness of Percy (with his amputated finger) is in our Historical Hall,—having been presented by Conway Robinson, who saw the original portrait in England. The name Petso, to which you allude, is only an abbreviation of " Petswo.," which was the old way of recording the word, as Norfolk was written " Norff.," or " Norfo."

8. ANTRIM.—This is the name of a parish in the county of Antrim, on the northeast coast of Ireland, of which Belfast is one of the principal towns, as also Lisburn and Carrickfergus,—all noted in the history of that great effort to Saxonize Ireland. It is the head-quarters of the Protestants and Scotch-Irish. It is an immense county of two hundred and seventy-one thousand inhabitants. Some descendant of the Scotch-Irish (as were the Lewises) gave one parish that name.

9. ST. JAMES'S NORTHAM.—Northam is a common name of a hundred places in England, (signifying north settlement,) and corresponds with Southam, Eastham, and Westham.

10. STRATTON MAJOR.—Stratton is the name of a town in Cornwall, England, and individuals took the name from the town. The Strattons came over to Virginia early and were scattered on the eastern and western shores of the Chesapeake. It was doubtless named by some minister who came over from Cornwall. That is to say, the minister suggested the name to the representative of the county, who proposed it in the House of Burgesses.

11. SHELBURNE.—Called after Lord Shelburne, who was prime minister in England for a short time, and was regarded as friendly to the Americans.

12. BLISLAND.—This is a common name in England, and is synonymous with " happy land." It is evidently applied from some local incident long lost, or from some place in England connected with some of its parishioners. The word was originally Bliss-land.

13. SAINT BRIDE.—This should have been printed "St. Bride's." It alludes to the spiritual marriage of St. Catharine, who, according to the Catholic legends, had the bridal ring placed on her finger by our Saviour in his childhood. Correggio—I think it is—has given us a superb painting of the scene. The picture (partly original) is at the house of the late Miss Ann Herson, a Catholic lady of Norfolk, who died during the yellow fever, and who was during her life a ministering angel to the poor,—bestowing her vast wealth freely in the cause of charity. As St. Catharine

was never married *corporeally*, she has been called the bride of Heaven,—that is, Saint Bride. We have a street in Norfolk called Catharine, named about the time of the erection of the parish of St. Bride.

14. BROMFIELD.—I overlooked Bromfield in its proper place. The term "brom," which signifies *wild oats*, is a common prefix in England; as, Bromley, Bromwich, Bromgrove, Bromton, (now Brompton,) &c.

There are seven different places in Staffordshire, England, called Bromley, and in Kent; and it is probable that some Staffordshire colonist or Kentish man suggested the name Bromfield, as appropriate to the position of the church in the county of Culpepper.

15. LYNNHAVEN.—This was so called from the port of Lynn in the county of Norfolk, England, and before Princess Anne, in which it now is, was set apart as a distinct county.

16. OVERWHARTON.—This name, like that of Stratton, is that of an English town in the first place, and, secondly, of an individual. It may have been called in honour of George Wharton, a native of Westmoreland, in England, who lost all during the civil wars, and who may have been a friend to the George Mason—the first of the name—who was a Staffordshire man and a royalist. Or it may have been called after the Marchioness of Wharton, who was a daughter of Sir Henry Lee, of Ditchley,—a great royalist,—and who inherited his wealth. If Stafford had not been settled by some strong Cavaliers, and the parish had been created after the Revolution of 1688, I would suppose it was called Wharton in honour of the author of the celebrated ballad of Lillibulero.

17. COPLE.—This should correctly be written Copple. The word is common in Cornwall and in the mining-counties of England, and means a vessel used in refining metals. It was common, three hundred years ago, to name taverns after instruments; as, the "Mortar and Pestle," the "Bell," &c. But I know of no place in England so called. If there were any mines in Westmoremand, the title would be appropriate enough.

18. WESTMORELAND.—This county was created between the years 1648 and 1653, near a century before any of its Revolutionary men were born; so the Northern writer cannot say properly that it was so called from its having produced so many great men in Virginia. The true meaning of Moreland is "greater land," from the comparative "more," which is used in the sense of great by Gower, Chaucer, and even as late as Shakspeare, who says, in King John, Act II. 5th sc., "a *more* requital." But, if Moreland is derived from the Celtic word "more," then Moreland signifies great land, or high land; as, Maccullum More is the Great Maccullum. "Gilmore" means the henchman of the *more* or great man. The name of Westmoreland was given originally without doubt to a scene of high land or a great stretch of land of some kind, and never had allusion to the men who were born or died in any place so called.

19. MARTIN'S BRANDON.—Brandon was so called from the town of Brandon, in Suffolk, England. It gives the British title to the Scotch

Duke of Hamilton. It is situated on the river Ouse, and its name was given, like that of Surrey, Sussex, and Suffolk, from emigrants from those parts of England. It appears from the appendix of Burke's History, vol. i. p. 334, that one John Martin brought out a patent from England of five hundred acres, which was located on the tract, or hundred, called Brandon, on Chapoke Creek; and, in the early enumeration of the different settlements or plantations in the Colony, the farm of John Martin was always called "Martin's Brandon." This was as early, I think, as 1630.

No. IV.

NAMES OF SOME OF THE OLD AND LEADING FAMILIES IN EASTERN VIRGINIA IN COLONIAL TIMES AND IMMEDIATELY SUCCEEDING THE REVOLUTION.*

[The following has been furnished by Mr. Francis Cabell, of Warminster, Va., to whom I am indebted for other valuable communications.]

Allen, Alexander, Ambler, Archer, Armistead, Atkinson, Aylett, Acril.

Bacon, Baker, Ball, Baldwin, Ballard, Bankhead, Banister, Bassett, Baylor, Baynham, Berkeley, Beverley, Birchett, Blair, Bland, Bolling, Bouldin, Booth, Bowyer, Bradley, Brent, Braxton, Bowdoin, Browne, Brooke, Broadnaxe, Burwell, Burnley, Butler, Buckner, Byrd, Baskerville, Branch, Booker, Blow.

Cabell, Calloway, Carr, Carrington, Carter, Cary, Catlett, Chamberlayne, Christian, Clopton, Claiborne, Clayton, Clarke, Cocke, Coleman, Coles, Colston, Cooper, Conway, Corbin, Custis, Crawford.

Dabney, Daniel, Davenport, Davis, Dandridge, Digges, Dulany.

Edmunds, Edwards, Eggleston, Eldridge, Ellis, Embry, Eppes, Everard, Eyre.

Fairfax, Farley, Faulcon, Field, Fitzgerald, Fitzhugh, Fleming, Fry.

---

* The above list of names is a copy of one which was drawn up for the writer's own use, and which, having grown by gradual accretion from a small nucleus, is still very imperfect. Especially is it defective in the names of many who resided in the lower counties, or in the Northern Neck, or the other necks between the large rivers. It is not pretended that these families were all of the ancient "aristocracy," so called, although most of them might have certain representatives among the gentry of the country. Some of them were "novi homines" within the memory of the living. They are here arranged in alphabetical order: those who are acquainted with our political and social history will know how to classify them according to another standard. Neither are they assigned to any determined locality. The original ancestral seats might be assigned to certain counties in most cases; but their posterity in many others is too widely dispersed.

Gay, Gibbon, Gilmer, Goode, Goodwyn, Graves, Grayson, Green, Griffin, Grymes, Grammar, Greenway, Garnett, Garland, Gaines, Gholson.

Hackley, Hansford, Hardaway, Harmer, Harrison, Harvie, Herbert, Hill, Holliday, Holmes, Hooe, Howard, Hubard, Hairston, Heath, Heth, Hicks, Hopkins, Hawkins, Hodges, Henderson, Haynes.

Innes, Irby.

Jefferson, Jennings, Johnson, Jones, Joynes.

Kennon, King.

Lanier, Lee, Lewis, Lightfoot, Littlepage, Littleton, Lomax, Ludwell, Lyons, Leftwich.

Mallory, Martin, Marshall, Marye, Mason, Massie, Matthews, Mayo, Meade, Mercer, Minor, Meredith, Merriwether, Michie, Minge, McCarty. Moore, Moseley, Munford, Morris, Morton, Mosby.

Nash, Nelson, Newton, Nicholas, Nivison, Norvell, Noland.

Page, Parke, Parker, Peachey, Pegram, Pendleton, Penn, Peter, Peyton, Phillips, Pierce, Pleasants, Pollard, Pope, Powell, Poythress, Prentiss, Price, Prosser, Posey.

Randolph, Reade, Riddick, Roane, Robertson, Robinson, Rose, Ruffin, Russell, Royall.

Savage, Saunders, Scarburgh, Selden, Shepherd, Short, Skelton, Skipwith, Slaughter, Spottswood, Stanard, Stevenson, Stith, Stokes, Steptoe, Strother, Swann, Syme, Spencer.

Tabb, Talbot, Taliafero, Tayloe, Taylor, Tazewell, Terry, Thornton, Todd, Travis, Trent, Tucker, Tyler.

Upshur, Upshaw; Venable, Vaughn.

Waller, Walker, Walton, Wade, Ward, Waryng, Washington, Watkins, Watson, West, Wickham, Webb, Whiting, Westwood, Wilkins, Wilcox, Willis, Winston, Williams, Withers, Wood, Woodson, Wise, Wormley, Wyatt, Wythe.

Yates, Yelverton.

A very few Scotch and Irish names are found in this list,—still more of Welsh; but the great body of them are English or British, (other than Saxon.)*

---

* *Welsh Names to be found in the United States and many of them in Virginia.*
Atkins, Adams, Apjohn, Apthorp, Aubrey.

Balch, Barlow, Bayly, Benlow, Bevan, Bowen, Boydell, Breese, Broadus, (Broadhurst,) Broughton, Bulkley.

Cadwallader, Catesby, Clements, Cloyd, Conway, Coates, Cobbs, Cerwin, Craddock, (Caradoc,) Crute, (Crwt,) Cunliffe.

Davis, Davies, Dawkins, Denby, Dickins, Dickinson, Dewey.

Edmunds, Edwards, Evans.

Fane, Fielding, Floyd, Fluellen.

Garland, Gerald, Glyn, Godwin, Griffin, Griffith, Gwathney, Gwillyn, Gwynn, Gwinnett, Graves.

Hawkins, Hanmer, Harris, Haskins, Hawkins, Havard, Haynes, Hopkins, Hoskins, Herbert, Hickes, Holland, Howell, Howland, Hughes, Humphreys, Hurst.

No. V.

EXTRACT FROM JOHN ROLF'S LETTER TO KING JAMES WHEN HE WAS IN ENGLAND WITH POCAHONTAS, CONCERNING THE FIRST PLANTATIONS OR SETTLEMENTS IN THE COLONY.

AT Henrico, on the north side of the river, ninety odd myles from the mouth thereof, and within fifteen or sixteen myles of the Falls or head of

Jenyns, Jenkyns, Judkins, Junkin, Jeffreys, Jefferson, Jacobs, James, Jones, Johnes, Isaacs.

Langhorn, Leigh, Lewis, Lewellyn, Lister, Lloyd, Ludlow, Lyman.

Maddock, (Madoc,) Matthews, Mansel, Meredith, Meyrick or Merrick, Morgan, Miles, Morris, Morse, Mosby, Mostyn, Middleton.

Nichols, Norris, Nevin or Nevins.

Owen, Owens.

Pannill, Par, Parry, Parkins, Perkins, Perkinson, Peacock, Peters, Penn, Pendergast, Pennant, Pickens, Phillips, Poole, Polwhell, Powell, Powys, Price, Pratt, Prichard, Pugh, Pym.

Richards, Rees or Reece, Rice, Rivers, Rowland, Roberts, Rogers, Ragland.

Stokes, Stanley, Stephens, Shelby, Simonds or Simmons, Snowden.

Thomas, Tompkins, Trevelyan, Trevor, Tudor, Tyndale or Tindall.

Vane or Fane, Vaughn.

Watkins or Gwatkin, Williams, Winn, Wilkins, Wilkinson, Watts, Walters or Waters, Wills, Willis, Wallis, Wall, Warner, Wayles, Wilks, Womack, Wootan, Wayne.

1. The following surnames are taken from those of the ancient princes of the country:—Cadwallader, Griffin, Gwynnett, (Gwynnedd,) Craddock, (Caradoc,) Howell, Lewellyn, Madoc, Owen, Rice, (Rhuys,) Tudor, (Tewdor.)

2. These by adding "s" to Scripture names,—viz.: Adams, Daniels, Davies, (Davids,) Ellis, (Elias,) Johnes or Jones, James, Isaacs, Jacobs, Matthews, Phillips, Stephens, Symonds, Peters, Thomas.

3. And these by adding "s" to common Christian names:—Clements, Edmunds, Edwards, Evans, Hughes, Humphreys, Jeffreys, (Geoffreys,) Richards, Roberts, Rowlands, Wills, Williams, Watts, Walters.

4. "Ap" or "ab" means son, and is often prefixed to other names; and the affix "kins" denotes a collateral relation: thus, Bevan is equivalent to Ap-Evan; Bowen, Ap-Owen; Breese, Ap-Rees; Parry, Ap-Harry; Powell, Ap-Howell; Pugh, Ap-Hugh; Price, Ap-Rice; Prichard, Ap-Richard; Penry, Ap-Henry. Atkins, (Arthurs'-kin,) Dickens-son, Dawkins, Haskins, Hawkins, Hopkins, Jenkins, Judkins, (Judas-kin,) Pickens, Perkins-son, Tomkins, Watkins, Wilkins.

5. Some of the above names may be Cornish, old British, or otherwise Celtic, rather than strictly Welsh; thus, the English have a proverb,—

"By Tre, Pol, and Pen
You may know the Cornish men."

6. It is curious to note how many of the original Puritans of New England, of the Quakers of Pennsylvania, of the Baptists of Virginia and elsewhere, of advocates of extreme republican opinions in matters of State, as well as of Revolutionary leaders, bore names to be found in the above list. Of very many of the citizens of the Piedmont district, in Virginia, the same may be said. Their ancestors may have been attracted thither from its resemblance to the Principality in its physical features.

that river, (being our furthest habitation within the land,) are thirty-eight men and boyes, whereof twenty-two are farmors, the rest officers and others, all whom maintayne themselves with food and apparrell. Of this towne one capten Smaley hath the command in the absence of capten James Davis. Mr. Wm. Wickham minister there, who, in his life and doctrine, give good examples and godly instructions to the people.

At Bermuda Nether Hundred, (seated on the south side of the river, crossing it and going by land, five myles lower then Henrico by water,) are one hundred and nineteen—which seate conteyneth a good circuite of ground—the river running round, so that a pale running cross a neck of land from one parte of the river to the other, maketh it a peninsula. The houses and dwellings of the people are sett round about by the river, and all along the pale, so farr distant one from the other, that upon anie alarme, they can succor and second one the other. These people are injoyned by a charter, (being incorporated to the Bermuda towne, which is made a corporacoun,) to effect and performe such duties and services whereunto they are bound for a certain tyme, and then to have their freedome. This corporacoun admit no farmors, unles they procure of the governor some of the colony men to be their servants, for whom (being no members of the corporacoun,) they are to pay rent corne as other farmors of this kind— these are about seventeen. Others also comprehended in the said number of one hundred and nineteen there, are resident, who labor generallie for the colonie; amongst whom some make pitch and tarr, potashes, charcole and other works, and are maintayned by the magazin—but are not of the corporacoun. At this place (for the most part) liveth capten *Peacdly*, deputy marshal and deputy governor. Mr. Alexander Whitaker, (sonne to the reverend and famous divine, Dr. Whitaker,) a good divine, hath the ministerial charge here.

At West and Sherley Hundred (seated on the north side of the river, lower then the Bermudas three or four myles,) are twenty-five, commanded by capten Maddeson—who are imployed onely in planting and curing tobacco,—with the profitt thereof to clothe themselves and all those who labor about the generall business.

At James Towne (seated on the north side of the river, from West and Sherley Hundred lower down about thirty-seven myles,) are fifty, under the command of lieutenant Sharpe, in the absence of capten Francis West, Esq., brother to the right ho'ble the Le. Lawarre,—whereof thirty-one are farmors; all theis maintayne themselves with food and rayment. Mr. Richard Bucke minister there—a verie good preacher.

At Kequoughtan (being not farr from the mouth of the river, thirty-seven miles below James Towne on the same side,) are twenty—whereof eleven are farmors; all those also maintayne themselves as the former. Capten George Webb commander. Mr. Wm. Mays minister there.

At Dales-Gift (being upon the sea, neere unto Cape Charles, about thirty myles from Kequoughtan,) are seventeen, under the command of one lieutenant Cradock; all these are fedd and maintayned by the colony. Their labor is to make salt and catch fish at the two seasons aforementioned.

So the number of officers and laborers are two hundred and five. The farmors 81; besides woemen and children, in everie place some—which in all amounteth to three hundred and fifty-one persons—a small nomber to advance so great a worke.

Theis severall places are not thus weakly man'd, as capable of no greater nomber, (for they will maintayne many hundreds more,)—but because no one can be forsaken without losse and detriment to all. If then so few people, thus united, ordered and governed, doe live so happily, every one partaking of the others labor, can keepe in possession so much ground as will feed a far greater nomber in the same or better condition; and seeing too, too many poore farmors in England worke all the yeare, rising early and going to bed late, live penuriously, and much adoe to pay their land-lord's rent, besides a daily karking and caring to feed themselves and families, what happines might they enjoy in Virginia, were men sensible of theis things, where they may have ground for nothing, more than they can manure; reape more fruits and profitts with half the labor, void of many cares and vexacions, and for their rent a matter of small or no moment, I leave to your singular judgment and consideracoun, nothing doubting, but He (who, by his infinite goodnes, with so small means, hath settled these poore and weake beginnings so happily,) will animate, stirr up and encourage manie others cheerfully to undertake this worke, and will assuredly add a daily strength to uphold and maintayne what he hath already begun.

Seeing then this languishing action is now brought to this forwardness and strength, no person but is provided for, either by their owne or others labors, to subsist themselves for food, and to be able to rayse commodities for clothing and other necessaries, envy it selfe, poysoned with the venom of aspes, cannot wound it.

Now, to drawe to a conclusion of this my poore oblacon, I would crave your Highnes' patience a little longer—and that you would turne your heart to a more heavenly meditacoun, wherein much joy and comfort is to be reaped and found, of all such as shall truly, sincerely and unfeynedly seeke to advance the honor of God, and to propagate his gospell. There is no small hope by pietie, clemencie, curtesie and civill demeanor, (by which meanes some are wonne to us alreadie,) to convert and bring to the knowledge and true worship of Jesus Christ thousands of poore, wretched and misbelieving people on whose faces a good christian cannot looke with-out sorrow, pittie and compsssion, seeing they beare the image of our Heavenlie Creator, and we and they come from one and the same mould, especiallie we knowing that they, merely through ignorance of God and Christ, doe run headlong, yea, with joy, into destruction and perpetuall damnation,—for which knowledge we are the more bound and indebted to Almightie God, (for what were we before the gospell of Christ shined amongst us?) and cannot better express our duties and thankfulness for so great mercies, then by using such meanes to them, as it pleased him to lend unto others to bring our forefathers and us into the waies of trueth, —it is much to be mourned and lamented how lightlie the workes of God are now a days generallie regarded, and less sought after; but the worke of the world, as though they were eternall, hungered for, and thirsted after with insatiable greedines. But should we well consider, examine and search into ourselves, what we were, and now are, there can be no heart, (if not hardened as the nether mill stone,) but would even break itself to pieces, and distribute to manie poore soules some parte thereof, to purge them from their lees of synne, and to sette them in the right pathes of holines and righteousnes, to serve the King of Heaven; by which meanes and God's holy assistance, no doubt they will soone be brought to abandon their old superstitions and idolatries, wherein they have been nursed and trayned from their infancies, and our greatest adversaries shall not taunt us with this reproach, "Whom of you have you wonne to christianitie?" What a crowne of glorie shalbe sett upon their heads who shall faithfullie labor herein, I leave to the enjoying of them, who shall endeavour un-feynedly to meritt the same. Finallie, as Caleb and Joshua in the verie heate of grudgings, murmurings, and assemblies of the children of Israell, stood stoutlie for the Lord's cause, commending the goodnes of the land they discovered, to the faces of their oppressors, and the easines to obtain it even to the perill of their lives, so many right ho'ble and worthie per-sonages, both here and in Virginia, (whom generallie the most parte with-drew themselves, that the action was almost sunck downe in forgetfulnes,) have mightilie upheld this christian cause—for God, even our owne God, did helpe them. For neither evill reports, nor slanders, nor murmurings, nor backbitings of others, nor any disaster, did once dismay or hinder them from upholding thereof with their good reports, incouragements, and meanes yearelie sent to the planters, to nourish life and being in this zeal-ous worke. I beseech God to raise up many more such, so zealous for God's glory, to forward the same—we have tasted of some fruits thereof. There are no great nor strong castles, nor men like the sons of Anack, to hinder our quiet possession of that land. God's hand hath been mightie in the preservacoun thereof hitherto; what need we then to feare, but to goe up at once as a peculiar people, marked and chosen by the finger of God, to possess it, for undoubtedly he is with us. And as for murmurers, slanderers and backsliders, a due porcoun shalbe given them for their re-ward. So the blessings of Caleb and Joshua shall fall upon all those that constantly persevere to the end. Thus, craving your gracious pardon for my rude boldnes, beseaching God to send you the fulnes of his blessings in this world and in the world to come, I rest,

Your highnes' most faithful and loyall subject,

JOHN ROLF.

No. VI.

THE following address and resolutions of the patriots of the Northern Neck of Virginia, in the year 1765, immediately after the passage of the Stamp Act, properly belongs to the article on Washington parish, Westmoreland. It was drawn up by Richard Henry Lee, whose name is first on the list. It is said to have been the first public association in the land for the resistance to that act.

Roused by danger, and alarmed at attempts, foreign and domestic, to reduce the people of this country to a state of abject and detestable slavery, by destroying that free and happy constitution of government under which they have hitherto lived,—We, who subscribe this paper, have associated, and do bind ourselves to each other, to God, and to our country, by the firmest ties that religion and virtue can frame, most sacredly and punctually to stand by, and with our lives and fortunes to support, maintain, and defend each other in the observance and execution of these following articles.

First.—We declare all due allegiance and obedience to our lawful Sovereign, George the Third, King of Great Britain. And we determine to the utmost of our power to preserve the laws, the peace and good order of this colony, as far as is consistent with the preservation of our constitutional rights and liberty.

Secondly.—As we know it to be the birthright privilege of every British subject, (and of the people of Virginia as being such,) founded on reason, law, and compact, that he cannot be legally tried, but by his peers, and that he cannot be taxed, but by the consent of a Parliament, in which he is represented by persons chosen by the people, and who themselves pay a part of the tax they impose on others. If therefore any person or persons shall attempt, by any action or proceeding, to deprive this colony of those fundamental rights, we will immediately regard him or them as the most dangerous enemy of the community; and we will go to any extremity, not only to prevent the success of such attempts, but to stigmatize and punish the offender.

Thirdly.—As the Stamp Act does absolutely direct the property of the people to be taken from them without their consent expressed by their representatives, and as in many cases it deprives the British American subject of his right to trial by jury; we do determine, at every hazard, and, paying no regard to danger or to death, we will exert every faculty to prevent the execution of the said Stamp Act in any instance whatsoever within this colony. And every abandoned wretch, who shall be so lost to virtue and public good, as wickedly to contribute to the introduction or fixture of the Stamp Act in this colony, by using stamp paper, or by any other means, we will, with the utmost expedition, convince all such profligates that immediate danger and disgrace shall attend their prostitute purposes.

Fourthly.—That the last article may most surely and effectually be executed, we engage to each other, that whenever it shall be known to any of this association, that any person is so conducting himself as to favour the introduction of the Stamp Act, that immediate notice shall be given to as many of the association as possible; and that every individual so informed shall, with expedition, repair to a place of meeting to be appointed as near the scene of action as may be.

Fifthly.—Each associator shall do his true endeavour to obtain as many signers to this association as he possibly can.

Sixthly.—If any attempt shall be made on the liberty or property of any associator for any action or thing done in consequence of this agreement, we do most solemnly bind ourselves by the sacred engagements above entered into, at the utmost risk of our lives and fortunes, to restore such associate to his liberty, and to protect him in the enjoyment of his property.

In testimony of the good faith with which we resolve to execute this association, we have this 27th day of February, 1766, in Virginia, put our hands and seals hereto.

Richard Henry Lee	William Sydnor
Will. Robinson	John Monroe
Lewis Willis	William Cocke
Thos. Lud. Lee	Willm. Grayson
Samuel Washington	Wm. Brockenbrough
Charles Washington	Saml. Selden
Moore Fauntleroy	Richd. Lee
Francis Lightfoot Lee	Daniel Tibbs
Thomas Jones	Francis Thornton, Junr.
Rodham Kenner	Peter Rust
Spencer M. Ball	John Lee, Jr.
Richard Mitchell	Francis Waring
Joseph Murdock	John Upshaw
Richd. Parker	Meriwether Smith
Spence Monroe	Thos. Roane
John Watts	Jas. Edmondson
Robt. Lovell	Jas. Webb, Junr.
John Blagge	John Edmondson
Charles Weeks	Jas. Banks
Willm. Booth	Smith Young
Geo. Turberville	Laur. Washington
Alvin Moxley	W. Roane
Wm. Flood	Rich. Hodges
John Ballantine, Junr.	Jas. Upshaw
William Lee	Jas. Booker

Thos. Chilton
Richard Buckner
Jos. Pierce
Will. Chilton
John Williams
John Blackwell
Winder S. Kenner
Wm. Bronaugh
Wm. Peirce
John Berryman
John Dickson
John Broone
Edwd. Sanford
Charles Chilton
Edwd. Sanford
Daniel McCarty
Jer. Rush
Edwd. Ransdell
Townshend Dade
John Ashton
W. Brent
Francis Foushee
John Smith, Jour.
Wm. Ball
Thos. Barnes
Jos. Blackwell
Reuben Meriwether
Edw. Mountjoy
Wm. J. Mountjoy
Thos. Mountjoy
John Mountjoy
Gilbt. Campbell
Jos. Lane

A. Montague
Rich'd Jeffries
John Suggett
John S. Woodcock
Robt. Wormeley Carter
John Beale, Junr.
John Newton
Will. Beale, Junr.
Chs. Mortimer
John Edmondson, Jr.
Charles Beale
Peter Grant
Thompson Mason
Jona. Beckwith
Jas. Samford
John Belfield
W. Smith
John Augt. Washington
Thos. Belfield
Edgcomb Suggett
Henry Francks
John Bland, Junr.
Jas. Emerson
Thos. Logan
Jo. Milliken
Ebenezer Fisher
Hancock Eustace
John Richards
Thos. Jett
Thos. Douglas
Max. Robinson
John Orr.

No. VII.

SYNOPSIS OF ASSEMBLY ACTS RELATING TO THE PROTESTANT EPIS-COPAL CHURCH.

IT was my intention to have written an article on the last years of the Protestant Episcopal Church of Virginia, beginning with the Act of Assembly in 1776, which suspended the salaries of the clergy, and ending with that which confiscated the glebes, in 1802. But I find the same so much better done in this and the two following numbers of this Appendix that I cannot hesitate between them. The summary of Acts and Memorials has been furnished me by my young friend, Mr. John Eston Cooke, of Richmond, Virginia, who, with great care, has examined all the documents on the subject which are laid up in the archives of the State, and presented the following result, for which my readers, as well as myself, will owe him many thanks :—

1. The first Act aimed at the Established Church was passed at a General Assembly begun and held at the Capitol, in Williamsburg, on the 7th. October, 1776,—the first year of the Commonwealth. This Act is interesting in an historical point of view, as the first public exhibition of the dislike of a large class of the community for the English Establishment. After reciting that much doubt existed touching the application of the laws of Parliament upon religious matters to the Commonwealth of Virginia, the Act proceeds to declare that all such laws "which render criminal the maintaining any opinions in matters of religion, forbearing to repair to church, or the exercising any mode of worship whatsoever, or which prescribe punishments for the same, shall henceforth be of no force or validity in this Commonwealth." After the passage of the Act, "all dissenters, of whatever denomination, from the said Church, shall be totally free from all levies, taxes, and impositions whatever, toward supporting and maintaining the said Church, as it now is or hereafter may be established, or its ministers." It is nevertheless provided that the vestries of the different parishes shall levy and assess upon the tithables, including dissenters, as before, all the salaries and arrearages due the ministers up to the first of the ensuing January. These assessments are also directed where the vestries, counting upon them, have made engagements; and the former provisions for the poor are directed to be continued, conformist and dissenting tithables contributing.

The fourth section reserves to the Church her glebe lands held at the time, her churches and chapels built or then contracted for, and all books, ornaments, and decorations used in worship; also, all arrearages of money or tobacco then due, and the "perpetual benefit and enjoyment" of all private donations.

The Act winds up with directions for taking a list of tithables, and ends by declaring that the old law of 22 George II., for the payment and support of the clergy, should be "suspended" until the termination of the next General Assembly.

The Assembly contented itself thereafter for several years with affirming simply this "suspension" of the old law

2. But at the session commencing October, 1779, it distinctly erased the old statute, declaring that this and "all and every other Act or Acts providing salaries for the ministers, and authorizing the vestries to levy the

same, shall be, and the same are hereby, repealed." The former provisions are made, however, for arrearages of salary, the performance of engagements, and the support of the poor. For these purposes all tithables, whether conformists or dissenters, are to be levied upon as before.

3. There was no new legislation then until the year 1784. In that year, in compliance with the petitions of the clergy, the Church was incorporated under the name of "The Minister and Vestry of the Protestant Episcopal Church"—in each parish. They were to hold and enjoy all which the old Act of 1776 permitted them to possess, and could sue or be sued like other corporations. An exception is made in the case of the glebe in the county of Augusta, where, until the Church was organized, the overseers of the poor were to receive and apply the proceeds for the repairing of the church, the grounds, &c., and the support of the poor.

The second clause directs that the vestries shall decide by vote,—the minister voting with the rest, and having no negative voice.

The third clause grants to the minister and vestry power to receive and hold every species of property, real and personal, for the Church, and to improve it as they think best; but the Church cannot derive from these tenements, in any case, more than eight hundred pounds income. They may use these proceeds in any manner they desire for the cause of religion and education.

The other clauses direct that the vestry shall consist of twelve "able and discreet men," to be elected by the members of the Church, "every third year forever;" that they shall, with the minister, present to the county court, triennially, a statement of all property held, real or personal, by the Church, verified by oath, failing to comply with which they shall forfeit to the Commonwealth one hundred pounds, and in case of further contumacy cease to be a body corporate. If the annual revenue exceeds eight hundred pounds, the subject shall be laid before the Assembly.

The Act ends by repealing all former laws touching the internal government of the Church, its liturgies, mode of worship, fasts, festivals, &c. All such are to be decided by Conventions, in which are vested all the powers of discipline, change, and general government.

At this same term of 1784, the vestry of South Farnham parish, in Essex, were declared "dissolved," having supplied vacancies in their body without consulting the freeholders. These latter were directed to meet and elect a vestry.

4. The foregoing is a summary of the Acts of the General Assembly touching the Established Church up to the time of the passage of the "Act for establishing Religious Freedom." This was passed December 16, 1785, and need not be recited.

5. In January, 1799, the Assembly declared that all the old legislation, above recited, in which the existence of a Governmental Church was directly or indirectly recognised, should thenceforth be repealed; that no such Establishment had legally existed since the Commonwealth; and that

the Act of "Religious Freedom" was the true exposition of the Bill of Rights and the Constitution.

6. The final legislation of the General Assembly was the Act "Concerning the glebe-lands and churches within the Commonwealth," passed January 12, 1802. The preamble declares that the Act of 1799, just referred to, "recognises the principle that all property formerly belonging to the said Church, of every description, devolved on the good people of this Commonwealth, on the dissolution of the British Government here, in the same degree in which the right and interest of the said Church was derived therein from them." The Assembly does not wish, however, to "disturb the possession of the present incumbents," though it has the "right of authorizing a sale of all such property indiscriminately." Therefore the overseers of the poor shall only sell such glebe-lands as are vacant or shall become so. Leases granted by the former officers of the Church shall be respected; but the overseers shall sue for and recover all moneys due from tenants, and shall receive all other moneys to which the Church is entitled. The proceeds of the sales, &c., shall be in all cases appropriated by the overseers for the benefit of the poor, or for any other purpose which a majority of the freeholders may elect: *Provided*, that these appropriations shall not be for "any religious purpose whatsoever."

Nothing in the Act, however, shall authorize a sale of the churches and their fixtures, furniture, or appliances, or the churchyards, nor affect any private donation prior to January 1, 1777, for Church or other purposes, where there is any person in being entitled to take the same, or affect the property of any kind "acquired by private donations or subscriptions by the said Church since the date last mentioned."

From the Manuscript Journal of the House of Delegates, 1773–74, and Manuscript Archives.

Thursday, the 12th of May, 14 *George III.*, 1774.—"A petition of sundry persons of the community of Christians called Baptists, and other Protestant dissenters, whose names are thereunto subscribed, was presented to the House and read, setting forth that the toleration proposed by the bill, ordered at the last session of the General Assembly to be printed and published, not admitting public worship except in the daytime, is inconsistent with the laws of England, as well as the practice and usage of the primitive Churches, and even of the English Church itself; that the night season may sometimes be better spared by the petitioners from the necessary duties of their callings, and that they wish for no indulgences which may disturb the peace of Government," &c.

The action of the House not discoverable.

On the 17th May, 1774.—"A petition of several members of the Presbyterian Church, in the county of Bedford, setting forth that many well-disposed persons of their community had made contributions, to which others are willing to add, for supporting their clergy in a method more convenient than the ordinary one by subscription, but that the pious intentions of such benefactors cannot be effectually carried into execution, the elders of the Church not being incorporated so as to be capable of taking and holding land and slaves for the use of the ministers, and therefore praying that the said elders may be enabled to take and hold land and slaves to such uses, under proper regulations."

No action, owing to political matters.

May 14, 1774.—"The vestry of the parish of Frederick ask leave to levy on the tithables, for the minister's salary, "one hundred and fifty pounds of current money of Virginia, in lieu of the tobacco and cask and the legal allowance for shrinkage."

The petition is granted,—Mr. Wood, Mr. Edward Pendleton, and Mr. Zane being directed to prepare the bill

On May 23, 1774.—The petitions of sundry inhabitants of the county and parish of Augusta, representing that "the parish is upward of ninety miles long and near eighty miles wide, and that there are between three and four thousand tithables in it, and but one church; therefore praying it may be divided."

On May 24, 1774.—"Ordered, That the members of this House do attend in their places at the hour of ten in the forenoon, on the first day of June next, in order to proceed with the Speaker and the mace to the church in this city, and that the Rev. Mr. Price be appointed to read prayers and the Rev. Mr. Gwatkin to preach a sermon suitable to the occasion."

Richard Henry Lee is to request Mr. G. to comply. Mr. G. has "a disorder in his breast," and Mr. Price preached. This was the day appointed by Parliament for the closing of Boston Harbour.

Many petitions ask the dissolution of vestries for malfeasance of various sorts,—that parishes may be altered, &c.

The first great Act aimed at the perpetuity of the Established Church was passed at the session commencing in October, 1776. I find a very striking paper among the archives, which seems to have had a large share in the passage of the subsequent Act. It is labelled "Dissenters' Pet'n, 1776, Oct. 24. Ref'd to Com. of Religion."

The petition is as follows :—

"To the Honourable the General Assembly of Virginia :—

"The memorial of the Presbytery of Hanover humbly represents, That your memorialists are governed by the same sentiments which inspire the United States of America, and are determined that nothing in our power and influence shall be wanting to give success to their common cause. We would also represent that the dissenters from the Church of England in this country have ever been desirous to conduct themselves as peaceable members of the civil government, for which reason they have hitherto submitted to several ecclesiastic burdens and restrictions that are inconsistent with equal liberty. But now, when the many and grievous oppressions of our mother-country have laid this continent under the necessity of casting off the yoke of tyranny and of forming independent governments upon equitable and liberal foundations, we flatter ourselves that we shall be freed from all the encumbrances which a spirit of domination, prejudice, or bigotry hath interwoven with most other political systems. This we are the more strongly encouraged to expect by the *Declaration of Rights,* so universally applauded for that dignity, firmness, and precision with which it delineates and asserts the privileges of society and the prerogatives of human nature, and which we embrace as the *magna charta* of our Commonwealth, that can never be violated without endangering the grand superstructure it was destined to sustain. Therefore we rely upon this *Declaration,* as well as the justice of our honourable Legislature, to secure us the *free exercise of religion according to the dictates of our consciences;* and we should fall short in our duty to ourselves and the many and numerous congregations under our care were we upon this occasion to neglect laying before you a statement of the religious grievances under which we have hitherto laboured, that they no longer may be continued in our present form of government.

"It is well known that in the frontier-counties—which are justly supposed to contain a fifth part of the inhabitants of Virginia—the Dissenters have borne the heavy burdens of purchasing glebes, building churches, and supporting the Established clergy, where there are very few Episcopalians, either to assist in bearing the expense or to reap the advantage; and that throughout the other parts of the country there are also many thousands of zealous friends and defenders of our State who, besides the invidious and disadvantageous restrictions to which they have been subjected, annually pay large taxes to support an Establishment from which their consciences and principles oblige them to dissent,—all which are confessedly so many violations of their natural rights, and in their consequences a restraint upon freedom of inquiry and private judgment.

"In this enlightened age, and in a land where all of every denomination are united in the most strenuous efforts to be free, we hope and expect that our representatives will cheerfully concur in removing every species of religious as well as civil bondage. Certain it is, that every argument for civil liberty gains additional strength when applied to liberty in the concerns of religion; and there is no argument in favour of establishing the Christian religion but what may be pleaded with equal propriety for establishing the tenets of Mahomed by those who believe the Alkoran; or if this be not true, it is at least impossible for the magistrate to adjudge the right of preference among the various sects that profess the Christian faith, without erecting a chair of infallibility, which would lead us back to the Church of Rome.

"We beg leave further to represent that religious establishments are highly injurious to the temporal interests of any community. Without insisting upon the ambition and the arbitrary practices of those who are favoured by Government, or the intriguing, seditious spirit which is commonly excited by this as well as every other kind of oppression, such establishments greatly retard population, and, consequently, the progress of arts, sciences, and manufactures. Witness the rapid growth and improvement of the Northern Provinces compared with this. No one can deny that the more early settlement and the many superior advantages of our country would have invited multitudes of artificers, mechanics, and all other useful members of society to fix their habitation among us, who have either remained in the place of their nativity, or preferred worse civil government and a more barren soil where they might enjoy the rights of conscience more fully than they had a prospect of doing it in this. From which we infer that Virginia might have now been the capital of America and a match for the British arms, without depending upon either for the necessaries of war, had it not been prevented by her religious Establishment.

"Neither can it be made appear that the Gospel needs any such civil aid. We rather conceive that when our blessed Saviour declares his *kingdom is not of this world* he renounces all dependence upon State power; and, as his *weapons were spiritual*, and were only designed to have influence upon the judgment and heart of men, we are persuaded that if mankind were left in the quiet possession of their unalienable religious privileges, Christianity, as in the days of the apostles, would continue to prevail and flourish in the greatest purity, by its own native excellence and under the all-disposing providence of God.

"We would also humbly represent that the only proper objects of civil government are the happiness and protection of men in their present state of existence, the security of the life, liberty, and property of the citizens, and to restrain the vicious and encourage the virtuous, by wholesome laws equally extending to every individual; but that the *duty which we owe our Creator, and the manner of discharging it, can only be directed by reason and conviction,* and is nowhere cognizable but at the tribunal of the Universal Judge.

"Therefore we ask no ecclesiastical establishment for ourselves, neither can we approve of them when granted to others: this, indeed, would be giving *exclusive or separate emoluments or privileges to one set* (or sect) *of men,* without any special *public services,* to the common reproach or injury of every other denomination. And, for the reasons recited, we are induced earnestly to entreat that all laws now in force in this Commonwealth which countenance religious domination may be speedily repealed,—that all of every religious sect may be protected in the full exercise of their several modes of worship, and exempted from all taxes for the support of any Church whatsoever, further than what may be agreeable to their own private choice or voluntary obligation. This being done, all partial and invidious distinctions will be abolished, to the great honour and interest of the State, and every one be left to stand or fall according to merit, which can never be the case so long as any one denomination is established in preference to others.

"That the Great Sovereign of the universe may inspire you with unanimity, wisdom, and resolution, and bring you to a just determination on all the important concerns before you, is the fervent prayer of your memorialists.

"Signed by order of the Presbytery.

"JOHN TODD, Moderator.
"CALEB WALLACE, P. Clerk."

On June 3, 1777, the Presbytery of Hanover petitioned the Assembly again. Thanking it for the late Act, (of 1776,) they proceed to remonstrate against "a general assessment" which was left to be decided by the next Assembly. If the Legislature have any power over religion and its ministers, it has all power, and might oppress and enslave. The memorialists declare that these consequences are "so entirely subversive of religious liberty, that, if they should take place in Virginia, we should be reduced to the melancholy necessity of saying, with the apostles in like cases, 'Judge ye whether it be best to obey God or man,' and also of acting as they acted."

Nov. 28, 1777.—The petition of the inhabitants of Christ Church parish, in the county of Lancaster, says that in 1759, by an Act of Assembly, a new vestry was elected in the parish, but death has now reduced them to four. These four have "elected into that office a person whom we think not friendly to the glorious cause we are now engaged in; and, as we are now declared a free and independent people, we think we have a right to the choice of a new set of rulers." They therefore pray a dissolution of the tory vestry and power to elect a new one. This petition is signed by one hundred and twenty-eight persons, apparently the principal men of the county. A counter-petition is filed, signed by seven persons, declaring that the vestryman in question—Mr. William Montague—is not a tory, though he had been so considered, and praying a refusal of the petition to dissolve the body. But the vestry was dissolved."

On the 26th November, 1778, various inhabitants of King William county (Protestant Episcopal) petition and say that the Act suspending the salaries of clergymen was regarded as temporary: they hope some provision will be made. They do not wish conscientious Dissenters to contribute to the support of the Church; "that men of such principles and persuasions should be exonerated from the support of a clergy so different in point of worship from them, must be confessed by all to be just and reasonable." The clergy are, however, men of real merit and fine education, and deserve some assistance from the Legislature. The Dissenters are declared to be, often, men of "disorderly and dissipated lives," who seduce the poor from their labour and negroes from their duties.

This memorial was "deferred" to the next Assembly.

Petitions from Amherst, Culpepper, Caroline, &c. for a general assessment. This last—Caroline—memorial, (Episcopal,) of date December 5, 1777, states that the memorialists "have seen an Act of the last session of Assembly, by which dissenters from the Church of England are exempted from all levies for the support of the said Church or its ministers, and highly approve thereof, as founded on principles of justice and propriety, and favourable to religious liberty: at the same time they beg leave to suggest that as, in their opinion, public worship is a duty we owe the Creator and Preserver of mankind, and productive of effects the most beneficial to society, it ought to be enjoined and regulated by the Legislature, so as to preserve public peace, order, and decency, without prescribing a mode or form of worship to any." It then declares that the voluntary-contribution system will cause difficulties between the clergy and people and discourage men of genius and injure religion. A general assessment is then prayed.

December 2, 1778, referred to next session.

November 6, 1778.—Sundry (Episcopal) inhabitants of the county of Cumberland declare that the Dissenters are seducing the ignorant and sowing "discontent between husbands and their wives." They have "seen meetings in the night of our slaves, without our consent, which could produce nothing but deeds of darkness," and the Dissenters had produced "disobedience and insolence to masters." They "wish to see a well-regulated toleration established," that men "may be permitted to serve God in their own way, without molestation. . . . But we wish also that these nightly meetings may be prohibited under severe penalties." Lastly, they pray that "some regulation may be adopted to make the clergy of the Established Church accountable for their conduct, and be removed for their misbehaviour."

This was rejected December 2, 1778.

October 29, 1778.—"Some of the people called Seceding Presbyterians" pray that they may thereafter make oath "by holding up the right hand" only; which petition was granted.

November 10, 1779.—"Divers of the freeholders and other free inhabitants of Amherst county"—who afterwards describe themselves as "composed of Church of England men, Presbyterians, Baptists, and Methodists"—" unanimously and with one voice declare their hearty assent, concurrence, and approbation of the Act of January, 1779, declaring all Church-laws null, and the Act of Religious Freedom the true exposition of the Bill of Rights." Signed by a great number. Many for and against.

May 12, 1780.—Sundry inhabitants of Amelia pray that marriage-licenses shall not continue to be directed, in the old form, to Episcopal ministers; that certain persons therefrom doubted the validity of marriages by other than the Episcopal clergy: they pray that the ceremony "without the use of the ring and the service" may be declared lawful. Successful. It led to the bill legitimizing children of all such marriages by Dissenting ministers. The Baptist Association at Sandy Creek, Charlotte, petition for the same. Also other Baptist associations.

November, 1780.—Petition and counter-petition of the inhabitants of Cumberland. The Presbyterians pray the Assembly to declare all non-juring clergymen incapable of preaching. The Episcopalians indignantly declare the Presbyterians "disorderly and turbulent, desirous of giving laws to all societies," and fond of noise and violence. The real object of their (the Presbyterians') petition, the memorialists say, is to ruin the Rev. Christopher MacRae, who, although prevented by conscientious scruples from taking the oath, is a most benevolent man, a pattern of piety, and one who wishes liberty and happiness to all mankind. The ruin of the Church in Cumberland is declared to be the ultimate object of the Presbyterians.

November 22, 1781.—Sundry inhabitants of Prince Edward county pray that all the old vestries may be dissolved by Act of Assembly and new ones elected by the body of the community at large, Dissenters to be equally competent with conformists to the post of vestrymen, and the sole proviso to be "attachment to the present form of government." Referred to next Assembly, and, June 9, 1782, rejected.

November 12, 1784.—The Hanover Presbytery pray that there may be no incorporations, and, if a general assessment is decided upon, that it may be as liberal as possible.

June 4, 1784.—The Protestant Episcopal clergy file their memorial.

From this time—that is to say, the date of the Act of "Religious Freedom"—the enemies of the Establishment redoubled their efforts to overthrow the last vestiges of its former power and usefulness. The petitions are throughout of this description, and need not be particularly referred to. The concessions of the Assembly had evidently given them hope and resolution, and they seem to have employed every possible means in their power to cast discredit on the Episcopacy.

During the same period, the petitions from parishes praying a dissolution of old, inanimate vestries and a sale of unoccupied glebes indicate that the Establishment was almost at its last gasp. There are great numbers of these petitions. The foregoing is the conclusion which will be arrived at from reading them. It is not necessary to publish them.

No. VIII.

Dr. Hawks's Opinion on the Glebe Case, taken from his Work on the Church of Virginia.

[I had intended to examine for myself the question of the constitutionality of the law for selling the glebes so far as to form and express an opinion on the subject, though it would have been of very little worth; but want of time, and the reading of this and the next number of the appendix, containing Dr. Hawks's candid statement of the case and Judge Story's able opinion, have led me to a course which will, I am sure, be greatly preferred by all my readers. I do not hesitate to say that I have always inclined to the belief that the Act was unconstitutional. I have long laboured, but in vain, to obtain the opinion of Judge Pendleton, which was to have been delivered the day after his sudden death, and which would have decided the question in favour of the Church. I hope it may yet be found. At the same time, I must declare that I have always rejoiced in that Act of the Assembly, so far as the Church was concerned. Such has also been the feeling of almost all our clergy and laity with whom I have ever conversed. Could we have had the glebes restored to us by a decision of the courts, or even by the Act of Assembly, we should have opposed the effort; it being injurious to the cause of religion in our own Church and in the State. The history of the glebes and glebe-houses in Virginia has, from first to last, been a most mortifying one. With comparatively few exceptions, as may be seen on the old vestry-books, they were not worthy of the residence of our ministers, and, for the most part, were rented out for very small sums of money—even for forty, thirty, and twenty shillings—or surrendered to vestries on condition that the casks or hogsheads for the tobacco were furnished. When the salaries were withdrawn, only a few of the glebes held out any inducement to the incumbents to remain, as the voluntary contributions were very small and often nothing at all. For these few the Episcopalians earnestly contended, and for their sale some other denominations as earnestly sought. I doubt not that there were those who advocated their sale from a sincere conviction that it was religiously and politically right, while it cannot be doubted that, in many instances, sectarian feeling and political ambition had much to do with it.]

As to the arguments by which a sale of the glebes was urged upon the Legislature, the principal were as follows :—

1. That most of the glebe-lands were originally purchased with money levied upon the people at large, and that, consequently, whenever a majority of the people desired a sale of the lands, they should be sold and the money applied to such other use as might seem best to them.

2. That if the Church was permitted to retain the property, a certain pre-eminence and superiority was thereby conferred, which was odious in a republic and inconsistent with its institutions.

3. That the fourth article of the Declaration of Rights of Virginia asserted, "That no man or set of men are entitled to exclusive or separate emoluments or privileges but in consideration of public services;" but the enjoyment of the glebes did confer upon the Church "exclusive emoluments from the community," and was consequently unconstitutional.

To the first of these arguments it was answered that some of the glebes were a private donation; that those which were purchased were bought many years before,—some of them more than a century,—and that the "people" with whose money the purchase was made were not Dissenters, (for there were few or none in the Colony at that day,) but were members of the Establishment, and perfectly content that their money should be thus applied; that, having been thus applied, the "people" had voluntarily divested themselves of it, and their descendants could not now take it back, any more than they could other moneys of which their ancestors had seen fit willingly to deprive themselves : it was also answered that, upon this principle of a restoration to the "people" of money which the "people" once gave, there should obviously be returned no more than such a part as would be proportionate to the original number of Dissenters among the people who purchased; for, if those who now asked for a sale of the glebes had, from conscientious motives, dissented from the faith of their fathers, they should thence learn that their fathers also had consciences, and with no justice or propriety could they seek to undo what their ancestors had done with a good conscience. But, as to Dissenters among the original purchasers, there were either none at all, or, at best, the number was very limited; and it was certain that there were no Baptists among them.

It was also asserted to be very questionable whether, considering the great emigrations to the Western country and to other States, there was one-third of the inhabitants remaining whose ancestors had contributed to purchase a glebe; that, if they were sold for the benefit of that third, it would be impossible to ascertain to whom the proceeds should be paid. If it should be urged that "the country" first purchased them, and that now they should be given back to "the country," then it was to be remembered that that country by a solemn Act had declared that "in all time coming" they should not be taken from the Church; and that if it would be unrighteous in an individual to take back by mere force that which he had once bestowed upon another, it required no small skill in casuistry to prove that similar conduct was righteous in a State.

As to the second argument, it was said in reply that the question of permitting the Church to retain the property was one of *right*, founded on law, which republics were emphatically bound to respect.   That by the very law which released Dissenters from all taxes to support the Episcopal Church, the Assembly of Virginia had pledged its legislative faith—the most solemn pledge and firmest sanction which a free State could give—that the property in dispute should "in all time coming" be saved and reserved to the use of the Episcopal Church.   That to order a sale of property thus solemnly reserved would tend to sap the foundation of those rights by which property in general is held, introduce into the Acts of the Legislature instability and uncertainty, exhibit a fluctuation in law unprecedented in Virginia, and overturn that confidence and security which the citizens of a republic should always feel in the stability of purpose avowed by their selected representatives.   It also said that, if pre-eminence and superiority in the Church were evils justly dreaded, a declared preference for any other religious denomination was no less to be deprecated; and that, if the glebes were sold to gratify any sect or party, a distinction would be so far manifested in its favour, and would tend to furnish it, in this patronage of the State, with the means of establishing its own creed upon the ruins of every other.

To the argument of unconstitutionality as deduced from the Declaration of Rights the answer was that "the community" under the Government established after the Revolution certainly had granted to the Church no exclusive emoluments," for it had granted nothing: it had only confirmed to the Church that which she had and owned and enjoyed for more than a century before.   But, in truth, the fourth article of the Declaration of Rights had no bearing upon the question, as was evident when the whole of it was viewed together.   The article declared "that no man or set of men are entitled to exclusive or separate emoluments or privileges from the community, but in consideration of public services; which, not being descendible, neither ought the offices of magistrate, legislator, or judge, to be hereditary,"—thus showing simply an intention to prevent *hereditary* honours, offices, or emoluments in the civil government.

These are the principal arguments and answers which from time to time were presented to the Legislature upon the question of a sale of the glebes generally : there are to be found also among the memorials and remonstrances some which concern the sale of a glebe in some particular parish only; and these afford additional considerations for and against the measure, founded upon the peculiar circumstances of each case, and possessing no general interest.

Bishop Madison, in the exercise of the discretion confided to him by the Convention of 1796, submitted to the Legislature of that year the memorial touching the sale of the property of the Church.   It was not acted upon by the Assembly; but the subject, according to some former precedents in matters concerning the Church already recorded, was submitted to the consideration of the people. Episcopalians began now to think that their only mode of saving the glebes was, if possible, with the concurrence of the Legislature, to draw the determination of the question from before that tribunal and submit its decision to the courts of law. With the concurrence of the standing committee, the Bishop therefore resolved to obtain professional advice, and an opinion was sought at the hands of some of the ablest jurists of Virginia. Bushrod Washington, Edmund Randolph, and John Wickham were consulted, and, as the result of their deliberations, stated:—

1. That the Protestant Episcopal Church was the exclusive owner of the glebes.

2. That so far was the title of the Church from being impaired by the Bill of Rights, that on no sound construction did they clash; but that the title of the Church stood upon precisely the same grounds with the rights of private property, which had been recognised and secured by the principles of the Revolution and by the Constitution.

3. That any question concerning the right of property in the glebes could constitutionally be decided by the judiciary alone.

Having obtained this opinion, the Bishop called together the Convention in December, 1797, and, in his address, directing their attention to the Church property, laid before them the opinion just recited.

The Convention appointed a committee to attend the discussion of their memorial before the Legislature, and instructed them to propose to that body that the controversy should be submitted to the decision of a proper tribunal of justice.

The task becomes truly painful of following through the ecclesiastical records of this period the gradual but sure descent of the Church from level to level, each a little lower than the former, and of witnessing effort after effort made in vain by her few remaining friends to stay her downward course. The picture presented by the Bishop, in one of his addresses about this time, offers to our contemplation a suffering clergy, temples in every stage of dilapidation and decay, and an increasing indifference to the interests of the Church, which told too plainly that the protracted struggle was fast driving Churchmen into the hopelessness of despair.

The last Conventional effort of which we have any record was made in 1799. By a resolution of that year, the Bishop was directed to employ counsel to defend the rights of the Church before the judiciary whenever it should be deemed most proper to bring the question before it; and it is to be presumed that the Church now sat down in patience to await the blow which probably was seen by all to be inevitable. The crisis came at last; and on the 12th of January, 1802, the Legislature passed the law by virtue of which the glebes of Virginia were ordered to be sold for the benefit of the public. The warfare begun by the Baptists seven-and-twenty years before was now finished : the Church was in ruins, and the triumph of her enemies was complete.

If there should be those who are disposed to view this law as an illegal encroachment upon the vested rights of the Church, it is proper to remind them of the reasons which satisfied those who enacted it that they were doing right. They supposed that from the beginning the *property* of the glebes was in the *people*, not in the *clergy;* and that, as the number of Episcopalians in the parishes which remained was not a majority of the people, therefore no injustice was done by the Act in question. Many who voted for the law felt compelled to do so by the force of popular opinion.

It was not long after the passage of the Act of 1802 before the Church found it necessary to bring the constitutionality of that law before the proper tribunal for consideration. This was done in the year 1804, in the celebrated case of Turpin et al. *vs.* Locket et al., commonly known as the Manchester case. The defendants, as overseers of the poor, had undertaken to sell the glebe-lands of the parish of Manchester, under the Act of 1802, and the plaintiffs—who were the churchwardens and vestrymen—filed a bill in Chancery to prevent the sale by an injunction.

The cause finally, by an appeal from the decree of Chancellor Wythe, came before the Court of Appeals,—the highest tribunal in Virginia,— which at that time was composed of Judge Pendleton, the President, with Judges Carrington, Lyons, Roane, and Fleming. The last-named gentleman, however, did not sit in the cause, because he considered himself interested in the decision.

As the principles involved in the case were of great importance and the property of the glebes was of much value, it may readily be supposed that the cause excited a deep interest; and, after an elaborate argument, the court declined then giving an opinion and held it under advisement. In the vacation which succeeded, Judge Pendleton prepared his opinion in writing. It was, that the Act of 1802 was unconstitutional, and that the glebes belonged to the Protestant Episcopal Church. But, on the night before the opinion was to have been pronounced, Judge Pendleton died; and, as Judges Carrington and Lyons were both known to be of a similar opinion, the judgment of the court, but for the death of its President, would have been rendered on the next day for the Church.

After the death of Judge Pendleton, Judge Tucker was appointed to succeed him, and the cause was again argued. The grounds taken were briefly these :—On the part of the defendants it was argued :—1. That if the Church had power to hold the glebes *before* the American Revolution, that event destroyed such power; and, upon a dissolution of the former political system, the glebes devolved upon the Commonwealth.

To this it was answered that, by various legislative acts adopted after the change in government, the very framers of the Constitution who adopted these acts conclusively showed that they did not suppose the Revolution had destroyed the Church: thus, on the very day after the declaration of independence, the Convention of Virginia altered the Book of Common Prayer, to accommodate it to the change of affairs; and it should here be added that Judges Carrington and Lyons—both of whom were members of the Convention of Virginia—declared in their opinion that the destruction of the Church was not supposed at the time to have resulted from the change of government. It was also answered that revolutions are intended to preserve rights, not to take them away; and that alterations in the form of a government do not affect the rights of private property.

2. It was urged that a distinction obtains between a natural person and an artificial body, such as a corporation; that even admitting the rights of the first to be unmolested by a revolution, yet the rights of the latter are thereby lost.

In reply it was said that, as all property was matter of civil institution, and the right to it was not natural, but in all cases created by law, the ground on which private property was held sacred applied as forcibly to a society as it did to an individual.

3. It was argued that the Church, as a society, lost its corporate existence by the Revolution: first, because the King—one of its integral parts—was gone; secondly, because incorporated religious societies were contrary to the sixteenth article of the Bill of Rights; and, thirdly, because the profits of the glebes were *emoluments,* which were forbidden by the fourth article.

It was answered that neither of these positions was true.

1. The King never was an integral part of the Established Church, even in England; but, if he were, then a society is not destroyed by the removal of one of its parts, provided enough be left to carry on its operations.

2. The sixteenth article of the Bill of Rights relates simply to the rights of conscience and the mutual charities due from man to man.*

3. The fourth article does not relate to *property* at all, but to emoluments and privileges subsequently to be created in favour of the great officers of government, and refers to magistrates, legislators, and judges only.

Upon the second argument, Judges Carrington and Lyons still retained their former opinion; Judge Tucker concurred in opinion with Judge Roane that the Act of 1802 was constitutional, and that the glebes might be sold; while Judge Fleming, who was known to agree with Judges Carrington and Lyons, still declined, for the reason before given, to sit in the case. Thus the court was equally divided, and, of course, the decree

---

* The article is in these words:—" That religion, or the duty which we owe to our Creator and the manner of discharging it, can be directed only by reason and conviction, not by force or violence, and therefore all men are equally entitled to the free exercise of religion according to the dictates of conscience ; and that it is the mutual duty of all to practise Christian forbearance, love, and charity toward each other."

below, from which an appeal had been taken, was affirmed; though it has never yet been determined by a majority of the Court of Appeal in Virginia that the law of 1802 is constitutional.

No. IX.

OPINION AND JUDGMENT OF THE SUPREME COURT WRITTEN AND DELIVERED BY JUDGE STORY IN THE CASE OF THE FAIRFAX GLEBE QUESTION AND IN CONTRADICTION TO THE DECISION OF THE VIRGINIA COURTS.

[IT is not known whether the decision was unanimous, or by what majority it passed. Chief-Justice Marshall was in favour of it, but requested Judge Story to draw up the opinion.]

Other considerations arising in this case, material to the title, on which relief must be founded, render an inquiry into the character and powers of the Episcopal Church indispensable.

At a very early period the religious establishment of England seems to have been adopted in the Colony of Virginia; and, of course, the common law upon that subject, so far as it was applicable to the circumstances of that Colony. The local division into parishes for ecclesiastical purposes can be very early traced; and the subsequent laws enacted for religious purposes evidently presuppose the existence of the Episcopal Church with its general rights and authorities growing out of the common law. What those rights and authorities are need not be minutely stated. It is sufficient that, among other things, the Church was capable of receiving endowments of land, and that the minister of the parish was, during his incumbency, seised of the freehold of its inheritable property, as emphatically *personia ecclesiæ*, and capable, as a sole corporation, of transmitting that inheritance to his successors. The churchwardens, also, were a corporate body clothed with authority and guardianship over the repairs of the Church and its temporal property; and the other temporal concerns of the parish were submitted to a vestry, composed of persons selected for that purpose. In order more effectually to cherish and support religious institutions, and to define the authorities and rights of the Episcopal officers, the Legislature from time to time enacted laws on this subject. By the statutes of 1661, ch. 1, 2, 3, 10, and 1667, ch. 3, provision was made for the erection and repairs of churches and chapels of ease; for the laying out of glebes and church-lands, and the building of a dwelling-house for the minister; for the making of assessments and trades for these and other parochial purposes; for the appointment of churchwardens to keep the church in repair, and to provide books, ornaments, &c.; and, lastly, for the election of a vestry of twelve persons by the parishioners, whose duty it was, by these and subsequent statutes, among other things, to make and proportion levies and assessments, and to purchase glebes and erect dwelling-houses for the ministers in each respective parish. See statute 1696, ch. 11; 1727, ch. 6; and 1748, ch. 28.—2 *Tucker's Blackst. Com. App. note M.*

By the operation of these statutes and the common law, the lands thus purchased became vested, either directly or beneficially, in the Episcopal Church. The minister for the time-being was seised of the freehold, in law or in equity, *jure ecclesiæ,* and during a vacancy the fee remained in abeyance, and the profits of the parsonage were to be taken by the parish for their own use.—*Co. Lit.* 340, *b;* 341, 342, *b.* 2 *Mass. R.* 500.

Such were some of the rights and powers of the Episcopal Church at the time of the American Revolution; and under the authority thereof the purchase of the lands stated in the bill before the court was undoubtedly made. And the property so acquired by the Church remained unimpaired, notwithstanding the Revolution; for the statute of 1776, ch. 2, completely confirmed and established the rights of the Church to all its lands and other property.

The statute of 1784, ch. 88, proceeded yet further. It expressly made the minister and vestry, and, in case of a vacancy, the vestry of each parish respectively, and their successors forever, a corporation by the name of the Protestant Episcopal Church, in the parish where they respectively resided, to have, hold, use, and enjoy, all the glebes, churches, and chapels, burying-grounds, books, plate, and ornaments, appropriated to the use of, and every other thing the property of, the late Episcopal Church, to the sole use and benefit of the corporation. The same statute also provided for the choice of new vestries, and repealed all former laws relating to vestries and churchwardens and to the support of the clergy, &c., and dissolved all former vestries; and gave the corporation extensive powers as to the purchasing, holding, aliening, repairing, and regulating the Church property. This statute was repealed by the statute of 1786, ch. 12, with a proviso saving to all religious societies the property to them respectively belonging, and authorizing them to appoint, from time to time, according to the rules of their sect, trustees, who should be capable of managing and applying such property to the religious use of such societies; and the statute of 1788, ch. 47, declared that the trustees appointed in the several parishes to take care of and manage the property of the Protestant Episcopal Church, and their successors, should, to all intents and purposes, be considered as the successors to their former vestries, with the same powers of holding and managing all the property formerly vested in them. All these statutes, from that of 1776, ch. 2, to that of 1788, ch. 47, and several others, were repealed by the statute of 1798, ch. 9, as inconsistent with the principles of the Constitution and of religious freedom. And by the statute of 1801, ch. 5, (which was passed after the District of Columbia was finally separated from the States of Maryland and Virginia,) the Legislature asserted their right to all the property of the Episcopal churches in the respective parishes of the State; and, among other things, directed and authorized the overseers of the poor, and their successors, in each parish wherein any glebe-land was vacant or should become so, to sell the same, and appropriate the proceeds to the use of the poor of the parish.

It is under this last statute that the bill charges the defendants (who are overseers of the poor of the parish of Fairfax) with claiming a title to dispose of the land in controversy.

This summary view of so much of the Virginia statutes as bears directly on the subject in controversy presents not only a most extraordinary diversity of opinion in the Legislature, as to the nature and propriety of aid in the temporal concerns of religion, but the more embarrassing consideration of the constitutional character and efficacy of those laws touching the rights and property of the Episcopal Church.

It is conceded on all sides, that at the Revolution the Episcopal Church no longer retained its character as an exclusive religious establishment. And there can be no doubt that it was competent to the people and to the Legislature to deprive it of its superiority over other religious sects, and to withhold from it any support by public taxation. But, although it may be true that "religion can be directed only by reason and conviction, not by force or violence," and that "all men are equally entitled to the free exercise of religion according to the dictates of conscience," as the Bill of Rights of Virginia declares, yet it is difficult to perceive how it follows, as a consequence, that the Legislature may not enact laws more effectually to enable all sects to accomplish the great objects of religion by giving them corporate rights for the management of their property, and the regulation of their temporal as well as spiritual concerns. Consistently with the Constitution of Virginia, the Legislature could not create or continue a religious establishment which should have exclusive rights and prerogatives; or compel the citizens to worship under a stipulated form or discipline, or to pay taxes to those whose creed they could not conscientiously believe. But the free exercise of religion cannot be justly deemed to be restrained by aiding with equal attention the votaries of every sect to perform their own religious duties, or by establishing funds for the support of ministers, for public charities, for the endowment of churches, or for the sepulture of the dead. And that these purposes could be better secured and cherished by corporate powers cannot be doubted by any person who has attended to the difficulties which surround all voluntary associations. While, therefore, the Legislature might exempt the citizens from a compulsory attendance and payment of taxes in support of any particular sect, it is not perceived that either public or constitutional principles required the abolition of all religious corporations.

Be, however, the general authority of the Legislature as to the subject of religion as it may, it will require other arguments to establish the position that, at the Revolution, all the public property acquired by the Episcopal churches under the sanction of the laws became the property of the State. Had the property thus acquired been originally granted by the State, or the King, there might have been some colour (and it would have been but a colour) for such an extraordinary pretension. But the property was, in fact and in law, generally purchased by the parishioners or acquired by the benefactions of pious donors. The title thereto was indefeasibly vested in the churches, or rather in their legal agents. It was not in the power of the Crown to seize or assume it, nor of the Parliament itself to destroy the grants, unless by the exercise of a power the most arbitrary, oppressive, and unjust, and endured only because it could not be resisted. It was not forfeited; for the churches had committed no offence. The dissolution of the regal government no more destroyed the right to possess or enjoy this property, than it did the right of any other corporation or individual to his or its own property. The dissolution of the form of government did not involve in it a dissolution of civil rights, or an abolition of the common law, under which the inheritances of every man in the State were held. The State itself succeeded only to the rights of the Crown, and, we may add, with many a flower of prerogative struck from its hands. It has been asserted, as a principle of the common law, that the division of an empire creates no forfeiture of previously-vested rights of property. Kelly *v.* Harrison, 2 *John. C.* 29. Jackson *v.* Lunn, 3 *John. C.* 109. Calvin's Case, 8 *Co.* 27. And this principle is equally consonant with the common sense of mankind and the maxims of eternal justice.

Nor are we able to perceive any sound reason why the Church lands escheated or devolved upon the State by the Revolution any more than the property of any other corporation created by the royal bounty or established by the Legislature. The Revolution might justly take away the public patronage, the exclusive cure of souls, and the compulsive taxation for the support of the Church. Beyond these we are not prepared to admit the justice or the authority of legislation.

It is not, however, necessary to rest this cause upon the general doctrines already asserted; for, admitting that by the Revolution the Church lands devolved on the State, the statute of 1776, ch. 2, operated as a new grant and confirmation thereof to the use of the Church.

If the Legislature possessed the authority to make such a grant and confirmation, it is very clear to our minds that it vested an indefeasible and irrevocable title. We have no knowledge of any authority, or principle, which could support the doctrine that a legislative grant is revocable in its own nature, and held only *durante bene placito*. Such a doctrine would uproot the very foundations of almost all the land-titles in Virginia, and is utterly inconsistent with a great and fundamental principle of a republican government,—the right of the citizens to the free enjoyment of their property legally acquired.

It is asserted by the Legislature of Virginia, in 1798 and 1801, that this statute was inconsistent with the Bill of Rights and Constitution of that State, and therefore void. Whatever weight such a declaration might properly have as the opinion of wise and learned men, as a declaration of what the law has been or is, it can have no decisive authority. It is, however, encountered by the opinions successively given by former Legislatures, from the earliest existence of the Constitution itself, which were composed of men of the very first rank for talents and learning. And this opinion, too, is not only a contemporaneous exposition of the Constitution, but has the additional weight that it was promulgated or acquiesced in by a great majority, if not the whole, of the very framers of the Constitution. Without adverting, however, to the opinions on the one side or the other, for the reasons which have been already stated, and others which we forbear to press, as they would lead to too prolix and elementary an examination, we are of opinion that the statute of 1776, ch. 2, is not inconsistent with the Constitution or Bill of Rights of Virginia. We are prepared to go yet further, and to hold that the statutes of 1784, ch. 88, and 1785, ch. 37, were no infringement of any rights secured, or intended to be secured, under the Constitution, either civil, political, or religious.

How far the statute of 1786, ch. 12, repealing the statute of 1784, ch. 88, incorporating the Episcopal churches, and the subsequent statutes in furtherance thereof of 1788, ch. 47 and ch. 53, were consistent with the principles of civil right or the Constitution of Virginia, is a subject of much delicacy, and perhaps not without difficulty. It is observable, however, that they reserve to the churches all their corporate property, and authorize the appointment of trustees to manage the same. A private corporation created by the Legislature may lose its franchises by a misuser or a nonuser of them; and they may be resumed by the Government under a judicial judgment upon a *quo warranto* to ascertain and enforce the forfeiture. This is the common law of the land, and is a tacit condition annexed to the creation of every such corporation. Upon a change of government, too, it may be admitted, that such exclusive privileges attached to a private corporation as are inconsistent with the new Government may be abolished. In respect, also, to public corporations, which exist only for public purposes, such as counties, towns, cities, &c., the Legislature may, under proper limitations, have a right to change, modify, enlarge, or restrain them; securing, however, the property for the uses of those for whom and at whose expense it was originally purchased. But that the Legislature can repeal statutes creating private corporations, or confirming to them property already acquired under the faith of previous laws, and by such repeal can vest the property of such corporations exclusively in the State, or dispose of the same to such purposes as they may please, without the consent or default of the corporators, we are not prepared to admit. And we think ourselves standing upon the principles of natural justice, upon the fundamental laws of every free government, upon the spirit and the letter of the Constitution of the United States, and upon the decisions of most respectable judicial tribunals, in resisting such a doctrine.

The statutes of 1798, ch. 9, and of 1801, ch. 5, are not, therefore, in our judgment, operative so far as to divest the Episcopal Church of the property acquired, previous to the Revolution, by purchase or by donation. In respect to the latter statute, there is this further objection, that it passed after the District of Columbia was taken under the exclusive jurisdiction of Congress, and, as to the corporations and property within that District, the right of Virginia to legislate no longer existed. And as to the statute of 1798, ch. 9, admitting it to have the fullest operation, it merely repeals the statutes passed respecting the Church since the Revolution; and, of course, it left in full force all the statutes previously enacted, so far as they were not inconsistent with the present Constitution. It left, therefore, the important provisions of the statutes of 1661, 1696, 1727, and 1748, so far as respected the title to the Church lands, in perfect vigour, with so much of the common law as attached upon these rights.

Let us now advert to the title set up by the plaintiffs in the present bill. Upon inspecting the deed, which is made a part of the bill, and bears date in 1770, the land appears to have been conveyed to the grantees as churchwardens of the parish of Fairfax, and to their successors in that office forever. It is also averred in the bill that the plaintiffs, together with two of the defendants, (who are churchwardens,) are the vestry of the Protestant Episcopal Church, commonly called the Episcopal Church of Alexandria, in the parish of Fairfax, and that the purchase was made by the vestry of said parish and church, to whom the present vestry are the legal and regular successors in the said vestry; and that the purchase was made for the use and benefit of the said church in the said parish. No statute of Virginia has been cited which creates churchwardens a corporation for the purpose of holding lands; and at common law their capacity was limited to personal estate. 1 *B. C.* 394. *Bro. Corp.* 77, 84. 1 *Roll. Abr.* 393, 4, 10. *Com. Dig. tit. Esglise, F.* 3. 12 *H.* 7, 27, *b.* 13 *H.* 7, 9, *b.* 27 *H.* 6, 30. 1 *Burns's Eccles. Law,* 290. *Gibs.* 215. It would seem, therefore, that the present deed did not operate by way of grant to convey a fee to the churchwardens and their successors; for their successors, as such, could not take; nor to the churchwardens in their natural capacity, for "heirs" is not in the deed. But the covenant of general warranty in the deed binding the grantors and their heirs forever, and warranting the land to the churchwardens and their successors forever, may well operate by way of estoppel to confirm to the Church and its privies the perpetual and beneficial estate in the land.

One difficulty presented on the face of the bill was, that the Protestant Episcopal Church of Alexandria was not directly averred to be the same corporate or unincorporate body as the church and parish of Fairfax, or the legal successors thereto, so as to entitle them to the lands in controversy. But upon an accurate examination of the bill, it appears that the purchase was made by the vestry "of the said parish and church" "for the use and benefit of the said church in the said parish." It must, therefore, be taken as true that there was no other Episcopal church in the parish; and that the property belonged to the Church of Alexandria, which, in this respect, represented the whole parish.   And there can be no doubt that the Episcopal members of the parish of Fairfax have still, notwithstanding a separation from the State of Virginia, the same rights and privileges as they originally possessed in relation to that church while it was the parish-church of Fairfax.

The next consideration is, whether the plaintiffs, who are vestrymen, have, as such, a right to require the lands of the church to be sold in the manner prayed for in the bill.   Upon the supposition that no statutes passed since the Revolution are in force, they may be deemed to act under the previous statutes and the common law.   By those statutes the vestry were to be appointed by the parishioners "for the making and proportioning levies and assessments for building and repairing the churches and chapels, provision for the poor, maintenance of the minister, and such other necessary purposes, and for the more orderly managing all parochial affairs;" out of which vestry the minister and vestry were yearly to choose two churchwardens.   As incident to their office of general guardians of the church, we think they must be deemed entitled to assert the rights and interests of the church.   But the minister also, having the freehold, either in law or in equity, during his incumbency, in the lands of the church, is entitled to assert his own rights as *persona ecclesiæ*.   No alienation, therefore, of the church lands can be made either by himself, or by the parishioners, or their authorized agents, without the mutual consent of both. And therefore we should be of opinion, that, upon principle, no sale ought to be absolutely decreed, unless with the consent of the parson, if the church be full.

If the statute of 1784, ch. 88, be in force for any purpose whatsoever, it seems to us that it would lead to a like conclusion.   If the repealing statute of 1786, ch. 12, or the statute of 1788, ch. 47, by which the Church property was authorized to be vested in trustees chosen by the Church, and their successors, be in force for any purpose whatsoever, then the allegation of the bill that the plaintiffs "have, according to the rules and regulations of their said society, been appointed by the congregation vestrymen and trustees of the said church," would directly apply and authorize the plaintiffs to institute the present bill.   Still, however, it appears to us that in case of a plenarty of the Church, no alienation or sale of the Church lands ought to take place without the assent of the minister, unless such assent be expressly dispensed with by some statute.

On the whole, the majority of the court are of opinion that the land in controversy belongs to the Episcopal Church of Alexandria, and has not been divested by the Revolution, or any Act of the Legislature passed since that period; that the plaintiffs are of ability to maintain the present bill; that the overseers of the poor of the parish of Fairfax have no just, legal, or equitable title to the said land, and ought to be perpetually enjoined from claiming the same; and that a sale of the said land ought, for the reasons stated in the bill, to be decreed, upon the assent of the minister of said church (if any there be) being given thereto; and that the present churchwardens and the said James Wren ought to be decreed to convey the same to the purchaser; and the proceeds to be applied in the manner prayed for in the bill.

The decree of the circuit court is to be reformed, so as to conform to this opinion.

No. X.

John Randolph's Recantation.

Norfolk, April 8, 1857.

Mr. John Randolph, of Roanoke, was at one time deeply impressed with religion, and in a pious frame of mind revised his copy of Gibbon's History of the Decline and Fall of the Roman Empire, which he had filled with notes approving the deistical views of the historian. These notes, or most of them, he obliterated, and on the celebrated fifteenth chapter, in which the historian gives an account of the rise of Christianity, on either side of the text of several pages, he wrote the following remarks, which I now copy for you from the book before me:—

"When the pencilled notes to this and the succeeding chapter were written, (and, indeed, all the notes, one excepted in volume tenth, page —,) the writer was an unhappy young man, deluded by the sophisms of infidelity. Gibbon seemed to rivet what Hume and Hobbes and Bolingbroke and Voltaire, &c. had made fast, and Satan—*i. e.* the evil principle in our (fallen) nature—had cherished; but—praised be His Holy name!—God sent the sense of sin and the arrow of the angel of Death, 'unless ye repent,' straight to his heart, and with it came the desire of belief; but the hard heart of unbelief withstood a long time, and fear came upon him and waxed great, and brought first resignation to his will, and after much refractoriness, (God be praised, but never sufficiently, that he bore with the frowardness of the child of sin, whose wages is death,) after a longer course of years, more than the servitude of Jacob for Rachel, God in his good time sent the pardon and the peace which passeth in the love which struck out fear. Allelujah."

The above is a true transcript from the original pencilled remarks of Mr. Randolph. His copy of Gibbon is in twelve volumes, printed in Dublin in 1784. The book belonged to Richard Randolph, the elder brother of John, and has Richard's name in it, with the endorsement "Matoax, 1790."   Hugh B. Grigsby.

To Bishop Meade.

No. XI.

THE REV. DAVID MOSSOM'S EPITAPH ON HIS TOMBSTONE, AT ST. PETER'S CHURCH, NEW KENT.

M. S.

REVERENDUS David Mossom prope Jacet,
Collegii St. Joannis Cantabrigiæ olim Alumnus,
Hujus Parochiæ Rector Annos Quadraginta.
Omnibus Ecclesiæ Anglicanæ Presbyteriis
Inter Americanos Ordine Presbyteratus Primus ;
Literaturâ Paucis Secundus.
Qui tandem Senio et Mœrore confectus
Ex variis rebus arduis quas in hac vita perpessus est,
Mortisq : in dies memor, ideo virens et valens,
Sibi hunc sepulturæ locum posuit et elegit,
Uxoribus Elizabetha et Maria quidem juxta sepultis
Ubi requiescat, donec resuscitatus ad vitam Eternam
Per Jesum Christum salvatorem nostrum.
Qualis erat, indicant illi quibus bene notus
Superstiles
　　　　　Non hoc sepulchrale saxum.
　　　　　　　　{ Londini Natus 25 Martii 1690.
　　　　　　　　{ Obiit 4° Jan[ii]. 1767.

No. XII.

THE ELLIS FAMILY.

[IN my article on Amherst I omitted any special notice of my old friend Mr. Richard Ellis, of Pedlar Mills or Red Hill.

The following communication from our worthy fellow-citizen, Mr. Thomas Ellis, of Richmond, will more than compensate for the omission.]

April 2, 1857.

The name of ELLIS appears at an early day in connection with the Colony of Virginia. David Ellis came out in the second supply of emigrants from England, and was one of the men sent by Captain Smith to build a house for King Powhatan at his favourite seat, Werowocomico, on York River. John Ellis was one of the grantees in the second charter of the Virginia Company.

My immediate family is of Welsh extraction, and my descent traced to JOHN ELLIS, who settled on Peters's Creek, a branch of Tuckahoe Creek, in Henrico county. He was born in the year 1661, and he appears at Varina, the county seat of Henrico, October 1, 1683. His wife was named Susannah, and their children were John, William, Thomas, Henry, James, Joseph, Mary, and Charles.

JOHN, the eldest son, married Elizabeth Ware, a relation of Baldwin and Ware Rockett, seafaring men, who owned the property in the city of Richmond since called "Rocketts'." He was a magistrate and sheriff of Henrico. His eldest son, who was also named John, inherited the family residence, and lived in it during his life. It still belongs to the family of one of his grand-daughters, who married John Bowles, of Louisa county. The land on which it is situated was patented to William Glover, April 28, 1691, and by him sold to John Ellis (the first named) for two thousand pounds of tobacco.

WILLIAM, the second son, lived to be eighty-three years of age, and died leaving four sons and four daughters. One of his grandsons, William Burton Ellis, who married Elizabeth West, is still living on Tuckahoe, in the seventy-sixth year of his age.

THOMAS, the third son, was inspector of tobacco at Shockoe Warehouse, and owned the coal-property since known as the "Edgehill Pits." He married Elizabeth Patterson, by whom he had two sons and three daughters, all of whom married and have left families.

HENRY, the fourth son, never married. He died in the year 1768.

JAMES, the fifth son, married, but died without issue.

JOSEPH, the sixth son, married Elizabeth Perkins and raised a very numerous family. He has a grandson, Daniel Ellis, born May 2, 1774, now living near Watkinsville, in Goochland county. The Ellises at this day on Tuckahoe Creek are principally the descendants of Joseph Ellis. His will, dated 11th June, 1785, is proved in court January 7, 1793.. His wife died about the year 1798.

MARY, the seventh child and only daughter, married John Smith, who owned the fine farm now belonging to Mr. Robert Edmond, of Richmond, called "Strawberry Hill."

CHARLES, the seventh son, (my great-grandfather,) was born in Henrico county in the year 1719, was married, by the Rev. William Stith, to Susannah Harding, daughter of Thomas Harding and Mary Giles, in the year 1739, and had issue two sons and eight daughters. He removed with his family to the county of Amherst, then the county of Albemarle, in the year 1754, and settled the original seat of the Ellises in that county, since called "Red Hill," on the waters of Pedlar River. He died May 4, 1759, and was buried in the family burying-ground at Red Hill. His widow lived to the ninety-fifth year of her age, and was buried by his side. The children of Charles Ellis and Susannah Harding were

Hannah, Edith, Susannah, Josiah, Mary Ann, Charles, Sarah, Bethena, Elizabeth, and Rosanna.

HANNAH married William Haynes.

EDITH married Devereux Gilliam.

SUSANNAH married Isaac Wright.

JOSIAH married Jane Shelton.

MARY ANN married Peter Carter.

CHARLES married—first, Elizabeth Waters, secondly, Sarah Tucker.

SARAH married John Harrison.

BETHENA married Thomas Leftwich.

ELIZABETH married William Gilliam.

ROSANNA married Charles Davis.

Josiah, (my grandfather,) above named, inherited the "Red Hill" estate, and lived and died there. His wife—a daughter of Richard Shelton—was born September 1, 1747. They were married on the 3d of April, 1766, and had issue John, Nancy, Charles, Richard Shelton, Josiah, Mary Wright, Thomas Harding, Jane Shelton, Lewis, Joshua Shelton, and Powhatan.

[The following letter, from the Rev. Mr. Caldwell, will be read with interest by all who were acquainted with Mr. Richard Ellis, of Red Hill, and his estimable family.]

RICHMOND, VA.

MY DEAR MR. ELLIS:—I fear that I shall be able to communicate very little in regard to the church on Pedlar. Your uncle Richard was one of the old-school, true Virginia gentlemen,—hospitable, unaffected, polite, courteous,—and as regardful of the rights and feelings of a servant as he was of the most favoured and distinguished that visited his house. I had not been in his house five minutes before I felt it to be what he and his delightful family ever afterward made it to me,—a *home*. I, however, experienced at their hands only what every clergyman of our Church who has been connected with the parish experienced.

Your uncle's hospitality was not, however, the most captivating trait of his character. The most captivating trait in his character was his simple-hearted piety and devotion to the Church. His devotion was the same when the ways of our Zion mourned, and when none came to her solemn feasts, and when her sanctuaries in his neighbourhood were levelled by the stranger and the spoiler. I think he told me that the first time the services of our Church were held in the Pedlar neighbourhood after the Revolution, the people met in a tobacco-house, and that many aged persons who had been accustomed to our services in their youth, when the clergyman repeated the sentences and exhortation, stood up and wept like children, big tears coursing their way down their cheeks in spite of every effort to restrain them. The confession following was made, by every one whose feelings did not stifle utterance, with a voice tremulous with emetion. Many an aged heart remembered and returned to its first love. The meeting in that tobacco-house was the beginning of the resuscitation of the church on Pedlar. Your uncle was the foremost and the most liberal in the effort at resuscitation. He gave largely—as he did to the end of life—both of his substance and of his time to the accomplishment of the object. He succeeded, but not without overcoming strong opposition. He applied, for a contribution toward building a church, to a good Christian man in the neighbourhood, who had been a soldier of the Revolution, to whom the old veteran replied, the fire of '76 flashing in his eye and speaking in the tones of his voice, "No! I drew my sword once to put that church down; and, if necessary, I will draw it again to keep it down." No one doubted either the old soldier's honesty or piety. And his reply only revealed the feelings in the minds of many in regard to the Episcopal Church. Their prejudices were as honestly as they were warmly entertained, and nothing but the unbounded confidence they had in the patriotism as well as piety of your uncle softened them. That confidence did soften them, first to tolerate, then to admire, and then to sustain, the Church whose cause he advocated. I am persuaded that the resuscitation of the church on Pedlar was owing altogether to the personal influence of your uncle; and what he was so instrumental in resuscitating he afterwards sustained with a liberality that was bounded only by his means, and a devotion that ended only with his life. His daughter Emily, who became a member of the Church while I was rector of the parish, was as like to her father in her devotion to the Church as a child could be like to a parent. Both she and her most excellent husband, David H. Tapscott, manifested the same fervid and hallowed spirit of devotion in their piety, as well as lively and liberal interest in the advancement of the Church. It grieves me to think that the·Church on earth has lost three such faithful soldiers and servants. And I should be doing violence to my feelings if I did not speak of Mrs Ellis, though a decided Presbyterian, in the same way. If I had been her own son she could hardly have treated me with more kindness. And she had been, I learned, equally kind to all the pastors of her husband. Indeed, I cannot think of any member of the family but with feelings of affectionate regard. I regret that my narrative is so limited and meagre: I hope, however, that it may not be altogether useless to you in accomplishing what you desire for Bishop Meade's Letters.

Truly and sincerely yours,

THOMAS H. ELLIS, ESQ.   DAVID CALDWELL.

No. XIII.

THE BAYLOR FAMILY.

[THE following account has been furnished me by a member of the same.]

JOHN BAYLOR the elder, and first of the name who came to the New World, was born at Tiverton, in England, where, from old Sellers, we learn that he was related to the Freres, Courtenays, Tuckers, Hedjers, Nortons, and others. His son John was born in 1650, and, emigrating to Virginia, was followed by his father, a very old man. He settled in Gloucester county, and was married to Lucy Tod O'Brien, of New Kent, in 1698. Large grants of land had been made to father and son in various parts of the Colony, and the latter, being of an enterprising character, embarked extensively in mercantile schemes, by which a large fortune for that day was amassed,—the inventory of his personal effects amounting to £6500. The books kept at his various counting-houses in Gloucester, King and Queen, and New Kent, from 1692 to 1722, are preserved, and not only attest his method and exactness, but afford an interesting comparison. The relative value of some articles of merchandise then and now is worthy of note. We find nails at four shillings sixpence per pound, cotton at one shilling sixpence per yard; and a Madagascar boy, "from on board ship Tiverton," in one place, is charged to Thomas Randolph at £6, and another at £10. Mention is made of between six and ten ships, belonging to him, at different times, engaged in trading with the Old World. To John Baylor the second and Lucy his wife were born two children,—John, on the 12th of May, 1705, and another whose fortunes we have no means of following. The Essex family of the same name originate here. John, the third of the name, married Lucy Walker at Yorktown, the 2d of January, 1744, several sons and daughters being the issue of this marriage. A sister of Lucy Walker married, at the same time and place, John Norton, of London, of whom we shall have occasion to speak hereafter. John the third (Colonel Baylor) was with Washington at Winchester. He represented the county of Caroline in the House of Burgesses from about 1740 to 1760. A list of the votes at one election is extant, and reveals his extensive popularity, as he received every vote in the county save one. Colonel Baylor moved to New Market— then King and Queen—in 1726, and occupied a grant of land which was made by Robert Tronsdale in behalf of the King the year before. This paper is also preserved. The year following Caroline was formed, and New Market remains in possession of the family, from which it has never been alienated. Extravagance and folly, unfortunately, leave few such instances of successive proprietorship, in the State, for so long a time. The Episcopal church at the Bowling Green was built by Colonel Baylor, and other gentlemen, between 1640 and 1660, where the family continued to worship until the death of the Rev. Mr. Waugh, after which time the church had no minister and the building, like many others in Virginia, was destroyed and the materials devoted to secular purposes. Colonel Baylor held several commissions, one of which, constituting him Lieutenant of the county of Orange, signed by Robert Dinwiddie at Williamsburg in 1752, is in the possession of the family. He too, like his father, was a man of great energy. New Market was in his time celebrated for a large and generous hospitality. John, the eldest son of Colonel Baylor, fourth of the name herein mentioned, was born at New Market on the 4th of September, 1750; was sent at twelve years of age to Putney Grammar-School, from which he was removed to Cambridge, and was a classmate and associate of Mr. Wilberforce. While in Europe, the Letters of Junius appeared, and, for some reason, he felt so deep an interest, either in the subject, style, or authorship, as to transcribe them as they were published,—the manuscript being now in a perfect state of preservation. The performance of a task so laborious as that involved in the copying of these famous letters from the Public Advertiser as they appeared, the numbers of which could have been as well preserved, presents a puzzle which has exercised the minds of his descendants to this day. This John Baylor the fourth was married, while in England, to Fanny, his cousin, only daughter of John and Courtenay Norton, of Gould Square, London, and returned to Virginia. They were followed by the brothers of Mrs. Baylor, John Hatley, George, and Daniel Norton, who married in Virginia, leaving issue. Several of their descendants have devoted their lives to the ministry. The Rev. John H. Norton, of Fauquier, is one of them. George, the second son of Colonel Baylor and Fanny Walker, was born at New Market the 12th of January, 1752. He was aid to General Washington at the battle of Trenton, and enjoyed the honour of presenting the colours then taken to the Congress at Philadelphia, and would doubtless have filled a large space in the stirring history of the times, had not a bayonet-wound through the chest, in a night-skirmish a short time after, disabled him so as to unfit him for the service. He died of pulmonary disease, from this injury, in Barbadoes in 1784. The regiment of horse which bore his name sprung into existence from his patriotic exertions and from the pecuniary aid of his elder brother, which was freely given.

Colonel George Baylor married, at Mansfield, Lucy Page, daughter of Mann Page, Esq., by whom he had one son,—John W. Baylor. Mrs. Baylor, widow of Colonel George Baylor, was married a second time, to Colonel N. Burwell, of Millwood, Frederick county, Virginia. Walker, fourth son of Colonel Baylor, was a captain in the Revolutionary army. He was also disabled, by a spent ball, which crushed his instep, at Germantown or Brandywine, which made him a cripple for life. He married Miss Bledsoe, and left several sons and daughters, one of whom—Judge R. E. B. Baylor—is now alive and is a prominent citizen of Texas. Robert, fourth son of Colonel Baylor, married Miss Gwinn, of Gwinn's Island. Lucy, third daughter of Colonel Baylor, was married to Colonel John Armistead, 17th of March, 1764. The sons by this marriage were all endued with martial spirit. Lewis was killed in battle in Canada; George defended Baltimore when attacked by the British in the war of 1812; and two other brothers occupied distinguished rank in the army of their country. John and Fanny Norton resided at New Market, and were the parents of two sons and five daughters, who intermarried with the Claytons, Upshaws, Foxes, Roys, &c. John Walker Baylor also left children. The Brents and Horners belong to this branch.

JOHN ROY BAYLOR, *of New Market, Caroline county.*

No. XIV.

THE PEYTON FAMILY.

[THE following limited account of this family has been sent me by a friend. In the civil and ecclesiastical lists the name may be found at an early day.]

JOHN PEYTON, Esq., of Stafford county, Virginia, who died in 1760, was twice married. By his first wife his children were Yelverton, Henry, and Ann Waye. By the second wife they were John Rowzee, and Valentine.

1. Yelverton had four sons and four daughters. One of the daughters—Elizabeth—married her cousin, John Peyton Harrison; and Catherine married Captain William Bronaugh, of Stafford, who moved to Kanawha and is the father of a numerous family, the most of whom now live in Missouri.

Of the sons of Yelverton, Henry was a pious Methodist preacher, and married a Miss Brent, of Fauquier; and another of his sons—Colonel Samuel Peyton—was the father of Yelverton, William, and Henry, all of whom were talented and pious ministers of the Methodist Church, and died young, leaving each one child.

2. Henry, the second son of John Peyton, married a Miss Fowke, and resided near the Plains, in Fauquier county. He was a pious member of the Episcopal Church. One of his sons—Dr. Chandler Peyton—married Eliza B. Scott, the eldest daughter of the Rev. John Scott; and another son—Yelverton—married Margaret, the youngest daughter of the Rev. Mr. Scott. She, after his death, married Mr. Charles Lee, and then Mr. Glassell.

3. Ann Waye, the daughter of John Peyton, married Mr. Thomas Harrison, of Stafford. She had a son named John Peyton Harrison, who

married his cousin, Elizabeth Peyton, and has left many descendants; and another son—Thomas—who was an Episcopal minister and the father of Philip Harrison, Esq., late of Richmond.

4. John Rowzee, the third son of John Peyton, was the father of John Howard Peyton, of Staunton, of General Bernard Peyton, of Richmond, and of Mr. Rowzee Peyton, who has moved to the State of New York.

5. Doctor Valentine Peyton, the fourth son of John Peyton, resided at the family seat, Tusculum, in Stafford, and was the father of Mrs. John Conway, of Stafford Court-House, and Mrs. Chichester, who resides near the Falls Church, in Fairfax county, and of many others.

No. XV.

MINISTERS AND VESTRYMEN OF ST. STEPHEN'S AND WICOMICO PARISHES, NORTHUMBERLAND.

[To the diligence of the Rev. Edmund Withers, minister of Lancaster county, I am indebted for the following lists, taken from an old vestry-book recently discovered by him.]

MINISTERS OF ST. STEPHEN'S (CALLED UPPER AND LOWER) PARISH, NORTHUMBERLAND COUNTY.

March 20, 1712,	Rev. John Span,	to	1722.
October 23, 1723,	" John Bell, for eight sermons at 450 pounds tobacco a-piece.		
1723,	" Lawrence De Butts,	to	1726.
1724,	" Mr. Lecharcey, for two sermons, 600 pounds tobacco.		
1726,	" John Blacknall.		
1727,	" William Wye,	to	1731.
1731,	" Francis Peart,	to	1742.
1742,	" Henry Christall,	to	1743.
1743,	" Moses Robertson,	to	——
——,	" David Morthland,	to	1754.
1754,	" Thomas Smith,	to	1758.
1758,	" James Crague,	to	——
1758,	" Adam Minzies,	to	1767.
1767,	" Benjamin Sebastian,	to	1777.
1779,	" Thomas Davis,	to	1786.
1792,	" Thomas Andrews	to	1794.

VESTRYMEN OF ST. STEPHEN'S PARISH, (UPPER AND LOWER,) NORTHUMBERLAND COUNTY.

1712. Col. Peter Hack,
Capt. Christopher Neale,
Capt. John Cralle,
Mr. John Clughton,
Mr. Richard Hull,
Capt. Richard Hews,
Capt. Francis Kenner,
Mr. Edward Coles.
1714. Mr. Griffin Fantleroy,
Capt. Richard Span,
Mr. John Opie,
Mr. David Straughan.
1716. Col. Peter Presley.
1720. Capt. Edward Sanders,
Mr. Thomas Hughlett,
Mr. Thomas Cralle.
1721. Capt. Richard Kenner.
1724. Mr. John Sharpleigh,
Mr. Samuel Bonom,
Mr. John Lewis,
Capt. Samuel Blackwell.
1728. Mr. Robert Clark,
Capt. John Waughop.
1731. Mr. John Foushee,
Mr. Thomas Gill,
Mr. Matthew Kenner,
Capt. John Hack.
1738. Mr. Travers Colston,
Mr. Spencer Ball
1742. Capt. Cuthbert Span,
Mr. Ellis Gill,
Capt. William Taite.
1749. Col. Presley Thornton.

1752. Mr. Newton Keane.
1754. Wynder Kenner.
1758. Parrish Garner,
Samuel Blackwell, Jr.,
Capt. Spencer Mottram Ball.
1763. Mr. Kenner Cralle,
Mr. Thomas Jones.
1770. Mr. Rodham Kenner,
John Williams,
Joseph Ball,
Edward Nelmes.
1772. James Ball.
1778. Matthew Neale,
William Eskridge.
1779. Joseph Williams,
Henry Boggess,
Elisha Harcum,
John Rogers,
Abram Beacham,
James Claughton,
Pemberton Claughton,
John Anderson.
1781. Walter Jones,
John Cottrell,
William Nelmes,
Peter Cox,
Thomas Hudnall,
Lindsey Opie,
Daniel Muse,
Hudson Muse,
Joseph Hudnall.
1794. Catesby Jones.

MINISTERS FOR WICOMICO PARISH, NORTHUMBERLAND COUNTY.

May 15, 1770, Rev. John Leland, to 1791.
1791, " John Bryan, to 1794, (expelled.)
1794, " David Ball, to 1799.
1799, " Duncan MacNaughton, to ——
1798, " John Seward, 50 pounds for services during this year.

VESTRYMEN OF WICOMICO PARISH, NORTHUMBERLAND COUNTY.

1770. John Eustace,
     Col. Thos. Gaskins,
     Capt. David Ball, Sr.,
     Capt. John Heath,
     Capt. David Ball, Jr.,
     Capt. Thos. Gaskins,
     Mr. Geo. Dameron,
     Mr. Wm. Taylor.
1772. Mr. Chas. Coppedge,
     Col. Chas. Lee.
1775. Mr. John Lawson,
1777. Mr. Kendall Lee.
     Capt. Wm. Nutt,
     Mr. Thos. Edwards,
     Capt. Wm. Davenport.
1784. Mr. Wm. Lee,
     Capt. Geo. Ingram,
     Mr. Isaac Baysie,

1784. Mr. Thos. Hurst,
     Capt. John H. Fallin,
     Mr. Mosley Nutt,
     Onesiphorus Harvey,
     Hopkins Harding,
     David Ball,
     Richard Hudnall,
     James Sutton,
     Chas. Lattimore,
     Capt. Geo. Ball.
1794. Thos. Hurst, Jr.,
     David Palmer.
1796. Henry L. Gaskins,
     Wm. Blackerby,
     Cyrus Harding,
     Henry Cundiff,
     Thos. W. Hughlett,
     Thos. Harvey.

No. XVI.

EXTRACTS FROM RALPHE HAMOR.

EDITION PRINTED AT LONDON BY JOHN BEALE, FOR WILLIAM WESLEY; DWELL-
ING AT THE SIGNE OF THE SWANNE, IN PAUL'S CHURCHYARD, 1615.

[MR. HAMOR was a man of high standing in the Colony. His residence
was at Bermuda Hundred, a few miles only from Henricopolis, where Sir
Thomas Dale and the Rev. Alexander Whittaker lived. He appears to
have been intimate with them both and to have partaken of their pious
spirit. It is one evidence of the estimation in which he was held, that
the severest punishment ever inflicted in the Colony was on a man who
uttered slanderous words against Mr. Hamor. Mr. Hamor's work, from
which we take the following extracts, was obtained by Mr. Conway
Robinson, of Richmond, on a late visit to England, and presented to the
Historical Society of Virginia. It is the most reliable and authentic
work on the early history of Virginia.

His religious character, and that of the age, is seen in the following
introductory passage.]

Sure, young though in years and knowledge, I may be said to be, yet
let me remember, to thee perhaps much knowing Reader, what the wisest

man that ever writ or spake (excepting him that was both God and man)
hath said, that such who bring others unto righteousnesse, shal themselves
shine as the stars in the firmament.   And doubtlesse I doe beleive even
amongst the rest of my Articles, when these poore Heathens shall be
brought to entertaine the honour of the name, and glory of the Gospell
of our blessed Saviour, when they shall testifie of the true and ever-living
God, and Jesus Christ to be their salvation, their knowledge so inlarged
and sanctified, that without him they confesse their eternal death : I do
believe I say (and how can it be otherwise ?) that they shal breake out and
cry with the rapture of so inexplicable mercie : Blessed be the King and
Prince of England, and blessed be the English Nation, and blessed forever
be the most high God, possessor of Heaven and earth, that sent these
English as Angels to bring such glad tidings amongst us.   These will be
doubtlesse the empaticke effects and exultation of this so Christian worke,
and may these nothing move !   Alas let Sanballat, and Tobiah, Papests
and Plaiers, Ammonites and Horonites, the scumme and dregges of the
people, let them mocke at this holy Businesse, they that be filthie, let
them be filthie still, and let such swine wallow in the mire, but let not
the rod of the wicked fall upon the lot of the righteous nor let them
shrinke back, and call in their helpes from this so glorious enterprise,
which the Prophet Isaiah cals, the declaring of God to the left hand, but
let them that know the worke, rejoice and be glad in the happie successe
of it, proclaiming that it is the everlasting God that raigneth in England,
and unto the ends of the world.

   [The following is the true and full account of the capture of Pocahontas
by Captain Argall.]

   It chaunced Powhatans delight and darling, his daughter Pocahuntas,
(whose fame hath even bin spred in England by the title of Nonparella
of Virginia,) in her princely progresse, if I may so terme it, tooke some
pleasure (in the absence of Captaine Argall) to be among her friends at
Pataomecke (as it seemeth by the relation I had) imploied thither, as
shopkeepers to a Fare, to exchange some of her fathers commodities for
theirs, where residing some three months or longer, it fortuned upon
occasion either of promise or profit, Captaine Argall to arrive there, whom
Pocahuntas, desirous to renew her familiaritie with the English, and delighting to see them, as unknowne, fearefull perhaps to be surprised, would
gladly visit, as she did, of whom no sooner had Captaine Argall intelligence,
but he delt with an old friend, and adopted brother of his, Japazeus, how and
by what means he might procure her captive, assuring him, that now or
never, was the time to pleasure him, if he intended indeede that love which
he had made profession of, that in ransome of hir he might redeeme some of
our English men and armes, now in the possession of her Father, promising
to use her withall faire, and gentle entreaty : Japazeus well assured that
his brother, as he promised would use her curteously promised his best

indevours and secresie to accomplish his desire, and thus wrought it, making his wife an instrument (which sex have ever bin most powerfull in beguiling inticements) to effect his plot which hee had thus laid, he agreed that himselfe, his wife, and Pocahuntas, would accompanie his brother to the water side, whether come, his wife should faine a great and longing desire to goe aboorde, and see the shippe, which being there three or four times, before she had never seen, and should be earnest with her husband to permit her : he seemed angry with her, making as he pretended so unnecessary a request, especially being without the company of women, which deniall she taking unkindly, must faine to weepe (as who knows not that women can command teares) whereupon her husband seeming to pity those counterfeit teares, gave her leave to goe aboord, so that it would please Pocahuntas to accompany her : now was the greatest labour to win her, guilty perhaps of her fathers wrongs, though not knowne as she supposed, to goe with her, yet by her earnest perswasions, she assented : so forthwith aboorde they went, the best cheere that could be made was seasonably provided, to supper they went, merry on all hands, especially Japazeus and his wife, who to express their joy, would ere be treading upō Capt. Argalls foot, as who should say tis don, she is your own. Supper ended, Pocahuntas was lodged in the Gunner's roome, but Japazeus and his wife desired to have some conference with their brother, which was onely to acquaint him by what strategem, they had betraid his prisoner, as I have already related : after which discourse to sleepe they went, Pocahuntas nothing mistrusting this policy, who nevertheles being most possessed with feare, and desire of returne, was first up, and hastened Japazeus to be gon. Capt. Argall having secretly well rewarded him, with a small copper kettle, and some other les valuable toies so highly by him esteemed, that doubtlesse he would have betraid his owne father for them, permitted both him and his wife to returne, but told him, that for divers considerations, as for that his father had then eight of our English men, many swords, peices and other tooles, which he had at severall times by trecherous murdering our men, taken from them, which though of no use to him, he would not redeliver, he would reserve Pocahuntas, whereat she began to be exceeding pensive and discontented, yet ignorant of the dealing of Japazeus, who in outward appearance was no les discontented, that he should be the meanes of hir captivity, much adoe there was to perswade her to be patient, which with extraordinary curteous usage, by little and little was wrought in her, and so to Jamestowne she was brought, a messenger to her father forthwith despatched to advertise him that his *only* daughter was in the hands and possession of the English : ther to be kept til such time as he would ransom her with our men, swords, peices and other tools treacherously taken from us : the news was unwelcome, and troublesom unto him, partly for the love he bare to his daughter, and partly for the love he bare to our men his prisoners, of whom though with us they were unapt for any imployment, he made great use : and those swords, and peices of ours, (which though of no use to him) it delighted him to view and look upon.

[The following is from the account of Sir Thomas Dale's visit to Powhatan at his residence, when he took Pocahontas with him and informed the king of the attachment between her and Mr. Rolfe, not long before their marriage. Mr. Hamor was of the party, and then presented Mr. Rolfe's letter to Thomas Dale, which we have published.]

Long before this time a gentleman of approved behaviour and honest cariage, Maister John Rolfe, had bin in love with Pocahuntas and she with him, which thing at the instant that we were in parlee with them, myselfe made known to Sir Thomas Dale by a letter from him, whereby he intreated his advise and furtherance in his love, if so it seemed fit to him for the good of the Plantation, and Pocahuntas herselfe, acquainted her brethren therewith : which resolution Sir Thomas Dale well approving, was the onely cause, hee was so milde amongst them, who otherwise would not have departed their river without other conditions.

The bruite of this pretended marriage came soon to Powhatans knowledge, a thing acceptable to him, as appeared by his sudden consent thereunto, who some ten daies after sent an old uncle of hirs, named Opachisco, to give her as his deputy in the church, and two of his sonnes to see the marriage solemnized, which was accordingly done about the fift of Aprill, and ever since we have had friendly commerce and trade, not onely with Powhatan himselfe but also with his subjects round about us; so as I now see no reason why the collonie should not thrive apace.

The Attempt of Sir Thomas Dale to get another Daughter of Powhatan, as a Surer Pledge of Peace.

It pleased Sir Thomas Dale (myselfe being much desirous before my retourne for England,) to visit Powhatan & his court, (because I would be able to speak somwhat thereof by mine own knowledge) to imploy myselfe, and an English boy for my Interpreter one Thomas Salvage (who had lived three years with Powhatan, and speakes the language naturally, one whom Powhatan much affecteth) upon a message unto him, which was to deale with him, if by any meanes I might procure a daughter of his, who (Pocahuntas being already in our possession) is generally reported to be his delight, and darling, (and surely he esteemeth her as his owne soule) for surer pledge of peace.

*Letter of Mr. Whittaker to his cousin, the Minister of Black-Friars'
Bridge, London, declaring the pious character of Sir Thomas Dale,
and confirming the fact of the baptism of Pocahontas before her
marriage. Taken from Mr. Hamor's book.*

To my verie deere and loving cosen M. G. Minister of the B. F. in
London.

Sir the colony here is much better. Sir Thomas Dale our religious
and valient Governour, hath now brought that to passe which never
before could be effected. For by warre upon our enemies, and kind usage
of our friends, he hath brought them to seek for peace of us which is
made, and they dare not breake. But that which is best, one Pocahuntas or Matoa the daughter of Powhatan is married to an honest and
descreete English Gentleman, Maister Rolfe, and that after she had
openly renounced her countrey Idolatry, confessed the faith of Jesus
Christ, and was baptized; which thing Sir Thomas Dale had laboured a
long time to ground in her.

Yet notwithstanding, are the vertuous deeds of this worthy Knight,
much debased, by the letters some wicked men have written from hence,
and especially by one C. L. If you heare any condemne this noble Knight,
or doe feare to come hither for those slanderous letters, you may upon
my word bouldly reprove them. You know that no malefactors can abide
the face of the Judge, but themselves scorning to be reproved, doe prosecute withal hatred, all those that labour their emendment. I marvaile
much that any men of honest life, should feare the sword of the magistrate, which is unsheathed onely in their defence.

Sir Thomas Dale (with whom I am) is a man of great knowledge in
Divinity, and of a good conscience in all his doings: both which bee rare
in a martiall man. Every Sabbath day we preach in the forenoone, and
chatechize in the afternoone. Every Saturday at night I exercise in Sir
Thomas Dales house. Our church affairs bee consulted on by the minister,
and foure of the most religious men. Once every month wee have a communion, and once a yeer a solemn Fast. For me, though my promis of
3 years service to my country be expired, yet I will abide in my vocation
here untill I be lawfully called from hence. And so, betaking us all unto
the mercies of God in Christ Jesus, I rest for ever

Your most deere and
loving cosen,
ALEX. WHITAKERS.

VIRGINIA, June 18, 1614.

No. XVII.

THE BROKENBROUGH AND FAUNTLEROY FAMILIES.

[AFTER supposing that my work was done, a box of papers has been sent me by a friend,* from which, and a brief notice by himself, I have drawn the following particulars concerning some members of the abovementioned families.]

Colonel William Brokenbrough, the first of the name in Virginia of whom we have any information, settled in Richmond county and married a Miss Fauntleroy. The Rev. Mr. Giberne married her sister. The sons of Colonel Brokenbrough were Austin, who married a Miss Champe, daughter of Colonel Champe, of King George. The children of Austin Brokenbrough were Champe, who married a Miss Bowie, of Port Royal, and left no sons. His surviving daughters are Mrs. Thornton, Mrs. Peyton, and Mrs. George Fitzhugh, of Port Royal. The other son of Austin Fitzhugh was John, who became an Episcopal clergyman,—a learned, amiable, but somewhat eccentric man. He left one son,—Austin, —who married a daughter of the late General Brown, of the United States Army. The daughters of the first Austin Brokenbrough were Lucy, who married a Mr. Alexander, of King George, and, at his death, a Captain Quarles, of Orange; Elizabeth, who married the Rev. James Elliott; Jane, who married Mr. Thomas Pratt, of King George, and was the mother of Mrs. William and Benjamin Grymes and Mrs. Dangerfield Lewis, of King George. At the death of Mr. Pratt, Jane married Mr. Taliafero, of Blenheim. Newman Brokenbrough, the second son of Colonel William Brokenbrough, left no children. More, the third son, was the father of the late Colonel William Brokenbrough, of Richmond county. John, the remaining son, was the father of the late Judge William Brokenbrough, of the Court of Appeals, Dr. John Brokenbrough, of Richmond, President of the Bank of Virginia, Thomas Brokenbrough, also of Richmond, Arthur Brokenbrough, of the University of Virginia, and of Dr. Austin Brokenbrough, of Tappahannock.

The first Austin Brokenbrough, son of Colonel William, was a man of no little notoriety in Virginia. He was in the English army with Washington, under General Braddock, but took a very different view of his obligation to the Crown from General Washington. He, like some of the old clergy, thought that he was perpetually bound by his oath of allegiance to the King. He wished, however, to remain in America, as he had a father, brother, children, and property here. He was willing to be passive and obey our laws, but could not unite in what he considered re-

---

* Mr. George Fitzhugh, of Port Royal.

bellion. This, however, did not suit the times and Virginia, especially the Northern Neck. In the year 1775, he sent in a petition to the Assembly, asking leave to remain in Virginia on the terms above mentioned, which was rejected. Nor only this, but not less than five companies of men from Richmond, Caroline, and Westmoreland counties came to his house, determined on some signal punishment, if not the taking of his life, which he avoided by flying to England in a vessel about to sail from Hobbs's Hole. His father and brother, though respecting his motives for adhering to the Crown, joined themselves to the American party. I have had access to a diary kept by this Austin Brokenbrough from the time he set sail in 1775 to the time of his return at the close of the war, and also to letters of the family. Although the diary is much mutilated, enough remains to enable us to form a just estimate of his character and a correct view of himself and companions in England during the war. Some of them had been officers in the army with him, but most of them were gentlemen from Virginia who sympathized with him. From his diary it would seem that they had a merry time of it while in England, especially in London, their chief place of rendezvous. But, in order to relieve the tedium of such a state of idleness and suspense, the American loyalists determined to form themselves into a company and offer their services to the King in case of a threatened invasion from France. When the time for electing officers arrived, a Lord Pepperell and John Randolph of Virginia, brother of Speaker Randolph, were the candidates for the captaincy. The former gained it by two votes. Major Grymes, who married Mr. Randolph's daughter, was made ensign of the company. The King most graciously accepted their offer. There was, however, no need of their services. Mr. Randolph, it is said, died of a broken heart, and made it his last request that his remains should be brought back to Williamsburg and deposited in the College chapel, which request was granted. Mr. Grymes also returned to Virginia. While in London the American loyalists seem to have had a merry time of it, dining and supping together at various inns, and having more private lodgings. Those who approved their principles and conduct were not wanting in hospitality to them,—especially Lord Dunmore, who either lived in London or was often there. Among those who consorted together I find the names not only of Randolph, Grymes, and Brokenbrough, but of Corbin, Beverley, Maury, Brackenridge, Kirkpatrick, Wormley, Madison, Burnley, Marshall, Norton, Gilmore, Innis, Steuart, Walker, Williamson, Richardson, Fitch, Rhoan, Delany, Loyd, Stephenson. All of them appear to have been Americans,—most of them Virginians. Whether they were all disaffected to the American cause, or whether other considerations may not have carried them thither, I know not. Mr. Brokenbrough seems to have been intimate with them all.

Time seems to have hung heavy on Mr. Brokenbrough's hands. He appears to have been more temperate than some of his companions, either

English or American, and more chaste in his speech, for he expresses himself quite shocked at some things in his intercourse with them; yet he speaks of taking two dinners at different taverns with one of them in the same day, and again two suppers the same night, and being quite drunk, with all the rest of his company, on one occasion. The manners and morals of London must have been very bad at that time. Mr. Brokenbrough exhibits a very varied character in his diary. At one time we have a humorous parody on a passage in Shakspeare; then one of Addison's hymns is copied into it. Now he visits the King's Chapel in the morning, dines with a friend, and, "after bottle, goes to St. Thomas's." Now he is in other churches, and speaks in praise of the sermons, and now at different theatres, and with a company of ladies at Vauxhall, all of whom, except the young ladies, drank too freely and were vociferous.

While in Glasgow he heard the celebrated Dr. Robertson, the historian, preach, and represents his delivery as the most inanimate and uninteresting, though his style was good and some sentences striking. Much of his time while in London was spent in hearing the debates in Parliament, especially those on American affairs. He was present when Lord Chatham delivered his last speech and fainted and was carried home. His account of it is quite good. After spending seven years in this manner, he becomes very desirous to return to Virginia. During his absence his father and youngest son died, and his property was wasting away through mismanagement and was in danger of confiscation. In the year 1782 he came over, and we find him in a vessel at Boyd's Hole, but is advised by his brother not to venture farther. After this he is in Charleston, S.C. At what time he actually resettled himself in Virginia does not appear. While at Boyd's Hole, on board the "Flag," he addresses a long letter to Mrs. Tayloe, of Mount Airy, whose husband died during the war. The letter is in reply to inquiries concerning some friends and relatives in England. An extract from it will be interesting to some of my readers.

"DEAR MADAM:—I received your favour by my brother, and should not have delayed returning my thanks for your kindness to my family and benevolent wishes to myself had it not been that I am under severe restrictions in a very small cabin. I lament the unhappy state of my native country and the causes which separated me from my family, and nothing is left for me but to be humbly content. It gives me pleasure that good people and those I respect sympathize with me. The prayers of such will, I hope, fly up to heaven. My prayers—God help me!—for seven long years have availed nothing; yet I shall still most cordially join them that Great Britain and America may be again cemented by mutual interests and that an honourable peace may soon take place. Should it be otherwise, I hope the din of war will never approach so near to Mount Airy as to produce the least disquietude or in any manner disturb your repose. May your son be a great comfort to you! I am told he very much resembles your papa, and I most sincerely wish that he may emulate his good qualities and eminent virtues. To surpass them can scarcely be expected,—that so rarely falling to the lot of man. I cannot, dear madam, help being highly interested in the welfare of a youth whose father always took pleasure in rendering my family his best services,* and laid me under particular obligation, and gave the most lively instances of generosity and humanity, unsolicited, at a time when party prejudices ran high and sorely against me, and in the moment when I was reduced to the most lamentable and critical situation that man could be driven into."

It seems that Colonel Tayloe, though on the American side, had gone as far as he could in behalf of Mr. Brokenbrough, and then warned him of his danger. The brothers of Mr. Brokenbrough were decidedly American, as is seen by their letters. The following extract from one of Mr. Newman Brokenbrough's shows that he took a religious view of the war:—

"The direful scene of war now carried on by Britain upon this continent is truly melancholy. No man could have thought that Englishmen and Christians could have so far degenerated from humanity as to be guilty of such barbarity as is acted upon the people of this continent. The most savage race in any age of the world would blush at it. However it may not be thought, on your side of the water, to be more severe than the nature of the offence deserves, yet I would beg leave to observe that people are never the sooner convinced of error by such measures, and that it rather incites them to revenge than deters them from war. Upon reflection we may plainly discover the cause of such calamity. The wickedness and impiety of the present profligate age requires an iron rod for chastisement. You are now in a country where iniquity abounds, and if you won't be wilfully blind you may discover the great degeneracy of the British nation from their ancient purity."

Mr. Austin Brokenbrough in his diary mentions one instance of this which shocks him,—viz.: the fact that the English Government sought, through Governor Johnson, of New York, to bribe some of the members of the American Congress. There was a nobleness of soul in him which revolted at this.

To the above gleanings from the fragments which have been sent me, I must add something concerning one member of this family from personal knowledge. With Dr. John Brokenbrough, of Richmond, President of the Bank of Virginia, I was long and intimately acquainted. His house was my home during many years whenever I visited Richmond, and we freely corresponded at other times. A more amiable man is not easily found. He took an active part in the building of the Monumental Church, and was during Bishop Moore's life the vestryman to whom he referred most frequently for council. And yet he was for a long time

---

* Colonel William Brokenbrough was a ward of Colonel Tayloe.

beset with skeptical opinions, and often lamented to me the difficulty of eradicating them. They were the result of the early teachings of Mr. Ogilvie, who did so much injury to the youth of Virginia. Mr. Austin Brokenbrough speaks of this gentleman in his diary as one with whom he became acquainted in England. How he came to Virginia I am unable to say, but he became a teacher in Tappahannock, and Dr. Brokenbrough either was his pupil, or heard those infidel lectures which he delivered in various parts of Virginia and which ruined so many of her young men. I have reason to believe that these unhappy doubts ceased to disturb the mind of Dr. Brokenbrough, and trust that he died in the true faith of the Christian.

THE FANTLEROY FAMILY, NOW SPELLED FAUNTLEROY.

This is a very ancient and numerous family of Virginia. The name is often found in the old vestry-books. I have not been able to get any genealogical account of it, but Henning's "Statutes at Large" makes frequent mention of Major Moore Fantleroy at a very early period, and I have recently received a document of some interest, dated 1651, in which he is one of the chief parties, which I shall present to the reader. Major Fantleroy lived in the Northern Neck, and kept the Indians in that region in order by his military talents. In the year 1651 he purchased a large tract of land from one of the tribes, as the following contract shows:—

At a machcomacoi held the 4th of April, 1651, at Rappahannock,—Accopatough, Wionance, Toskicough, Coharneittary, Pacauta, Mamogueitan, Opathittara, Cakarell James, Minniaconaugh, Kintassa-hacr.

To all people to whom these presents shall come, both English and Indians, know ye that I, Accopatough, the right-born and true king of the Indians of Rappahannock Town and Townes, and of all the land thereto belonging, do hereby, for and in consideration of ten fathom of peake and goods, amounting to thirty arms'-length of Rohonoke already in hand received, and for the love and affection which I the king, and all my men, do bear unto' my loving friend and brother, Moor Fantleroy, who is likewise now immediately to go with me unto Pasbyhaies unto the governor, and safely to convey me and my men back again hither unto Rappahannock, for which and in consideration thereof I do hereby bargain and sell, give, grant, and confirm, and by this present indenture have bargained, sold, given, granted, conveyed, and fully confirmed unto the said Fantleroy, his heirs and assigns forever, a certain p'cell of land situate, lying, and being in two necks on the north side of Rappahannock Creek, beginning for breadth at the southernmost branch or creek of Macaughtions bay or run, and so up along by the side of the said river of Rappahannock, unto a great creek or river which run—Totosha or Tanks Rappahannock Town; for length extending easterly with its full breadth unto the bounds of the Potowmack River at the uttermost bounds of my land. To have, hold, and enjoy all and singular the aforesaid lands and waters, with all and every part and parcel thereof, lying and being as aforesaid, unto the said Fantleroy, his heirs, executors, administrators, and assigns forever, so long as the sun and moon endureth, with all the appurtenances, rights, liberties, commodities, and profits whatsoever thereunto belonging, in as full and as ample manner as ever I, the said king, or any of my predecessors, ever had or could have had, by for me. My heirs and successors fully assuring the said Fantleroy, his heirs and assigns, forever peaceably and quietly to enjoy all and every part and parcel of the said land without any manner of lett, losses, molestations, or disturbance whatsoever proceeding from me or any Indian or Indians whatsoever, now or hereafter, may or shall belong unto me or any of my heirs, assigns, or successors, hereby giving unto my said brother full power, leave, license, and authority to punish, correct, beat, or kill any Indian or Indians whatsoever, which shall contrary to the intent of this my act and deed presume to molest, harm, or offer any manner of harm, wrong, injury, or violence upon the said land, or any part of it, unto the said Fantleroy, his heirs, executors, administrators, or assigns, or any whomsoever he or they shall seat, place, or put upon any part or parcel of the abovesaid land hereby given, and granted, and alienated as aforesaid. In witness whereof, and to the true and full intent and meaning is hereof, with a full knowledge and understanding of this present act and deed, I, the said king, in the presence of my said great men and divers others of my Indians, have hereunto signed and sealed, the fourth day of April, one thousand six hundred and fifty-one. Signed, sealed, and possession given by tree and turf,

ACCOPATOUGH, (SEAL.)

JOHN EDGECOMBE,   NATHA BATSON,
ALEXANDER CAMPLER,   FRANC: MARSH.

This eleventh of May, one thousand six hundred and fifty-one, we, Touweren, the great King of Rappahannock and Moratoerin, do hereby fully ratify and confirm the above said act and deed unto our loving brother Fantleroy, his heirs and assigns. Witness our hand and seals the day above written.

Witnesses: TOUWEREN,   MACHAMAP.
WILLIAM FOOTE,   (SEAL.)   (SEAL.)
FRAN. MARSH,
NATHA BATSON
    (A copy.)   (Teste.)   WILSON ALLEN, C. G. C.

Colonel Fantleroy was probably a man of high and fearless temper. It is on record that on a certain occasion, when he was a member of the House of Burgesses, something occurred which greatly displeased him, and led to such strong denunciation of the Assembly that he was expelled for insulting its members. On the following morning, however, he was reinstated.

The following extract from a communication from Dr. Henry Faunt Le Roy, of Naylor's Hole, Richmond county, furnished at my request, is added to what has been said about the Faunt Le Roys.

The family is of French origin. After their increase they became dispersed, and, from what I can gather, had something to do with the struggles between the Catholics and Huguenots or French Protestants. Some remained in their native land, some crossed the Channel, and one came to America and settled in Virginia at an early period. The last-named, Moore Faunt Le Roy, purchased from the aborigines a very large tract of land on the Rappahannock River, above and below the creek of the same name, and located. How many children he had, I know not. The only written record which I have is in an old family Bible, in which appears the name of my great-grandfather, whose name was William. He was born in 1684, was married to Apphia Bushrod, had three sons and seven daughters, and died in 1757. The sons were William, Moore, and John. The first-named was my grandfather, and was born in 1713 and died in 1793. The second was born in 1716; death not mentioned. His children moved from the Northern Neck to King and Queen, where their descendants now live. The third was born in 1724 : when he died is not mentioned. My grandfather (who was called Colonel William Faunt Le Roy) was twice married. By the first wife he had one daughter, (Elizabeth,) who became the wife of Mr. Adams, of James River, after having refused her hand to General George Washington. By his second union (with Miss Murdock) he had seven sons and three daughters. One married Colonel Turner, near Leedstown, another Mr. Carter, of Amherst; a third died single. The eldest two of the sons (William and Moore) as was customary in the good old days of the aristocracy, received the greatest share of attention, and, in accordance with the usages of the times, were sent to Europe (home, as it was then called) to be educated. They were medical students at Edinburgh and Aberdeen,—one fourteen and the other seven years. William died soon after his return. Moore lived for some time after his return in Tappahannock, Essex county. On account of bad health, he did not do much professionally. He died in Charleston, S. C., in 1802, at the house of the Rev. Wm. Wilson Henry. The youngest son but my father was very chivalrous in character, enlisted in the Revolutionary army, and became a favourite with the commander-in-chief. He was killed in the battle of Monmouth, N.J., in June, 1777, on the anniversary of his natal day, aged twenty-one years. My father (Robert) was born in 1758, and was married to Sarah Ball, a daughter of Colonel James Ball, of Lancaster county, and had five children. His life was marked by a great non-conformity to the world, which made him offensive to some who did not understand him, but by those who knew him and his motives he was highly esteemed and duly appreciated. He embraced religion in 1806, and was a Christian in the Scripture sense of the word.

He died, peaceful and happy, on the 29th of October, 1832. His last words were, "I want to die; come, Lord Jesus," and he entered into his rest. "Mark the perfect man, and behold the upright, for the end of that man is peace."

It would seem from the foregoing, and from what may be read in my notice of Mr. Edward Ambler and his wife, and what Mr. Irving and other writers have conjectured concerning Miss Grymes, of Middlesex, and perhaps one other lady in the land, that General Washington in his earlier days was not a favourite with the ladies. If the family tradition respecting his repeated rejections be true,—for which I would not vouch,—it may be accounted for in several ways. He may have been too modest and diffident a young man to interest the ladies, or he was too poor at that time, or he had not received a college or university education in England or Virginia, or, as is most probable, God had reserved him for greater things, —was training him up in the camp for the defence of his country. An early marriage might have been injurious to his future usefulness.

No. XVIII.

THE BEVERLEY FAMILY.

[THE following extract from a letter of Mr. William B. Beverley, of Blandfield, Essex county, Virginia, is all I have received concerning this widely-extended family. The reference made to what is said in Henning's "Statutes at Large" is well worthy of attention.]

DEAR SIR:—In replying to your letter from Tappahannock, I am sorry to have to say to you that I am in possession of no papers that can be useful to you in your notices relative to the Church, &c. in Virginia. I have always understood that my ancestors were attached to the Protestant Episcopal Church from their first settlement in this new world. They were all well-educated men, and all business-men, generally filling public offices down to the Revolution. It is highly probable my grandfather— who died in April, 1800, and who, I was told, was a regular attendant at and supporter of the church of which Parson Matthews was the pastor— did leave papers that might have been useful to you. But in the division of his estate his library and papers not on business were divided out among his many sons, and, no doubt, like the other property left them, scattered to the four winds. My uncle, Carter Beverley, qualified first as his executor, and so took all papers on business—and, it is probable, many others—to his home in Staunton, and, he told me, lost every thing of the kind by the burning up of his house.

My father, Robert Beverley, married Miss Jane Taylor, of Mount Airy, Richmond county. My grandfather, Robert Beverley, married Miss Maria Carter, of Sabine Hall. My great-grandfather, William Beverley, married Miss Elizabeth Bland,—the sister, I have heard, of the distinguished Colonel Richard Bland, of the Revolution. My great-great-grandfather, Robert Beverley, (the historian,) married Miss —— Byrd, of Westover, I have heard. His father—the first of the name in the Colony of Virginia—settled at Jamestown about the year 1660, and from thence moved to Middlesex county. He was a long time Clerk of the House of Burgesses, a lawyer by profession, and a prominent actor in Bacon's Rebellion, commanding, I think, the King's troops as major. I have never heard the name of the lady he married in Hull, England. I have heard she was the daughter of a merchant of that town. He brought her to Virginia with him. For a more particular account of this individual I must refer you to the third volume of Henning's "Statutes at Large," from page 541 to the end. You will there see an authentic account of some of his services and persecutions. You will also find in vol. viii. of the same work, page 127, an act which gives, I presume, the only true account of the male branch of the family now extant: the act was obtained by my grandfather for the purpose of changing an *entail* from an estate in Drysdale parish, King and Queen county, (where the historian lived and died,) to one of more value in Culpepper.

I am sorry I have nothing more interesting to communicate.

With much respect, your ob't serv't,
WM. B. BEVERLEY.

REV. BISHOP MEADE, *Millwood.*

No. XIX.

THE PHILLIPS AND FOWKE FAMILIES.

[THE following communication concerning two families whose names are to be seen on the old vestry-books has been sent me by one of the descendants.]

Mr. James Phillips (sometimes spelled Philipps) was a native of the South of Wales. He came to this country early in the eighteenth century, and settled in that part of Virginia known as the county of Stafford. He married a Miss Griffin. Colonel William Phillips, their only child, was born about the year 1746, was High-Sheriff of Stafford, and died about the year 1797. Colonel William Phillips married Miss Elizabeth Fowke, a daughter of Gerard Fowke, Esq., and Miss Elizabeth Dinwiddie, (Miss Dinwiddie was a daughter of Mr. Lawrence Dinwiddie, Provost of Glasgow, Scotland, and was a niece of Robert Dinwiddie, Governor of Virginia,) by whom he had twelve children, six of whom are now living, the eldest of those living (Mrs. Jones) being eighty-three, and the youngest (Colonel William Fowke Phillips) being sixty-two, years of age. Colonel William Fowke Phillips married his cousin, Sarah Edith Cannon, of Prince William county, Virginia, by whom he had seven children,—Laura and Mary Caroline, (now dead,) William Fowke, Jr., Laura E. S., (married to Mr. Wm. B. Carr, of Loudon county, Virginia,) Dinwiddie Brazier, (married Miss Nannie F., daughter of William Walden, Esq., of Rapp county, Virginia,) Virginia Edith, and Roberta Gustavia. Colonel Gerard Fowke was the first of his name who came to this country. He was Colonel in the British army, and Gentleman of Privy Chamber to Charles I. He came to Virginia about the time that his unfortunate monarch was beheaded. One of his sons settled in Maryland. His son, Chandler Fowke, Esq., settled in King George county, Virginia. He had three sons,—Chandler, Gerard, and Richard. Chandler married a Miss Harrison, Gerard married a Miss Dinwiddie, and Richard married a Miss Bumbary. Their sister, Elizabeth Fowke, married a Mr. Z. Brazier, (son of Robert Brazier, of Isle of Thanet, Kent county, England.) Chandler, the eldest of the children, had three sons,—viz.: William, John, and Thomas. William married his first-cousin, Jenny Fowke, of Maryland, and John went to the South with his sister Jenny.

Mr. Gerard Fowke (the second brother) had issue also,—Chandler and Roger, who went South, Gerard, William, (William married a Miss Bronaugh,) Robert Dinwiddie, (Robert Dinwiddie married a Miss Peachy,) Elizabeth, (who married Colonel William Phillips, of Stafford,) and another daughter, (who married a Mr. Johnston, who resided in Kentucky.) Richard Fowke, Esq. died in the army. He also left a family.

Elizabeth Brazier had a daughter,—Sarah Harrison Brazier. She married Mr. John Cannon, son of Mr. L. Cannon, of Ireland. They left four children,—Grandison, (now dead,) Elizabeth, (dead,) and Sarah Edith, who married Colonel William Fowke Phillips, the present Auditor of Treasury for the Post-Office Department. She is now dead also.

Most of those named in this short and in some respects deficient history were members of the English and Episcopal Churches. Of the others, two were members of the Methodist Episcopal Church, and some few were not communicants in any.

No. XX.

FURTHER AND MORE ACCURATE INFORMATION CONCERNING POHICK CHURCH.

[MR. ALFRED MOSS, the present clerk of Fairfax county, having carefully examined all its records, furnishes me with the following statement. The church at Pohick must have been completed in the year 1772, since a certain number of its pews were sold in that year by order of the vestry. A copy of one of the deeds is presented to the reader as probably the first of the kind ever executed in Virginia. I have met with no hint of any such thing in all my researches. The example was in a measure followed, a year or two after, in Christ Church, Alexandria, as has been already stated. It appears from the court-records that General Washington was vestryman in 1763. George Mason was elected first in 1749. Some objection was made to him on the ground that he was not a resident in the parish, but it did not avail. The Rev. Charles Green was the minister from 1738 until his death in 1765. He came from Ireland, and in his will recommended his wife to return thither. They do not appear to have had children. Mr. Moss informs me that Payne's Church must have been built some time before Pohick, as there is an old man now living in the neighbourhood who is ninety-nine years old and who was baptized in it.]

This indenture, made the twenty-fourth day of February, in the year of our Lord one thousand seven hundred and seventy-four, between the vestry of Truro parish, in the county of Fairfax, of the one part, and Daniel McCarty, of the same parish and county, gentleman, of the other part: whereas, the said vestry did, on the fifth day of June, in the year 1772, order sundry pews in the new church on the upper side of Pohick to be sold, at the laying of the next parish levy, to the highest bidder for the benefit of the parish, pursuant to which order the said pews were sold accordingly by the vestry at the laying of the said next parish levy, on the 20th day of November, in the same year; and the said Daniel McCarty, party to these presents, then purchased one certain pew in the said church for the price of fifteen pounds ten shillings current money,—to wit: the pew numbered 14, situate on the north side of the said church, and adjoining the north wall and the rector's pew, being the second pew above the pulpit, as by the proceedings and records of the said vestry, reference being thereunto had, may more fully and at large appear. Now this indenture witnesseth that the said vestry, for and in consideration of the said sum of fifteen pounds ten shillings current money, to them in hand paid, for the use of the said parish, by the said Daniel McCarty, before the sealing and delivery of these presents, the receipt whereof is hereby confessed and acknowledged, have granted, bargained, and sold, aliened and confirmed, and by these presents do grant, bargain, and sell, alien and confirm, unto the said Daniel McCarty, the said pew in the said new church lately built on the upper side of Pohick, in the said parish of Truro and county aforesaid, numbered and situated as above mentioned, to have and to hold the said pew above described unto the said Daniel McCarty, his heirs and assigns, to the only proper use and behoof of him, the said Daniel McCarty, his heirs and assigns forever. And the said vestry, for themselves and their successors, (vestrymen of Truro parish,) do covenant and grant to and with the said Daniel McCarty, his heirs and assigns, that he, the said Daniel McCarty, his heirs and assigns, shall, and may forever hereafter, peaceably and quietly have, hold, and enjoy the said pew above mentioned and described, without the lawful let, hindrance, interruption, or molestation of any person or persons whatsoever. In witness whereof the vestry now present (being a majority of the members) have hereunto set their hands and affixed their seals the day and year first above written.

> G. MASON,
> GEO. WASHINGTON,
> ALEX. HENDERSON,
> F. ELLZEY,
> THOS. WITHERS COFFER,
> THOS. FORD,
> J. A. WAGENER,
> MARTIN COCKBURN.

Signed, sealed, and delivered in the presence of
> WM. TRIPLETT,
> WM. PAYNE,
> JOHN BARRY,
> JOHN GUNNELL,
> THOMAS TRIPLETT.

At the close of this deed is a receipt to Mr. McCarty for fifteen pounds ten shillings, the price of the pew. General Washington's pew in Christ Church, Alexandria, cost thirty-six pounds ten shillings.

No. XXI.

The Inscription on Commissary Blair's Tombstone in the Old Graveyard at Jamestown, furnished by Mr. Hugh Blair Grigsby, a Descendant of Commissary Blair's Brother.

My dear Sir:—I send you the inscription on the stone of the old Commissary in as perfect condition as I could procure it. I also send a translation, filling the blanks and chasms with my own knowledge of the events of the Commissary's life. If you look critically at the Latin and at my paraphrase, you will perceive that I have rarely missed the mark. One thing it is proper to say. In the line " Evangeli—Preconis" there may be a mistake of the transcriber. If the word "Preconis" be correct, then it is figurative, and means to compare the Commissary with John the Baptist. But I think the word " Preconis" is wrong, and was written *"Diaconi," "* Deacon," as the *number of years* shows that it was in his combined character of Evangelist, Deacon, and Priest, to which allusion is made; that is, to his whole ministerial services, which were precisely fifty-eight years.

To another topic I would invite your attention. The concluding lines in which theology is mentioned are imperfect, and cannot convey the exact meaning intended, and so I translate them as referring to pious youth who may seek instruction in sacred things; but they certainly lead us to suspect that the good old man left his books *to theological students as a class,* and that he had in view to endow by his will an ecclesiastical professorship. His will in the Clerk's Office, and the statute or order of the faculty accepting his books, would ascertain the fact.

I wish the remains of the Commissary could be removed to the chapel of the College, and there, with appropriate services, deposited beneath the chancel.

With affectionate regards, I am, as ever, reverently and faithfully yours,
HUGH B. GRIGSBY.

Bishop Meade.

H. S. E. (Hic sepultus est)
Vir Reverendus et Honorabilis
JACOBUS BLAIR, A.M.
In Scotia natus,
In Academia Edinburgensi nutritus,
Primo Angliam deinde Virginiam
venit :
In qua parte tenarum
Annos LVIII. Evangeli, Preconis
LIV. Commissarii
Gulielmi et Mariæ Præsidis,

e Britanniæ Principum
Consiliarii
Concilii Præsidis,
Coloniæ Prefecti,
munera sustinuit :
ornavit
um oris venusti Decus,
ate hilari sine (?) hospitali
munificent
issimo egenis largo.
omnibus comi
superavit.
Collegio bene diversam
fundaverat
ens Bibliothecam suam
id alendum Theologiæ studiosum
juventutem pauperiorem instituendam
Testamento legavit
Cal. Maii in die*
MDCCXLIII
ætat : LXXXVIII
am desideratissimi
Senis Laudem
is nepotibus commendabunt
pene marmore perenniora.

Here lies buried
The Reverend and the Honourable
James Blair, A.M.,
who was born in Scotland, was educated in the College of Edinburgh,
and emigrated to England, and thence to Virginia, in which Colony
he spent fifty-eight years as an Evangelist, Deacon, and Priest of the

---

* The word "Maii" must be a mistake of the gentlemen who transcribed one of
the fragmentary inscriptions from which I have made out the above skeleton. **Dr.**
Blair died, I believe, on the 3d of August, 1743. Some of the words, apparently
perfect in my notes, are certainly wrong; but I have done the work as thoroughly
as my materials will allow me. The two transcripts before me were made, one of
them by the Rev. George W. McPhail, of Easton, Pa., the other by William Lamb,
Esq., of Norfolk. I have made a translation, filling up the chasms with my own
suggestions; and I feel confident that, however much we may regret the loss of
the inscription as a whole, and however unable we may be to judge of it as a work
of taste in its present dilapidated state, I have incorporated every important sentiment which it contained in the transcript which I send you on the opposite leaf.
I am ashamed to say that I have lost—or, rather, put too carefully away—the fragments of the inscription which you transmitted to me.

Church of England, and fifty-four years as Commissary of the Bishop of London.

He was the Founder and first President of William and Mary College, a member of the Council, and, subsequently, its President; and, as such, in the absence of the representative of the King, the Governor of the Colony.

He sustained his various offices with the approbation of his fellow-men, while he illustrated in his life those graces which adorn the Christian character.

He had a handsome person, and in the family circle blended cheerfulness with piety.

He was a generous friend of the poor, and was prompt in lending assistance to all who needed it.

He was a liberal benefactor of the College during his life; and, at his death, bequeathed to it his library, with the hope that his books—which were mostly religious—might lead the student to those things that pertain to salvation.

He died on the — day of the Calends of May, [August, rather,] in the year 1743, aged eighty-eight years, exhibiting to the last those graces which make old age lovely, and lamented by all, especially by his nephews, who have reared this stone to commemorate those virtues which will long survive the marble that records them.

No. XXII.

Episcopal High School.

This institution, the diocesan school for boys, is situated at Howard, in Fairfax county, three miles west of Alexandria, and within a quarter of a mile of the Theological Seminary. The situation is perfectly healthy at all seasons of the year, and from its elevation commands a beautiful view of the Potomac, the cities of the District of Columbia, and the surrounding country for many miles. The play-grounds are extensive and adorned with trees of inviting shade. They are immediately adjoining the school, and with the fields of the enclosure (containing about seventy acres) afford ample room for exercise and recreation. The Potomac and other small streams in the neighbourhood furnish opportunities for bathing and skating. The buildings, erected expressly for the purposes of the school, are large, furnished with every convenience for the wants of the students, and capable of accommodating about eighty boys.

The object of the Church in establishing the High School was to provide an institution of learning, where youth could be thoroughly educated on Christian principles, and where their morals and habits could be preserved from the dangers of evil association. Students can here fully complete their studies; or they can be prepared for advanced classes—the junior and senior—at any of the colleges or universities of the country; or be fitted to enter upon the study of a profession or the active business of life During their entire course, the most wholesome moral and religious influences are sought to be exercised over them.

It is a fixed and unvarying rule, that every branch taught at the school is to be studied faithfully and well. To effect this object, every effort is made to insure ability and faithfulness on the part of the instructors and diligence and improvement on the part of the scholars. Great pains are taken, by the internal regulations of the school, in each particular department, to train the students to habits of method, neatness, and punctuality, so important in every business or profession and so indispensable to the comfort and convenience of individuals.

Education of the mind, however, and the formation of business-habits, are by no means the sole or most important aim of the school. Whilst these receive constant and proper attention, it is at all times borne in mind that the morals and the manners of the students are by no means to be neglected.

To make mere scholars or exact men of business is not the sole duty of the Christian teacher. He has much nobler ends in view. No exertions are to be spared to secure those just named; but at the same time he is to be diligent to bring those intrusted to his care under the influence of religious principle. He is not only to labour to make them useful men, but, so far as in him lies, he is to endeavour to make them Christian gentlemen,—gentlemen as well in feelings and principles as in outward conduct and manners.

For these important ends the school was established by the trustees of the Theological Seminary, in 1839, in obedience to a resolution of the Diocesan Convention, and placed under the care of the Rev. William N. Pendleton, who opened it in October of that year. The number of pupils soon became large; and, besides superior intellectual training, the blessings of divine grace were very richly bestowed upon them, about forty having in the first few years made a creditable profession of religion, and some of these having afterward entered the ministry of the Church. This prosperity continued until the years 1843–44, when, chiefly through a general pecuniary embarrassment, which injured almost every literary institution in the country and ruined some, it became necessary to close the High School for one year.

In the fall of 1845 it was reopened by the Rev. E. A. Dalrymple, who had been appointed its rector at the Convention in May preceding, and whose energy and skill, under the blessing of a good Providence, soon restored it to its former prosperity. After a most laborious devotion to his duties for about seven years, the failure of his health constrained him to resign, leaving the institution in a condition promising permanent success.   In the summer of 1852, the Rev. John P. McGuire, its present rector, was appointed his successor, and is now nearly at the close of his fifth session.   The number of pupils—between seventy and eighty—is about what it has been for years; it is still among the very first as an institution of learning; the fruits of grace are still gathered to an encouraging extent, some twenty having been added to the Communion of the Church during the last session, and others now expecting soon to be confirmed,—thus in the highest sense accomplishing the purpose for which the school was originally established.

No. XXIII.

FURTHER STATEMENTS CONCERNING THE RELIGIOUS CHARACTER OF WASHINGTON AND THE QUESTION WHETHER HE WAS A COMMUNICANT OR NOT.

EXTRACT from a letter of the Rev. Dr. Berrian, of New York, to Mrs. Jane Washington, of Mount Vernon, in answer to some inquiries about General Washington during his residence in New York as President of the United States :—

"About a fortnight since I was administering the Communion to a sick daughter of Major Popham, and, after the service was over, happening to speak on this subject, I was greatly rejoiced to obtain the information which you so earnestly desired.

"Major Popham served under General Washington during the Revolutionary War, and I believe he was brought as near to him as their difference of rank would admit, being himself a man of great respectability, and connected by marriage with the Morrises, one of the first families in the country.   He has still an erect and military air, and a body but little broken at his advanced age.   His memory does not seem to be impaired nor his mind to be enfeebled."

To the above I can add my own testimony, having in different ways become acquainted with the character of Major Popham, and having visited him about the same time mentioned by Dr. Berrian.

Extract from Major Popham's Letter to Mrs. Jane Washington.

NEW YORK, March 14, 1839.

MY DEAR MADAM :—You will doubtless be not a little surprised at receiving a letter from an individual whose name may possibly never have reached you; but an accidental circumstance has given me the extreme pleasure of introducing myself to your notice. In a conversation with the Rev. Dr. Berrian a few days since, he informed me that he had lately paid a visit to Mount Vernon, and that Mrs. Washington had expressed a wish to have a doubt removed from her mind, which had long oppressed her, as to the certainty of the General's having attended the Communion while residing in the city of New York subsequent to the Revolution. As nearly all the remnants of those days are now sleeping with their fathers, it is not very probable that at this late day an individual can be found who could satisfy this pious wish of your virtuous heart, except the writer. It was my great good fortune to have attended St. Paul's Church in this city with the General during the whole period of his residence in New York as President of the United States. The pew of Chief-Justice Morris was situated next to that of the President, close to whom I constantly sat in Judge Morris's pew, and I am as confident as a memory now labouring under the pressure of fourscore years and seven can make me, that the President had more than once—I believe I may say often—attended at the sacramental table, at which I had the privilege and happiness to kneel with him. And I am aided in my associations by my elder daughter, who distinctly recollects her grandmamma—Mrs. Morris—often mention that fact with great pleasure. Indeed, I am further confirmed in my assurance by the perfect recollection of the President's uniform deportment during divine service in church. The steady seriousness of his manner, the solemn, audible, but subdued tone of voice in which he read and repeated the responses, the Christian humility which overspread and adorned the native dignity of the saviour of his country, at once exhibited him a pattern to all who had the honour of access to him. It was my good fortune, my dear madam, to have had frequent intercourse with him. It is my pride and boast to have seen him in various situations,—in the flush of victory, in the field and in the tent,—in the church and at the altar, always himself, ever the same.

Letter from General Lewis, of Augusta county, Virginia, to the Rev. Mr. Dana, of Alexandria.

LEWISTOWN, December 14, 1855.

REVEREND AND DEAR SIR :—When (some weeks ago) I had the pleasure of seeing you in Alexandria, and in our conversation the subject of the religious opinions and character of General Washington was spoken of, I repeated to you the substance of what I had heard from the late General Robert Porterfield, of Augusta, and which at your request I promised to reduce to writing at some leisure moment and send to you. I proceed now to redeem the promise. Some short time before the death of General Porterfield, I made him a visit and spent a night at his house. He related many interesting facts that had occurred within his own observation in the war of the Revolution, particularly in the Jersey campaign and the encampment of the army at Valley Forge. He said that his official duty (being brigade-inspector) frequently brought him in contact with General Washington. Upon one occasion, some emergency (which he mentioned) induced him to dispense with the usual formality, and he went directly to General Washington's apartment, where he found him on his knees, engaged in his morning's devotions. He said that he mentioned the circumstance to General Hamilton, who replied that such was his constant habit. I remarked that I had lately heard Mr. —— say, on the authority of Mr. ——, that General Washington was subject to violent fits of passion, and that he then swore terribly. General Porterfield said the charge was false; that he had known General Washington personally for many years, had frequently been in his presence under very exciting circumstances, and had never heard him swear an oath, or in any way to profane the name of God. "Tell Mr. —— from me," said he, "that he had much better be reading his Bible than repeating such slanders on the character of General Washington. General Washington," said he, "was a pious man, and a member of your Church, [the Episcopal.] I saw him myself on his knees receive the Sacrament of the Lord's Supper in —— Church, in Philadelphia." He specified the time and place. My impression is that Christ Church was the place, and Bishop White, as he afterward was, the minister. This is, to the best of my recollection, an accurate statement of what I heard from General Porterfield on the subject.

I am, sir, with great respect, very truly yours,   S. H. LEWIS.

[In relation to what is said about the paroxysms of passion and terrible swearing of General Washington, we have something very special to say.

We have heard of this many years since, and think we are able to trace it to its true source.

The following extract from a late synopsis of General Washington's private letters to his secretary,—Mr. Tobias Lear,—by the Hon. Richard Rush, of Philadelphia, will throw some light on the subject:—]

"An anecdote I derived from Colonel Lear shortly before his death in 1816 may here be related, showing the height to which his [General Washington's] passion would rise, yet be controlled. It belongs to his domestic life which I am dealing with, having occurred under his own roof, whilst it marks public feeling the most intense and points to the moral of his life. I give it in Colonel Lear's words as nearly as I can, having made a note of them at the time.

Toward the close of a winter's day in 1791, an officer in uniform was seen to dismount in front of the President's in Philadelphia, and, giving the bridle to his servant, knock at the door of his mansion. Learning from the porter that the President was at dinner, he said he was on public business and had despatches for the President. A servant was sent into the dining-room to give the information to Mr. Lear, who left the table and went into the hall, when the officer repeated what he had said. Mr. Lear replied that, as the President's secretary, he would take charge of the despatches and deliver them at the proper time. The officer made answer that he had just arrived from the Western army, and his orders were to deliver it with all promptitude, and to the President in person; but that he would wait his directions. Mr. Lear returned, and in a whisper imparted to the President what had passed. General Washington rose from the table and went to the officer. He was back in a short time and made a word of apology for his absence, but no allusion to the cause of it. He had company that day. Every thing went on as usual. Dinner over, the gentlemen passed into the drawing-room of Mrs. Washington, which was open in the evening. The General spoke courteously to every lady in the room, as was his custom. His hours were early, and by ten all the company had gone. Mrs. Washington and Mr. Lear remained. Soon Mrs. Washington left the room. The General now walked backward and forward slowly for some minutes without speaking. Then he sat down on a sofa by the fire, telling Mr. Lear to sit down. To this moment there had been no change in his manner since his interruption at table. Mr. Lear now perceived emotion. This rising in him, he broke out suddenly:—"It's all over! St. Clair's defeated,—routed; the officers nearly all killed, the men by wholesale; the rout complete. Too shocking to think of;—and a surprise into the bargain!" He uttered all this with great vehemence. Then he paused, got up from the sofa, and walked about the room several times, agitated, but saying nothing. Near the door he stopped short and stood still for a few seconds, when his wrath became terrible. "Yes," he burst forth, "here, on this very spot, I took leave of him. I wished him success and honour. 'You have your instructions,' I said, 'from the Secretary of War: I had a strict eye to them, and will add but one word,—beware of a surprise! I repeat it, beware of a surprise; you know how the Indians fight us.' He went off with that as my last solemn warning thrown into his ears. And yet to suffer that army to be cut to pieces, hacked, butchered, tomahawked, by a surprise,—the very thing I guarded him against! O God! O God! he's worse than a murderer! How can he answer it to his country? The blood of the slain is upon him,—the curse of the widows and orphans,—the curse of Heaven!" This torrent came out in tones appalling. His very frame shook. "It was awful," said Mr. Lear. More than once he threw his hands up as he hurled imprecations upon St. Clair. Mr. Lear remained speechless, awed into breathless silence. The roused chief sat down on the sofa once more. He seemed conscious of his passion, and uncomfortable. He was silent. His warmth beginning to subside, he at length said, in an altered voice, "This must not go beyond this room." Another pause followed,—a longer one,—when he said, in a tone quite low, "General St. Clair shall have justice: I looked hastily through the despatches, saw the whole disaster, but not all the particulars.

I will receive him without displeasure; I will hear him without prejudice; he shall have full justice." He was now (said Mr. Lear) perfectly calm. Half an hour had gone by. The storm was over; and no sign of it was seen in his conduct or heard in his conversation. The whole case was investigated by Congress. St. Clair was exculpated, and regained the confidence Washington had in him when appointing him to command. He had put himself into the thickest of the fight, and escaped unhurt, though so ill as to be carried on a litter and unable to mount his horse without help.

In relation to the above, let it be granted that Mr. Lear, (who did not sympathize with General Washington's religious opinions,) after the lapse of more than twenty years, retained an accurate recollection of all his words, and that Mr. Rush fully understood them and truly recorded them, as doubtless he did: yet what do they amount to? Is the exclamation "O God! O God!" under his aroused feeling, that swearing since imputed to him, but which from his youth up he had so emphatically condemned in his soldiers as impious and ungentlemanly?*

If it be said that some doubt still rests on the question of General Washington's being a communicant, by reason of the testimony of Bishop White, as mentioned in a previous part of this book, such doubt may be removed in the following manner:—Here are two most respectable officers under General Washington, who testify to the fact of having seen him commune in New York and Philadelphia. He may have communed in Philadelphia on some occasion and yet not been seen by Bishop White, who had the care of two or three churches, at which he officiated alternately in conjunction with one or more ministers. He may have retired, and doubtless did, at other times, and was seen by Bishop White. If it be asked how we can reconcile this leaving of the church at any time of the celebration of the Lord's Supper with a religious character, we reply by stating a well-

---

* The Rev. Dr. McGuire, of Fredericksburg, while preparing his volume on the Religious Opinions and Character of Washington, having heard this report emanating from some of the enemies of Washington and too readily admitted by some of his friends, made a particular personal inquiry of Mr. Robert Lewis, of Fredericksburg, and Mr. Laurence Lewis, of Woodlawn, two gentlemen as competent to know the private habits of Washington as any others in the land. They were nephews of General Washington. The former lived in the family of Washington for some time as private secretary: the latter was his near neighbour, living on a farm given him by the General. Both of them were men of the highest character, and pious members of our Church, and both declared that they had never heard an oath from the lips of their uncle. To this testimony, and those of General Porterfield and Major Popham, is to be opposed that of Mr. Tobias Lear's account of one of Washington's paroxysms, as given above, and which, according to his own showing, was never to go beyond the room in which it occurred. The testimony of one who had betrayed a sacred trust of Washington on another occasion besides this should be received with doubt.

known fact,—viz: that in former days there was a most mistaken notion, too prevalent both in England and America, that it was not so necessary in the professors of religion to communicate at all times, but that in this respect persons might be regulated by their feelings, and perhaps by the circumstances in which they were placed. I have had occasion to see much of this in my researches into the habits of the members of the old Church of Virginia. Into this error of opinion and practice General Washington may have fallen, especially at a time when he was peculiarly engaged with the cares of government and a multiplicity of engagements, and when his piety may have suffered some loss thereby.

No. XXIV.

THE VIRGINIA ALMINACK FOR THE YEAR OF OUR LORD GOD 1776.

The right Honourable John Earl of Dunmore, Governor.

Members of his Majesty's Council.
Honourable.

Thomas Nelson, Esqr., Presid
Richard Corbin, Esqr.
William Byrd, Esqr.
John Tayloe, Esqr.
Robert Carter, Esqr.
Robert Burwell, Esqr.

George William Fairfax, Esqr.
Ralph Wormley, jun., Esqr.
Rev'd. John Camm.
John Page, Esqr.
Gawin Corbin, Esqr.

Governors and Visitors of the College.

Nathaniel Burwell, Esqr., Rector.

Hon. Thomas Nelson, Esqr.
  "   Richard Corbin, Esqr.
  "   Wm. Byrd, Esqr.
  "   John Page, jun., Esqr.
  "   Ralph Wormley, Esqr.
Rev. James Maury Fontaine.
Rev. Thomas Field.
Peyton Randolph, Esqr.
Robert Carter Nicholas, Esqr.
Mann Page, Esqr.

Thomas Nelson, jun., Esqr., (afterwards General Nelson).
Richard Bland, Esqr.
Dudley Digges, Esqr.
Charles Carter, Esqr., Corotoman.
Richard Randolph, Esqr.
John Blair, Esqr.
Robert Beverley, Esqr.
Benjamin Harrison, Esqr.

The foregoing shows who were the leading persons in the government of the State and College in the year 1776. The Mr. Nathaniel Burwell who was rector of the College was probably of Isle of Wight, and the ancestor of many of that name. The Thomas Nelson who was President of the Council was one of the sons of the first Thomas Nelson, and usually called Secretary Nelson, because generally Secretary of the Colony. His brother William, who was generally President of the Council, being now dead, Thomas succeeded to his office as President.

No. XXV.

Blissland Parish, New Kent County.

Since the first edition of this book I have received a fragment of the vestry-book of this parish, beginning in the year 1721, and ending in 1786. During this period of sixty-five years, there were only three ministers: the Rev. Daniel Taylor, who continued from 1721 to 1729; the Rev. Chickerley Thacker, from 1729 to 1763; the Rev. Price Davies, from 1763 to 1786. Their continuance in office for such periods speaks well for their character. The Rev. Mr. Davies was one selected by the House of Burgesses to take part in the services at Williamsburg, at the beginning of our Revolutionary struggle,—which indicates his patriotic principles. The services of the ministers of this parish are supposed to have been divided between Warren Church, so called from the swamp of that name about ten miles below New Kent Court-House, which has entirely disappeared, and Hickory Neck Church, in James City county, which is still standing, though not used by Episcopalians. We hear of some movement towards the re-establishment of Episcopal worship there. It is about ten miles distant from Williamsburg, and was sometimes visited by Bishop Madison. Eltham, the seat of the Bassetts, in New Kent, was within this parish, and the Honourable Burwell Bassett, as well as his father, William Bassett, were long the vestrymen of it. The following is a list of the names of the vestrymen from 1721 to 1786 :—Bassett, Thornton, Slater, Cox, Morris, Richardson, Alderley, Armstead, Keeling, Holdcroft, Kenney, Hockaday, Doran, Williams, Woodward, Dickson, Allen, Mackain, Sherman, Clough, Henley, Radcliffe, Terrel, James, Hogg, Power, Goddin, Macon, Dandridge, Hankin, Prince, Russell, Timberlake, Bridges, Banks, Lewis, Baker. In the above, how many of the families in Virginia and elsewhere may find the names of their ancestors!

THE END.

WISE'S
DIGESTED INDEX

AND

GENEALOGICAL GUIDE

TO

BISHOP MEADE'S

Old Churches, Ministers and Families

OF

VIRGINIA,

Embracing 6,900 Proper Names.

COMPILED BY

JENNINGS CROPPER WISE,

Member of the Virginia
Historical Society.

RICHMOND, VA.
PRINTED FOR SUBSCRIBERS,
MCMX.

PREFACE.

The genealogy of Virginian families has, for obvious reasons, been regarded to be of peculiar interest. It would hardly be too much to say that Bishop Meade's "Old Churches and Families of Virginia" is a corner-stone in the edifice of American genealogical lore, and that there has been no "long-felt want" more pressing than that for a satisfactory index and digest of this great work.

The compiler of the following pages lays claim to no credit beyond that which is due to the accurate performance of an uncommonly laborious task. So great, in Bishop Meade's work, is the number of names to be included in even the simplest index that the making of this would be no slight matter, and this labor has been vastly increased by the compiler's design to identify the individuals mentioned and to present, along with the index, a digest of important facts recorded in the book. It is matter of regret that students have not had, from the beginning, access to a full and accurate digested index to this work; not so much because of the time wasted for want of such a help as for the reason that most of them, lacking this guide, have largely forborne to attempt to use the well-nigh boundless treasure of personal and public history within these pages. It will surely, then, be matter of congratulation to all who are interested in historical research and its results that now, at last, such a digested index is presented, as it is a matter of gratification to the compiler that he now proffers to the thirsty a "seasoned gourd" with which they may dip from another's spring the sweetest water of which is often beyond the reach of the casual passer-by.

I wish to acknowledge my indebtedness to my friend, Mr. John Hart, of Richmond, Va., who has given me valued assistance at every point of this work.

JENNINGS CROPPER WISE.

Richmond, Virginia, January 1st, 1910.

WISE'S DIGESTED INDEX

AND

GENEALOGICAL GUIDE

TO

Bishop Meade's Old Churches, Ministers and Families of Virginia.

Armistead, Wm.—Vol. I. 230, 235, 236, 326.

Armistead, Wm., of Hesse—Vol. I. 326.

Armistead, Miss, of Hesse, m. John Dangerfield—Vol. I. 406.

Armstrong, the elder, of Wheeling—Vol. I. 39.

Armstrong, T. H.—Vol. II. 336.

Armstrong, Saml.—Vol. II. 253.

Armstrong, Geo.—Vol. II. 337.

Armstrong, Rev. John—Vol. II. 332, 333, 336, 349.

Armstrong, Rev. Wm.—Vol. II. 336, 337, 338, 339, 348, 350.

Arnold, Gen.—Vol. I. 299.

Arnold, Rev. Mr.—Vol. II. 43.

Arnold, Isaac—Vol. II. 186.

Ascough, John—Vol. I. 324.

Ashburn, Jno.—Vol. I. 289.

Arthurs—Vol. II. 315.

Ashley, Mr. William—Vol. I. 276.

Ashton—Vol. I. 240; Vol. II. 348.

Ashton, Mr.—Vol. II. 185.

Ashton, Henry A.—Vol. II. 192.

Ashton, John—Vol. II. 436.

Ashton, Laurence—Vol. II. 186.

Ashby, John—Vol. II. 281.

Assawaman Church—Vol. I. 266.

Aston, Walter—Vol. I. 446.

Atkinson—Vol. II. 428.

Atkinson, Bishop—Vol. I. 221.

Atkinson, Guy—Vol. II. 268.

Atkinson, James—Vol. II. 268.

Atkinson, Roger, of Mannfield—Vol. I. 220, 221, 444, 446, 452, 487.

Atkinson, Rev. Thomas—Vol. I. 275, 281; Vol. II. 17.

Atkinson, Thos.—Vol. II. 349.

Atkinson, Thos. C.—Vol. II. 268.

Atkins—Vol. II. 429.

Atterburg, W. B.—Vol. II. 337.

Aubrey—Vol. II. 206, 429.

Aubrey, Henry—Vol. I. 404; Vol. II. 172.

Augusta County and Parishes—Vol. II. 317.

Austin, Chas.—Vol. II. 72.

Avens, Rev. Archibald—Vol. I. 325; Vol. II. 273.

Avery's Church—Vol. II. 21.

Aylett—Vol. II. 428.

Aylett, Miss, 1st wife of Richard Henry Lee—Vol. II. 139.

Aylett, Miss (wife of Thomas Ludwell Lee)—Vol. II. 139.

Ayrfield—Vol. II. 154, 157.

Aylott—Vol. I. 178.

Aylmer, Rev. Justimian—Vol. I. 230, 231.

Ayrs, Rev. Mr.—Vol. I. 267.

Baber, Col.—Vol. II. 159.

Back Creek Church—Vol. II. 301.

Bacon—Vol. I. 353, 354; Vol. II. 428.

Bacon's Rebellion—Vol. I. 93, 112, 252, 262, 305; Vol. II. 482.

Bacon, the rebel—Vol. I. 93, 94, 112, 136, 305; Vol. II. 290.

Bacon, Rev., of Maryland—Vol. II. 355.

Bacon, Edmund—Vol. I. 387.

Bacon, Edmund P.—Vol. I. 487.

Bacon, Lyddall—Vol. I. 483, 486.

Bacon, Col. Nathaniel (Uncle of Rebel), m. Elizabeth Kingswell—Vol. I. 200, 353; Vol. II. 290.

Bagge, Rev. Jno.—Vol. I. 396, 397; Vol. II. 393, 396, 397, 401-405.

Bagnal, Mrs. (Miss Selden)—Vol. I. 140.

Bagnal, W. D., of Norfolk—Vol. I. 140.

Bagwell—Vol. I. 279.

Bahannon, Joseph—Vol. I. 405.

Bailey—Vol. II. 13.

Bailey, Capt. of "Rosegill"—Vol. I. 373.

Bailey, Mrs. Capt.—Vol. I. 373.

Bailey, Jeremiah G.—Vol. II. 153.

Baker—Vol. I. 298; Vol. II. 428, 496.

Baker, Jerman—Vol I. 451.

Baker, Laurence—Vol. I. 304.

Baker, Nicholas—Vol. I. 230.

Baker, Richard—Vol. I. 289-291.

Baker, Rev. Thos.—Vol. I. 325; Vol. II. 65.

Balch—Vol. II. 429.

Balch, Rev. Lewis—Vol. II. 303.

Baldwin—Vol. I. 365; Vol. II. 428.

Baldwin, Judge Briscoe G.—Vol. II. 323, 424.

Baldwin, Joseph—Vcl. II. 289.

Balfour, Col.—Vol. II. 359.

Balfour, Rev.—Vol. I. 289.

Balinger's Church—Vol. I. 401.

Ball—Vol. I. 192; Vol. II. 82, 124, 126, 128, 180, 428.

Ball, Col. Burgess, son of Jeduthun —Vol. II. 127.

Ball, Rev. David—Vol. II. 123, 132, 468, 469.

Ball, David, son of Wm. 2nd—Vol. II. 127.

Ball, Capt. David, Sr.—Vol. II. 469.

Ball, Capt. David, Jr.—Vol. II. 469.

Ball, Fayette—Vol. II. 276, 277.

Ball, Flexmer, son of Joseph, of Ditchley—Vol. II. 135.

Ball, Capt. Geo.—Vol. II. 469.

Ball, Hannah, m. Daniel Fox—Vol. II. 126.

Ball, Hannah, m. Rowleigh Travers —Vol. II. 204, 205.

Ball, Maj. James—Vol. II. 125.

Ball, Col. Jas., of Bewdley, m. Fanny Downman—Vol. II. 124, 125, 127, 128, 468, 480.

Ball, Mrs. Col. James (Fanny Downman)—Vol. II. 127.

Ball, Mrs. Col. James (Lettuce Lee) —Vol. II. 127.

Ball, James, m. Mary Conway—Vol. II. 127, 468.

Ball, Mrs. James (Mary Conway)— Vol. II. 127.

Ball, James, son of James and Mary Conway—Vol. II. 125, 127, 468.

Ball, Jeduthun, son of Wm. 2nd— Vol. II. 127.

Ball, Jesse—Vol. II. 125, 127.

Ball, Joseph (Uncle of Geo. Washington), m. Miss Ravenscroft— Vol. II. 128, 129, 468.

Ball, Joseph, of Ditchley—Vol. II. 132, 133-136.

Ball, Joseph, son of Wm. 2nd— Vol. II. 125, 126, 127.

Ball, Mrs. Mary Ann (Miss Betrand)—Vol. II. 127.

Ball, Mary (mother of Geo. Washington)—Vol. II. 127, 204.

Ball, Mildred—Vol. II. 127.

Ball, Samuel—Vol. II. 74, 77.

Ball, Sarah, m. Robt. Fauntleroy— Vol. II. 480.

Ball, Spencer—Vol. II. 468.

Ball, Capt. Spencer Mottram—Vol. II. 435, 468.

Ball, Col. Wm. 1st (Emmigrant)— Vol. II. 126, 127.

Ball, Capt. Wm. 2nd, son of Col. Wm. 1st—Vol. II. 125-127.

Ball, Wm.—Vol. II. 50, 78, 436.

Ballantine, Jno., Jr.—Vol. II. 435.

Ballard—Vol. I. 240; Vol. II. 428.

Ballard, Benj.—Vol. II. 72.

Ballard, Jno.—Vol. I. 487.

Ballard, Col. Thos.—Vol. I. 178.

Ballard, Hon. Thos.—Vol. I. 178.

Ballenger, Richard—Vol. II. 58.

Ballenger's Church, Warren—Vol. II. 48, 49, 51.

Balmaine, Rev. Alexander, m. Lucy Taylor—Vol. I. 20, 21, 31, 36, 42, 54; Vol. II. 95, 98, 99, 141, 282, 285-287, 303, 310, 319, 321, 324.

Balmaine, Mrs. Alexander (Lucy Taylor)—Vol. II. 86, 94.

Bancroft (Historian)—Vol. II. 144.

Bancroft's Washington—Vol. II. 236.

Bangor Church—Vol. II. 346.

Banister—Vol. II. 22, 428.

Banister, Rev.—Vol. I. 475.

Banister, T. R.—Vol. II. 22.

Bankhead—Vol. II. 428.

Bankhead, Gen'l—Vol. I. 404.

Bankhead, Wm.—Vol. II. 94.

Banks—Vol. II. 13, 206, 496.

Banks, Jas.—Vol. II. 435.

Banks, Sir Joseph—Vol. I. 293.

Banks, Dr. R. G.—Vol. I. 236.

Banks, Tunstall—Vol. I. 405.
Bannister—Vol. I. 446.
Bannister, Jno., m. Miss Bland—Vol. I. 444, 445, 447.
Baptism, Public—Vol. II. 366.
"Baptists of Virginia" by Semple—Vol. I. 429.
Barber—Vol. I. 452; Vol. II. 82, 173, 240.
"Barber, Caesar," (Jno. Hope)—Vol. I. 201.
Barber, James—Vol. I. 179; Vol. II. 74, 77.
Barber, Capt. Wm.—Vol. II. 173.
Barbour—Vol. II. 94, 103.
Barbour, Gov.—Vol. II. 90, 94.
Barbour, Judge—Vol. II. 90, 94.
Barbour, Richard—Vol. II. 95, 98.
Barbour, Thos.—Vol. II. 90, 98.
Barclay, Rev.—Vol. I. 484; Vol. II. 261.
Barksdale, Dr. Jno., of Halifax—Vol. I. 451.
Barksdale, Wm.—Vol. II. 42.
Barksdale, Wm., Jr.—Vol. II. 22.
Barksdale, W. J.—Vol. II. 22.
Barlow—Vol. II. 429.
Barlow, Rev.—Vol. II. 375.
Barlow, Rev. Edward—Vol. I. 258.
Barlow, Rev. Henry—Vol. I. 248, 249, 303.
Barnard, Robt.—Vol. I. 326.
Barnard, Wm.—Vol. I. 324.
"Barnelms," (Berkeley)—Vol. I. 371; Vol. II. 278.
Barnes—Vol. II. 173.
Barnes, Mr., of Bermuda Hundred —Vol. I. 253.
Barnes, Rev.—Vol. II. 224.
Barnes, James—Vol. II. 34.
Barnes, Thos.—Vol. II. 436.
Barnett, Jas.—Vol. II. 284.
Barnett, Rev. Jno.—Vol. II. 89, 98.
Barnett, Richard—Vol. I. 324.
Barnit, Wm.—Vol. II. 34.
Barns, Rev.—Vol. I. 421.
Barns, Jno.—Vol. II. 284.
Barr, D. M.—Vol. II. 349.
Barracks in Albemarle—Vol. II. 49.

Barradale, Edward—Vol. I. 179.
Barradale, Edward, Jr.—Vol. I. 179.
Barradall—Vol. I. 198.
Barraud—Vol. I. 468.
Barrett, Rev., of Louisa—Vol. I. 401.
Barrett, Mrs. (Miss Maury)—Vol. II. 44.
Barrett, Chas.—Vol. II. 42.
Barrett, Rev. Robt.—Vol. I. 420, 430; Vol. II. 43.
Barron, Commodore Jas.—Vol. I. 235, 237.
Barrow—Vol. II. 173.
Barry, Jno.—Vol. II. 226, 485.
Barry, Robt.—Vol. I. 304.
Bartlett, Rev. Hobart—Vol. I. 267, 443.
Baskerville—Vol. I. 489; Vol. II. 428.
Baskerville, Jno.—Vol. II. 34.
Bass, Arch.—Vol. I. 451.
Bassett—Vol. I. 185, 240; Vol. II. 428, 490.
Bassett, Col.—Vol. I. 386.
Bassett, Miss, m. Gawin Corbin—Vol. II. 146.
Bassett, Miss, m. Benj. Harrison, Jr.—Vol. I. 311.
Bassett, Burwell—Vol. I. 185-187, 388; Vol. II. 496.
Bassett, F.—Vol. II. 337.
Bassett, G. W.—Vol. II. 73.
Bassett, Wm.—Vol. I. 386; Vol. II. 146, 496.
Bates—Vol. I. 461.
Bates, Jno.—Vol. II. 13.
Batherst—Vol. I. 406.
Bath Parish—Vol. I. 469, 471, 479.
Batley's Quarter Church, St. Mark's —Vol. II. 76.
Batson, Natha.—Vol. II. 479.
Battaile—Vol. I. 410, 412.
Battaile, Hay.—Vol. I. 410.
Battaile, Capt. Jno.—Vol. I. 404.
Battaile, Lawrence—Vol. I. 410.
Battaley, Wm.—Vol. II. 72.
Batte—Vol. I. 446.
Batte, Wm.—Vol. I. 479.
Baughan, Jas.—Vol. I. 404.

Beverley, Robt. 3rd, m. Maria Carter —Vol. I. 398; Vol. II. 482, 495.

Beverley, Robt. 4th, m. Jane Taylor —Vol. I. 403, 405; Vol. II. 182, 482, 495.

Beverley, Capt. Wm., m. Elizabeth Bland—Vol. I. 393, 401, 405, 446, 482; Vol. II. 140.

Beverley, Wm. B., of Blandfield— Vol. II. 481.

"Bewdley" (Ball)—Vol. II. 128.

Bibber, Jas.—Vol. I. 326.

Bickersteth, Mr.—Vol. II. 365.

Bier, P.—Vol. II. 336.

Big Lick Church, Roanoke—Vol. II. 65.

Biglow, J., of Boston—Vol. II. 244.

Billop—Vol. I. 326.

Billop, Jno.—Vol. I. 326.

Billups, Jno.—Vol. I. 487.

Birchett—Vol. I. 446; Vol. II. 428.

"Bishop's Neck" (Lee)—Vol. II. 145.

Black, Rev.—Vol. I. 320; Vol. II. 58.

Black, Rev. Jas.—Vol. I. 328.

Black, Rev. Wm.—Vol. I. 264, 265, 269; Vol. II. 393.

Blackburn—Vol. II. 215, 236.

Blackburn, Miss, m. Bushrod Washington—Vol. II. 236.

Blackburn, Miss Christian—Vol. II. 208, 236.

Blackburn, Edward—Vol. II. 227, 268.

Blackburn, Jane and Polly—Vol. II. 236.

Blackburn, Judy, m. Gustavus Alexander—Vol. II. 208, 236, 237.

Blackburn, Col. Richard 1st, of Rippon Lodge—Vol. II. 208, 236.

Blackburn, Richard 2nd—Vol. II. 236.

Blackburn, Thos., m. Miss Sinclair —Vol. II. 208, 236.

Blackburn, Mrs. Thos. (Miss Sinclair)—Vol. II. 236, 237.

Blackerby, Wm.—Vol. II. 469.

Blackford—Vol. II. 315.

Blackford, W. M.—Vol. II. 73.

"Black Jack"—Vol. II. 222.

Blacknal, Chas.—Vol. I. 326.

Blacknal, Rev. Jno.—Vol. I. 325; Vol. II. 467.

Blackwater—Vol. I. 201, 299, 310.

Blackwell—Vol. I. 64.

Blackwell, Jno.—Vol. II. 436.

Blackwell, Jos.—Vol. II. 436.

Blackwell, Capt. Sam'l—Vol. II. 468.

Blackwell, Sam'l., Jr.—Vol. II. 468.

Bladen, Miss, m. Robt. Carter 2nd— Vol. II. 111.

Blaford—Vol. II. 103.

Blagge, Jno.—Vol. II. 435.

Blagrove, Rev. Benj.—Vol. I. 310, 320, 386, 438; Vol. II. 265.

Blagrove, Henry—Vol. I. 487.

Blair—Vol. I. 192, 218; Vol. II. 428.

Blair, Archibald—Vol. I. 179.

Blair, David—Vol. II. 72.

Blair, Rev. James, Commissary and Pres. of Wm. and Mary College— Vol. I. 42, 94, 114, 136, 150, 154, 155, 157, 158, 159, 160-164, 167, 180, 195, 302, 304, 318, 385, 394, 398, 419, 432, 456, 457; Vol. II. 28, 291, 393, 395, 397, 400-402, 405, 412, 413, 420, 486, 487.

Blair, Mrs. James—Vol. I. 114.

Blair, Rev. Jno.—Vol. I. 285, 286.

Blair, Jno.—Vol. I. 165, 179; Vol. II. 495.

Blair, Miss, m. Jno. Bolling—Vol. I. 80.

Blair's Sermons—Vol. I. 22, 25, 54.

Blakely, Miss, m. Mr. McClaurine— Vol. II. 33.

Blanchard, Mr. C. B., of Norfolk— Vol. II. 425.

Bland—Vol. I. 192, 405, 444, 446; Vol. II. 428.

Bland, Miss, m. Mr. Haynes—Vol. I. 447.

Bland, Miss, m. Mr. Ruffin—Vol. I. 447.

Bland, Miss, m. Mr. Bannister—Vol. I. 447.

Bland, Elizabeth, m. Wm. Beverley —Vol. I. 113; Vol. II. 482.

Bland, Frances, m. (1) Jno. Randolph, (2) St. Geo. Tucker—Vol. I. 447.

Bland, Giles—Vol. I. 446.

Bland, Jno.—Vol. I. 446; Vol. II. 436.

Bland, Maria, m. Robert Munford—Vol. I. 449.

Bland, Miss, m. Henry Lee—Vol. II. 140.

Bland, Col. Richard, m. (1) Miss Swan, (2) Elizabeth Randolph—Vol. I. 446, 447; Vol. II. 320, 321, 482, 495.

Bland, Richard, m. Miss Poythress —Vol. I. 446, 447.

Bland, Theodoric 1st, of Westover—Vol. I. 446.

Bland, Theodoric 2nd—Vol. I. 446.

Bland, Theodoric 3rd, son of Richard 1st, m. Miss Bolling—Vol. I. 446, 447.

Bland, Col. and Dr. Theodoric, son of Theodoric 3rd—Vol. I. 148, 152, 171, 183, 221, 295, 445-447; Vol. II. 49.

Bland, Rev. Wm.—Vol. I. 113, 169, 238, 273.

Bland Papers—Vol. I. 295.

"Blandfield" (Bland)—Vol. I. 393; Vol. II. 481.

Blandford Church, Petersburg—Vol. I. 231, 439, 441, 442, 444, 452.

Blandford, Town of—Vol. I. 442, 444.

Blandford, derivation of name—Vol. I. 444.

Bledsoe, Miss, m. Walker Baylor, son of Col. Jno. Baylor—Vol. II. 465.

"Blenheim" (Taliafero)—Vol. II. 474.

Blewer, Rev. Thos.—Vol. II. 173.

Blick, Benj.—Vol. I. 479.

Blind Preacher, Famous (Mr. Waddell)—Vol. II. 87, 88, 95, 129.

Blissland Parish, New Kent—Vol. I. 383, 388; Vol. II. 496.

Bloomfield, Gen.—Vol. II. 154.

Bloomfield, Capt. Sam'l—Vol. I. 404; Vol. II. 172.

Bloomfield Parish—Vol. II. 77, 102, 103, 214.

Blow—Vol. I. 280; Vol. II. 428.

Blunt, Rev. Benjamin—Vol. I. 308.

Boggess, Henry—Vol. II. 468.

Boggs, Rev. Hugh Coran—Vol. I. 416, 420; Vol. II. 73, 91.

Bolithor—Vol. I. 248.

Boisseau—Vol. I. 468.

Boisseau, J.—Vol. I. 445.

Bolling—Vol. I. 139, 446; Vol. II. 428.

Bolling, Miss, m. Jas. Murray—Vol. I. 79.

Bolling, Miss, m. Thomas Eldridge —Vol. I. 79.

Bolling, Miss, m. Dr. Wm. Gay—Vol. I. 79.

Bolling, Miss, m. Col. Fleming—Vol. I. 79.

Bolling, Miss, m. Richard Randolph, of "Curls"—Vol. I. 138.

Bolling, Miss, m. Theodoric Bland —Vol. I. 447.

Bolling, Alexander—Vol. I. 446.

Bolling, Archibald, m. Miss Cary—Vol. I. 455.

Bolling, Drury—Vol. I. 445.

Bolling, Maj. Jno., son of Col. Robt. m. Miss Kennon—Vol. I. 79, 80, 458, 461.

Bolling, Col. Jno., son of Maj. Jno., m. Miss Blair—Vol. I. 79, 461.

Bolling, Pocahontas, m. Joseph Cabell—Vol. II. 62.

Bolling, Col. Robt., m. Miss Rolph—Vol. I. 79, 444-446; Vol. II. 62.

Bolling, Thomas—Vol. I. 446, 451, 461.

Bolling, Wm., of Bolling Hall, m. Miss Randolph—Vol. I. 80, 461, 462.

"Bolling Hall" (Bolling)—Vol. I. 80.

Bolton—Vol. I. 240.

Bolton, Rev. Dr.—Vol. I. 145.

Brackenridge—Vol. II. 475. (See Breckenridge.)

Braddock, Gen.—Vol. II. 43, 129, 246, 247, 252, 326, 474.

Braddock's War—Vol. I. 241.

Bradford—Vol. I. 240.

Bradford, Alexander—Vol. II. 347.

Bradley—Vol. II. 428.

Bradley, Rev.—Vol. I. 36.

Brady, S.—Vol. II. 337, 338.

Brafferton Professorship—Vol. I. 288.

Braidfoot—Vol. I. 280.

Braidfoot, Rev. Wm.—Vol. I. 279, 280; Vol. II. 314.

Bragg—Vol. I. 446, 452.

Branch—Vol. I. 452; Vol. II. 428.

Brand, Alexander—Vol. II. 35.

"Brandon" (Harrison)—Vol. I. 239, 357, 369, 398. (See upper and lower Brandon.)

Brandon Church, Old—Vol. I. 438.

Brandon, Rev. Jno.—Vol. II. 18.

Branham, D.—Vol. II. 72.

Branham, Vincent—Vol. II. 176.

Brassem, Mr. Jno.—Vol. I. 306.

Braxton—Vol. II. 111, 428.

Braxton, Miss, m. Robert Page—Vol. I. 340.

Braxton, Carter, m. Miss Corbin—Vol. I. 378, 380; Vol. II. 146.

Braxton, Carter, Jr.—Vol. I. 380.

Bray—Vol. I. 199.

Bray, Commissary—Vol. I. 158.

Bray, Mr.—Vol. I. 178.

Bray, David—Vol. I. 178.

Bray, David, Jr.—Vol. I. 179.

Bray, Jas.—Vol. I. 178.

Bray, Jas., Jr.—Vol. I. 179.

Bray, Richard—Vol. I. 376.

Bray's, or Leed's Church—Vol. II. 162-164.

Brazier, Robt.—Vol. II. 483.

Brazier, Sarah Harrison, m. Jno. Cannon—Vol. II. 483.

Brazier, Z., m. Elizabeth Fowke—Vol. II. 483.

Breckenridge—Vol. II. 61, 62. (See Brackenridge.)

Breckenridge, Anne, m. Robert Carter—Vol. II. 62.

Breckenridge, Elizabeth, m. Col. Wm. J. Lewis—Vol. II. 62.

Breckenridge, Gen. James—Vol. II. 62, 65.

Breckenridge, Jno., m. Mary Cabell—Vol. II. 62.

Breckenridge, Jno., Robt. and Wm.—Vol. II. 62.

Breckenridge, Joseph Cabell, m. Caroline Smith—Vol. II. 62.

Breckenridge, Letitia, m. (1) Mr. Grayson, (2) Gen. P. B. Carter—Vol. II. 62.

Breckenridge, Robt.—Vol. II. 318.

Breese—Vol. II. 429.

Breghin, Jas. Rev.—Vol. II. 393.

"Bremo" (Randolph and Cocke)—Vol. I. 139.

Brent—Vol. II. 206, 230, 428, 466.

Brent, Capt., of Stafford County—Vol. I. 93, 230; Vol. II. 205.

Brent, Mr.—Vol. II. 40.

Brent, Mr., m. Miss Euphan Mann Washington—Vol. II. 230.

Brent, Miss, of Fauquier, m. Henry Peyton—Vol. II. 466.

Brent, Daniel Carroll, m. Miss Lee—Vol. II. 205.

Brent, Geo. and Robt.—Vol. II. 205.

Brent, Jas.—Vol. II. 125.

Brent, Wm., m. Eliza Ambler—Vol. I. 98.

Brent, W.—Vol. II. 436.

Brentsville Church—Vol. II. 215.

Brewster, Cases—Vol. I. 118.

Briarly, Richard—Vol. II. 289.

"Brick Church"—Vol. I. 248.

Brick, or Middle Church, St. Thos. Parish—Vol. II. 84-88, 95.

Bridger—Vol. I. 303, 304.

Bridger, Widow, m. Col. Josiah Parker—Vol. I. 305.

Bridger, Jas.—Vol. I. 304.

Bridger, Joseph—Vol. I. 305.

Bridger, Gen. Joseph, son of Joseph—Vol. I. 305.

Bridger, Wm.—Vol. I. 304.

2

Brooke, Jno. T.—Vol. I. 402; Vol. II. 205.
Brooke, Richard, of King William, m. Maria Mercer—Vol. II. 205.
Brooke, Rev. Zachariah—Vol. I. 39, 386, 419, 459, 467.
Brooke County—Vol. II. 327.
Brooke's Bank—Vol. I. 404.
Brooking, Robt.—Vol. II. 85.
Brooking, Wm.—Vol. I. 324.
Brooks, Capt. Christopher—Vol. II. 242.
Brooky, Robt.—Vol. I. 405.
Broomscale, Rev.—Vol. I. 386.
Broone, Jno.—Vol. II. 436.
Brough, Robert—Vol. I. 230.
Brough, Wm.—Vol. I. 236.
Brougham, Lord—Vol. II. 160.
Broughton—Vol. II. 429.
Browinge—Vol. I. 240.
Brown—Vol. I. 280; Vol. II. 111, 201, 206.
Brown, Rev.—Vol. I. 236, 274; Vol. II. 103, 104, 307.
Brown, Old Mrs., of Charlestown—Vol. II. 297.
Brown, Miss, m. Rev. Samuel Low—Vol. I. 275.
Brown, Gen., of U. S. A.—Vol. II. 474.
Brown, Dr., m. Miss Scott—Vol. II. 208
Brown, Mrs. (Miss Scott)—Vol. II. 208.
Brown, Rev. Benj.—Vol. I. 234, 386.
Brown, Dr. Gustavus, m. Frances Fowke—Vol. I. 400; Vol. II. 198, 199, 201, 205.
Brown, Mrs. Frances (wife of Dr. Gustavus Brown—Vol. II. 199, 205.
Brown, Gustin—Vol. II. 201.
Brown, H. D.—Vol. II. 337.
Brown, Jas.—Vol. II. 72.
Brown, Jno., m. Hannah Cooke—Vol. II. 205.
Brown, Jno. and Danford—Vol. II. 333.
Brown, Nicholas—Vol. I. 230.

Brown, Sarah, m. Rev. Jas. Scott—Vol. II. 199, 208.
Brown, Rev. Templeman—Vol. II. 258.
Brown, Thos. and wife, Quakers—Vol. I. 255.
Brown, Rev. Thompson L.—Vol. II. 344, 348.
Brown, Richard—Vol. II. 13.
Brown, Rev. R. T.—Vol. II. 344.
Brown, W.—Vol. I. 387, 446.
"Brownsville" (Brown)—Vol. I. 255.
Browne—Vol. II. 206, 428.
Browne, Wm.—Vol. II. 268.
Brownell, Bishop—Vol. II. 378.
Bruce Chapel—Vol. II. 348.
Bruce—Vol. II. 13.
Bruce, Mrs. (Miss Cabell)—Vol. II. 62.
Bruce, Mrs. Eliza—Vol. II. 348.
Bruce, G. W.—Vol. II. 350.
Bruce, Wm.—Vol. II. 186.
Brunskills, Rev. Jno.—Vol. I. 167, 200, 409, 413, 430, 483; Vol. II. 20, 21, 24, 393, 401, 412.
Brunskill, Rev. Joseph—Vol. II. 217.
Brunswick County and Parishes—Vol. I. 469, 476; Vol. II. 183, 187, 203.
Bruton Parish—Vol. I. 146, 297; Vol. II. 400.
Bryan, Anne Butler (Lady Spottswood), wife of Gov. Alexander Spottswood—Vol. I. 166.
Bryan, Frederick—Vol. I. 179.
Bryan, J. R.—Vol. I. 329.
Bryan, Rev. Jno.—Vol. II. 287, 340, 468.
Bryant, Mr.—Vol. II. 40.
Bryant, Jno.—Vol. II. 215.
Bryant, Rev. Wm.—Vol. II. 66, 124, 287.
Bryce—Vol. I. 461.
Buchan—Vol. I. 446.
Buchan, Earl of—Vol. II. 109.
Buchan, Rev. Robt.—Vol. II. 59, 202, 204, 205.

Burwell, Mr., m. Miss Digges—Vol. I. 239.

Burwell, Miss, m. P. B. Whiting—Vol. I. 353.

Burwell, Miss, m. Rev. Lee Massey—Vol. II. 240.

Burwell, Miss, m. Philip Nelson—Vol. II. 290.

Burwell, Armistead—Vol. I. 179.

Burwell, Bacon—Vol. I. 353.

Burwell, Miss Betty, m. Jno. Page—Vol. I. 339.

Burwell, Carter, of "Grove," m. Lucy Grymes—Vol. I. 353, 371; Vol. II. 290.

Burwell, Elizabeth, m. Benj. Harrison—Vol. I. 311.

Burwell, Elizabeth, m. Pres. Nelson—Vol. I. 205; Vol. II. 290.

Burwell, Fanny, or Frances, m. Gov. Page—Vol. I. 334; Vol. II. 290.

Burwell, Fanny, Ariana—Vol. II. 290.

Burwell, Geo., of Carter Hall—Vol. II. 289.

Burwell, Jane—Vol. I. 353; Vol. II. 290.

Burwell, Maj. Lewis, 1st., of Carter's Creek, m. (1) Miss Higginson—Vol. I. 98, 106, 179, 339, 353; Vol. II. 290.

Burwell, Maj. Lewis, 2nd. m. Abigail Smith—Vol. I. 158, 311, 354; Vol. II. 65, 290, 291.

Burwell, Martha (Widow Cole)—Vol. I. 353, 354.

Burwell, Mr. Lewis 2nd, m. Abigail Smith—Vol. I. 353.

Burwell, Lewis 3rd., son of Lewis 2nd., of King's Mill—Vol. I. 332, Vol. II. 290.

Burwell, Lewis, son of Nathaniel 1st—Vol. II. 290.

Burwell, Pres. Lewis—Vol. I. 398, 477, 483; Vol. II. 290.

Burwell, Lewis, of Richmond—Vol. I. 353.

Burwell, Mary, daughter of Lewis 2nd—Vol. I. 353.

Burwell, Nathaniel 1st., son of Lewis 1st, m. Elizabeth Carter—Vol. I. 183, 353, 380; Vol. II. 111, 289, 290.

Burwell, Widow (Elizabeth Carter), m. George Nicholas—Vol. I. 183.

Burwell, Col. Nathaniel, of Carter's Hall, m. Susan Grymes—Vol. I. 147, 301, 370; Vol. II. 64, 288, 290, 293.

Burwell, Mrs. Susan—Vol. I. 370.

Burwell, Col. Nathaniel, of Frederick, m. Lucy Page—Vol. I. 339; Vol. II. 64, 289, 465, 495.

Burwell, Nathaniel, of Isle of Wight—Vol. II. 290, 495.

Burwell, Mrs. Nathaniel, of Saratoga (Miss Nelson)—Vol. I. 340.

Burwell, Philip—Vol. II. 289.

Burwell, Rebecca, m. Jaqueline Ambler—Vol. I. 98, 101, 106.

Burwell, Robt.—Vol. I. 304; Vol. II. 495.

Burwell, Robt. Carter—Vol. I. 353; Vol. II. 289, 290.

Burwell Graveyard—Vol. II. 281, 289, 290.

Bush, Philip—Vol. I. 102; Vol. II. 284.

Bushrodd, or Bushrod—Vol. I. 240, 407; Vol. II. 151.

Bushrod, Apphia (Mrs. Jno. Bushrod)—Vol. II. 151.

Bushrod, Apphia, m. Wm. Fauntleroy—Vol. II. 480.

Bushrod, Jno., son of Richard, m. Hannah Keene—Vol. II. 151, 153.

Bushrod, Mr., m. Jenny Corbin—Vol. II. 146.

Bushrod, Richard—Vol. II. 151.

Butler—Vol. I. 303; Vol. II. 215, 428.

Butler, Mrs. Ann, m. Chas. Carter, of Shirley—Vol. II. 112.

Butler, Jas., Duke of Ormond—Vol. I. 166.

Butler, Jane, m. Gov. Spottswood—Vol. I. 166.

Butler, Mr., of Miss. or La., m. Miss Lewis—Vol. II. 232.

Butler, Rev. Samuel, Pres. of Jockey Club—Vol. I. 310.

Butler's Analogy—Vol. II. 356.

Butt—Vol. I. 280.

Butterwood Church, Bath Parish—Vol. I. 471.

Butts, Mark—Vol. II. 271.

Butts, Thos.—Vol. I. 387.

Byrd—Vol. I. 318, 319, 330; Vol. II. 428.

Byrd, Miss, m. Chas. Carter—Vol. II. 111.

Byrd, Jane, m. Jno. Page—Vol. I. 339.

Byrd, Jno., m. Molly Page—Vol. I. 340.

Byrd, Maria, m. Landon Carter—Vol. II. 111.

Byrd, Ursula, m. Robt. Beverley—Vol. II. 482.

Byrd, Thos.—Vol. II. 289.

Byrd, William, of Williamsburg—Vol. I. 113.

Byrd, Col. Wm., of Westover—Vol. I. 53, 82, 158, 160, 218, 271, 282, 283, 285, 289, 292, 311, 315, 318, 396, 444; Vol. II. 68, 74, 75, 495.

Byrd, Mrs. Wm.—Vol. I. 319.

Cabell—Vol. II. 26, 29, 59, 60, 61, 428.

Cabell, Gen'l., of Danville—Vol. II. 61, 62.

Cabell, Prof., of W. Va., grandson of Col. Nicholas Cabell—Vol. II. 63.

Cabell, Miss, daughter of Wm. 2nd. m. Judge W. H. Cabell—Vol. II. 61.

Cabell, Miss, m. Mr. Bruce—Vol. II. 61.

Cabell, Miss, m. Mr. Rives—Vol. II. 61.

Cabell, Miss, daughter of Frederick 1st. m. (1) Hecter Cabell, (2) Judge Daniel—Vol. II. 63.

Cabell, Anne, daughter of Joseph 1st. m. Robert Carter Harrison—Vol. II. 62.

Cabell, Col. Edward A., son of Wm. 3rd—Vol. II. 58, 62.

Cabell, Elizabeth, daughter of Joseph 1st. m. Col. Wm. J. Lewis —Vol. II. 62.

Cabell, Francis, of Warminister, son of Col. Nicholas Cabell—Vol. II. 63.

Cabell, Frederick 1st, son of Col. Jno. 1st—Vol. II. 63.

Cabell, Frederick 2nd, son of Fred. 1st—Vol. II. 63.

Cabell, Dr. Geo., son of Col. Jno. 1st—Vol. II. 61, 62.

Cabell, Hannah and Henningham, daughters of Col. Nicholas Cabell —Vol. II. 63.

Cabell, Hecter, m. Miss Cabell—Vol. II. 63.

Cabell, Col. Jno. 1st., son of Wm. 1st. m. Paulina Jordan—Vol. II. 60, 61, 62, 63.

Cabell, Dr. Jno. 2nd., son of Col. Jno. 1st—Vol. II. 63.

Cabell, Col. Joseph 1st., son of Wm. 1st. m. Miss Hopkins—Vol. II. 60, 61, 62.

Cabell, Joseph, 2nd., son of Joseph 1st. m. Pocahontas Bolling—Vol. II. 62.

Cabell, Joseph C. Col., son of Nicholas—Vol. II. 61.

Cabell, Landon, son of Wm. 3rd. m. Miss Rose—Vol. II. 62.

Cabell, Mary, daughter of Joseph 1st. m. John Breckenridge—Vol. II. 62.

Cabell, Mayo, son of Wm. 3rd—Vol. II. 62.

Cabell, Col. Nicholas, of Liberty Hall, son of Wm. 1st. m. Hannah Carrington—Vol. II. 29, 60, 61, 63.

Cabell, Paulina, daughter of Wm. 3rd. m. (1) Major Edmund Read, (2) Rev. Legrand—Vol. II. 62.

Cabell, Dr. R. Henry, son of Landon —Vol. II. 62.

Cabell, Col. Samuel Jordan, son of Wm. 2nd. m. Sarah Lyme—Vol. II. 62.

Cabell, Dr. Wm. (Emigrant)—Vol. II. 60-62.

Cabell, Col. Wm. 2nd., son of Wm. 1st., of Union Hill, m. Margaret Jordan—Vol. II. 30, 60-62.

Cabell, Col. Wm. 3rd, son of Wm. 2nd. m. Anne Carrington—Vol. II. 61, 62.

Cabell, Judge W. H., son of Col. Nicholas, m. Miss Cabell—Vol. II. 61.

Cabell, Wm. I.—Vol. II. 58.

Cabel—Vol. I. 401.

Cabin Point, Church, Surrey—Vol. I. 310.

Cadwallader—Vol. II. 429.

Caines, Miss Frances, of London— Vol. I. 142, 201, 232, 233.

Ca-Ira Church—Vol. II. 35, 38.

Caison, Rev. Jean—Vol. I. 466.

Caldwell, Judge Alexander—Vol. II. 337, 338.

Caldwell, Rev. David—Vol. I. 281, 386; Vol. II. 18, 19, 58, 275, 462, 463.

Caldwell, E. H.—Vol. II. 350.

Caldwell, Joseph—Vol. II. 337, 338.

Call, Daniel, m. Lucy Ambler—Vol. I. 99.

"Callands"—Vol. II. 15.

Callaway, Rev.—Vol. II. 224, 307.

Calloway—Vol. II. 428.

Calloway, Jas.—Vol. II. 58.

Calloway, Thos.—Vol. II. 13.

Calloway's Church—Vol. II. 59.

Calmes, Marquis—Vol. II. 284.

Calvert, Rev. Cornelius, Jr.—Vol. I. 249.

Calvert, Capt. Jno.—Vol. I. 276.

Calvin, Jno.—Vol. I. 259.

Cambden, Lord—Vol. I. 222; Vol. II. 14.

Camden Parish, Pittsylvania—Vol. II. 14.

Cameron, Lord—Vol. II. 106.

Cameron, Anna M.—Vol. I. 486.

Cameron, Judge Duncan—Vol. I. 486; Vol. II. 371, 373.

Cameron, Dr. Jno.—Vol. I. 443, 453, 479, 485-488; Vol. II. 23, 37.

Cameron, Thos. M.—Vol. I. 487.

Cameron, Wm. Rev.—Vol. I. 443, 453.

Cameron Parish, Loudoun—Vol. II. 225, 271, 272, 273.

Camm, Rev. Jno. (Commissary)— Vol. I. 173, 176, 202, 203, 208, 214, 216, 218, 219, 225, 242, 304, 401; Vol. II. 495.

Camp, Geo.—Vol. II. 13.

Camp, Rev. Ichabod—Vol. II. 48, 57.

Campbell—Vol. I. 192; Vol. II. 94, 159-161.

Campbell, Rev., m. Miss Percy— Vol. II. 359.

Campbell, Rev., m. Miss Brown— Vol. II. 199.

Campbell, Miss, m. Judge Wayne— Vol. II. 160, 161.

Campbell, Alexander 1st—Vol. II. 159, 160.

Campbell, Alexander 2nd. m. Miss Fitzhugh—Vol. II. 161.

Campbell, Anna, m. Dr. Tennant— Vol. II. 161.

Campbell, Rev. Archibald 1st. m. (1) Rebecca Stuat, (2) Miss Mc-Coy—Vol. II. 158, 159-162, 164; Vol. II. 422.

Campbell, Archibald 2nd. m. Miss Hughs—Vol. II. 161.

Campbell, Chas., (The Historian)— Vol. I. 65, 130, 139, 336, 396; Vol. II. 144, 326.

Campbell, Eliza, m. Mr. Leland— Vol. II. 161.

Campbell, Emily, m. Robert Mayo— Vol. II. 161.

Campbell, Ferdinand, Prof. W. & M. —Vol. II. 160, 161.

Campbell, Frederick, son of Rev. Archibald—Vol. II. 160.

Campbell, Gilbert—Vol. II. 436.

Campbell, J.—Vol. I. 446.

Campbell, Jas.—Vol. I. 393.

Carrington, Mary, daughter of Paul 2nd—Vol. II. 29.

Carrington, Mayo, son of Geo. 1st—Vol. II. 29, 35.

Carrington, Nathaniel, son of Geo. 1st—Vol. II. 29.

Carrington, Paul 1st. (Emigrant), m. Miss Henningham—Vol. II. 28-30.

Carrington, Judge Paul 2nd, son of Geo. 1st. m. (1) Miss Read, (2) Priscilla Sims—Vol. I. 483; Vol. II. 29, 30, 62, 450, 451.

Carrington, Judge Paul 3rd, son of Paul 2nd—Vol. II. 29, 450-451.

Carrington, Robert, son of Paul 2nd —Vol. II. 29.

Carrington, William, son of Geo. 1st—Vol. II. 29.

Carter—Vol. I. 183, 218, 319, 364, 422, 461; Vol. II. 52, 82, 105, 110, 111, 116, 123, 173, 181, 206, 221, 279, 298, 428.

Carter, Mr., of Amherst, m. Miss Fauntleroy—Vol. II. 480.

Carter, Councellor of "Nomini," son of Robert 2nd—Vol. II. 111-112.

Carter, Miss, daughter of Chas., of Fredericksburg, m. Robert Page, of Hanover—Vol. I. 339.

Carter, Ann, daughter of Cleave Carter, m. John Carter 1st—Vol. II. 110, 121.

Carter, Ann, daughter of King Carter, m. Benj. Harrison, of Berkley—Vol. II. 111.

Carter, Chas. 1st, son of Jno. 1st—Vol. II. 110.

Carter, Chas. 2nd., son of King Carter, m. (1) Miss Walker, (2) Miss Byrd, (3) Miss Taliafero—Vol. II. 111.

Carter, Chas., of Corotoman and Shirley, m. (1) Mary ——, (2) Ann Butler Moore—Vol. I. 318, 382; Vol. II. 112-114, 122, 125, 283, 495.

Carter, Mrs. Mary, wife of Chas., of Corotoman—Vol. II. 122.

Carter, Chas., of Fredericksburg, m. Elizabeth Lewis—Vol. I. 339; Vol. II. 72, 186, 187, 202, 232.

Carter, Chas. L.—Vol. II. 72.

Carter, Cleave—Vol. II. 110, 121.

Carter, Dale—Vol. II. 125.

Carter, Edward—Vol. II. 58.

Carter, Eleanor, daughter of Jno. 1st—Vol. II. 110, 121.

Carter, Elizabeth, daughter of King Carter, m. (1) Nathanial Burwell, (2) Dr. Geo. Nicholas—Vol. I. 153; Vol. II. 111.

Carter, Geo. 1st, son of Jno. 1st—Vol. II. 110, 121.

Carter, George 2nd., son of King Carter—Vol. II. 111, 215.

Carter, Henry—Vol. I. 396; Vol. II. 125.

Carter, James—Vol. I. 325.

Carter, Rev. Jesse—Vol. I. 390, 414; Vol. II. 33.

Carter, Jno. 1st., of Lancaster. m. (1) Jane Glyn, (2) Ann Carter, (3) Sarah Ludlowe—Vol. II. 110, 116, 117, 121, 123, 227.

Carter, Jno. 2nd, son of Jno. 1st, m. (1) Elizabeth Wormley, (2) Miss Loyd—Vol. II. 110, 116, 123.

Carter, Jno. 3rd., son of King Carter. m. Miss Hill—Vol. II. 111.

Carter, Judith, daughter of King Carter, m. Mann Page—Vol. I. 339; Vol. II. 111, 122.

Carter, Joseph—Vol. II. 125.

Carter, Landon, of Sabine Hall, son of King Carter, m. (1) Elizabeth Wormley, (2) Maria Byrd, (3) Miss Beale—Vol. II. 111, 178.

Carter, Landon, of Richmond County, m. Catherine Tayloe—Vol. II. 182.

Carter, Lucy, daughter of King Carter, m. Henry Fitzhugh—Vol. II. 111.

Carter, Maria, daughter of Landon, m. Robt. Beverley—Vol. II. 482.

Carter, Mary, daughter of King Carter—Vol. II. 111.

Carter, Peter, m. Mary Ann Ellis—Vol. II. 462.

Carter, Robert (King) 1st. son of Jno. 1st. m. (1) Judith Armistead, (2) Betty Landon (widow Willis)—Vol. I. 205, 218, 311, 324, 339, 345-347, 351, 353; Vol. II. 110, 111, 113, 116, 117-119, 121, 122, 124, 125, 153, 290, 495.

Carter, Robert 2nd. of Nomini, son of King Carter, m. Miss Bladen—Vol. I. 458; Vol. II. 111, 153.

Carter, Robt. Wormeley—Vol. II. 436.

Carter, Sarah, daughter of Jno. 1st—Vol. II. 110, 121.

Carter, Sarah, Betty and Ludlow—Vol. II. 122.

Carter, Thos.—Vol. II. 34.

"Carter Hall" (Burwell)—Vol. I. 353, 370; Vol. II. 289, 293.

Cartersville Church—Vol. II. 38.

Caruthers—Vol. I. 227, 294.

Cary, or Carey—Vol. I. 97, 139, 238, 303, 326, 330, 364, 414, 455; Vol. II. 39, 108, 109, 428.

Cary, Miss, m. Archibald Bolling—Vol. I. 455.

Cary, Miss, m. Thos. Isham Randolph—Vol. I. 455.

Cary, Miss, m. Thos. Mann Randolph—Vol. I. 455.

Cary, Miss, m. Joseph Kincade—Vol. I. 455.

Cary, Miss, m. Benj. Watkins—Vol. I. 451.

Cary, Miss, m. Geo. Wm. Fairfax—Vol. I. 108.

Cary, Archibald, of Amphill—Vol. I. 340, 455; Vol. II. 34.

Cary, Col. G. A.—Vol. I. 236.

Cary, Henry, m. Miss Randolph—Vol. I. 179, 455.

Cary, Jno., of Bristol, England—Vol. I. 455.

Cary, Jno.—Vol. I. 236, 326.

Cary, Mary, m. Edward Jaqueline 1st—Vol. I. 101, 108-110.

Cary, Miles—Vol. I. 236, 455.

Cary, Polly, m. Carter Page—Vol. I. 340, 455.

Cary, Richard—Vol. I. 238.

Cary, Robt.—Vol. I. 326.

Carey, Col. Wilson, of "Celeys"—Vol. I. 101, 108, 185.

Cary, Wilson Miles, of "Carysbrook"—Vol. I. 109, 235, 236, 242.

"Carysbrook" (Cary)—Vol. I. 242.

Caslett, Capt. Jno.—Vol. I. 404.

"Castle Hill" (Rives)—Vol. II. 46.

Castleman, Rev. Robt. A.—Vol. II. 317, 342, 343.

Castleman, Rev. Thos.—Vol. I. 475.

Catesby—Vol. II. 429.

Cathcart, Robt. "Moderator"—Vol. I. 432.

Catlett—Vol. I. 330; Vol. II. 428.

Catlett, Chas.—Vol. II. 259.

Catlett, Jno., m. E. Gaines—Vol. II. 77, 96.

Catlett, Rebecca, m. Francis Conway—Vol. II. 96.

Catlett, Judith and Elizabeth—Vol. II. 97.

Cattail Church, King William—Vol. I. 381, 382.

"Causons" (Bland)—Vol. I. 446, 447.

Caves—Vol. II. 82, 94.

Cave, Benj.—Vol. II. 74, 85.

Cave, David—Vol. II. 76.

Cave, William—Vol. II. 77.

Caw, Thos.—Vol. II. 42.

Cazenove, Lewis A.—Vol. II. 268, 271.

Cazenove, Wm. G.—Vol. II. 268.

Cecils (Religious Sect)—Vol. II. 360.

Cedar Creek Chapel (Fred.)—Vol. II. 283.

"Cedar Grove" (McCall)—Vol. II. 180.

"Celeys" (Cary)—Vol. I. 108.

Cennick, Mr.—Vol. I. 429.

Cerwin—Vol. II. 429.

Cewling, Mr. Jas.—Vol. I. 305.

Chadouin—Vol. I. 468.

Chalmers (writer)—Vol. II. 144.

Chamberlain, Sam'l—Vol. II. 336.

Chamberlain—Vol. I. 277.

Chamberlaine, Richard—Vol. II. 15.

Chamberlayne—Vol. II. 428.

Chamberlayne, Edward—Vol. I. 380.

Chamberlayne, Wm.—Vol. I. 387.

Chambers, Rev.—Vol. II. 322.

Chambers, Thos.—Vol. I. 487.

Chambliss—Vol. I. 446.

Champe—Vol. II. 111.

Champe, Col., of King George—Vol. II. 474.

Champe, Jno.—Vol. II. 187.

Champe, Miss, m. Austin Brokenbrough—Vol. II. 474.

Chandler, Rev. Dr.—Vol. I. 168; Vol. II. 351.

Chandler, Robt.—Vol. II. 15.

Change in Service, Proposal by Bishops—Vol II. 373.

"Chantilly" (Lee)—Vol. II. 140, 143, 171.

Chapin, Rev. Sewar—Vol. I. 318, 320.

Chapline, Josiah—Vol. II. 336, 337.

Chapline, Moses W.—Vol. II. 336.

Chapline, W., Sr.—Vol. II. 337.

Chapline, Wm., Jr.—Vol. II. 336, 337.

Chapman—Vol. II. 206.

Chapman, Dr.—Vol. I. 407.

Chapman, Edmund—Vol. I. 416.

Chapman, Capt. Henry—Vol. I. 247.

Chapman, Wm.—Vol. II. 268.

"Chappawamsic" (Harrison)—Vol. II. 214.

Charles City County and Parish— Vol. I. 314, 437.

Charles, or Charles River Parish, York County—Vol. I. 239.

Charles City Hundred—Vol. I. 314.

Charlotte Parishes and County— Vol. I. 482.

Charlottesville Church—Vol. II. 52.

Charlton—Vol. I. 259, 261.

Charlton, Bridget, m. Mr. Foxcroft —Vol. I. 256, 258.

Charlton, Elizabeth—Vol. I. 256.

Charlton, Mr. Henry—Vol. I. 254.

Charlton, Mr. Stephen—Vol. I. 253, 254.

Chase, Bishop, his college in Ohio— Vol. II. 306, 336.

Chase, Rev.—Vol. I. 267.

Chasteen—Vol. I. 468.

Chasteen, Isham—Vol. II. 13.

"Chatham" (Fitzhugh)—Vol. II. 183, 195, 202.

Chatham, Lord—Vol. I. 412; Vol. II. 476.

Chattelux—Vol. I. 211.

"Chatterton" (Tayloe)—Vol. II. 182.

"Chattsworth" (Randolph)—Vol. I. 139.

Cheesecake Church—Vol. I. 197.

"Chellowe" (Bolling)—Vol. II. 62.

Chesley, Capt.—Vol. I. 178.

Chesley, Rev.—Vol. I. 489; Vol. II. 162.

Chesley, Robt.—Vol. II. 192.

Chesterfield County and Parishes— Vol. I. 125, 448.

Chevers, Jno. M.—Vol. I. 259.

Chevers, Rev. Mark L.—Vol. I. 231, 237; Vol. II. 23.

Chew—Vol. II. 94.

Chew, Miss Alice—Vol II. 97, 98.

Chew, James—Vol. II. 98.

Chew, Jno.—Vol. II. 72.

Chew, Larkin—Vol. II. 72, 97.

Chew, Miss Milly—Vol. II. 97. 98.

Chew, Robt. I.—Vol. II. 72.

Chew, Thos.—Vol. II. 72.

Chewming—Vol. I. 364, 365.

Chewning, Robt.—Vol. II. 127, 359, 360, 373.

Chewning, Wm.—Vol. II. 125.

Chicawane, or Northumberland— Vol. II. 131.

Chichely, Sir Henry (Baronet)— Vol. I. 364, 372; Vol. II. 116.

Chichely, Lady Agatha—Vol. I. 357.

Chichester—Vol. I. 364; Vol. II. 233.

Chichester, Geo. M.—Vol. II. 238, 276, 277.

Chichester, Mrs. (Miss Peyton)— Vol. II. 467.

Chichester, Richard—Vol. II. 125.

Clark, Robt.—Vol. II. 42, 468.

Clark, Thos.—Vol. II. 13.

Clarke—Vol. I. 452; Vol. II. 428.

Clarksburg Churches—Vol. II. 336, 340.

Clarkson, Peter—Vol. II. 43.

Clarksville Church, Mecklenburg—Vol. I. 487.

Claughton, Jas.—Vol. II. 468.

Claughton, Pemberton—Vol. II. 468.

Claughton, Wm.—Vol. II. 132.

Clay—Vol. I. 192.

Clay, Rev. Chas—Vol. II. 48-51, 61.

Clay, Henry, (Statesman)—Vol. II. 48.

Clay, Obadiah—Vol. I. 487.

Clay, Rev. Paul—Vol. I. 453.

Clayborne—Vol. I. 240; Vol. II. 111.

Clayborne, Mr., of Dinwiddie—Vol. I. 475.

Clayborne, Miss, m. Rev. Jarratt—Vol. I. 475.

Claybourn—Vol. I. 259.

Clayton—Vol. II. 428, 466.

Clayton, Rev. Daniel—Vol. I. 388.

Clayton, Jno.—Vol. I. 179.

Clayton, Mr., m. Miss Pendleton—Vol. II. 298.

Clayton, Philip—Vol. II. 77, 78.

Clayton, Sam'l—Vol. II. 78.

Clayton, Wm.—Vol. I. 387.

Cleck, Jas. Rev.—Vol. II. 393.

Clements—Vol. II. 172, 429.

Clements, Jno.—Vol. I. 393, 405.

Clements, Maco—Vol. I. 405.

Clerical Associations—Vol. I. 42.

Clift—Vol. II. 206.

"Clifton" (Harrison)—Vol. II. 62.

Clopton—Vol. II. 428.

Clopton, Rev. Reuben—Vol. I. 380.

Clopton, Walton—Vol. I. 387.

Clopton, W.—Vol. I. 387.

Clough—Vol. II. 496.

Clover, Rev. Lewis P.—Vol. I. 87; Vol. II. 39.

Cloyd—Vol. II. 429.

Clughton—Vol. II. 468.

Coakley, Jno.—Vol. II. 73.

Coalsmouth Church—Vol. II. 346.

Coates—Vol. II. 429.

Cobb, Ambrose—Vol. I. 179.

Cobb, Robt.—Vol. I. 178, 524.

Cobb, Samuel—Vol. I. 440; Vol. II. 24.

"Cobbs" (Lee)—Vol. II. 136, 145.

Cobbs—Vol. I. 39, 40; Vol. II. 52, 429. (Cobb.)

Cobbs, Mr. Edward—Vol. II. 50.

Cobbs, Rev. Nicholas—Vol. II. 18, 19, 443, 444; Vol. II. 50, 53, 65, 262.

Cobbs, Thos.—Vol. I. 179.

Cock—Vol. I. 364.

Cock, Richard—Vol. I. 359.

Cockburn, Admiral—Vol. II. 148, 241.

Cockburn, Martin, m. Miss Bronaugh—Vol. I. 174; Vol. II. 226, 229, 241, 485.

Cockburn, Mrs. Martin (Miss Bronaugh)—Vol. II. 229.

Cocke—Vol. I. 303, 311, 461; Vol. II. 428.

Cocke, Bowler—Vol. I. 141.

Cocke, Henry—Vol. I. 479.

Cocke, Jno. R.—Vol. II. 13.

Cocke, Gen. Philip, St. George—Vol. II. 40, 51.

Cocke, Wm.—Vol. II. 435.

Cofer, Rev.—Vol. II. 18, 39, 66.

Coffer, Thos. Withers—Vol. II. 226, 270, 485.

Coffin, Rev.—Vol. II. 177, 181.

Coghill, Jesse—Vol. I. 451.

Coharneittary (Chief)—Vol. II. 478.

Cohoon, Samuel—Vol. I. 290.

Coke, Bishop—Vol. II. 353.

Cole—Vol. I. 192, 243, 461.

Cole, M., of Matchoactoke River—Vol. II. 131.

Cole, Rev.—Vol. I. 356, 438; Vol. II. 103.

Cole, Gulielmi—Vol. I. 244. (See Wm.)

Cole, Jno.—Vol. II. 48, 52.

Cole, Rev. Jno.—Vol. I. 310, 329; Vol. II. 82.

Cowper, the poet—Vol. I. 55, 87, 100.

Cox—Vol. I. 192, 280; Vol. II. 298, 301, 496.

Cox, Fleet—Vol. II. 153.

Cox, Jno.—Vol. I. 486.

Cox, Peter—Vol. II. 468.

Cox, Presley—Vol. II. 268.

Coxe, Miss, m. Lorenzo Lewis—Vol. II. 232.

Coxe, Wm.—Vol. II. 50.

Cox, Rev.—Vol. I. 240.

Crabb, Jno.—Vol. II. 153.

Craddock (Carodoc)—Vol. II. 429.

Craddock, Elizabeth, m. Jno. Jaqueline—Vol. I. 104.

Craddock, Granville—Vol. II. 13.

Craddock, Lieut.—Vol. II. 432.

Craford, David—Vol. I. 387.

Cragne, Rev. Jas—Vol. II. 467.

Craig—Vol. I. 192.

Craig, Jas.—Vol. I. 484, 485.

Craig, Rev. Jas—Vol. II. 10, 217, 218.

Craig, Rev. Jno.—Vol. I. 344, 345, 347.

Craig, Rev. Wm.—Vol. I. 490.

Craik, Rev.—Vol. II. 344, 347, 348.

Craioby, Wm.—Vol. II. 24.

Cralle, Capt. Jno.—Vol. II. 468.

Cralle, Kenner—Vol. II. 468.

Cralle, Thos.—Vol. II. 468.

Crashaw, Rev.—Vol. I. 67, 69, 74, 76, 121.

Crawford—Vol. II. 428.

Crawford, Rev. Chas.—Vol. II. 57-59.

Crawford, David—Vol. II. 58.

Crawford, Nelson—Vol. II. 58.

Crawford, Col. Wm.—Vol. I. 278, 280.

Crawford, Rev. Wm.—Vol. II. 51, 59.

Crawford, W. S.—Vol. II. 58.

Crawley, Robt.—Vol. I. 178.

Crease, Anthony—Vol. II. 268

Crease, J. H.—Vol. II. 268.

Creel, Dr. D.—Vol. II. 249.

Crews, Thos.—Vol. II. 58.

Crocker, Dr., of Providence—Vol. II. 362.

Crockford, Jno.—Vol. II. 268.

Croes, Rev. Robt—Vol. I. 143, 144.

Cromley, Jas.—Vol. II. 281.

Cromwell—Vol. I. 189; Vol. II. 106-108.

Cromwell, Oliver—Vol. I. 291, 370; Vol. II. 137, 229, 253, 300, 352.

Cromwell, Thos., of Putney—Vol. I. 291.

Crooper—Vol. I. 270.

Crosk, Edward—Vol. I. 404.

Croswell, Rev. Dr., of New Haven—Vol. II. 362.

Crowley, Nathaniel—Vol. I. 179.

Cruden, Rev. Alexander—Vol. I. 390, 401.

Crump—Vol. II. 215.

Crump, Jno.—Vol. II. 72.

Crump, Richard—Vol. II. 34.

Crumples, Wm.—Vol. I. 304.

Crusoe, Robinson—Vol. I. 283.

Crutcher—Vol. II. 206.

Crutcher, Thos.—Vol. II. 72.

Crutchfield, Maj.—Vol. I. 236.

Crute (Crwt)—Vol. II. 429.

Crute, Robt.—Vol. II. 13.

Culpeper—Vol. II. 106, 110.

Culpepper, Lord Thos.—Vol. II. 105. 106, 108. 193, 282, 398.

Culpepper County—Vol. II. 74.

Cumberland County and Parishes—Vol. I. 98, 139; Vol. II. 33.

Cumberland Parish, Lunenburg Co.—Vol. I. 482; Vol. II. 179.

Cummings, Rev. Geo.—Vol. I. 145, 276, 281.

Cunliff, Henry—Vol. II. 469.

Cunliffe—Vol. II. 429.

Cunningham—Vol. I. 489, 461; Vol. II. 82.

Cunningham, J. A.—Vol. I. 461.

Cunningham Chapel—Vol. II. 281, 283, 288.

Curd—Vol. I. 461.

Curdsville Church—Vol. II. 39.

Cureton, Jno.—Vol. I. 487.

Curle, Thos.—Vol. I. 230.

Curle, Wilson, of Hampton—Vol. I. 292.

"Curls" (Randolph)—Vol. I. 80, 136, 138, 139, 140, 293, 294, 398.

Curls Church—Vol. I. 137.

Currie, Geo.—Vol. II. 13.

Currie, Rev. David—Vol. I. 123.

Currie, Rev. E., of Lancaster—Vol. II. 112, 113.

Currie, Mrs.—Vol. II. 112.

Curtis—Vol. I. 330, 364, 365.

Curtis, Rice—Vol. II. 72.

Curtis, Rice, Jr.—Vol. II. 72.

Curtis, Z. B.—Vol. II. 337.

Cushing, Mr.—Vol. II. 30.

Custis—Vol. I. 259, 262, 270; Vol. II. 428.

Custis, Daniel Parke—Vol. I. 387.

Custis, Edmund—Vol. I. 326.

Custis, Edmund, of London, son of Jno. 1st—Vol. I. 262.

Custis, Geo. Washington Parke, of "Arlington"—Vol. I. 180, 196; Vol. II. 169, 231.

Custis, Mrs. G. W. P., of Arlington (Miss Fitzhugh)—Vol. II. 196.

Custis, Jno. 1st. (Emigrant)—Vol. I. 22, 34, 180, 255, 262.

Custis, Jno. 2nd., of Arlington, son of Jno. 1st. m. (1) —— ——. (2) Miss Scarborough—Vol. I. 262.

Custis, Jno. 3rd., son of Jno. 2nd—Vol. I. 262.

Custis, Maj. Jno. 4th., son of Jno. 3rd., m. Miss Parke—Vol. I. 179, 257, 262.

Custis, Joseph, son of Jno. 1st—Vol. I. 262.

Custis, Robert, of Rotterdam, son of Jno. 1st—Vol. I. 262.

Custis, Thos., of Baltimore, Ireland, son of Jno. 1st—Vol. I. 262.

Custis, Wm., son of Jno. 1st—Vol. I. 262.

Custis, Mr., son of Mrs. Washington —Vol. II. 184, 185.

Custis, Mrs., m. Dr. Daniel Steuart —Vol. II. 231.

Custis, Miss, daughter of Jno. Custis, m. Col. Argal Yeardley— Vol. I. 262.

Custis, Miss, wife of Lawrence Lewis—Vol. II. 231.

Cutchins, Thos.—Vol. I. 306.

Cutter, Rev.—Vol. II. 275.

Cypress Chapel—Vol. I. 289.

Dabnee, Cornelius—Vol. I. 387.

Dabney—Vol. I. 330; Vol. II. 428.

Dabney, Benjamin—Vol. I. 325.

Dabney, Mr. Wm.—Vol. I. 380.

Dade—Vol. I. 240; Vol. II. 185, 206, 256.

Dade, Baldwin—Vol. II. 192, 258, 268.

Dade, Cadwaller I.—Vol. II. 190, 192.

Dade, Horatio—Vol. II. 186.

Dade, Langhorne—Vol. II. 190, 192.

Dade, Townshend—Vol. II. 186, 190, 191, 258, 268, 270, 436.

Dagleish, Alexander—Vol. I. 325.

Daily—Vol. I. 489.

Dale's Gift—Vol. I. 123; Vol. II. 431.

Dale's attempt to get another daughter of Powhatan—Vol. II. 472.

Dale's Chapel—Vol. I. 278.

Dale Parish, Chesterfield—Vol. I. 439, 440, 448, 450, 451, 453, 455.

Dale—Vol. I. 278.

Dale, Commodore Richard—Vol. I. 278, 279; Vol. II. 357.

Dale, Sir Thomas—Vol. I. 75, 77-79, 81-85, 118, 123, 124, 125, 126, 136, 137, 253, 338, 439, 448; Vol. II. 425, 469, 472, 473.

Dalcho, Rev. Mr. (His History)— Vol. II. 352, 356.

Dalrymple, Rev. E. A.—Vol. II. 489.

Dalrymple, Rev. Mr.—Vol. I. 382, 386.

Dalton, John—Vol. II. 268, 270.

Dalton, Tristam—Vol. II. 268.

Dalton, Wm.—Vol. II. 43.

Dame, Rev. Mr.—Vol. II. 16, 30.

Dameron, Geo.—Vol. II. 469.

Dana, Rev. Mr.—Vol. II. 165, 262, 491.

Danton, W.—Vol. I. 259.

Dandridge—Vol. I. 282; Vol. II. 298, 428, 496.

Dandridge, Mrs. (Miss Pendleton)— Vol. II. 299.

Dandridge, John—Vol. I. 387.

Dandridge, Mary, m. John Spottswood—Vol. I. 166.

Dandridge, Nathaniel—Vol. I. 166.

Dangerfield—Vol. I. 405.

Dangerfield, Miss, m. G. C. Tarberville—Vol. II. 146.

Dangerfield, Col. John, m. Miss Merriwether—Vol. I. 405-406; Vol. II. 146, 405.

Dangerfield, John 1st. (Emigrant) —Vol. I. 405, 406.

Dangerfield, John, son of Col. Wm., m. (1) Miss Southall, (2) Miss Armstead—Vol. I. 406.

Dangerfield, LeRoy—Vol. I. 405, 406.

Dangerfield, Wm., m. Miss Fauntleroy—Vol. I. 405, 406; Vol. II. 72.

Dangerfield, Capt. Wm.—Vol. I. 393.

Dangerfield, Col. Wm., m. Miss Willis—Vol. I. 405, 406.

Daniel—Vol. I. 364; Vol. II. 94, 206, 428.

Daniel, Judge—Vol. II. 63, 204.

Daniel, J.—Vol. II. 90, 276.

Daniel, Peter, m. Sarah Travers— Vol. II. 198, 205.

Daniel, P. V.—Vol. II. 205.

Daniel, Sarah (Miss Travers)—Vol. II. 205.

Daniel, Travers, m. Frances Moncure—Vol. II. 205.

Darden, John—Vol. I. 304.

Darke, Genl.—Vol. II. 308.

Darne, Henry—Vol. II. 268.

Darneile, Rev. Mr. Isaac—Vol. II. 51, 59, 61.

Dashiel, Rev.—Vol. I. 38; Vol. II. 18, 147, 159, 261.

Dauson, Mr.—Vol. II. 24.

Davenport—Vol. II. 428.

Davenport, Biskett—Vol. II. 81.

Davenport, I. J. C.—Vol. II. 349.

Davenport, Rev. Joseph—Vol. I. 204, 239.

Davenport, Richard—Vol. II. 50.

Davenport, Thos.—Vol. II. 13, 34.

Davenport, Capt. Wm.—Vol. II. 469.

Davenport, Wm.—Vol. II. 132.

Davies—Vol. II. 429.

Davies, Mr., President of Princeton College—Vol. I. 15; Vol. II. 280.

Davies, Arthur B.—Vol. II. 58.

Davies, A. B., Jr.—Vol. II. 58.

Davies, Dr. H. L.—Vol. II. 58.

Davies, James—Vol. II. 58.

Davies, Capt. J.—Vol. II. 58

Davies, Nicholas—Vol. II. 34.

Davies, Rev. Price—Vol. I. 388; Vol. II. 496.

Davies, Rev. Samuel—Vol. I. 220, 385, 425, 429, 432, 433, 434, 435; Vol. II. 27, 30, 353, 354.

Davies, Whiting—Vol. II. 58.

Davies, Rev. Wm.—Vol. II. 184.

Davis—Vol. I. 280; Vol. II. 63, 69, 173, 428, 429.

Davis, Mrs. (Miss McGuire)—Vol. II. 150, 151.

Davis, Rev. Mr.—Vol. I. 168; Vol. II. 52, 358.

Davis, Chas., m. Rosanna Ellis—Vol. II. 462.

Davis, Isaac—Vol. II. 42, 43.

Davis, Capt. James—Vol. II. 431.

Davis, Mr. James—Vol. I. 305.

Davis, John—Vol. I. 304.

Davis, Rev. Richard—Vol. II. 307.

Davis, Robert—Vol. I. 404.

Davis, Rev. Peter—Vol. I. 310.

Davis, Samuel—Vol. I. 304.

Davis, Mr. Thomas—Vol. I. 129, 238, 259, 272, 274; Vol. II. 70, 132, 174, 260, 467.

Davis, William—Vol. I. 318, 320; Vol. II. 97, 184.

Dawkins—Vol. II. 429.

Dawley, Dennis—Vol. I. 249.

3

"Edgehill Pits"—Vol. II. 461.

Edloe, Jno.—Vol. I. 486.

Edmond, Robert, of Richmond—Vol. II. 461.

Edmonds—Vol. II. 221.

Edmondson, Jas.—Vol. II. 435.

Edmondson, Jno.—Vol. II. 435.

Edmondson, Jno., Jr.—Vol. II. 436.

Edmonson, James—Vol. I. 393.

Edmonson, Jno.—Vol. I. 393.

Edmonds—Vol. II. 428, 429.

Edmonds, Miss, of Brunswicke, m. Rev. Clement Read—Vol. II. 28.

Edmonds, Henry—Vol. I. 479.

Edmonds, Nicholas—Vol. I. 479.

Edmonds, Thos.—Vol. I. 479.

Edmundson—Vol. II. 13.

Edmunson, Thos.—Vol. I. 404.

Edrington—Vol. II. 206.

Edwards—Vol. I. 54, 280; Vol. II. 428, 429.

Edwards, Mr.—Vol. II. 125.

Edwards, Mrs.—Vol. I. 114.

Edwards, Rev.—Vol. II. 397.

Edwards, Nathaniel—Vol. I. 479.

Edwards, Thos.—Vol. II. 469.

Edwards, Wm.—Vol. I. 476, 479.

Education Society—Vol. I. 41.

Education of Indian, Negro and Mulatto Children—Vol. I. 265.

Edyard, Rev.—Vol. II. 186.

Effingham, Lord—Vol. I. 148, 150; Vol. II. 410.

Eggleston—Vol. II. 20, 21, 22, 428.

Eggleston, Mrs. (Miss Maury)—Vol. II. 44.

Eggleston, Chas.—Vol. II. 22.

Eggleston, Joseph, Sr.—Vol. II. 20-22.

Eggleston, Joseph, Jr.—Vol. II. 20-22.

Eggleston, Richard—Vol. II. 22.

Eggleston, Wm.—Vol. II. 20, 21.

Eldridge—Vol. II. 461; Vol. II. 428.

Eldridge, Mr. Thomas—Vol. I. 79.

Eley, Jno.—Vol. I. 304.

Elizabeth City—Vol. I. 92.

Elizabeth Parish—Vol. I. 140.

Elizabeth City County and Parish—Vol. I. 197, 229.

Elizabeth River Parish—Vol. I. 271, 272, 276, 279.

Elk Run Church (Fauquier)—Vol. II. 216.

Ellidge, Francis—Vol. I. 486.

Elligood, Capt. Jacob—Vol. I. 248.

Elligood, Mr. Wm.—Vol. I. 247.

Elliot—Vol. I. 364.

Elliott, Rev. James, m. Elizabeth Brokenbrough—Vol. I. 324; Vol. II. 147, 154, 474.

Elliott, Jno. T.—Vol. I. 259.

Elliott, Richard—Vol. I. 479.

Elliott, Robert—Vol. I. 326.

Ellis—Vol. II. 63, 428, 460-462.

Ellis, Bethena, m. Thos. Leftwich—Vol. II. 462.

Ellis, Wm. Burton, m. Elizabeth West—Vol. II. 461.

Ellis, Chas., son of Jno. 1st, m. Susannah Harding—Vol. II. 461.

Ellis, Chas., m. (1) Elizabeth Waters, (2) Sarah Tucker—Vol. II. 462.

Ellis, Daniel, of Goochland—Vol. II. 461.

Ellis, David (Emigrant)—Vol. II. 460.

Ellis, Edith, m. Devereux Gilliam—Vol. II. 462.

Ellis, Elizabeth, m. William Gilliam—Vol. II. 462.

Ellis, Ellison—Vol. I. 487.

Ellis, Hannah, m. Wm. Haynes—Vol. II. 462.

Ellis, Henry, son of Jno. 1st—Vol. II. 461.

Ellis, Jas., son of Jno. 1st—Vol. II. 461.

Ellis, Jno.—Vol. I. 141; Vol. II. 58.

Ellis, Jno. 1st, of Peter's Creek, m. Susannah ———Vol. II. 460, 461.

Ellis, Jno. 2nd, son of Jno., of Peter's Creek, m. Elizabeth Ware—Vol. II. 461.

Ellis, Jno. 3rd, son of Jno. 2nd—Vol. II. 461.

Ellis, Joseph, son of Jno. 1st, m. Elizabeth Perkins—Vol. II. 461.

Ellis, Josiah, m. Jane Shelton—Vol. II. 58, 462.

Ellis, Mary, daughter of John 1st, m. Jno. Smith—Vol. II. 461.

Ellis, Mary Ann, m. Peter Carter—Vol. II. 462.

Ellis, Richard—Vol. II. 58, 460, 462.

Ellis, Rosanna, m. Chas. Davis—Vol. II. 462.

Ellis, Sarah, m. Jno. Harrison—Vol. II. 462.

Ellis, Susannah, m. Isaac Wright—Vol. II. 461, 462.

Ellis, Thos., of Richmond—Vol. II. 460.

Ellis, Thos., son of John 1st, m. Elizabeth Petterson—Vol. II. 461.

Ellis, Thos. H., Esq.—Vol. II. 463.

Ellis, Wm., son of Jno. 1st—Vol. II. 461.

Ellis, children of Josiah and Jane Shelton—Vol. II. 462.

Ellsworth, Mr.—Vol. II. 251.

Ellzey, F.—Vol. I. 415; Vol. II. 485.

Ellzey, Thos.—Vol. II. 226.

Ellzey, Tomison—Vol. II. 270.

Ellzey—Vol. II. 277.

Elsey—Vol. II. 215.

"Eltham" (Bassett)—Vol. II. 496.

Embra, Henry—Vol. I. 479; Vol. II. 28.

Embra, Miss, m. Col. Isaac Read—Vol. II. 28.

Embry—Vol. II. 428.

Embry, Wm., of Embra—Vol. I. 487.

Emmanuel Church, Southam Parish —Vol. II. 33.

Emmerson, Rev. Arthur—Vol. I. 265, 480.

Emmerson, Rev. Arthur, Jr.—Vol. I. 280, 291.

Emerson, Jas.—Vol. II. 436.

Ennises—Vol. I. 330.

Entwisle, James—Vol. II. 271.

Eoff, Beverley, M.—Vol. II. 338.

Eoff, Jno.—Vol. II. 336.

Eppes—Vol. II. 428.

Eppes, Daniel—Vol. I. 23, 475.

Eppes, Isham—Vol. I. 441.

Eppes, Peter—Vol. I. 487.

Eppes, W.—Vol. I. 445.

Epps—Vol. I. 452.

Episcopal High School—Vol. II. 120, 488.

Episcopal Sunday School Union—Vol. II. 375.

Epitaph of Rev. David Mossom—Vol. II. 460.

Eskridge, Geo.—Vol. II. 152.

Eskridge, Sarah, wife of Willowby Newton—Vol. II. 152.

Eskridge, Wm.—Vol. II. 468.

Essex, Earl of, Prime Minister—Vol. I. 130, 131, 133.

Essex County and Parishes—Vol. I. 389, 396, 404.

Etheridge—Vol. I. 280.

Eubank, Jno. E.—Vol. II. 58.

Eubank, Thos. N.—Vol. II. 58.

Eustace,—Vol. II. 206.

Eustace, Hancock—Vol. II. 436.

Eustace, John—Vol. II. 469.

Eustace, Wm.—Vol. II. 124.

Evans—Vol. I. 259; Vol. II. 429.

Evans, Jno.—Vol. I. 324.

"Evelington" (Byrd)—Vol. I. 319.

Evelyn, Mr.—Vol. I. 180.

Evelyn, Miss, m. Daniel Parke—Vol. I. 180.

Everard—Vol. I. 291; Vol. II. 428.

Everard, Gov., of N. C.—Vol. I. 292.

Everard, Thos.—Vol. I. 179.

Everett, Sir Richard—Vol. I. 286.

Eversham Parish—Vol. II. 212.

Ewell—Vol. II. 215.

Ewell, Dr. Benj.—Vol. I. 178.

Ewell, Jesse—Vol. II. 214.

Ewell. Solomon—Vol. II. 125.

Extract from paper written by Edmund Randolph—Vol. I. 182.

Eyre—Vol. I. 259; Vol. II. 428.

Eyre, John—Vol. I. 259, 260.

F. T. Church, at Slate Mills—Vol. II. 103.

Fackler, Rev. D. M.—Vol. I. 250.

Fauntleroy, Miss, m. Mr. Carter—Vol. II. 480.

Fauntleroy, Miss, m. Wm. Dangerfield—Vol. I. 406.

Fauntleroy, Elizabeth, m. Mr. Adams—Vol. II. 480.

Fauntleroy, Griffin—Vol. II. 176, 468.

Faunt Le Roy, Dr. Henry, of Naylor's Hole—Vol. II. 480.

Fountleroy, Jno.—Vol. II. 174, 176, 480.

Fauntleroy, Maj. Moore 1st—Vol. II. 478-480.

Fauntleroy, Moore, m. Margaret Micon—Vol. I. 406; Vol. II. 179, 435.

Fauntleroy, Dr. Moore, of Tappahannock—Vol. II. 480.

Fauntleroy, Robert, m. Sarah Ball—Vol. II. 480.

Fauntleroy, Wm., m. Apphia Bushrod—Vol. II. 480.

Fauntleroy, Col. Wm., of Naylor's Hole, m. (1) —————, (2) Miss Murdock—Vol. II. 172, 186, 480.

Fauntleroy, Wm.—Vol. I. 404.

Fauntleroy, Dr. Wm.—Vol. II. 480.

Fauquier, Lieut Gov.—Vol. I. 217, 377, 478; Vol. II. 247.

Fauquier County—Vol. II. 216.

Female Missionary Society of Fredericksburg—Vol. I. 416.

Fendall, Benj. I.—Vol. II. 271.

Fendall, Philip R.—Vol. II. 268.

Fenton—Vol. I. 240.

Fentress, Anthony—Vol. I. 249.

Ferguson—Vol. I. 461; Vol. II. 215.

Ferguson, John—Vol. II. 186.

Ferguson, Robt.—Vol. I. 443.

Ferrar—Vol. I. 238.

Ferrar, Jno.—Vol. I. 67, 70, 71.

Ferrar, Nicholas—Vol. I. 67, 70-72, 85.

"Ferry Chapel," near the "Falls"—Vol. I. 439, 440.

Ferth, Daniel—Vol. I. 486.

Ficklin,—Vol. II. 206.

Ficklin, J. B.—Vol. II. 73.

Field—Vol. II. 82, 428.

Field, James—Vol. I. 444, 446.

Field, Henry—Vol. II. 74, 77, 78.

Field, Henry, Jr.—Vol. II. 77.

Field, Theophilus—Vol. I. 445.

Field, Rev. Thos.—Vol. I. 325; Vol. II. 495.

Fielding—Vol. II. 429.

Fife, Rev. Wm.—Vol. I. 231, 232.

Fincastle Church—Vol. II. 65.

Finlason, Jno.—Vol. II. 74.

Finlason, W.—Vol. II. 77.

Finley, Rev. Mr.—Vol. I. 432.

Finney—Vol. I. 270.

Finney, Rev. Wm.—Vol. II. 393, 401, 402.

Finnie—Vol. I. 451.

Finnie, Mrs. (Miss Leigh), of Powhatan—Vol. I. 450, 451.

Finnie, Rev. Alexander—Vol. I. 437, 438, 451, 458.

Finnie, Wm., of Amelia—Vol. I. 451.

Fisher—Vol. I. 259.

Fisher, Rev.—Vol. II. 33.

Fisher, Mrs. (Anne Ambler)—Vol. I. 98.

Fisher, Geo., m. Anne Ambler—Vol. I. 99.

Fisher, Chas.—Vol. I. 445.

Fisher, Ebenezer—Vol. II. 436.

Fitch—Vol. II. 475.

Fitzgerald—Vol. II. 428.

Fitzgerald, Wm.—Vol. II. 13.

Fitzhugh—Vol. I. 400, 402, 412; Vol. II. 173, 192, 193, 194, 206, 215, 221, 230, 428.

Fitzhugh, Mr.—Vol. I. 401.

Fitzhugh, Mr., m. Miss Digges—Vol. I. 239.

Fitzhugh, Miss, wife of Alexander Campbell, then married Rev. Dr. Kollock—Vol. II. 161.

Fitzhugh, Ann, of Stafford, m. Rev. Robt. Rose—Vol. I. 402; Vol. II. 193.

Fitzhugh, Burdett—Vol. II. 349.

Fitzhugh, Daniel—Vol. II. 192.

Fitzhugh, Drury B.—Vol. II. 192.

Foote's Sketches—Vol. II. 27, 28.

Foote, Rev. Mr.—Vol. I. 431, 434; Vol. II. 27, 28.

Foote, Richard—Vol. II. 192.

Foote, Wm.—Vol. II. 479.

Forbes—Vol. I. 192; Vol. II. 206.

Forbes, Miss, m. Robert Eden Scott —Vol. II. 213.

Forbes, Rev. Alexander—Vol. I. 301, 303; Vol. II. 393.

Forbes, Murray—Vol. II. 72.

Forbes, Sir William—Vol. II. 213.

Forbes, Rev. Mr.—Vol. I. 386.

Forbs, Mr.—Vol. I. 163.

Force, Peter—Vol. II. 230.

Ford, Mr.—Vol. I. 323.

Ford, Mordecai—Vol. II. 43.

Ford, Thos.—Vol. II. 226, 270, 485.

Forge Church—Vol. I. 401; Vol. II. 48, 49, 51.

Fork Chapel, St. Mark—Vol. II. 74, 77, 83.

Fork Church (Hanover)—Vol. I. 420, 423, 435.

Fork of Roanoke Church—Vol. I. 482.

Forster, Mr.—Vol. I. 387.

Fort Cumberland—Vol. I. 166.

Fort James—Vol. I. 121.

Fort McHenry (Baltimore)—Vol. II. 156.

Foster,—Vol. II. 27.

Foster, Joel.—Vol. I. 326.

Foster, Jno.—Vol. I. 376; Vol. II. 42.

Foster, Thomas—Vol. I. 376.

Fouace, Rev. (same as Rev. Fowace) —Vol. I. 159; Vol. II. 291.

Fouch, Thos.—Vol. II. 277.

Fouches (Fouche)—Vol. I. 226, 468; Vol. II. 215.

Fouchee, Wm.—Vol. I. 141.

Fouke, Wm.—Vol. II. 277.

Foulis, Jas.—Vol. II. 10.

Four-Mile-Creek-Church—Vol. I. 136, 137.

Foushee, Francis—Vol. II. 436.

Foushee, Jno.—Vol. II. 468.

Fowace, Rev. (same as Rev. Fouace)—Vol. I. 159; Vol. II. 291.

Fowkes of Gunster Hall, Eng.—Vol. II. 199.

Fowke—Vol. II. 206, 482.

Fowke, Elizabeth, m. Z. Brazier— Vol. II. 483.

Fowke, Miss, m. Henry Peyton— Vol. II. 466.

Fowke, Miss, wife of Dr. Gustavus Brown—Vol. II. 199.

Fowke, Miss, m. Mr. Johnston, of Ky.—Vol. II. 483.

Fowke, Chandler, Esq., son of Gerard—Vol. II. 483.

Fowke, Chandler, m. Miss Harrison —Vol. II. 483.

Fowke, Elizabeth, m. Col. Wm. Phillips—Vol. II. 483.

Fowke, Col. Gerard, 1st of name— Vol. II. 483.

Fowke, Gerard, of Md.—Vol. II. 199.

Fowke, Gerard, Esq., m. Elizabeth Dinwiddie—Vol. II. 483.

Fowke, Jenny, m. Wm. Fouke—Vol. II. 483.

Fowke, Jerard—Vol. II. 192.

Fowke, John—Vol. II. 483.

Fowke, Richard, m. Miss Bumbary —Vol. II. 483.

Fowke, Robert Dinwiddie, m. Miss Peachy—Vol. II. 483.

Fowke, Roger—Vol. II. 483.

Fowke, Thos.—Vol. II. 483.

Fowke, William, m. Miss Bronaugh —Vol. II. 483.

Fowke, Wm., m. Jenny Fowke—Vol. II. 483.

Fowle, Wm.—Vol. II. 268, 271.

Fowle, Wm. H.—Vol. II. 271.

Fowlkes, Jno. A.—Vol. II. 13.

Fox—Vol. I. 412; Vol. II. 206, 466.

Fox, Daniel—Vol. II. 126.

Fox, David—Vol. II. 127.

Fox, Rev. John—Vol. I. 325, 328, 329, 354; Vol. II. 20.

Fox, Mary and Susannah—Vol. I. 354.

Graves, Wm.—Vol. I. 179.

Gray—Vol. I. 412.

Gray, Rev. Dan'l—Vol. I. 359, 370, 385.

Gray, Geo.—Vol. I. 415.

Gray, Dr. J.—Vol. II. 277.

Gray, James—Vol. II. 215.

Gray, Jno., of Traveller's Rest—Vol. II. 169.

Gray, Jno.—Vol. II. 72, 78, 81.

Gray, Rev. Sam'l—Vol. II. 65.

Gray, Sam'l—Vol. I. 387.

Gray, W.—Vol. II. 336.

Gray, Wm. F.—Vol. II. 72.

Gray, W. H.—Vol. II. 277.

Grayson—Vol. I. 192; Vol. II. 206, 215, 429.

Grayson, Senator—Vol. II. 62.

Grayson, Ambrose—Vol. II. 72.

Grayson, Benj.—Vol. II. 276.

Grayson, Rev. Spence—Vol. II. 205, 213, 214, 259, 273.

Grayson, Wm.—Vol. II. 72, 435.

Grayson, Mr. (son of Senator). m. Letitia Breckenridge—Vol. II. 62.

Great Bridge Chapel—Vol. I. 276, 295.

Great Massacre—Vol. I. 198.

Great Wycomico Parish—Vol. II. 134, 135.

Green—Vol. I. 192; Vol. II. 13, 82, 206, 429.

Green, Gen.—Vol. I. 98.

Green, Rev.—Vol. II. 202, 484.

Green, James—Vol. II. 271.

Green, Maj. John—Vol. II. 78, 81.

Green, L.—Vol. I. 445.

Green, Robt. II. 74, 77.

Green, Thomas—Vol. I. 324.

Green, Wm.—Vol. II. 77, 78.

Greene, Ralph—Vol. I. 324.

Greenbrier Parishes—Vol. II. 57, 64.

"Greenfield" (Dangerfield)—Vol. I. 405, 406.

Greenleaf, Jno.—Vol. II. 284.

Grenhow, Jno.—Vol. I. 199.

Greenhow, Sam'l—Vol. II. 72.

Green Mountain Congregation—Vol. II. 47-49, 51.

"Green Spring" (Berkeley)—Vol. I. 94, 95, 113-114, 414; Vol. II. 136.

Greenway—Vol. II. 429.

"Greenway Court" (Fairfax)—Vol. II. 250, 283.

Greensville County—Vol. I. 480.

Greer, J. R.—Vol. II. 337.

Crew—Vol. I. 280.

Gregorie, Jno.—Vol. I. 289.

Gregory, Mrs. Mildred—Vol. II. 242.

Gregory, R.—Vol. I. 446.

Gregory, Richard—Vol. I. 326.

Gregory, Roger—Vol. I. 376.

Griffin—Vol. I. 226; Vol. II. 173, 429.

Griffin Miss, m. Jas. Phillips—Vol. II. 482.

Griffin, Mr. Chas.—Vol. I. 284, 287-289, 302, 307.

Griffin, Cyrus—Vol. II. 125.

Griffin, Col. LeRoy—Vol. I. 404; Vol. II. 172.

Griffin, Thos.—Vol. II. 125.

Griffith—Vol. I. 240; Vol. II. 148, 429.

Griffith, Rev. Dr.—Vol. I. 17, 32, 415, 460; Vol. II. 259, 262, 263, 264, 265, 267, 273-274.

Grisby, Hugh Blair, and His Work—Vol. I. 183, 311, 312, 455, 480; Vol. II. 29, 60, 206, 425, 459, 486.

Grimes, Miss, m. Walker Maury—Vol. I. 273.

Grimkys—Vol. I. 465.

Grimsley, Jno.—Vol. II. 186.

Griswold Bishop—Vol. I. 269; Vol. II. 262, 362, 363, 379.

Griswold, Rev. Geo.—Vol. II. 262.

"Grove," The (Carter and Burwell)—Vol. I. 242, 330; Vol. II. 290.

Groves, Miss, m. Edward Randolph—Vol. I. 138.

Grubb, J.—Vol. II. 268.

Grubhill Church—Vol. II. 20-22.

Ground-Squirrel Bridge—Vol. I. 109.

Hale, Sir Matthew—Vol. I. 486; Vol. II. 242.

Halifax County—Vol. II. 9.

Hall—Vol. I. 192.

Hall, A.—Vol. I. 445.

Hall, Clement—Vol. I. 286, 287.

Hall, Elisha—Vol. II. 72.

Hall, Rev. Jno.—Vol. I. 385, 459.

Hall, Wm.—Vol. I. 376.

Halliday—Vol. I. 298, 413.

Halson, Rev. Geo.—Vol. I. 231, 236, 249.

Halyburton, Dr.—Vol. I. 175.

Ham Chapel—Vol. II. 34.

Hamar, Mr.—Vol. I. 253.

Hamilton—Vol. I. 192; Vol. II. 173.

Hamilton, Alexander—Vol. I. 295, 296; Vol. II. 300, 492.

Hamilton, Rev. Arthur—Vol. I. 323, 325, 374.

Hamilton, Geo.—Vol. II. 72.

Hamilton, Jas.—Vol. II. 276.

Hamilton Parish, Faquier—Vol. II. 197, 198, 207, 216, 217, 218, 220, 221, 224.

Hamlin, Wm.—Vol. I. 445.

Hammond—Vol. I. 446.

Hammond, J.—Vol. II. 176.

Hamner, Nicholas—Vol. II. 50.

Hamor, Ralphe, and His Work—Vol. II. 469, 472.

Hampden-Sydney College—Vol. I. 191; Vol. II. 27, 31.

Hampshire Parishes and County—Vol. II. 309.

Hampton—Vol. I. 192.

Hampton, Rev. Thomas—Vol. I. 92, 200.

Hampton Parish—Vol. I. 229, 235.

Hancock, Jno.—Vol. I. 249.

Hancock, Miss Mary Ann, of Princess Ann—Vol. I. 140.

Hankin—Vol. II. 496.

Hanner—Vol. II. 429.

Hanover County and Parishes—Vol. I. 97, 419, 426.

Hanover Parish, King George—Vol. II. 183, 184-186, 203.

Hansford—Vol. I. 280; Vol. II. 429.

Hansford, Wm.—Vol. I. 178, 324; Vol. II. 72.

Hanson, Thos. H.—Vol. II. 73.

Hanson, Rev. Wm.—Vol. II. 154.

Hanson, Rev. W. D.—Vol. I. 480.

"Happy Dick"—Vol. I. 294.

Harcum, Elisha—Vol. II. 468.

Hardaway—Vol. I. 446, 452; Vol. II. 429.

Hardaway, D.—Vol. I. 446.

Hardaway, Daniel—Vol. II. 22.

Hardin—Vol. I. 364.

Harding—Vol. II. 206.

Harding, Cyrus—Vol. II. 469.

Harding, Hopkins—Vol. II. 469.

Harding, Jno. I.—Vol. II. 277.

Harding, Susannah, m. Chas. Ellis —Vol. II. 461.

Harding, Thos., m. Mary Giles—Vol. II. 461.

Harding, Wm.—Vol. I. 487.

Hardy, Mr.—Vol. II. 132.

Hardy, Covington—Vol. I. 487.

Harewoods—Vol. I. 330.

Hargrave, Rev.—Vol. I. 84, 85.

Harmer—Vol. II. 429.

Harmer, Jno.—Vol. I. 179.

Harmonson, J. H.—Vol. I. 259.

Harper, Robert Goodloe—Vol. II. 213.

Harpold, H.—Vol. II. 349.

Harris—Vol. I. 413, 461, 468; Vol. II. 52, 111, 429.

Harris, Mrs. (Miss Leigh)—Vol. I. 450, 451.

Harris, Miss, m. Rev. Mr. Christopher Macrae—Vol. II. 36.

Harris, Benj.—Vol. II. 34, 268.

Harris, Daniel—Vol. II. 318.

Harris, Jno.—Vol. II. 36, 50.

Harris, Marshall—Vol. II. 58.

Harris, Robt.—Vol. II. 42.

Harris, Sam'l—Vol. II. 13.

Harris, Thos.—Vol. I. 416.

Harris, Tyree, or Tyrce—Vol. II. 42.

Harrison—Vol. I. 139, 311, 319, 438; Vol. II. 206, 214, 215, 324, 429.

Harrison, Miss, m. Mr. Randolph—Vol. I. 311.

Harrison, Miss, m. Mr. Copeland—Vol. I. 311.

Harrison, Miss, m. Chandler Fowke—Vol. II. 483.

Harrison, Miss, m. Philip Ludwell (2d)—Vol. II. 139.

Harrison, Mr. Archy—Vol. II. 40.

Harrison, B. W.—Vol. II. 227.

Harrison, Hon. Benj., Esq., (1) of Surrey—Vol. I. 158, 310, 311, 312, 319.

Harrison, Benj. (2) (Speaker), of Berkeley, m. Elizabeth Burwell—Vol. I. 311-312, 320.

Harrison, Benj. (3), m. Miss Carter—Vol. I. 311.

Harrison, Gov. Benj. (4), m. Miss Bassett—Vol. I. 114, 152, 221, 295, 311; Vol. II. 252, 320-321, 495.

Harrison, Benj. (5)—Vol. I. 311.

Harrison, Benj. (6), of Berkeley—Vol. I. 311, 320.

Harrison, Benj., of Southam Parish—Vol. II. 34.

Harrison, Benj., son of Nathaniel (2), of Brandon, m. (1) Betsey Page, (2) Miss Byrd—Vol. I. 311, 320, 339.

Harrison, Burr, of Chappawamsie, son of Cuthbert—Vol. II. 214.

Harrison, Burr, son of Burr—Vol. II. 214, 284.

Harrison, Carter, of "Clifton"—Vol. II. 62.

Harrison, Carter B., son of Benj. (5)—Vol. I. 311.

Harrison, Carter Henry, son of Benj. (3)—Vol. I. 311, 461; Vol. II. 34.

Harrison, Gen. Charles, son of Benj. (3)—Vol. I. 311.

Harrison, Mr. Colier, of Kettiuvan—Vol. I. 320.

Harrison, Colin, son of Benj. (3)—Vol. I. 311.

Harrison, Cuthbert—Vol. II. 214.

Harrison, E.—Vol. I. 446.

Harrison, T. K.—Vol. I. 461.

Harrison, Geo., of Lower Brandon, son of Benj., of Brandon—Vol. I. 242, 311.

Harrison, H. T.—Vol. II. 227.

Harrison, Henry, son of Benj. (3)—Vol. I. 311.

Harrison, Henry, of Brunswick—Vol. I. 476.

Harrison, Henry, of Nansemond—Vol. I. 290.

Harrison, Herman—Vol. I. 312.

Harrison, Jane and Seth—Vol. II. 214.

Harrison, Gov. Jno.—Vol. I. 312.

Harrison, Jno., m. Sarah Ellis—Vol. II. 462.

Harrison, Jno. Peyton, m. Elizabeth Peyton—Vol. II. 466.

Harrison, Julian—Vol. I. 461.

Harrison, Mrs. Mary, wife of Nathaniel (2) (Mary Digges)—Vol. I. 241, 242.

Harrison, Nathaniel (1), son of Benj. (1)—Vol. I. 311, 476.

Harrison, Nathaniel (2), son of Nathaniel (1), m. Mary Digges—Vol. I. 239, 242, 311.

Harrison, Nathaniel, of Wakefield, son of Benj. (3) (m. Miss Digges)—Vol. I. 311.

Harrison, Philip, of Richmond, son of Rev. Thomas—Vol. II. 214, 467.

Harrison, Randolph—Vol. I. 461.

Harrison, Robert Carter, m. Anne Cabell—Vol. II. 62.

Harrison, Col. Robert Hanson, m. Miss Johnston—Vol. II. 240.

Harrison, Rev. Thomas—Vol. II. 214, 277, 333, 467.

Harrison, Thos. of Stafford, m. Ann Wage Peyton—Vol. II. 466.

Harrison, Thos., of Richmond County—Vol. II. 172, 209, 210, 404.

Harrison, Pres. William Henry, son of Benj. (5)—Vol. I. 308, 311.

Harrison, Rev. Wm.—Vol. I. 441, 443.

Harrison, William, of Upper Brandon, son of Benj., of Brandon—Vol. I. 242, 310, 311.

Harrop Parish—Vol. I. 92, 195, 240.

Hart—Vol. I. 413; Vol. II. 298.

Hart, Rev.—Vol. I. 143.

Hart, Archibald—Vol. II. 73.

Hart, Jno.—Vol. II. 72.

Hart, Robert, m. Miss Dick—Vol. I. 416.

Hartwell, Rev.—Vol. I. 442.

Harwood—Vol. I. 240.

Harvey, Mrs. Gen.—Vol. II. 223, 224.

Harvey, Oneriphorus (Onesiphorus) —Vol. II. 132, 469.

Harvey, Thos.—Vol. II. 132, 469.

Harvie—Vol. II. 429.

Harvie, Jno.—Vol. II. 42, 43.

Haskin's Creed—Vol. II. 34.

Haskins, Edward—Vol. II. 34.

Hassell, Rev. Thomas—Vol. I. 306.

Hastewood, Jno.—Vol. I. 359.

Hat Creek Church—Vol. II. 59.

Hatch, Rev.—Vol. II. 47, 51-53, 92.

Hatcher—Vol. I. 468.

Hatcher, Wm.—Vol. I. 243.

Hatcher's Run Church, Bath Parish —Vol. I. 471.

Havard—Vol. II. 429.

Havield, Capt. L.—Vol. I. 305.

Hawkins—Vol. II. 429.

Hawkins, Thos.—Vol. I. 487; Vol. II. 168.

Hawks, Dr. and His Work—Vol. I. 13, 116, 171, 187, 188, 189, 202, 315, 328, 465, 466; Vol. II. 10, 144, 351, 446.

Hawley, Rev. Wm.—Vol. II. 82, 91, 92.

Hay, Rev. Alexander—Vol. I. 489, 490; Vol. II. 10, 11.

Hay, Jno., m. Miss Maury—Vol. I. 273.

Hay, Mrs. John (Miss Maury)—Vol. II. 44.

Hay, Dr. Jno., m. Anne Robinson—Vol. I. 378.

Hay-Market Church—Vol. II. 215.

Hayes, Jno.—Vol. I. 326.

Hayes, Thos.—Vol. I. 326.

Haynes—Vol. II. 429.

Haynes, Mr., m. Miss Bland—Vol. I. 447.

Haynes, Erasmus—Vol. I. 249.

Haynes, Jno.—Vol. II. 13.

Haynes, Joseph—Vol. II. 13.

Haynes, Wm., m. Hannah Ellis—Vol. II. 462.

Hays, Patrick—Vol. II. 318.

Heale—Vol. II. 173, 200.

Heale, Joseph—Vol. II. 125.

Heath—Vol. II. 429.

Heath, Rev.—Vol. II. 297.

Heath, Capt. Jno.—Vol. II. 469.

Hedgeman—Vol. II. 206.

Hedgeman, Jno., m. Miss Grayson —Vol. II. 205.

Hedges—Vol. II. 298, 301.

Hedge, Rev. C. J.—Vol. I. 301.

Hedgeville Church—Vol. II. 297, 300, 301.

Hedjers—Vol. II. 464.

Hefferhon, Rev.—Vol. I. 361, 362.

Heiskell, Godlove—Vol. II. 72.

Heiskell, W. H.—Vol. II. 337.

Hempstone, C.—Vol. II. 277.

Henderson—Vol. II. 220, 221, 429.

Henderson, Gen., of Wash., son of Alexander, Emigrant—Vol. II. 223.

Henderson, Rev.—Vol. I. 204, 486; Vol. II. 347.

Henderson, Alexander—Vol. II. 226, 233, 485.

Henderson, Anne, Mrs. (Miss Henderson)—Vol. II. 233.

Henderson, David—Vol. II. 72.

Henderson, Jane—Vol. II. 233.

Henderson, Jno., Alexander and James, of W. Va., sons of Alexander—Vol. II. 233, 270.

Henderson, Mary, m. Inman Horner—Vol. II. 233.

Henderson, Richard, of Leesburg, son of Emigrant Alex.—Vol. II. 233.

Jones, Rev. Emanuel—Vol. I. 323, 360; Vol. II. 393, 400-402, 408-409.

Jones, Rev. Emanuel, Jr.—Vol. I. 279.

Jones, Frederick—Vol. I. 178.

Jones, Genl. G.—Vol. II. 350.

Jones, Gabriel—Vol. II. 281, 324, 325.

Jones, Mrs. Gabriel—Vol. II. 325.

Jones, George—Vol. I. 386.

Jones, Rev. Hugh—Vol. I. 160; Vol. II. 393, 400-402, 405, 408, 411, 413.

Jones, Jno., Esq.—Vol. I. 230, 479.

Jones, Rev. John—Vol. II. 318, 319.

Jones, James—Vol. II. 125.

Jones, Joseph—Vol. II. 72, 186.

Jones, J. W.—Vol. I. 236.

Jones, Matthew—Vol. I. 304.

Jones, Morias—Vol. II. 42.

Jones, Orlando—Vol. II. 50.

Jones, Rev. Owen—Vol. I. 409; Vol. II. 393.

Jones, Paul—Vol. I. 278.

Jones, Maj. Peter—Vol. II. 24.

Jones, Mr. Peter—Vol. I. 444, 445-446.

Jones, Rice—Vol. I. 405.

Jones, Richard—Vol. I. 325; Vol. II. 24.

Jones, Rev. Rowland—Vol. I. 146, 147, 148, 194.

Jones, Mr. Skelton—Vol. I. 147.

Jones, Strother, of Frederick—Vol. II. 287, 289, 325.

Jones, Thos.—Vol. I. 179, 444-446; Vol. II. 435, 468.

Jones, Rev. Walter—Vol. II. 158.

Jones, Gen. Walter, m. Ann Lee—Vol. II. 143.

Jones, Walter—Vol. II. 468.

Jones, Wm.—Vol. I. 415; Vol. II. 276.

Jones, Rev. Wm. G., of Orange—Vol. I. 267; Vol. II. 47, 92-93.

Jones, Sir Wm.—Vol. I. 293.

Jones, Col. Wilson W.—Vol. I. 237.

Jones, Wood—Vol. II. 24.

Jone's Hole Church—Vol. I. 441.

Jordan—Vol. I. 461, 468; Vol. II. 173.

Jordan, Edward—Vol. I. 487.

Jordan, James—Vol. I. 129.

Jordan, John—Vol. II. 50.

Jordan, Margaret, m. Wm. Cabell—Vol. II. 62.

Jordan, Paulina, m. John Cabell—Vol. II. 62.

Jordan, Col. Sam'l—Vol. II. 62.

Jordan, Samuel, m. Sarah Syme—Vol. II. 62.

Jordan, Maj. Thomas—Vol. I. 306.

"Jordans" (Blands)—Vol. I. 446, 447.

Jouette—Vol. I. 468.

Journal of House of Delegates, the 1st—Vol. I. 129.

Joy, Capt. James—Vol. I. 278.

Joy Creek Church—Vol. I. 409.

Joynes—Vol. I. 270; Vol. II. 429.

Joynes, Mr. Levin—Vol. I. 265.

Joynes, T. R., Sr.—Vol. I. 265, 266.

Judkins—Vol. II. 430.

Julian, Jno.—Vol. II. 72.

Junis, Hugh—Vol. II. 13.

Junkin—Vol. II. 430.

Kall, Wm.—Vol. I. 446.

Kanawha Churches—Vol. II. 344.

Kater, Mrs. Phœbe—Vol. I. 393.

Kay, or Key—Vol. II. 179.

Kay, Rev. Mr.—Vol. II. 178, 179.

Kay, James—Vol. II. 186.

Kay, Rev. Wm.—Vol. I. 483, 484, 490.

Keans—Vol. I. 413.

Kearne, Capt. B.—Vol. I. 306.

Kearns—Vol. I. 280.

Keastleys—Vol. II. 103.

Keech, Alexander—Vol. II. 192.

Keeling—Vol. II. 496.

Keeling, Henry—Vol. I. 250.

Keeling, Rev. Jacob—Vol. I. 291.

Keeling, Solomon S.—Vol. I. 250.

Keeble, Walter—Vol. I. 326.

Keeling, Mr. Wm.—Vol. I. 248.

Keene, Elizabeth, wife of William Keene—Vol. II. 152.

Kingswell, Richard—Vol. I. 200.

King and Queen County and Prishes —Vol. I. 374, 379, 381.

King William Parishes and County —Vol. I. 374, 379, 381, 463; Vol. II. 69.

Kilbee—Vol. I. 364.

Kilpatricke—Vol. I. 240.

Kilmarnock Church, Lancaster— Vol. II. 124.

Kincade, Joseph—Vol. I. 455.

Kincheloe—Vol. II. 215.

Kinchin, William—Vol. I. 304.

Kinckle, Rev. Wm. H.—Vol. II. 17, 35.

"Kinlock" (Meade)—Vol. I. 403.

Kinnaird, A. L.—Vol. II. 349.

Kinney, Nicholas C.—Vol. II. 323.

Kinsolving, Rev. Mr.—Vol. II. 18, 342.

Kiok, James—Vol. II. 125.

Kirby, B.—Vol. I. 446.

Kirby, John—Vol. I. 446.

Kirk, Thos.—Vol. II. 349.

Kirk, Mr.—Vol. II. 185.

Kirk-Alloway—Vol. II. 155.

Kirkland, Rev. Wm., of Boston— Vol. II. 245.

Kirkpatrick—Vol. II. 475.

"Kirnan" (McCoy)—Vol. II. 161.

Kiskiacke—Vol. I. 197.

Kittle Stick Church—Vol. I. 477.

Klug, Rev. Jno.—Vol. I. 361.

Knight, Wm.—Vol. II. 58.

Knight's of the Horse Shoe—Vol. II. 317.

Knowles, Sands—Vol. I. 326.

Knox—Vol. II. 82.

Knox, C. D.—Vol. II. 336.

Knox, Thos. F.—Vol. II. 73.

Knox, W. A.—Vol. II. 72.

Kohn, Mr.—Vol. I. 41.

Kollock, Rev. Dr., m. widow of Alexander Campbell (Miss Fitzhugh)—Vol. II. 161.

Koones, Chas.—Vol. II. 271.

Korker, Wm.—Vol. I. 178.

Kosciusko, Genl.—Vol. I. 98.

Krew, Rev. Mr.—Vol. I. 390.

Kuhm, Jacob—Vol. II. 72.

Lacy, Theodoric—Vol. II. 15.

La Fayette, Marquis de—Vol. I. 109, 213; Vol. II. 253.

Laidley, Alexander T.—Vol. II. 337.

Lamb, Wm., of Norfolk—Vol. II. 487.

Lamb's Creek Church—Vol. II. 187, 190, 191.

Lamkin, Peter—Vol. I. 487.

Lamon, Rev.—Vol. II. 103.

Lancaster County and Parishes— Vol. I. 356; Vol. II. 115.

Lance, Rev.—Vol. II. 362.

Landon—Vol. II. 122.

Landon, Betty, m. (1) —— Willis, (2) King Carter—Vol. II. 110, 121-122.

Landon, Mary, wife of Thomas, of England—Vol. II. 122.

Landon, Thomas, of England, m. Mary —— —Vol. II. 110, 122.

Lane—Vol. II. 206.

Lane, Joseph—Vol. II. 276, 436.

Lane, J. W.—Vol. II. 23.

Lane, Richard—Vol. II. 337.

Lane, W. S.—Vol. II. 350.

Lang—Vol. I. 240.

Lang, Rev.—Vol. I. 385, 386.

Langford, Thos.—Vol. I. 376.

Langhorn—Vol. II. 430.

Langhorne—Vol. I. 240.

Langhorne, Maurice—Vol. II. 34.

Langley, Capt. Samuel—Vol. I. 278.

Lanne, Capt. Christopher—Vol. I. 130.

Lanni's Plantation—Vol. I. 130.

Lanier—Vol. I. 468; Vol. II. 429.

Lanier, Nicholas—Vol. I. 479.

Lanier, Samson—Vol. I. 479.

Lanier, Thos.—Vol. I. 487.

Lansdowne, Marquis, of—Vol. II. 28.

Latane—Vol. I. 192, 468; Vol. II. 172.

Latane, Jno., m. Mary Allen—Vol. I. 393.

Latane, Rev. Lewis, m. Mary Dean
—Vol. I. 389, 392, 393, 394, 395,
401, 403, 465.
Latane, Wm.—Vol. I. 393, 405.
Latham, Miss, m. Andrew Meade—
Vol. I. 292.
Latham, Edward—Vol. II. 268.
Latimer, Jas.—Vol. I. 236.
Latimer, Thos.—Vol. I. 236.
Latimer, Wm.—Vol. I. 236.
Lattimore, Chas.—Vol. II. 469.
Laud, Bishop—Vol. I. 71; Vol. II.
352, 354.
Laurence, Mr.—Vol. II. 251.
Laurence, W. H.—Vol. II. 350.
Laurens—Vol. I. 295, 465.
Lavillon, Susannah Countess, m.
Bartholomew Dupuy—Vol. I. 467.
Law, Mr., m. Miss Custis—Vol. II.
231.
Laware, Lord (De la War)—Vol.
I. 121; Vol. II. 431.
Lawn's Creek Parish—Vol. I. 308,
309, 312.
Lawrence—Vol. I. 259.
Lawson, Henry—Vol. II. 125.
Lawson, John—Vol. II. 469.
Lawson, Thomas—Vol. I. 249; Vol.
II. 125.
Lay, Rev. Henry—Vol. I. 250.
Leacock, Rev. B. B.—Vol. II. 191.
Leading Families of Eastern Va.—
Vol. II. 428.
Leake—Vol. I. 461.
Lear, Jno.—Vol. I. 306.
Lear, Col. Tobias—Vol. II. 492, 493,
494.
Leatherbury—Vol. I. 259.
Leavell, Rev.—Vol. I. 319; Vol. II.
102, 103, 104.
Leavills—Vol. I. 413.
Lecharcey, Rev.—Vol. II. 467.
Lecock—Vol. I. 308.
Lee—Vol. I. 95, 139, 141, 191; Vol.
II. 111, 135, 136, 140, 144, 145,
156, 159, 163, 170, 180, 206, 215,
429.
Lee, Miss, m. Wm. Byrd Page—Vol.
I. 339.

Lee, Miss, wife of Wm. Fitzhugh,
2nd—Vol. II. 138.
Lee, Miss, m. Edmund I. Lee—Vol.
II. 269.
Lee, Miss, widow of Wm. Fitzhugh
2nd—Vol. II. 193.
Lee, Ann, m. Gen. Walter Jones—
Vol. II. 143.
Lee, Ann, m. Chas. Lee—Vol. II.
143.
Lee, Arthur—Vol. II. 136, 139, 141,
285.
Lee, Cassius F., of Fairfax—Vol.
II. 268.
Lee, Genl. Chas.—Vol. II. 263, 308.
Lee, Col. Chas.—Vol. II. 114, 140,
208, 466, 469.
Lee, Chas., m. Anne Lee—Vol. II.
143.
Lee, Chas. H.—Vol. II. 268.
Lee, Cornelia, m. John Hopkins—
Vol. II. 136.
Lee, Dan'l—Vol. II. 289.
Lee, Edmund I. Lee, m. Miss Lee—
Vol. II. 143, 268, 269, 337.
Lee, Eleanor (Mrs. Alexander)—
Vol. II. 143.
Lee, Flora, wife of Ludwell Lee,
of Loudoun—Vol. II. 139.
Lee, Francis, son of Richard 1st—
Vol. II. 145.
Lee, Francis, son of Richard 2nd—
Vol. II. 138.
Lee, Francis Lightfoot, m. Rebecca
Tayloe—Vol. I. 267; Vol. II. 136,
139, 180, 182, 435.
Lee, George, son of Richard 3rd, m.
(1) Miss Wormly, (2) Miss Fair-
fax—Vol. II. 138, 153, 277.
Lee, Hancock, m. Miss Allerton—
Vol. II. 134, 136, 140, 405.
Lee, Hannah, m. Gawin Corbin—
Vol. II. 146.
Lee, Hannah, wife of Corbin Wash-
ington—Vol. II. 143.
Lee, Sir Henry, of Ditchley—Vol.
II. 427.

Lee, Henry 1st, son of Richard 2nd, m. Miss Bland—Vol. I. 446; Vol. II. 138, 140.

Lee, Henry 2nd, son of Henry 1st, m. Miss Grymes—Vol. II. 140.

Lee, Gen. Henry, m. Matilda Lee—Vol. II. 139, 140, 170, 244.

Lee, Jno., son of Richard 1st—Vol. II. 137, 145.

Lee, Jno., of Md.—Vol. II. 140.

Lee, Jno., son of Jno., of Md.—Vol. II. 140.

Lee, Jno., son of Hancock—Vol. II. 140.

Lee, Jno.—Vol. I. 405; Vol. II. 131, 198.

Lee, Jno., Jr.—Vol. II. 435.

Lee, Jno. H.—Vol. II. 94.

Lee, Jno. P.—Vol. I. 405.

Lee, Kendall—Vol. II. 469.

Lee, Lancelot, Esq., of England—Vol. II. 136.

Lee, Lettuce, m. Mr. Corbin—Vol. II. 127, 138.

Lee, Ludwell, of Loudoun, m. Flora Lee—Vol. II. 139, 143, 268.

Lee, Martha, m. Mr. Turberville—Vol. II. 138.

Lee, Mary, wife of Col. W. A. Washington—Vol. II. 143.

Lee, Matilda, wife of Gen. Henry Lee—Vol. II. 139.

Lee, Philip—Vol. II. 138.

Lee, Philip Ludwell, m. Miss Steptoe—Vol. II. 139.

Lee, Portia, m. Wm. Hodgson—Vol. II. 136.

Lee, Col. Richard 1st, m. Anna ——Vol. II. 136, 137, 144, 152.

Lee, Richard 2nd, m. Miss Corbin—Vol. II. 137, 138, 145, 146, 152.

Lee, Richard, m. Miss Silk—Vol. II. 138.

Lee, Richard, of Ditchley—Vol. II. 127, 435.

Lee, Squire Richard, of Lee Hall, m. Miss Poythress—Vol. II. 140, 151, 153.

Lee, Richard Bland—Vol. II. 140.

Lee, Col. Richard Henry, m. (1) Miss Aylett, (2) Mrs. Pinkard—Vol. I. 152, 171, 174, 218, 221, 267, 414; Vol. II. 99, 136, 139, 140, 141, 142, 144-146, 163, 164, 251, 285, 320, 321, 434, 435, 440.

Lee, Richard Henry, grandson of Col. R. H. Lee—Vol. II. 139.

Lee, Robt., of Gloucester—Vol. I. 324.

Lee, Theodoric—Vol. II. 140.

Lee, Thos., of Stratford, m. Hannah Ludwell—Vol. II. 138-139.

Lee, Col. Thos. Ludwell, m. Miss Aylett—Vol. II. 139, 163, 170, 205, 435.

Lee, Thos., son of R. H. Lee—Vol. II. 143.

Lee, Wm., of London, m. Miss Ludwell—Vol. II. 136, 139, 145, 170.

Lee, Rev. Wm. F.—Vol. II. 143, 144, 460; Vol. II. 22, 23, 33, 66, 143, 340, 344, 349.

Lee, Wm. Ludwell, of Greenspring —Vol. I. 39, 40, 42, 112, 415; Vol. II. 136, 435, 469.

"Lee Hall" (Lee)—Vol. II. 151, 157.

Lee Parish—Vol. II. 136.

Leech, Wm.—Vol. II. 127.

Leeds, or Bray's Church—Vol. II. 162, 163, 164, 171.

Leeds Parish, Fauquier—Vol. II. 216, 218, 220, 221, 223, 224.

Leeds Academy, Wakefield, Yorkshire—Vol. I. 105, 108.

"Leeds Manor" (Farrow)—Vol. I. 103.

Leedstown Church—Vol. I. 404.

Leesburg Presbyterian Church—Vol. II. 273, 275, 276, 278.

"Leetown" (Lee)—Vol. II. 308.

Leetown Church—Vol. II. 307, 308.

Lefevre, Chas. Shaw—Vol. I. 104.

Leftwich—Vol. II. 429.

Leftwich, Thos., m. Bethena Ellis—Vol. II. 462.

Legare—Vol. I. 259, 465.

Legg, Jno.—Vol. II. 72.

Lewis, Laurence, m. Miss Custis—Vol. II. 231-233 ; 271, 494.

Lewis, Lorenzo, m. Miss Coxe—Vol. II. 232.

Lewis, Nicholas—Vol. II. 42.

Lewis, Gen. Robt., of Wales, Emigrant to Gloucester —Vol. II. 232.

Lewis, Robert 2nd, son of Emigrant—Vol. II. 232.

Lewis, Robert 4th, son of Col. Fielding—Vol. II. 232.

Lewis, Robt., of Fredericksburg—Vol. II. 42, 72, 494.

Lewis, Gen. Sam'l, of Port Republic, son of Chas.—Vol. II. 324, 326, 491, 492.

Lewis, Thos., of Rockingham, son of John—Vol. II. 319, 321, 324, 325.

Lewis, Thos., of Loudoun—Vol. II. 276.

Lewis, Wm., son of Jno. 1st—Vol. II. 319, 325.

Lewis, Col. Wm. J., of Campbell, m. Elizabeth Cabell—Vol. II. 62.

Lewis, Z.—Vol. II. 72.

Lexington Parish—Vol. II. 57, 58, 59.

Liberty Church, Russell, Parish—Vol. II. 18.

Licking Hole Church—Vol. I. 459, 460.

Lidford, Rev. Matthew—Vol. I. 359.

Lightfoot—Vol. I. 139, 319; Vol. II. 82, 429.

Lightfoot, Miss, m. Col. Isaac Coles—Vol. II. 15.

Lightfoot, Mrs. (Miss Maury)—Vol. II. 44.

Lightfoot, Goodrich—Vol. II. 72, 74, 77, 78.

Lightfoot, Henry—Vol. I. 304.

Lightfoot, Philip—Vol. I. 324.

Ligleport, Jno.—Vol. I. 479.

Ligon—Vol. I. 468.

Lincoln, Gen.—Vol. I. 293.

Linton—Vol. II. 206, 215.

Lindsey, Jno.—Vol. II. 281.

Linsay, W. K.—Vol. II. 337.

Linsey, Capt.—Vol. II. 44.

Lippitt, Rev.—Vol. I. 39; Vol. II. 307.

Lipscomb, Thos.—Vol. II. 13.

List of Vestrymen, Hampton Parish, 1751, 1826—Vol. I. 235.

Lester—Vol. II. 430.

Littemburne Parish—Vol. I. 404; Vol. II. 167, 172.

Little Falls Church, Fairfax—Vol. II. 256, 257, 258.

Little Fork Chapel—Vol. II. 77, 78.

Little Roanoke Chapel—Vol. I. 482.

Littleboy, J. M. Sen.—Vol. II. 349, 250.

Littlepage—Vol. II. 429.

Littlepage, Miss, m. Rev. Jas. Stephenson—Vol. II. 71.

Littlepage, Richard—Vol. I. 387.

Littleton—Vol. I. 259; Vol. II. 429.

Littleton, Col. Southey—Vol. I. 480.

Littleton Parish, Cumberland—Vol. II. 34, 35, 38.

Lively, Capt. Robt.—Vol. I. 236, 237.

Livingston, Jno.—Vol. I. 376.

Llandaff, Bishop of—Vol. II. 235.

Lloyd—Vol. I. 260; Vol. II. 430.

Lloyd, Jno.—Vol. II. 268, 284.

Lloyd, Jno. J.—Vol. II. 268.

Lochart, Jas.—Vol. II. 318.

Locke, Rev. Jno.—Vol. I. 325; Vol. II. 17.

Locke, Rev. Thos.—Vol. I. 486; Vol. II. 17.

Lockwood, Rev.—Vol. II. 258.

Logan—Vol. I. 461; Vol. II. 13.

Logan, Thos.—Vol. II. 436.

Logwood, Edmund—Vol. II. 34.

Lomax—Vol. I. 406; Vol. II. 429.

Lomax, Mr.—Vol. I. 401.

Lomax, Col. Jno., m. Miss Wormly—Vol. I. 404-406.

Lomax, Judge Jno. T.—Vol. I. 405; Vol. II. 54, 72.

Lomax, Lundford, m. Judith Micou—Vol. I. 406.

Lomax, Thos., of Caroline, m. Anne Corbin Tayloe—Vol. I. 406; Vol. II. 182.

Lomax, T. L.—Vol. II. 192.

London, Jno., Lord Bishop of Loudon—Vol. II. 295.

Lord, Mr. Jno.—Vol. I. 380.

Loring, Henry—Vol. II. 58.

Loudoun County—Vol. II. 271.

Loughty, Francis—Vol. I. 257.

Louisa County—Vol. II. 41.

Loury, Wm.—Vol. I. 236.

Louther, Miss, of N. Y.—Vol. I. 334.

Lovall, Mr.—Vol. II. 185.

Lovell, Mrs. Col.—Vol. II. 344, 345.

Lovell, Robt.—Vol. II. 435.

Lovell, Wm.—Vol. II. 72.

Low, Rev. Jno.—Vol. II. 185.

Low, Rev. Samuel—Vol. I. 274; Vol. II. 71, 124, 132.

Lowe—Vol. I. 39.

Lowe, Rev. Enoch—Vol. I. 42, 275; Vol. II. 307, 340.

"Lower Brandon"—Vol. I. 242, 311.

Lower Church, King and Queen—Vol. I. 375, 382.

Lower Church, Louisa County—Vol. II. 43.

Loyd—Vol. II. 475.

Loyd, Miss, 2nd wife of Jno. Carter 2nd—Vol. II. 110.

Loyd, Gov. Edward, of Md.—Vol. II. 182.

Loyd, Col. Wm.—Vol. I. 404; Vol. II. 172.

Lucas, Z.—Vol. II. 72.

Ludlow—Vol. II. 430.

Ludlow, Mr., of Greenspring—Vol. I. 180.

Ludlowe, Gabriel—Vol. II. 110, 121.

Ludlowe, Sarah, 3rd wife of Jno. Carter 1st—Vol. II. 110, 121.

Ludwell—Vol. II. 138, 429.

Ludwell, Miss, m. Col. Parke—Vol. II. 139.

Ludwell, Miss, m. Wm. Lee—Vol. II. 136.

Ludwell, Frances—Vol. II. 139.

Ludwell, Hannah, m. Thos. Lee—Vol. II. 138, 139.

Ludwell, Hannah Phillippa—Vol. II. 139.

Ludwell, Jno. Secty—Vol. II. 138.

Ludwell, Lucy—Vol. II. 139.

Ludwell, Lucy, wife of Col. Grymes —Vol. II. 139.

Ludwell, Philip 1st, Gov. of N. C., m. widow of Wm. Berkeley—Vol. II. 138, 139.

Ludwell, Philip 2nd, son of Gov., m. Miss Harrison—Vol. II. 139.

Ludwell, Philip 3rd, m. Sarah Grymes—Vol. I. 113, 114, 146, 178, 195; Vol. II. 139.

Ludwell, Sarah (Sarah Grymes)—Vol. I. 113.

Ludwell, Secty. Thos.—Vol. I. 146, 178, 195.

Luke—Vol. I. 280.

Lunan, Rev. Patrick—Vol. I. 290, 478.

Lund, Capt. Francis—Vol. I. 247, 249.

Lundie, Rev.—Vol. I. 478, 479.

Lunenburg Parishes and County—Vol. I. 482; Vol. II. 172, 173, 176, 178, 179, 181.

Lunsford, Sir Thomas, Knight—Vol. I. 195.

Lurin, Edmund—Vol. II. 127.

Lydall, Jno.—Vol. I. 387.

Lyde, Mrs. Elizabeth, m. Jno. Tayloe—Vol. II. 181.

Lyell, Rev. Dr., of N. Y.—Vol. II. 362.

Lyman—Vol. II. 430.

Lyne, Wm.—Vol. II. 376, 414.

Lynhaven Parish—Vol. I. 246, 271; Vol. II. 17.

Lynn, Adam—Vol. II. 271.

Lynton, Wm.—Vol. II. 227, 270.

Lyon, Rev. Jno., of Rhode Island—Vol. I. 266.

Lyons—Vol. I. 192; Vol. II. 429.

Lyons, Judge—Vol. I. 220; Vol. II. 450, 451.

Macawleys—Vol. I. 226.

"Macclesfield" (Parker)—Vol. I. 299, 304, 305.

Mackamap, Chief—Vol. II. 479.

Machem, or Mitchem, Thos.—Vol. II. 215.

Machen, ,Wm.—Vol. I. 479.

Machen, Frederick—Vol. I. 479.

Machipungo Chapel—Vol. I. 258.

Machodoc Meeting-House—Vol. II. 166.

Mackaim—Vol. II. 496.

Mackall, Jno., of Md.—Vol. II. 324.

Mackay—Vol. I. 192.

Mackay, Rev. Wm.—Vol. II. 173, 174, 186.

Mac Math, Jno.—Vol. II. 74.

Mac Naughton, Duncan, Rev.—Vol. II. 468.

Macon—Vol. II. 496.

Macon, Col. Gideon—Vol. I. 178, 187, 387.

Macon, Mr. Wm. Hartwell—Vol. I. 388.

Macon, Henry—Vol. II. 34.

Macon, Mrs. Thos. (Sarah Madison) —Vol. II. 98.

Macon, Wm.—Vol. I. 387.

Macrae, Rev. Christopher, m. Miss Harris—Vol. II. 35, 36, 37, 445.

Macrae, A.—Vol. I. 446.

Maddeson, Captain—Vol. II. 431.

Maddock (Madoc)—Vol. II. 430.

Maddocks—Vol. II. 206.

Madin, Mrs. (Polly Payne)—Vol. II. 164.

Madison—Vol. II. 94, 96, 475.

Madison, Bishop Jas., Pres. of Wm. and Mary College—Vol. I. 17, 21, 22, 27, 28, 30, 34, 37, 39, 42, 95, 96, 113, 173, 176, 194, 203, 211, 212, 225, 291, 324, 325, 352, 473, 474; Vol. II. 57, 65, 70, 73, 91, 99, 175, 176, 257, 267, 268, 272, 274, 304, 322, 324, 346, 422, 496.

Madison, Mr., son of Bishop—Vol. II. 65.

Madison, Ambrose, m. Frances Taylor—Vol. II. 89, 96-98.

Madison, Elizabeth—Vol. II. 98.

Madison, Mrs. Ambrose (Frances Taylor)—Vol. II. 86, 89.

Madison, Frances—Vol. II. 97.

Madison, Frances Taylor (Mrs. Rose)—Vol. II. 98.

Madison, Catlett—Vol. II. 97.

Madison, Dolly (Dolly Payne, widow Todd)—Vol. II. 96.

Madison, James, Sen. (father of Pres.), m. Nelly Conway—Vol. II. 96, 97.

Madison, Pres. James, m. Mrs. Todd (nee Dolly Payne)—Vol. I. 20, 50, 480; Vol. II. 30, 86, 87, 89, 92, 94-101, 159, 160, 161.

Madison, Jno. 1st—Vol. II. 96.

Madison, Jno. 2nd—Vol. II. 96.

Madison, Jno.—Vol. II. 424.

Madison, Jno., clerk of Augusta County (father of Bishop)—Vol. II. 318, 324.

Madison, Nelly (Mrs. Hite)—Vol. II. 97.

Madison, Reuben—Vol. II. 98.

Madison, Sarah (Mrs. Thos. Macon) —Vol. II. 98.

Madison, Thos.—Vol. II. 97.

Madison, Wm.—Vol. II. 97.

Madison County—Vol. II. 96.

Madison County Churches—Vol. II. 102.

Madison Courthouse Church—Vol. II. 103.

Maffit, Rev., m. Harriet Washington—Vol. II. 143.

Magill, Mrs. Henry, of Leesburg— Vol. II. 231.

"Main Church"—Vol. I. 113.

Maintenon, Madame—Vol. I. 464.

Maitland, D.—Vol. I. 446.

Malbone, Peter—Vol. I. 248, 249.

Mallory—Vol. II. 429.

Mallory, Rev.—Vol. I. 230, 231.

Mallory, Wm.—Vol. I. 235, 236.

Mamoqueitan (Chief)—Vol. II. 478.

Manchester Parish—Vol. I. 448, 450, 453, 454.

Mangochick Church, King William —Vol. I. 381.

Marye, Rev. Jas., Sr.—Vol. I. 400, 467; Vol. II. 69, 242.

Marye, Rev. Jas., Jr., m. Letitia Staige—Vol. II. 69, 89, 97, 98.

Marye, Robt. B., Esq.—Vol. II. 89.

Massamon, Rev.—Vol. I. 467.

Massey—Vol. II. 206.

Massey, Chas.—Vol. II. 190, 192.

Massey, Rev. Lee, m. (1) Miss Johnston, (2) Miss Burwell, (3) Miss Bronaugh—Vol. II. 225-227, 233, 238, 239, 247, 254.

Massey, Maj. Thos.—Vol. II. 285.

Massie—Vol. I. 461; Vol. II. 64, 429.

Massie, Rev.—Vol. I. 174, 475.

Massie, Maj., of Nelson—Vol. II. 64.

Massie, Chas.—Vol. I. 387.

Massie, Thos.—Vol. I. 387; Vol. II. 64.

Mastellar, Ferdinand (Marstellar?) —Vol. II. 271.

Masters, Solomon—Vol. II. 268.

Mason—Vol. I. 141; Vol. II. 186, 206, 225, 228, 229, 230, 241, 429.

Mason, Gen. Jno.—Vol. II. 204, 268.

Mason, Rev. Dr.—Vol. II. 358.

Mason, Euphan, m. (1) Bailey Washington, (2) Mr. Brent—Vol. II. 230.

Mason, Col. Geo., of Stafford—Vol. I. 93; Vol. II. 193, 206, 229, 230, 241, 425, 427.

Mason, Mrs. Col. Geo.—Vol. I. 93.

Mason, Hon. Geo., of Gunston—Vol. I. 152, 174; Vol. II. 99, 100, 201, 202, 225, 226, 227, 229, 238, 240, 241, 270, 484, 485.

Mason, Jno. Thompson, m. Mrs. Elizabeth Westwood Wallace—Vol. II. 204, 230.

Mason, Mrs. Jno. Thompson—Vol. II. 230.

Mason, Richard C.—Vol. II. 268.

Mason, Stephen Thompson—Vol. II. 276.

Mason, Temple, of Loudoun—Vol. II. 230.

Mason, Thos., brother of Geo.—Vol. II. 241.

Mason, Thompson—Vol. II. 436.

Mason, Wm., brother of Emigrant Geo.—Vol. II. 229.

Mason, W. T. T.—Vol. II. 277.

Mattapony Church—Vol. II. 68.

Matram, Jno.—Vol. II. 131.

"Matholic," or "Mount Pleasant" (Lee)—Vol. II. 145.

Matoax, Pocahontas's real name— Vol. I. 79.

Mathews—Vol. I. 407.

Mathews, Mr., of Caroline—Vol. I. 415.

Mathews, Baldwin—Vol. I. 178, 179.

Mathews, Jno.—Vol. I. 405.

Mathews, Mary, m. Dr. Alexander Somervail—Vol. I. 407.

Mathews, Mr., of S. C.—Vol. II. 251.

Mathews, Thos.—Vol. I. 403, 407.

Mathews County—Vol. I. 325.

Matthews—Vol. I. 280; Vol. II. 429, 430.

Matthews, Capt. Geo.—Vol. II. 319.

Matthews, Rev. Jno., m. (1) ————, (2) Miss Smith—Vol. I. 390, 402, 406, 407, 481.

Matthews, Jno.—Vol. II. 318.

Matthews, Samson—Vol. II. 319.

Maulsby, B.—Vol. II. 277.

Maupin—Vol. I. 280, 468.

Maury—Vol. I. 192, 316, 328, 465, 468; Vol. II. 475.

Maury Children and Descendants— Vol. II. 44.

Maury, Miss Anne—Vol. I. 202, 315, 328, 465.

Maury, Fontaine—Vol. II. 44, 72.

Maury, Rev. Jas., m. Miss Walker —Vol. I. 219, 220, 273, 428, 429, 465; Vol. II. 44, 97.

Maury, Matthew, from Gascony, m. Mary Ann Fontaine—Vol. I. 316.

Maury, Rev. Matthew—Vol. I. 273, 465; Vol. II. 44.

Maury, Mrs. Matthew—Vol. I. 317.

Maury, R. B.—Vol. II. 73.

Maury, Strother, from Gascony, m. Anne Fontaine—Vol. I. 465.

Maury, Rev. Walker, m. Miss Gaines —Vol. I. 272, 273, 401.

Maxey—Vol. I. 468.

May, Dr. Jno., m. Susan Tenant— Vol. II. 161.

Mayo—Vol. II. 29, 429.

Mayo, Anne, m. Geo. Carrington— Vol. II. 29.

Mayo, Jno., m. Louisa Campbell— Vol. II. 34, 161.

Mayo, Joseph, from Barbadoes— Vol. II. 29.

Mayo, Robert, m. Emily Campbell— Vol. II. 161.

Mayo, Wm., of Goochland—Vol. II. 29, 34, 37.

Mays, Jas. R.—Vol. II. 349.

Mays, Rev. Wm.—Vol. II. 431.

Mazarin, Cardinal—Vol. I. 464.

Mazzei, Philip—Vol. II. 50.

Meade—Vol. I. 139, 294, 297; Vol. II. 21, 27, 429.

Meade, Mrs. Col. (Miss Grymes)— Vol. I. 371.

Meade, Andrew, of Kerry, m. Mary Latham—Vol. I. 283, 289, 290, 291, 292, 293, 295, 479.

Meade, Ann, m. Richard Randolph —Vol. I. 80, 293.

Meade, Miss Ann R., m. Matthew Page—Vol. I. 340.

Meade, Benj. L.—Vol. II. 22.

Meade, David, m. Miss Waters— Vol. I. 291, 293.

Meade, David, m. Susannah Everard —Vol. I. 289, 290, 292-293.

Meade, Gen. Everard—Vol. I. 293; Vol. II. 30.

Meade, Hodijah—Vol. II. 22.

Meade, Jno.—Vol. I. 293.

Meade, Mary, m. Col. Walker—Vol. I. 293.

Meade, Priscilla, m. Wilson Curle— Vol. I. 292.

Meade, Col. R. K., m. Miss Grymes —Vol. I. 80, 293; Vol. II. 64, 285.

Meade, Rev. R. K.—Vol. I. 281; Vol. II. 53.

Meade, Bishop Wm.—Vol. I. 33, 116, 117, 119, 121, 250, 268; Vol. II. 92, 93, 154, 160, 385, 459, 463, 482, 486.

Mead, Rev. Zachariah—Vol. II. 47, 51, 53.

Meadville Church—Vol. II. 13.

Meale, C. J.—Vol. II. 350.

Meare—Vol. I. 84.

Meaux, Dr. Thos.—Vol. II. 22.

Mecklenburg Chapel, Shepherdstown—Vol. II. 283, 285, 295-296.

Mecklenburg Parishes and County —Vol. I. 482.

Medical College of N. Y.—Vol. I. 176.

Medley, Isaac—Vol. II. 13.

Meherrin Church—Vol. I. 477.

Meherrin Parish, Greensville—Vol. I. 280, 480.

Meldrum, Rev.—Vol. II. 285, 302.

Memorial and Commission of Bishops—Vol. II. 382.

Mercer—Vol. II. 206, 429.

Mercer, Gen.—Vol. II. 232.

Mercer, Mr.—Vol. I. 401.

Mercer, Miss, widow of Muscoe Garnett—Vol. II. 205.

Mercer, Ann, widow of Samuel Selden—Vol. II. 205.

Mercer, Chas. Fenton—Vol. II. 205, 277, 348, 358.

Mercer, Col. Geo.—Vol. II. 205.

Mercer, Hugh—Vol. II. 72.

Mercer, Judge James—Vol. II. 205.

Mercer, Jno., of Ireland—Vol. II. 205.

Mercer, Gov. Jno. Francis—Vol. II. 198, 205.

Mercer, Miss Margaret—Vol. II. 275.

Mercer, Maria, m. Richard Brooke —Vol. II. 205.

Mercer, Robert., of Fredericksburg —Vol. II. 205.

Merchant's Hope, Old Church—Vol. I. 438.

"Meredith"—Vol. I. 375; Vol. II. 429, 430.

Meredith, Rev.—Vol. II. 35, 39.

Meredith, Samuel—Vol. II. 58.

Meriwether, Miss, of Batherst, m. John Dangerfield—Vol. I. 406.

Meriwether, Chas.—Vol. II. 13.

Meriwether, Francis—Vol. I. 405.

Meriwether, Jno.—Vol. II. 42.

Meriwether, Nicholas, m. Margaret Douglas—Vol. I. 458; Vol. II. 42, 43.

Meriwether, Reuben—Vol. II. 436.

Meriwether, Thos.—Vol. I. 404.

Meriwether, T.—Vol. II. 42.

Meriwether, Wm. D.—Vol. II. 43.

Merrick (Meyrick)—Vol. II. 430.

Merriwether—Vol. I. 387; Vol. II. 429.

Merryman, Jno.—Vol. II. 127.

Metcalf—Vol. I. 376; Vol. II. 173.

Metcalfe, Jno.—Vol. II. 72.

Methodist Female College—Vol. II. 39.

Meuse, Hudson—Vol. II. 132.

Meyer, Anne Barbara, m. Gen. Peter Muhlenberg—Vol. II. 313.

Meyrick (Merrick)—Vol. II. 430.

Michaux—Vol. I. 468.

Michaux, Anne, m. Richard Woodson—Vol. II. 31.

Michie—Vol. II. 429.

Michie, Mrs. (Miss Maury)—Vol. II. 44.

Michie, William—Vol. II. 43.

Micklejohn, Rev. Geo.—Vol. I. 488.

Micou—Vol. I. 405; Vol. II. 172.

Micou, Jas. Roy, m. Fanny Matthews—Vol. I. 407.

Micou, Judith, m. Lunsford Lomax —Vol. I. 406.

Micou, Paul (Emigrant)—Vol. I. leroy—Vol. II. 179.

Micou, Paul (Emmigrant)—Vol. I. 405, 406; Vol. II. 179.

Middle Church, Albemarle—Vol. II. 43.

Middle. or Brick Church, St. Thomas—Vol. II. 84-88, 95.

Middle Chapel, Nansemond—Vol. I. 289.

Middle Plantation—Vol. I. 94, 146, 195.

Middleburg Free Church—Vol. II. 274, 275, 276, 278.

Middlesex Parish and County—Vol. I. 146, 202, 356, 364.

Middleton—Vol. II. 430.

Middleton, Benedict—Vol. II. 153.

Middleton, H. O.—Vol. II. 72.

Middleton, Robt.—Vol. II. 153.

Middletown Parish—Vol. I. 240, 287, 288.

Middletowne—Vol. I. 195.

Midge—Vol. I. 364.

Miles—Vol. I. 364; Vol. II. 430.

Miles, David—Vol. II. 121.

Mileston, W. A.—Vol. II. 22.

Milhado—Vol. I. 280.

Military Names of Va.—Vol. I. 192.

Military Institute, at Lexington— Vol. II. 66.

Mill Creek Church, 1st in Valley— Vol. II. 302, 303, 304.

Mill Prison—Vol. I. 278.

Miller—Vol. I. 364, 412, 461; Vol. II. 16.

Miller, Mr., of Brookes Bank—Vol. I. 404.

Miller. Rev. B. M.—Vol. I. 281.

Miller, Thos.—Vol. I. 324.

Miller, Wm.—Vol. I. 324.

Millfield Church, Southampton— Vol. I. 308.

Milliken, Jo.—Vol. II. 436.

Mills, Jas.—Vol. I. 393.

Mills, David—Vol. II. 42.

Millwood Church, Clarke—Vol. II. 288.

Milner, Rev.—Vol. I. 304.

Milnor, Dr.—Vol. I. 33; Vol. II. 362.

Milton, Mrs. (Miss Washington)— Vol. II. 282.

Milton, Jno.—Vol. II. 285.

Minegerode. Rev.—Vol. I. 145, 438; Vol. II. 276.

Minge—Vol. I. 319; Vol. II. 429.

Miner, Hon. Chas.—Vol. I. 417, 418.

McGuire, Rev. J. P.—Vol. I. 39, 40, 380, 391, 403, 416, 417; Vol. II. 71, 72, 189, 262, 490

McGuire, Rev. Wm.—Vol. II. 71, 72, 147, 162.

McIlwaine, Bishop—Vol. II. 305, 367.

McKay (or Mackay)—Vol. II. 161, 174.

McKensie, Rev.—Vol. I. 304.

McKnight's Commentary on Epistles—Vol. II. 292.

McLean, Anthony—Vol. II. 271.

McLean, Daniel—Vol. II. 271, 272.

McMahon, Mr., of Traphill—Vol. II. 282.

McMechin, Rev.—Vol. II. 341, 342, 349.

McNaughton, Rev. Daniel—Vol. II. 124.

McNaughton, Rev. Duncan—Vol. II. 132, 380.

McPhail, Rev. Geo. W.—Vol. II. 487.

McQuerr, Rev.—Vol. II. 260.

McRoberts, Rev. Archibald—Vol. I. 448, 449, 450, 473; Vol. II. 24-25.

M'Millon—Vol. II. 215.

"Mock Neck"—Vol. II. 145.

Moir—Vol. I. 286.

Monacans—Vol. I. 141.

Moncure—Vol. I. 192, 468; Vol. II. 206.

Moncure, Miss, widow of Gen. Wood—Vol. II. 198, 212.

Moncure, Frances, m. Travers Daniel—Vol. II. 205.

Moncure, Rev. Jno., m. Miss Brown —Vol. I. 400, 465; Vol. II. 198, 199, 201, 202, 204, 205, 209.

Moncure, Mrs. Rev. Jno.—Vol. II. 201.

Moncure, Judge R. C. L.—Vol. II. 73, 203, 204.

Monford, Robt., m. Miss Bland— Vol. I. 446.

Monroe—Vol. I. 192.

Monroe, Col., of Westmoreland— Vol. I. 458.

Monroe, Pres. James—Vol. I. 294, 458; Vol. II. 159, 160, 161.

Monroe, Mr. James, m. Miss Douglas—Vol. I. 458.

Monroe, Rev. Jno.—Vol. I. 258.

Monroe, Jno.—Vol. II. 435.

Monroe, Spence—Vol. II. 435.

Monro, Andrew—Vol. I. 405.

Monro, Rev. Jno. (Monroe)—Vol. II. 393, 401, 412, 413.

Monro, Jno.—Vol. I. 304.

Montague—Vol. I. 330, 364.

Montague, Captain—Vol. I. 210.

Montague, Abraham—Vol. I. 393; Vol. II. 436.

Montague, Wm.—Vol. I. 366, 392, 405; Vol. II. 124, 125, 443.

Montgomery, Rev. Dr.—Vol. I. 279; Vol. II. 357, 358, 362.

Montgomery Parish—Vol. II. 57, 64.

"Monticello" (Jefferson)—Vol. II. 52.

"Montpelier" (Madison)—Vol. II. II. 89, 92, 99.

Montrose Parish—Vol. II. 162.

Monumental Church, of Richmond —Vol. I. 38, 144, 145; Vol. II. 221, 477.

Moon, Mr.—Vol. I. 470.

Moore—Vol. II. 94, 111, 348, 429.

Moore, Bishop—Vol. I. 38, 40-42, 45, 47, 49, 57, 61, 143, 144, 187, 235, 237, 362, 420, 453, 461, 486; Vol. II. 51, 91, 92, 132, 133, 135, 217, 224, 304, 309, 310, 362, 477.

Moore, Ann Butler, m. Chas. Carter —Vol. II. 122.

Moore, Gen. Bernard, m. Catherine Spottswood—Vol. I. 166.

Moore, Cason—Vol. I. 249.

Moore, Rev. David—Vol. I. 143.

Moore, Francis—Vol. II. 95.

Moore, Jacob—Vol. II. 50.

Moore, Jeremiah—Vol. II. 215.

Moore, Jno.—Vol. I. 236; Vol. II. 97.

Moore, Sir Jno.—Vol. I. 301.

Moore, Miss Lucy, m. Rev. Henry Skyren—Vol. I. 381.

Mount Laurel Church—Vol. II. 12

"Mount Pleasant" (Lee)—Vol. II. 145, 152, 171.

"Mount Vernon" (Washington)— Vol. I. 98, 297; Vol. II. 60, 109, 208, 225, 227, 231, 236, 237, 246, 247, 249, 250, 263, 270, 281.

Mount Vernon, or Pohick Church— Vol. II. 225, 226, 227, 231, 233, 236, 237, 247, 257, 270.

Mower, Rev.—Vol. I. 479.

Moxley, Alvin—Vol. II. 435.

Muddy Creek Church—Vol. II. 187.

Muhlenburg, Rev. Dr. (father of Gen.)—Vol. II. 311, 312, 313, 362, 364, 365.

Muhlenburg, Frederick—Vol. II. 311.

Muhlenburg, Henry—Vol. II. 311.

Muhlenburg, Rev. Gen. Jno. Peter Gabriel, m. Ann Barbara Meyer— Vol. I. 20; Vol. II. 250, 283, 311, 312, 313, 314, 315.

Mulberry Island Parish Church— Vol. I. 94, 95, 240, 241.

Muncaster, Jno.—Vol. II. 268.

Mundell, Jno. Vol. II. 72.

Munford, Vol. I. 139, 468; Vol. II. 429.

Munford, Robt.—Vol. I. 445, 449.

Murdaugh, Rev. Edmund—Vol. I. 417, 438, 458.

Murdock, Rev., of Goochland—Vol. I. 467.

Murdock, Miss, m. Col. Wm. Fauntleroy—Vol. II. 480.

Murdock, J. R.—Vol. II. 350.

Murdock, Jos.—Vol. II. 186, 435.

Murphy, Mr., of Ayrfield—Vol. II. 148, 154, 157.

Murray, Jas., m. Miss Rolph—Vol. I. 79.

Murray, Rev. M. J.—Vol. I. 438, 445.

Murray, Wm.—Vol. II. 22.

Muscoe, Capt. Salvator—Vol. I. 405.

Muse, Dan'l—Vol. II. 468.

Muse, Hudson—Vol. II. 468.

Mushrow—Vol. I. 280.

Mustin, Henry—Vol. II. 192.

Mylne, Rev. Francis—Vol. II. 393, 401, 402, 412.

Names, Military and Civil, of Va.— Vol. I. 192.

Names of Parishes, Origin of—Vol. II. 425.

Names, Welsh, in U. S. and Va.— Vol. II. 429, 430.

Nansemond County and Parish— Vol. I. 123, 282, 289.

Nantaquaus—Vol. I. 81.

"Nantypyron"—Vol. II. 112.

Napier—Vol. II. 52.

Napier, Jno.—Vol. II. 51.

Napier, Patrick—Vol. II. 50.

Nash—Vol. I. 277; Vol. II. 27, 429.

Nash, Rev., of Ohio—Vol. II. 44.

Nash, Miss, m. Rev. Jno. Cameron —Vol. I. 488.

Nash, Rev. F. B.—Vol. II. 124, 347.

Nash, Rev. Norman—Vol. II. 124, 309, 310.

Nash, Sylvester—Vol. II. 310.

Nash, Thomas—Vol. I. 271, 487.

Nash, Mr. Wm.—Vol. I. 276.

Nassawattocks Church—Vol. I. 252, 254.

Nassawattocks Parish—Vol. I. 252.

National Institute at Washington —Vol. II. 45.

Navisons—Vol. I. 192.

Navison, John—Vol. I. 480.

Neale—Vol. II. 180.

Neale, Christopher—Vol. II. 271, 468.

Neale, G. B.—Vol. II. 350.

Neale, Henry C.—Vol. II. 268.

Neale, J. J.—Vol. II. 350.

Neale, Matthew—Vol. II. 468.

Necostin's Town, or Georgetown, D. C.—Vol. II. 131.

Needler, Benj., m. Alice Corbin— Vol. I. 376; Vol. II. 146.

Needler, Dan'l—Vol. I. 179.

Neil, Lewis—Vol. II. 281.

Neil, Sam'l—Vol. II. 337.

Nelmes, Edward—Vol. II. 468.

Nelmes, Wm.—Vol. II. 468.

Newman—Vol. I. 285.

Newport, Gov.—Vol. I. 118.

Newport Parish—Vol. I. 201, 299, 303, 305.

"Newstead" (Campbell)—Vol. II. 160.

Newton—Vol. II. 144, 151, 152, 173, 429.

Newton, Augustin—Vol. II. 271.

Newton, Col. Geo.—Vol. I. 278.

Newton, Jno.—Vol. II. 151, 153, 436.

Newton, Maj. Nathaniel—Vol. I. 249.

Newton, Mrs. Sarah, m. Willowby Newton—Vol. II. 152, 157.

Newton, Thomas—Vol. I. 278.

Newton, Wm.—Vol. II. 186.

Newton, Wm., m. Sarah Eskridge —Vol. II. 145, 151-153.

Newton, Writings of—Vol. II. 295.

Newtons (Evangelist), Sect.—Vol. II. 355, 356, 360.

Niblett, Sterling—Vol. I. 487.

Nicholas—Vol. II. 52, 206, 429.

Nicholas, Bishop, of St. David's— Vol. II. 78.

Nicholas, Anne—Vol. I. 185.

Nicholas, Geo.—Vol. I. 179-446; Vol. II. 43, 62.

Nicholas, Dr. Geo., of Williamsburg —Vol. II. 111.

Nicholas, Robert Carter, Col.—Vol. I. 109, 148, 174, 179, 183, 184, 267; Vol. II. 140, 292, 495.

Nicholas, Mrs. (wife of R. C.)— Vol. I. 185.

Nicholas, Miss, m. Edmund Randolph—Vol. II. 184.

Nicholas, Lewis, John, Geo.—Vol. I. 184.

Nicholas, Philip Norbonne—Vol. I. 184.

Nicholas, Wilson Cary—Vol. I. 184.

Nicholls, Jas. B.—Vol. II. 271.

Nicholls, Jas. P.—Vol. II. 268.

Nichols—Vol. II. 430.

Nichols, Rev.—Vol. I. 144.

Nicholson—Vol. I. 259, 330.

Nicholson, Gov.—Vol. I. 149, 150, 151, 158, 159, 160, 164, 197, 306, 323, 367, 383, 384; Vol. II. 123, 128, 291, 407, 408.

Nicolson—Vol. I. 226.

Nicolson, Mr., m. Miss Diggs—Vol. I. 239.

Niern, Rev.—Vol. I. 466, 467.

Nimmo, Mr. Jas.—Vol. I. 248, 249.

Nivison—Vol. I. 280; Vol. II. 429.

Nivison, Rev. Jno.—Vol. I. 280.

Nixon, Rev. Wm.—Vol. I. 231.

Noland—Vol. II. 429.

Noland, Wm. Loudoun—Vol. II. 278.

"Nomini" (Carter)—Vol. II. 111.

Nominy (Nomini) Church—Vol. II. 148, 171.

Norbourne Parish—Vol. II. 284, 295, 296, 297, 302, 307.

Norfleet, Edward—Vol. I. 289.

Norfleet, Christopher—Vol. I. 289.

Norfleet, Jno.—Vol. I. 289.

Norfolk County and Parishes—Vol. I. 271.

Norman—Vol. II. 206.

Norris—Vol. II. 430.

Norris, Rev. Alexander—Vol. I. 319, 403; Vol. II. 162, 188.

Norris, George—Vol. II. 289.

Norris, Rev. Oliver—Vol. I. 34, 38, 39, 41, 46, 403; Vol. II. 162, 188, 261, 262.

Norsworthy, Col. George—Vol. I. 306.

North—Vol. I. 280.

North, Lord—Vol. I. 191.

"North End" (Page), Gloucester— Vol. I. 339.

North Farnham Parish—Vol. II. 160, 173, 178, 181.

North Garden Church, Albemarle— Vol. II. 52.

Northampton County and Parishes —Vol. I. 180, 252.

Northington, Lord—Vol. I. 219.

"Northumberland House" (Thornton)—Vol. II. 143.

Northumberland County and Parishes—Vol. II. 131.

Orr, Jno.—Vol. II. 436.

Orr, Dr. Jno. Dalrymple—Vol. II. 205.

Osborne—Vol. I. 452.

Osbourne, J.—Vol. I. 446.

Osbourne's, or Ware Bottom—Vol. I. 450.

Osburn—Vol. II. 206.

Osgood, Rev.—Vol. II. 17, 39.

"Ossian Hall" (Steuart)—Vol. II. 231.

Otter River Church—Vol. I. 482.

Ousley, Thos.—Vol. II. 276.

Overton, Wm.—Vol. I. 487.

Overwharton Parish—Vol. II. 183, 197, 198, 202, 207, 214.

Owen—Vol. II. 430.

Owen, Rev. Gronon—Vol. I. 478.

Owen, Hobson—Vol. I. 141.

Owen, Jno.—Vol. II. 13.

Owens—Vol. II. 430.

Ownes, Jno.—Vol. I. 178.

Page—Vol. I. 139, 194, 330, 339, 423; Vol. II. 298, 429.

Page, Alice, m. Mann Page 3rd (Alice Grymes)—Vol. I. 352-353.

Page, Alice, m. Jno. Page—Vol. I. 196.

Page, Rev. Bernard—Vol. II. 259, 297.

Page, Betsey, m. Benj. Harrison, of Brandon—Vol. I. 339.

Page, Byrd—Vol. I. 339.

Page, Carter—Vol. I. 339.

Page, Carter, of Cumberland, m. (1) Polly Cary, (2) Lucy Nelson— Vol. I. 339, 455.

Page, Carter B.—Vol. I. 340.

Page, Cartherine, m. Benj. Walker —Vol. I. 340.

Page, Chas.—Vol. II. 271.

Page, Chas. Rev.—Vol. I. 32, 39, 40, 42, 339; Vol. II. 58, 59, 124.

Page, Rev. Chas. Henry (Missionary)—Vol. II. 340, 344, 346, 347, 349.

Page, Elizabeth, daughter of Matthew 1st—Vol. I. 350.

Page, Elizabetham—Vol. I. 199.

Page, Capt. Francis, m. Mary Digges —Vol. I. 178, 196.

Page, Mrs. Mary, m. Capt. Francis Page (Mary Digges)—Vol. I. 196, 197.

Page, Sir Gregory—Vol. I. 147.

Page, Gwinn—Vol. I. 339.

Page, Rev. James—Vol. II. 124, 342.

Page, Jane—Vol. I. 339.

Page, Jane, m. Nathaniel Nelson— Vol. I. 340.

Page, Jane, m. Edmund Pendleton —Vol. I. 339.

Page, Rev. Jno.—Vol. I. 231, 385; Vol. II. 124.

Page, Jno., Sir and Col., of Williamsburg—Vol. I. 146, 147, 178, 181, 195, 196, 331, 339, 425.

Page, Gov. Jno., of Rosewell, son of Mann 3rd, m. Fanny Burwell— Vol. I. 147, 152, 178, 183, 195, 329, 331, 333, 334, 336, 339, 341, 348, 351, 352, 414; Vol. II. 99, 289, 290, 292, 293, 495.

Page, Mrs. Gov. Jno. (Fanny Burwell)—Vol. II. 206, 334.

Page, Jno., of North End, m. Jane Byrd—Vol. I. 178, 339, 340, 414; Vol. II. 289.

Page, Jno., son of Jno., of North End, m. Betty Burwell—Vol. I. 178, 339, 414; Vol. II. 289.

Page, Jno., of Page Brook, son of Robert, of Broadneck, m. Miss Byrd—Vol. I. 178, 340; Vol. II. 289.

Page, Jno. White, son of Robert, of Broadneck—Vol. I. 340; Vol. II. 289.

Page, Judith, m. Lewis Burwell— Vol. I. 339.

Page, Judith, m. Col. Hugh Nelson —Vol. I. 340.

Page, Judith, m. Jno. Waller—Vol. I. 340.

Page, Lucy, m. Frank Nelson—Vol. I. 340.

Page, Lucy, m. (1) Col. Geo. Baylor, (2) Col. N. Burwell, of Frederick —Vol. I. 339; Vol. II. 465.

Page, Mrs. Mary, of Pagebrook— Vol I. 297.

Page, Mrs. Mary (Mary Mann)— Vol. I. 351.

Page, Mann 1st, of Rosewell, son of Matthew 1st—Vol. I. 147, 331, 339; Vol. II. 495.

Page, Mann, Jr., 2nd, m. (1) Judith Wormley, (2) Judith Carter— Vol. I. 339, 340, 351; Vol. II. 495.

Page, Mann 3rd, of Rosewell, m. (1) Alice Grymes, (2) Ann Corbin Tayloe—Vol. I. 339, 353; Vol. II. 181, 495.

Page, Mann 4th, of Mannsfield, m. Mary Tayloe—Vol. I. 339, 350, 351, 353; Vol. II. 72, 182, 465, 495.

Page, Mann, son of Jno., of North End, m. Miss Selden—Vol. I. 339; Vol. II. 495.

Page, Mann A., of Orange—Vol. II. 94.

Page, Mrs. Mann, of Shelley—Vol. I. 322, 336.

Page, Matthew 1st, son of Jno. 1st, m. Mary Mann—Vol. I. 339, 147, 195, 331, 350, 351, 387.

Page, Matthew, Mary and Ann, children of Matthew 1st—Vol. I. 351.

Page, Matthew, son of Jno., of North End (died unmarried)— Vol. I. 340, 387.

Page, Matthew, of Hanover Town (unmarried)—Vol. I. 339, 350, 351.

Page, Matthew, of Annfield, son of Robt., of Broadneck (Ann R. Mead)—Vol. I. 340, 387.

Page, Matthew, of Frederick—Vol. I. 221; Vol. II. 289.

Page, Molly, m. Jno. Byrd—Vol. I. 340.

Page, Robert 1st, of Janeville, m. Miss Braxton—Vol. I. 296, 340; Vol. II. 289.

Page, Robert, 2nd., of Janeville, m. Sarah Page—Vol. I. 296, 340; Vol. II. 289.

Page, Robert, of Hanover Town, m. Miss Carter—Vol. I. 339.

Page, Robert, of Broadneck, m. Sarah Walker—Vol. I. 339, 340; Vol. II. 45.

Page, Sarah, m. Robert Page, of Broadneck—Vol. I. 340.

Page, Tom, m. Mildred Pendleton— Vol. I. 340.

Page, Walker—Vol. I. 340.

Page, William, son of Jno., of North End, m. Miss Jones—Vol. I. 339.

Page, Wm. Byrd, of Frederick, m. Miss Lee—Vol. I. 339; Vol. II. 289.

Page, W. C.—Vol. II. 268.

"Page Brook" (Page)—Vol. I. 297.

"Pageland" (Page)—Vol. I. 331.

Paine—Vol. II. 221.

Paine, Tom (Author)—Vol. II. 235.

Paine's "Age of Reason"—Vol. II. 12, 235.

Paisley, Wm.—Vol. I. 387.

Palmer—Vol. I. 192, 200; Vol. II. 298.

Palmer, Chilton—Vol. II. 13.

Palmer, David—Vol. II. 469.

Palmer, Jno.—Vol. I. 179.

Palmer, Rev. Thos.—Vol. I. 254, 257.

Palmer, Wm.—Vol. II. 176.

Pannell—Vol. II. 103.

Pannill—Vol. II. 430.

"Paper Marker's Neck" (Lee)—Vol. II. 145.

Par—Vol. II. 430.

"Paradise" (Lee)—Vol. II. 145.

"Parish Church" (Bermuda Hundred—Vol. I. 439.

Parishes, Origin of Names of—Vol. II. 425.

Park, Jno.—Vol. I. 387.

Park, Jno., Jr.—Vol. I. 387.

Parke—Vol. II. 429.

Parke, Col. Gov., of Leeward Islands, m. Miss Ludwell—Vol. II. 138.

Parke, Col. Daniel, m. Miss Evelyn —Vol. I. 178, 180, 181, 200, 257, 262.

Parke, Daniel, Jr.—Vol. I. 178.

Parke, Miss Jane S.—Vol. II. 192.

Parker—Vol. I. 240, 259, 270, 280, 303, 304; Vol. II. 27, 156, 173, 429.

Parker, Judge, of Westmoreland— Vol. I. 406.

Parker, Miss, m. Leroy Dangerfield —Vol. I. 406.

Parker, Abraham—Vol. I. 290.

Parker, Alexander—Vol. I. 393, 401, 405, 406.

Parker, Gen'l Alexander—Vol. II. 155.

Parker, Dan'l—Vol. II. 13.

Parker, George—Vol. I. 259.

Parker, Hardey—Vol. II. 290.

Parker, Mrs. Rev.—Vol. II. 124.

Parker, Col. Josiah—Vol. I. 299, 305.

Parker, Richard—Vol. II. 435.

Parker, Severn E.—Vol. I. 259.

Parker, Thos.—Vol. I. 304.

Parker, Gen. Thos.—Vol. II. 288, 289.

Parkersburg Churches—Vol. II. 344, 349.

Parkins—Vol. II. 430.

Parks, Rev.—Vol. I. 275.

Parks, Wm.—Vol. I. 179.

Parr, Dr.—Vol. I. 293.

Parrish, Jno.—Vol. I. 487.

Parry—Vol. II. 430.

Parsons, Jas.—Vol. II. 256, 257.

Parsons, Rev. Jno.—Vol. II. 188, 189, 191.

Parsons, Dr. Robt.—Vol. II. 192.

Parsons, Wm.—Vol. I. 236.

Parson's Road—Vol. II. 160.

Pasamour (Paramour)—Vol. I. 270.

Paramour—Vol. I. 270.

Pascauta (Chief)—Vol. II. 478.

Pasteur—Vol. I. 468.

Pasteur, Rev. Jas.—Vol. I. 276, 279, 469.

Pate, Jno.—Vol. I. 324.

Pate, Thos.—Vol. I. 324.

Patterson, David—Vol. I. 387, 453.

Patterson, Elizabeth, m. Thos. Ellis —Vol. II. 461.

Pattison—Vol. I. 240.

Patton, James—Vol. II. 318.

Patton, Robt.—Vol. II. 72.

Patrich Parish—Vol. II. 16.

Paulding—Vol. I. 205.

Paulett, Thos.—Vol. II. 42.

Payne—Vol. II. 163.

Payne, Bishop, of Africa—Vol. II. 164.

Payne, Dr., of Lexington—Vol. II. 165.

Payne, Daniel—Vol. II. 165, 166.

Payne, Miss Dolly, m. (1) Mr. Todd, (2) James Madison—Vol. II. 96.

Payne, Edward—Vol. II. 270.

Payne, Geo.—Vol. II. 125.

Payne, Geo. and Elizabeth—Vol. II. 165.

Payne, Jno.—Vol. II. 164.

Payne, Merryman—Vol. II. 125.

Payne, Polly (Mrs. Madin)—Vol. II. 164.

Payne, Richard—Vol. II. 164, 186.

Payne, Richard, of Warrenton—Vol. II. 164-166.

Payne, Thos.—Vol. II. 164.

Payne, Sir Wm.—Vol. II. 164.

Payne, Capt. Wm.—Vol. II. 164, 165, 485.

Payne, Wm., m. Fanny Woodville— Vol. II. 82, 165.

Payne, Wm., Jr.—Vol. II. 226, 229, 268, 270.

Payne's Church—Vol. II. 241, 484.

Peachly, Capt.—Vol. II. 431.

Peachey—Vol. II. 429.

Peachy—Vol. II. 173.

Peachy, Miss, m. Robt. Dinwiddie Fowke—Vol. II. 483.

Peachy, Leroy—Vol. II. 176.

Peachy, Samuel—Vol. I. 393, 404, 405; Vol. II. 172.

6

Poplar Spring Church—Vol. I. 321-323.

Poppingham, Ensign—Vol. I. 130.

Population of Va. before Protectorate—Vol. I. 189.

Porson, Jno.—Vol. I. 304.

Portan—Vol. I. 111.

Porter—Vol. I. 280.

Porter, Gen. P. B., of N. Y., m. Letitia Breckenridge (widow Grayson)—Vol. II. 62.

Porterfield, Gen. Robert—Vol. II. 491, 492, 494.

Porteus, Beilby—Vol. I. 206, 207, 322; Vol. II. 238.

Porteus, Bishop—Vol. I. 25, 26, 169, 172, 203, 322.

Porteus, Edward—Vol. I. 324.

Porteus, Robert—Vol. I. 324.

"Port Micou" (Micou)—Vol. II. 179.

Portsmouth Parish, Norfolk County —Vol. I. 272, 279.

Posey—Vol. II. 429.

Posey, Jno.—Vol. II. 270.

Potomac Church, Old—Vol. II. 203, 204.

Potter—Vol. I. 364, 468.

Potter, Christopher—Vol. I. 378.

Potter, Elizabeth, m. Jno. Robinson —Vol. I. 378.

Pott-House Church—Vol. II. 274.

Potts, Hezekiah—Vol. II. 192.

Poulson—Vol. I. 270.

Povey, Mr.—Vol. I. 158.

Pow, Rev. Wm.—Vol. I. 469, 477.

Powell—Vol. II. 214, 277, 429, 430.

Powell, Mr., m. Miss Digges—Vol. I. 239.

Powell, Rev.—Vol. II. 287.

Powell, Alfred—Vol. II. 277, 289.

Powell, Capt. Ambrose—Vol. II. 98.

Powell, Burr—Vol. II. 277.

Powell, Col., of Loudoun, m. Miss Harrison—Vol. II. 277.

Powell, Cornelius—Vol. II. 58.

Powell, Cuthbert—Vol. II. 127, 227, 268, 277.

Powell, Levin—Vol. II. 276, 277.

Powell, Mary—Vol. I. 255.

Powell, Prosser—Vol. II. 58.

Powell, Richard—Vol. II. 58.

Powell, Robert—Vol. II. 268.

Powell, Thos.—Vol. II. 127.

Powell, W. A.—Vol. II. 277.

Powell, Capt. Wm.—Vol. I. 129.

Powell, W. .H—Vol. II. 276.

Powell, Wm. L.—Vol. II. 268.

Powell's Fort—Vol. II. 315.

Power—Vol. II. 496.

Power, Jno.—Vol. I. 179.

Powhatan, King—Vol. I. 77-79, 83, 86, 135, 141, 243, 335, 336, 337, 349, 350, 463, 466; Vol. II. 29, 460, 475, 472, 473.

"Powhatan" (Mayo)—Vol. II. 29.

Powlett, Mr.—Vol. I. 129.

Pownal, Rev. Benj.—Vol. II. 393, 401, 402.

Powys—Vol. II. 430.

Poythress—Vol. I. 446; Vol. II. 144, 429.

Poythress, F.—Vol. I. 445.

Poythress, Miss, m. Thos. Rolfe— Vol. I. 80.

Poythress, Miss, m. Richard Bland —Vol. I. 447.

Poythress, Miss, m. Richard Lee— Vol. II. 151.

Poythress, Wm.—Vol. I. 445.

Pratt—Vol. II. 430.

Pratts (Religious Sect)—Vol. II. 360.

Pratt, Jno.—Vol. I. 324.

Pratt, Thomas, m. Jane Brokenbrough—Vol. II. 192, 474.

Prentiss—Vol. II. 429.

Prentiss, Mr., of Suffolk—Vol. I. 297.

Prentiss, Jno.—Vol. I. 179.

Prentiss, Wm.—Vol. I. 179, 446.

Presley—Vol. II. 144.

Presley, Mr.—Vol. II. 143.

Presley, Col. Peter—Vol. II. 468.

Presley, Wm.—Vol. II. 131.

Prestman, Rev.—Vol. II. 203.

Preston—Vol. I. 192, 259.

Randolph, Beverly, Gov. of Va.—Vol. I. 139, 295.

Randolph, Brett—Vol. II. 35.

Randolph, David Meade, Marshall of Va.—Vol. I. 139.

Randolph, Edmund, Gov. of Va.—Vol. I. 139, 141, 174, 182, 183, 184, 218; Vol. II. 292, 293, 320.

Randolph, Edward, m. Miss Groves—Vol. I. 138.

Randolph, Elizabeth, m. Col. Richard Bland—Vol. I. 446.

Randolph, Henry—Vol. I. 138, 445.

Randolph, Isham, of Dungeness, m. Miss Rojers—Vol. I. 138, 139, 455.

Randolph, Jane, m. Col. R. K. Meade—Vol. I. 294.

Randolph, Sir Jno., m. Miss Beverly—Vol. I. 137-139, 147, 179, 181, 371.

Randolph, Jno., Att'y Gen'l—Vol. I. 181, 371; Vol. II. 292, 475.

Randolph, Jno., m. Frances Bland—Vol. I. 447.

Randolph, Jno., of Roanoke—Vol. I. 23, 24, 33, 83, 139, 294, 324, 334, 451, 489; Vol. II. 459.

Randolph, Judith, of Tuckahoe, m. Wm. Stith—Vol. I. 138-139.

Randolph, Peter, Attn'y Gen'l, m. Mary Spottswood—Vol. II. 139, 166.

Randolph, Hon. Peyton—Vol. I. 139, 152, 179, 181, 182, 221; Vol. II. 140, 292, 320, 321, 495.

Randolph, Col. Richard, of "Curls" m. (1) Miss Bolling, (2) Anne Meade—Vol. I. 79, 80, 110, 124, 137, 138, 139, 242, 293, 294, 455; Vol. II. 28.

Randolph, Richard—Vol. II. 459, 495.

Randolph, Col. Robert, of Fauquier—Vol. I. 139, 140, 295.

Randolph, Theodoric—Vol. I. 334.

Randolph, Thomas, of Tuckahoe, m. Miss Fleming—Vol. I. 138-139.

Randolph, Thomas—Vol. II. 464.

Randolph, Thomas, English Poet—Vol. I. 139.

Randolph, Thos. Isham, of Dungeness, m. Miss Cary—Vol. I. 455.

Randolph, Thomas Mann, m. Miss Cary—Vol. I. 139, 140, 455, 458, 460, 461.

Randolph, Wm. 1st, of Turkey Island, m. Mary Isham—Vol. I. 136-139, 218, 333, 461.

Randolph, Wm. 2nd, m. Miss Beverley—Vol. I. 461; Vol. II. 34.

Randolph, Wm., of Chattsworth—Vol. I. 295, 461.

Rankin, Mrs. (Miss Scott)—Vol. II. 208.

Ramsdell, Edward—Vol. II. 436.

Ransford, Rev.—Vol. I. 396.

Ransom, Jas.—Vol. I. 326.

Ransom, Peter—Vol. I. 326.

Rappahannock Academy—Vol. I. 410.

Rappahannock Parishes and County—Vol. I. 404; Vol. II. 96, 102.

Rathbone, W. P.—Vol. II. 350.

Rattlesnake Chapel—Vol. I. 477.

Ravenscroft, Bishop—Vol. I. 39, 486, 487-489; Vol. II. 11, 12, 50, 367.

Ravenscroft, Miss, m. Joseph Ball—Vol. II. 128.

Ravenscroft, Jno.—Vol. I. 441.

Ravenscroft, Thos.—Vol. I. 440.

Ravenscroft, Town of—Vol. I. 444.

Ravenswood Church—Vol. II. 344, 348.

"Ravensworth" (Fitzhugh)—Vol. II. 194.

Rawles, Mr.—Vol. I. 289.

Rawlings—Vol. I. 413.

Rawson, Jas.—Vol. I. 259.

Ray, P.—Vol. II. 336.

Read—Vol. II. 26-28, 31.

Read, Col. Clement, m. Miss Hill—Vol. I. 479, 483, 486; Vol. II. 28-30, 62.

Read, Rev. Clement, m. Miss Edmunds—Vol. II. 28.

Read, Rev. Duell—Vol. I. 358, 359.

Rivers—Vol. II. 430.

Roan, Chas.—Vol. I. 324.

Roane—Vol. II. 429.

Roane, Thos.—Vol. I. 393, 405; Vol. II. 435, 450, 451.

Roane, Thos., Jr.—Vol. I. 405.

Roane, Wm.—Vol. I. 393, 405; Vol. II. 435.

Roane, Wm. R.—Vol. II. 58.

"Roanoke" (Randolph)—Vol. I. 139.

Roanoke Church—Vol. I. 477.

Robert, Rev.—Vol. I. 308, 480.

Roberts—Vol. I. 280; Vol. II. 430.

Roberts, Benj.—Vol. II. 77.

Roberts, Christopher—Vol. I. 290.

Roberts, Edmund—Vol. I. 326.

Roberts, Jno.—Vol. II. 268.

Roberts, Michael—Vol. II. 13.

Robertson—Vol. I. 192; Vol. II. 429.

Robertson, the Historian—Vol. II. 144, 160, 476.

Robertson, Mr.—Vol. II. 100.

Robertson, Rev.—Vol. II. 287.

Robertson, Christopher—Vol. I. 487.

Robertson, Rev. Eleazer—Vol. I. 443.

Robertson, Geo.—Vol. I. 451.

Robertson, Rev. Geo.—Vol. I. 439, 440.

Robertson, Rev. Jas.—Vol. II. 393, 401.

Robertson, Rev. Jno.—Vol. I. 430, 442; Vol. II. 33.

Robertson, Jno. R.—Vol. II. 22.

Robertson, Rev. Moses—Vol. II. 467.

Robertson, Wm.—Vol. I. 179, 394, 446.

Robins—Vol. I. 252, 259, 330.

Robins, Major—Vol. I. 254, 255.

Robins, T. N.—Vol. I. 259.

Robinson—Vol. I. 192, 270, 364, 365, 369, 378, 405, 423; Vol. II. 173, 298, 301, 429.

Robinson, Commissary—Vol. I. 222, 290, 375; Vol. II. 179.

Robinson, man named—Vol. I. 362.

Robinson, Miss, m. Benj. Grymes—Vol. I. 371.

Robinson, Agatha—Vol. I. 378.

Robinson, Anne, m. Dr. Jno. Hay—Vol. I. 378.

Robinson, Maj. Benj., m. Miss King—Vol. I. 376, 378, 404, 405; Vol. II. 172.

Robinson, Christopher 1st, m. Miss Bertram—Vol. I. 378.

Robinson, Christopher 2nd, m. Miss Wormley—Vol. I. 378.

Robinson, Clara, m. James Walker—Vol. I. 378.

Robinson, Conway—Vol. I. 65, 84, 126, 129; Vol. II. 426, 469.

Robinson, Rev. Geo.—Vol. II. 393, 400.

Robinson, Henry, m. Miss Waring—Vol. I. 378.

Robinson, James—Vol. I. 249.

Robinson, Jno. (Emigrant), m. Elizabeth Potter—Vol. I. 378.

Robinson, Dr. Jno., Bishop of London—Vol. I. 378.

Robinson, Jno., Pres. of Council, m. Catherine Beverley—Vol. I. 360, 376, 378, 393, 380; Vol. II. 72.

Robinson, Jno., Speaker and Treas.—Vol. I. 360, 375, 376, 378, 380, 393; Vol. II. 72.

Robinson, Jno.—Vol. II. 337.

Robinson, Mrs. Mary—Vol. I. 84.

Robinson, Maxmilian—Vol. II. 186, 436.

Robinson, Michael—Vol. II. 72.

Robinson, Rev. Needler—Vol. I. 279, 451.

Robinson, Thos. A.—Vol. II. 94.

Robinson, Rev. Wm.—Vol. I. 167, 168, 172, 374, 377, 378.

Robinson, Wm., Clerk of Council—Vol. II. 408, 435.

Robinson, Wm.—Vol. II. 72, 186.

Rochester, Jno.—Vol. II. 153.

Rockbridge Parishes—Vol. II. 57, 64.

Rockett, Baldwin and Ware—Vol. II. 461.

"Rocketts"—Vol. II. 461.

Rockfish Church, Nelson—Vol. II. 52, 59, 64.

Royall, Jno.—Vol. II. 21.

Royster, Littlebury—Vol. II. 13.

Royster, Jno.—Vol. I. 325.

Royston, Thos.—Vol. I. 324.

Rucker—Vol. II. 94, 103.

Rucker, Ambrose—Vol. II. 58.

Rucker, Benj.—Vol. II. 58.

Rucker's Church—Vol. II. 58.

Ruckersville Church—Vol. II. 84.

Rudd, Wm.—Vol. I. 306.

Ruddell, Jno.—Vol. II. 284.

Ruffin—Vol. II. 429.

Ruffin, Mr., m. Miss Bland—Vol. I. 447.

Ruffin, Edmund—Vol. I. 294, 437.

Ruffin, Jas.—Vol. I. 380.

Ruffin, Jno.—Vol. I. 446.

Ruffin, Robt.—Vol. I. 444.

Rumney, Rev.—Vol. II. 147.

Rush, Dr. Benj.—Vol. II. 332.

Rush, Jeremiah—Vol. II. 436.

Rush, Hon. Richard, of Phila.—Vol. II. 492.

Rushworth—Vol. I. 267.

Russell—Vol. II. 429, 496.

Russell, Rev. Joseph A.—Vol. II. 191, 192.

Russell, Wm.—Vol. II. 77.

Russell Parish, Bedford County—Vol. II. 17, 18.

Russul, Jas., of England—Vol. II. 138.

Rust—Vol. II. 180, 215.

Rust, Peter—Vol. II. 435.

Rust, Samuel—Vol. II. 153.

Rutherford, Thos.—Vol. II. 284.

Rutledge—Vol. I. 465.

Rutledge, Rev. D.—Vol. II. 10.

Ryland—Vol. I. 240.

"Sabine Hall" (Carter)—Vol. II. 111, 173, 181.

Safford, E. D.—Vol. II. 350.

Sale, Jas.—Vol. I. 405.

Sale, Rev.—Vol. II. 18, 19, 58.

Salines, Churches in the—Vol. II. 345.

Sallie, Mr.—Vol. I. 190.

Sally, Abraham—Vol. II. 34.

Salter, Wm.—Vol. I. 304.

Salvage, Thos.—Vol. II. 472.

Samford, Jas.—Vol. II. 436.

Sample, Rev. Robt. and his History —Vol. I. 52, 429.

Sampson—Vol. I. 461.

Sands, Robt. C.—Vol. I. 268.

"Sandy Point" (Lightfoot)—Vol. I. 319.

Sanders, Capt. Edward—Vol. II. 468.

Sandy River Church—Vol. I. 449; Vol. II. 25, 26.

Sandys, Sir Edwin—Vol. I. 67, 85, 122, 239.

Sandys, Sir Geo.—Vol. I. 239.

Sanford, Edwd.—Vol. II. 436.

Sanford, Patrick—Vol. II. 153.

Sanford, Richard—Vol. II. 268, 270.

Sanford, Samuel—Vol. I. 264, 265.

Sanky, Mr.—Vol. I. 449.

Saponey Church, Old—Vol. I. 442, 450, 452, 471, 476.

Saponi Indians—Vol. I. 284.

Saunders—Vol. I. 192; Vol. II. 429.

Saunders, H.—Vol. II. 277.

Saunders, Rev. Hyde—Vol. II. 33.

Saunders, Rev. Jno. Hyde—Vol. I. 95.

Saunders, Robert—Vol. I. 178, 187, 188, 348.

Satchell—Vol. I. 270.

Satchell, Thos.—Vol. I. 259.

Satchell, Wm.—Vol. I. 259.

Satchwell—Vol. I. 280.

Savage—Vol. II. 429.

Savage, Mrs. Susan—Vol. II. 72.

Saville, Sir Jno.—Vol. I. 239.

Sayer, Mr. Chas.—Vol. I. 247.

Sayres, Mrs. (Miss Grymes)—Vol. I. 371.

Scale—Vol. I. 84.

Scandrith, Isaac—Vol. I. 393.

Scarborough—Vol. I. 259, 364.

Scarborough, Col. Edmund—Vol. I. 252-256, 257, 262.

Scarbrough—Vol. I. 270.

Scarburgh—Vol. II. 429.

Seldon (Selden?)—Vol. II. 206.

Seddon—Vol. II. 206.

Semmes, Douglas R.—Vol. II. 268.

Semmes, Thos.—Vol. II. 268.

Semple, Rev. Jas.—Vol. I. 386, 388.

Serapis—Vol. I. 278.

Servant, Mr. Richard B.—Vol. I. 236, 238.

Servant. Richard C.—Vol. I. 236.

Settlement of Eastern Shore—Vol. I. 85.

"Seven Islands" (James River)— Vol. II. 62.

Severn—Vol. I. 259.

Sewall, Mr., of N. H.—Vol. II. 244.

Seward, Rev.—Vol. I. 259; Vol. II. 132, 176, 468.

Seymour—Vol. I. 270.

Shackleford—Vol. I. 375.

Shackleford, Jno.—Vol. I. 376.

Shackleford, Lyne, Jr. and Sr.— Vol. I. 376.

Shackleford, Richard—Vol. I. 376.

Shadwell Mills—Vol. II. 43.

Shaife, Rev. Jno.—Vol. II. 393, 400, 401. (See Skaife.)

Shapespeare—Vol. I. 238, 282.

Sharp—Vol. I. 192.

Sharp, Rev. Thos.—Vol. I. 385.

Sharpe, H.—Vol. II. 72.

Sharpe, Samuel—Vol. I. 129.

Sharpe, Rev. Thos.—Vol. II. 393, 401.

Sharpe, Thos.—Vol. II. 72.

Sharpleigh, Jno.—Vol. II. 468.

Shaw, Rev. George—Vol. I. 104.

Shaw, Thos.—Vol. II. 268.

Shaw's Mount and Devil's Run Church—Vol. II. 77.

Shearman, Martin—Vol. II. 124, 125.

Shelburne, Lord—Vol. II. 426.

Shelburne Parish—Vol. II. 262, 270, 272, 273, 275, 276.

Shelby—Vol. II. 430.

"Shelly" (Page)—Vol. I. 243, 322, 330, 335, 336, 350.

Shelley, Mr. Walter—Vol. I. 130.

Shelton—Vol. I. 280; Vol. II. 16, 63.

Shelton, Abraham—Vol. II. 15.

Shelton, Crispin—Vol. II. 15.

Shelton, Edwin—Vol. II. 58.

Shelton, Jane, m. Josiah Ellis— Vol. II. 462.

Shelton, Ralph C.—Vol. II. 58.

Shelton, Richard—Vol. II. 58, 462.

Shelton, Sam'l—Vol. II. 50.

Shelton, Wm.—Vol. II. 58.

Shenandoah County and Parishes— Vol. I. 20; Vol. II. 309.

Shephard, Captain—Vol. I. 422.

Shepherd—Vol. I. 423; Vol. II. 94, 298, 429.

Shepherd, Mrs.—Vol. II. 297.

Shepherd, Abraham—Vol. II. 295.

Shepherd, Andrew—Vol. II. 86, 98.

Shepherd, Baldwin—Vol. I. 236.

Shepherd, Jas.—Vol. II. 94.

Shepherd, Rev. Jno.—Vol. I. 357, 358, 372.

Shepherd, Moses—Vol. II. 336, 337.

Shepherd, Solomon—Vol. I. 291.

Shepherd, Thos.—Vol. II. 295.

Shepherd, Wm.—Vol. I. 250.

Sherley Hundred—Vol. II. 431.

Sherlock—Vol. II. 173.

Sherman—Vol. II. 496.

Sherman, Joseph—Vol. II. 215.

Sherman, Michael—Vol. I. 387.

Sherred, Jacob, of N. Y.—Vol. II. 371.

Shield—Vol. I. 226.

Shield, Rev. Chas.—Vol. I. 417.

Shield, Rev. Robt.—Vol. I. 239.

Shield, Rev. Samuel—Vol. I. 210, 414, 415, 417, 418; Vol. II. 224, 267.

Shield, Dr. Wm. H.—Vol. I. 227, 228.

Shields, Nathaniel—Vol. I. 179.

Shinn, Stephen—Vol. II. 271.

Shiraz, Rev.—Vol. II. 287.

"Shirley" (Carter)—Vol. I. 320; Vol. II. 112, 283.

Shirmon, Jno.—Vol. I. 325.

Shocco, or Richmond—Vol. I. 444.

Shockoe Warehouse—Vol. II. 461.

Shore—Vol. I. 452.

Shore, Jno.—Vol. I. 446.

Smith, Dr., of Phila—Vol. II. 263, 369.

Smith, Miss, m. Rev. Jno. Matthews —Vol. I. 407.

Smith, A. I.—Vol. II. 42.

Smith, Abigail, m. Maj. Lewis Burwell—Vol. I. 353, 354; Vol. II. 290.

Smith, Rev. Adam—Vol. II. 64, 317.

Smith, Mr. Alexander, of Wythe County—Vol. II. 64.

Smith, Ann—Vol. I. 254.

Smith, Rev. Armistead—Vol. I. 325, 326.

Smith, Rev. Aristides—Vol. I. 291.

Smith, Arthur—Vol. I. 304.

Smith, Rev. Augustine—Vol. I. 40, 176, 322, 324; Vol. II. 147, 268.

Smith, Augustus—Vol. II. 72.

Smith, Bishop B. B.—Vol. I. 39, 42; Vol. II. 307, 340, 348.

Smith, Benj.—Vol. II. 174, 176.

Smith, Beverley—Vol. II. 350.

Smith, Miss Caroline, m. Joseph Cabell Breckenridge—Vol. II. 62.

Smith, Chas.—Vol. I. 487; Vol. II. 25, 176, 283, 384.

Smith, Rev. Chas.—Vol. I. 272, 279.

Smith, Col. Edward, of Frederick— Vol. I. 98, 101; Vol. II. 285-289.

Smith, Miss Elizabeth, wife of Harry Turner—Vol. II. 186.

Smith, Col. Francis H., of Lexington —Vol. II. 30, 66.

Smith, Capt. Francis—Vol. I. 393.

Smith, Francis—Vol. I. 405.

Smith, Francis L.—Vol. II. 271.

Smith, Rev. Franklin G.—Vol. II. 17.

Smith, G.—Vol. I. 445.

Smith, George—Vol. I. 387.

Smith, Rev. George—Vol. I. 39.

Smith, Rev. Geo. A.—Vol. I. 275; Vol. II. 82, 92.

Smith, Rev. Guy (Gay)—Vol. II. 393, 401, 402, 412.

Smith, Maj. Henry—Vol. I. 404; Vol. II. 172.

Smith, Isaac—Vol. I. 259.

Smith, Jaqueline—Vol. II. 288.

Smith, Jas.—Vol. I. 487.

Smith, Rev. Jonathan—Vol. I. 267, 301.

Smith, Capt. Jno.—Vol. I. 64, 66, 68, 77, 81, 82, 86, 112, 124, 141, 188, 229, 243, 335, 336, 338, 349, 350; Vol. II. 421, 460.

Smith, Jno., of Augusta and Rockingham—Vol. II. 318.

Smith, Gen. Jno., of Frederick— Vol. I. 98, 101; Vol. II. 251, 284.

Smith, Capt. Jno., of Gloucester— Vol. I. 324.

Smith, Jno., of Lynnhaven—Vol. I. 249.

Smith, Jno., of "Strawberry Hill," m. Mary Ellis—Vol. II. 176, 461.

Smith, Jno., of Westmoreland, m. Maty Jaqueline—Vol. I. 98, 101.

Smith, J. B.—Vol. II. 27.

Smith, J. M.—Vol. II. 124, 336.

Smith, Jno., Jr.—Vol. II. 72, 436.

Smith, Rev. Leonidas—Vol. I. 281, 291.

Smith, Luke—Vol. I. 486.

Smith, Marsden—Vol. I. 174.

Smith, Merriwether—Vol. I. 393, 405; Vol. II. 435.

Smith, Nicholas—Vol. I. 324, 393, 405; Vol. II. 186.

Smith, Philip—Vol. I. 324.

Smith, Richard C.—Vol. II. 268.

Smith, Maj. Gen. Robt.—Vol. I. 357, 358.

Smith, Gov. Sam'l, of Baltimore— Vol. I. 185.

Smith, Sam'l Stanhope, Pres. of Princeton—Vol. II. 27, 62.

Smith, Sands—Vol. I. 326.

Smith, Col. Thos.—Vol. I. 328, 329.

Smith, Capt. Thos.—Vol. I. 326.

Smith, Rev. Thos.—Vol. II. 132, 147, 342, 348, 349, 467.

Smith, Thos.—Vol. I. 301, 304, 326; Vol. II. 192.

Smith, Thos. B.—Vol. II. 42.

Spottswood, Dorethea, m. Nathaniel Dandridge—Vol. I. 166.

Spottswood, Capt. Jno., m. Mary Rouzey—Vol. I. 166.

Spottswood, Jno., m. Mary Dandridge—Vol. I. 166; Vol. II. 72.

Spottswood, Mary, m. Peter Randolph—Vol. I. 166.

Spottswood, Sir Robert—Vol. I. 165, 166.

Spottswood, Robert—Vol. I. 166.

Spottsylvania County—Vol. II. 68, 73.

Spotwoods—Vol. I. 139.

Spratt, Maj. Henry—Vol. I. 248.

Sprigg, Rev. D. F.—Vol. I. 480; Vol. II. 307.

Spring, Robt.—Vol. I. 178.

Sproull—Vol. I. 280.

Squire, Rev. Richard—Vol. I. 385.

St. Andrew's Church, Boydton—Vol. I. 487.

St. Andrew Church (Camden Parish)—Vol. II. 16.

St. Andrew's Church, Phila.—Vol. II. 306.

St. Andrew's Church, Essex—Vol. I. 312.

St. Andrew's Parish, Brunswick—Vol. I. 476, 479, 480.

St. Anne's Parish, Albemarle—Vol. II. 38, 39, 47-51, 57.

St. Anne's Parish, Essex—Vol. I. 160, 390, 391, 393, 396, 399, 401, 403, 404; Vol. II. 395-396. 412.

St. Asaph Parish—Vol. I. 409, 413, 414.

St. Brides Parish—Vol. I. 272, 279.

St. David's Parish, King William—Vol. I. 379, 380, 381.

St. George's Church, Fredericksburg—Vol. II. 81.

St. George's Church, Windsor, Eng.—Vol. II. 210.

St. George's Parish, Accomac—Vol. I. 264, 266, 267, 269.

St. George's Parish, Spottsylvania County—Vol. II. 68, 69, 72, 73, 84, 89.

St. James Church, Accomac—Vol. I. 264.

St. James Church, Richmond—Vol. I. 145, 177.

St. James Northam Parish—Vol. I. 456.

St. James Southam Parish—Vol. I. 456; Vol. II. 33-35, 39.

St. James Parish, Jefferson County—Vol. II. 331.

St. James Parish, Mecklenburg—Vol. I. 482, 485, 487, 488.

St. John's Church, on Richmond Hill—Vol. I. 141, 142, 143, 461; Vol. II. 190.

St. John's Church, Baltimore—Vol. I. 302.

St. John's Church, Brooke County—Vol. II. 327, 331, 332, 333.

St. John's Church, Columbia—Vol. II. 40.

St. John's Church, Cumberland Parish—Vol. I. 486.

St. John's Church, East Wheeling—Vol. II. 338, 339-340, 347.

St. John's Church, Hampton—Vol. I. 230.

St. John's Church, Moore Parish—Vol. II. 17.

St. John's Church, Washington—Vol. II. 96, 180.

St. John's Parish, King William—Vol. I. 379-381, 383, 438.

St. Luke's Church, Newport Parish—Vol. I. 301-307.

St. Luke's Church, Southam Parish—Vol. II. 33, 34.

St. Luke's Church, Mecklenburg—Vol. I. 487.

St. Luke's Parish, Southampton—Vol. I. 299, 307, 308.

St. Margaret's Parish, King William—Vol. I. 379, 409, 410, 413, 416, 417.

Sumner, Jacob—Vol. I. 290.

Sumner, Jethro—Vol. I. 289.

Sumner, Thomas—Vol. I. 289.

Sumpter, Gen.—Vol. I. 98.

Sunday School, Union—Vol. II. 375.

Superiors, Rev.—Vol. I. 358.

Surrey Church, Old—Vol. I. 310.

Surrey County and Parishes—Vol. I. 308, 314.

Sussex County and Parishes—Vol. I. 312, 314.

Sutton, Jas.—Vol. II. 469.

Swain, Mr. (Architect of St. Paul's, Norfolk)—Vol. I. 277.

Swan—Vol. I. 413.

Swan, Miss, m. Richard Bland—Vol. I. 446.

Swan, Capt. Alexander—Vol. II. 173.

Swann—Vol. II. 33, 429.

Swann, Maj. Thos.—Vol. I. 305; Vol. II. 34, 268.

Swearingen, Eli B.—Vol. II. 337.

Swearingen, Thos.—Vol. II. 281, 284.

Swearingen, Van—Vol. II. 284, 285.

Sweny, Mr. Chas.—Vol. I. 276, 278.

Sweny, Merit—Vol. I. 235.

Swift—Vol. I. 280.

Swift, Rev.—Vol. I. 467; Vol. II. 39.

Swift, Dean—Vol. I. 173; Vol. II. 239.

Switty, Thos.—Vol. I. 479.

Sydnor—Vol. I. 451; Vol. II. 173.

Sydnor, Epaphroditus—Vol. II. 176.

Sydnor, Jno.—Vol. II. 174, 176.

Sydnor, Wm.—Vol. II. 125, 435.

Syles, Wm.—Vol. II. 268.

Syme—Vol. II. 429.

Syme, Rev. Andrew—Vol. I. 231, 274, 390.

Syme, Col. Jno., of Hanover—Vol. II. 62.

Syme, Sarah, m. Samuel Jordan—Vol. II. 62.

Symes, Rev.—Vol. I. 259.

Syndor, Beverly—Vol. II. 13.

T. Church, Charlestown—Vol. II. 296.

Tabb—Vol. I. 326, 330; Vol. II. 20-22, 429.

Tabb, Edward—Vol. I. 326.

Tabb, Humphrey Joye—Vol. I. 326.

Tabb, Jno.—Vol. I. 235.

Tabb, Robt.—Vol. I. 326.

Tabb, Thos.—Vol. I. 326, 328, 487; Vol. II. 20, 24.

Tabb, Thos. G.—Vol. II. 23.

Tabb, Mrs. Tom (Miss Smith)—Vol. I. 328.

Tabb, Wm.—Vol. I. 326.

Taite, Capt. Wm.—Vol. II. 468.

Talbot—Vol. II. 429.

Talbot, Matthew—Vol. I. 483, 486.

Taliafero—Vol. I. 328, 330, 376, 412; Vol. II. 63, 94, 173, 298, 429.

Taliafero, B. B.—Vol. II. 58.

Taliafero, Benj. Franklin—Vol. II. 94.

Taliafero, Rev. Dr. Chas.—Vol. I. 328, 330, 486; Vol. II. 307.

Taliafero, Chas.—Vol. II. 58.

Taliafero, Francis—Vol. I. 404; Vol. II. 72, 86.

Taliafero, F.—Vol. II. 72.

Taliafero, Horace D.—Vol. II. 94.

Taliafero, Jaqueline P.—Vol. II. 94.

Taliafero, Jno.—Vol. I. 404; Vol. II. 72, 94, 186.

Taliafero, Lawrence H.—Vol. II. 94.

Taliafero, Mr., of Blenheim, m. Mrs. Pratt (Jane Brokenbrough)—Vol. II. 474.

Taliafero, Miss (Mrs. Chas. Carter, 2nd.)—Vol. II. 111.

Taliafero, Norborne—Vol. I. 415.

Taliafero, Philip—Vol. I. 376.

Taliafero, Richard—Vol. I. 325.

Taliafero, Col. Wm.—Vol. II. 97.

Taliafero, Wm.—Vol. I. 376.

Taliafero, Wm. F., m. Mary Turberville—Vol. II. 146.

Tallant, Henry—Vol. II. 338.

Tally, Rev., of Gloucester—Vol. I. 183.

Talley, Rev. Elkanah—Vol. I. 420; Vol. II. 35.

Tankard—Vol. I. 280.

Tankersley, Geo.—Vol. II. 186.

Tanner—Vol. I. 452.

Tanner, Jas.—Vol. II. 337.

Tanner's Creek Chapel—Vol. I. 276.

Tapp, Vincent—Vol. II. 323.

Tapscott, D. H.—Vol. II. 58.

Tarent, Mr.—Vol. I. 401.

Tarleton, Col.—Vol. I. 299, 455; Vol. II. 322.

Tarlton—Vol. I. 461.

Tarplay—Vol. II. 173.

Tarpley, Dr. Thos.—Vol. II. 181.

Tarry—Vol. I. 489.

Tasker—Vol. II. 111.

"Tasso's Jerusalem Delivered"—Vol. II. 107.

Tatum, Capt. Trimagon—Vol. I. 276.

Taverner—Vol. II. 173.

Tayloe—Vol. II. 65, 173, 180, 181, 186, 429.

Tayloe, Col., of Loudoun—Vol. II. 276.

Tayloe, Capt.—Vol. II. 125.

Tayloe, Ann Corbin, m. Mann Page—Vol. I. 339, 352; Vol. II. 181.

Tayloe, Anne Corbin, m. Thos. Lomax, of Caroline—Vol. II. 182.

Tayloe, Benj. Ogle—Vol. II. 182, 192.

Tayloe, Miss Betty, m. Richard Corbin—Vol. II. 146, 181.

Tayloe, Catherine, m. Landon Carter—Vol. II. 182.

Tayloe, Eleanor, m. Ralph Wormly—Vol. II. 182.

Tayloe, Elizabeth, m. Gov. Edward Loyd, of Md.—Vol. II. 182.

Tayloe, Henry, of Alabama—Vol. II. 182.

Tayloe, Jane, m. Robt. Beverly, of Essex—Vol. II. 182.

Tayloe, John, 1st., son of Wm., 1st., m. Mrs. Elizabeth Lyde (Elizabeth Gwyn)—Vol. II. 18.

Tayloe, Col. Jno., of "Mount Airy," m. Rebecca Plater—Vol. I. 339, 371; Vol. II. 125, 139, 146, 180-182, 477, 495.

Tayloe, Mrs. Col., of Mt. Airy—Vol. II. 476.

Tayloe, Jno., 3rd., m. Anne Ogle—Vol. II. 182.

Tayloe, Lieut. Jno., 4th.—Vol. II. 182.

Tayloe, Jno., of "Chalterton"—Vol. II. 182.

Tayloe, Mary, m. Mann Page—Vol. II. 182.

Tayloe, Rebecca, m. Francis Lightfoot Lee—Vol. II. 139, 182.

Tayloe, Sarah, m. Col. Wm. A. Washington—Vol. II. 182.

Tayloe, Wm., the Emigrant of London, m. Anne Corbin—Vol. II. 181.

Tayloe, Wm., son of Jno.—Vol. II. 181.

Tayloe, Wm., Edward and Geo., sons of B. O. Tayloe—Vol. II. 182.

Taylor—Vol. I. 192, 218, 410, 423, 452, 461; Vol. II. 94, 96, 98, 298, 429.

Taylor, Bishop—Vol. I. 14.

Taylor, Mrs.—Vol. II. 237.

Taylor, Mrs. Alice (Miss Smith)—Vol. I. 272.

Taylor, Bennett, m. Miss Randolph Vol. II. 293.

Taylor, Rev. Daniel—Vol. I. 385; Vol. II. 393, 496.

Taylor, Edmund—Vol. I. 487; Vol. II. 284.

Taylor, Elizabeth, m. —— Glassell —Vol. II. 98.

Taylor, Erasmus—Vol. II. 85, 95, 97, 98.

Taylor, Frances, m. —— Burnley— Vol. II. 96-98.

Taylor, Col. Geo.—Vol. II. 96-98.

Taylor, Capt. Geo.—Vol. I. 404; Vol. II. 172, 173, 268.

Taylor, Geo. Keith—Vol. I. 446.

Taylor, Henry, of Bunker's Hill—Vol. II. 165.

Taylor, Jas. (Emigrant)—Vol. II. 85, 97, 98.

Taylor, Rev. Jas.—Vol. I. 291, 414, 415.

Taylor, Dr. James, m. Miss Smith—Vol. I. 272.

Taylor, Mrs. James—Vol. II. 86.

Taylor, Mrs. Jane—Vol. II. 97.

Taylor, Jane, m. Robt. Beverley—Vol. II. 482.

Taylor, Rev. Jeremiah—Vol. I. 230, 231, 291.

Taylor, Jno., of Norfolk—Vol. I. 276.

Taylor, Judge John, of Miss.—Vol. II. 98.

Taylor, Jno., of Berryville—Vol. II. 288.

Taylor, Col. Jno., of Caroline—Vol. I. 410, 415; Vol. II. 98.

Taylor, Jno., m. Miss Pendleton—Vol. II. 98, 127, 298, 349.

Taylor, Lawrence B.—Vol. II. 268.

Taylor, Miss Lucy, m. Rev. Mr. Balmaine—Vol. II. 95.

Taylor, Martha—Vol. II. 97.

Taylor, Mary, m. —— Pendleton—Vol. II. 98, 298.

Taylor, Miss Milly—Vol. II. 97.

Taylor, Richard—Vol. I. 446; Vol. II. 98.

Taylor, Robert, m. Miss Pendleton—Vol. II. 86, 98, 298.

Taylor, Mrs. Sarah—Vol. II. 98.

Taylor, Thos.—Vol. I. 178.

Taylor, Wm.—Vol. I. 487; Vol. II. 72, 469.

Taylor, Gen. Zachary—Vol. II. 85, 98.

Taylor, Zachary—Vol. II. 85, 98, 186.

Taylor's Church, Fauquier—Vol. II. 219.

Tazwell—Vol. I. 480; Vol. II. 429.

Tazwell, Henry, m. Miss Waller—Vol. I. 478,-479.

Tazwell,-Littleton—Vol. I. 477, 479, 480.

Tazwell,-Littleton Waller—Vol. I. 480.

Tazwell, Wm., m. Miss Littleton—Vol. I. 480.

Teackle—Vol. I. 192.

Teackle, Rev. Mr. Thos.—Vol. I. 255, 257, 266.

Teagle—Vol. I. 270.

Tear, or Tar Wallett Church—Vol. II. 33, 34, 36, 38.

Tebault, A. G.—Vol. I. 250.

Tebbs, Mr., of Culpeper, m. Miss Skyren—Vol. I. 382.

Temple—Vol. I. 260, 381, 413.

Temple, Mr., m. Miss Bowdoin—Vol. I. 260.

Temple, Col. Benj.—Vol. I. 380, 382; Vol. II. 247.

Temple, Henry—Vol. I. 289.

Temple, Jno., m. Mary Latane—Vol. I. 393.

Temple, Peter—Vol. II. 176.

Temple, Robt., of Ampthill, m. Elizabeth Skyren—Vol. I. 382.

Temple, Mr. Wm.—Vol. I. 380.

Temple, Young—Vol. I. 394.

Temple, Rev. Mr.—Vol. I. 403.

Temple Farm—Vol. I. 202, 226, 227.

Templeman, Sam'l—Vol. II. 153.

Templeton, Rev., of Warm Springs—Vol. I. 347.

Tenant, Rev. James—Vol. I. 247, 248; Vol. II. 393.

Tenant, Lucy, m. Taliafero Hunter—Vol. II. 161.

Tenant, Maria, m. Thos. Hunter—Vol. II. 161.

Tenant, Susan, m. Dr. Jno. May—Vol. II. 161.

Tenant's Church—Vol. II. 77.

Tenbroeck, Rev. Dr., of Portland, Me.—Vol. II. 362.

Tenent, M.—Vol. II. 192.

Tennant, Dr., m. Miss Campbell—Vol. II. 161.

Tennant, Mercer, m. Miss Grymes—Vol. II. 161.

Thornton, James—Vol. II. 58.

Thornton, Jno.—Vol. II. 72.

Thornton, Joseph—Vol. II. 271.

Thornton, Meaux—Vol. I. 325.

Thornton, Presley—Vol. II. 143, 468.

Thornton, Rowland—Vol. II. 186.

Thornton, Seth—Vol. I. 324.

Thornton, Sterling—Vol. I. 325.

Thornton, Rev. Thos.—Vol. II. 69, 70, 202.

Thornton, William—Vol. I. 324, 325, 479; Vol. II. 186, 192.

Thoroughgoods—Vol. II. 229.

Thorougood, Jno.—Vol. I. 250.

Thorp, or Thorpe—Vol. I. 198.

Thorp, Col. Geo.—Vol. I. 136, 146.

Thorp, Catherine, m. Capt. Thos.—Vol. I. 198.

Thorp, Hugh—Vol. I. 178.

Thorp, Maj. Thomas—Vol. I. 198.

Thorpe, Capt. Otho—Vol. I. 178, 198.

Thorpe, Thos.—Vol. I. 376.

Thrasher, Samuel—Vol. I. 404.

Threlheld, Elijah—Vol. II. 205.

Throckmorton—Vol. I. 326, 328, 330.

Throckmorton, Albion—Vol. I. 324.

Throckmorton, Jno.—Vol. I. 325.

Throckmorton, Wm.—Vol. I. 324.

Thruston—Vol. I. 330.

Thruston, Rev. and Col.—Vol. I. 20; Vol. II. 285.

Thruston, Judge, of Wash., D. C.—Vol. II. 285.

Thruston, Capt. Chas. Minn—Vol. I. 323, 325.

Thruston, Jno.—Vol. II. 285.

Thweats—Vol. I. 452, 468.

Tibbs, Daniel—Vol. II. 153, 435.

Tilghman, Chas.—Vol. I. 304.

Tillotson—Vol. I. 25, 401; Vol. II. 354, 355, 356.

Tillotson Parish, Buckingham County—Vol. II. 38, 39.

Timberlake—Vol. II. 496.

"Timberneck" (Mann)—Vol. I. 195, 349, 351, 352.

Tims, Wm.—Vol. II. 43.

Timson, Samuel—Vol. I. 178, 179.

Timson, Wm.—Vol. I. 178.

Timson, Wm., Jr.—Vol. I. 179.

Tingle, G. C.—Vol. II. 337.

Tinker, Jno.—Vol. II. 268.

Tinsley—Vol. II. 63.

Tinsley, Dr.—Vol. I. 200.

Tinsley, David—Vol. II. 58.

Tinsley, Martin—Vol. II. 58.

Tinsley, Reuben—Vol. II. 43.

Tinsley, Zachariah D.—Vol. II. 58.

Titmassie—Vol. I. 441.

Tizzard, Rev., of Chesterfield—Vol. I. 452, 467.

Todd—Vol. I. 303; Vol. II. 429.

Todd, Chas.—Vol. I. 415.

Todd, Mrs. Dolly (Miss Payne), m. James Madison—Vol. II. 96.

Todd, Jno. (Moderator)—Vol. II. 443.

Tolson—Vol. II. 206.

Tomlin—Vol. II. 173, 180.

Tomlin, Mr.—Vol. II. 119.

Tomlin, Walker—Vol. II. 174, 176.

Tomlin, Wm.—Vol. I. 404.

Tomlinson, Benj.—Vol. I. 487.

Tompkins—Vol. I. 413; Vol. II. 52, 430.

Tompkins, Rev.—Vol. II. 17, 333, 342, 348.

Tompkins, Mrs. Col. (Miss Smith) —Vol. I. 328.

Tompkins, Chas.—Vol. I. 325.

Tompkins, Miss Elizabeth—Vol. I. 326.

Tompkins, Humphrey—Vol. I. 326.

Tompkins, Robt.—Vol. I. 416.

Tompkins, Wm.—Vol. I. 326.

Toot, Adam—Vol. II. 13.

Toparchia—Vol. I. 119.

Torian, Icare—Vol. II. 13.

Torian, Sceevor—Vol. II. 13.

Toslicough (Chief)—Vol. II. 478.

Totten, Rev. Dr.—Vol. I. 110.

Towns, Jno., Jr.—Vol. II. 22.

Touweren, King—Vol. II. 479.

Towles, Rev.—Vol. II. 16, 215.

Turkey Run Church, Fauquier—Vol. II. 216, 217, 218.

"Turkey Island" (Randolph)—Vol. I. 137-139.

Turnbull, George—Vol. I. 444.

Turnbull, R.—Vol. I. 446.

Turner—Vol. I. 461; Vol. II. 186, 220, 298.

Turner, Dr., the Emigrant—Vol. II. 186.

Turner, Prof.—Vol. II. 365.

Turner, Mr. (Sir Gregory Page)—Vol. I. 147.

Turner, Harry, m. Elizabeth Smith—Vol. II. 186.

Turner, Mrs. Eliza—Vol. II. 170.

Turner, Jno. P.—Vol. II. 347.

Turner, Henry, m. Miss Blackburn—Vol. II. 58, 208. 236.

Turner, Mrs. Henry—Vol. II. 208.

Turner, Henry, Thos. Richard, Geo.—Vol. II. 186.

Turner, Reuben—Vol. I. 410.

Turner, Col. Thos., m. Miss Fauntleroy—Vol. II. 186, 480.

Turpin, Thos.—Vol. II. 34, 35.

Turpin, et al. vs. Locket, et al.—Vol. II. 450.

Turretine (Works of)—Vol. I. 459.

"Tusculum" (Peyton)—Vol. II. 467.

Tutt, Jas.—Vol. II. 72.

Tutt, Richard—Vol. II. 72.

Tuttle, Rev. Mr.—Vol. II. 162.

Twitty, Jno.—Vol. I. 483, 486.

Two Springs Church, St. Mark's—Vol. II. 76.

Twyman, Anthony—Vol. II. 94.

Tyler—Vol. I. 319; Vol. II. 429.

Tyler, Elizabeth, m. Jno. Greenhow—Vol. I. 199.

Tyler, Jno.—Vol. I. 199.

Tyler, Henry—Vol. I. 178; Vol. II. 198.

Tyler, Henry, Jr.—Vol. I. 179.

Tyler, Richard, Jr.—Vol. I. 405.

Tyler, R. R.—Vol. I. 416.

Tyndale (Tindall)—Vol. II. 430.

Tynes, Thomas—Vol. I. 304.

Tyng, Rev. Dudley—Vol. II. 307.

Typerios, Rev. Michael—Vol. I. 325.

Ufford, John—Vol. I. 259.

Underwood—Vol. I. 461.

Underwood, Mr. Wm.—Vol. II. 115, 173.

"Union Hill," or "Collecton" (Cabell)—Vol. II. 60, 61.

University of Early Va.—Vol. I. 84.

"Upper Brandon"—Vol. I. 242, 311.

Upper Church, Richmond County—Vol. II. 180.

Upper Church, King and Queen—Vol. I. 375.

Upperville Church—Vol. II. 275.

Upshaw—Vol. II. 172, 429, 466.

Upshaw, James—Vol. I. 405; Vol. II. 435.

Upshaw, John—Vol. I. 393, 405; Vol. II. 435.

Upshaw, Wm.—Vol. I. 324.

Upshur—Vol. I. 255, 259, 270; Vol. II. 429.

Upshur, Abel P.—Vol. I. 259.

Upshur, James—Vol. I. 259.

Upshur, John—Vol. I. 259.

Upshur, Littleton—Vol. I. 259.

Urmston—Vol. I. 285.

Urquhart, Chas.—Vol. II. 72.

Vail—Vol. I. 294.

Valley Church—Vol. I. 461; Vol. II. 313.

Vanbibbers—Vol. I. 330.

Vanbibber, Mrs.—Vol. I. 330.

Vandergrift, Henry W.—Vol. II. 268.

Vane (or Fane)—Vol. II. 430.

Vashon—Vol. I. 461.

Vass, Mr., m. Miss Pendleton—Vol. II. 298.

Vass, Henry—Vol. I. 393.

Vass, Jno.—Vol. I. 393.

Vaughan, Edmund—Vol. II. 35.

Walker, Lucy, m. Col. Jno. Baylor —Vol. II. 464.

Walker, Robt.—Vol. II. 58.

Walker, Sarah, m. Robt. Page, of Broadneck—Vol. I. 340.

Walker, Dr. Thos. (Discoverer of Ky.)—Vol. I. 382, 465; Vol. II. 42, 43.

Walker's Church, Albemarle—Vol. II. 43, 45, 47, 51, 87, 92.

Wall—Vol. II. 430.

Wall, Jno.—Vol. I. 479.

Wall, Rev.—Vol. II. 204.

Wallace—Vol. I. 192; Vol. II. 206.

Wallace, Caleb—Vol. II. 443.

Wallace, Jas.—Vol. I. 235, 236.

Wallace, Mrs. Margaret (Miss Henderson)—Vol. II. 233.

Wallace, Mr., m. Elizabeth Westwood—Vol. II. 230.

Waller—Vol. II. 111, 206, 429.

Waller, Benj., m. Catherine Page— Vol. I. 179, 340.

Waller, Jno., m. Judith Page—Vol. I. 340; Vol. II. 72.

Waller, Jno., Jr.—Vol. II. 72.

Waller, Miss, m. Henry Tazwell— Vol. I. 480.

Waller, Wm.—Vol. I. 290; Vol. II. 58, 63, 72.

Wallingford Parish—Vol. II. 314-316.

Wallington—Vol. I. 280.

Wallis—Vol. II. 430.

Wallop's Road Church—Vol. I. 266.

Walter, Geo.—Vol. I. 479.

Walters (Waters)—Vol. II. 430.

Walthall—Vol. I. 446.

Walthall, Arch.—Vol. I. 451.

Walthall, Thos.—Vol. II. 23.

Waltham—Vol. I. 259.

Walton—Vol. II. 429.

Walton, Geo.—Vol. I. 486.

Walton, Thos.—Vol. I. 304.

"War Captain's Neck" (Lee)—Vol. II. 145.

Ward—Vol. I. 452; Vol. II. 429.

Ward, Rev. Jacob—Vol. I. 385.

Ward, Rowland—Vol. II. 22.

Ward, Rev. Wm. N.—Vol. I. 413, 417; Vol. II. 73, 147, 153, 154, 177, 181, 340, 341, 344.

Warden—Vol. I. 192.

Warden, Chas.—Vol. I. 487.

Ware—Vol. I. 192, 376.

Ware, Edward—Vol. I. 376.

Ware, Elizabeth, m. Jno. Ellis—Vol. II. 461.

Ware, Jas.—Vol. II. 58.

Ware, Jno.—Vol. I. 376; Vol. II. 50.

Ware, Valentine—Vol. I. 376.

Ware, Wm.—Vol. II. 58.

Ware Bottom, or Osbourne's—Vol. I. 450.

Ware Church—Vol. I. 354.

Ware Parish—Vol. I. 321, 323, 328, 329, 334.

Waring—Vol. II. 172.

Waring, Ann, m. Wm. Latane—Vol. I. 393.

Waring, Francis—Vol. I. 405; Vol. II. 435.

Waring, Miss, m. Henry Robinson— Vol. I. 378.

Waring, Payne, m. Lucy Latane— Vol. I. 393.

Waring, Robt. Payne—Vol. I. 405.

Waring, Capt. Thos.—Vol. I. 405.

Waring, Maj. Thos.—Vol. I. 405.

"Warminister" (Cabell)—Vol. II. 63.

Warner—Vol. I. 355; Vol. II. 430.

Warner, Hon. Augustine—Vol. I. 321, 322.

Warner, Rev. Geo. K.—Vol. II. 340.

Warner, Miss, m. —— Washington, son of 1st. Jno.—Vol. I. 355.

Warren Church, New Kent—Vol. II. 496.

Warrington—Vol. I. 192.

Warrington, Commodore Louis— Vol. I. 201, 204, 232-234, 237.

Warrington, Rev. Thos., of Hampton—Vol. I. 204, 218, 219, 231, 232, 235, 239.

Warrington, Susannah (Mrs. Riddle)—Vol. I. 201, 234.

Warrosquoyacke, or Warrosquijoake —Vol. I. 92, 299, 300, 301.

Warwick—Vol. I. 364.

Warwick, Robt.—Vol. II. 58.

Warwick County and Parish—Vol. I. 97, 238.

Warwicksqueake Parish—Vol. I. 299, 301, 304.

Waryng—Vol. II. 429.

Washington—Vol. I. 103, 355; Vol. II. 109, 156, 158, 159, 163, 164, 166, 169, 206, 215, 228, 230, 348, 429.

Washington, Miss, daughter of Warner, m. (1) Mr. Nelson, (2) Mr. Milton—Vol. II. 282.

Washington, Miss, daughter of Warner, m. Mr. Whiting—Vol. II. 282.

Washington, Anne, daughter of Jno., 1st.—Vol. II. 167.

Washington, Ann, daughter of Laurence, 1st.—Vol. II. 168.

Washington, Armistead—Vol. II. 13.

Washington, Augustine—Vol. I. 166.

Washington, Bailey, of Stafford, m. Euphan Mason—Vol. II. 230.

Washington, Betty, m. Col. Fielding Lewis—Vol. II. 231.

Washington, Judge Bushrod, m. Jane Blackburn—Vol. II. 208, 236.

Washington, Mrs. Bushrod (Jane Blackburn)—Vol. II. 208, 236, 490, 491.

Washington, Chas., brother of George—Vol. II. 72, 296, 435.

Washington, Corbin, m. Hannah Lee —Vol. II. 143.

Washington, Elizabeth, m. Gen. Alexander Spottswood—Vol. I. 166.

Washington, Fairfax—Vol. II. 289.

Washington, Gen'l, m. Widow Custis (Martha Dandridge)—Vol. I. 20, 21, 32, 34, 98, 101, 108, 109, 147, 152, 166, 167, 174, 213, 221, 260, 262, 293, 295, 296, 318, 378, 386,

405, 411, 447, 460; Vol. II. 28, 43, 60, 70, 106, 108, 109, 127, 128, 129, 131, 140, 141, 159, 161, 162, 165, 166, 169, 184, 185, 204, 208, 225, 226-229, 231, 233-238, 240, 242, 256, 257, 259, 260, 263, 270, 282, 283, 292, 296, 308, 314, 315, 316, 320, 321, 326, 348, 465, 474, 480, 481, 484, 485, 490, 491, 492, 493-495.

Washington, Religious Character— Vol. II. 242-255.

Washington's Wrath with St. Clair —Vol. II. 493.

Washington, Mrs. Gen'l (Martha Dandridge), widow of John Custis —Vol. I. 98, 180, 424; Vol. II. 184, 196, 225, 230, 231, 236, 237, 228, 254, 282, 493.

Washington, Harriet, m. (1) Geo. Turberville, (2) Rev. Mr. Moffit —Vol. II. 143.

Washington, Henry T.—Vol. II. 192.

Washington, Col. Jno., 1st. (Emigrant—Vol. I. 322, 355; Vol. II. 131, 166, 167, 168.

Washington, Col. Jno., 2nd., son of Jno., 1st., m. Miss Warner—Vol. I. 324; Vol. II. 167, 186.

Washington, Jno., son of Laurence, 1st.—Vol. I. 324; Vol. II. 168, 186, 192.

Washington, Jno. Augustine, brother of George—Vol. II. 153, 236, 252, 268, 436.

Washington, Jno. T.—Vol. II. 192.

Washington, J. K.—Vol. II. 192.

Washington, Laurence, 1st. (Emigrant), m. (1) ———, (2) Miss Fleming—Vol. II. 166, 168.

Washington, Laurence, son of Jno., 1st.—Vol. II. 167, 186, 192.

Washington, Laurence, brother of George, m. Miss Fairfax—Vol. II. 169, 186, 192, 225, 246, 259, 435.

Washington, Laurence—Vol. II. 161.

Washington, Mary, daughter of Laurence, 1st.—Vol. II. 168.

Washington, Needam—Vol. II. 192.

Washington, Mrs. Polly (Miss Blackburn)—Vol. II. 208.

Washington, Robt.—Vol. II. 192.

Washington, Sam'l—Vol. II. 192, 435.

Washington, Thos.—Vol. II. 192.

Washington, Warner, son of Col. Jno., 2nd., m. Hannah Fairfax—Vol. I. 322, 325; Vol. II. 282, 284, 289.

Washington, Mrs. Warner (Hannah Fairfax)—Vol. II. 282.

Washington, Col. Wm. Augustine, m. (1) Mary Lee, (2) Sarah Tayloe—Vol. II. 143, 182.

Washington Academy—Vol. II. 260.

Washington's Family Seat—Vol. II. 169.

Washington's Vault—Vol. II. 237.

Washington Parish—Vol. II. 158, 159, 162, 167, 190, 191, 434.

Waterbury, Dr.—Vol. I. 155.

Waters (Walters)—Vol. II. 430.

Waters, Miss, m. David Meade—Vol. I. 293.

Waters, Elizabeth, m. Chas. Ellis—Vol. II. 462.

Watkins—Vol. I. 240, 450, 451, 461, 468; Vol. II. 26, 27, 29, 31, 32, 82, 429-430.

Watkins, Miss, m. Rev. Leigh—Vol. I. 451.

Watkins, Benj., m. Miss Cary—Vol. I. 450, 451.

Watkins, Edward—Vol. I. 450.

Watkins, Francis, of Prince Edward—Vol. I. 450.

Watkins, Geo.—Vol. II. 13.

Watkins, Hannah, m. Wm. Finnie—Vol. I. 451.

Watkins, Hannah, m. Dr. Jno. Barksdale—Vol. I. 451.

Watkins, James (Emigrant)—Vol. I. 450.

Watkins, Col. Joel, of Charlotte—Vol. I. 451.

Watkins, Mary, m. Judge Wm. Leigh—Vol. I. 451.

Watkins, Rebecca, m. Benj. Watkins Leigh—Vol. I. 451.

Watkins, Thos., of Henrico, son of Edward—Vol. I. 450.

Watkins, Thos., of Swift Creek, Powhatan—Vol. I. 450, 451.

Watkins, Thos., of Chickahominy, son of Thos., of Swift Creek—Vol. I. 450.

Watkins, Thos., son of Benjamin, m. Rebecca Selden—Vol. I. 451.

Watkins, Wm.—Vol. I. 487.

Watkins Church Chapel—Vol. II. 25.

Watson—Vol. II. 429.

Watson, Alexander—Vol. I. 479.

Watson, Jonathan—Vol. I. 325.

Watson, Wilkins—Vol. II. 58.

Wattington, Jno.—Vol. II. 13.

Watts, Dr.—Vol. I. 348.

Watts, Gen.—Vol. II. 65.

Watts—Vol. II. 430.

Watts, Jno.—Vol. II. 435.

Watts, Sam'l—Vol. I. 236, 237.

Watts, Thos.—Vol. I. 236.

Waugh—Vol. II. 95, 206.

Waugh, Rev. Abner—Vol. I. 409, 412; Vol. II. 71, 465.

Waugh, Alexander—Vol. II. 95.

Waugh, Guary—Vol. II. 205.

Waugh, George Lee—Vol. II. 205.

Waugh, Jno.—Vol. II. 81, 192.

Waugh, Robt.—Vol. II. 205.

Waughop, Capt. Jno.—Vol. II. 468.

Wayles—Vol. II. 430.

Wayne—Vol. II. 430.

Wayne, Judge, m. Miss Campbell—Vol. II. 160, 161.

Wayne, Mrs. (Miss Campbell)—Vol. II. 161.

Webb—Vol. I. 192; Vol. II. 429.

Webb, George—Vol. I. 387.

Webb, Capt. Geo.—Vol. II. 431.

Webb, James—Vol. I. 278, 393.

Webb, Jas., Jr.—Vol. II. 435.

Webb, Merry—Vol. II. 13.

Whitaker, Rev. Alexander—Vol. II. 431.

White—Vol. I. 192; Vol. II. 94.

White, Bishop—Vol. I. 34, 47, 170, 219, 221, 460; Vol. II. 73, 236, 254, 255, 267, 328, 330, 352, 356, 361, 362, 365, 371, 372, 494.

White, Rev. Alexander—Vol. I. 379, 380; Vol. II. 314.

White, Alexander—Vol. II. 284.

White, Joseph—Vol. I. 178.

White, Richard—Vol. II. 94.

White, Solomon—Vol. I. 248.

White, Wm.—Vol. I. 249.

White Chapel Church, St. Mary's—Vol. II. 125, 126.

"White Chimney's Tavern"—Vol. II. 235.

"White's Memoirs"—Vol. II. 371.

Whitefield and his Works—Vol. I. 32, 459; Vol. II. 295, 356, 360.

Whitehead, Rev. Jas.—Vol. I. 273, 274.

Whitehead, Jno.—Vol. I. 249.

"White House"—Vol. I. 386.

"White Marsh" (Burwell)—Vol. I. 106.

Whiting—Vol. I. 375; Vol. II. 429.

Whiting, Miss Betsy—Vol. II. 305.

Whiting, Beverley—Vol, II. 242, 305.

Whiting, Henry—Vol. I. 325.

Whiting, Jno.—Vol. I. 376.

Whiting, Kemp—Vol. I. 326.

Whiting, Mrs. (Miss Washington) —Vol. II. 282.

Whiting, Peter B., m. Miss Burwell —Vol. II. 277.

Whiting, Mrs. Peter B. (Miss Burwell)—Vol. I. 353.

Whittaker—Vol. I. 192, 240.

Whittaker, Rev. Alexander—Vol. I. 70, 74-78, 84, 85, 87, 125, 134-136, 442, 448; Vol. II. 469, 473. (See also Whitaker.)

Whittingham, Bishop—Vol. II. 375.

Whittle, Rev. Francis—Vol. I. 461; Vol. II. 287, 344.

Whittle, Jas.—Vol. II. 15.

Wickes, Rev.—Vol. I. 275.

Wickham—Vol. I. 423; Vol. II. 429.

Wickham, Rev. Wm.—Vol. I. 77, 84, 136, 442, 448; Vol. II. 431.

Wickliffe—Vol. II. 215.

Wickliff Parish—Vol. II. 208, 287, 288.

Wicomico Parish, Northumberland —Vol. II. 369, 467, 468.

Wigton, Grammar School—Vol. I. 411.

Wilberforce, Rev.—Vol. I. 25, 26; Vol. II. 355, 361, 465.

Wilberforces (Religious Sect)—Vol. II. 360.

Wilcox—Vol. I. 319; Vol. II. 429.

Wilcoxon, Rev. H. T.—Vol. I. 301, 307.

Wildman, Jno.—Vol. II. 227.

Wiley, Mr.—Vol. II. 260.

Wiley, Rev.—Vol. I. 296.

Wiley, Jno.—Vol. II. 22.

Wilkins—Vol. II. 429, 430.

Wilkins, Geo. F.—Vol. I. 259.

Wilkin's Chapel—Vol. I. 479.

Wilkinson—Vol. I. 138, 192; Vol. II. 430.

Wilkinson, Nathaniel—Vol. I. 141.

Wilkinson, Richard—Vol. I. 304.

Wilkinson, Rev. Thos.—Vol. I. 443; Vol. II. 23.

Wilkinson, William—Vol. I. 304.

Wilks—Vol. II. 430.

Will of Gen. Chas. Lee—Vol. II. 308.

William and Mary College—Vol. I. 17, 21, 29, 40, 95, 99, 113, 134, 136, 138, 140, 150, 154, 157, 165, 167, 175, 186, 188, 191, 201, 206, 208, 225, 284, 288, 318, 370, 405, 450, 485; Vol. II. 28, 99, 121, 122, 160, 272, 488.

William and Mary College Convention, Proceedings at, 1719—Vol. II. 393.

William and Mary Parish, Md.—Vol. II. 190.